GERMAN RULE, AFRICAN SUBJECTS

GERMAN RULE, AFRICAN SUBJECTS

State Aspirations and the Reality of Power in
Colonial Namibia

Jürgen Zimmerer
Translated by Anthony Mellor-Stapelberg

First published in Southern Africa by Jacana Media (Pty) Ltd in 2022
10 Orange Street
Sunnyside, Auckland Park
Johannesburg, 2092
+27(11) 628 3200
www.jacana.co.za

This edition has been sponsored by the Rosa Luxemburg Stiftung with funds
of the Federal Ministry for Economic Cooperation and Development of the
Federal Republic of Germany.

The content of the publication is the sole responsibility of the author and
publisher and does not necessarily reflect a position of the Rosa Luxemburg
Stiftung.

The publishers wish to thank The Johannesburg Holocaust & Genocide
Centre for their kind support.

First published by Berghahn Books in 2021
www.berghahnbooks.com

Originally published in German as Deutsche Herrschaft über Afrikaner:
Staatlicher Machtanspruch und Wirklichkeit im kolonialen Namibia

ISBN: 978-1-4314-3228-8

Also available as an ebook.

Cover image: Unveiling of the 'Reiterdenkmal' in Windhoek, 27 January
1912. Photo: Albrecht © Bildbestand der Deutschen Kolonialgesellschaft in der
Universitätsbibliothek Frankfurt am Main.
Set in Palatino Linotype 10/12.5pt
Printed by Tandym Print, Cape Town
Job no. 003871

See a complete list of Jacana titles at www.jacana.co.za

To Clara, Rebecca and Amélia

Contents

Illustrations

Diagrams

Tables

Preface to the English Edition

There is something very special about getting a new edition of a book of one's own published twenty years after it first appeared – and what is more, translated into another language. It is a matter for great pleasure and pride; but it also immediately confronts you, as the author, with questions as to how you have developed academically in the meantime, how your field of study has developed, and how much impact your own work has had on that development.

When my book *Deutsche Herrschaft über Afrikaner: Staatlicher Gewaltanspruch und Wirklichkeit im kolonialen Namibia* first appeared in 2001, any preoccupation with German colonial history was languishing in a mere niche of the academic world, to a large extent banished to the field of Area Studies – for example, African History. The dominant themes of historical studies in general at that time, only ten years after German reunification, were, on the one hand, the history of the German Democratic Republic, and on the other, the Holocaust and the war of annihilation 'in the East', in the aftermath of the controversy stirred up by the *Wehrmachtsausstellungen*, the exhibitions devoted to the role played in this by the German army – to name only those subjects positioned in the fields of modern and contemporary history. Hardly anybody was interested in German colonial history: there were still barely any breaks in the mist of 'colonial amnesia', as I labelled the phenomenon when I drew attention to it in 2013.[1]

Despite this, the book ran through three editions within just a few years. That in itself showed that the volume, and the subject matter it dealt with, must have struck a chord, and that there was a degree of interest in the topic after all. This is confirmed by the way the book was received; the echo was enormous for something that had started life as a dissertation, not only in the academic press but also in the general-interest media. Already, English-language reviewers were calling for the book to be translated into English; but it was not possible to fulfil those requests at that time.

Since then, a lot has changed. Over the last twenty years there has been a steady increase in the amount of attention being paid to German colonial history. And the segment of this topic that has attracted the largest part of this attention is the German colonial history of Namibia, Germany's only settler colony, not least as a result of the political controversies surrounding the genocide inflicted on the Herero and Nama by German imperial forces between 1904 and 1908. As early as 2004 the then minister Heidemarie Wieczorek-Zeul apologized for this genocide, even if this did not lead to much in the way of concrete results. Ten years later, in 2015, the German government started negotiating with the Namibian government about a recognition of this event as a case of genocide, an official apology and also possibilities of (financial) compensation. At the same time, representatives of the Herero and the Nama have brought a legal action in New York for the payment of reparations, which has now reached the appeal stage. As of July 2020, its outcome is still uncertain.

Meanwhile, the debate on the colonial legacy has been expanded to take in additional regions and other topics as well. The question of the origin of colonial collections in German and European museums is firmly on the agenda, as is the question of their restitution. The whole issue of colonialism and its consequences, including for Germany and Europe, is being discussed over a broad spectrum. For the first time in the history of the Federal Republic of Germany, the task of subjecting the colonial legacy to reappraisal has even been adopted as an element of government policy: the programme of the fourth Merkel government states that 'it is part of the fundamental democratic consensus in Germany that the Nazi reign of terror, the SED dictatorship and Germany's colonial history need to be reappraised and come to terms with'.[2]

Despite this, the debate is concentrated on a narrow range of topics: for example, war crimes and genocide, and whether particular objects in museums were legally acquired. That colonialism in itself was structurally criminal gets lost sight of. For it is indeed the case that not merely were crimes committed under colonialism, as is generally conceded, but rather that colonialism itself is criminal. There is a distinct lack of awareness of this.

A favourite method of approaching the issue is to draw up a balance sheet: aspects of colonialism that are considered to have been positive – the 'civilizatory achievements' – are set off against the excessively violent episodes. In this way, war crimes are transformed into exceptional events: the genocide committed against the Herero and Nama, for example, is above all laid at the door of the commanding general, Lothar von Trotha. This is alarmingly reminiscent of the strategy with which German colonial officials sought to justify particularly brutal events in German South West Africa, as is depicted in my book. The blame always lay only with individuals; nobody called the racist colonial system itself into question. Pointing the finger at individuals who bore a particular degree of blame serves to push the structurally racist and structurally criminal nature of colonialism into the background.

That the colonial situation was criminal in itself, that the racism underlying colonial rule could not but lead inevitably to systematic oppression: these factors are the subject of my book. It also highlights the fact that German South West Africa was the first attempt in German history to erect a 'racist state', with strict segregation between the 'races' and the attempt to transform the African population into an amorphous class of Black workers and servants, to the benefit and advantage of members of the German 'master race'.

It is a microstudy of everyday and bureaucratically exercised colonial violence, and of the views of humanity and racist ideology prevalent among the Wilhelminian colonial officials and military officers that gave rise to it. It shows clearly how all other considerations were subordinated to the idea of comprehensive economic 'development' of the settler colony, and how racist atrocities were interpreted merely as temporary side effects of this process, for which the Africans themselves or German settlers drawn from the 'underclass' were to blame. What there was no sign of was any self-critical attitude on the part of the officials towards their own actions and policies.

German Rule, African Subjects: State Aspirations and the Reality of Power in Colonial Namibia, as this English-language edition is entitled, was one of a number of works that stood at the beginning of a development which, looking back, represented the beginning of the final breaking down of the colonial amnesia that had prevailed in Germany up until then. It was not the only such study, and – how could it be otherwise in the academic world? – it was able to build upon other seminal studies that had appeared in the 1960s, as a glance at the bibliography and at the introduction chapter, which is reproduced unrevised in this edition, will show. However, whereas in the 1990s and early 2000s the focus was on the national, Namibian, perspective, *German Rule, African Subjects* viewed and views events from the perspective of colonial history. This perspective, however, is not limited to the discourse that took place in the 'home country', but focuses on the impact of colonial rule in the colony itself. It goes without saying that this story could also be told from the perspective of the Herero, Nama, Damara, Ovambo or San; indeed, it needs to be told from these perspectives as well. But that would be a completely different book, and the present author would not be the ideal person to write it. The time is now past when history was written for Africans by Whites. But this book does lay a basis for the telling of their history too, at least to the extent that it relates to the colonial state. Its theoretical and methodological approach is, however, grounded in the history of German violence and bureaucratic rule – which nevertheless should in no way be taken as providing a basis for claiming any primacy of that perspective over others.

German Rule, African Subjects sketches out the nature of everyday life in the racist state, the inevitable transmutation of a legal system based on racial distinctions into structural and individual exploitation and barbarity. It shows that it was this racist state, the core features of which had already been established before 1904, that endowed German colonial rule with its characteristic features, and that together with the genocide was responsible for its gravest after-effects. It corrects both the false image of German colonial rule as having been exercised benevolently before 1904, and that of a 'peace of the graveyard' (Drechsler) after the genocide.

Against the background of an analysis of this racist state, with its intention to implement uniform economic development over a vast area (i.e. to subordinate all concerns, interests and rights, especially those of the African population, to the new economic order that was to be created throughout such an area), parallels to and continuities with the crimes of the National Socialists become apparent. I formulated these in the years after 2001, and published my findings in book form in 2011 under the title *Von Windhuk nach Auschwitz? Beiträge zum Verhältnis von Kolonialismus und Nationalsozialismus*. Both the question of whether a case of genocide had occurred and the issue of the relationship between colonialism and the crimes of the Third Reich led to intensive debate.[3]

The actual analysis of the 'racist state' and the 'society of racial privilege', on the other hand, evoked hardly any disagreement, so no revisions of the content were necessary.[4] That is another reason why it is worthwhile to produce a new edition. To understand colonialism, it is absolutely essential to have a knowledge of the micromechanisms through which it exercised control. Only against the background of the everyday nature of the violence inflicted can its impact, and African reactions to it, be appropriately evaluated.

For these two reasons – namely, that the book is still up to date in its essential analysis, and that it has itself, through the debates that it has helped to initiate, become a historical document – I have decided to have it translated in unaltered form. Any revision of individual aspects would inevitably have led to a completely new book. Only linguistically have I carried out cautious adaptations.[5] Here too, it is the case that, after twenty years of intensive discussion precisely on the topic of language and racism, I would today write the book differently. The fundamental problem, however, remains: how can one write about sources that are full of racist language without perpetuating that racism, but also without ignoring the violence inherent in them?

It gives me particular pleasure that an English translation will now allow the book to become more widely known in Namibia itself, beyond the circle of specialists on the German colonial period. My thanks are due first and foremost to the publishers, Berghahn Books, and their staff; to my translator Anthony Mellor-Stapelberg; and to my research assistants Dr Elisabeth Murray, Cäcilia Maag, Nils Schliehe and Dr Julian zur Lage, who helped at different times with the task of producing an English-language version ready for publication and to Lara Mia Padmanaban and Rosa Jung for the preparation of the index.

This book is dedicated to Clara, Rebecca and Amélia.

Notes

1. See Zimmerer, 'Kolonialismus und kollektive Identität', 9.
2. Cf. Coalition Agreement between CDU, CSU and SPD for the 19th Parliament, March 2018, lines 7954–57.
3. Zimmerer, *Von Windhuk nach Auschwitz?* An English-language edition under the title 'From Windhoek to Auschwitz? Reflections on the Relationship between Colonialism and National Socialism' will be published in 2021. Both the translation and an upcoming new German-language edition will contain a bibliography to cover the subsequent debates of the years 2011–2020.
4. In relation to this, see the supplementary bibliography that has been added to this edition.
5. In relation to this, see also the Glossary.

Abbreviations

BA-MA	Bundesarchiv-Militärarchiv Freiburg (German Federal Archives, Military Archives, Freiburg)
BAL	Bundesarchiv Berlin-Lichterfelde (German Federal Archives, Lichterfelde, Berlin)
betr.	*betreffend* = concerning
BKE	*Bezirksamt Keetmanshoop* (archive shelfmark: Keetmanshoop District Office)
BLU	*Bezirksamt Lüderitzbucht* (archive shelfmark: Lüderitzbucht District Office)
BOM	*Bezirksamt Omaruru* (archive shelfmark: Omaruru District Office)
BRE	*Bezirksamt Rehoboth* (archive shelfmark: Rehoboth District Office)
BSW	*Bezirksamt Swakopmund* (archive shelfmark: Swakopmund District Office)
BWI	*Bezirksamt Windhuk* (archive shelfmark: Windhoek District Office)
CSW	Commander (in Chief) of the Schutztruppe, Windhoek
DKG	*Deutsche Kolonial-Gesetzgebung* (see Bibliography)
DO	District Office (*Bezirksamt* or *Distriktamt*)
DOK	*Distriktsamt Okahandja* (archive shelfmark: Okahandja District Office)
DOs	District Offices (*Bezirksämter* and *Distriktämter*)
ELCIN	Archives of the Evangelical-Lutheran Church in the Republic of Namibia, Windhoek
esp.	especially

FO	Foreign Office
FO-CD	Foreign Office, Colonial Department
GCG	German Consulate General
Gen.	Generalia
GLU	*Bezirksgericht Lüderitzbucht* (archive shelfmark: Lüderitzbucht District Court)
GSW	*Bezirksgericht Swakopmund* (archive shelfmark: Swakopmund District Court)
GSWA	German South West Africa
GWI	*Bezirksgericht Windhuk* (archive shelfmark: Windhoek District Court)
ICO	Imperial Colonial Office
IGW	Imperial Governor's Office, Windhoek
ITP	Inspectorate of the Territorial Police
M	marks (German currency)
MF	microfilm
NAW	National Archives, Windhoek
NC	Native Commissioner
NCO	Native Commissioner's Office
n.d.	no date
n.p.	no page number
SNC	Schutztruppe, Northern Command
Spec.	Specialia
spec. pag.	special pagination [=insertion into the file]
SSC	Schutztruppe, Southern Command
sten. rec.	stenographic records of Proceedings in the German Reichstag
Vol., vol.	Volume
w.f.b.	with free board
ZBU	*Zentralbureau des kaiserlichen Gouvernements* (archive shelfmark: Central Office of the Imperial Governor)

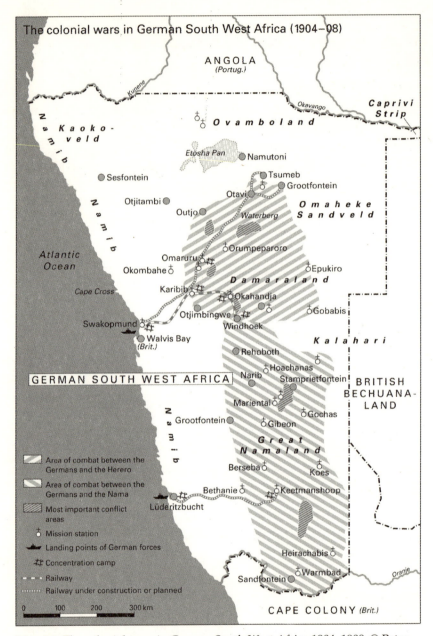

Map 0.1 The colonial wars in German South West Africa 1904–1908. © Peter Palm, Berlin. Reproduced with permission.

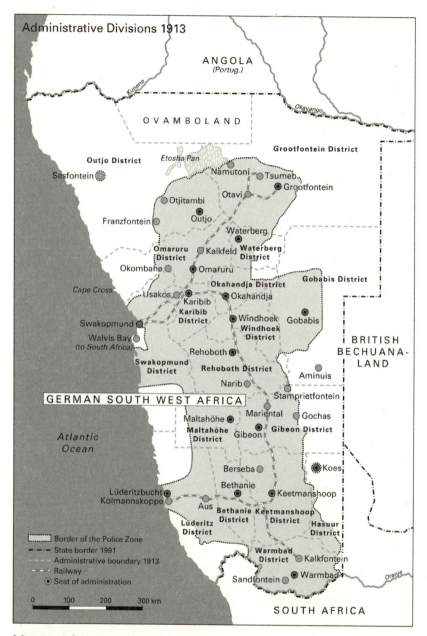

Map 0.2 Administrative Divisions, 1913. © Peter Palm, Berlin. Reproduced with permission.

Introduction

European rule over Africans is a key topic in the history of European colonial rule, since colonialism, according to the definition laid down by Wolfgang Reinhard, is 'control exercised by one nation over another, foreign, one, involving the economic, political and ideological exploitation of the differential between the two in their degrees of development'.[1] In the modern colonial state, the need to regulate this relationship led to the development of a separate field of policy within the Colonial Administration, concerned exclusively with relations between the colonizers and the colonized population: the field of Native Policy. The aim of this study is to investigate this area, taking as an example German colonial rule in South West Africa, today's Namibia.

Native Policy is to be understood to include all measures taken by the colonial state to determine its relationship with the colonized population, including regulations governing how the White population was to deal with the latter. This includes the behaviour of private individuals towards 'natives' only to the extent that certain administrative measures gave rise to visible manifestations in this area, or allow conclusions to be drawn as to the way the colonial officers involved carried out their duty of supervision. Despite this, the term Native Policy covers a wider field than merely the day-to-day dealings of the administration with the local population; it also covers the concept, fundamental to German policy, of a *Herrschaftsutopie*, a 'governmental and administrative utopia'[2] that extended beyond the conceptions of colonial rule prevailing at any given moment, i.e. of how to deal with the day-to-day business of Native Policy. In the field of Native Policy, the concept of 'governmental and administrative utopia' relates to a system of relationships with the local population that the colonial officials sought to achieve as the ideal permanent situation.

Much space in this work is devoted to the issue of the role played by the modern state and its representatives, the colonial officers, in Native Policy. This arises out of the fact that the period of German colonial rule, albeit relatively short (1884–1915), was long enough for colonial rule to become firmly established, the foundations of a settler society to be laid, the greater part of the African-owned land to be transferred into the possession of the colonial state, and the traditional economic and social structures of the African communities to be largely destroyed. Within a few years, the African population had ceased to be free inhabitants of their own country, able to engage in independent economic activity, and were transformed into subjects of the German Reich who lacked all possessions and were obliged to rely on dependent employment in order to survive. This process of oppression and of depriving the population of the colony of its rights took place in South West Africa at a speed that can only be explained by the extent to which the long arm of the State's bureaucratic administration attempted to reach down into all areas of the lives of ordinary people. In this study, the focus is on the years 1905 to 1915, when the German administration, subsequent to the genocidal war against the Herero and Nama (1904–08) with its thousands of victims among the African population and the resulting shifts in power relationships, was able to throw overboard all the restraints practised before the war and to implement direct rule over the Africans.

At the centre of these considerations stand above all the colonial 'practitioners' on the spot; that is to say, the Colonial Government in Windhoek and the local administrations of the Districts, since they were not only the ones essentially responsible for shaping and implementing Native Policy but were also in a position to observe directly the consequences arising out of it. This does not, however, exclude investigation of the part played by the *Reichskolonialamt*, the Imperial Colonial Office in Berlin, in developing the concepts behind this Native Policy.

This nuanced examination in itself implies the abandonment, which is fundamental to this study, of a view that regards the colonial bureaucracy as a homogeneous structure in which all officials shared the same values and pursued the same intentions. On the contrary, it emphasizes the fact that such a complex organization as the Colonial Administration was inevitably composed of individuals who entertained divergent opinions with regard to their objectives and the ways in which these were to be achieved. The assumption underlying this study, as a prerequisite for any investigation of the multifaceted processes out of which the formulation and implementation of Native Policy evolved, is that 'all those involved acted as subjects of history'; in other words – again borrowing from Trutz von Trotha – the admission that those players acted with self-awareness, and the assumption that each individual colonial officer performed his tasks in a competent and rational way: he 'set himself objectives and weighed up the means he needed to employ to realize those objectives', and he was able 'to put forward understandable reasons for acting as he did',[3] even if those reasons appear to us today to be false or irrational.

For the field of Native Policy, this means posing the question as to how the bureaucrats perceived themselves, and how they perceived others. How did the individual colonial officer regard the duties attached to his office, how did he see himself in the colonial environment, and what factors contributed to the perceptions he had of both the Africans and the White population? Not only are the answers to these questions important in respect of the development and implementation of Native Policy; they are also able to contribute to an analysis of the significance of racism and of the self-image of Wilhelminian officialdom. In this way, the insights obtained hold a significance going beyond the specific context of South West Africa. This offers a good example of the extent to which the history of German colonial rule is also a part of German history in general, though admittedly a part that took place above all in Africa.

Alongside the general attitude of the people concerned, however, their specific personal interests in matters both internal and external to their bureaucratic activities are of essential importance in the design of Native Policy. Pierre Bourdieu has pointed out in a carefully nuanced manner that players forming part of an organization always, consciously or unconsciously, pursue not only unselfish but also egotistical goals.[4] Indeed, these may run thoroughly counter to those of the collective player that the individual is part of – in this case, the Administration – and hinder the effective implementation of the policy concerned. The pursuit of one's own personal career is an obvious example of this, but so is the adoption of positions held by specific groups in society, such as, for example, the mining companies or the farmers' associations. Colonial officials lived in a social environment that bore the clear imprint of particular interests in the field of Native Policy, and the social pressures exerted by these could well lead to officials adopting positions that displayed a conflict of interest with the general policy of the Administration.

But the work of the lobbyists also impacted directly on the Government itself. In German South West Africa this is apparent above all in the competition for influence between the mining industry and the farmers. This in itself gave rise to a situation in which the bureaucracy was forced to take sides, or at the very least to weigh up and consider whether it should take sides, and it points to the fact that it is not as easy to determine the actual degree of influence of particular lobby groups as the Marxist theory of history in particular would have us believe. This work therefore takes as its starting point the assumption that, as Trutz von Trotha has formulated it in respect of Togo, the actions of the colonial bureaucracy were not driven merely by 'structural constraints' determined 'by social and economic forces'.[5] This should not, however, be taken to mean that there was no overlap between the interests of specific colonialist groups and the objectives of the German Administration; because if German South West Africa was to be turned into a settler colony it was essential, for example, to pay due regard to the farming community. The economic development of the colony too could only be achieved by providing support to both agriculture and the mining companies. There is nevertheless no question of the bureaucracy having responded in a reflex-like manner to whatever demands were made on them by these interest groups.

This leads on directly to a further problem: that of the relationship between the legal provisions as promulgated and the legal reality. From the fact that regulations existed in the field of Native Policy, it cannot be concluded that these were comprehensively implemented. There were numerous hindrances to this. Among them were a shortage of staff, inadequacies in the infrastructure and the unrealizable nature of certain measures, as well as active and/or passive resistance on the part of the African population. Of equal importance is the issue of the degree of cooperation that was forthcoming from the White population. Native Policy was formulated in such detail and in such convoluted regulations that it was simply impossible for the administration and its executive organs alone to make the resources available that would have been required for their implementation. Cooperation from the White population was essential. The extent to which this was forthcoming, the areas in which it was not (because the objectives of the settlers diverged from those of the Administration), and the impact that these factors had on Native Policy are questions that need to be investigated.

But even the assumption that the officials basically all pulled together, and that when implementing a policy they set aside any differences of opinion that might have come to light during its formulation, is, as I have already mentioned, questionable. Particularly the District Officers, who were scarcely or not at all involved in creating the regulations and ordinances, found that they had substantial leeway to bring their own views into play, as it were retrospectively, when interpreting the provisions that had been promulgated. Any historical analysis must therefore pay careful attention to colonial practice, and take due account of how individual officers behaved. This study attempts to deal with this problem, which has been neglected up until now, by not only describing how the Native Policy ordinances and regulations came into being, but also concerning itself with how they were then applied in practice.

Native Policy, as an expression of the State's administrative activity, is codified in the form of laws, ordinances and decrees that originated in the form of individual drafts, memoranda and statements of position in the course of a bureaucratic process. Over and above this, it is expressed in the decisions taken in individual cases by the Colonial Government and the local authorities. Due consideration needs to be given to all of these.

The situation with regard to the sources from which answers to the questions raised may be extracted is extraordinarily favourable, since the entire archives of the Central Office of the Imperial Governor in Windhoek have not only been preserved, but have also, since Namibia's independence, been made freely accessible for academic research. This makes it possible for the first time to examine Native Policy from the point of view of those people who were themselves active in the colony. Since, in addition, the Central Office acted as an intermediate level of administration between the Imperial Colonial Office in Berlin and the District Offices distributed throughout the colony, the relevant correspondence is to be found in its entirety in these files, in the form either of originals or of copies of the outgoing documents. These sources embrace all fields of Native Policy, from education, taxation policy and employment matters to classified military documents, and all the way to files relating to civil legal cases and the records of the criminal courts. To supplement this body of evidence, I have also drawn upon the archives of the Imperial Colonial Office – deposited previously in the Central State Archives of the GDR in Potsdam, but now to be found in the Federal Archives in Lichterfelde, Berlin – and the records of individual District Offices and of the Native Commissioners' Offices, which today are preserved in the Namibian National Archives in Windhoek. Only in respect of the *Schutztruppe*, the military force stationed in the colony, are there significant gaps, as the relevant archives have been destroyed. According to information given by Archive staff, the *Schutztruppe* documents located in the colony were burnt by the Germans themselves when South African forces marched into the territory in 1915, while the corresponding archives in Germany were destroyed in a Red Army air raid shortly before the end of the Second World War. The German Federal Archives – Military Archives in Freiburg hold some individual source documents relating to the war against the Herero and Nama.

I have investigated and analysed these. To supplement the source documents originating from state institutions, I have in individual cases also made use of documents from the Rhenish Missionary Society, which are preserved in the archives of the Evangelical Lutheran Church in the Republic of Namibia.

The user of these sources is, however, confronted with a certain degree of difficulty as a result of the way the records were kept during the German colonial period. Although vast quantities of source documents were archived, they were often filed in a completely haphazard manner, and so the researcher cannot always rely on the classification of files by subject matter. Often, a volume of documents will be found to contain only some of the documentation relating to a particular event or administrative procedure, in which case it may be necessary to work through many such volumes in order to be able to reconstruct the topic completely. For this reason, a much smaller number of files may have been referred to and quoted in the text than I actually worked through.

Thus the sources that this work is based on are, in the overwhelming majority of cases, administrative files containing documents written personally by the people concerned. The advantage that they thereby afford direct access to the actions of those people must be weighed against the disadvantage that they were themselves parties to any dispute that may have arisen with regard to what policy would be correct. As is ultimately always the case with historical sources, these administrative documents must be examined individually for clues that indicate the intentions of the specific writer concerned. But precisely as a result of this, it is possible to obtain insights into how the administration functioned and into the objectives being pursued in the field of Native Policy; these go far beyond anything that was set out in generalized policy documents or in published articles seeking to give overviews of contemporary events. Even less reliable than the latter as indicators of the intentions that were actually being pursued are the memoirs written by some of those involved, or the programmatic articles by colonial propaganda-mongers that are to be found in the numerous colonialist periodicals. For this reason, these have been drawn upon only in exceptional cases. The most outstanding example of the dangers inherent in taking the programmatic writings of colonialist theoreticians to represent the historical reality is to be found in the case of Paul Rohrbach. As he occupied the position of Settlement Commissioner in South West Africa from 1903 to 1906, he was considered to be a major authority on the aims of the German Colonial Administration. What was overlooked, however, was the fact that he was ultimately obliged to give up his office in South West Africa precisely because the settlement policy he stood for conflicted with the view prevailing in the Colonial Government.[6]

Considering the importance of German Native Policy in the history of Namibia after 1905, it is surprising that no soundly based analysis of it has yet appeared. The two works that continue to be of fundamental importance in respect of German rule in South West Africa, namely the monographs by Horst Drechsler[7] and Helmut Bley,[8] dating from 1966 and 1968 respectively, devote little space to any portrayal of Native Policy after 1905. In particular, Drechsler's statement that the period after 1905 was characterized by 'the peace of the graveyard' was largely adopted uncritically by other commentators, apparently blocking any more precise study of the last ten years of German colonial rule. This is in spite of the fact that Drechsler does draw attention to continuities between the prewar and postwar periods; but his Marxist approach, which only admitted economic interests as motivations for German policy, obscured his view of other motivations arising out of the ideologies or mentalities of the people involved. As he regards German Native Policy as a uniform phenomenon supported by all Germans both in South West Africa itself and at home in the Reich, he is unable to do justice to the dynamics and internal contradictions of a settler colony within which there emerged several disparate elements with divergent interests.

Fritz Wege's[9] study, despite its wealth of content, is also subject to similar theoretical and ideological limitations. His work focuses on the economic and social situation of the Africans, and he describes in detail the importance of the shortage of labour in the formulation of German policy. But he scarcely concerns himself with the process of opinion-forming within the German Administration – a result, among other things, of the sources he draws upon. The crucial documents of the authorities on the spot in South West Africa, which are so important to any analysis of policy as it was practised on the level of the local administration, were available to him only to the extent that they were to be found in the then Central Archives in Potsdam. This led to a one-sided emphasis on the way the German Administration was instrumentalized by German business circles.

Helmut Bley's approach is fundamentally more complex. He analyses in detail developments within the White population, and points out the plurality of interests and the tensions, in particular precisely in the 'native question', on the one hand between the Colonial Administration in South West Africa and the Imperial Colonial Office, and on the other hand between the Governor and the

White population. Yet he scarcely goes into the various positions held
by different members of the German Administration in the colony;
and, furthermore, he overlooks the fundamental continuity in Native
Policy from the early years of German colonial rule under Governor
Leutwein up to the period after the war against the Herero und Nama.
As a result, his (brief) analysis of Native Policy after 1905 is lacking
in historical depth. Despite this, Bley's work essentially represents
the state of research that has remained current up to the present day.
Gert Sudholt's[10] study of German Native Policy down to 1904 does not
manage to add to what Bley had already presented, and in addition
displays some apologetic tendencies.

Some valuable insights into the discrepancy between the legal
provisions defining German Native Policy after 1905 and the day-
to-day reality of their implementation are provided by Johannes
Müller[11] in his 1984 MA thesis. On the basis of a careful analysis of the
published texts of laws and ordinances, of contemporary monographs
and of newspapers and periodicals, he succeeds in shaking to the
foundations the view of the last ten years of German colonial rule that
had prevailed until then. For he points out that the various Native
Ordinances were often not, and indeed could not be, rigorously
implemented. With the sources available to him, however, which do
not include any official archives, Müller was able neither to draw
any well-founded conclusions with regard to the motivations and
background factors underlying Native Policy, nor to gain any in-depth
insights into colonial practice. His work reveals clearly how essential
it is for German Native Policy in the period concerned to be examined
in the light of the files archived in Windhoek. Müller's research and
the questions he raises form the starting point for my own study, even
if our interpretations diverge widely in some areas. As his study was
never published, its reception in the academic world remained very
limited. Wolfgang Reinhard[12] further developed Müller's ideas, and
called into question the picture that had prevailed up until then of an
African population subjected to total control. This work takes up on
his theme of the discrepancies between the Native Policy regulations
valid in law and the day-to-day reality of their implementation.

Since 1995, two smaller-scale studies devoted to individual issues
have appeared. Peter Scheulen[13] has examined the image of the 'native'
in South West Africa. He is able to show how the view of the African
population disseminated by publications was very much determined
by stereotypes that were often racist by nature. However, in view of
his concentration on colonial periodicals he was not able to answer the
more intriguing question as to whether these stereotypes were also to

be found among the colonial officials on the spot, and whether they changed over the course of time. Jürgen Zimmerling[14] has devoted himself to the complex of problems surrounding the administration of criminal justice in relation to Africans, examining above all the legal provisions governing this field; his very brief survey of how criminal justice was in fact administered is unfortunately limited to a listing of the sentences of corporal punishment imposed, as found in the official statistics. From this, it is not possible to gain any deeper insights into the day-to-day reality of Native Policy in the field of criminal justice.

One reason for the lack of any new examination of German Native Policy after the war of 1904–08 is the shift in perspective that has occurred in the field of non-European history, with colonial history giving way to African history. In bringing about this shift, the historical sciences have made an important contribution to mental decolonization, with Africans no longer being perceived as 'peoples without writing and without history'.[15] In the case of Namibia too, some authors have addressed themselves to the history of the African population. This shift in perspective was initiated by two editions of the diaries of the Nama *Kaptein* (Chief) Hendrik Witbooi, produced by Wolfgang Reinhard[16] and Brigitte Lau[17] respectively, these diaries being the only large-scale source originating from an African during the period of German rule. With her work on southern and central Namibia in the mid-nineteenth century, which appeared in 1987 but was written in 1982, Brigitte Lau[18] has also provided a first contribution to the history of the Nama in precolonial times. Gerhard Pool[19] approached the history of the Herero under German rule with his biography of Samuel Maharero, who after initially collaborating with the Germans finally led his people into the 1904–08 war against them. This book offers valuable source documents, particularly ones relating to the German conduct of the war, as Pool had access to the private archives of the von Trotha family. The study by Jan Bart Gewald[20] provides a comprehensive portrayal of the history of the Herero between 1890 and 1923; it turns the focus onto the social dynamics within Herero society and the interplay between these and the process of establishing of German colonial rule.

The Ovambo, who lived in the north of the colony, have also been the subject of attention. The work of Regina Strassegger[21] has proved to be of particular relevance to this study. She has provided an extensive description of the system of migrant labour, but does not manage to go beyond clichés in respect of the attitude of the German Administration. Without any in-depth analysis of the constraints that the Administration was subject to in its actions, she displays a curious belief in its omnipotence. She does not show any awareness of the fact that the Administration, even in its dealings with other European protagonists such as the mining companies, was bound by law. The very choice of subject makes it impossible for the book to provide a comprehensive analysis of German Native Policy that takes into account the whole complex of motives that governed the modus operandi of the German Administration. Despite this, a merit of her work is doubtless the fact that she does not portray the Ovambo merely as passive victims of German policy, but shows them to be autonomous players who skilfully exploited the options for action that were open to them. Martti Eirola's[22] examination of the archives of the Finnish Mission, which are available only in Finnish, represents a significant contribution to our understanding of the relationship between the Ovambo and the Germans. Above all, he too is able to show that the Ovambo were not only an object of German policy, but were an independently active force that the Germans were not able to control. However, as German administration did not extend to Ovamboland, this present work deals with the Ovambo only to the extent that they migrated to the centre or south of the colony to work.

Against the background of the shift in perspective mentioned above, the question naturally arises as to why my work, contrary to the current trend in the academic world, focuses on the colonial bureaucracy. This comes from my conviction, which to me goes without saying, that the impact of colonial rule and the interactions between the colonial 'masters' and the colonized can only be comprehended on the basis of a precise knowledge of colonial policy, and above all of Native Policy. But there are considerable gaps in our knowledge of this field, which this work attempts to close. Furthermore, it seems to me that the shift of perspective in respect of African history has brought with it a negative side-effect: German colonial rule has been detached from German history, and responsibility for it transferred to a small circle of specialists in African history. The history of colonial rule, however, lies at the interface between European and non-European history. It is always the history of two countries: on the one hand of the colony itself and the people living there, and on the other hand of its colonial mother country. I therefore regard this work as being first and foremost a contribution to German history, even though the subject matter is a chapter of German history that took place in Africa. This does not mean that the fate of the colonized is to be completely left on one side; again and again, I point out the consequences of German actions for the African population, and the Africans' reactions to them. In view of my primary research interest, however, these matters are not at the centre of my study.

In the first chapter I deal with the formal establishment of the *Schutzgebiet* (as the German colonies were officially known), the first twenty years of German colonial rule and the genocidal war against the Herero and Nama. Although several academic studies exist in this field, a revised treatment of it has become necessary: in particular, a fundamental reassessment of the intentions and policies of Governor Leutwein and his staff with regard to Native Policy is called for, since a degree of continuity, previously overlooked but now apparent, links the periods before and after the war. The Native Policy pursued after the war represents not a fundamentally new beginning but the realization of objectives that had already existed in the prewar period. In a following section, the war against the Herero and Nama, the genocidal quality of which is indisputable and is not confined purely to combat situations or to the person of General von Trotha, is dealt with in respect of both the conduct of hostilities and the treatment of prisoners of war. Already in this context it becomes clear that the German side by no means acted monolithically. In respect of German Native Policy, however, the war represented an exceptional phase, a state of emergency, as the murder and expulsion of the African population was in fact contrary to that policy's true objectives.

In the second chapter, the focus turns to the legal consolidation of German Native Policy. This includes the expropriation of land and measures aimed at achieving racial segregation, as well as the codification of various measures of Native Law dating from the prewar period, which were now for the first time to apply throughout the colony (with the exception of its most northerly and south-easterly regions). The focus, in addition to the issues of the nature of the decision-making process, precursor measures from the prewar period and the specific people responsible in each individual case, also extends to the question of the intentions behind the measures. Particularly in the case of the Native Ordinances, which were central to the structure of the system of control, the analysis extends to the reactions and statements of opinion that were forthcoming from the District Officers – that is to say, from those people who, although they were not involved in the decision-making process that had led to the formulation of the ordinances, were responsible for implementing them in their everyday contacts with Africans. This gives rise to a more complex picture of the *Herrschaftsutopie* (governmental and administrative utopia) that the German colonial regime sought to create: the society of racial privilege and the 'semifree labour market'. It also makes clear that the establishment of a cohesive Native Policy was to no small extent the outcome of the efforts of only four persons, namely von Lindequist,

Golinelli, Tecklenburg and Hintrager, some of whom had worked in the colony's administration as early as under Leutwein, and from 1905 onwards occupied a variety of key positions in the colony or in the Imperial Colonial Office.

The third chapter contains a brief sketch of the essential demographic, economic and institutional developments and changes in the period after the war. These include, in addition to the changes in the population figures brought about by the war and by White immigration, the discovery of diamonds and the resulting tensions between agriculture and the mining industry, the massive reduction in the size of the colonial armed forces and the build-up of a territorial police force under the sole command of the civilian authorities, and the first steps towards creating an autonomous Native Administration, with the setting up of a Department of Native Affairs in the Governor's Office and the appointment of 'Native Commissioners' in selected districts.

As the adoption of Native Policy laws and ordinances does not tell us anything about how they were implemented or their effects, the reality of colonial rule is analysed in two separate chapters devoted to specific central themes: the securing of colonial rule and the labour market. In the fourth chapter, the focus is on the practical realization of the all-embracing system of control. The ways in which registration and control were implemented are examined in detail, as are the difficulties arising out of various factors: logistical problems, the reluctance of the White population to cooperate and the inadequate functioning of the bureaucratic apparatus. It was precisely the failure of 'total surveillance' that led the settlers to put forward ever more radical demands – such as for any Africans who attempted to escape from the control system to be tattooed. But it also demonstrates that it did not prove possible at any time for the African population to be reduced to mere objects of the actions of the German Administration, and it helps to create an understanding of the ways in which they succeeded in upholding their own traditions in the face of all the colonial state's efforts and intentions to re-educate them. Although they never fundamentally endangered German colonial rule, the small number of cases in which Africans organized themselves into so-called 'gangs' in order to undertake campaigns against their oppressors triggered growing hysteria among the White population, leading to rapid military reactions, the employment of all available means to expedite the extradition of Africans who had fled to South Africa, and a revival of plans to compulsorily resettle whole ethnic groups. The detailed analysis of individual extradition proceedings in particular demonstrates the need for a reassessment of the view that there was always smooth cooperation between the British or South African and the German colonial administrations.

The fifth chapter, which is devoted to the labour market, examines a further key element of the 'governmental and administrative utopia' that the German authorities aimed to create, namely the attempt to recruit the entire African population into dependent employment and to incorporate it into the 'semifree' labour market. This was based upon a compulsion to enter into an employment relationship, but was at the same time intended to promote the stability of such employment relationships and thus of the entire system of colonial rule by securing minimum rights for the Africans. With regard to the origins of the African labourers, three groups can be distinguished: the workers from the Police Zone (i.e. predominantly Herero and Nama), those from Ovamboland and those from South Africa. As there were significant distinctions between these three groups – firstly with regard to the manner of their recruitment, as it was only the workers from the Police Zone who were subject to a direct compulsion to undertake employment, whereas the other two groups had to be recruited outside the area of direct German rule; and secondly with regard to the fields in which they were employed – they are dealt with in separate sections of the chapter. The different ways in which they were recruited led to there being significant distinctions between South Africans, Ovambo and Africans from the Police Zone with regard to the wages they were required to be paid, which in turn led to the worst paid being those who worked on the farms, whilst those entitled to better remuneration could only be employed in the mines and in railway construction. In each case, the study concentrates primarily on the recruitment of workers and the part played in this by the Administration, and on the conditions of the employment relationships. In particular, it asks how far the authorities were able and willing to guarantee minimum rights, and whether they duly fulfilled their duty of supervision. In the case of workers from the Police Zone, the question of how far the District Offices fulfilled their protective functions in respect of the African workers is also investigated, whereas in respect of the Ovambo in the diamond fields it is the Native Commissioner who plays an important role. The section of the chapter dealing with the South African workers contains among other things descriptions of the Wilhelmstal Massacre, in which fourteen workers were shot dead by the colonial armed forces, and of the strategies adopted by the German military and civil administrations to sweep the matter under the carpet; it also deals with the difficulties for the German side occasioned by the fact that the workers concerned were of foreign origin, leading to a foreign power being able to interfere in South West African affairs. In addition, each of the three sections of the chapter goes into the topic of the constant competition between employers for the available workers, as well as the employers' attempts to persuade the Administration to act in ways that would be of benefit to them.

A solid foundation for the modern colonial state that the German authorities sought to create was to be achieved through a process of social disciplining, through which the Africans were to 'learn' to accept their own position at the bottom end of the social order. Among the factors intended to contribute to this, in addition to the compulsion to enter into dependent employment, were schooling and subjection to taxation. The sixth and final chapter is devoted to these two factors. Schooling is examined not only with regard to its extent and curricula, but also in respect of the Administration's attempts to subject the Missionary Societies, as the providers of education, to state supervision in that area. This furnishes a good example of the sometimes strained relationships between the state Administration and the missions. In addition to 'educating the Africans to work', schooling was seen as a way of fulfilling the 'mission to spread civilization'.

The purpose and usefulness of imposing direct taxation on the Africans, and the form such taxation should take, were topics of heated dispute. In addition to being a way of indirectly intensifying the compulsion to undertake employment, the tax was also intended to promote the development of a cash economy. Apart from the fact that this would increase the degree of control that the Administration would be able to exercise over employment relationships between Whites and Africans, it was also seen, as was taxation in general, as a step towards creating a 'modern' society and economy. Not the least important aspect was that the Africans were to be made to contribute directly to the financing of the colonial project. The intensely controversial manner in which the debate on a Native Tax was conducted, not only within the territorial Administration and the Colonial Government but also in the Imperial Colonial Office, affords profound insights into the manner of thinking of the officials involved, and into the strategies that were used, consciously or unconsciously, to legitimize colonial rule. The fact that it proved impossible, in the face of resistance from the White population, to implement a uniform tax throughout the colony is indicative of the shift in the political framework conditions brought about by the introduction of local self-government for the Whites.

Notes

1. Reinhard, *Kleine Geschichte des Kolonialismus*, 1.
2. [Translator's note: This phrase is used in this work to translate the term *Herrschaftsutopie*, borrowed from Trutz von Trotha]. Von Trotha, *Koloniale Herrschaft*, 12.
3. Ibid., 6.
4. For a summary of Bourdieu's theses, see Bourdieu, *Praktische Vernunft*.
5. Von Trotha, *Koloniale Herrschaft*, 7.
6. Rohrbach, *Aus Südwestafrikas schweren Tagen*, 276–79. His major work on South West Africa is: Rohrbach, *Deutsche Kolonialwirtschaft*, Vol. 1, *Südwest-Afrika*.
7. Drechsler, *Südwestafrika unter deutscher Kolonialherrschaft*, Vol. I.
8. Bley, *Kolonialherrschaft und Sozialstruktur*.
9. Wege, 'Zur Entstehung und Entwicklung der Arbeiterklasse'.
10. Sudholt, *Die deutsche Eingeborenenpolitik in Südwestafrika*.
11. Müller, 'Die deutsche Eingeborenenpolitik'.
12. Reinhard, 'Eingeborenenpolitik in Südwestafrika'.
13. Scheulen, *Die 'Eingeborenen' Deutsch-Südwestafrikas*.
14. Zimmerling, *Die Entwicklung der Strafrechtspflege für Afrikaner*. This can be well supplemented by Schröder's portrayal, as he also goes into the origins and practice of the 'parental power of (corporal) chastisement' over Africans. Schröder, *Prügelstrafe und Züchtigungsrecht*.
15. Such is the title of a study by Christoph Marx that examines the attitudes of numerous ethnologists, *'Völker ohne Schrift und Geschichte'*. For too long, historians shared the attitude of the ethnologists.
16. Reinhard, *Hendrik Witbooi*.
17. Lau, *The Hendrik Witbooi Papers*.
18. Lau, *Southern and Central Namibia in Jonker Afrikaner's Time*.
19. Pool, *Samuel Maharero*.
20. Gewald, *Towards Redemption*.
21. Strassegger, 'Die Wanderarbeit der Ovambo'.
22. Eirola, *The Ovambogefahr*.

1

The Establishment of the *Schutzgebiet* and 'Native Policy' up until 1907

One striking feature of the German colonial period in South West Africa was the glaring mismatch between the aspirations of the Colonial Government and the resources – that is to say, the levels of both military and administrative personnel – that the representatives of that government actually had available for the realization of those aspirations. These inadequate resources relative to the objectives had a constant impact on Native Policy throughout the period of German colonial rule, whether during the initial twenty years, the genocidal colonial war from 1904 to 1908, or the period subsequent to the war. The compromises and tactical constraints that the administration had to submit to, particularly during the early period, initially obscured the true aim of the German administration, namely that of making the Africans living in the '*Schutzgebiet*'[1] directly subject to the German legal and administrative machinery of ordinances and regulations. It was not until after the military victory in the war against the Herero and Nama that direct rule was implemented, at least over the African population living in the central and southern areas of the colony – a development that represented the eventual fulfilment of a policy that had been initiated under Governor Theodor Leutwein (1894–1905).[2]

The objective of bringing not only administrative but also, and indeed above all, military means to bear in order to advance the interests of the young colonial power in respect of the African population was one that Leutwein shared with his predecessor Curt von François (1891–94). Compared to von François, however,

Leutwein was much more skilful in exploiting the differences and tensions within the African population in order to achieve his aims, and in compensating for his military weakness by using diplomacy and by drawing on assistance from African collaborators.[3] Moreover, he had a clear concept of the kind of 'native policy' that he wanted to establish in the colony. He was not able to realize his objectives himself, since he lacked the necessary military force; but he had already conceived them in outline. His plans did not become reality, however, until after the crushing defeat of the Herero in August 1904, when the administration under his successor Friedrich von Lindequist (1905–07) created a uniform Native Policy for the entire *Schutzgebiet* by means of the three so-called *Eingeborenenverordnungen* (Native Ordinances) of 1907. Academic research has not in the past paid sufficient attention to the extent to which these represented the implementation of a policy originating under Leutwein; rather, it has presented the period after the war as marking the beginning of a completely new phase in Native Policy, one characterized by immobility. The situation that appeared to prevail was one of the 'peace of the graveyard', to use the phrase coined by Horst Drechsler[4] and constantly echoed by subsequent writers. Helmut Bley declared that it was scarcely possible to trace any derivation of postwar conditions from approaches apparent before the war,[5] thereby reinforcing the perception of a strict division into three periods: that of the establishment of colonial rule up to the outbreak of the war of conquest (1884–1904); the genocidal war (1904–08); and the postwar phase (1908–14) with its completely new approach to Native Policy. This division into phases is only pertinent, however, in respect of the technique of domination – in other words, the policy of 'divide and rule' practised before the war and the simultaneous dependency on the collaboration of local leaders. As will be shown, it is not tenable either in respect of the objective of colonial rule, which even under Leutwein was directed towards establishing an ever stronger direct German influence on the African population, or with regard to the way Native Policy developed in terms of concrete measures, since all the basic features of Native Policy after 1905 are rooted in considerations and approaches that had already existed before the war. They thus represent a direct continuum from the position under Leutwein, and this was further reinforced by continuity in respect of the personnel concerned, as the men who essentially formulated postwar policy had also been involved as subordinate officials in the administration of South West Africa in the period before the war.

But such a view of the situation changes the significance to be attributed to the war in the context of the history of German South

West Africa. The outbreak of war on 12 January 1904 represented the failure of the policy that Leutwein had pursued until then of constantly extending German influence – with the objective of establishing a modern state on the basis of European models – through indirect rule (i.e. through the collaboration of African elites), while at the same time avoiding driving the Africans into desperate acts of resistance by gradually accustoming them to foreign rule. The genocidal intentions of some elements in the German military command, intentions that determined the manner in which the war was fought, were thus out of line with the fundamental objectives of the Administration; as a result, the war period became a 'state of emergency', during which a large proportion of the African population were completely stripped of their rights and became liable to arbitrary extermination. The significance of the war for postwar Native Policy thus lay in the fact that, for the first time, it brought about a shift in the power relationships in favour of the German colonizers, and thus may be considered to have been a catalyst that allowed prewar concepts to be implemented while eliminating the need to pay any regard to the African population in doing so.

The Establishment of German Colonial Rule

Even though the desire of the Germans to have colonies of their own predated the establishment of the German Empire in 1871,[6] the colonial movement in Germany gained an increasing measure of support after unification.[7] The enthusiasm for it was nourished 'by a whole bundle of motives, with arguments drawn from socio-economics, nationalist ideology and socio-Darwinism, and a belief in a national mission and vocation to promote the spread of civilization all standing alongside each other'.[8] These cannot simply be dismissed as ideologies presented in self-justification by particular groups in society, even if at times they also fulfilled that function, but were the expression of a profound sense of insecurity evoked in their protagonists by the crises to which the young Reich was subject, and embodied a longing for security and for the German Empire to be able to occupy what was seen as its rightful place among the Great Powers. It was thought that colonies would provide a safety valve against the threat of overpopulation, and would also offer a market for the overproduction of German industry, as well as being a visible symbol documenting the country's aspiration to exercise the role of a world power. It was a further respect in which the country's bourgeoisie sought to emulate its great model, Great Britain.

The discussion was dominated by slogans such as those of a 'German India' in Africa or a 'German Hong Kong' in China. If Germany had its own colonial possessions, it was claimed, this would ensure that in future 'our sons and grandsons' would be able 'to bestride the earth as members of a master race', as Robert Faber, the publisher of the liberal nationalist newspaper *Magdeburger Zeitung*, formulated it.[9] The possession of colonies appeared to be a necessity, according to the logic of the socio-Darwinist interpretation of the rivalry between the emerging imperialistic industrialized countries, and to be a debt owed to subsequent generations. It was for their benefit that it had to be ensured that they would have a place among the winners in this contest, in which, as was widely believed, it was a matter of the 'survival of the fittest'. If large parts of the country's bourgeoisie were convinced that they belonged to a superior people, even among the nations of Europe, then the same applied all the more in comparison with non-European civilizations. This was expressed in the idea of a 'civilizing mission': those who saw themselves as occupying a superior position among the nations believed themselves to be called to 'civilize' the inhabitants of the world outside Europe, 'backward' and 'primitive' as they were presumed to be, and thus they had a ready-made positive justification for any striving for colonial possessions.[10]

Whereas for a long time German colonialist propaganda had envisaged the acquisition of colonies in Latin America, the Middle East or the Far East, in the 1870s public attention also began to concern itself with the possibility of establishing a colonial empire in Africa.[11] What later became South West Africa appeared a particularly favourable prospect, as it was one of the few areas of Africa to which no other colonial power had yet asserted formal claims. At the same time, it afforded the purveyors of colonialist propaganda an ideal arena. Whether as a source of exploitable natural resources, a suitable environment for White colonists to settle in or an area offering plenty of scope for the civilizing mission, South West Africa appeared to be a place that could make all such colonial dreams and fantasies come true.

Yet it was only hesitantly and half-heartedly that Germany began to seek to claim a seat at the table with the other colonial powers. What it was that caused Chancellor Otto von Bismarck, previously a strict opponent of any formal acquisition of colonies,[12] to modify his policy continues to be the subject of lively debate between historians. Both domestic and foreign policy considerations and also economic arguments[13] were involved when he declared Angra Pequeña to be under German protection on 24 April 1884.[14] In doing so, he was responding to a request from the Bremen tobacco merchant Adolf

Lüderitz, who a year previously had acquired Angra Pequeña Bay and the surrounding area from Joseph Fredericks, who ruled over the Nama of Bethanie.[15] His intention was to set up a 'trading post' there, to carry on trade, exploit the natural resources that he believed were to be found there and open up significant markets for German industry.[16]

Lüderitz's private involvement in South West Africa seemed to Bismarck to offer the opportunity to implement a change of course in respect of a German colonial empire, but in line with his own ideas on the subject, which were based on the concept of 'chartered companies' – that is to say that a given territory should be administered by a private company under a charter granted to it by the state. The territories to be acquired, for which Bismarck coined the term *Schutzgebiet* as an equivalent to the English 'protectorate' in order to avoid using the term *Kolonie* (colony),[17] were 'to remain as far as possible the responsibility of the commercial overseas interests'.[18] Bismarck himself justified this principle by stating that in the overseas possessions it should be 'the governing merchant and not the governing bureaucrat …, not the governing army officer and not the Prussian civil servant' who was in charge.[19]

Because the costs to Lüderitz of opening up the territory he had acquired and of the expeditions he was sending into the interior of the country soon proved to be beyond his means, and as in addition his hopes of quickly finding gold and diamonds had been dashed, he was obliged as early as 4 April 1885 to sell his possessions to the Deutsche Kolonialgesellschaft für Südwestafrika [German Colonial Society for South West Africa].[20] This was a company specially formed for the purpose at the urging of Bismarck and his banker Gerson von Bleichröder.[21] The investors do not appear to have expected any great economic return from this colonial undertaking, but rather felt it to be their duty to get involved 'out of patriotic interest and in order to support the Chancellor's colonial policy'.[22] Thus there was now in South West Africa a landowning company with a gigantic estate of some 240,000 sq. km, but no charter company.[23] So Bismarck's hopes of being able to undertake colonial expansion at the expense of colonial trading companies were torpedoed by the unwillingness of the Deutsche Kolonialgesellschaft für Südwestafrika to 'exercise sovereign rights involving any financial risks'.[24] But by then it was too late to reverse the original decision to embark on a colonialist policy. Neither in terms of domestic nor of foreign policy would it have been conceivable to admit failure: the country's prestige was at stake.

The fact that Bismarck's turnaround in adopting a colonialist policy was only half-hearted, and that it did not reflect any genuine interest in the colonies as such, did influence the way in which German rule was built up in South West Africa, since the Imperial Government was extremely hesitant about committing human resources, and did so only on a very low level. An official representative of the German Empire did arrive in the colony as early as May 1885, in the person of Imperial Commissioner Heinrich Göring,[25] in order to lend the force of international law to the declaration of German protection by the establishment of a nominal administration; however, it must have been clear to everybody in German administrative circles that the three civil servants originally sent out would not be in a position to set up any really functional administration for this vast territory, which is estimated to have been populated at the end of the nineteenth century by some 90,000–100,000 Ovambo, 70,000–80,000 Herero, 15,000–20,000 Nama, 30,000–40,000 Berg Damara and San, and 3,000–4,000 Basters.[26]

In late 1888, the Herero chief Maharero,[27] having realized that the three civil servants were not in a position to afford him the military assistance he had hoped to receive from the German Empire in his conflict with Hendrik Witbooi,[28] drove Göring and his two colleagues out of the territory into British-ruled Walvis Bay.[29] Although Bismarck would have much preferred to abandon the colony, he saw himself constrained by the colonial movement and by concerns for his own domestic standing, which was now firmly tied to the establishment of a colonial empire; in order to avoid any appearance of yielding ground to Great Britain,[30] he decided to send military reinforcements to South West Africa under the command of Captain Curt von François.[31] But whereas Göring had demanded an expeditionary force of some four to five hundred men with five or six light field guns in order to re-establish German rule,[32] the two dozen soldiers who were in fact dispatched[33] were not capable of undertaking a military operation of any size. The symbolic significance of the measure, however, was much more far-reaching, as von François himself recognized:

> Small though the force was, the step that the colonial authorities had taken in sending it was all the more important, since it represented an admission that the Deutsche Kolonialgesellschaft für Südwestafrika was not capable of exercising rights of sovereignty in the colony. This was the second important fundamental step, following the sending out of a government Commissioner in 1885, in the transformation of the 'company colony' into a Crown Colony.[34]

The dispatch of von François was also characteristic of another process that in its essence was to be repeated quite frequently up until the 1904–08 Herero and Nama War: namely, that the sending of official representatives of the German Empire resulted, as soon as they got into difficulties, in further and larger commitments of manpower by the Imperial Government,[35] since for nationalistic and propagandistic reasons it was inconceivable that the possibility of suffering a defeat in South West Africa should even be entertained.

Contrary to his instructions, however, which were to abstain from any hostilities directed against the Herero, von François aroused their anger against him so quickly and to such an extent that he was forced, in a military stalemate, to 'dig in' within the confines of his camp. Although the Herero were not able to drive him and his soldiers out of there, neither were they able to decide the conflict in their own favour. The Herero increasingly feared that as soon as the German reinforcements arrived they would join with the Witbooi in a campaign against them, so in May 1890 Maharero accepted the *Schutzvertrag* (Protection Treaty) with the German Empire that he had rejected two years before, hoping to exploit German power – which, however, he still very much overestimated – to his own ends.[36] But this submission to the German Empire did not bring him any military advantage, as only two months later, when the Witbooi attacked again, von François denied him assistance – this time standing on his instructions, which required him to keep out of 'native affairs'. During the conquest of Otjimbingwe by the Nama there were even scenes of open fraternization between Nama and German officers.[37]

On 7 October 1890 Maharero died; and the dispute that then broke out as to who was to succeed him eroded still further the united Herero front against both Hendrik Witbooi and the Germans. Under Herero inheritance law, which provided for both matrilineal and patrilineal succession, there were five people – Samuel Maharero, Riarua, Kaviseri, Nicodemus Kavikuna and Tjetjo – competing for the late chief's legacy, which encompassed not only his material possessions but also the dignity of ruler over Okahandja, and thus a certain degree of paramountcy over the other leaders. It was ultimately Riarua who succeeded to this position, as well as gaining possession, jointly with Kaviseri and Tjetjo, of what remained of Maharero's cattle after Hendrik Witbooi's raids. Samuel Maharero, who was largely excluded from the succession because he had been baptized a Christian, retained only his father's house. He was, however, able to gain the support of the missionaries and of the White traders who had settled in Okahandja for his other claims, which were much more far-reaching. In order to secure his claim to lordship over Okahandja he asked von François for his support, deliberately setting his hopes on the fact that under German concepts of inheritance law he would be regarded as the legitimate heir, being Maharero's eldest son. And von François did indeed confirm Samuel Maharero's claims, without however committing himself to affording him any actual aid for enforcing them. But this meant that Samuel Maharero, under constant threat from Hendrik Witbooi and lacking recognition from his own people, had placed himself in a dangerous state of dependency on the Germans.[38]

In 1892 an understanding was reached between Samuel Maharero and Hendrik Witbooi, since both had realized that the German 'Schutztruppe' – the so-called Protection Force that was in effect a colonial army – represented a greater danger to both of them than they did to each other.[39] Although this understanding really meant that von François' original mission of bringing about 'pacification' had been accomplished, at the beginning of 1893 the Colonial Administration in Berlin increased the strength of the Schutztruppe to two hundred men and instructed the Imperial Commissioner to 'maintain German rule under all circumstances'. Whether this was to be achieved by defensive or offensive action was left to him.[40]

Thus the objective of keeping the peace had been superseded by that of maintaining German rule. Von François was therefore able to regard himself as acting in accordance with the intentions of the Colonial Administration in Berlin when on 12 April 1893, in the face of a situation in which the common front that had been formed by the Herero of Okahandja and the Witbooi could indeed be seen as a threat to German rule, he attacked Hendrik Witbooi's fortified Hoornkrans camp without any prior warning.[41]

This massacre[42] marked the beginning of a guerrilla war lasting almost two years, which von François was not able to win.[43] Furthermore, successful attacks by the Witbooi on German military positions and traders seriously damaged the reputation of the Schutztruppe with the African population, so that Hendrik Witbooi 'appeared as the victor both in his own and in other people's eyes, simply because he had succeeded in keeping up his resistance for so long'.[44]

The Consolidation of German Rule: Chiefs, 'Pacification' and a Modern Administration

It was not, however, in the interests of the German government to enter into a long-drawn-out colonial war. Although Chancellor von Caprivi, addressing the Reichstag on 1 March 1893, had come down definitively on the side of permanent possession of South West Africa and had distanced himself from earlier plans to hold the colony merely as a bargaining counter for use in negotiating settlements with other European powers, he was nevertheless unwilling to contemplate the use of armed force to impose the progressive colonization of the territory: 'We do not want to wage war; we want to gain mastery over the country progressively and consolidate our rule without bloodshed. We do have South West Africa; it is now German territory and must remain German territory'.[45] This position presumably reflected not so much humanitarian reservations against waging war as concern about the costs that a military operation would occasion. The German Empire was not, however, prepared to remain passive in the face of the humiliation of its forces, and in 1893 it sent out to South West Africa on a fact-finding mission the man who was to do most to shape the affairs of the colony in the following eleven years: Theodor Leutwein. On him too, Chancellor von Caprivi impressed the need to pay due attention to the limited resources:

> Your Excellency should always keep in mind the consideration that our position of power with regard to the natives is to be maintained under all circumstances and more and more consolidated. ...

> I would be interested to receive proposals that are susceptible of enhancing the effectiveness of our forces. But everything possible must be done to avoid expending more resources than those provided for in the draft budget for 1894–95.[46]

The dispatch of Leutwein prepared the way for the withdrawal of von François;[47] Leutwein's task was to initiate the extension of colonial control to cover the whole of the territory, but without violent conquest. But he too saw this in terms of the deployment of military power, as he was of the opinion that the government had already hesitated 'for almost too long ... to demonstrate its power to the natives'. What Bismarck had once said about the merchant going ahead and the soldier and administrator following might be a well-turned formulation; 'but nevertheless, particularly when we are faced with such warlike natives as are to be found in South West Africa, the soldier must not be too far behind'. It was not possible, Leutwein maintained, to operate with the concept of the 'governing merchant' alone.[48]

Although the responsible authorities in Berlin would have preferred, for reasons of cost, to bring the campaign that von François was conducting to a peaceful conclusion, they were not prepared to endanger the reputation of the army or jeopardize German rule. Where this was threatened they gave their backing to military operations, despite that being contrary to the orders that had originally been issued, and dispatched reinforcements. But by doing so, they lost control over military activities to the commanders on the spot, whose readiness to undertake military operations drew the German government more and more deeply into the existing conflicts.

Leutwein's most important task was to subdue Hendrik Witbooi, since his continuing resistance was endangering German rule itself. He succeeded in doing this surprisingly quickly after the arrival of further reinforcements, 200 man strong, with a contingent of 40 Basters from Rehoboth also fighting on the German side.[49] After some intense combat, and in order to avoid the danger of a renewed, long-drawn-out and expensive guerrilla war, Leutwein accepted Hendrik Witbooi's offer of submission.[50] Although some elements among the settlers were demanding that he should be shot, Hendrik Witbooi retained his office as *Kaptein* – 'Captain' or 'Chief' – of his people.[51] The war was ended by the conclusion of a Protection Treaty, with an additional protocol in which Hendrik Witbooi even committed himself to providing military assistance to the Germans.[52]

It was only by skilfully exploiting the tensions and power rivalries existing within the African population that Leutwein was able to fulfil his instructions to enforce the German claim to sovereignty in the territory, despite not being able to expect any notable strengthening of his forces. But he did not restrict himself to securing German rule: he also systematically extended German influence. In contrast to von François, his concept of the establishment of colonial rule was something that went beyond a purely military victory. Being a far more skilful diplomat and political tactician than his predecessor, he developed a technique of government that left the traditional African elites still formally occupying their positions, as long as they were willing to submit to the principles of keeping the peace and of the state monopoly on the use of force – principles that he considered to be indispensable to any modern rule over a territory. Hostilities within the African population, feuds between different nations and cattle raiding were thus things that could not be tolerated in the modern state that he sought to establish, as it would only be through internal stability that the country could be made attractive to settlers and investors, who in their turn were essential for the economic development of the colony.

The perfect opportunity to gain control over the majority of the Herero more or less fell into Leutwein's lap even before his victory over Hendrik Witbooi. As soon as the threat to the Herero from the Nama had been eliminated, Samuel Maharero, who, as already described, had usurped the position of Paramount Chief of the Herero in succession to his father contrary to the tradition of his people, came under pressure from the other Herero leaders he had displaced. In

June 1894 supporters of Riarua drove him and his followers out of Okahandja. Faced with imminent defeat, Samuel Maharero appealed to Leutwein for assistance.[53] Leutwein reacted promptly, since 'such a favourable opportunity to intervene in the affairs of the Herero was not likely to arise again in the near future'.[54] Although Leutwein was well aware of the fact that according to Herero tradition Samuel Maharero was not his father's rightful successor, he exploited the 'favourable opportunity' to give him his support, as he thought it would be much more advantageous to the German cause for the Herero to be divided in future than for them to be united. Ultimately it was Leutwein who decided the conflict in Samuel Maharero's favour by military means.[55]

As a result, Samuel Maharero was able to secure for himself considerable prosperity and the status of leader of all the Herero;[56] but at the same time he made himself dependent on the Germans. As he had to rely on his alliance with the colonial power to preserve his position as Paramount Chief, his freedom of manoeuvre in respect of the German administration was severely limited. Leutwein was now able to implement his 'divide and rule' policy, leaving the Germans holding the balance between the various local factions: 'Even if the Paramount Chief had little power himself, any sub-chief who was planning to rebel nevertheless had to reckon with him, and this would always ensure that Samuel's direct supporters were on our side.'[57] As a clear and visible sign of this change in the power relationships, Samuel Maharero was obliged to agree to the erection of a German fort in Okahandja,[58] whereby 'the most important place in Hereroland was incorporated into the sphere in which the colonial authorities exercised effective power'.[59]

However, it is also clear that the frictions existing within Herero society were a decisive factor in the success of this policy. As the Herero had not yet completed the establishment of their own polity, or at least that polity was not yet consolidated, insofar as a multiplicity of leaders were competing to attain the position of Paramount Chief, it was not all that difficult to achieve this success. But the Africans were by no means purely passive victims of a policy of promoting divisions directed at them from outside; rather, it was Samuel Maharero himself who drew upon German support to satisfy his own personal ambition, and thus made it possible for the Germans to attain a position in which they were able to play a decisive role despite the inadequacy of their military strength.[60]

Leutwein was not, however, content with a superficial 'pacification' of the country and the formal recognition of German rule. He also set about actively involving himself in ensuring that the peace was kept and the state monopoly on the use of force upheld.[61] Any disputes between individual African leaders had to be submitted to arbitration by the German governor. If any African chief ignored this rule, he had to expect drastic sanctions to be taken. For example, Leutwein had the leader of the Khauas Nama, Andreas Lambert, condemned to death by a court martial and executed. This allowed Leutwein to demonstrate that he would take rigorous measures against any breach of the peace; in addition, the official court procedure was intended to show that German rule was not arbitrary but was based on law and order,[62] even though this order was grounded on military force and not voluntary submission. Andreas Lambert's successor was appointed only provisionally, and was forced to sign a Protection Treaty. Only a month after the execution of Lambert, Leutwein was able to compel the Fransman Nama under Simon Kopper to enter into a Protection Treaty as well; so that by the end of 1894 he had succeeded in getting the whole of southern and central Namibia to submit to formal German sovereignty.[63]

Leutwein and Samuel Maharero, working in close cooperation, now set about asserting in practice the latter's position as Paramount Chief of all the Herero, which the other Herero leaders had acknowledged only under compulsion, and weakening the rival centres of power that still existed.[64] The initiative for such activities came sometimes from the one side and sometimes from the other. Between 1894 and 1896 Herero leaders were humiliated before the very eyes of their followers by demonstrations of military might, and forced into submission. Everywhere they had to accept the redrawing of the boundaries of their territories; this generally involved ceding areas to Samuel Maharero, who in turn placed part of his newly acquired land at the disposal of the German settlers who were now coming into the territory in increasing numbers. The Herero who had traditionally lived on these lands were forcibly expelled and some of their livestock was confiscated, the proceeds from the sale of the animals being shared equally between Samuel Maharero and the German administration. In this way, Hereroland was for the first time given fixed borders laid down by treaty, while land was simultaneously made available for German settlement. Thus the original claim of the Herero to possess the whole country was replaced by partition – an area for White settlement and then African land. This had far-reaching social consequences: the acceptance of German rule that was associated with Leutwein's 'divide and rule' policy, which was forcefully imposed by his readiness, conspicuously demonstrated, to make use of military force, together with the compulsion to keep the peace and to recognize the monopoly on the use of force of the fledgling colonial state, undermined the positions of the African rulers. The voluntary or forced cession of land to the settlers who were now flooding into the colony, and the associated resettlement of Herero from those areas now earmarked for German settlement into the remaining Herero areas, diminished in size as they were, resulted in the overpopulation and general impoverishment of these areas. The curtailment of the chiefs' traditional sources of income meant that they were no longer in a position to compensate for this impoverishment and to maintain their systems of patronage. As a result, the loyalty of their respective clienteles declined, leading to enormous tensions within traditional societies. The limitation on the extent of each Chief's territory prevented the emigration of impoverished or disaffected Herero to more distant areas, a phenomenon that in the past had contributed to diffusing tensions within societies without bloodshed. The requirement to keep the peace made it impossible for any ruler affected to compensate for the loss of prosperity, either by expanding the territory under his control or by acquiring new resources through cattle raids.

Leutwein was concerned to achieve a balance, a stalemate, between the newly installed Paramount Chief and those rivals of his who, although their claims had been passed over, were still influential and were also not to be underestimated in terms of their military potential. He was therefore very careful to ensure that the drastic measures taken to enforce the newly concluded border treaties and the civil peace that he had imposed were implemented with the support of the ruler of Okahandja. On tour he was always accompanied by Samuel Maharero or an emissary of his. Herero auxiliary contingents not only reinforced Leutwein's military might, but also diverted some of the discontent generated by the measures in the direction of the Paramount Chief. In this way, Leutwein forestalled the formation of an alliance of all the Herero against him, and kept Samuel Maharero constantly dependent on support from the German Schutztruppe. The reason Leutwein's policy of 'divide and rule' was so successful was that superficially its objectives coincided with those of Samuel Maharero; and he in his turn was by no means merely a puppet in the hands of the German governor, but sought to instrumentalize him for his own purposes.

The excessive levels of human population and livestock that many districts had to support as a result of Leutwein's and Samuel Maharero's policies were also in part responsible for the devastating consequences of the major natural disaster that shook African society at the end of the nineteenth century and accelerated the catastrophic sequence of events leading to full-scale war in the years 1904 to 1908: the rinderpest epidemic of 1897.[65]

Rinderpest appeared in Africa in the late 1880s, and by 1892 had already reached present-day Zambia. After its advance had been held up by the Zambezi for a few years, it was introduced into the colony by ox treks linking the trading centre on Lake Ngami in the Bechuanaland Protectorate with the colony, and also by wild animals. It then spread quickly throughout the territory. In view of the density of the population, which in some places had already led to all the available grazing land being put to intensive use, there was no way in which infected herds could be placed in quarantine when the epidemic broke out.

The disastrous impact of rinderpest led to far-reaching changes in the social and economic structures of the Herero. A large proportion – in some cases up to 95 per cent – of livestock died, cattle prices collapsed, and many Herero saw their livelihoods destroyed. 'Effectively in the space of a few months Herero society was completely bankrupted and the Herero transformed into paupers.'[66]

The rinderpest outbreak also triggered other epidemics that spread rapidly. The contamination of watering places by the decomposing bodies of cattle, the eating of cattle that had died of disease and ubiquitous undernourishment promoted outbreaks of sicknesses, which raged among the Herero between March and August 1898 and claimed thousands of victims, especially in the overpopulated areas along the Swakop, Okahandja and Nossob Rivers where the recently dispossessed Herero had settled.[67] The drought that prevailed between 1899 and 1902 further reduced any chance the Africans might have had of conducting autonomous agriculture. The economic and patronage systems that had supported the traditional elites collapsed completely. This erosion of their social and political structures also diminished the Herero's ability to defend themselves against the ever-increasing encroachments and attacks by Whites. Due to their general impoverishment, the Herero were also compelled for the first time to sell their labour on a large scale to White farmers and entrepreneurs, and to the Colonial Administration.

The reduction of the Herero to destitution also substantially enhanced their willingness to undertake acts of desperation; and this meant that Leutwein's policy of gradually accustoming the Africans to German rule had failed. The African population no longer had the time it needed to adapt to the new situation. The rinderpest outbreak accelerated a line of development that ultimately led to the African nations having to give up their traditional way of life and independent economic status, to be gradually transformed into an army of labourers for the colonial state and its newly arrived settlers. At least for a large proportion of the Herero, this was the final act in a process that had begun in 1884 with the inconspicuous arrival of three German civil servants.

But it was not only the limitation of the power of the chiefs or the social disintegration resulting from loss of territory, resettlement and rinderpest that led to the erosion of the Africans' traditional way of life; it was also the increasing penetration of the country by the German administration. Contrary to the superficial image of the 'Leutwein system', the Administration did from the very beginning undertake measures and issue legal instruments and regulations that had an immediate impact on the Africans' lives, since the building up of a German administration covering all areas of the territory was a central component of the modern state that Leutwein was seeking to create. As early as 1894, after his victory over Hendrik Witbooi, Leutwein and the then chief official of Otjimbingwe District, Friedrich von Lindequist, drew up a civil administration plan under which the colony was divided into the three *Bezirke* of Keetmanshoop, Windhoek und Otjimbingwe. Each was administered by an authority called the *Bezirkshauptmannschaft* (District Captaincy) and headed by an official called the *Bezirkshauptmann* (District Captain): these were renamed *Bezirksamt* (District Office) and *Bezirksamtmann* (District Officer) respectively in 1898.[68] By 1903 the number of *Bezirke* had already increased to six,[69] the various administrative centres being established to take account of military exigencies.[70] The Administration was headed by the Governor, who was at one and the same time the head of the civil administration and the Commander in Chief of the Schutztruppe.

Since more and more Africans were being employed by Whites, their working conditions needed to be regulated. As Africans could not bring any kind of legal proceedings against Whites, it was the Administration that had to deal with any complaints when there were differences of opinion as to whether a contract of employment had been violated. While the agreements with the individual chiefs to determine the boundaries of their jurisdictions and the subsequent resettlement measures had created zones in which the traditional African authorities no longer had any influence and where German farmers could be settled, the need for labour brought African workers back into these areas – where, however, they were now directly subject to the German administration. Although it was still possible, thanks to the fact that the colonial state did not have the resources that it needed to impose its will, for these workers to leave the farms and flee to the areas ruled by their chiefs, the claim of the German authorities to exercise direct jurisdiction over them could no longer be made to go away.

While at the top of the hierarchy Governor Leutwein was pursuing his strategy of indirect rule, which followed the British model by involving the traditional chiefs, at a lower level, namely that of the District administrations, a development towards direct rule was taking place that would find its full expression, after the end of the Herero and Nama War, in the Native Ordinances of 1907. Under pressure from the settlers, and confronted with everyday problems of coexistence between Africans and Whites and of how they could work together, District officials were advocating ordinances that reinforced the claim to exercise direct jurisdiction over Africans as well. In individual districts, for example, Pass Ordinances were promulgated which were intended to make it possible to control the movements of the African population, and also Master and Servant Ordinances to regulate conditions of employment, as well as Labour Ordinances that already anticipated the introduction of a compulsion to enter into an employment relationship. These developments will be analysed more closely in Chapter 2, which covers the Native Ordinances of 1907.

Leutwein accepted these measures, even though he did not yet introduce them throughout the territory. The fact that he did not is likely to have had something to do with the power relationships within the colony, which on the one hand led him to expect that there would be resistance to the measures, and on the other meant that there were still sufficient areas that Africans could withdraw to in order to be out of reach of the Germans. This was also, for example, the reason that Leutwein gave as late as 1903 for rejecting proposals to introduce a universal Native Poll Tax, although he expressly emphasized that it would be 'a nice idea to use this type of tax to force the natives to work'. He was afraid that those Africans who had already entered German service would be able to go back and rejoin their communities; he did, however, say that he would like to reconsider the matter of a Native Tax later, when the cattle disease epidemics had been overcome.[71]

Whereas Leutwein had effectively turned the Chiefs into agents of the German Empire, exercising its sovereign powers, the actual civil servants were busy issuing legal instruments and regulations intended to place the African population directly within the reach of the German administration. As a result, conflicts were constantly arising, and it was only the Herero and Nama War of 1904–08 that led to direct rule prevailing.

It is easy to see the effects of these tensions in the administration of justice. If administrative measures were transmitted indirectly to the 'ordinary' Africans through their traditional rulers, this meant that the Chiefs also retained formal legal jurisdiction over their subjects. But this coexistence of two legal systems was a mere fiction. The principle that Whites were only to be tried by other Whites could not fail to lead to collisions with this type of indirect rule whenever there were legal disputes between Whites and Africans. Jurisdiction in such cases lay with the German Administration or the German courts, although the Protection Treaties that governed this did in some cases provide for African assessors to take part in the proceedings.[72] In the reporting year 1902/03, for example, 799 sentences were pronounced against Africans in criminal cases, with 473 people being sentenced to corporal punishment and 326 to imprisonment.[73] The effect of such massive interference in the sphere of authority of the African leaders, who had previously been the supreme judges of their subjects, was intensified even more by the fact that Leutwein, right from the beginning of his period of office, quite deliberately used cases in which Whites had been killed by Africans as pretexts for his policy of subjugation and to justify his interventions in African affairs.

Murders of Africans by Whites were also taken into the jurisdiction of the German administration. Between 1894 and 1900 the deaths of four African men and one African woman at the hands of Whites were punished by prison terms of between three months and three years, although the frequent imposition of corporal punishment is likely to have led to far more deaths,[74] while fifteen Africans were sentenced to death for the killings of six Whites.[75] As Leutwein himself later admitted, 'the life of a white man was judged to be worth more ... than that of a native'. In retrospect, the punishment of the Whites appeared to him to have been 'indisputably too lenient', which he attributed to the fact that 'the white judges always found reasons to be lenient towards their fellow whites, and considered the offences to be merely manslaughter'. This, he went on, was a distinction that the Africans would not have been able to understand, since for them 'murder and manslaughter [were] one and the same thing'.[76]

The fact that the African rulers were deprived of any way of dealing themselves with assaults on their people, and thereby of affording them protection, represented a serious weakening of their position. Furthermore, the removal of such assaults from the legal jurisdiction of the Africans, and the resulting leniency, consolidated the 'position of mastery over the natives that the whites assumed they held',[77] and thus provoked an increase in the number of such assaults, including upon

African women. As a result of the almost 'complete lack of rights of the Africans in respect of the Germans',[78] African men were no longer able to protect their wives and daughters against abuse by White men, cases of which were constantly on the increase as a result of the shortage of White women. When Africans were killed defending their families the German authorities did not generally proceed against the murderers, while at the same time the courts and the Administration completely ignored the sexual abuse of African women.[79]

The African population was similarly disadvantaged in civil litigation between Whites and Africans, such as arose especially in connection with credit transactions. In cases relating to debt the responsible administrative authorities generally ordered the distraint of the Africans' livestock and land, thereby accelerating the transfer of both into White ownership.[80]

For the Africans, the principle of security under the law propagated by Leutwein as a necessary precondition for economic development, which implied the application of German law throughout the colony, meant submission to a foreign legal system that did not even pretend to be able to take any account of the conceptual differences that prevailed between the legal systems of the Herero, the Nama and other African nations. In legal disputes between Whites and Africans – the latter's ignorance of German law made it rare for them to bring legal action to enforce their rights – ultimate jurisdiction always lay with a German court, which generally rated African witnesses as possessing a very low level of credibility; legal security for Whites therefore inevitably meant a high measure of legal insecurity for Africans. Thus even before the war of 1904–08, the African population was already effectively, albeit in a covert and undeclared manner, subject to German laws and regulations in important areas of their lives, despite the fact that superficially their traditional social structures still appeared to be intact.

The opportunity to completely substitute direct rule for indirect rule was then provided by the outbreak of war against the Herero in 1904. The threat of military humiliation in this war caused the German government to massively increase its commitment, and so at last made it possible for the colonial authorities to deploy the military strength required for the implementation of direct rule. The newly arrived troops were concerned only to achieve a quick military victory, without paying any regard to the victims among the African population. Furthermore, like their commander General von Trotha, they had in their heads a stereotyped concept of a 'race war' that could only end with the annihilation of their opponents.

'Native Policy' in a State of Emergency: The Herero and Nama War

The creeping but constant loss of territory, the deliberate humiliation of traditional leaders, the breakdown of inherited social structures as a result of the population being restricted to an ever-diminishing area of land, and the economic disaster of the rinderpest outbreak: all these factors had a severe negative impact on internal cohesion within Herero society. In addition, the settlers who were entering the country in ever-greater numbers were increasingly conducting themselves as members of a 'master race', who sought confrontation instead of coexistence and who violated the property or even took the lives of Africans without the chiefs having any way of obtaining recourse against them. The disaffection triggered within local societies by these circumstances only required a spark to ignite desperate acts of resistance. This point was reached at the turn of the year 1903/04, when a local conflict with the Bondelswarts in the south of the territory set a train of events in motion that ultimately culminated in the genocidal war.

The Herero and Nama War differed from previous conflicts not only in respect of its scale – with the greater part of the Herero and Nama entering into hostilities against the Germans as the war proceeded – but also in that the German war aims had changed. Instead of seeking to bring about the submission of the defeated enemies and their integration into the structures of indirect rule, the objective now was to totally destroy the hostile African polities and to expel from the colony, or even kill, all who belonged to them. Responsibility for achieving this genocidal objective lay with the army commanders who had come to the country in the course of the massive reinforcement of the Schutztruppe, and above all with Lieutenant General Lothar von Trotha. He was in complete ignorance of the situation within the colony; he had no respect at all for African life or African culture and no regard even for the needs of the colonial economy, which was dependent on African labour. Filled with the idea that a 'race war' had now broken out, he initiated the genocide. Although he was prevented by his superiors in Berlin from completing his work of extermination, the genocide continued in the prison camps. These camps were also symbolic of the new direction of Native Policy, signifying as they did the most direct subjection of the previously free African population to whatever directives were issued by the representatives of the German state. Thus despite the fact that a certain degree of moderation crept back into the legal codification of Native Policy that was undertaken at the same time, nothing was done to reverse the fundamental change from the indirect rule practised by Leutwein to the new direct German rule.

The war aims debated among White settlers, colonial administrators and military personnel during the war – namely the alternatives of complete annihilation or forced labour – continued to provide the framework for the political discourse when the war was over. In the face of the measures actually implemented, which ranged from internment in labour camps to deportation to arbitrary shootings, any scruples that might previously have existed about the need to pay at least some regard to the Africans' interests were swept away, leaving the action to be taken to be determined by the most extreme White positions. On the German side, the last taboos were broken with regard to what was permissible in respect of the African population. Thanks moreover to the vast number of victims on the African side, the war at last created the requisite conditions under which a policy drawn up by bureaucrats as a theoretical model could now be implemented free of all inhibitions.

The Genocidal Conduct of the War

The chain of events that ultimately led to the almost complete destruction of Herero and Nama society was triggered by what should have remained a limited conflict in the south of the colony, where the Bondelswarts started to undertake resistance in October 1903 after the German administration had interfered in their internal affairs; in the course of this, the District Officer of Warmbad, Lieutenant Walter Jobst, and two other Germans were shot dead.[81]

Although Leutwein condemned the actions of the German Administration that had given rise to the incident, he could not allow the killing of German officials by the Bondelswarts to remain unatoned. He declared a State of War, and put a reward on the head of each of the Bondelswarts who had been involved. Extremist settlers and representatives of the land concession companies publicly demanded the abolition of the office of Kaptein of the Bondelswarts and the resettlement of this small ethnic group in reservations; some even spoke of the opportunity to destroy them – a style of rhetoric that remained prevalent during the war of the following years, and made a major contribution to the spread and radicalization of the conflicts.

Despite aspects foreshadowing those paradigms that would prevail during subsequent conflicts,[82] the political and military dimensions of the dispute itself were kept within limits and the matter was soon brought to an end, since the officer exercising command in the area until Leutwein reached Keetmanshoop, Captain Johannes von Fiedler, had already arranged a ceasefire before Leutwein arrived. Although this meant that Leutwein was not able to achieve his war aim of 'eliminating the enemy in Warmbad District',[83] for which reason he was anything but pleased with this rapid cessation of hostilities, he had no choice but to enter into peace negotiations with the Bondelswarts;[84] for in the meantime war had broken out with the Herero, requiring his immediate return to the central area of the colony.[85]

There, the fact that Hereroland had been left denuded of German troops as a result of their having largely been redeployed to the south was a major factor contributing to the outbreak of the Herero War. Scholars disagree as to who fired the first shot.[86] What is certain, however, is that Samuel Maharero and his people launched an unexpectedly successful offensive on 12 January 1904, and within a few days had occupied the whole of Hereroland except for the military posts. In the process they had killed over a hundred German men, and in a few cases also women and children, on the farms; but they failed to exploit these initial successes to achieve a rapid and decisive victory over the Schutztruppe, who were still ensconced in their fortified positions,[87] and so allowed the Germans to strengthen their forces in Hereroland by bringing back the units that had been redeployed to the south, or replacing them with additional manpower from Germany.[88]

But not all the Herero were yet involved in the hostilities. It was the numerous attacks and massacres carried out by the German side in response to the first reports of the outbreak of war, attacks that were directed indiscriminately even against Herero who had taken no part in the fighting until then, that aroused fear among them that the Germans would nevertheless hold them responsible too. In addition, there were numerous threats from German settlers and army personnel, which caused the missionary August Elger to make his bleak prediction in February 1904: 'There is no doubt but that the Germans will exact a terrible revenge.'[89] It was ultimately the fear that the Germans were about to launch a large-scale offensive that drove even chiefs who were critical of the war into active participation in the fighting on Samuel Maharero's side.[90]

Samuel Maharero did not, however, succeed in gaining allies from outside the Herero. Only the Ovambo Chief Nehale of Oshitambi was involved in the fighting for a short time, after an emissary from Samuel Maharero had called upon him and his brother Kambonde to join in the resistance. On 28 January 1904 his troops fell upon Fort Namutoni and captured it, the German garrison having fled the fortress precipitately after the first attack. But his primary intention was not in fact to support the Herero but to destroy Namutoni, in order to regain control himself over the copper deposits at Tsumeb and prevent the Germans from establishing a bridgehead from which they would be able to conquer Ovamboland. Once he had achieved this objective, he took no further part in the fighting. King Kambonde, on the other hand, distanced himself from this operation and maintained neutrality throughout the war. Nor did the other Ovambo join in the fighting in Hereroland, even though in subsequent years supplies and ammunition reached the Africans fighting in the south via Ovamboland, and numerous fugitives, above all Herero, found refuge among the Ovambo.[91]

Samuel Maharero's attempts to win over the Baster Kaptein Hermanus van Wijk and the Nama leader Hendrik Witbooi as allies[92] were equally unsuccessful. Not only did they both refuse to support him in the way he had hoped; they even took part in the war on the other side. As during the conflict with the Bondelswarts, in which Witbooi Nama and Rehoboth Basters had supported the German forces,[93] so too their contingents of auxiliaries now fought on the German side. Samuel Maharero, by contrast, found no one to support him, even though his threat to declare war on the Basters if they continued to give refuge to Germans led to the expulsion of Germans from some Baster settlements where they were living.[94]

It was only thanks to the Marines from the cruiser *Habicht*, who landed in Swakopmund on 18 January 1904, having been summoned by telegraph from Cape Town on 11 January, one day before the outbreak of hostilities,[95] and the Naval Expeditionary Corps that arrived from Germany on 9 February,[96] that the Germans were able to avert the impending defeat. As the mood of hysterical fanaticism among the settlers and the attention that the war had quickly attracted in Germany now prevented Governor Leutwein from achieving the rapid peace agreement he would have liked to have concluded in order to avoid having to conduct a campaign of annihilation,[97] the war began to gain a fateful momentum of its own.

Immediately after the outbreak of hostilities demands were heard from the settlers for a fundamental revision of Leutwein's Native Policy, which in their view was much too lenient. If there had already been criticism of this policy earlier, the opportunity now seemed to have arisen to bring about radical changes in power and property relationships. In the demand for the 'complete disarmament' of the Africans and the 'confiscation of all their lands and livestock', in order to 'enable calm and confidence to be restored among the whites',[98] the desire for retribution was mixed up with the prospect of direct economic benefit for the colonial state and its settlers. The farmers and entrepreneurs hoped that such a change in policy would bring them not only land and livestock but also cheap labour, as the local population, having been dispossessed in this way, would have no alternative but to seek dependent employment. But the horror at the deaths of so many settlers was also reflected in more extreme demands: many now spoke of 'clearing up with them, hanging them, shooting them down to the very last man, with no mercy', as the missionary August Elger of the Rhenish Mission reported.[99]

Demands for the destruction of the Africans' political structures and of their autonomous economic existence on the one hand, and for the physical destruction of the entire nation on the other, became the two poles around which the formulation of war aims orbited. While the latter could be argued for on the basis of the ideological concept of German South West Africa as a settler colony to be created 'purely for whites', and as far as possible without an African population, the former focused on the importance of African labour to the economic development of the territory.

During the first few months of the war, the extremist demand for genocidal measures became so strong that Leutwein, who was himself demanding the unconditional surrender of the Herero, found himself having to warn against 'ill-considered voices … that now want to see the Herero completely annihilated'; since a nation of 60,000–70,000 people 'could not be exterminated just like that', and in any case the Herero were still needed as 'small-scale cattle breeders and particularly as labourers'. He did, however, agree that they should be rendered 'politically dead', that their political and social organization should be destroyed, and they should be concentrated in reservations 'that would be just barely sufficient for their needs'. Africans who had not taken part in the resistance would also have to submit to disarmament and to 'confinement in reservations'. All African prisoners were to be brought before courts martial for punishment, and if they were 'found guilty of having pillaged farms, or even of having murdered peaceful residents, in every case be punished with death'.[100]

Leutwein regarded the Herero involved in the fighting not as legitimate combatants, but as bandits guilty of murder and pillage who could not expect any leniency even if they surrendered. Only where it was a question of whether the death penalty should be imposed was the level of individual guilt to be examined. During the first few months of the war, however, there were no fair legal proceedings, and many of the captured Africans were simply shot, with or without trial. In addition, the settlers who had been conscripted as soon as the war broke out gave no quarter when on patrol;[101] and the Marines from the cruiser *Habicht* who had arrived in haste in January to assist the resident forces had committed massacres that had struck terror into the hearts of the Herero, and thus driven even Herero who had not been involved in the war until then to take up arms.[102]

With this mood prevailing, prisoners were seldom taken. Although Leutwein, in May 1905, denied the allegation that there was an order stating that no prisoners were to be taken, he nevertheless had to admit that after everything that had happened, German soldiers would 'not be particularly indulgent' in their manner of proceeding, and that up to that point no unwounded prisoners had in fact been taken. Even Africans who were captured 'as cattle thieves and marauders away from the actual conflict' were regularly sentenced to death by the courts.[103] But in a war in which there were no formally constituted combatant units on the African side, almost anyone could be considered to be a 'marauder'.

Leutwein was increasingly finding that power was slipping out of his grasp. As early as 9 February 1904 an order had reached him stating that the Great General Staff in Berlin had taken over the direction of the campaign.[104] Scarcely two weeks later he was forbidden to conduct any peace negotiations without the express authorization of the Emperor.[105] The fact that, contrary to the practice during earlier, smaller conflicts, the General Staff in Berlin had immediately taken control of the campaign meant that both the Colonial Department of the Foreign Office in Berlin and the Administration in Windhoek were deprived of their influence over the conduct of the war and the war aims.[106] The circumstance that events were no longer being determined in accordance with the principles of colonial policy that had been pursued up until then represents a decisive departure from the way that previous military operations had been conducted.

Lieutenant General Lothar von Trotha[107] was appointed Commander in Chief. He was responsible directly to the Emperor, receiving his instructions through the Chief of the General Staff. Theodor Leutwein remained Governor, but no longer had any means of exerting influence on the further conduct of the campaign, since von Trotha was not even required to consult with him.[108]

Lieutenant General von Trotha had no knowledge of either the country or its people, but was obsessed with the idea of a coming 'race war' that would end in the annihilation of one of the belligerent parties, but in which there was no room for any humane treatment of the enemy. His view was that Africans would 'yield only to force', and it was his intention to exercise that force 'with blatant terrorism and even cruelty', and to annihilate 'the rebellious tribes with rivers of blood'.[109] Even with hindsight he continued to justify his brutal policy, since, as he said, a war in Africa simply could not 'be conducted in accordance with the rules of the Geneva Convention'.[110]

Von Trotha's intention to annihilate the enemy was manifested right from the beginning in his uncompromising attitude to the matter of prisoners of war. Enemy warriors were to be shot immediately. Even while he was still on his way to the territory, on board the steamer *Eleonore Woermann*, he declared a State of War pursuant to Article 68 of the Constitution of the German Empire, and decreed that every commanding officer was authorized 'to have coloured inhabitants of the country who are caught in the act of carrying out treasonable activities against German troops, for example all rebels who are found under arms with belligerent intent, shot without any prior court proceedings, as has been customary practice in this war up to now'. All other Africans 'arrested by German military personnel on suspicion of punishable activities' were to be 'sentenced by special field courts'.[111] Thus all warriors were to be executed, and only unarmed Africans who were not involved in the fighting could be taken prisoner. With this proclamation, von Trotha gave his retrospective approval to the shooting of prisoners, which had already been practised on the German side from the earliest days of the war. Even if it is possible to attribute, as Leutwein did, such conduct by German soldiers to the panic prevailing after the outbreak of war, and even if the soldiers were able to believe that their actions were covered by the laws of war, the same cannot be said of von Trotha's manner of conduct. Whereas the laws of war aim to mitigate the effects of hostilities, von Trotha's motivation was completely the opposite, in that he extended the circle of those affected by the hostilities to include practically all his opponents. His order to shoot prisoners made massacres and terrorism into systematic instruments in the German conduct of the war. Anyone who offered resistance to the Germans was to be shot. But the fact that von Trotha's orders superficially provided for due legal process no doubt contributed to the degree of acceptance of his extermination policy among his officers.

With the appointment of von Trotha, the idea of the war of annihilation prevailed over the possibility of settling a conflict without an all-out bloodbath. The reasons put forward by Leutwein for practising leniency towards the Herero no longer counted for anything, as von Trotha remained insensible to all humanitarian arguments – and to all economic ones as well, for example that of how important 'native' labour was to the colony. Nothing counted for him except what he considered to be the military exigencies. He dismissed

Leutwein's appeals to conduct the war in such a way 'that the Herero nation is preserved', and insisted that the Governor must allow him 'to conduct the campaign as [he] saw fit'.[112] Pointing out that South West Africa was the one colony 'in which a European can himself work to provide for his family',[113] he simply set aside the views of a Governor who had occupied that office since 1894. He also ignored the opinion of other people who had known South West Africa for many years, and who pleaded for the capitulation of any Herero leaders who were ready to submit to be accepted. When, for example, the Herero leader Salatiel Kambazembi, who right from the beginning had not wanted to fight against the Germans, responded to a peace proposal from Leutwein and tried to negotiate a surrender, being encouraged to do so by Schutztruppe officers such as von Estorff and Böttlin, who had been serving in the country for some considerable time, von Trotha forbade any negotiations with the words: 'Won't help him at all: fought together, caught together, hanged together.'[114]

The battle that von Trotha was so longing for finally took place on 11 August 1904 at the Waterberg mountain, some 250 km to the north of Windhoek, where the Herero, clearly expecting an offer of peace, had assembled together with their womenfolk and children, and their herds of cattle. Although this battle brought military victory to the Schutztruppe, some of the Herero broke out of the encirclement and fled into the largely waterless Omaheke Desert in the east of the colony, which von Trotha then had sealed off by his troops.[115] At the beginning of October, in his notorious Proclamation, von Trotha ordered that all Herero returning from the desert should be shot:

> The Hereros have ceased to be German subjects.
>
> They have murdered and robbed, have cut off the ears and noses and other bodily parts of wounded soldiers, and are now too cowardly to want to go on fighting. I say to that people: whoever delivers one of their Kapteins to one of my posts as a prisoner will be given 1,000 marks; whoever brings Samuel Maharero will be given 5,000 marks. But the Herero people must quit this country. If they do not, I will compel them to do so with the Great Cannon.
>
> Within the borders of German territory, any Herero, with or without a firearm, with or without livestock, will be shot; nor will I give refuge to women or children any more. I will drive them back to their people or have them fired upon.[116]

He clarified this in an 'order of the day' by stating that 'for the sake of the reputation of the German soldier', the order to fire upon women and children is to be understood in such a way that shots are to be fired over their heads, in order to force them to run away. I definitely assume that this Proclamation will lead to no further male prisoners being taken, but will not degenerate into atrocities against women and children. They will doubtless run away, if shots are fired over their heads a couple of times.[117]

But there was nowhere they could run to except into the desert, where thousands died of thirst in consequence of this order.

In the weeks after the Battle of Waterberg, German troops patrolled the perimeter of the desert, with individual patrols also pursuing the Herero into the Omaheke. 'Like wild animals harassed half to death in the hunt' the enemy were 'chased from waterhole to watering place, until they fell into a state of complete apathy, victims of the nature of their own country'. In this way, the 'waterless Omaheke was to complete what German arms had started: the annihilation of the Herero nation'.[118]

What is described in such elegiac tones in the official historical record of the Herero War cost the lives of thousands of people, and must have caused more casualties than the fighting itself. In the end, the brutal procedures aroused criticism even from individual German officers. Ludwig von Estorff, for example, who even before the Battle of Waterberg had been one of the group of officers who sought to avoid a campaign of extermination, described the scenes witnessed by the pursuers as follows:

> I followed their tracks, which led me to a number of wells where I beheld terrible scenes. All around them lay heaps of cattle that had died of thirst, having reached the wells with their last remaining strength, but not having being able to drink in time. The Herero continued to flee before us into the *sandveld*. The terrible spectacle was repeated over and over again. The men had worked with feverish haste to dig wells, but the water had become more and more sparse, the waterholes scarcer and scarcer. They fled from one to the next, losing almost all their cattle and very many people. The nation was shrunk to meagre remnants, which gradually fell into our hands, though both then and later some escaped through the *sandveld* into British territory. The policy of shattering the nation in this way was as foolish as it was cruel; many of them and their wealth of cattle could still have been saved if they had now been shown mercy and received back; they had been punished enough. I proposed this to General von Trotha; but he wanted them completely exterminated.[119]

But it was not only the animals that suffered under their ever-increasing thirst. In some cases, the Herero slit the throats of their cattle in order to drink their blood, or squeezed the last remnants of moisture out of the content of the stomachs of dead animals.[120] But many could not save themselves even in this way, and thousands if not tens of thousands died, even though no precise figure can be given for the number of victims.[121] In addition, the flight into the Omaheke resulted in the disintegration of social structures, since the traditional leaders were either dead or on the run.[122]

Nevertheless, von Trotha's strategy was ultimately defeated by the sheer vastness of the country and by the epidemics of typhoid and malaria that were rampant among the troops,[123] making it impossible for the whole of the desert perimeter to be kept under observation for any length of time. Time and again, small groups of Herero managed to get through the German lines and secretly return to the colony.[124] The danger they represented could only be eliminated by the procurement of their voluntary submission, linked with their internment until the end of the war. It became more and more important to the Germans that the Herero should surrender, as 'the whole misguided operation against that unhappy people ... was keeping strong military forces tied down in a thankless task' – forces that were now needed to fight against the Nama.[125]

Although Hendrik Witbooi had still supported the Germans at the Battle of Waterberg by sending auxiliary troops, in October 1904 – when the Herero War had already been decided in military terms – it was now the Nama's turn to attack the Germans. This decision was precipitated above all by the demands circulating among the settlers that now there were strong forces in the country the Nama too should be disarmed and finally subjugated.[126] Learning from the mistakes of the Herero – they had seen what dire straits the Schutztruppe had got into trying to pursue the fleeing Herero[127] – they avoided a set-piece battle and launched a guerrilla war. The Nama's better knowledge of the country and their greater mobility were enough to outweigh the Schutztruppe's advantages of size and better equipment; they were able to keep the war going for a long time, tying down large forces and gradually wearing them out and grinding them down.[128] Their will to resist did not flag even after the death of Hendrik Witbooi on 25 October 1905; his fellow leaders Cornelius Stuurmann, Jakob Morenga, Johannes Christian, Abraham Morris and Simon Kopper continued with their resistance, so that the conflict dragged on until 1908. But the fighting was confined to the south of the country,[129] where the Nama were again and again able to retreat into the Kalahari or across the border into the British Cape Colony. It was not until 20 September 1907 that Jakob Morenga was shot dead on British territory by the Cape Police in an action closely coordinated between the Germans and the

British. The colonial government ultimately had to resort to paying an annual pension to Simon Kopper in return for his agreeing to terminate hostilities. And the only way to end the resistance of the Bondelswarts, which had also flared up again during the hot phase of the war, was to conclude a separate peace with them against the will of the civilian Administration, which now, in a reversal of its earlier position, favoured the elimination of all centres of potential resistance.[130]

Prisoner-of-War Camps and Deportations

The U-turn in policy with regard to the war aims thus arose above all out of tactical necessity, since the opening up of a new theatre of war in the southern part of the colony meant that German troops had to be redeployed away from the centre. Because of this, the Chief of the General Staff, Alfred von Schlieffen, was finally compelled to seek the revocation of von Trotha's Extermination Order in order to be able to initiate negotiations with the Herero – even though he continued to agree with the substance of von Trotha's attitudes, as he wrote to Chancellor von Bülow:

> His intention to annihilate the whole nation, or to drive it out of the country, is a matter in which one can agree with him. ... The race war that has broken out can only end with the annihilation or else the complete subjugation of the one party. But the latter course is one that cannot be sustained in the long term, given current attitudes. One is therefore able to approve General v. Trotha's intentions; the only thing is that he does not have the power to implement them.[131]

In the end, von Bülow was able to persuade Wilhelm II to revoke the Waterberg proclamation. Von Trotha thereupon modified his order to state that Herero who surrendered would be allowed to live, but that they would have to serve as forced labourers in chains. In addition, he wanted to have a nonremovable metal tag attached to each prisoner, bearing the letters 'G.H.' for *Gefangene Herero* – 'Herero prisoner'. And should they not be willing to reveal where they had hidden their weapons, one of them was to be shot each week.[132]

As this so-called 'Chain Order' (*Kettenbefehl*) was no more susceptible than the Extermination Order to persuade the Herero to surrender voluntarily, the Emperor yielded to pressure from von Bülow and revoked this order as well in December 1904. With the approval of the General Staff and of the Governor Designate, Friedrich von Lindequist, von Bülow proposed that 'those Herero who surrender', including women and children, should with the assistance of the Rhenish Missionary Society be accommodated 'in concentration camps[133] at various points in the country' and forced 'to work under guard'.[134] The colony's civil administration also supported this new policy, although the senior administrative officer, Hans Tecklenburg, would have liked to have delayed the publication of the call to surrender until the Witbooi had 'sustained even more losses', as otherwise the Herero might think that 'we do not believe we are capable of dealing with the uprising'.[135]

Von Trotha continued to refuse to display any greater degree of leniency than was absolutely necessary to satisfy the requirements laid down in Berlin. When the Rhenish Mission intervened with a proposal that the Herero should be re-established as a 'tribe' and enabled to pursue their traditional forms of economic activity, he replied:

> His Majesty the Emperor and King has moderated my intentions through his command to the extent that those Herero who surrender voluntarily, with the exception of ringleaders and murderers, should be granted their lives. The Chancellor has revoked my order that all Herero who surrender should perform labour in chains for an indefinitely long period of time. I know of no other orders modifying mine, so that they remain in force, to the effect that
>
> 1. all the Herero's livestock shall be taken from them,
>
> 2. men and women who are capable of working shall be made use of at places where they are needed, in return for their board, but without wages,
>
> 3. that courts of law under an authority to be established by me shall investigate the cases of murder.[136]

The decision to set up prisoner-of-war camps in which the prisoners were to perform forced labour represented both a concession to humanitarian misgivings and economic considerations – von Trotha's brutal methods had attracted considerable criticism in Germany, while there had also been complaints from within South West Africa about the shortage of labour, which was making itself felt ever more acutely – and was also a way of meeting the military exigencies. Furthermore, military power could now be used to prepare for the postwar period by 'educating' the prisoners in the camps to work, as von Lindequist wrote:

> Getting the Hereros to work while they are prisoners of war is a very salutary matter for them; indeed they may regard themselves as being very fortunate in that they can learn to work before full freedom is restored to them, since otherwise they would probably continue to wander around the country avoiding work, and, since they have lost their entire cattle stocks, lead wretched lives.[137]

Thus the only prospect remaining for Herero who surrendered voluntarily was an existence as completely destitute labourers. All attempts on the part of moderate officers to persuade the Herero to abandon their resistance by offering them more lenient conditions, and in particular by promising them that they would not be deported to the camps but would be allowed to settle again in the areas where they had formerly lived, were forbidden by von Trotha. And he broke promises of that kind that had already been made by his officers.[138]

The new policy produced rapid results: by March 1905 there were already 4,093 prisoners in German hands, including 1,413 women and 1,576 children,[139] and two months later this figure had almost doubled to 8,040, less than a quarter of these being men.[140] Nevertheless, at the end of 1905 there were still thousands of Herero in hiding and in places of refuge. The new civilian Governor, Friedrich von Lindequist, who had arrived in the colony subsequent to the recall of von Trotha (which occurred on 19 November 1905) and the restoration of civil administration, therefore reissued the call to surrender. He hoped that with the assistance of the Rhenish Mission, which continued to enjoy a large measure of trust among the Africans, he would be able to persuade more Herero to surrender voluntarily. He offered the prospect of an early end to the State of War and the release of the prisoners of war, though making these things dependent on the success of his call to surrender. The Herero were to report to assembly points set up by the Mission, where they would be supplied with food. The women and children were even to be allowed to keep some of their small livestock, whilst those men who were strong enough would be forced to 'work' (i.e. enter into dependent employment), though they would receive a small amount in wages. No soldiers were to be stationed at these assembly points, and the soldiers in the army posts were to be ordered not to shoot at Herero any more. In addition, no more Herero settlements were to be sought out and destroyed by the Schutztruppe after 20 December.[141]

The Mission therefore set up four collection camps at Omburo, Otjosazu, Otjihaenena and later Otjozongombe, and also tried to persuade the Herero who were still holding out in the Omaheke Desert to surrender.[142] The missionaries also sent out patrols of their own to try to trace groups in hiding, with 'Big Men' of the Herero sometimes accompanying these expeditions in order to persuade their people to give themselves up. While many of the refugees were too weak through hunger and as a result of their wretched living conditions to flee from the patrols or to come to the camps of their own accord, others were still so hostile to the Germans that they threatened to kill the people who brought them the offer of peace. Others fled before the patrols, since wild rumours had spread that they were continuing to shoot those Herero they were able to find.[143]

Despite all this, the Rhenish Mission's collection camps were a success from the German point of view, as by 31 March 1907 a further 12,000 to 15,000 Herero had reported to them.[144] If the 8,800 prisoners taken by the Schutztruppe up to the end of 1905 are added to this number,[145] the total number of Herero in German captivity amounted to some 21,000 to 24,000.

Those Nama who managed to survive the extermination strategy, which was now being pursued against them as well – the German side were attempting to occupy the watering places in order to destroy their enemies through thirst, as they had already done in the Omaheke Desert[146] – were now being captured in ever greater numbers and also brought to the Schutztruppe's prisoner-of-war camps. As, like the Herero, they also had women and children travelling with them in their troops, every Nama was considered an enemy. To prevent the guerrilla forces from receiving support from the population, even peace agreements were violated. Ludwig von Estorff, for example, in view of the drawn-out nature of the guerrilla war and the difficulty of 'actually getting one's hands' on the Nama, had promised the Nama Kaptein Samuel Isaak life and liberty if he were to surrender with his people. When he then did so on 24 November 1905, together with 139 followers including 63 women and children, the Supreme Command of the Schutztruppe disregarded the agreement, even though the area concerned – that around Gibeon – was quickly 'pacified' as a result. A complaint by von Estorff to the Imperial Colonial Office[147] that his good name had been besmirched was ignored.[148] Samuel Isaak and his people were immediately sent to the prisoner-of-war camp on Shark Island, off Lüderitzbucht.[149]

Between 1904 and 1908 prisoner-of-war camps were set up throughout the colony to provide for the custody of prisoners. The internees were used as forced labour on both military and civil projects.[150] From April 1905 onwards civilians could also ask to be assigned forced labourers,[151] for which they might under certain circumstances have to pay a fee per head to the Administration.[152] While smaller employers would collect 'their' prisoners every day and take them to work in their businesses, larger enterprises such as the Woermann shipping line even set up camps of their own.[153] Women and children, and also sick people who were unable to work, were to be found not only in the state camps but in these private camps as well.[154]

The situation in the state camps in particular was catastrophic, with inadequate rations and a disease-ridden atmosphere leading to horrendous mortality rates. To some extent, this was intentional. Deputy Governor Hans Tecklenburg, pointing out that food was required for the German soldiers and settlers, expressed his disagreement with any measures to improve the rations of the prisoners of war.[155] Ideas of retribution and of the need to discipline the prisoners also played their part in this:

> The more the Herero people now experience the consequences of rebellion in terms of their own physical suffering, the less desire they will have to seek to repeat the rebellion for generations to come. Our military successes in themselves have made less of an impression on them. I expect the time of suffering they are now having to endure to have a more sustained effect, though in expressing this view it is by no means my wish to take up cudgels on behalf of Lieutenant General Trotha's Proclamation of 2 October of last year. From an economic point of view, though, the death of so many people does represent a loss.[156]

The conditions at Swakopmund that Tecklenburg was referring to were in no way exceptional, however. Conditions were even worse in the concentration camp on Shark Island off Lüderitzbucht, which was the biggest of the prison camps. Both Herero and Nama were interned there and left to their fate. Imprisonment on Shark Island meant certain death for many, simply in view of the harsh climatic conditions and the inadequate rations provided by the Germans. An eyewitness, the missionary Emil Laaf from Lüderitzbucht, described the conditions as follows:

> At that time [early 1906] there were about 2,000 Herero prisoners of war interned at the very far end of Shark Island. … As long as the people were in good health, they were given work by the forces or by other whites who lived nearby. They were allowed to leave Shark Island to go to work, but came back every evening. … As a result of the great hardships and deprivations that the prisoners had suffered while they were out in the veld they were very weak, and there was great misery and much sickness among them. And in addition to all that, they found the wet, harsh sea climate hard to endure at first; and in any case they had been completely taken away from their accustomed way of life.[157]

The situation became even more acute in September 1906, when a further seventeen hundred prisoners were brought in. In particular, the food provided did not meet requirements, since the flour distributed was unsuitable for bread making, there was no fresh meat, and the pulses that were distributed could not be cooked at all due to a lack of fuel. Many prisoners went down with scurvy or typhoid.

But even more than these miserable conditions, their isolation at the very far end of Shark Island played its part in destroying the people's will to live. They gradually became quite apathetic in the face of their wretched state. They were separated from the outside world by three high barbed-wire fences. ...

The number of the sick increased day by day. In order to keep the people profitably occupied, the tribes had initially been put to work on a major blasting operation, with a view to building a quay on the side facing Roberts Harbour. At first, almost 500 men were employed on this blasting work. But within a short time this number had dwindled to such an extent that the blasting work had to be suspended. There was scarcely a *pontok* [hut] without one or more sick people in it. A hospital unit was set up in a few large rooms, created by hanging up sacks. But the rations provided were in no way adapted to the needs of the sick. The food was simply put down in front of the people suffering from scurvy, and then it was a matter of 'Eat it or die!' If a sick person had no sympathetic relative to help him, he could easily starve to death. ...

The mortality rate was horrifyingly high at that time. Sometimes as many as twenty-seven people died on a single day. The dead were taken to the cemetery by the cartload.[158]

Not even the need for labour led to the prisoners of war being given better care; rather than do that, the risk was accepted that construction work might have to be suspended. Criticism of the conditions came above all from the missionaries. In the end, the situation became so wretched that the two missionaries Emil Laaf and Hermann Nyhof were able to convince the commandant of Lüderitzbucht, Captain von Zülow, that the catastrophic conditions had to be improved. According to Laaf's account, von Zülow then asked Colonel Berthold von Deimling, the commander of the forces in the Southern Region, if it would not be better to remove the prisoners from Shark Island and intern them on the mainland, since 'in his view they had no will to live any more'; to which von Deimling replied that 'as long as he, von Deimling, was in charge, no Hottentot would be allowed to leave Shark Island alive'.[159]

Thus despite the revocation of von Trotha's Proclamation, the treatment of the Herero and Nama in the camps represented a continuation of his extermination policy. The dispute between von Trotha and Leutwein at the beginning of the war with regard to the need to keep the Herero as labour was continued in the struggle between the concept of making use of the prisoners of war as labour and that of decimating them through intolerable conditions.

The inhuman treatment of prisoners of war on Shark Island did not, however, meet with the approval of all officers. Ludwig von Estorff, who in the meantime had been made Commander of the Schutztruppe for German South West Africa, regarded the prevailing practice as offending against his honour as an officer. He therefore did not want to continue to take responsibility for 'hangman's work of this kind', which he could not conscientiously delegate to his officers either, particularly as there were some among the prisoners to whom he himself had promised better treatment when they surrendered. After von Zülow had reported to him that between September 1906 and April 1907 as many as 1,032 out of 1,795 prisoners had died, and that of the 245 men interned there only 25 were periodically capable of working, while the others could only get about on crutches, he issued an order on 8 April 1907 that the camp was to be relocated to the mainland.[160] He did this against the declared opposition of the Government in Windhoek, as Deputy Governor Oskar Hintrager considered that it was only the camp's location on Shark Island that offered security against the prisoners escaping.[161] Owing to a hysterical fear of Africans even when they were sick, combined with feelings of revenge, even the need for manpower in the future had to take a back seat.

Whereas from October 1906 to March 1907 between 143 and 276 prisoners had died every month,[162] the relocation of the camp led to a significant drop in the mortality rate. This confirmed Emil Laaf's assessment that with better treatment, and in particular 'with good nursing of the sick, a high percentage … could have been saved'.[163] All in all, according to figures compiled by the Schutztruppe, 7,682 prisoners,[164] that is to say between 30 and 50 per cent, died between October 1904 and March 1907.

When the State of War was officially ended on 31 March 1907, the civil authorities took over the supervision of the Herero and Nama prisoners of war. But they remained interned and had to perform forced labour even after the war had come to an end.[165] It was not until 27 January 1908, the Emperor's birthday, that they were officially released from captivity.[166]

In addition to this confinement in prisoner-of-war camps within the territory, there were also, right from the beginning, deportations to other German colonies and to South Africa. From the outbreak of war on 12 January 1904, all Herero were regarded as enemies. As early as 15 January, therefore, six hundred Herero who had been working on the construction of railways were interned on the ships *Helen Woermann* and *Eduard Bohlen* at Swakopmund.[167] Of these, half were sent to Cape Town on 21 January 1904 in order to work in the mines in South Africa. This export of valuable manpower to British colonies met with opposition, however, and suggestions soon arose that the

Herero prisoners should be deported to other German colonies. The governor of Cameroon, Jesko von Puttkamer, wrote to the Foreign Office Colonial Department as early as April 1904 that a competent person with a good knowledge of South West Africa had proposed resettling the Herero in Cameroon. There was not in fact any shortage of labour on the plantations there at the time, but with a view to the building of the railway, 'which will require thousands of labourers', an 'influx of manpower would be something to be greeted with delight'. In Cameroon the Herero would be able to 'work under the eyes of the government, and if they proved their worth, even only to a moderate extent, then it would at any rate be better to relocate them here than to deport them en masse to the British colonies'.[168] To von Puttkamer, the African population was the property of the colonial power, and so could be disposed of freely and kept available for the German colonies. But von Trotha's extermination policy prevented any large number of prisoners being taken during the Herero War, so that in fact no deportation of Herero to Cameroon took place.

When the Nama War started, the idea of deportation was taken up again. Immediately after the outbreak of hostilities, eighty Witbooi, who until only very recently had been fighting on the German side in the war against the Herero, were disarmed and interned at Swakopmund. As Deputy Governor Tecklenburg was afraid they might escape to the British territory of Walvis Bay, he applied to Berlin for these prisoners to be deported to Cameroon or Togo.[169] He considered it to be 'urgently necessary' that they should be deported, since 'the natives would find it easier to understand if we were to finish off these eighty Witboois than if we went on feeding them at the state's expense'. And he thought it was out of the question to use them as labour within the colony because of the danger of escape.[170] Only two days later he received Colonial Department approval for the Witbooi to be deported,[171] even before Governor Julius von Zech of Togo had declared himself to be in agreement with the transfer, which he did the following day.[172] Together with thirty-nine other Nama,[173] the Witbooi were dispatched to Togo on 28 October 1904.[174]

In Togo, however, doubts now arose about the status of the Witbooi, since the officers accompanying the transport informed the Administration in Togo that 'these people are not really prisoners of war, but were fighting on the German side against the Herero until very recently, some as soldiers on active service, others as irregular auxiliary troops, and have only been disarmed and deported to be on the safe side now that the Witboi tribe [*sic*] has become rebellious'. Governor von Zech therefore asked the Colonial Department for instructions as to the basis on which the people were to be treated, 'and in particular whether they should be paid wages, in which respect they have already asked for a hearing'. Up until then they had received prisoners' rations, supplemented on the basis of a medical report by 250 grams of meat twice a week and 25 grams of coffee every day, and were employed on lighter work, namely the clearance of bush land, in Lomé and the surrounding area.[175]

The Director of the Colonial Department of the Foreign Office, Oskar Wilhelm Stübel, confirmed that the Witbooi who had been sent to Togo were 'native auxiliaries' who had fought against the Herero. When the Nama War broke out they had been taken into custody in order to prevent them from joining the resistance:

> Since it is beyond doubt that the people concerned would have followed the call of their Kaptein to fight against us, as was to be concluded from the desertion of some individual Witboois shortly before the outbreak of the Witboi [sic] rebellion, the situation described above cannot be a hindrance to our treating the Witboois who have been sent to you as if they were prisoners of war.[176]

Despite the special rations on medical grounds, the deportation with its associated hardships and the unaccustomed climate in Togo claimed dozens of victims among the Witbooi. In July 1905, therefore, the Colonial Department, having received a report from Togo that fifty-four of the prisoners had already died, ordered that the survivors should be sent back to South West Africa.[177] This met with determined opposition from Tecklenburg and von Trotha. Tecklenburg saw the high level of mortality as being 'retribution for the rebellion', and proposed that the prisoners should be sent to Germany instead, but 'under no circumstances' back to South West Africa. His inhuman reference to taking revenge for the war did not, however, meet with unqualified approval in the Colonial Department, as can be deduced from the question mark placed in the margin at this point by the official dealing with the communication.[178]

The Colonial Department was not convinced by Tecklenburg's objection, and instructed the Government of Togo to notify it when the next opportunity would be to send the Nama home. In the meantime they were to wait for further instructions, and not implement the repatriation order for the time being.[179] When General von Trotha also declared himself to be 'resolutely' opposed to the Nama being brought back to Swakopmund, as the camp there was overflowing, and suggested transferring the prisoners to Cameroon if necessary,[180] the Colonial Department at first played for time, requesting further details of the incidence of mortality among the prisoners and asking whether relocation to the interior of the country might bring an improvement from a medical point of view.[181]

A few days later the Colonial Department had come to the conclusion that it was absolutely essential to remove the Witbooi from Togo, but that in the opinion of the doctors it was impossible to transfer them to Cameroon. It asked the Government in Windhoek to examine whether, 'in view of the constraints we are under and of the small number of Hottentots who are still alive, it might not be possible after all to intern the Nama at an inland camp in South West Africa'.[182]

Caught in a dilemma between the categorical refusal of General von Trotha to intern the Nama somewhere inland in South West Africa or to confine them on the coast 'but not in chains'[183] (which, however, he was forbidden to do), and the still horrendous mortality rate being reported from Togo (no fewer than sixty-three had already died and many others were sick),[184] the Colonial Department finally decided after all to deport the prisoners onwards to Cameroon.[185]

This decision, in the making of which the welfare of the Witbooi themselves was clearly only a minor concern, is also likely to have been influenced by overdramatization on the part of von Trotha, who in his telegram to the Colonial Department monstrously exaggerated the threat emanating from the fifty-six survivors and wrote: 'The death of every German who is shot by one of these Witbois [*sic*] that are to be sent back here will be on the head of whoever orders their return.'[186] Nobody in the Colonial Department was prepared to take on this degree of responsibility for the sake of the prisoners, and all the less so since the Government in Cameroon had declared itself willing to take them.[187] The medical concerns relating to their being sent to Cameroon that had been expressed only a very short time before were apparently swept aside.

Von Puttkamer, the Governor of Cameroon, had indicated his willingness to take prisoners of war from South West Africa as early as April 1904, and did not want to allow the opportunity to obtain a large number of cheap workers to slip through his fingers. So just at the time when von Trotha and the Colonial Department were debating the removal of the Nama from Togo he wrote to the Colonial Department again with concrete proposals as to how the deportees might be used.[188]

His expectations with regard to an influx of workers from Togo, however, were disappointed, since of the forty-seven Nama[189] who arrived in Cameroon on 19 September 1905, thirteen had to remain in Victoria because they were sick. The thirty-four prisoners who were sent on to Buea also appeared to be 'scarcely able to work', and made 'a pitiable impression in their present state', so that they could only be given lightish work to do. Moreover, they had to be accommodated separately from the local Africans, in order to avoid making a 'bad impression' on these. Von Puttkamer wrote that if the Nama did not recover and get fit for work soon, he would want to send them back to South West Africa.[190] This alarmed the Colonial Department, and the head of the South West Africa desk, Angelo Golinelli, immediately pointed out to the Government in Cameroon that in view of the high costs that had already been incurred sending the Witbooi there and of the refusal of the Governor of South West Africa to allow them to return, the Administration in Cameroon needed to take urgent measures to ensure that they would be able to stay there. Their being unable to work, Golinelli maintained, was no grounds for deportation, as sending them back to South West Africa would not make them any more able to do so. The only reasons that might be acceptable would be climatic ones, but the Administration should take steps to see that the deportees were accommodated 'at a place that would be good for their health, in order if at all possible to avoid their having to live under conditions that are more unfavourable to them than those in South West Africa'.[191] Only when the Government in Windhoek at last abandoned its rejectionist stance in February 1906[192] were the forty-two surviving Nama able to set out for South West Africa again.[193]

This experience with the Witbooi deported to Togo and Cameroon had shown how catastrophic the consequences of deportation could be for prisoners; but despite this, neither the military nor the civil wings of the German administration would distance themselves from this option. The new civilian Governor, Friedrich von Lindequist, had originally intended to deport some largish groups of Nama once the State of War had been ended. But the new Commander of the Schutztruppe, Berthold von Deimling, who had been appointed in July 1906, pressed for deportations to begin straight away, while the war was still going on. As Witbooi-Nama prisoners of war were constantly escaping from the camps, von Lindequist accepted his view and proposed to the Colonial Department that 'the entire tribe of the Witbooi should be deported to Samoa, and the followers of Cornelius of Bethanie and those of Simon Kopper's people who have been taken prisoner to Adamaua' [in Cameroon]. As long as a State of War continued, he expressly did not want the deportation to be restricted to 'Big Men'.[194] Altogether, 1,599 Witbooi, including nine 'Big Men' and 501 other men, and 191 Bethanie people, including eight 'Big Men' and 107 other men, were scheduled for deportation.[195] Since the Nama concerned were already interned in camps in Windhoek and Karibib,[196] there was no immediate reason why they should be deported. This fact and also the numbers involved indicate that it was a matter of carrying out an experiment in the economic distribution of the African population, with an eye to how South West Africa might develop after the war.

The plans of von Lindequist and von Deimling were thwarted by opposition from the Colonial Department in Berlin, which rejected the removal of whole 'tribes' and permitted only the deportation of the 'Big Men' to Adamaua.[197] Von Lindequist refused to be content with that, however, and requested the Colonial Department to allow him to deport not only the 'Big Men' but also other influential men and their families – a total of forty-two people.[198] In the end, after the Government of Cameroon had refused to accept the Nama and political reservations had also been expressed about deporting them to Togo,[199] the Colonial Department decided that the Nama concerned and their families should be sent to one of the Mariana Islands, where they would be able to pursue arable farming and animal husbandry without any danger of their escaping, being liberated by the inhabitants of other islands or inciting the islanders to resist.[200] But the planned deportation did not ultimately take place. This was doubtless partly due to the fact that the matter no longer seemed so urgent, as the Nama concerned had in the meantime, at von Deimling's insistence, been interned on Shark Island, and even von Lindequist considered them to be safely confined there. He also thought that it might be possible later on to reduce the number of people to be deported, thereby saving costs.[201]

A number of private individuals who were enthusiastic followers of developments in the colonies, apparently prompted by reports in the German press about the increasing numbers of Herero and Nama prisoners of war, were also involved in putting forward plans as to how they could beneficially be used in other colonies. The animal feed manufacturer Ludwig Boldt from Stettin, for example, wrote to Director Stübel of the Colonial Department, enclosing with his letter a newspaper cutting that told of over four thousand prisoners, eight hundred of them men, and proposing that the more dangerous ones among them should be settled in German East Africa and employed in railway construction. Language difficulties would see to it that their revolutionary ideas could not take root there, whereas in South West Africa they would remain a danger after their release. Boldt thought, however, that they could equally well be sent to other German colonies, the important thing being that this would fulfil a double purpose, 'keeping their labour while at the same time cleansing the country'.[202]

But it was not only the labour shortage in the colonies that was to be remedied by making use of supposedly 'surplus' Africans from

Namibia: there were also ideas as to how they could be made use of in Germany itself. In 1907 a certain Adolf Hentze suggested to the Colonial Secretary and head of the Imperial Colonial Office, Bernhard Dernburg, that the sixteen thousand African prisoners of war who, according to newspaper reports, were having to be guarded by the Schutztruppe in South West Africa, thereby occasioning costs for both their food and for their internment, should be brought to Germany to relieve the labour shortage in agriculture. In Germany they would learn 'good behaviour, the language and how to till the soil', and be 'educated to work'. In this way, they could replace the Russians and Poles who had previously been employed there, and who 'truly do nothing to enhance our population'. So that the prisoners would not be deprived of the hope of ultimately returning home, the landowners who employed them would be obliged to put a part of their earnings aside to pay for their repatriation.[203] In this way, the fulfilment of the mission to 'advance the level of civilization' of the Africans was linked to benefits for the Germans. This idea, extreme though it doubtless was, of bringing in Africans in order to be able to restrict the immigration of Russians and Poles shows how virulent racist ideas were, even beyond the simple distinction between White and Black. Hentze will scarcely have imagined the Africans doing anything to 'enhance' the German population either, but must rather have envisaged the creation of a Black 'helot class', which would have been prevented from having too close contact with the German population simply through the racist stigmatization of their darker skin colour.

The various proposals for the compulsory relocation of the Herero and Nama remained thoroughly in accord with von Trotha's radical war aims of either exterminating the Africans who were involved in the war or else at least driving them out of the core area of South West Africa that was earmarked for German settlement. The deportations, even though they were only actually implemented in a few individual cases, quickly developed from being a military measure into a way of shifting the population in order to ensure that the colony could develop peacefully after the ending of the State of War. This is the true significance both of the deportations that actually took place and of von Lindequist's further plans for the Witbooi and Bethanie Nama. A concept was developed that could be, and was, taken out of the drawer again in peacetime. The proposals put forward not only by the authorities but also by private individuals in Germany to resettle whole population groups in other German colonies, and even in Germany itself, demonstrate how widespread the idea was that the African population could be disposed of at will in accordance with the economic and political interests of the colonial state, and show that the inhuman resettlement policy that was implemented during and after the war was not simply something conjured up by individual administrators or army officers. But the attitude of the Colonial Department in rejecting von Lindequist's proposals also shows that the idea of large-scale resettlement was not undisputed, even though this may have been for reasons of political opportunism or because of the associated costs.

The deportations and the prisoner-of-war camps, with their catastrophic consequences for the local population, were the consequences of a war waged not only against African warriors but against women and children too; a war that on the German side was initially conducted with genocide as its aim, and which even after the revocation of von Trotha's orders to commit mass murder still pursued the intention of destroying the defeated enemy's social and political structures in their entirety. This German brutality, however, was also a reaction to the amazing successes of the Africans, which had left the German military largely helpless. In the end they resorted to countering it by means of the widespread internment not only of combatants but of women and children as well. It was the nature of the war as waged by Germany that also determined the nature of the treatment meted out to prisoners afterwards, and 'race war' meant a war of annihilation in which it was intended, or at least accepted as a consequence, that thousands should perish. The concentration of prisoners into prison camps distributed across the whole of the colony, and their deployment as forced labour, represents a compromise between the two predominant war aims. If there were some who saw in these measures the basis for a new labour order in which the Africans would be totally available to the Germans as manpower, there were others who sought to continue to pursue their murderous policy of extermination in the context of the camps, though by other means – namely, through disease and neglect.

For the Africans, the everyday experience of the war meant constant mortal danger, flight to Bechuanaland or northwards into Ovamboland, or a life spent in hiding under the constant threat of being captured and put into a prison camp. There, all that awaited them were further privations and forced labour. All individual rights were suspended; every possibility of making decisions of their own on how they wished to live their lives was taken away from them. For the German administration, this created an opportunity and also a necessity to undertake the codification of Native Policy.

Notes

1. [Translator's note: The German colonies were officially called *Schutzgebiete* (Protectorates); however, contrary to the use of the term 'Protectorate' in British imperial history, the German *Schutzgebiete* had no status that distinguished them from colonies, and the two terms are in effect interchangeable (cf. the terms 'Kolonialabteilung' and 'Reichskolonialamt' designating the responsible government department)].
2. The name of the office was changed from *Kaiserlicher Kommissar* (Imperial Commissioner) to *Kaiserlicher Landeshauptmann* (Imperial Administrator) in 1893, and to *Kaiserlicher Gouverneur* (Imperial Governor) in 1898. On the development of the Colonial Administration, see Hubatsch, *Grundriß zur deutschen Verwaltungsgeschichte*, 424–50. A list of the Commissioners, Administrators and Governors can also be found in Gründer, *Kolonien*, 249.
3. With regard to the importance of cooperation between local elites and colonizers in enabling the European colonial powers to become firmly established on other continents, see Robinson, 'Non-European Foundations of European Imperialism'.
4. 'Ruhe des Friedhofs', the title of a chapter in Drechsler, *Südwestafrika unter deutscher Kolonialherrschaft*, Vol. I, 221–36. Prein has pointed out that the image of the passive African victim implicit in this title requires reconsideration; see Prein, 'Guns and Top Hats'.
5. Bley, *Kolonialherrschaft und Sozialstruktur*, 193.
6. Fenske, 'Ungeduldige Zuschauer'.
7. For a more exhaustive discussion of the origins and motives of the German colonial movement, see Gründer, *Kolonien*, 25–50.
8. Ibid., 33.
9. Faber at the constitutive assembly of the Deutsche Evangelische Missions-Hilfe (German Protestant Mission Aid) on 6 December 1913, quoted according to Gründer, *Christliche Mission*, 110. Similarly, Carl Peters too had expressed his motives for pursuing colonial acquisitions in terms of his wish to be a member of a 'master race', in order to be on equal terms with the British. Gründer, *Kolonien*, 31.
10. Ibid., 33.
11. Ibid., 79.
12. Since colonies would mean that the German Empire was also vulnerable to attack overseas, he saw them as an albatross around the neck of foreign policy: Hildebrand, *Das vergangene Reich*, 86–87.
13. For a presentation of the opinions of individual scholars in this field, see Gründer, *Kolonien*, 51–62.
14. Drechsler, *Südwestafrika unter deutscher Kolonialherrschaft*, Vol. II, 19.
15. Gründer, *Kolonien*, 80. In addition, in the August of the same year he had purchased a strip of land stretching twenty miles inland at the mouth of the Orange River. 'Misunderstanding or duplicity' led to Fredericks assuming British statute miles were meant (equivalent to 1.6 km), while Lüderitz successfully claimed 'geographical miles' corresponding to 7.4 km. Reinhard, *Kleine Geschichte*, 250.

16. Wehler, *Bismarck und der Imperialismus*, 265. He was apparently also planning to get involved in arms trading; this exposed him to criticism from Friedrich Fabri, who not only held an extremely gloomy view of the company's economic prospects but was also of the opinion that this would only pour further oil onto the flames of the hostilities in South West Africa. Riehl, *Der 'Tanz um den Äquator'*, 396–97.

17. Reinhard, *Kleine Geschichte*, 251. Gründer, *Kolonien*, 58.

18. Gründer, *Kolonien*, 58. The idea was that the administration of the overseas territories by private companies would not only save the government money but would also prevent the Reichstag from being able to influence colonial affairs through its budgetary prerogative. Reinhard, *Kleine Geschichte*, 251.

19. Bismarck before the Reichstag on 28 November 1885, sten. rec. 86, quoted according to Gründer, *Kolonien*, 59.

20. Ibid., 80. It was presumably because of his financial difficulties that Lüderitz was never granted a charter. See also Drechsler, *Südwestafrika* II, 8.

21. Drechsler, *Südwestafrika* II, 27.

22. Such was the resolution adopted by the Company's constitutive meeting on 14 March 1885: quoted according to Drechsler, ibid., 21. Drechsler also draws attention to the difficulty of finding sufficient subscribers to allow the Company to be established at all. It was only by dint of great efforts that the promoters were able to raise the sum of M300,000 required for this purpose. Thus the Company's level of capitalization was completely inadequate. Even the amount of equity eventually raised, M800,000, was still too little, if one recalls that Friedrich Fabri had estimated the initial capital required by a company that was to be in a position to govern the country by its own efforts at M5 million. The willingness of von Bleichröder and his fellow bankers to invest was more a matter of 'being well disposed towards prevailing currents in public opinion and influences from official circles' than of expectations of financial profit, as Bismarck himself noted in a press release in 1889. For an extensive treatment of this problem, see ibid., 21–29, 26.

23. Whereas the Deutsch-Ostafrikanische Gesellschaft [German East Africa Company] and the Neuguinea-Compagnie [New Guinea Company], which were both set up in the same year, were granted charters, the Deutsche Kolonialgesellschaft für Südwestafrika never applied for one. Indeed, the two companies named remained the only ones to be granted charters, as no entity interested in having a charter could be found for Togo or Cameroon either. Ibid., 8–9.

24. Gründer, *Kolonien*, 81.

25. Ibid., 81.

26. These were Theodor Leutwein's estimates for the year 1892. Leutwein, *Elf Jahre Gouverneur*, 11. The figures more or less correspond to those arrived at by modern scholars. Only for the Ovambo have higher estmates of up to 150,000 been made; the range of variation is especially large in their case because in both contemporary and more recent statistics the Ovambo living on Angolan territory are sometimes also included. See Drechsler,

Südwestafrika I, 28–29; Eirola, *The Ovambogefahr*, 31; Strassegger, 'Die Wanderarbeit der Ovambo', 21. All in all, the figures given are based on very rough estimates made by travellers, colonial officials and missionaries, and give a better impression of the distribution of the population as between the various ethnicities than of the actual size of the population. This also explains the substantial divergencies between the upper and lower levels of the estimates in some cases – for example, in Drechsler, *Südwestafrika* I, 28. With regard to the population figures for the Herero, Brigitte Lau has pointed out that they are based on very imprecise estimates made by missionaries in the 1870s, and that in the precolonial time and the early years of colonial rule there was no way in which 'such intimate knowledge of a country and its population could have existed as is necessary for accurate population estimates. The size of the prewar Herero population is simply not known' – Lau, 'Uncertain Certainties', 43. Much the same applies to the rest of the population too. Further information on the history, culture and political organization of the African population on the eve of German colonization is also to be found in the literature mentioned.

27. Maharero was the son of Tjamuaha, who died in 1861, and the father of Samuel Maharero, who succeeded him in 1890.
28. On the conflict between the Witbooi and the Herero, see Reinhard, *Hendrik Witbooi*, 35–48. This book also gives some valuable insights into Hendrik Witbooi's conflicts with the Germans, though seen exclusively from his point of view since it reproduces his diary and other complementary sources. See also Lau, *Hendrik Witbooi Papers*.
29. Gewald, *Towards Redemption*, 38–39. See also Gründer, *Kolonien*, 81.
30. Reinhard, 'Eingeborenenpolitik in Südwestafrika', 548.
31. Gründer, *Kolonien*, 81.
32. Drechsler, *Südwestafrika* I, 54–55. Peter Heinrich Brincker, the superintendent of the Herero Mission, also pointed out in a letter to Bismarck dated 13 March 1889 that control of Damaraland could not be established through treaties or the local leaders, but was only possible if at least 400 soldiers equipped with artillery were to be stationed there. Gewald, *Redemption*, 39.
33. Gründer, *Kolonien*, 81.
34. C. von François, *Deutsch-Südwestafrika*, quoted according to Drechsler, *Südwestafrika* I, 56. On the significance of this measure for the establishment of 'formal direct rule of the territory', see also Gründer, *Kolonien*, 81–82.
35. Bismarck himself had had a premonition of the inauspicious momentum that colonial adventures could take on when he rejected the plans submitted to him at the same time by the Africa explorer Eugen Wolf for a military mission to rescue Emin Pasha, the German explorer and Governor of Egypt's Equatoria Province, and to establish a German sphere of influence in northern Africa. He gave his reasons as follows: 'If I send a Prussian lieutenant out there, then I may have to send several more out after him, to get him out again'. Wolf, *Vom Fürsten Bismarck*, quoted according to Gründer, *Kolonien*, 59.
36. Gewald, *Redemption*, 39–45.
37. Ibid., 46.

38. Ibid., 47–52.
39. Ibid., 59.
40. Leutwein, *Elf Jahre*, 15.
41. Reinhard, *Witbooi*, 174–75.
42. According to Hendrik Witbooi himself, who fled with his soldiers as soon as the raid began and surrendered the camp to the Germans undefended, ten men and seventy-five women were killed. Gewald, *Redemption*, 60–61. Bley even speaks of von François waging a 'war of annihilation' (*Vernichtungskrieg*) against the Witbooi. Bley, *Kolonialherrschaft*, 19.
43. Gewald, *Redemption*, 59–61.
44. Leutwein, *Elf Jahre*, 16.
45. Von Caprivi in the Reichstag on 1 March 1893, sten. rec. 128, quoted according to Bley, *Kolonialherrschaft*, 18.
46. Quoted according to Leutwein, *Elf Jahre*, 17.
47. Bley, *Kolonialherrschaft*, 20.
48. Leutwein, *Elf Jahre*, 18.
49. Reinhard, *Witbooi*, 174. This was the origin of a military cooperation with the Germans that was to last until 1915. It was not until the so-called 'Baster rebellion', when the Basters refused to support the Germans during the 1915 South African invasion in order to avoid being drawn into the war between the Germans on the one hand and the British and South Africans on the other, that the cooperation ended and gave way to hostilities.
50. Reinhard, *Witbooi*, 200.
51. Bley, *Kolonialherrschaft*, 52.
52. The Protection Treaty and the Protocol are reproduced in Reinhard, *Witbooi*, 205–9.
53. Gewald, *Redemption*, 62.
54. Leutwein, *Elf Jahre*, 60.
55. Gewald, *Redemption*, 62–65.
56. Ibid., 63–64.
57. Leutwein, *Elf Jahre*, 61.
58. 'Samuel then took up with joy the suggestion that was made to him that he should ask for a German garrison to be stationed in Okahandja, for his own protection' – Leutwein, *Elf Jahre*, 60. Hendrik Witbooi too had had to accept a German garrison in Gibeon as a sign of his submission. *Schutz- und Freundschaftsvertrag zwischen dem Deutschen Reich und Hendrik Witbooi* (Treaty of Protection and Friendship between the German Empire and Hendrik Witbooi) of 15 September 1894, reproduced in Reinhard, *Witbooi*, 205–8.
59. Leutwein, *Elf Jahre*, 61.
60. The fact that between 14,000 and 19,000 German soldiers were required to defeat the Herero and Nama in the war of 1904–08 makes it clear how insufficient Leutwein's military resources were for the systematic conquest of the country. The cannons may have terrified the Africans at first, but there were too few of them to count for much in the unequal distribution of force between Germans and Africans.
61. On this, see Bley, *Kolonialherrschaft*, 18–106.

62. The formal aspects of the ·court proceedings, during which twenty Bechuana and the murdered trader's cattle drover gave evidence against Lambert, were intended to counter any reproach of arbitrariness. The real problem, however, lay in the issue of the legitimacy of the court itself. Ibid., 24–30.

63. For a contemporary German interpretation of the Protection Treaties, see Hesse, *Die Schutzverträge in Südwestafrika*.

64. Gewald has set out in detail the interplay between Leutwein's objectives and those.of individual Herero leaders – the most important of these being Samuel Maharero. Gewald, *Redemption*, 36–137.

65. On rinderpest and its impact on Herero society, see ibid., 138–68.

66. Ibid., 147.

67. Ibid., 147–49. Gewald, drawing on the details given by the missionary Jakob Irle, puts the number of deaths at ten thousand.

68. Sudholt, *Eingeborenenpolitik*, 125.

69. These six Bezirke with the Distrikte included in them were: Outjo Bezirk with Sesfontein Distrikt, Omaruru Bezirk with Karibib Distrikt, Swakopmund Bezirk, Windhoek Bezirk with Rehoboth and Okahandja Distrikte, Gibeon Bezirk with Maltahöhe Distrikt, and Keetmanshoop Bezirk with Bethanie and Warmbad Distrikte; there were also the two autonomous Military Districts of Gobabis and Grootfontein. Rafalski, *Vom Niemandsland zum Ordnungsstaat*, 45. Sudholt, *Eingeborenenpolitik*, 125–26. As the administration continued to develop, the number of Bezirke and Distrikte continued to increase; many of the latter, however, were autonomous (i.e. not part of a Bezirk but directly responsible to the Governor), while the Bezirke, as larger administrative units, might continue to be divided into non-autonomous districts [Translator's note: Accordingly, and for the sake of simplicity, both *Bezirk* and *Distrikt* are translated as 'District' in this work]. On the structure of the Administration, see also Hubatsch, *Verwaltungsgeschichte*, 424–50, and Map 0.2 in the Front Matter to this book.

70. Sudholt, *Eingeborenenpolitik*, 126–27. Leutwein did, however, make efforts to eliminate the military aura attaching to the Administration, which was expressed among other things in the appointment of soldiers to some positions in the District Offices, and to convert the still extant remnants of the military administration into a civil administration.

71. IGW to FO-CD, 26 September 1903, ZBU W.II.I.1. Vol. 1, 1da–1ea (special pagination).

72. Leutwein, *Elf Jahre*, 243–44.

73. Ibid., 245.

74. Reinhard, *Eingeborenenpolitik*, 551.

75. See the list given in Leutwein, *Elf Jahre*, 431. Leutwein presented these statistics in an attempt to answer the charge that his Native Policy had been too lenient.

76. Ibid., 431.

77. Ibid., 430. Leutwein actually wrote '*die scheinbare Herrenstellung der Weißen über die Eingeboren*' [the position of mastery that the whites appeared to hold over the natives]; but he presumably meant rather that they acted as if they were entitled to such mastery.

78. Drechsler, *Südwestafrika* I, 132. Drechsler assumes that the Africans were completely without rights; but this is contradicted by the fact that there were convictions and sentencings of Europeans as well.
79. Ibid., 133.
80. On the rise in the number of cases of credit abuse, and the government's efforts to bring them under control, see Leutwein, *Elf Jahre*, 246–48, 559–68.
81. On the conflict with the Bondelswarts, see Drechsler, *Südwestafrika* I, 115–19.
82. Among these aspects, apart from the demand made by the Emperor Wilhelm II that the Schutztruppe should be reinforced and placed directly under the command of the General Staff in Berlin, was the fact that in the course of hostilities both German troops and Bondelswart contingents violated the border with British South Africa, thereby providing a precedent for occurrences during the later guerrilla war. Ibid., 117–18.
83. Leutwein to Fiedler, 3 January 1904, BAL R-1001/2154, quoted according to Drechsler, *Südwestafrika* I, 119.
84. These culminated in the peace treaty concluded in Kalkfontein on 27 January 1904, under which the Bondelswarts submitted, agreeing to give up their weapons, hand over the guilty parties and cede land to the Crown. Ibid.
85. IGW to CSW (transcript of a telegram), 3 February 1904, BA-MA RM 3/v. 10263, 35a.
86. Gewald has recently questioned the traditional interpretation that the Herero resistance was a planned action. In his view, the war arose out of German attacks on Herero resulting from the Germans' hysterical fear of hostile acts on the part of the Africans. He also rejects the theory that the outbreak of hostilities was a complete surprise, pointing out that rumours of such a thing had been circulating since at least December 1903. Gewald, *Redemption*, 178–201. However, the fact that Leutwein marched off southwards is sufficient proof that he was not expecting war with the Herero at that moment.
87. Leutwein, *Elf Jahre*, 491.
88. For a detailed overview of the military units deployed, the individual episodes in the fighting and the sequence of operations during the war, see *Die Kämpfe der deutschen Truppen*.
89. Elger to the Rhenish Mission, 10 February 1904, BAL R1001/2114, quoted according to Drechsler, *Südwestafrika* I, 146–47.
90. Gewald, *Redemption*, 196–201. See also Pool, *Samuel Maharero*, 223–24.
91. Eirola, *Ovambogefahr*, 163–76, 181–85.
92. Samuel Maharero wrote letters to both Kapteins in the January, seeking to persuade them to join him in concerted action against the Germans in order to drive the colonialists out of the country. Hermanus van Wijk handed over all the letters – including those addressed to Witbooi, which had initially been sent to him – to the German administration. The precise dating of these letters is a matter of dispute between scholars. In the past they were believed to date from the days immediately before the outbreak of war, and were seen as proof that Maharero had been planning the war

over a long period and had regarded it as a united war of liberation of all Africans; but Gewald advances plausible reasons for believing that they were not written until after the fighting had started and represent a desperate call for assistance on Maharero's part. Gewald, *Redemption*, 191–96. The letters are reproduced in Leutwein, *Elf Jahre*, 468–69.

93. K. Schwabe, *Der Krieg in Deutsch-Südwestafrika* (Berlin: Weller, 1907), 52–54.
94. This can be seen from a report of the Stud Administration in Windhoek, which tells of the case of an NCO named Herpolsheimer who had to remove his livestock from land belonging to the Baster Dirk van Wijk because of threats from the Herero. After the Battle of Waterberg he was able to send his cattle back, but had to remove them again a short time later when Witbooi warriors were making the neighbourhood unsafe. Board of the Stud Adminstration Windhoek to IGW, 15 March 1905, ZBU W.II.C.3. Vol. 3, 147a f.
95. Gewald, *Redemption*, 188. *Kämpfe*, Vol. 1, 33.
96. *Kämpfe*, Vol. 1, 61.
97. Gewald, *Redemption*, 201–5.
98. Commander of SMS *Habicht* to the Chief of the Admiralty Staff (transcript), 4 February 1904, BA-MA RM 3/v. 10263, 38a.
99. Elger to the Rhenish Mission, 10 February 1904, BAL R1001/2114, quoted according to Drechsler, *Südwestafrika* I, 146–47.
100. IGW to FO-CD, 23 February 1904, BAL R-1001/2113, quoted according to Drechsler, *Südwestafrika* I, 149–50.
101. Bley, *Kolonialherrschaft*, 217.
102. Gewald, *Redemption*, 199–201.
103. IGW to FO-CD, 17 May 1905, BAL R-1001/2115, quoted according to Drechsler, *Südwestafrika* I, 153–54.
104. Leutwein, *Elf Jahre*, 495–96.
105. Drechsler, *Südwestafrika* I, 149.
106. Bley, *Kolonialherrschaft*, 196.
107. Born on 3 July 1848 as the son of a Prussian officer, he too joined the army and took part in the Austro-Prussian and Franco-Prussian Wars. Between 1894 and 1897 he was the Commander of the Schutztruppe in German East Africa, where he gained military renown through his suppression of the 'Wahehe Uprising'. Thereafter he took part voluntarily, as Commander of the First East Asian Infantry Brigade, in the campaign to suppress the 'Boxer Rebellion' in China. Pool, *Maharero*, 260–61.
108. Imperial Order (*Allerhöchste Kabinettordre*) of 19 May 1904, NAW ZBU *Geheimakten* (Classified Documents) IX.A. Vol. 1, 1a. After Leutwein's recall in November 1904, von Trotha also took over the office of Governor. Hintrager, *Südwestafrika in der deutschen Zeit*, 61.
109. Von Trotha to Leutwein, 5 November 1904, BAL R-1001/2089, quoted according to Drechsler, *Südwestafrika* I, 156.
110. Article by von Trotha in *Die deutsche Zeitung*, 3 February 1909, quoted according to Pool, *Maharero*, 293.
111. Proclamation by von Trotha, June 1904, NAW ZBU *Geheimakten* IX.A. Vol. 1, 1b.

112. Quoted according to Drechsler, *Südwestafrika* I, 155.
113. Von Trotha's diary, quoted according to Pool, *Maharero*, 265.
114. '*Wird ihm wohl nichts helfen, mitgegangen, mitgefangen, mitgehangen.*' Von Trotha's diary, quoted according to Pool, ibid., 266–67.
115. Gewald, *Redemption*, 205–7.
116. The intentions behind this Proclamation and von Trotha's entire extermination strategy have been subjects of controversy between scholars. On the critics of the thesis of a war of extermination, see Lau, *Uncertain Certainties* and G. Spraul, 'Der "Völkermord" an den Herero', *Geschichte in Wissenschaft und Unterricht* 39 (1988), 713–39. A provisional summing up of the debate is to be found in T. Dedering, 'The German-Herero War of 1904. Revisionism of Genocide or Imaginary Historiography?', *Journal of Southern African Studies* 19 (1993), 80–88.
117. Proclamation by von Trotha, Osombo-Windhoek (transcript), 2 October 1904, BAL R 1001/2089, 7a f. This document is a transcript. A further transcript of the Proclamation is to be found in the Military Archive of the Federal Archives (*Bundesarchiv-Militärarchiv*) in Freiburg. This is identical in content, but gives the place of issue as Osombo-Windembe. Proclamation by von Trotha, Osombo-Windembe (transcript), 2 October 1904, BA-MA RW 51/2. 1a. The copy in the National Archives in Windhoek mentioned by Gewald is also a transcript. Gewald, *Redemption*, 207.
118. *Kämpfe*, Vol. 1, 211.
119. Von Estorff, *Wanderungen und Kämpfe*, 117.
120. Pool, *Maharero*, 282.
121. In view of the lack of any precise figures regarding either the prewar population – estimates vary between 70,000 and 100,000 – or the postwar population, which is estimated at between 17,000 and 40,000, no exact indication of the extent of the losses during the war can be made. No precise figures are available for the strength of the Schutztruppe either; but there must have been between 14,000 and 19,000 soldiers in action. On the various estimates and the problems relating to the figures in general, see Lau, *Uncertain Certainties*, 39–52.
122. After the war, however, the Herero people did succeed in reorganizing themselves, so that the attempt to destroy them as a distinct ethnicity failed. On the beginnings of this process after the war, see Gewald, *Redemption*, 241–75.
123. Poewe has pointed out that the level of mortality among German soldiers was high as well, as a result of the extreme climatic and other health-endangering conditions of the operation; in addition to which a significant number of suicides also occurred. Poewe, *Namibian Herero*, 75–77. The number of casualties had to be kept secret from the home arena, where a rapid military victory was expected. In some cases, the families of soldiers killed in action no longer received notification; some learnt of the deaths of their sons, brothers or husbands from the press. Cutting from the *Schleswig-Holsteinische Volkszeitung*, 8 October 1904, BA-MA RM 3/v. 10263, 66a.
124. Von Estorff, *Wanderungen*, 117.

125. Ibid.
126. Drechsler, *Südwestafrika* I, 172.
127. Von Estorff, *Wanderungen*, 116.
128. Ibid., 120.
129. Bley, *Kolonialherrschaft*, 191. See also Drechsler, *Südwestafrika* I, 187–220. Wishing to draw particular attention to the resistance of the Herero and Nama, Drechsler exaggerates the extent of the hostilities.
130. Drechsler, *Südwestafrika* I, 194–206.
131. Von Schlieffen to von Bülow, 23 November 1904, BAL R-1001/2089, quoted according to Drechsler, ibid., 166.
132. Ibid., 167–69.
133. The term 'concentration camp' had first been used by the Spanish during the war in Cuba in 1896, and reappeared only two years later during the American war in the Philippines. The expression became familiar throughout the world during the South African War (1899–1902). However, the use of the same name should not lead to the conclusion that there were any structural similarities to the Nazi concentration camps. Kaminski, *Konzentrationslager*, 34–35.
134. Imperial Chancellor to IGW, 13 January 1905, BAL R 1001/2087, 116a–117a.
135. IGW to FO, 10 December 1904, BAL R 1001/2087, 60a f.
136. Von Trotha to the missionary Kuhlmann, 18 February 1905, BAL R-1001/2089, quoted according to Bley, *Kolonialherrschaft*, 208.
137. IGW to FO-CD, 17 April 1906, BAL R 1001/2119, 42a–43b.
138. Gewald, *Redemption*, 218–20.
139. Von Trotha to General Staff, 10 March 1905, BAL R 1001/2117, 139a.
140. Von Trotha to Imperial Chancellor, 8 June 1905, BAL R 1001/2118, 122a–124a. The number of men among the prisoners was 1,853.
141. Leutwein, *Elf Jahre*, 523–24.
142. Gewald, *Redemption*, 221. On the activities of the Rhenish Mission in the collection camps, see also Glocke, *Zur Geschichte der Rheinischen Missionsgesellschaft*, 271–87.
143. The missionary Diehl to IGW, 15 February 1906, NAW ZBU D.IV.l.2 Vol. 5, 54a f.
144. Bley gives the figure as 12,000. Bley, *Kolonialherrschaft*, 208. Gewald says 15,000. Gewald, *Redemption*, 242.
145. Gewald, *Redemption*, 242.
146. Von Estorff, *Wanderungen*, 121–22.
147. The newly formed *Reichskolonialamt* (Imperial Colonial Office – ICO) took over the responsibilities of the former *Kolonialabteilung im Auswärtigen Amt* (Colonial Department of the Foreign Office – FO-CD) in May 1907.
148. Von Estorff, *Wanderungen*, 123.
149. *Chronik der Gemeinde Lüderitzbucht* (Chronicle of Lüderitzbucht Parish), ELCIN V. 16, 23.
150. Gewald, *Redemption*, 220.
151. Ibid., 222.
152. Arthur Koppel A.G. – Otavi Eisenbahnbau to Pahl, IGW Financial Officer, 5 December 1905, NAW ZBU *Geheimakten* VI.A. Vol. 1, 23a–26a.

153. Gewald, Redemption, 222.
154. The Otavi-Minen- und Eisenbahn-Gesellschaft (Otavi Mining and Railway Company), for example, was allocated 2,220 prisoners for the construction of the Otavi Railway, of whom 700 were women and 620 children. Drechsler, *Südwestafrika* II, 299. According to the Koppel Company, there were even as many as three or four non-working people to every worker. Arthur Koppel A.G. – Otavi Eisenbahnbau to Pahl, IGW Financial Officer, 5 December 1905, NAW ZBU *Geheimakten* VI.A. Vol. 1, 23a–26a.
155. IGW to FO-CD, 3 July 1905, BAL R 1001/2118, 154a–155a. Von Trotha too had already defended his Extermination Order as follows: 'Taking in women and children, on the other hand, when both of these groups are for the most part sick, represents an eminent danger to the troops, while providing them with food is simply impossible. I therefore consider it better that the nation should perish among themselves, and not also infect our soldiers and compromise their water and food supplies'. Von Trotha's diary, quoted according to Pool, *Maharero*, 292.
156. IGW to FO-CD, 3 July 1905, BAL R 1001/2118, 154a–155a.
157. *Lüderitzbucht Chronicle*, ELCIN V. 16, 21–26.
158. Ibid.
159. Ibid., 26–27.
160. Von Estorff to Schutztruppe, 10 April 1907, BAL R 1001/2140, 88a f.
161. Hintrager to FO-CD, 10 April 1907, BAL R 1001/2140, 87a. Hintrager had replaced Tecklenburg as Deputy Governor in 1907.
162. Drechsler, *Südwestafrika* I, 212.
163. *Lüderitzbucht Chronicle*, ELCIN V. 16, 27.
164. Drechsler, *Südwestafrika* I, 213.
165. Swakopmund DO to the Local Commandant of the Schutztruppe, Swakopmund, 19 July 1907, NAW ZBU W.III.F.4. Vol. 1, 2b.
166. Circulated Order, IGW, 18 January 1908, BAL R 1001/2235, 49a.
167. File memo relating to a telegram of 15 January 1904, n.d., unsigned, BAL R 1001/2090: 2a. See also Commander of SMS *Habicht* to Admiralty Staff (transcript of telegram), 21 January 1904 (date received), BAL R 1001/2111, 62a. The figures differ in the two sources between 500 and 600.
168. Government of Cameroon to FO-CD, 6 April 1904, BAL R 1001/2090, 4a f.
169. On the fate of the Witbooi in Togo and Cameroon, see also Drechsler, *Südwestafrika* I, 181–83.
170. Tecklenburg to FO (telegram), 21 October 1904, BAL R 1001/2090, 5a f.
171. FO-CD to IGW (telegram), 23 October 1904, BAL R 1001/2090, 7a.
172. Government of Togo to FO-CD (telegram), 24 October 1904, BAL R 1001/2090, 8a.
173. This figure can be derived from the confirmation of the Woermann company's invoice for the costs of passage for 119 Witbooi. Commissariat of the Schutztruppe for German South West Africa to FO-CD, 19 April 1905, BAL R 1001/2090, 17a. The sources give no indication as to who these additional 39 Witbooi were.

174. Memo relating to a telegram from von Trotha dated 28 October 1904, stating that the Witbooi had been dispatched. Memorandum, FO-CD, n.d., BAL R 1001/2090, 9a.
175. Government of Togo to FO-CD, 12 December 1904, BAL R 1001/2090, 11a.
176. FO-CD to Government of Togo, 7 January 1905, BAL R 1001/2090, 12a f.
177. FO-CD to IGW (telegram), 3 July 1905, BAL R 1001/2090, 21a.
178. IGW to FO-CD (telegram), 4 July 1905, BAL R 1001/2090, 22a.
179. FO-CD to Government of Togo (telegram), 4 July 1905, BAL R 1001/2090, 23a.
180. Von Trotha to FO-CD (telegram), 5 July 1905, BAL R 1001/2090, 24a.
181. FO-CD to Government of Togo (telegram), 14 July 1905, BAL R 1001/2090, 27a.
182. FO-CD to IGW (telegram), 20 July 1905, BAL R 1001/2090, 30a.
183. Von Trotha to FO-CD (telegram), 24 July 1905, BAL R 1001/2090, 34a f.
184. FO-CD to Government of Cameroon, 29 July 1905, BAL R 1001/2090, 35a.
185. FO-CD to IGW, 8 August 1905, BAL R 1001/2090, 40a.
186. Von Trotha to FO-CD (telegram), 24 July 1905, BAL R 1001/2090, 34a f.
187. Government of Cameroon to FO-CD (telegram), 4 August 1905, BAL R 1001/2090, 39a.
188. Government of Cameroon to FO-CD, 21 July 1905, BAL R 1001/2090, 41a–42a.
189. It is not known what became of the other nine Nama.
190. Government of Cameroon to FO-CD, 23 December 1905, BAL R 1001/2090, 45a–46b.
191. FO-CD to Government of Cameroon, 16 November 1905, BAL R 1001/2090, 47a f.
192. IGW to FO-CD, 11 February 1906, BAL R 1001/2090, 58a.
193. Government of Cameroon to FO-CD, 28 June 1906, BAL R 1001/2090, 61a.
194. IGW to FO-CD (telegram), 10 July 1906, BAL R 1001/2090, 62a.
195. IGW to FO-CD (telegram), 23 July 1906, BAL R 1001/2090, 71a.
196. Memo, Section 10, FO-CD, 29 August 1906, BAL R 1001/2090, 85a–86a.
197. FO-CD to IGW (telegram), 28 July 1906, BAL R 1001/2090, 72a. This decision was taken at a meeting attended by Rose, Conze, Golinelli and Quade. Hohenlohe, who signed the message to von Lindequist, was merely informed of the meeting's outcome and thereupon approved it.
198. IGW to FO-CD (telegram), 12 August 1906, BAL R 1001/2090, 74a.
199. Memo by Richter, 29 August 1906, BAL R 1001/2090, 85a–86a.
200. Memo by Richter, 23 August 1906, BAL R 1001/2090, 78a–79a.
201. Drechsler, *Südwestafrika* I, 211.
202. Ludwig Boldt, of Boldt-Futterfabriken, Stettin, to FO-CD, 31 March 1905, BAL R 1001/2090, 16a. Newspaper cutting, ibid., 16b (n.d., no source given). Drechsler gives further examples in *Südwestafrika* I, 147.
203. Adolf Hentze, Hanover, to ICO, 1 March 1907, BAL R 1001/2090, 109a f.

2

THE CODIFICATION OF 'NATIVE POLICY' AFTER 1905

Under von Trotha the civil administration of the colony was unable to exert more than a minor influence on Native Policy, as the General had taken control of all executive functions and, after Leutwein's recall in November 1904, of the remaining aspects of gubernatorial business as well. It was not until the arrival of the new Governor, Friedrich von Lindequist, and von Trotha's departure on 19 November 1905 that the civil administration was able to reassert its decision-making competences in all matters of Native Policy, as long as they did not relate to purely military issues.[1]

The civil administration now set about drawing up a comprehensive rule book to govern relationships between the African and the White populations. This had been made possible by the German military victory, which had eliminated the necessity to pay any regard to power relationships with the Africans or between the different groups making up the African population. Purchased at the price of the deaths of thousands and the almost complete destruction of the social and political structures of the vanquished, this victory had opened up the way towards a reorientation of Native Policy. Such a reorientation was in any case essential, since after the war there was no desire, and nor would it have been feasible, to continue with the policy of indirect rule. Instead, with the structures of African society in ruins, indirect rule was replaced by the direct subjection of the individual African to German administration.

Preparatory work on drawing up a concept for this had already been done by Deputy Governor Hans Tecklenburg, who had remained in South West Africa throughout the war. In addition, since mid-1905, Governor Designate von Lindequist and the head of the South West Africa desk in the Colonial Department of the Foreign Office in Berlin, Angelo Golinelli, had been engaged with others in discussions on the future shape of Native Policy – discussions which had taken place in Berlin under the chairmanship of the Director of the Colonial Department, Oskar Wilhelm Stübel.[2]

The objective that Tecklenburg, von Lindequist and Golinelli were pursuing was that of achieving a comprehensive codification of Native Policy, and to do so they drew upon preparatory studies dating from the prewar period. So it was not the individual provisions that were new, but the bundling of them into ordinances that were basically intended to be applicable throughout the colony to every individual African, even if their implementation had to be limited for the time being to the central and southern areas of the Colony – the so-called 'Police Zone'.

The regulations concerned encompassed the following areas: the land issue; the system of state control envisaged in the Control and Pass Ordinances; the employment relationships between Whites and Africans set out in the so-called Master and Servant Ordinance, which meant the latter being compelled to work for the former; and measures to promote racial segregation.

The first of these issues to come back onto the agenda was that of the distribution of land ownership as between Whites and Africans, which had already been hotly debated before the war. The restraint that had been practised under Leutwein was no longer found to be necessary, as the Herero and Nama had been defeated and their livestock had perished or had been confiscated by the Germans. Many people had lost their lives, others were on the run or being held prisoner. So it was a question of taking advantage of this situation, which provided (from the German point of view) an incomparably favourable opportunity to confiscate all the land of the vanquished enemies and any livestock they had managed to retain, with the intention of breaking down the communal organizations of the Herero and Nama and giving formal effect to their elimination as 'political power factors'.[3] Parallel to this, the task was to cement the new power relationships on the basis of the subordinate status of the Africans.

The three Native Ordinances of 1907 set out a system of rigorous control over the African population. They created a basis on which the Africans could be subjected to social discipline, and could be obliged to work for Whites. Employment regulations were mainly intended to give effect to this compulsion to work; however, they went beyond this in that they did also provide for some minimum rights for the employee. This minimal degree of protection arose out of the realization that only the 'proper' treatment of African workers could guarantee harmonious labour relations and prevent acts of desperation such as had been experienced during the war. At the same time, this attempt to create a 'semifree' labour market also took account of modern ideas of the 'free play of market forces' in the way it provided for manpower to be distributed among employers who were in competition with each other – that is to say, above all, the farmers, the mining industry and the railway construction companies.

The whole system was backed up by accompanying measures to promote racial segregation, intended to make sure that there was no opportunity to climb the ladder into the privileged upper strata of society. Apart from the political objectives of such measures, ideas of 'racial hygiene' increasingly came to the fore, with their proponents seeking to prevent any miscegenation between Whites and Africans.

These various thematic complexes will be dealt with one by one in this chapter, their precursors identified, the way they arose in their various contexts described and the intentions associated with them set out, with the most detailed consideration being accorded to the three Native Ordinances of 1907, as it was these that subsequently came to form the core of codified Native Law.

The Expropriation of African Land

The military defeat of the Herero and Nama, the fact that their social and political organizations had largely been destroyed, the loss of their herds and the way they were dispersed in prison camps located throughout the colony: all these were factors that made it possible to settle the land question once and for all. Already under Governor Leutwein, areas had been designated as being available for White settlement, and these had been further extended in treaties made with Samuel Maharero and other chiefs. The process had been accompanied by discussions between the settlers, the Rhenish Missionary Society and the Governor's Office on the issue of how much of the land should be used for this purpose.[4] It had originally been intended to declare 75 per cent of the land as government land, while the Africans were to retain 25 per cent;[5] but such 'restraint' now proved to be no longer necessary.

The occasion to look more closely at the land issue arose out of a dispute between the Colony's Revenue Administration and the

Deutsche Kolonialgesellschaft, which had nothing at all to do with the war against the Herero and Nama.[6] Adolf Lüderitz, to whom the Deutsche Kolonialgesellschaft was the legal successor, had bought land from the Oorlam under Jan Jonker Afrikaner, and had agreed to pay them an annual royalty for the mining rights. When this community disappeared from the map, having being absorbed into the Nama population in the last third of the nineteenth century,[7] the Deutsche Kolonialgesellschaft refused to recognize the German Empire as the legal successor to the Oorlam and therefore to pay the mining royalties to the South West Africa Revenue Administration, as the Imperial Government demanded it should.[8] The debate on this problem that was carried on between the colonial administrators in Berlin and Windhoek furnished a precedent for the land expropriations of the following years, in particular to the extent that it related to the position of the Chiefs and their possible legal successors. In the course of the debate the German Administration's claims became more and more far-reaching, ultimately embracing almost all the land that was not already in the hands of Whites. The responsible people in the Colonial Department in Berlin and in the Governor's Office in Windhoek exploited the opportunity afforded by the war to expropriate all the Herero and a large proportion of the Nama. Apart from the motives of revenge and of punishing the Africans for resisting, there was also a fear that the settlers might pursue claims for compensation. The official expropriation of land was intended to ensure that it was the Revenue Administration that emerged from the chaos of the war as the owners of the land, and not the White settlers.

The Colonial Administration took the view, as Oskar Hintrager formulated it in March 1905, that Jan Jonker Afrikaner had sold the area to the merchant Adolf Lüderitz in his capacity as *Kaptein* of the Oorlam and not as a private person. When German protection was established over the territory, the German Empire had allowed him and the other chiefs to retain certain rights of sovereignty, such as the powers of the Captaincy, the rights of legal jurisdiction and the right to receive duties payable on the sale of land. But Germany had only agreed to them for certain practical reasons, among which had been its lack of effective means of exercising power, a lack of knowledge of the rights and customs of the Africans, and the desire to make the chiefs more inclined to accept German protection. It had not been the intention, Hintrager maintained, that the Kapteins should retain these rights for all time: rather, they had been invested in the person of the Kaptein holding office at the time, and would not automatically be inherited by his successor. This limitation on the sovereign power of the German state would be forfeited if the Kaptein concerned were to be guilty of abusing his office, in particular by resisting or by ceding his rights of sovereignty to foreigners, or if the position of chief were to cease to exist altogether, as had happened in the case of Jan Jonker Afrikaner's Oorlam. But if the limitations on the powers of the protecting state were to be removed, those powers would revert to the Colonial Government. And it was by virtue of this situation that the German Empire had already taken possession of the private property of members of Jan Jonker Afrikaner's group when it was dissolved, and had become his legal successor.[9]

In this way, Hintrager provided the legal argumentation, going beyond the concrete case at issue, for the expropriation of those groups involved in the Herero and Nama Wars. Since the way the Deutsche Kolonialgesellschaft had challenged the Revenue Administration's claims meant that the issue had now 'become of practical importance', he recommended that it should be 'regulated by an Ordinance', which could then be used 'to sequestrate the land of those now in rebellion',[10] thereby initiating a debate on an extensive confiscation of African property.

In March 1905 Golinelli accepted Hintrager's opinion and demanded that the matter should be settled by a new legal instrument, as he expected challenges to the Revenue Administration from other companies as well as from the Kolonialgesellschaft. He pleaded for an ordinance to be promulgated on the basis of which the land of resisting communities could be declared 'Crown Land', and which would provide 'that the payments and royalties contractually paid to the Kapteins of these areas in the past, and still to be paid in future, [would] be paid to the South West Africa Revenue Administration'.[11] It was already foreseeable at this juncture that one of the consequences of the war would be the dissolution of the 'tribes'.

Golinelli immediately prepared the draft of an Ordinance under which the Colonial Government could sequestrate, with the Revenue Authority as beneficiary, the 'movable and immovable property of such natives as have taken part in hostilities and belligerent acts against the German government or against non-natives or natives of the colony of South West Africa', or had 'provided direct or indirect support for such acts' or 'entered into any other form of relationship directed against the German government with the hostile natives'.[12]

Golinelli took account of the original occasion for this measure by also including a regulation providing for confiscation in the case of any groups 'that have lost their tribal organization', even if they had not themselves taken part in belligerent activities. He emphasized explicitly that 'capital amounts, interest, rental payments, postal service charges, payments in consideration of land or mineral rights, and all other sums owed to those affected by such sequestration' should be paid to the State Revenue Administration.[13] In this way he wanted to prevent settlers or the land concession and mining companies from exploiting the situation created by the war to quietly free themselves of their debts. Where Whites had claims upon Africans, these were to be satisfied only if they related to the Africans' private property, but not to communal assets.

Over and above the need to deal with the original Oorlam case and the effects of the war, Golinelli also wanted to make it possible to confiscate property in cases in which 'the number of members of a tribe is in such disproportion to its area of land that it is not possible for the tribe to actually exploit such land'. In such cases, however, only 'such part of the tribal area as is not required for the maintenance of the tribe may be sequestered'.[14] With this provision, Golinelli made the Sequestration Ordinance applicable to all the remaining 'tribes' in the future, irrespective of whether their members had been involved in resistance activity or not, and so created a legal basis for deciding what was to be regarded as state property in the colony. The decision as to whether or not the land was in fact adequately exploited would be made by the Germans alone. In this way Golinelli introduced the criterion of economic efficiency into the debate, a criterion derived from the Germans' colonial objective of achieving the best possible economic exploitation of the land. This represented an important element in the legitimation of colonial rule, which was based on the one hand on the 'cultural improvement' of the Africans, and on the other hand on the supposed need to pursue development in the colonies.

The draft ordinance was thus directed not only against the Africans, but also against the claims of the settlers and the land concession companies. This makes clear the legalistic character of German rule, which was not willing or able to allow itself to be satisfied by the appropriation of the Africans' land as it had de facto already occurred. It was essential to have a watertight legal framework in order to be able to reject claims from Whites. This was necessary because of the self-imposed restraint of the German colonial bureaucracy in legal matters, and because while the Africans themselves, in the situation they were in after their defeat, were in no position to pursue any claims in court, German settlers and the land concession companies were able to exploit the regulations that had previously existed. The German colonial bureaucracy was bound by statutes and regulations, and as Native Policy always impacted on the rights of the Whites as well, measures relating to it were also subject to monitoring by the courts of law.

Even the reservations that had been set up before the war were to be explicitly subject to possible sequestration – an indication of the fundamental manner in which Golinelli was seeking to reverse the existing ownership situation. In 1903 (i.e. before the turbulent months of the war), nobody was yet interested in taking over this 'tribal' land, and only 10 per cent (36,000 sq. km) of the area earmarked for German settlement had so far been sold off to settlers.[15]

Under Golinelli's proposals, not only 'tribal' assets but also the private property of Africans were to be subject to possible confiscation. Where only certain members of a 'tribe' had been guilty of the offences listed, it was to be possible for both the individual property of the guilty parties and also a proportion of their communal assets to be expropriated.

It was not Golinelli's intention, however, to deprive the Africans of all possibility of pursuing autonomous economic activity. He explicitly proposed that the Governor should 'take the measures necessary for the resettlement and economic preservation of the natives affected by the sequestration.' It was therefore to be made possible for Africans to be economically independent. This point was so important to him that he pointed out again elsewhere in the text that even when it was a matter of satisfying the claims of Whites against Africans, 'those assets are to be exempt from attachment by creditors that are essential to the maintenance of the economic existence of the debtor and his family.'[16] Thus the ideas contained in the draft ordinance did not originally stem from a desire to destroy the basis of the Africans' economic existence as a convenient way of forcing them to enter into employment. But this was to change in the course of the discussion of the Sequestration Ordinance, above all through the influence of Tecklenburg.

Although the Foreign Office Colonial Department approved Golinelli's draft, it requested the Governor's Office in Windhoek to put forward a draft of its own without first initiating the officials there into what Golinelli had proposed.[17] The Colonial Department apparently wanted to get a second independent proposal from them, as they were the ones who were most familiar with the drastically changed situation resulting from the war. Here too the focus was to be on a general settlement of the land question that went beyond the concrete current issues. Windhoek was explicitly requested to state its views on the question of 'how due regard is to be paid to the economic survival of the natives affected by sequestration'.[18]

An analysis of the detailed position paper drawn up by Deputy Governor Tecklenburg and sent by him to the Colonial Department on 17 July 1905, together with a draft Ordinance written in collaboration with Local Court Judge and Deputy Chief Justice Dr Meyer, demonstrates the substantially more radical position held by this 'man on the spot'. His document contains proposals for a future Native Policy that go far beyond the direct expropriation of land, and that in part anticipate key features of the Native Ordinances promulgated in 1907.[19]

Tecklenburg's attitude had been shaped by the experience of the war, which had destroyed his faith in a Native Policy built on the assumption that the Africans were loyal. The fact that not all Africans had taken part in the war did nothing to alter this: 'Those among the natives that have not yet joined the rebellion have desisted from it not through loyalty to the Germans, but because they consider us to be the stronger party, and that the prospects for booty and reward are better on our side'.[20] His assessment of the Africans' 'unreliability' was reflected in far-reaching proposals for expropriation. Going beyond the confiscations planned by Golinelli and the Colonial Department, he declared himself to be in favour of complete expropriation, even in those cases where only some members of a community had taken part in the resistance. As his only concession to the neutrality maintained by the Kapteins concerned, he envisaged 'allowing them to keep part of their former tribal area without charge for the lifetime of the Kaptein concerned or as long as political considerations make it expedient, for the use of those who did not rebel'. So they too would be de jure dispossessed, and the State would be able to take possession of their land at any time. In Tecklenburg's opinion it would be 'a display of weakness that would come bitterly home to roost if we were to allow the present opportunity to declare all native land to be Crown Land to slip out of our hands unused'. Only the Rehoboth Basters would be permitted to retain ownership of their land for the time being; but even in their case expropriation was to be admissible 'for reasons of public interest'. In including this provision, Tecklenburg was thinking of the plans to build a railway from Windhoek to Rehoboth, the route of which would cross land owned by the Rehoboth Basters.[21]

There was thus to be no possibility of any remaining property rights coming into conflict with the Colonial Administration's development aims. Since in any individual case it would be the Colonial Administration that decided what was necessary in the public interest – that is to say, in the interests of opening up the country for the benefit of the colonizers – Tecklenburg's proposal even undermined the property rights of the Basters, which were still officially recognized but which he himself regarded as being only provisional.

Whereas Golinelli's proposal had focused on establishing an unassailable legal solution to the land issue, Tecklenburg was concerned to bring about a fundamental change in African social and economic structures. He not only favoured more rigorous measures than Golinelli, but also endowed expropriation with a completely new objective: apart from punishing the resisters and settling the question of compensation, he wanted to exploit the opportunity to force Africans to accept work as dependent employees by destroying the basis of their previous economic existence. In the draft produced by Golinelli and the Colonial Department, expropriation was to be limited by the requirement to ensure the Africans' economic survival, whereas Tecklenburg sought to eliminate precisely that. His proposals went beyond the question of land ownership: because it was his intention 'to get the matter of the tribes and tribal areas sorted out once and for all'. Going beyond the complete expropriation of the Africans' land, he also proposed a fundamental prohibition on their keeping cattle, 'since the natives cannot be left in charge of the amount of land that would then be required for grazing'. Only for those Africans who had not been involved in the war, especially the Rehoboth Basters and the Ovambo, were temporary exceptions to be made. It was also to be generally forbidden for Africans, except for the Rehoboth Basters, to acquire plots of land; and African workers were to live directly on the farms where they worked or else in larger settlements close to the centres of population. For these residential areas they were to pay a rental charge, which could gradually 'be developed into a general tax on the natives'. Only farmworkers would be exempted from this rental payment, so that there would be an incentive for Africans to seek employment on the farms. *Werfs* (African settlements) 'located in out-of-the-way places in an attempt to escape the attentions of the police' should 'not be tolerated', as 'memories of tribal organization and ownership of land would find nourishment there'. In Tecklenburg's view, no largish community of Africans 'should be able to exist as an independent entity closed off from the outside world'. And in addition, freedom of movement was to be abolished and a requirement to carry a pass introduced. These far-reaching measures, anticipating the later Native Ordinances, were in Tecklenburg's view 'unavoidably necessary in the interests of our community of settlers'.[22]

With the demand that farmers who had suffered 'losses of assets that could not be made good' as a result of the war should have their liabilities towards resisting Africans (that is to say, payments still due for the purchase of their farms) remitted, to the extent that they had not previously received compensation from the Revenue Administration, Tecklenburg placed himself completely on the side of the settlers:

> It will never be possible to make it clear to the settler that he cannot set off what he owes to the rebellious native Tom against what he is owed by the equally rebellious native Dick or Harry. He will always point out that the Revenue Administration, having already confiscated the natives' entire possessions, is able to suck the natives' white debtor dry, whilst the white man has to forfeit his claims against the native.[23]

This was Tecklenburg's expression of support for general debt relief to the farmers with regard to the liabilities they had entered into when buying their farms. His point of view was that as the farmers for their part were no longer able to collect loans they had made to 'natives', the Revenue Administration, which now held the expropriated African land, ought to compensate them for their losses by granting favourable prices when selling farms to them.

Judge Meyer formulated a draft ordinance out of Tecklenburg's proposals. It would be possible for the 'tribal' assets of all 'Herero and Hottentots [Nama] who had lived in tribal organizations until the outbreak of the disturbances' to be sequestrated without limitation. This would apply also to Chief Nehale's Ovambo, who had attacked Namutoni in 1904;[24] this would be the first time that the German colonizers had attempted to get their hands on the property of the Ovambo in the north of the Colony, who until then had largely managed to avoid attracting the attention of the authorities. However, the Colonial Department did not accept the demand for the Ovambo to be expropriated, presumably because they did not want to make it incumbent upon themselves to intervene in Ovamboland, which would have been quite impossible for them to do.

As far as the Colonial Department was concerned, the proposals made by Tecklenburg and Meyer went too far, and so on 10 November 1905, in collaboration with the Imperial Office of Justice, they worked out a compromise between Golinelli's draft and Meyer's.[25] This was promulgated on 26 December 1905 as the 'Imperial Ordinance concerning the Sequestration of Native Assets in the Colony of South West Africa',[26] thus creating the formal conditions for the expropriation to take place. It provided that, by a decree of the Governor, the communal assets of those Africans 'who had taken part in hostilities and belligerent acts against the Government, against non-natives or against other natives', or who had 'provided direct or indirect support' for such acts, could be sequestrated. Even if only some of the 'tribe' had taken part in such acts, that would be sufficient. Thus the demand for an ordinance dealing with the issue in a fundamental manner was fulfilled in a way that also provided the basis for dealing with any other possible cases of expropriation in the future. In addition, the land of 'such native tribes as have lost their tribal organization', or whose numbers were 'so low in relation to the size of the tribal land that it does not appear to be possible for the tribe to exploit its whole tribal area economically', was in danger of being declared Crown Land. The only land that had to be excepted was the amount that appeared essential to maintain the 'tribal' organization. And as it was the Governor's Office itself that decided whether land was indeed being utilized economically, this was a warrant for any expropriation that might be intended. Even the 'tribal' reservations that had already been established had the explicit threat of sequestration hanging over them as well.

On 23 March 1906, as 'the settlement activity that is now getting under way makes it urgent to clarify as soon as possible the ownership situation with regard to land',[27] Governor von Lindequist made use of the Ordinance for the first time to sequestrate the 'movable and immovable tribal assets' of all Herero north of the Tropic of Capricorn, and also of the Swartbooi Nama of Fransfontein and the Topnaar Nama of Sesfontein.[28] This measure became legally effective on 7 August 1906.[29]

However, von Lindequist had to give up the idea of immediately extending the Ordinance to apply to the other Nama as well, as he was afraid that 'the necessity they would then be faced with of having to earn their living in future by working, without any tribal possessions of their own', would further inflame the will of the guerrilla fighters, who had not yet been finally beaten, to resist. As long as 'a leader of the resourcefulness and influence of a Morenga is not yet in our power', he wanted to avoid anything 'that might contribute to reawakening the rebellion and to strengthening his ability to resist'. With regard to the 'provisos attached to the Sequestration Ordinance requiring the natives to be allocated as much of their livestock as is essential for their livelihood', he intended to 'make use of this provision in a way that is appropriate to each individual case'. He laid particular stress on the fact that the livestock would remain formally the property of the Revenue Administration, in order to prevent 'creditors from taking it away from the natives in satisfaction of their claims, of which there would otherwise be a very great danger'.[30]

On 8 May 1907 von Lindequist repeated the procedure in respect of the Witbooi, Bethanie, Fransman and Veldskoendraer Nama, the Red Nation of Hoachanas and the Bondelswarts including the

Swartmodder Nama.[31] For the Bondelswarts and the Stuurmann people, who in November and December 1906 had concluded a treaty of submission and a peace treaty respectively with the Germans, the exceptions laid down in those treaties applied,[32] but this made no more than a minor difference to the overall extent of the expropriations. The Bondelswarts were given the western part of Warmbad, Hab, Gabis, Draihuk and Wortel as places to settle in, together with goats, sheep and hens, while Cornelius Stuurmann was settled at Spitzkopp and provided with goats and two oxcarts.

Once these confiscations too had become legally unchallengeable after the expiry of the period for raising objections on 11 September 1907,[33] the ownership situation had been fundamentally transformed. All the 'tribal' land in South West Africa, except in Ovamboland and the Caprivi Strip and with the exception of the land belonging to the Rehoboth Basters and the Berseba Nama, was now in German ownership.[34] In this way, von Lindequist had almost completely realized his intention of doing away with 'the independent existence of all the native tribes who took part in the rebellion for all time, in order to prevent any future unrest'.[35]

Although the impetus for the Sequestration Ordinance had arisen out of an individual case that had nothing to do with the war against the Herero and Nama, the responsible people in the Colonial Department and in government in South West Africa had taken advantage of the 'favourable' circumstances after the military defeat of the Herero and Nama to confiscate all the land of their defeated enemies, and even the livestock they had managed to retain. What is more, the confiscations by the state meant that it was virtually impossible for private individuals to claim compensation from Africans, so that it was first and foremost the Revenue Administration that was able to satisfy its demands out of their assets. Making the colonial state into the legal successor to the African nations secured for the colony's treasury the income from the royalties that the mining companies had contractually agreed to pay to the Africans.

While the Sequestration Ordinance was successful to the extent that it brought the communal land of the communities involved in the resistance into the ownership of the State, it was less successful with regard to the State's desire to also take possession of land owned privately by Africans. This was to become apparent a few years later when problems arose in connection with the Vilander people, a small Baster group that no longer existed.

In 1910 a dispute arose between two Whites who both claimed ownership of the Koichas farm, one of them maintaining that he had bought it directly from the Vilander people. In order to eliminate the legal uncertainty, the Governor's Office proposed to expropriate the Vilander people retrospectively.[36] This proposal was reiterated by Hintrager a year later, since 'considerable uncertainty currently exists with regard to the ownership situation in relation to land' and 'it is necessary to give future purchasers an unimpeachable title to the Vilander farms that are currently ownerless'.[37]

A legal opinion drawn up within the Imperial Colonial Office[38] showed, however, that it was not possible in this case to expropriate the property on the basis of the Sequestration Ordinance of 26 December 1905. Although the original draft of the Ordinance had envisaged the confiscation of private property too, this clause had been deleted from the final text since there was no desire to free Africans from the debts they owed to White creditors. It had been all the easier to omit this provision because it was assumed that only the Rehoboth Basters had any private property, that of all the other Africans having been destroyed in the war.[39] But as David Vilander, the last Kaptein of the group, had distributed his people's communal property to the members of the group in the form of individual farms,[40] under German law this real estate was private property and its expropriation was therefore not legally permissible.[41] But this also removed the legal basis for all expropriations, particularly in South West Africa, since there, in contrast to all the other German colonies in Africa, there was no applicable Crown Land Ordinance under which 'all land for which no rights of ownership can be proved by any natural person, legal entity, family or association of families or local or tribal community is ownerless and subject to the exclusive right of the Revenue Administration to take possession of it'.[42]

The legal opinion already quoted did, however, offer a wildly bizarre solution to the problem, which even drew upon traditional African law in its argumentation. Although it was impossible to sequestrate the farms as long as they were in private ownership, it might be admissible if the farms – for example, after the death of their Baster owners – had reverted to the community in accordance with Baster law. This would be the case if one were to assume that the distribution of the property by Vilander represented a 'development of traditional law in accordance with the principles of German property law, analogous to the way in which Germanic law, which had been based on communal relationships, was developed on an individualistic basis by Roman law'. Since it continued to be the case that 'at the time [of the distribution of the property by David Vilander] it was provided for that in certain circumstances, e.g. the death of the

Baster owner, a property should revert to the tribe', then 'particularly since the individualistic influences of German or English law can only have been very minor in the Vilander tribe in 1889', it might be the case that 'the distribution as private property was only to be regarded as a temporary phenomenon'. In this case, 'merely taking possession might suffice', since 'land that had not actually been inhabited by a tribe for ten years' could be 'regarded as ownerless land'.[43]

Thus despite the fact that the handling of the expropriation issue was presented as being strictly in conformity with the rule of law, the experts from the Imperial Colonial Office were quite prepared to make use of intricate legal constructions and to resort selectively to traditional law where this served the interests of the colonizers.

In the end, the Governor's Office decided to take the easiest option and did not impose a formal confiscation, in order to avoid the possibility that this might be 'exploited by undesirable elements in the neighbouring border areas of the Union of South Africa as a pretext for agitation against alleged legal uncertainty in the colony, which it is essential to avoid'. In January 1914, therefore, Hintrager instructed the responsible District Office in Hasuur to treat the Vilander communal area as 'effectively ownerless land', and gave his approval for the District Office to take possession of the area in question on behalf of the colony's Revenue Administration.[44]

The 'Native Ordinances' of 1907

As a result of the expropriations, most of the Herero and Nama living in the centre and the south of the Colony had lost their political and social organization, and the African societies had ceased to exist as political power factors. This meant that the policy towards the chiefs that had been practised until the outbreak of the war (i.e. the use of local elites as intermediaries between the German administration and the individual Africans) had lost its raison d'être. It was now replaced by the direct subjection of every individual African to the German administration and to German laws and regulations. Precisely in view of the anarchic conditions that had prevailed while von Trotha had been in charge, with the comprehensive and indiscriminate internment of thousands of Africans in prison camps and an unknown number of refugees living in hiding in inaccessible areas of South West Africa, the Colonial Administration saw itself obliged to create a new legal framework for its day-to-day dealings with the African population – one that would, as the Administration saw it, meet the needs that had arisen after a time of great change. Moreover, the military victory of the Schutztruppe had created conditions under which a reorientation of Native Policy was possible. This reorientation was intended to institutionalize the subjugation of the Africans that had been achieved by military means, and to cement their subordinate position. The German Colonial Administration had already, before 1904, been in search of ways to effect the direct subjection of all Africans to German prewar legal instruments and regulations, only to find that it lacked the strength it would have needed to put this through, or at least that it would only able to do so in certain districts. It therefore renewed its efforts in this direction and set about pushing ahead with the codification of those instruments into a unified legal structure. The core of this Native Legislation consisted of the three Native Ordinances of 1907: the Control Ordinance,[45] the Pass Ordinance[46] and the so-called Master and Servant Ordinance (*Gesindeverordnung*).[47] Outlining the debates and measures that had preceded them will serve to demonstrate conclusively that there was continuity with the Native Policy of the prewar period. It is therefore essential, in order both to be able to draw conclusions about their intentions and also to examine how they were actually implemented in the everyday life of the colony, to analyse their origins and their content in detail.

How the Ordinances Came into Being

Initial steps to bring the Africans under state surveillance and control, to restrict their freedom of movement and to control by law the employment contracts concluded between Whites and Africans had already been taken before the turn of the century. As early as 1892 the Colonial Department of the Foreign Office had attempted to prescribe that state agencies employing Africans should make a written contract with every individual employee, which was to contain 'the name of the person recruited, the date of the beginning of his service, the nature of the employment and the wage at which he is employed'. In particular, this contract, which was to be executed in duplicate, was to list 'the payments made, any advances made, any disciplinary measures imposed and any deductions from wages', and the date of termination of the contract. The document containing these proposals had been drawn up in connection with a series of disputes over wage claims from Africans who, having been employed temporarily to provide services, in particular on expeditions, had afterwards made claims for wage payments that they said they had been promised verbally.[48] Although this obligation to make a written contract was only intended to apply to state offices and agencies, the form of the contract envisaged anticipated that of the later *Dienstbuch* (employment record or logbook), particularly to the extent that any disciplinary measures or punishments were to be recorded in it. The Administration itself saw the document as being the first stage in the process of drawing up a Master and Servant Ordinance.[49]

An initial step towards the general regulation of the conditions under which Africans were employed had been undertaken in 1894 by the District Officer of Otjimbingwe, the later Governor of South West Africa and Colonial Secretary in the Imperial Colonial Office, Friedrich von Lindequist. In a 'District Police Ordinance concerning the Relationship between Employers and Workers' for his District he laid down that in the event of any dispute arising out of an employment contract that had either been concluded in writing or witnessed by the police, both parties were entitled to request the local police to adjudicate. The police were then obliged to initiate proceedings in relation to any alleged breaches of contract, and to 'do everything in their power to bring runaway workers back to their employers'. In this way, von Lindequist got an organ of the state executive involved in private contractual relationships between employers and employees. He accorded employers 'parental powers of (physical) chastisement' (*elterliches Züchtigungsrecht*) with regard to workers who were under the age of eighteen; but he appears to have been well aware of the danger that the right to inflict corporal punishment might be abused by Whites, for he provided for a fine of up to 500 marks or a prison sentence of up to one month for cases of 'excesses relating to the right of chastisement'. Also of great significance was his introduction of a compulsion on unemployed people to take up work, which was also incorporated into the later Native Ordinances in the form of the so-called Vagrancy Section: this provision stated that any individuals without visible means of support – 'persons who are not able to demonstrate that they are able to provide for themselves out of their own means or by undertaking work, and who roam around the country from place to place without working' – were to be 'assigned work by the police authorities against the provision of board, clothing or cash payment', and could also be handed over to a private employer. Such people were, however, to be remunerated at a rate to be determined by the police, but amounting to at least one mark per day.[50]

This measure introduced by von Lindequist immediately found Leutwein's approval: he saw in it a promising instrument to 'relieve the very acute shortage of labour' and to 'gradually accustom the unpropertied natives, in particular the Berg Damaras and the

Hottentots, to working'. Moreover, he reported that similar provisions were under consideration in Windhoek District as well.[51]

Almost two years later, Gibeon District Office followed von Lindequist's example and promulgated a similar Ordinance. As in Otjimbingwe, the registration of a contract that had been concluded was voluntary; but the contract had to have a term of at least one month. Only if the contract had been registered could the police intervene in the event of any dispute. The worker had to observe a fourteen-day period of notice, and could then leave his employment as long as he had no debts to be worked off. If his employer still had claims against him, these had to be reported to the police; this provision was intended to stop employers from arbitrarily preventing a worker from giving notice. If the employee failed to comply with the formal requirements for giving notice, any claims against his employer would be void and he could, 'on application, be punished by the police for running away [i.e. leaving his workplace without permission], and brought back to his employer'. With this measure, the Gibeon District Officer, Henning von Burgsdorff, like von Lindequist before him, had moved in the direction of criminalizing breaches of private contracts. The African, by contrast, was much less well protected against dismissal: 'If the worker performs his duties badly or makes impudent demands, any employer shall be entitled to dismiss his servant immediately, or, if the contract has been registered with the police, first to request the assistance of the police'. In contrast to von Lindequist, von Burgsdorff rejected any idea either of employers taking the law into their own hands or of any 'right of physical chastisement' on the part of employers, and emphasized that 'misdemeanours' and 'disputes' were to be adjudicated by the police, whose duty it would be to exercise supervision over any punishment of the Africans.[52]

These Ordinances having been promulgated in Otjimbingwe and Gibeon, the Governor appears to have considered introducing a similar measure to cover the whole of the Colony; and he asked the head of the Southern District, a position occupied at the time by the later Colonial Department official Angelo Golinelli, to submit a formal opinion.[53] Golinelli was well disposed towards the idea of the Governor issuing a Master and Servant Ordinance, since he himself was being confronted with a wave of complaints about bad treatment, in particular about the inadequate rations provided to Africans by White employers. In Golinelli's view, such an ordinance ought to make it possible for the authorities to exercise surveillance over working conditions, and in particular to lay down minimum standards for board and appropriate wages. He linked the obligation to register contracts of employment with the police to the idea of control and surveillance of the Africans: every African employed by Whites was to be given a numbered 'service token' when he entered into his contract of employment, which would also identify the 'issuing police authority':

> Every police station shall keep a list of the tokens issued, in which the date of issue, the name of the recipient and the file number of the contract of employment is to be entered. In this way the station will be in a position to exercise surveillance over the native concerned, and to issue him with a legitimation document. The native shall wear the service token attached to his clothing or his loincloth.[54]

This was to allow the heads of the Districts 'to get a picture of the work being performed by the natives belonging to their Districts, and where necessary to intervene with a view to stirring up their desire to work'. In order to promote 'zeal in respect of work', state payments were to be granted to reward 'long and faithful service with the same employer'. As it was in the Government's interest 'that the natives should be engaged in regular work and that their nomadic instincts should be subdued', employment contracts should have a term of at least one year. He did not consider it practicable to prohibit chastisement by employers, but pleaded for strict limitations on its legal application, for example to cases of 'negligence, disobedience, drunkenness, the stealing of food, leaving the workplace without permission etc.' However, he was against allowing employers to inflict 'more than ten strokes of the cane per person per day', to deprive employees of their liberty, to make deductions from wages on their own authority or to 'impose the punishment of reducing or withholding rations', since he feared that 'unscrupulous employers' would abuse such a right 'in order to benefit their larders'. Like von Lindequist and von Burgsdorff, he recommended criminalizing breaches of civil contracts, wishing to introduce punishments for Africans who committed such breaches.[55] The 'service tokens' and the lists recording details of their issue clearly foreshadow the pass tokens and Native Registers introduced later.

It seems it did not prove possible to establish uniform regulations governing the employment of African workers before the outbreak of war, as it was not until the promulgation of the Master and Servant Ordinance of 1907 that this area was regulated uniformly throughout the Colony. Apart from the similarities in content, the simple fact that two of the people principally involved in drawing up the 1907 Native Ordinances, namely Golinelli and von Lindequist, had already been involved in discussions on a Master and Servant Ordinance between

1894 and 1896 is sufficient proof of the continuity between the earlier and the later measures.

The German Administration's efforts to subject the African population directly to German law are also apparent in the debate surrounding the introduction of a general obligation on Africans to register and obtain a pass. Leutwein had sent a draft ordinance covering these matters to the individual District Officers in August 1900, and asked them to state their opinions. This draft ordinance required every African to carry a pass if he wished 'to cross the border of the area assigned to his tribe by the Government' or to leave his place of residence, if this was outside the communal area. The pass was to contain its date of issue, the name of the person issuing it, the name of the African, his 'tribal' affiliation, his place of residence, his reason for leaving it, the nature of his work and where appropriate the name of his employer and the office where or the person to whom the pass was to be handed in again. The police were entitled to inspect the pass at any time, and it had to be handed in to the person or authority named when the African reached his destination. The issue of a pass could be refused for 'security or other well-founded reasons'.[56]

While the aim of the Ordinance was primarily to impose strict surveillance on the African population, the restriction on freedom of movement could also be used to control the distribution of the available workers. The fact that not only purely security aspects but the labour issue too was a factor in the provisions of the Ordinance can be deduced from two further sections, which laid down that 'natives who are found outside their tribal areas ... or away from their places of residence ... without a pass shall be taken into temporary police custody and assigned work against board or cash payment'. In such a case they could also, on application and in return for 'remuneration to be determined by the police authority', be compulsorily assigned to Whites for employment.[57]

As far as the District Officers were concerned, there did not appear to be anything really new about the pass requirement. Gibeon District Office, for example, reported that it had already been customary for the Witbooi 'to get themselves a pass if they wished to travel any distance outside the tribal area, in order to be able to prove their identities if necessary'. As a result, the District Officer reported, Kaptein Hendrik Witbooi and Kaptein Simon Kopper, with whom the matter had been discussed, had not raised any essential objections to the new Ordinance.[58]

Swakopmund District Office too reported that groups of African workers who were, for example, on their way to their place of work had in the past been given a collective authorization document (*Begleitschein*). The District Office also saw the Pass Ordinance that was under discussion as offering the opportunity to provide Africans with a certain degree of protection. It would be a good thing, the officials argued, if the pass were to contain the dates of the start of employment and its agreed end, as this would prevent employers from arbitrarily extending contracts and thereby keeping Africans in the unaccustomed coastal climate 'until they fall victim to the sicknesses peculiar to the coastal area'. Furthermore, the harsh working conditions in Swakopmund also led the District Office to suggest that further protective measures should be included in the Pass Ordinance as well: 'medical care' should be made 'obligatory', as should a requirement to send sick people inland by train, 'as the change of climate would make it more likely they would recover, and it would be easier for them to return home'. Minimum levels of rations should also be laid down for them.[59]

The Outjo District Officer also welcomed the Ordinance as being 'very opportune', but considered it to be 'very difficult to implement', since the African workers would simply not collect their passes as long as they had not yet rid themselves of their habit of leaving their places of work clandestinely and moving away. In order to make it easier for the police to maintain surveillance, he recommended that every incoming African should be given 'a metal token to be worn visibly around his neck', which he was to hand in again when he left.[60] The information shown in the pass should also include distinguishing features allowing easier identification and details of any previous punishments inflicted on the worker, so that the police would be able to impose a more severe penalty if the offence was repeated.[61] In other words, the requirement to carry a pass was in future no longer merely to serve the purposes of monitoring the Africans' travel habits and possibly imposing restrictions on their freedom of movement, but was also to be an instrument of surveillance in their everyday lives. This and the proposal to introduce a metal tag that was to be worn visibly, which basically corresponded to Golinelli's ideas on the introduction of a 'service token' formulated in 1896, proved to be significant in the further development of a surveillance and control system covering all Africans.

But the prospective requirement for Africans to be registered did not meet with approval in all quarters. The District Offices in Keetmanshoop and Omaruru declared themselves to be opposed to a Pass Ordinance. District Officer Hansen of Keetmanshoop seems to have been influenced in this by his annoyance that the District Officers had not been invited to participate in formulating the draft ordinance. Without explaining his reasons in any more detail, he condemned the obligation to carry a pass as an 'extremely dubious experiment'.[62]

The head of Omaruru District, First Lieutenant von Seifert, on the other hand, set out his objections very explicitly. He saw no need for a Pass Ordinance, since 'no inconveniences' had arisen in the past out of the Africans' existing freedom of movement. More fundamental was his objection that in view of the vast area of Hereroland it would not be possible to provide the degree of police control necessary to implement the Pass Ordinance. It seemed to him to be 'premature' to 'promulgate a general ordinance' as long as 'the prerequisites for strict implementation do not exist', even though it might, under certain circumstances, be 'expedient within certain local areas'. It would be difficult to determine which Africans were away from their places of residence or 'tribal' areas; and in any case, as he added ironically, Africans who absented themselves illegally from their 'tribal' areas were not in the habit of calling in at police stations to report this. Where it appeared expedient in individual cases to issue passes, this had already been done. Employers in Swakopmund, for example, and the Railway Command had issued authorization documents to those Ovambo whose employment had been terminated, since they would often come into contact with police stations on their way home. In this case, controls 'could be carried out up to a certain extent' – as had indeed actually been done, 'as it is easy for anyone to recognize Ovambos'.[63] Von Seifert's reference to the problems of carrying out checks was pertinent, as experience in the period after 1908 (i.e. after the war) demonstrated. But it nevertheless remains the case that with the exceptions mentioned there was a general feeling as early as 1900 of there being a need for stricter direct surveillance of Africans and for the regulation of employment relationships. As no separate Master and Servant Ordinance came to be promulgated at that time, measures such as the introduction of the compulsion to work were incorporated into Leutwein's draft Pass Ordinance in the form of the Vagrancy Section. In addition, the abolition of freedom of movement, the issue of pass tags that had to be worn visibly and the subjection of the local African population to constant surveillance were all important elements of the debate on the Pass Ordinance that reappeared as major factors in relation to the three 1907 Native Ordinances.

In the end, the Pass Ordinance did not come to be put into effect before the outbreak of the Herero and Nama War. It was only in the changed political situation after the outbreak of war that some of the District Offices issued local pass regulations. Swakopmund District Office, for example, issued an Ordinance on 18 May 1904 introducing a universal pass requirement,[64] followed on 7 October 1904 by Keetmanshoop[65] together with Lüderitzbucht, which at the time was still a subordinate and not an autonomous District Office.[66] On 9 February 1905 it was the turn of Grootfontein,[67] on 8 November 1905 of Windhoek[68] and on 16 January 1906 of Karibib[69] to issue Pass Ordinances for their respective Districts. The District Office at Outjo also introduced a pass requirement.[70] Thus even before the promulgation of the 1907 Native Ordinances, there were regulations of this type already in force in all Districts except Gibeon, Gobabis, Rehoboth and Okahandja. These measures drew upon the proposals that had been put forward by the Governor's Office four years before the outbreak of the Herero and Nama War.

In many places, however, these local Pass Ordinances existed only on paper, or were implemented only to a very limited extent. In Grootfontein, for example, the authorities soon had to give up registering Africans again, because they did not have enough pass tokens available – a shortage that they were not able to eliminate until 1907[71] and that was to reoccur when the pass requirement was introduced throughout the colony. In Outjo District too, the regulation could be implemented only to a certain extent: pass tokens were issued only to those 'natives' resident in Outjo and to the Swartboois of Fransfontein, and it was only in respect of these people that registers were kept;[72] the pass requirement does not appear to have been implemented in Windhoek District either.[73]

Parallel to the introduction of these local Pass Ordinances, a debate also began on reshaping Native Policy in a uniform manner for the whole Colony. Deputy Governor Hans Tecklenburg had submitted a series of proposals to the Foreign Office Colonial Department in Berlin from April 1904 onwards, drawing its attention to his ideas as to how the Africans should be treated in future.[74] He took up on the discussion concerning the direct subordination of Africans to German law outlined above: the demands that he raised for the issue of pass tokens and the abolition of freedom of movement – in addition to those for the expropriation of land, the prohibition on keeping large livestock and the creation of centralized settlements for Africans close to their employers – had formed part of the debate on the Pass Ordinance. The Native Ordinances were thus devised in the context of a discussion going back more than ten years on how the German authorities could get a more direct grip on the African population.

In September 1905, a commission set up in connection with the measures of land expropriation also discussed the future direction of Native Policy. Its members – in addition to representatives of the Colonial Department, namely its Director, Oskar Stübel, and the head of the South West Africa desk, Angelo Golinelli, and to high-ranking representatives of the Rhenish Missionary Society – also included Chief Justice Richter of Windhoek and the Governor Designate of South West Africa, Friedrich von Lindequist.[75] After von Lindequist had taken up his post in the colony in November 1905, the three Ordinances were formulated in Windhoek and then presented to the Colonial Department for scrutiny. The drafts were approved on 8 January 1907, with a few amendments by Bernhard Dernburg, who had been appointed Director of the department in September 1906.[76] It is astonishing that Dernburg, with his reputation as a colonial reformer, was so directly involved in the Ordinances that were planned for South West Africa.[77] Not only did he accept the drastic measures proposed, but the amendments that he approved, even if they were only minor, all without exception increased the severity of the Ordinances.

It was not until after the draft ordinances had been accepted by Dernburg that the Governor's Office sent them out to the District Offices on 13 May 1907, calling on them to submit 'statements of their views on implementation' in order to draw upon the practical experience that many Districts already had with the 'systematic registration of their natives and with the Pass Ordinances', which had been introduced some considerable time before.[78] The advice and comments submitted by the Districts, however, were scarcely regarded; and if they were taken into account at all, which at best was only marginally, it was not in the Ordinances themselves but in the Circulated Decree[79] from the Governor that accompanied them.[80] The three Ordinances came into force on 18 August 1907.[81]

The Content of the Ordinances

The codification of Native Policy in the 1907 Ordinances placed relations between Whites and Africans in South West Africa on a new legal basis. The Ordinances set their definitive stamp on the reshaping of African societies, subjected them to a new social discipline and laid the foundations for a new order on the labour market that relegated Africans to the status of a labour pool that was freely available to any White who wished to draw on it. The Native Ordinances represent an attempt to develop a social structure which from the German point of view could be regarded as modern and efficient and which promised to guarantee public order and the rule of law – an attempt that at one and the same time was influenced by the traumatic experiences of the war and was orientated towards an objective of colonial policy that displayed utopian traits.

The three Ordinances intermeshed with each other in many ways, in order as far as possible to bring all areas of the Africans' lives under control. Although they set up an inhuman apparatus of oppression, they also contained sections designed to protect the Africans. The main purpose of the Ordinances was doubtless to secure colonial rule by setting up a seamless system of surveillance and control. They were intended to make it possible for the Administration to determine how many Africans were present in a particular District at any particular time, who they were, where they lived and whether and how they were employed. To ensure that all Africans living in South West Africa were covered, their details were to be entered in Native Registers that were to be kept by the 'Supervisory Authority for Native Affairs', namely the responsible District Office (Sec. 3 and 5, Control Ordinance). Unambiguous identification was to be made possible by requiring all Africans aged over seven to have passes (Sec. 1, Pass Ordinance),[82] and to carry their pass tokens on their persons at all times and produce them on demand to the police or to 'any white person' (Sec. 2, Pass Ordinance). The original draft of the Ordinance had provided for children aged fourteen or over to be subject to the pass requirement; but the age was reduced to seven by the Foreign Office Colonial Department. This not only enabled control to be exercised over a larger proportion of the population, but also increased the number of people available for work.[83] In order to ensure that there were no gaps in the system of surveillance, any pass tags that had been lost or were no longer legible had to be replaced immediately – with a penalty of one mark to be paid as well (Sec. 8, Pass Ordinance). The pass tags or travel passes of deceased persons were to be handed in without delay by their employers or relatives (Sec. 9, Pass Ordinance).

The form of the pass token also represented an act of social disciplining. It was to consist of 'a metal disc to be worn visibly', and was to bear not only the Imperial Crown and the name of the District but also the serial number under which the holder was listed in the Native Register (Sec. 10, Pass Ordinance). Thus it could be seen from a distance if an African was without his pass tag; while at the same time the tag gradually became part of the bearer's identity.

The pass token made it possible to determine at any time whether an African had left his District illegally. Every pass was valid only for a particular District (Sec. 12, Pass Ordinance). If an African wanted to leave the District he lived in (i.e. was registered in) for a limited time, he had to obtain a travel pass from the responsible police station,[84] which he then had to hand in again on his return (Sec. 3, Pass Ordinance). The travel pass was valid only for 'the time and route stated in it' (Sec. 12, Pass Ordinance), and would only be issued if the African could demonstrate that he was no longer in employment or if his employer had given his permission in writing (Sec. 7, Pass Ordinance). Furthermore, he had to obtain confirmation of his arrival at his destination: from a White person, if he was visiting one, or else from an official (Sec. 13, Pass Ordinance); or if there was no official available, then 'from any other white person' (Sec. 13, Pass Ordinance). In addition, anybody could be 'forbidden for good cause to leave his District, and refused the issue of a travel pass' (Sec. 5, Pass Ordinance). Being subject to watertight surveillance, Africans were to have no opportunity to move around freely.

If an African wanted to settle in a different District, he had to obtain a travel pass for the journey and exchange this for a new pass token when he arrived at his new place of residence (Sec. 3, Pass Ordinance). Any African subject to the pass requirement but who had no valid pass token or travel pass might not 'be given employment, accommodation, maintenance or any other support that might aid and abet the native's infringement of the pass regulations' (Sec. 14, Pass Ordinance).[85] Thus he was caught between the rock of the Pass Ordinance and the hard place of the Control Ordinance: without a pass, an African could not work for Whites, but he was forbidden, without the express permission of the Governor, to keep the large livestock or riding animals that he would have needed for economic independence (Sec. 2, Control Ordinance).[86] Furthermore, most land had already been expropriated, and the acquisition of plots of land also required permission (Sec. 1, Control Ordinance). The Africans were therefore prevented from regaining their economic independence, or at least their doing so was subject to surveillance by the Administration and could be stopped at any time. The only choice remaining for Africans was therefore to seek employment with Whites, as otherwise they were in danger of being punished as 'vagrants' – the punishment that threatened all Africans found 'roaming around … without any demonstrable means of support' (Sec. 4, Control Ordinance).

The passes also served to control the distribution of the population. The Administration was making a deliberate attempt to provide, in the most efficient manner possible, for an adequate supply of labour throughout the colony, by making sure that there was a regular distribution of workers. In order to keep the African workers under control and ensure that they were evenly spread out over the country,[87] not more than ten families or individuals were allowed to live in a private *werf*, that is to say in an African settlement on private land, without special authorization (Sec. 7, Control Ordinance). In order to make it possible for the Administration to have an overview of the number of Africans present within a district at any time, the owner of the land[88] had to report all werfs to the responsible supervisory authority, stating the number of families or individual persons living there (Sec. 6, Control Ordinance). In addition, a register was to be kept listing the names and employment of each werf's inhabitants, and the numbers of their pass tokens (Sec. 12, Control Ordinance). The supervisory authority could determine both the location and the size of any werfs not situated on 'land that is inhabited and economically exploited', this applying in particular to werfs that were to be established close to large centres of population (Sec. 8, Sub-sec. 1 and 2, Control Ordinance). These public settlements could be made subject at any time to a curfew lasting from nine o'clock in the evening until four in the morning (Sec. 8, Sub-sec. 3, Control Ordinance). The hope was obviously, as was later the case with the townships in South Africa, to supply the towns with labour while keeping it largely out of sight and accommodating it in places that were easy to control.

The intention that all Africans should be employed by Whites made it essential to bring about a legal codification of conditions of employment too. At the same time the Administration was able to supplement the system of surveillance by extending it to include information on employment. It was, for instance, laid down that employment contracts with terms of more than one month concluded with Africans over fourteen years of age were not effective until a *Dienstbuch*, an employment logbook, had been handed out to the employer by the responsible police authority. In addition, the conclusion of a contract of employment was to be recorded against the name of the African concerned in the Native Register (Sec. 1, Sub-sec. 2, Master and Servant Ordinance).

The Employment Logbook was to contain not only the name and 'tribal' affiliation[89] of the employee and the number of his pass token but also the name of the employer, the date on which employment commenced, the term of the contract, the period of notice (if any had been agreed), and the 'amount and type of remuneration to be granted to the native' (Sec. 2, Master and Servant Ordinance). In this way, the pass token became the connecting link between the Register, any travel pass document and the Employment Logbook. The last mentioned was intended to provide a complete record of all the jobs an African had had, and of the reasons for any dismissals, and to document the extent to which he was considered to be a willing worker. The inclusion of the period of notice demonstrates that the Administration did recognize contracts of employment as valid contracts under civil law. Africans were not regarded as being totally deprived of all rights and subject to the whims of their employers; at least in theory they could negotiate their conditions of employment themselves. In practice, however, this was vitiated by their lack of familiarity with the European legal system and by the fact that they were to all intents and purposes compelled to undertake dependent employment. The extent to which they were actually able to insist on their rights, minimal as they were, depended on the attitude of the individual local administrative officer responsible.

Before handing out the Employment Logbook, the police were supposed to check whether the African was still bound by any previous employment contract. Whites who employed a worker knowing that he was still subject to some previous employment were threatened with a penalty of up to 600 marks (Sec. 11, Master and Servant Ordinance). This is a clear indication of a recognition on the part of the Administration that, due to the intensifying labour shortage, White employers might try to poach each other's workers or use force to compel them to change their employer, and that this could jeopardize the proper functioning of the labour market. If a worker was not able to obtain an Employment Logbook from the police because the nearest police station was too far away, then a Decree could be issued by the Governor allowing the logbook to be replaced by 'a written contract signed by the employer and the employee', of which the African too was to be given a copy. If the African did not understand the employer's language, the content of the contract had to be explained to him through an interpreter.[90] This was to be 'recorded by the employer at the bottom of the contract document', and a transcript of the contract had to be submitted to the responsible District Office for approval (Sec. 3, Master and Servant Ordinance). Police officers were explicitly required to ascertain before issuing an Employment Logbook 'that the content of the contract had been made adequately comprehensible to the employee, and agreed to by him' (Sec. 1, Sub-sec. 1, Master and Servant Ordinance). Like the conclusion of the contract, its termination too had to be reported to the authorities, and the reasons stated (Sec. 4, Sub-sec. 2, Master and Servant Ordinance).

This mandatory approval by the authorities of all employment contracts with a term of more than one month was not merely an instrument of surveillance, but also had the function of 'protecting' the

Africans: it was intended to ensure minimum standards of working and living conditions, and so help to mitigate the problem of the frequent occurrence of Africans 'running away' (i.e. deserting their workplaces) because of the wretched conditions they were subject to there.[91] In this way, it was hoped, the Africans would in the long term become better reconciled to their new status as wage earners, and a degree of stability would be achieved in labour relations.

Employment contracts were not allowed to have a term of more than one year, but the contract was deemed to have been automatically renewed if the employment was continued beyond the agreed end of the contract. An endorsement to this effect was to be entered in the Employment Logbook and signed by the employer and the African (Sec. 5, Master and Servant Ordinance). The permissible grounds for terminating the contract strengthened the position of the employer immeasurably: premature termination by the employer was explicitly allowed 'for good cause', which included circumstances such as 'repeated disobedience', 'incitement to disobedience', 'theft', 'desertion', 'inability to work over a considerable period of time occasioned by the worker's own fault', or 'sickness lasting more than four weeks' (Sec. 6, Master and Servant Ordinance). The African, by contrast, was permitted to terminate the contract without notice only for reasons of 'gross maltreatment' or 'gross violation of the obligations incumbent on the employer by virtue of this Ordinance or of the Contract of Employment' (Sec. 7, Master and Servant Ordinance).

Among the obligations incumbent on the employer was that of providing an African who fell ill while in his service 'with the requisite medicines and dressings, and the customary board free of charge' until the end of the employment, although in such a case he was entitled to make corresponding deductions from the worker's wages (Sec. 8, Master and Servant Ordinance). If the African was improperly dismissed before the end of his contract, he was entitled to appropriate compensation (Sec. 10, Master and Servant Ordinance). How he was supposed to enforce his claim to this in practice was not explained, however.

The fact that the duties of the Africans were set out very precisely in the Ordinances, but their rights only rather vaguely – although in this case too, more precise details were contained in a Circulated Decree from the Governor, albeit not widely disseminated[92] – illustrates a fundamental principle of colonial domination: although the administration showed itself prepared to afford Africans a minimum level of protection, the Africans were not to be put in a position in which they could take the initiative to claim this for themselves.[93] The protection of the Africans was to be perceived as a paternalistic act, graciously accorded, and not as a right that those concerned could enforce by taking legal action.

The vagueness of the permissible grounds for termination made the Africans vulnerable to arbitrary interpretation on the part of the responsible administrative officers. Furthermore, in order to give effective notice they were obliged, even when they were the victims of illegal treatment, to follow formal rules that they were unaware of. If they failed to do so, they would find themselves entangled in an impenetrable net of legal provisions and could only too easily make themselves guilty of the offence of 'desertion'. But if they left their employment 'without legal cause' before the ending of their contracts, they could, on application from their employers, be 'made to continue their work through measures of compulsion exercised by the authorities', even if in the meantime they had found other work (Sec. 9, Master and Servant Ordinance). Nowhere is the unfair manner in which European legal principles were imposed on the African population to be seen more clearly than in these bureaucratic subtleties. This did not necessarily mean that Africans would inevitably be treated in ways that violated the law; but the likelihood that there would be a feeling of solidarity between the officials and the settlers left the door wide open to abuse.

Quite apart from the fact that in case of doubt the officials would consider the White 'masters' to have greater credibility than the Africans, within the proposed apparatus of control the employers were clearly on the side of the authorities. The cooperation of the White settlers was an essential factor in ensuring that the control apparatus functioned efficiently. Every settler who had a werf on his land was required to exercise supervision over it (Sec. 11, Control Ordinance), attending to issues of health and hygiene and the maintenance of order, and ensuring that the provisions of the Ordinance were observed by the Africans (Sec. 12, Control Ordinance). In addition, the Native Ordinances allowed every White person to exercise numerous public order functions in respect of the Africans, which should really have been matters for the police:

> Any native who is subject to the pass regulations may be stopped by any white person and, if he is found to be without a pass, handed over to the nearest police officer. If there is no police officer nearby and the detained person is therefore released again, he is to be reported to the nearest police station or police patrol at the earliest opportunity. (Sec. 16, Sub-sec. 1, Pass Ordinance)[94]

A clearer example of the division of society in South West Africa into an underclass of Africans largely deprived of rights and an upper class composed – as the Africans were bound to see it – of the administration *and* the settlers could hardly be found. In a general process of imposing social discipline, the Africans could not but regard obedience to state authority and obedience to private employers as being more or less one and the same thing.

But the White employers themselves were also to be subjected to controls. The extremely sceptical and ever more strained attitude of the settlers towards the Administration found its corollary in the fundamental mistrust that the authorities felt towards the settlers, which was expressed in control measures directed against Whites, including with regard to how they treated their African employees. Despite this, the Administration was by no means prepared to allow Africans to entertain any doubts with regard to the superiority of the culture and power of all White people. For example, the District Offices were supposed to investigate the people whose task it was to supervise the werfs, and were entitled and required 'to subject the conditions of the natives in a private werf to close examination at certain intervals, and to ensure that any irregularities are dealt with' (Sec. 14, Control Ordinance). But such inspections were on no account to undermine the authority of the White employer in any way:

> Tours of inspection and searches of private werfs, which are to be implemented as often as the situation in the District allows, are generally to be carried out together with the employer of the inhabitants of the werf concerned in a considerate manner which will not excite or frighten the natives. Except in cases in which for legal, political or similar reasons it is necessary to keep the search secret from the employer, exceptions to this rule are to be made only if, in the view of the official carrying out the inspection, it is to be feared that the presence of the employer will influence the natives or otherwise lead to the true conditions in the werf being obscured.[95]

As a rule, this reduced the inspection visits to no more than a joint tour of the werf by the official and the employer. This demonstrative closeness to the authorities could only reinforce the authority of the werf owner. Nevertheless, legal instruments to discipline the Whites as well did exist, and it depended on the individual official how intensively he made use of them.

Basically it was the responsibility of the supervisory authority to issue 'in particular such instructions as are in the general public interest to regulate conditions of employment, to establish a good level of public health and to maintain order among the natives' (Sec. 9,

Control Ordinance);[96] in the draft document as originally drawn up by the Governor's Office, however, this obligation had been formulated as follows:

> to issue such instructions as are in the general public interest for the purposes of establishing a good level of health among the natives, and of maintaining order and contentment among them; in particular, also in order to maintain the latter, to pay attention to the working conditions of the natives, but to refrain, as must also the local supervisory persons, from any interference in the purely internal affairs of the natives, unless they themselves request an adjudication.[97]

It is not just the change in the order in which the various objectives are listed that shows the differing priorities between the Colonial Department in Berlin under Dernburg on the one hand and the Governor's Office on the other, but also the deletion of the criterion of the 'contentment' of the Africans. The 'general public interest' which alone was still included in the final text of the document was the interest of the White colonizers, whose primary concern was to properly 'regulate conditions of employment'.

In summary, the Native Ordinances drawn up under the immediate impression of the war formed the basic legal framework for Native Policy until South West Africa came under South African rule in 1915. They provided for the construction of a seamless and perfectionist system of surveillance and control, and signified the introduction of a requirement to enter into dependent employment. At the same time, they laid down the basis for a completely new type of social structure in which there was no longer any room for the African communities and their traditional way of life, with the extensive utilization of land and livestock that was typical of the Herero in particular. South West Africa was to be transformed into a uniform economic area in which the African population was evenly distributed in order to serve as labour. The strict regulation and control of employment contracts was intended to achieve a degree of constancy in employment relations which, taking account of supply and demand, would ensure the adequate availability of manpower to all farms and businesses, and guarantee the maintenance of 'law and order' by granting employees a minimum level of rights.

Reactions from the District Officers to the 1907 'Native Ordinances'

As the introduction of new laws and regulations is by no means synonymous with their implementation, the first question to be asked is how the provisions of the three Native Ordinances were interpreted by German officials. An initial indication can be found in the way the District Officers responded to them. These officials had not been involved in the process of formulating the Ordinances – it was not until May 1907, after the drafts had been approved by Dernburg, that the Governor's Office sent them out to the Districts in order to obtain reactions as to how they might best be implemented[98] – and a number of the officers grasped the opportunity to confront the Governor with their fundamental opinions of the Ordinances. Their interpretations of the measures open up some revealing insights into the thinking and aims of the people who were actually involved in administering Native Policy and had to implement the provisions.

Basically, the Ordinances were met with a broad measure of approval[99] and were regarded as being 'useful and necessary'.[100] The District Officers considered them to be 'very important',[101] and were of the opinion that registration and the permanent control and surveillance of the African population would enable the colony to develop in an orderly manner. The fact that the requirement for all Africans to take up employment was given the force of law was generally considered to be a decisive factor in this. Some of the officials, however, also expressed doubts about the effectiveness of purely coercive measures, and welcomed the Ordinances because of the protection they felt they afforded to the African workers. For these officers it was above all the legal security they saw as being gained in the field of labour relations that represented progress, since it seemed to guarantee long-term employment relationships:

> The Ordinance relating to Employment Contracts with Natives is to be welcomed as a great step forward, in the interests both of the whites and of the natives themselves. The provision in Sec. 5, Sub-sec. 1 will prove to be a particular blessing. The native will lose the feeling of being practically a slave and deprived of all rights in respect of his employer, and if he is treated well and paid in accordance with his performance will consider it expedient to keep his employer satisfied, so that he will extend the contract when it has run its term. The employer for his part will treat his natives better than is often the case at present if he knows that they not only have duties towards him but also rights, above all the right to decide for themselves, within the provisions of the Ordinance, how they wish to dispose of their labour. Once the Ordinance is in force, natives will desert from their places of work much less often than they do at present.[102]

This assessment from the District Office in Swakopmund was also shared by the Outjo office. District Officer Victor Franke's deputy, Senior Medical Officer Hungels, saw the introduction of the Employment Logbook as 'serving the interests of both the employer and the employee in equal measure', and proposed, on the basis of his knowledge of the actual situation on the farms, that the Ordinances should be supplemented by a detailed catalogue of measures to protect the Africans:

> As has already been set out in the Annual Report, a need has been felt in this District too for the rights and duties of both employees and employers to be laid down in law, and for written agreements between the contractual parties to be introduced for the same purpose. The introduction of the Employment Logbook serves the interests of both the employer and the employee in equal measure. This is the only way to prevent workers from running away and to protect them against maltreatment and exploitation.
>
> In respect of <u>Sec. 2, No. 4</u>: In the view of the District Office, a provision must be added to the Ordinance that the remuneration consists of a monthly [*word illegible*] wage payable *in cash*. In this region the undesirable practice known as the 'truck system' is widespread, by which the native is paid not in cash but in kind, or is compelled to purchase goods only from his employer's shop. Both of these practices are equally reprehensible abuses, in that they make it more difficult or impossible for the supervisory authority to exercise control, open the doors wide to the native's being cheated and arouse the distrust of the native, who in any case never ceases to be on his guard. ... Similarly, the District Office is of the opinion that the amount of rations to be provided free of charge should be precisely laid down in the contract. Generalized expressions such as 'as is customary in the area' should be avoided.[103]

The reason for setting out these considerations in such detail appears to be that there were indeed frequent cases of Africans being cheated. This was made possible by the use of such vague expressions of quantity as 'a beakerful' in the details of the rations to be provided by the employer. The size of the beaker was not defined, and the employer would use a smaller one, or else would measure the food out only after it had been boiled, thereby increasing its volume, as the District Officer was able to report from experience.[104]

In order to ensure that the labour market regulations outlined in the Master and Servant Ordinance, which allowed the person seeking employment to freely choose his employer,[105] did actually work properly, Hungels demanded that they should be supplemented by a provision 'stating that existing debts are no reason to prevent the worker from leaving his employment', since 'experience shows that unscrupulous employers keep diligent workers, whom they are unwilling to allow to leave, artificially in debt by furnishing them with goods – often against the will of the natives concerned – and so prevent them from moving to another job'.[106] While this suggestion could still be seen as serving to ensure that all Whites had equal access to labour, which was becoming more and more scarce,[107] the proposal from the District Office in Gibeon that farmers should be under an obligation to 'bring a native who is liable to be dismissed due to extended sickness to the responsible medical practitioner, at the same time informing the responsible police station ... insofar as the native is not able, in view of the seriousness of his sickness, to report to the doctor for treatment himself without assistance',[108] marks the first stirrings of a feeling that there needed to be a scheme to provide for the welfare of the Africans. Even if these proposals themselves did not find their way into the Native Ordinances,[109] they nevertheless clearly demonstrate that there were some District Officers who did not regard the Ordinances as being purely and simply instruments of exploitation.

None of those questioned, however, rejected the requirement to enter into employment that the African population was now to be subjected to by law, or even so much as expressed surprise at the way this coercion was being imposed. The shortage of labour that every District Officer had to try and deal with in his administrative work simply appeared too pressing. The head of Keetmanshoop District, Hugo Blumhagen, even wanted to extend the Vagrancy Section to cover 'workshy natives who, despite orders from the police, refuse appropriate work opportunities that are offered to them without any convincing reason'. His argument was that in Keetmanshoop 'at least a third of the men who are capable of working and almost all the women do not deign to do any work, since they live on money they are furnished with inappropriately by the troopers'.[110] Other District Officers had already practised a strict system of compulsory labour even before the Ordinances were promulgated. The head of Gobabis District, Kurt Streitwolf, for example, saw the way he had acted in the past now legalized by the Native Ordinance: 'Of course, *no* Klippkaffir living out on the veld will comply with the order to collect a token. But that is no matter: I have already in the past always had people going out after these vagrant Klippkaffirs, in order to force them into work, so there will now be a legal provision allowing for this procedure'.[111] Thus the provisions for Africans to be compulsorily given over to employers did not represent any fundamental new direction in Native Policy, but simply confirmed what was already the practice in many cases.

Despite this, the Ordinances were not yet comprehensive enough for Streitwolf's liking. He was critical of the lack of any precise provisions with regard to Africans living on the mission stations. Since the Missions believed 'that all the natives living there belong to them', and every mission station 'always seeks to collect and keep as many natives as possible', thereby depriving employers of 'the last few labourers who are available', they were a hindrance to 'every effort at settlement and cultivation'.[112] As a precautionary measure he wanted to see any such potential loopholes closed. The Governor's Office accepted this suggestion, and ordered that no mission station should be allocated more than ten African families except under the condition 'that if a shortage of workers should occur anywhere in the colony the mission station concerned ... should cause its superfluous natives to take up employment away from the mission'.[113] As the labour shortage in fact persisted throughout the entire period of German rule, this gave the German Administration legal access to the African population living on Missionary Society land at any time.

District Officer Rudolf Böhmer of Lüderitzbucht was equally of the opinion that the Ordinances did not go far enough, and sought to give the network of controls an even finer mesh. It was his intention to entrust two police sergeants with the surveillance of the nineteen hundred Africans present in the District, one of them to be concerned with Lüderitzbucht itself and the other with the workers on the railway and on the farms. Every African was to be checked at least once a month, as proposed by the Governor's Office. The District Officer would have liked to have seen the control registers kept by these two police officers checked against an overall register in his office, in which the police officers were to 'record all changes on a weekly basis'. Someone in the Governor's Office recognized Böhmer's zeal for the cause by writing 'Very good' in the margin. However, his suggestion that the public order competences granted to Whites by the Native Ordinances should be revoked again in the near future – a suggestion arising out of his deep mistrust of the settlers – was rejected. He felt uneasy about the fact that, particularly in the south of the country, there were 'many foreign and not even purely white farmers in whom <u>as little trust as possible</u> should be placed'. This was a view that struck a chord in government circles, as is testified by the 'Quite right!!' entered in the margin.[114] Rehoboth District Office also criticized the transfer of fundamental competences of the state to the settlers, and proposed that the right of Whites to check Africans' passes should apply only on their own private land.[115] Keetmanshoop District Office wanted to restrict the right of Whites to check passes to places outside built-up areas, as in populated areas the police would have enough manpower to do it themselves. The reason given was that 'in <u>inhabited</u> places, whites would use the mask of acting on behalf of the police to abuse the provision'.[116]

The officers of the Administration, although always fundamentally convinced that Europeans were morally and culturally superior, were not prepared to trust the Whites any further than was absolutely necessary. Many officials were worried above all by the social origins of the settlers:

> It is absolutely essential that those whites who supervise private werfs should themselves be subject to supervision, since there are some specimens among our settlers, coming mainly from very modest backgrounds at home, who are easily inclined to exploit improperly any position of power granted to them.[117]

This reveals the class consciousness of the Wilhelminian civil service in respect of the subjects of the Empire, particularly those from the lower social classes. The same inhumanly contemptuous and arrogant language as was used in dealings with the African population was also apparent, even if in a much-diluted form, in discourse concerning the lower classes of White society.

Böhmer's support for the planned registration of the African population was not, however, purely a matter of the practical requirements for exercising control, but also stemmed from an interest in obtaining ethnographical insights:

> I consider it very opportune to have a measure under which every arrival and departure, every birth and every death is to be reported immediately. In order to be able to assess conditions among the natives it is essential to obtain an overview of population movements; apart from which, the statistics obtained with regard to a population at this level of civilization are also very likely to be of scientific interest.[118]

In this he was alone among the District Officers. But his statement does show the wide range of the reactions to the Native Ordinances, and is an indication of the ethnological investigations that were increasingly being carried out by colonial officials and officers of the Schutztruppe.[119] The people in the Governor's Office did not think much of this interest in ethnology; they placed their emphasis on the main purpose of the provision, as is indicated by a marginal note added to Böhmer's report, 'especially in order to be able to keep track of the growth or decline in the number of workers'.[120]

Another thing that Böhmer disapproved of was the fact that the Rehoboth Basters were to be exempted from the pass requirements. He would have liked to have reduced the number of people originally benefiting from this provision by making a hair-splitting legal distinction: he proposed that instead of the Basters of Rehoboth, only the 'Basters in Rehoboth' should be exempted.[121] From this, he explained, it would follow 'that if Basters of Rehoboth left the District of Rehoboth without ceasing to have their place of residence there, they would need to have a pass',[122] so that they could be subject to the control provisions at least outside the district. The Rehoboth District Officer took up this problem as well, requesting that the existing practice should be maintained: 'For the Basters, the most practical thing in the future would probably be if they were to be given a written identity document when they left the district, as has been the case in the past'.[123] The Governor's Office agreed to this recommendation, and had it included in the implementation regulations.[124] The attention that was devoted to this numerically small group[125] indicates the perfectionism that went into drawing up the Ordinances. As they were to be the fundamental legislation on which future Native Policy was to be based, every conceivable case needed to be covered by them.

Böhmer in his comments even considered the case of those Basters with foreign nationality, who were not required to have a pass under the Pass Ordinance if they were not considered to be 'natives' under the law of their own country.[126] In this case too, he considered it to be necessary for them 'to be furnished with an identity document showing their nationality, which they can present to the responsible administrative authority, so that this authority can notify the police. This will make it easier to make a clean distinction between white and coloured, which is particularly necessary in the South'.[127] Böhmer apparently feared that some Basters might not be recognized as such from their external appearance, and mistakenly be treated as Whites.

Even at this early stage, ideas were put forward as to how the Ovambo who went south as migrant workers could be brought into the control and surveillance system. District Officer von Eschstruth of Grootfontein proposed that they should be issued with pass tokens when they crossed the border at Namutoni or Okaukweyo, which they would have to hand in again when they crossed back. As any such measure was doomed to failure as long as only these two major crossing points were manned and 'it is possible for the migrating Ovambo to avoid these places', he pleaded for the boundary to be placed under more comprehensive surveillance.[128] This would, of course, have required an enormous level of manpower. But as von Eschstruth also complained in the same letter about the undermanning and inadequate training of the police, his report is in many ways typical of the attitude of the administrative officials: called upon to give their opinion, they made abstract proposals for improvements aimed at building up a theoretically watertight system of control which totally disregarded the level of manpower that they in fact had at their disposal, while at the same time bemoaning the fact that the forces they actually had available were so limited. In von Eschstruth's case, this contradiction between aspiration and reality culminated in his admission of the problems associated with implementation: 'In my view it would be a good idea to wait with the introduction of the Ordinance until about a year's experience of dealing with the <u>draft</u> version has been gathered in the various parts of the country'.[129] And so the heads of the Districts went on putting forward more and more suggestions as to how the control network could be made even more sophisticated, although in fact they lacked even enough people to implement the basic measures. In the same way, their proposals for the implementation of the Ordinances often paid no regard at all to what was feasible in practice. This mental compartmentalization, whereby the theoretical development and refinement of the instructions coming from their superior authorities was kept quite separate in their minds from the practical realities on the ground, is typical of the way German Native Policy was created, but makes it impossible to simply equate the regulations adopted with their practical application.

Apart from von Eschstruth, only Streitwolf in Gobabis and Hungels in Outjo were brave enough to draw the attention of the Governor's Office to some of the difficulties that were to be expected: 'Bushmen [*San*] cannot be kept under control' was Streitwolf's terse summary, a conclusion that was often to recur as a stereotype in reports from other offices as well during the following years. With regard to the Herero and Nama, on the other hand, he did not as yet see any problems.[130] Hungels took due account of the shortage of personnel and admitted that in his District, that 'vast and sparsely populated area', there would be difficulties attached to implementing the Pass and Control Ordinances, which

> can probably not be completely implemented until the settlement of the country has progressed, since it is also in the country's interests to gain the confidence of the natives living out on the veld, who are in any case timid by nature and have been even more intimidated by the war (Berg Damaras, Ovambos and Bushmen), so that they come to trust the authorities.[131]

He thought it would be impossible for 'a policeman to ride around all the places where there are natives every month'. For Sesfontein District he proposed 'limiting the introduction of the measures to those natives who can be reached by the District Office, since it can hardly be in the interests of the colony to bother the Himba living to the north of Sesfontein'.[132] He also considered it would be impossible to implement the intended procedure of tracking down the scattered Africans and incorporating them into the available labour force, which was one of the main objectives of the Ordinances. But his references to the need to gain the confidence of the Africans, and to the Himba who had better not be 'bothered', show that he was keenly aware of the limited degree to which it was feasible, in view of his district's sheer distance from the centre, to implement administrative measures based on pure coercion.

Although only three of the District Officers were brave enough to admit that there were difficulties, it was soon to become apparent that these were not limited to their three districts. Other officials appear to have been aware of the problems that were inevitably going to arise as well, even though they had not dared to mention them directly in their responses. Indirectly, however, the proposal from Lüderitzbucht that 'any identifying features of the native' should be recorded in the Employment Logbook, as otherwise 'even the requirement to wear the pass token will not serve to prevent individuals from exchanging their books and tokens',[133] is a further indication that District Officer Böhmer was well aware of the difficulties that would attend the implementation of the Ordinance. A similar proposal was also made by the District Officer of Keetmanshoop, who recommended that the travel pass should include a space for 'distinguishing marks', since these could 'be very important in checking the identity of travellers'.[134]

The arguments for changing a provision that was really only of secondary importance, namely that providing for a penalty of five marks for the loss of the pass token and the issue of a replacement,[135] were also derived from the negative effects it would have on the implementation of the Pass Ordinance as a whole. Since this amount corresponded to a whole month's wages, anyone who lost his tag would 'attempt to conceal the loss',[136] or, as Outjo District Office feared, might even succumb to the temptation 'to run away into the veld'.[137] Thus there was an awareness that it would ultimately not be possible to prevent Africans from escaping the German control machinery. But that the Governor's Office even considered imposing such a high penalty shows how little idea the Colonial Government in Windhoek had of the social situation of the Africans.

The broad measure of agreement to the Native Ordinances on the part of the District heads and their optimism with regard to the possibility of implementing them quickly and smoothly shows their complete disregard for the impact that the measures could be expected to have. Nobody expressed fundamental objections to the regulations or posed the question of whether it really made any sense at all to introduce such measures – a question that had been raised during the discussion of the first draft of a Pass Ordinance in 1900. The reasons for this were to be found first of all in the experience of the war – the enormous numbers of troops deployed had made anything seem possible – and secondly in the fact that the administrative officers now had direct responsibility for the African population, which made it necessary for the relationship to be regulated by law.

In 1900 Leutwein's policy of ruling through and in cooperation with the African chiefs had still been functional, and the German administrative officers hardly had any direct contact with the African population. The intact structures of the various groups with their Kapteins and traditional leaders had still protected their members from any excessively ruthless exploitation, although these traditional structures had already begun to be eroded, as was apparent from the increasingly frequent attacks on and abuse of Africans, and above all African women, by Whites. But it had still been possible for 'native affairs' to be largely regulated with the assistance of just a few African leaders who influenced their subjects in accordance with the wishes of the Germans.

But the war and the destruction of traditional social structures had brought about radical changes in these conditions. The African leaders were now replaced by German administrative officers, whose task it was to make the Africans available as labour to White employers. But this also meant that they were confronted directly with the brutal behaviour of some of the Whites, who mistreated workers and raped women. They therefore welcomed the Native Ordinances, which from their point of view created the kind of legal basis for their day-to-day interactions with Africans that they saw as being necessary after a time of great changes. For the Africans, hardly anything changed. Having being deprived of all rights and exposed to amorphous violence from the Schutztruppe and the Administration during the war, they now found this replaced by a more predictable kind of violence in a legally institutionalized form.

The exploitation of African workers was precisely regulated by the Ordinances. Even if the Africans were no longer to be required to 'labour in chains for indefinite periods of time',[138] and were even to be paid wages, they were nevertheless completely at the mercy of the Whites after the destruction of their traditional way of life. Although the Ordinances provided for a minimum level of protection, how conscientiously the individual District officials performed their duty of care was entirely up to them. As has already been shown from the statements submitted by the District Offices in response to the Native Ordinances, they had widely varying attitudes. They certainly did not see the Native Ordinances purely as measures of oppression, but as providing a basis for the restoration of 'public order and security', with the 'public order' aspect being particularly important to them. The very idea of an African population that was able to move around freely, unregistered and uncontrollable, appeared an incalculable threat after the experiences of the Herero rising, which had been so traumatic for both sides. No other future system was conceivable to them but one in which the Africans were registered and integrated into a legal framework, defined in detail, of duties and a few rights. There was nevertheless one essential distinction from a system of forced labour. The Africans had to work, it is true; but the intention was that they should have a voice in the conditions under which they worked, for example in the choice of employer or the level of wages. This was supposed to make the requirement to work more tolerable for them, and thus to create a basis for long-term employment relationships. At the same time, it offered a modern system whereby the distribution of labour was to be determined by market forces. The availability of labour may have been maintained by coercion, but its distribution was regulated by demand, so that it is possible to talk of a 'semifree' labour market.

From the point of view of political theory, the Native Ordinances were based on the same conception of a modern state with a monopoly on the use of force and administered under the rule of law that can already be seen in Leutwein's attempts to impose the keeping of the peace (*Landfriede*) throughout the country, and to replace the Africans' traditional mechanisms for regulating conflicts by the European idea of the state monopoly on the use of force.

The administrative officers were unable to act at all except on the basis of laws or regulations, and such a basis for Native Policy was created by the three Ordinances. The Administration was unable to think in any other terms than those of an autocratic and authoritarian state, and accordingly the Native Ordinances were beyond the reach of any fundamental criticism simply because they had already been approved by the superior authority. But in terms of their content too, the District heads were in agreement with the Ordinances. The supreme objective of their activities was to establish a new social order in South West Africa, which can best be described as a society of racial privilege. Within this system the Africans were assigned the role of providing cheap labour, which the colonizers considered to be an essential resource for economic development and for the establishment of a settler colony. The officials were unable to perceive any contradiction between this and the civilizatory task that they saw themselves as fulfilling: education for and through work was seen as complementary to that mission. The registration of the Africans and the watertight system of control exercised over them were seen as social disciplining, and thereby as serving both the supposed mission to 'educate the natives' and the direct economic interests of the settlers in having cheap labour available.

Racial Segregation

In the second year of the war, at the same time as he produced his position statement on the reorientation of Native Policy, Tecklenburg implemented the legal prohibition on marriages between Whites and Africans, thereby decisively determining the future orientation of policy with regard to racial segregation. The battle against sexual relations between Whites and Africans, and the intensification of discrimination against their offspring, represented the consummation – at least in the field of lawmaking and regulation – of the society of privilege, as they made it impossible to climb the ladder into the privileged strata. Considerations relating to safeguarding the power of the privileged were allied to racist ideas of a hierarchy of status and value as between the various races, and to dubious views regarding the purity of the 'white race' and the danger of its 'degenerating' as a result of miscegenation or 'interbreeding'.

The same people who were principally involved in drawing up the Sequestration Ordinance and the Native Ordinances – von Lindequist, Tecklenburg and Golinelli – were also responsible for the legal implementation of racial segregation. Here too they took up and responded to demands that had already been aired under Leutwein.

The question of whether 'mixed' marriages should be permitted, and in particular the status of the children born out of relationships between White men and African women – 'mixed-race' people, or 'coloureds' as they were known in South Africa – had preoccupied the German Administration right from the start. Many of the unmarried men entered into relationships with African women.[139] Although, as the Rhenish Mission observed, they fundamentally looked down on them as being members of an 'inferior race', the fact that there were no White women available caused them to push this fact to one side. In addition, marriages to African women, who generally came from the leading families, offered numerous economic advantages. On the one hand, many of these women contributed substantial dowries, often in the form of land ownership, while on the other hand the support given to the wife by her relatives represented valuable assistance from an economic point of view. Some of the men wanted to enter into legal marriages with the women they already regarded as their wives. The Rhenish Missionary Society in particular was in favour of this, as it set out in an 1887 Memorandum on the issue. It rejected extramarital relationships on moral grounds, and was concerned about the social consequences of the irresponsible behaviour of many men. It was common practice for a man, once he had made his fortune, to leave the colony again and simply abandon his partner and her children there; and the Missionary Society saw in this a danger to law and order within the Colony, since they feared that the illegitimate children, 'being superior to the fellow members of their tribes in terms of their natural abilities and cultivation', might 'everywhere become their leaders in their opposition to the race of the heartless fathers'. In order to avert this threat, the Rhenish Missionary Society pleaded for legal marriage between Whites and Africans to be permitted, and even to be deliberately promoted. Proper settled family relationships freed from social stigma could serve to defuse the threatening danger:

> Such people of mixed race, who have been brought up by their white fathers and so are able to count themselves, and like to count themselves, as being in every respect part of the 'white' community, will strengthen the German element in the colonies, and that increasingly as time goes by; and increasingly as time goes by, the native population, whose leading families are related by marriage to the settlers, will truly feel themselves happy and at ease as subjects of the German Empire and enjoying its protection.[140]

But over and above any moral or political considerations, the desire to develop the national economy also seemed to favour the promotion of marriages between the colonizers and the colonized, since the missionaries believed that the offspring of such marriages, being intent on emulating the Whites in language and lifestyle, would be 'eager consumers of the products of German industry'. And they in their turn would be eagerly emulated by their African relatives, keen 'to put on at least the superficial appearance of belonging to the higher race'. Furthermore, the Missionary Society hoped that 'mixed' marriages would also facilitate the cultural mission of 'civilizing the natives':

> The introduction of foreign blood, even if initially only in small measure, will moreover also be of the greatest significance to the overall development of civilization in Africa. The native, left to himself, will hardly be able to create a new and more highly civilized way of life in Africa by his own efforts, just as the white man will hardly ever find himself in the position of being able to prevail against the nature of the country without the coloured population. The gradual development of

a new race, standing between the … natives and the higher nature of the outsiders, will work a marvellous transformation of the wretched conditions that exist at present. People of mixed race, endowed with a new level of drive and with almost unlimited opportunities to further improve themselves, will be in a position to open up their far-off countries completely to the German nation.[141]

Although not convinced with regard to the 'moral, political and economic consequences' thus outlined, since he considered the number of 'mixed' marriages that were likely to occur to be small, Imperial Commissioner Heinrich Göring had conceded the admissibility of marriages between Whites and Africans; but in view of the circumstances prevailing in South West Africa he had believed that the best way would be for such marriages 'to be neither restricted nor encouraged'. He had, however, wished to see 'the regard in which people of mixed race and natives are held in German colonies' enhanced.[142]

Under Theodor Leutwein, however, a policy of preventing, as far as possible, legally legitimized unions between Whites and Africans came to prevail. For such marriages Leutwein conceded only the possibility of a church ceremony, but not the civil register office wedding that had in the meantime been made compulsory for marriages between Whites. This had far-reaching legal consequences, because under the 'Act on the Acquisition and Loss of Imperial and State Nationality' of 1 June 1870, only 'children born in wedlock to a German man acquire the nationality of the father by birth, even if this takes place abroad'. This applied equally if the mother was a 'native', as the Colonial Department informed Leutwein in 1897.[143]

Leutwein, in his reply to the letter from the Colonial Department, did concur with the basic principle that 'the children of German nationals, even if their mothers are natives, are themselves automatically nationals of the German Empire and are not to be treated as bastards'; but at the same time he insisted on his own view that this applied only to children born of duly registered civil marriages. And as it was not possible for couples from different races to enter into an official civil marriage in South West Africa, it followed that the children of 'mixed' marriages could not be German nationals. He thought it was right to consider these children as 'bastards', as he did not consider 'the promotion of such marriages' to be 'in the interests' of the colony. He hoped this would have a deterrent effect: no small number of Germans would be put off marrying African women simply by the knowledge that their children would be considered to be 'bastards'. Leutwein did not, however, exclude the possibility of individual exceptions, as long as the power to decide on them lay with the Governor in the Colony.

He considered this to be reasonable, since there were 'significant differences' between Africans 'with regard to the level of civilization they have attained to', and some women among the Rehoboth Basters in particular could not be placed on a par with 'any mere Hottentot or Herero girl' – apart from which, there were distinctions to be made between the White fathers as well. One would attempt 'to raise his children up out of the sphere of the native mother, while another allows himself to be dragged down into it, together with his children'.[144]

The Colonial Department in Berlin was not, however, willing to accept Leutwein's contrariness, and pointed out to him in 1899 that it was not open to question but that 'a marriage can still be entered into within the Colony of South West Africa, pursuant to the Imperial Ordinance on Marriages and the Registration of Marital Status of 8 December 1892, even if only one of the bridal couple is a non-native'. Leutwein was therefore instructed to ensure that the application of the Prussian national Wilhelm Panzlaff to be permitted 'to conclude a civil marriage with the Baster Magdalena van Wyk should at any rate no longer be rejected on the grounds that the latter person is a native, and furthermore that future cases should proceed in accordance with this basic principle'.[145] This rendered the civil celebration of 'mixed' marriages possible. The African wife and the issue of such marriages automatically obtained German citizenship, and were therefore removed from the sphere of applicability of the nascent Native Law.

The Administration in the colony was not prepared to let things rest there, however. Even though a mere forty-two 'mixed' marriages in all had been concluded in the time up to 1 January 1903, Leutwein and others saw them as representing a threat to the 'German character' of the colony. In the following years Tecklenburg in particular became the driving force behind attempts to get such marriages prohibited altogether. As early as 1903 he came out against the social integration of the offspring of these relationships, thus no longer basing the assessment of which 'race' a particular person belonged to on their degree of assimilation:

> Panzlaff's Hottentot woman is now taking up a lot of space alongside our German ladies at the festivities of the Soldiers' and Marksmen's Associations (*auf Krieger- und Schützenvereinsfesten*), although still without managing to form much in the way of relationships with them. This would change if two or three more such women were to gain admittance to the circle. English law with regard to their black brethren is a good example of how not to go about things: the numbers of Cape Boys and Cape Girls have already almost reached plague proportions. The example of the Boers, among whom there was very seldom any social

mixing with natives, and every one of whom shows a rare skill in the art of always playing the master in respect of the natives, is unfortunately one we are simply not able to emulate. So we have no other alternative than to get legislation in place while there is still time that will erect a strong barrier between non-natives and natives, even if this represents a hard blow to some mixed-race individuals or people married to mixed-race individuals, and it initially leads to something of an increase in the number of illegitimate children.[146]

Apparently contrary to the wishes of the (male) White population, who sought to keep the option of marrying African women open for themselves, and who also by no means rejected social intercourse with people of 'mixed' heritage,[147] Tecklenburg attempted to impose his policy of racial segregation by introducing new rules and regulations. In contrast to many of the settlers,[148] he was not concerned to regulate by law 'how natives can be accepted into the ranks of the Europeans', but rather to 'protect the ranks of the Europeans against penetration by coloured blood'.[149]

Up until 1903, no definition of who was a 'native' had existed, and this opened the door wide to arbitrary decision-making by individual officials. It had, for example, been known to occur that a person initially considered to be German suddenly found himself reclassified as a 'native' by a new District Officer who had drawn on different categorizations as the basis for his decisions.[150]

Tecklenburg pleaded for an Ordinance that would place the issue of 'mixed' marriages or the offspring of 'mixed' non-marital relationships on the same legal footing as 'natives'. It would be possible for the Governor to permit exceptions, the necessity of which he had to admit in order to avoid 'hard cases', but only if 'the prospective beneficiary is to be regarded as at least ¾ non-native by blood, and is worthy to benefit in terms of upbringing, intellectual powers, character and position in life'.[151] He was not yet able to prevail with his position; and Governor Leutwein, in a statement in response to Tecklenburg's report, declared that he was unable to accept his views and that he did not regard an overhaul of the law relating to 'mixed' marriages as being 'a matter of any urgency'.[152]

This situation underwent a radical change as a result of the outbreak of war against the Herero and Nama, and the consequences of that war.[153] Above all, the presence of several thousand German soldiers, and the associated increase in the size of the 'mixed'-heritage population, provided Tecklenburg and Hintrager[154] with the pretext they required to ignore the instructions of the Colonial Department in Berlin, which had been binding on them until then, and to put into effect their own ideas concerning racial segregation. Tecklenburg's 1903 document quoted above is proof that it was not the war that triggered the introduction of legal measures of racial segregation, even though the circumstances accompanying the war now made it appear to be 'a matter of urgency' after all.

The concrete occasion for the prohibition of 'mixed' marriages was an enquiry from District Officer Stübel of Rehoboth, who in July 1905 requested the Governor's Office in Windhoek to decide on applications made to him by two members of the Schutztruppe who were shortly to be discharged to be allowed to enter into civil marriages with Baster women. Tecklenburg thereupon instructed all register offices 'not to solemnize such marriages until further notice', as 'mixed' marriages were to be regarded as 'undesirable in view of their legal, political and social consequences'[155] – thereby creating facts that decided the smouldering conflict between the Governor's Office in Windhoek and the Colonial Department in Berlin in favour of radical racial segregation. In order to justify his position, which deviated from the Colonial Department's 1899 instructions, he invoked the amendment of the *Schutzgebietsgesetz*, the Colonies Act, dated 10 November 1900,[156] under which German laws were to apply to the African population as well only if such applicability was explicitly declared in an Imperial Ordinance. In the case of the *Indigenatsgesetz*, the Nationality Act, which provided the basis for the position that 'mixed' marriages were admissible, this had not been done.[157]

Apart from his fundamental rejection of any integration across the 'barriers of race', Tecklenburg also justified his attitude in terms of the endangerment of German colonial rule that would result from it. This was an argument that could claim to be only too credible after the recent experiences in the Herero and Nama War:

> Males of mixed race will be liable to serve in the forces, will be capable of occupying public offices, and will be beneficiaries of the right to vote, which is likely to be introduced at some time in the future, and of other rights attached to nationality. These consequences are extremely alarming, and in view of the present situation in German South West Africa they represent a grave danger. They will not only compromise the maintenance of the purity of the German race and of German civilization to a major extent, but also put the white man's entire position of power in jeopardy.

> As far as the first of these matters is concerned, it is an old fact of experience, evident not only in Africa, that a white man who lives together permanently with a member of the lower race does not draw the latter up to his level, but is drawn down to hers; he 'goes native' or

'goes kaffir', as they say here. Similarly, experience teaches us that such relationships do not improve the race, but debase it: the offspring are as a rule physically and morally weak, they unite in themselves the bad qualities of both parents and by their nature take more after the native mother in their language and behaviour than after the white father. If the government were to give its sanction to all these consequences by legally permitting marriages between non-natives and natives, it would be acting against its own interest, which is to make this colony into a country of German culture and way of life. It is true that the legal prohibition of marriages between whites and natives will not prevent sexual relations between them and thus the begetting of children of mixed race; but such sexual relationships should be outside the law, and their progeny should be excluded from entitlement to the rights of children born in wedlock and should not be allowed to exert any influence on the fortunes of the country. If the matter is handled in this way, it will also influence the social attitudes of our settlers, which are often very immature in this respect, to an extent that is by no means to be underestimated.[158]

In this, Tecklenburg believed himself to be completely at one with the lessons to be drawn from the history of European expansion, which seemed to him to be confirmed by the fall of the Spanish and Portuguese colonial empires, as compared to the way the British Empire was flourishing and to the rise of the United States:

The experience of other nations in this important issue speaks for itself: one sees on the one hand the consequences of the degeneration of the European race in the former Spanish and Portuguese colonies in America and in Portugal's African possessions, and on the other hand those of the strict segregation of the races as between Caucasians and coloured Africans that is practised in the United States of America and in the British colonies. In particular, the attitude of the British in the neighbouring British colonies is the same as that of the Boers.[159] The Boers, who have the longest experience in dealing with the South African natives, will never forgive a white man who marries a coloured woman. If any does, no Boer will cross his threshold ever again. The British too consider strict segregation to be necessary.[160]

The imminent threat of a rapid growth in the number of sexual relationships between Whites and African women, arising out of the large number of soldiers in the country, seemed to Tecklenburg to make immediate action necessary, and at the same time afforded him the pretext for a U-turn in policy on 'mixed' marriages. The chaotic conditions and the confused decision-making competences during the war are likely to have contributed whatever else was necessary to make the Administration think it would be able to prevail with the new policy, even against opposition from Berlin. Tecklenburg's prohibition of marriages between Whites and Africans was then implemented two months before his statement of position on the expropriation of land and on Native Policy, and made a major contribution to the creation of a privileged society for Whites in that it represented an attempt to cut the African population off from any chance of moving up in society.

In August 1906 Governor von Lindequist confirmed Tecklenburg's decision, explicitly stating that he shared his reasoning and declaring that he would do everything in his power 'to counter the threat arising out of miscegenation'. If persons of 'mixed' heritage were to be recognized by law as having equal rights, 'a great gulf would open up between the law and popular attitudes', which would be highly embarrassing for the Government.

> It would be very difficult to deny the child of a German national who has concluded a civil marriage with a native woman access to the Government School, while the great majority would certainly refuse to allow their children to continue attending the school under such conditions. Compulsion applied against the great majority of the white inhabitants of the country in such a delicate matter as the race question would be dangerous to the highest degree, would evoke the greatest possible degree of bitterness towards the mother country, and sooner or later lead to separation from it.[161]

Von Lindequist makes it quite clear why, in this case, he invokes the feelings of the White population: 'in this case' they had come to the right conclusion 'in having decided, half consciously and half unconsciously, that this country, which is in every respect a suitable one for whites to live and work in, must in the first place support a ruling white population and secondly remain German'. Permitting 'miscegenation', on the other hand, would pose 'the imminent threat that … the colony could very soon forfeit its German character'. Von Lindequist therefore recommended a return to the earlier practice of 'handling relationships between whites and natives under Native Law' (i.e. not permitting register office marriages). In order to refute the reproach voiced in Protestant missionary circles that 'to deny people civil marriage would promote concubinage', he expressed himself in favour of allowing the missionaries to celebrate church marriages. He could not see any injustice or hardship in the prohibition of civil marriage – the only form of marriage legally recognized by the State – as he felt it was only fair 'that anyone who lowers himself to the extent of entering into a relationship with a native woman who is so far beneath him' should be placed on the same legal footing, in particular with regard to inheritance law, as the 'natives'. He would 'merely have to bear the consequences of his own actions', and it would be better 'for the individual to have to suffer in this respect, than for damage to be inflicted on the community as a whole'.[162]

Both Tecklenburg and von Lindequist were following completely in the tradition of Leutwein, who had seen the growth of 'a tribe of bastards forming part of a white nation' as a worrying development, 'which one could not simply stand and watch with one's arms folded' if one did not wish to expose oneself to the danger that 'in fifty years' time there would be no German colony any longer, but a bastard colony'. For in Leutwein's view this would have meant the loss of the Colony itself in the long term. Just as not so long before, the cry of 'Cuba for the Cubans' had made itself heard, so the Germans, at some time in the future, would hear the cry of 'South West Africa for the Africans'. History taught that sooner or later all colonies felt the inclination to turn their backs on their mother countries, which they no longer needed. And this inclination was particularly strong wherever the colony was prevented from maintaining its 'racial community with the motherland'.[163]

In September 1907, Windhoek District Court reinforced the efforts of Tecklenburg and von Lindequist with its judgment in the divorce case Leinhos v. Leinhos, in which the register office marriage between the couple was retrospectively declared invalid. Ada (aka Ida) Maria Leinhos, the daughter of the Englishman Frederik Thomas Green and the Herero woman Kaipukire, had petitioned for divorce from her husband, a German citizen named Kaspar Friedrich Leinhos whom she had married on 22 May 1904 before the Registrar in Okahandja, on the grounds of adultery. Windhoek District Court rejected the petition on the grounds that she was a 'native', a circumstance that was not affected by the fact that her father was an Englishman. In the grounds of the judgment the Court declared:

> Whether a person is a native or a member of the white race is a question of fact, not a question that can be answered by reference to legal provisions. In the view of this Court, the law intends the term native to be understood as referring to the blood members of the primitive or semi-civilized peoples who are or have been settled in the German colonies or neighbouring territories – since it designates other elements of the non-white population as members of foreign coloured tribes. Natives are all the blood members of a primitive people, including the progeny of native women that they have borne to men of the white race, even if there should have been miscegenation with white men over a period of several generations. As long as descent from a member of the primitive people can be proved, the descendant is, by reason of his blood, a native.[164]

Under Sec. 7 of the Colonies Act, however, a 'native' could not enter into a 'civil marriage with a white person',[165] and 'any marriage entered into contrary to this provision' was therefore 'null and void, and the contracting of the marriage a meaningless formal act'. The entry in the Marriage Register made no difference either. So 'a civil marriage has never existed between the parties, but a community that is to be evaluated under Native Law and does not require any recourse to the Court to dissolve it'. Mrs Leinhos's petition was therefore dismissed.[166] With this judgment the Windhoek District Court too took up a position against the conclusion of civil marriages – notwithstanding the fact that these had been tolerated by the German Colonial Administration in South West Africa until 1905 in accordance with the instructions of the Colonial Department – and retrospectively declared all 'mixed' marriages concluded before the Registrar to be invalid.

The responsible people in the Governor's Office saw this as welcome confirmation of their policy on 'mixed' marriages, which aimed at achieving strict racial segregation; and Hintrager personally took action to make sure that the judgment was disseminated as widely as possible, emphasizing in so doing that the judgment established a precedent. It was on his recommendation[167] that the Chief Justice circulated it to all courts in the colony,[168] and Hintrager himself sent the relevant extracts from the grounds of the judgment to all District Offices, in order to let them know how much value those marriages 'between natives and members of the white race' that had been entered into prior to Tecklenburg's prohibition possessed in law.[169]

Tecklenburg having already forbidden the conclusion of any further 'mixed' marriages before Registrars, marriages entered into before that prohibition had now also been declared null and void retrospectively. This was a highly questionable procedure in view of the nature of the German Empire as a state under the rule of law, as contemporaries did not fail to notice. The most prominent critic of the judgment only a short time later was Governor Bruno von Schuckmann, who took the view that the Government 'could not simply treat these marriages, which were properly entered into under the authority of the State, as being null and void', and pointed to the 'bitterly hard cases' that this new legal situation gave rise to. However, instead of himself undertaking anything to counter this glaring injustice, he merely contented himself with the declaration that he was 'in no way to blame for the situation that has arisen'.[170]

This decision also impinged, as no other measure of Native Policy ever did, on the affairs of German citizens, and the German husbands of African women were by no means willing to accept without protest the declaration that their marriages were in fact extramarital relationships, since it turned their children into illegitimate offspring, depriving them of their citizenship and also, which was an even more serious matter for many parents in the private context, of their right of inheritance. Many colonial officials too doubted whether this policy made sense or was admissible. The District Officer of Keetmanshoop, Karl Schmidt, for example, complained that the judgment had suddenly made White men into 'natives' of illegitimate birth, even if, like the son of the trader Krabbenhöft of Gibeon, they had recently served as 'white riders' – mounted troopers – with the Schutztruppe during the war. He prophesied a wave of actions challenging the judgment, some of which he wished every success.[171]

The judicial authorities in the colony remained unmoved by such considerations, however, and on 10 November 1909 Windhoek Superior Court rejected Ada Maria Leinhos's appeal against the decision of Windhoek District Court, explicitly declaring marriages between 'natives' and 'non-natives' to be legally invalid in view of the lack of an Imperial Ordinance permitting them. The definition of a 'native' contained in the original judgment was also confirmed: although the Superior Court admitted that the 'term "native" … [had] in the past been nowhere legally defined', it declared that it was understood 'by common consent' as referring to everyone 'whose genealogy can be traced back to a native on either the paternal or the maternal side'.[172] The colony's highest court had thereby declared the practice of recognizing 'mixed' marriages that had applied since 1899 to be illegal, and sanctioned their retrospective annulment. The fact that in reality no such unambiguous 'common consent', as the court had declared there to be existed with regard to who was to be regarded as an African, but that this had been interpreted in various ways in the course of time, did not concern the court any further. In their acceptance of the principle that who was an African was to be defined in terms of descent, the judgments of the Windhoek District and Superior Courts marked an important stage in the general substitution of a biological concept of race for the cultural one. The degree of assimilation was no longer the criterion.

However, far from being content with the fact that the prohibition of 'mixed' marriages deprived the children of such unions of their German citizenship, and thereby eliminated the supposedly dangerous consequences that such citizenship involved, the Colonial Government sought to go further and to limit the growth of a 'mixed'- heritage population by preventing all sexual relations between Whites and Africans.[173] In launching this attack, the Government set its sights on the figure of the White father. He was to be socially stigmatized and punished for his lack of racial consciousness by being deprived of his rights of citizenship. The Colonial Government thought it saw a suitable starting point for this operation in the *Selbstverwaltungsverordnung* (Local Self-Government Ordinance) of 1909,[174] which afforded the German population of South West Africa a limited degree of political involvement in the administration of the colony through the election of District and Regional Councils and a *Landesrat* (Territorial Council):[175] all men who 'are married to a native or live in concubinage with such a person' were explicitly excluded from the right to vote for or be elected to these bodies, both rights that all German citizens aged over twenty-five were otherwise entitled to exercise.[176] Whereas the exclusion of men married to Africans was entirely in line with the campaign against 'mixed' marriages outlined above, that of men living in concubinage was obviously aimed at furthering the strictest possible social segregation, for reasons of the much-invoked 'racial purity'.

In the original draft of the Local Self-Government Ordinance, which was drawn up by the Imperial Commissioner for Self-Government, Wilhelm Külz, in consultation with Governor von Schuckmann, there had not yet been any mention at all of the 'mixed' marriage issue.[177] As early as March 1908, however, it was the unanimous view within the Imperial Colonial Office[178] that both marriage to and concubinage with African women were to be regarded as reasons for depriving men of the right to vote. One of the people mainly responsible for this change of political course was clearly Angelo Golinelli, who added passages dealing with the issue to von Schuckmann's draft.[179] Thus the fourth member of the group primarily responsible for the expropriation of African land and for the Native Ordinances, alongside Tecklenburg, von Lindequist and Hintrager, was also involved in the implementation of racial segregation.

In August 1908 the Imperial Colonial Office informed the Colonial Government in Windhoek that it had approved the Local Self-Government Ordinance, and drew attention to the changes it had made with regard to the issue of 'mixed' marriages:

> Furthermore it appears expedient to exclude from the right to vote not only those members of the community who are living in concubinage with a native, but also those who are married to a native.[180] The view that the State has tolerated these marriages is in no way a barrier to such members of the community being treated under public law as being disqualified from voting, in particular as experience shows that they are

drawn down by such marriages. This measure may also be presumed to be in harmony with the views of the majority of the white population of the Colony, who regard those whites who are married to native women as having forfeited something of the reputable standing they would otherwise enjoy.[181]

In fact, though, the attitude of the White settlers in South West Africa to this issue was far from being as clear-cut and unambiguous as the Imperial Colonial Office tried to make out. Among the men disqualified by the Local Self-Government Ordinance there were settlers who enjoyed high regard. They defended themselves against the stigmatization, and were supported in this by other citizens. Moreover, by constantly making submissions to the highest levels of the Administration, the men concerned succeeded in keeping the issue on the boil, so that in the end even the Reichstag was forced to devote time to the problem.[182]

In Windhoek, Governor von Schuckmann had not yet given up his opposition to the discriminatory treatment of men married to African women either. On 2 May 1910, at his request,[183] the Territorial Council applied to the Imperial Colonial Office for the Governor to be granted the right to confer voting rights upon individual Whites who had entered into either register office or church marriages with Africans before 1 January 1909.[184] This was only to be permissible, however, in cases where the marriage 'is such as to admit particular recognition from the moral point of view, and where the entire way of life of the family concerned is such as to place beyond all doubt the worthiness of the paterfamilias to enjoy civic rights'.[185]

In his covering letter that accompanied the Territorial Council's resolution when it was sent to the Imperial Colonial Office, however, Deputy Governor Hintrager torpedoed the intentions of Schuckmann and the Territorial Council by expressing his own negative attitude to the matter. In his opinion, there was no reason at all in the 'already very bastardized colony' to amend the Local Self-Government Ordinance, and he feared that the Administration, were it to comply with the wishes of those persons 'who have been forgetful of their race', would only encourage others to imitate them in this matter, which related to 'nothing less than the maintenance of racial purity and racial consciousness'. But his mention of how important it was that the Administration should maintain a strict stance against the 'still regrettably lax attitudes of the settlers in this respect' was nothing less than an admission on his part that the White population was not unanimously behind him in the matter of racial segregation.

It was not until two years later that the Imperial Colonial Office fulfilled the Territorial Council's request and amended the Local Self-Government Ordinance, allowing the Governor

> to confer voting rights upon members of the community who married a native woman in a religious ceremony before 1 January 1893 or in a civil wedding before 1 October 1905, to the extent that the woman's way of life and that of her family admit special recognition of their conjugal life from a moral point of view, and vouch for their worthiness to be invested with civic rights.[186]

The dates of reference laid down by the Imperial Colonial Office were more restrictive than those proposed by the Territorial Council, showing that this measure by no means represented an authorization of 'mixed' marriages, but was merely intended to clean up the mess arising out of the withdrawal of civil rights on the basis of the retrospective annulment of such marriages, which was extremely questionable from a legal point of view. Register office marriages that had taken place since 1905, however, were not covered.

In May 1912 the Colonial Government, now headed by Governor Theodor Seitz, once again intensified its struggle against extramarital sexual relationships between White men and African women by extending the stigmatization and social ostracism of the father of a child born of such a relationship to the mother as well, and promulgating an Ordinance 'concerning the Mixed-Race Population'.[187] This made it mandatory for the births of children whose fathers were 'non-natives' but whose mothers were Africans to be registered in separate registers at the District Offices. While the register entries, containing the name, 'tribal' affiliation, status or occupation and pass number of the mother – no details of the father were asked for[188] – were still completely in the tradition of the way illegitimate German children were registered within the Empire,[189] Sec. 3 of the Ordinance was clearly directed towards criminalizing such relationships. This section states:

> Where the extramarital cohabitation of a non-native man with a native woman gives rise to a public nuisance, the police may require them to separate, and to the extent that the period set for compliance expires without such compliance, may force such a separation.

> Similarly, the immediate ending of a contract of employment and the removal of the mother of a half-white child may be required if the father of the child is the employer or a relative or employee of the employer forming part of his domestic community.[190]

This measure had two declared objectives. One was to facilitate the compilation of reliable statistics on the development of the 'mixed'-heritage population in order to provide an indication of whether stricter measures were necessary to prevent a further increase in its numbers; the other was to produce a socially disciplinary impact on African women. In a Circulated Decree Hintrager instructed the District Officers to conduct the registration proceedings in such a way that they would have the effect of 'deterring the coloured mothers ... through the disgrace involved', and make them aware of the fact that it was 'a transgression against their nation to become involved with a white man'.[191] Above all, everything was to be done to prevent the registration from being regarded as an honour. The assistance of the Missionary Society and of the elders of the werf was to be sought in order to ensure this. The same point of view was also to be put over vigorously to White men, among whom a 'regrettably lax attitude' was frequently to be found.[192] Implicitly underlying this Ordinance as well, as had already been the case with the other state measures against miscegenation, was an admission that racial consciousness was by no means as well developed in the colony as the proponents of strict racial segregation within the Governor's Office would have liked it to be.

Hintrager was able to feel himself confirmed in his attitude, however, by a Memorandum from the missionary Carl Wandres of the Rhenish Mission, whom he had asked to give a formal statement of opinion as an 'old and experienced connoisseur of the country'.[193] In his statement, Wandres rejected all sexual relations between White men and African women, and spoke in favour of strict control. White men, for example, should be subjected to surveillance by secret police, while checks should be made on African women by the headmen of the werfs with the assistance of African informers, who were to report to the police any women who associated with White men: 'Such women ought to be subjected to compulsory medical examinations and placed under control, <u>because they are prostitutes</u>'. To provide for the punishment of such women, Wandres even pleaded for the reintroduction of corporal punishment for women. Wandres himself admitted that it would be very difficult to prevent relationships between White men and African women: 'Only serious moral racial consciousness can help in this respect. We must adopt the same point of view as the Boers: "Any white man who lives with a native woman is to be despised". He should therefore be deprived of his civil rights and honourable status'.[194]

Two years later, Wandres, who was the head of the Synod, reiterated his views:

Mixed marriages are not only undesirable, but are truly immoral and a slap in the face for Germanness …

Mixed marriages are always a sin against racial consciousness. A nation that sins against its own honour in this way definitely sinks to a lower level and, as can be seen from the Latin nations, is not capable of carrying out any thorough colonization …

As far as people of mixed race are concerned, we have to say on the basis of widespread experience that these people are a calamity for our colony. These pitiable creatures are almost all very severely impaired genetically. All that is to be seen among them are lies and deceit, sensuosity and stupid pride, an inclination to dishonesty and to alcoholism, and last but not least they are almost without exception syphilitic. And it could scarcely be otherwise, as their fathers are not good for very much, and their mothers for nothing at all.[195]

This support in his battle for racial segregation was very opportune to Hintrager, and he circulated the Memorandum to all District Offices.[196]

The attempts to define the term 'native' initially arose out of the different legal systems applying to Whites and Africans. Racial segregation completed the society of privilege by defining precisely who was to belong to the privileged and who to the nonprivileged group. If at the beginning of German colonial rule this was still based on the view that the Africans were culturally inferior, but that they could overcome this 'inferiority' by assimilation, from the turn of the century onwards biological concepts came to dominate more and more. The purity of the blood was to be preserved, relationships between Whites and Africans were to be forbidden, and the development of a 'mixed'-heritage population prevented out of racist motivation.

Notes

1. Von Lindequist had apparently received assurances to this effect during the negotiations before he took office. IGW to FO Berlin, 29 November 1905, ZBU *Geheimakten* (Classified Documents) IX.A. Vol. 1, 2a. As the Commander in Chief of the *Schutztruppe* (German colonial forces), Colonel Dame, was unwilling to accept this, von Lindequist asked Berlin to confirm the extent of his competences. By an Imperial Order of 9 January 1906 Wilhelm II decreed that, for the duration of the State of War the Commander of the Schutztruppe was to 'keep the Governor constantly informed of the progress of combat operations and to notify him of all significant applications to be addressed to the home country'. Before implementing any measures not confined entirely to the military sphere, the Commander of the Schutztruppe was to communicate with the Governor in order to

obtain his prior approval. The latter was also to determine the conditions for accepting Africans' submission. This is evident from the following telegram: ICO to IGW and Colonel Dame (telegram), 12 January 1906, ZBU *Geheimakten* IX.A. Vol. 1, 10a–11b. See also Bley, *Kolonialherrschaft*, 200.

2. Bley, *Kolonialherrschaft*, 209.
3. Gründer, *Geschichte der deutschen Kolonien*, 122. See also Bley, *Kolonialherrschaft*, 194.
4. Drechsler, *Kolonialherrschaft* I, 120–27.
5. Gründer, *Kolonien*, 118.
6. Drechsler fails to mention this concrete occasion, and also the proposed ordinance drafted by Golinelli in response to it. As a result, on the one hand the importance of the war as a factor is overemphasized, while on the other hand the various instances within the Colonial Administration are presented as being of one mind with regard to the intention of using the ordinance to compel the Africans to take up dependent employment, which was not the case. Drechsler, *Südwestafrika* I, 214–17.
7. On the Oorlam, see Reinhard, *Hendrik Witbooi*, 26–27. They had emigrated from South Africa at the beginning of the nineteenth century, and by the middle of the century had attained a position of hegemony over the Nama and the Herero, before gradually merging with them, particularly with the Nama. Jonker Afrikaner had been succeeded as ruler of the Oorlam first by Christian Afrikaner and then by Jan Jonker Afrikaner.
8. Deutsche Kolonialgesellschaft to FO-CD (transcript), 31 December 1904, BAL R 1001/1220, 3a f.
9. Expert opinion of Hintrager's, 1 March 1905, BAL R 1001/1220, 4a–9b.
10. Memorandum of Hintrager's relating to his expert opinion, 1 March 1905, BAL R 1001/1220, 9b.
11. Statement of opinion by Golinelli, 2 March 1905, BAL R 1001/1220, 10a f.
12. Golinelli, *Verordnungsentwurf betr. Einziehung des Stammesvermögens der Eingeborenen* [Draft Ordinance concerning the Sequestration of the Natives' Tribal Assets – the 'Draft Sequestration Ordinance'], 7 April 1905, BAL R 1001/1220, 14a–17b. Golinelli prefaced his draft with some explanatory notes. Ibid. 12a–13b. He found a model in the French Sequestration Order for Algiers of 31 October 1845.
13. Golinelli, *Verordnungsentwurf*, 14a–17b.
14. Ibid.
15. Gründer, *Kolonien*, 118.
16. Golinelli, *Verordnungsentwurf*, 14a–17b.
17. It was at the suggestion of an official called von der Decken that the Colonial Department decided not to send Golinelli's draft ordinance to Tecklenburg, but to request him to compile a draft of his own. Memo by von der Decken on Golinelli's draft, 14 April 1905, BAL R 1001/1220, 12a–13b.
18. FO-CD to IGW, 9 May 1905, BAL R 1001/1220, 25a–27a. Extracts from the text are reproduced in Drechsler, *Südwestafrika* I, 215–16; however, Drechsler omits any mention of a number of aspects of the content.
19. IGW to FO-CD, 17 July 1905, BAL R 1001/1220, 28a–35b. Meyer's draft ordinance is to be found ibid., 36a–39a. Extracts from Tecklenburg's statement are reproduced in Drechsler, *Südwestafrika* I, 215–17.

20. IGW to FO-CD, 17 July 1905, 28a–35b.
21. Ibid.
22. Ibid.
23. Ibid.
24. Meyer, *Verordnungsentwurf betr. Einziehung des beweglichen und unbeweglichen Vermögens Eingeborener zu Gunsten des Fiskus des südwestafrikanischen Schutzgebietes* [Draft Ordinance concerning the Sequestration of the Movable and Immovable Assets of Natives in favour of the Revenue Administration of the Colony of South West Africa], n.d., BAL R-1001/1220, 36a–39a.
25. Record of the meeting of 10 November 1905, n.d., unattributed, BAL R 1001/1220, 57a–59a. Golinelli took part in this meeting. Von Lindequist too had taken part in a preliminary meeting on 2 and 3 October 1905.
26. *Kaiserliche Verordnung, betr. Einziehung des Stammesvermögens der Eingeborenen* [Imperial Ordinance concerning the Sequestration of the Natives' Tribal Assets]), 26 December 1905, BAL R 1001/1220, 65a–66b. *Begründung der Verordnung* [Grounds for the Ordinance], ibid., 67a–69a. The Ordinance is reproduced in *Die Deutsche Kolonial-Gesetzgebung* (DKG), Vol. 9 (Berlin: Mittler, 1905), 284–86.
27. IGW to FO-CD, 25 April 1906, BAL R 1001/1220, 131a–134a.
28. IGW, *Bekanntmachung betr. Einziehung des Stammesvermögens der Herero, Swartbooi- und Topnaar-Hottentotten* [Proclamation concerning the Sequestration of the Tribal Assets of the Herero and of the Swartbooi and Topnaar Hottentots], 23 March 1906, reproduced in DKG 10 (1906), 142–43.
29. IGW, *Bekanntmachung betr. Einziehung des Stammesvermögens der Herero, Swartbooi- und Topnaar-Hottentotten* ('Proclamation concerning the Sequestration of the Tribal Assets of the Herero and of the Swartbooi and Topnaar Hottentots'), 8 August 1906, reproduced in DKG 10 (1906), 298.
30. IGW to FO-CD, 25 April 1906. See also Drechsler, *Südwestafrika* I, 216–17.
31. IGW, *Bekanntmachung betr. Einziehung des Stammesvermögens der Witbooi-usw. Hottentotten, sowie der Roten Nation und der Bondelszwarts – einschließlich der Swartmodder-Hottentotten* [Proclamation concerning the Sequestration of the Tribal Assets of the Witbooi and other Hottentots and of the Red Nation and the Bondelswarts, including the Swartmodder Hottentots], 8 May 1907, reproduced in DKG 11 (1907), 233–34.
32. *Unterwerfungsabkommen zwischen Oberstleutnant von Estorff und den Bondelszwarts-Hottentotten, mit Zustimmung des Oberst von Deimling abgeschlossen am 23.12.06* [Submission Agreement between Lieutenant Colonel von Estorff and the Bondelswart Hottentots, concluded on 23 December 1906 with the consent of Colonel von Deimling], reproduced in DKG 11 (1907), 234. *Friedensverhandlungen zwischen der deutschen Regierung und Cornelius Stürmann, vereinbart am 21.11.06* [Peace negotiations between the German Government and Cornelius Stuurmann, agreed on 21 November 1906], reproduced ibid., 235.
33. IGW, *Bekanntmachung betr. Einziehung des Stammesvermögens der Witbooi-usw. Hottentotten, sowie der Roten Nation und der Bondelszwarts – einschließlich der Swartmodder-Hottentotten* [Proclamation concerning the Sequestration of the Tribal Assets of the Witbooi and other Hottentots and of the Red

Nation and the Bondelswarts, including the Swartmodder Hottentots], 11 September 1907, reproduced in DKG 11 (1907), 370–71.

34. Gründer, *Kolonien*, 122. Gründer's statement is basically true, although there were a few other, if rare, cases of Africans owning land privately.

35. IGW to FO-CD, 25 April 1906.

36. IGW to ICO, 19 July 1910, BAL R 1001/1220, 158a–159b.

37. IGW to ICO, 12 November 1912, BAL R 1001/1220, 164a–165b.

38. The newly formed *Reichskolonialamt* (Imperial Colonial Office – ICO) had taken over the responsibilities of the former *Kolonialabteilung im Auswärtigen Amt* (Colonial Department of the Foreign Office – FO-CD) in May 1907.

39. Expert opinion of ICO Section 6 for Section 3, ICO, 13 February 1913, BAL R 1001/1220, 175a–177b.

40. IGW to ICO, 19 July 1910.

41. Expert opinion ICO, 13 February 1913.

42. ICO to IGW, 22 March 1913, BAL R 1001/1220, 178a–179b.

43. Expert opinion ICO, 13 February 1913.

44. IGW to Hasuur DO (transcript), 31 January 1914, BAL R 1001/1220, 185a–186a.

45. IGW, *Verordnung betr. Maßregeln zur Kontrolle der Eingeborenen* [Ordinance concerning Regulations for the Control and Surveillance of Natives – the Control Ordinance], 18 August 1907, NAW ZBU W.III.A.1. Vol. 1, 61a–62b. Typewritten text with handwritten corrections. The text with corrections corresponds to the version in DKG 11 (1907), 345–47.

46. IGW, *Verordnung betr. die Paßpflicht der Eingeborenen* [Ordinance concerning the Pass Requirement for Natives – the 'Pass Ordinance'], 18 August 1907, NAW ZBU W.III.A.1. Vol. 1, 63a–65b. Typewritten text with handwritten corrections. The text with corrections corresponds to the version in DKG 11 (1907), 347–50.

47. IGW, *Verordnung betr. Dienst- und Arbeitsverträge mit Eingeborenen* [Ordinance concerning Employment and Service Contracts with Natives – the 'Master and Servant Ordinance'], 18 August 1907, NAW ZBU W.III.A.1. Vol. 1, 66a–68a. Typewritten text with handwritten corrections. The text with corrections corresponds to the version in DKG 11 (1907), 350–52.

48. FO-CD to imperial commissioner, 5 May 1892, ZBU W.III.N.1. Vol. 1, 1a f.

49. This is demonstrated by the fact that this document is the first in the file that also contains the various drafts of the 1907 Master and Servant Ordinance. NAW ZBU W.III.N.1. Vol. 1.

50. Otjimbingwe DO, *Verordnung betr. das Verhältnis der Arbeitgeber zu den Arbeitern* [Ordinance concerning the Relationship between Employers and Workers] (transcript), 3 July 1894, NAW ZBU W.IV.A.3. Vol. 2, 5a–7a, reproduced in DKG 2 (1893–97), 104. What is notable about von Lindequist's District Police Ordinance is that it always speaks of employees in a quite neutral manner. It is only from the context that it is apparent that it is intended to apply to Africans; at the Deutsche Kolonialgesellschaft, for example, it was filed under the heading 'Legal relationships with Natives'. DKG 2 (1893–97), 104.

51. Imperial Administrator to Imperial Chancellor, 26 July 1894, NAW ZBU W.IV.A.3. Vol. 2, 2a–3a.

52. Gibeon DO, *Verordnung betr. Regelung der Dienstboten-Verhältnisse* [Ordinance concerning the Regulation of Master and Servant Relationships] (transcript), 23 March 1896, NAW ZBU W.IV.A.3. Vol. 2, 41ea–41fa (spec. pag.). Emphases (underlining) as in the original (underlined by the processing officer in the original, with a question mark in the margin).

53. Keetmanshoop District Captaincy to IGW, 28 August 1896, NAW ZBU W.IV.A.3. Vol. 2, 42aa–42ka (spec. pag.).

54. Ibid.

55. Ibid.

56. IGW, *Verordnungsentwurf betr. die Paß- und Meldepflicht der Eingeborenen* [Draft Ordinance concerning Pass and Registration Requirements for Natives], August 1900, NAW ZBU W.III.K.1. Vol. 1, 7a–8a.

57. Ibid.

58. Gibeon DO to IGW, 30 November 1900, NAW ZBU W.III.B.1. Vol. 1, 8a.

59. Swakopmund DO to IGW, 5 November 1900, NAW ZBU W.III.B.1. Vol. 1, 5a–6a.

60. This proposal apparently went too far for the Governor's Office, to judge from the large question mark somebody placed in the margin.

61. Outjo DO to IGW, 21 December 1900, NAW ZBU W.III.B.1. Vol. 1, 7a f.

62. Keetmanshoop DO to IGW, 17 December 1900, NAW ZBU W.III.B.1. Vol. 1, 9a.

63. Omaruru DO to IGW, 3 January 1901, NAW ZBU W.III.B.1. Vol. 1, 10a–11a.

64. *Bestimmungen, betr. die Paßpflicht der Eingeborenen im Bezirk Swakopmund* [Provisions concerning the Pass Requirement for Natives in Swakopmund District], 18 May 1904, NAW ZBU W.III.K.1. Vol. 1, 53a–55a. See also Swakopmund DO to IGW, 8 June 1907, NAW ZBU W.III.A.1. Vol. 1, 26a–27a.

65. *Bestimmungen, betr. die Paßpflicht der Eingeborenen im Bezirk Keetmanshoop* [Provisions concerning the Pass Requirement for Natives in Keetmanshoop District], 7 October 1904, NAW ZBU W.III.K.1. Vol. 1, 62a–63b. See also Keetmanshoop DO to IGW, 10 June 1907, NAW ZBU W.III.A.1. Vol. 1, 28a–29a.

66. However, the provisions of this ordinance were not implemented. Lüderitzbucht DO to IGW, 12 July 1907, NAW ZBU W.III.A.1. Vol. 1, 33a–36a.

67. *Bestimmungen, betr. die Paßpflicht der Eingeborenen des Bezirks Grootfontein* [Provisions concerning the Pass Requirement for Natives in Grootfontein District] (transcript), 9 February 1905, NAW ZBU W.III.K.1. Vol. 1, 92a f.

68. *Bestimmungen, betr. die Paßpflicht der Eingeborenen im Bezirk Windhuk* [Provisions concerning the Pass Requirement for Natives in Windhoek District] (transcript), n.d., NAW ZBU W.III.K.1. Vol. 1, 97a–98a.

69. *Bestimmungen, betr. die Paßpflicht der Eingeborenen im Bezirk Karibib* [Provisions concerning the Pass Requirement for Natives in Karibib District] (transcript), 16 January 1906, NAW ZBU W.III.K.1. Vol. 1, 101a–103a (came into force on 1 February 1906).

70. Outjo DO to IGW, 27 May 1907, NAW ZBU W.III.A.1. Vol. 1, 21a–24a. This ordinance is undated.

71. Grootfontein DO to IGW, 26 August 1907, NAW ZBU W.III.A.1. Vol. 1, 69a–70a.

72. Outjo DO to IGW, 27 May 1907.
73. This is indicated by the fact that in his Circular to the DOs the Governor recommends taking the procedure for the implementation of the Ordinance planned by Windhoek as a model, but says nothing about the experience already gained with it. Circular from the Governor to the DOs, 13 May 1907, NAW ZBU W.III.A.1. Vol. 1, 15a–18a.
74. IGW to FO-CD, 17 July 1905, BAL R 1001/1220, 28a–35b. Extracts from the text are reproduced in Drechsler, *Südwestafrika* I, 215–16.
75. Bley, *Kolonialherrschaft*, 210.
76. Approved versions of the three Ordinances with corrections made by hand were received at IGW on 8 February 1907, having been signed off by Dernburg on 8 January. NAW ZBU W.III.A.1. Vol. 1, 6a–14b. The drafts submitted and the corrections are also to be found, together with exhaustive explanations, in BAL R 1001/2235, 3a–22b. Dernburg's alterations are considered in more detail below.
77. On Dernburg as a reformer of Native Policy, see Schiefel, *Bernhard Dernburg*, 108–20. Schiefel's thesis that Dernburg brought about a change of direction in German Native Policy is by no means apparent, however, in relation to South West Africa.
78. Circular, IGW to DOs, 13 May 1907, NAW ZBU W.III.A.1. Vol. 1, 15a–18a.
79. IGW, Circulated Decree accompanying the *Verordnungen, betr. die Kontrolle und Paßpflicht der Eingeborenen sowie die Dienst- und Arbeitsverträge mit diesen* [Ordinances concerning the Control of and Pass Requirement for Natives and Employment and Service Contracts with them], 18 August 1907, reproduced in DKG 11 (1907), 352–57.
80. IGW to ICO, 10 October 1907, BAL R 1001/2235, 23a–24b. Von Lindequist's successor as Governor, Bruno von Schuckmann, confirmed that the Native Ordinances had come into force on 10 October 1907, with only editorial corrections as against the versions approved by Dernburg.
81. In order to ensure their dissemination among the African population, the three Ordinances were translated into the Nama and Herero languages by the missionaries Carl Wandres and Friedrich Bernsmann in August and September respectively. Transcripts of the translations are to be found in NAW ZBU W.III.A.1. Vol. 1, 78a–107a.
82. Exceptions continued to made with regard to 'the Basters of Rehoboth, as long as they are still resident within the District' and 'such Basters as possess the nationality of a foreign state and are not regarded as natives under the law of their own state' (Sec. 1, Sub-sec. 2 and 3, Pass Ordinance).
83. In his Circulated Order accompanying the dispatch of the three Native Ordinances to the District Officers on 13 May 1907, the Governor expressly pointed out that where there was any difficulty in estimating age, any 'natives ... who are already able to work are to be regarded as being over fourteen years of age'. IGW, Circulated Order, 13 May 1907. This appears to relate to the drafts of the Ordinances before the insertion of Dernburg's corrections, as it still assumes that Africans would be subject to the pass requirement from the age of fourteen. In a letter to the Swakopmund DO, the Governor's Office once again confirmed the criterion of being

old enough to work. IGW to Swakopmund DO, 22 June 1907, NAW ZBU W.III.A.1. Vol. 1, 26a.

84. The only exemption from the mandatory travel pass was if the African was travelling on behalf of or accompanied by his White employer: in that case, however, he required a letter of authority (*Begleitschreiben*) whose 'form and content' corresponded to those of the travel pass (Sec. 4, Pass Ordinance).
85. Nor might they be sold either train or ship tickets (Sec. 15, Pass Ordinance).
86. The only exemption from this restriction was that of the Basters of Rehoboth 'insofar as they are resident and have their livestock in Rehoboth District' (Sec. 2, Sub-sec. 2, Control Ordinance).
87. IGW, Circulated Decree accompanying the Native Ordinances of 18 August 1907.
88. Or possibly a responsible tenant farmer or farm manager. IGW, Circulated Decree accompanying the Native Ordinances of 18 August 1907.
89. This requirement for the 'tribal' affiliation to be stated – unambiguous identification apparently not being possible without it – is particularly surprising as it was bound to perpetuate awareness of a group identity.
90. Failure to translate the content of the contract for the employee was punishable by a fine of up to 150 marks (Sec. 12, Master and Servant Ordinance).
91. For example, Outjo DO to IGW, 27 May 1907.
92. The fact that the Circulated Decree had not been widely disseminated is apparent from a letter from Rehoboth DO to IGW, in which the District Officer proposes integrating the precise provisions of the Circulated Decree into the texts of the Ordinances, as the farmers had these, but not the Decree, in their possession. Rehoboth DO to IGW, 28 October 1908, NAW ZBU W.III.A.3. Vol. 1, 36a–41a. It may therefore be assumed that the text of the Decree was even less widely disseminated among Africans, particularly as the Circulated Decree, unlike the three Ordinances, was not translated into African languages.
93. The Governor's Office laid down explicitly in September 1909 that 'as long as no Native Commissioners have yet been appointed', applications by Africans for criminal prosecutions to be brought against Whites 'are to be filed by the District Officers or by their Deputies on behalf of the natives as their legal representatives', but not by the affected individuals themselves. IGW, Circulated Decree to DOs, 13 September 1909, NAW ZBU W.III.A.1. Vol. 1, 141a. The occasion for this had been a letter from the Superior Court in Windhoek, in which the Court had expressed its concern about a number of cases in which Africans in the south of the colony had applied for criminal prosecutions to be brought against Whites. The Court was alarmed by this, as Africans 'are not to be assessed more highly in terms of their intellectual development and powers of judgement than whites who are under eighteen years of age', and who therefore required a legal representative to act on their behalf. The Court was extremely disturbed by the fact that officials were obliged 'to accept and pass on any application for a prosecution made by a native without any scrutiny as to whether it

was justified'. It feared that the Africans would soon discover 'that they have it in their hands to bring about the prosecution of a white man, and that this would lead to numerous unjustified applications'. Windhoek Superior Court to IGW, 9 August 1909, NAW ZBU W.III.A.1. Vol. 1, 140a f. The Governor's Office accepted the Court's view.

94. Although it was already laid down in Sec. 2 of the Pass Ordinance, the Governor's Office formulated this paragraph in order to explicitly confirm this control function once again.

95. IGW, Circulated Decree accompanying the Native Ordinances of 18 August 1907.

96. This description of the tasks originates from Dernburg, or at least was explicitly approved by him as a modification to the draft submitted by the Governor's Office.

97. Draft of the Control Ordinance as approved by Dernburg. NAW ZBU W.III.A.1. Vol. 1, 10a–11b.

98. IGW, Circular to DOs, 13 May 1907, NAW ZBU W.III.A.1. Vol. 1, 15a–18a.

99. Responses of the DOs to the IGW's Circular of 13 May 1907, NAW ZBU W.III.A.1. Vol. 1, 21a–31b, 33a–41b, 69a–70a.

100. Outjo DO to IGW, 27 May 1907.

101. Lüderitzbucht DO to IGW, 12 July 1907.

102. Swakopmund DO to IGW, 8 June 1907, NAW ZBU W.III.A.1. Vol. 1, 26b–27a.

103. Outjo DO to IGW, 27 May 1907. Emphasis (underlining) as in the original.

104. Ibid.

105. Governor von Schuckmann explicitly drew attention once more to the worker's right to choose his employer freely in connection with the release of the Herero prisoners of war in 1908: 'From the said day [1 April 1908] onwards the Herero are subject in every respect to the Ordinances of 18 August 1907 and all other provisions applying to natives. In particular they may no longer, except in the case set out in Sec. 4 of the Control Ordinance, be assigned to work for a particular employer, but it must be left to them to decide with whom they wish to conclude a contract of employment.' IGW, *Verfügung betr. Aufhebung der Kriegsgefangenschaft der Herero* [Order concerning the Release of Herero Prisoners of War], 26 March 1908, extracts reproduced in DKG 12 (1908), 38.

106. Outjo DO to IGW, 27 May 1907.

107. This attitude also led him to favour the prohibition of large private werfs: 'Re Sec. 7. The restriction on the number of families living in a private werf appears very advantageous for this District in particular, in order to combat abuse by farmers who keep natives simply as hunters.' Outjo DO to IGW, 27 May 1907.

108. Gibeon DO to IGW, 19 July 1907, NAW ZBU W.III.A.1. Vol. 1, 38a–40b.

109. The document bears a marginal note: 'Was rejected by the Governor's Council. The relatives will have to take care of the sick.' Gibeon DO to IGW, 19 July 1907.

110. Keetmanshoop DO to IGW, 10 June 1907.

111. Gobabis DO to IGW, 17 June 1907.

112. Gobabis DO to IGW, 17 June 1907.
113. IGW, Circulated Decree accompanying the Native Ordinances of 18 August 1907.
114. Lüderitzbucht DO to IGW, 12 July 1907. Emphasis (underlining) as in the original.
115. Rehoboth DO to IGW, 28 October 1908.
116. Keetmanshoop DO to IGW, 10 June 1907. Emphasis (underlining) as in the original.
117. Outjo DO to IGW, 27 May 1907.
118. Lüderitzbucht DO to IGW, 12 July 1907.
119. On the ethnological studies carried out by colonial officials, see Marx, *'Völker ohne Schrift und Geschichte'*, 172.
120. Lüderitzbucht DO to IGW, 12 July 1907.
121. This prompted a reader in the Governor's Office to write 'Good' in the margin. Lüderitzbucht DO to IGW, 12 July 1907. Emphasis (underlinings) as in the original.
122. Lüderitzbucht DO to IGW, 12 July 1907.
123. Rehoboth DO to IGW, 22 July 1907, NAW ZBU W.III.A.1. Vol. 1, 37a.
124. IGW, Circulated Decree accompanying the Native Ordinances of 18 August 1907.
125. It was a matter of some four thousand people in all, of whom two thousand lived in Rehoboth. Dove, article 'Bastards', in Schnee, *Deutsches Kolonial-Lexikon*, Vol. I, 140–41.
126. IGW, Pass Ordinance, 18 August 1907.
127. Lüderitzbucht DO to IGW, 12 July 1907.
128. Grootfontein DO to IGW, 26 August 1907.
129. Ibid. Emphasis (underlining) as in the original.
130. Gobabis DO to IGW, 17 June 1907.
131. Outjo DO to IGW, 27 May 1907.
132. Ibid.
133. Lüderitzbucht DO to IGW, 12 July 1907.
134. Keetmanshoop DO to IGW, 10 June 1907.
135. The amount had already been reduced to one mark by FO-CD. Pass Ordinance, NAW ZBU W.III.A.1. Vol. 1, 12a–14b. However, the version circulated to the DOs by the Governor's Office was not the one that FO-CD had approved, but its own draft.
136. Gibeon DO to IGW, 19 July 1907.
137. Outjo DO to IGW, 27 May 1907.
138. Von Trotha to the missionary August Kuhlmann, 18 February 1905, BAL R-1001/2089, quoted according to Bley, *Kolonialherrschaft*, 208.
139. As of 1 January 1903 there were 4,640 Whites living in South West Africa, of whom 3,391 were men. Leutwein, *Elf Jahre*, 232. The Colonial Administration and groups in Germany enthusiastic about colonialism sought to mitigate this problem by deliberately promoting the emigration of women of marriageable age to South West Africa. On this see Smidt, 'Germania'.
140. Rhenish Missionary Society, *Denkschrift betr. die Schließung von Ehen zwischen Weißen und Farbigen in den deutschen Schutzgebieten* [Memorandum

on the Conclusion of Marriages between Whites and Coloured Persons in the German Colonies] (transcript), 1887, NAW ZBU F.IV.R.1., 3a–6b.

141. Ibid. Emphases (underlinings) as in the original. In the Rhenish Missionary Society's view, as early as the 1885 negotiations with the African chiefs in South West Africa, the prospect of a legal settlement of the marriage question had been one of the main factors inducing the Africans to sign Protection Treaties. The Society also believed that this was a major positive factor in relation to the acceptance of German rule, as the expected readiness on the African side to accept the competency of German registrars – whose functions could also be exercised by missionaries – would also lead to a more general acceptance of 'other arrangements made by German colonial officials'.

142. Imperial Administrator to Imperial Chancellor, 17 September 1887, NAW ZBU F.IV.R.1., 7a–8b.

143. FO-CD to IGW, 17 August 1897, NAW ZBU F.IV.R.1., 14a–15b. Children born out of wedlock had the nationality of the mother. Where a legal marriage existed, on the other hand, the wife too was granted the nationality of the husband. *Gesetz über die Erwerbung und den Verlust der Bundes- und Staatsangehörigkeit* [Act on the Acquisition and Loss of Federation and State Nationality], 1 June 1870: this was a law of the North German Federation, which was taken over into imperial German law one year later. It is reproduced in Meyer, *Reichs- und Staatsangehörigkeitsgesetz*, 235–72, esp. 237 and 242.

144. IGW to FO-CD, 22 August 1898, NAW ZBU F.IV.R.1., 15b–17a.

145. FO-CD to IGW, 3 August 1899, NAW ZBU F.IV.R.1., 21a f. Panzlaff had applied to FO-CD for the authorization of his civil marriage to the Baster Magdalena van Wyk.

146. Report by Tecklenburg (transcript), 24 September 1903, NAW ZBU F.IV.R.1., 61ca–61ea (spec. pag.).

147. The IGW pointed out explicitly that Panzlaff's children were attending the 'Government School for Non-Natives' in Windhoek, 'without this causing offence to anybody'. IGW to FO-CD, 20 February 1904, NAW ZBU F.IV.R.1., 61fa–61ga (spec. pag.).

148. The Windhoek citizen Friedrich Gentz, for example, demanded that lists should be drawn up of those people of 'mixed race' who were regarded as Europeans and enjoyed all the privileges of Whites. In this way he sought to eliminate legal uncertainty and to facilitate the differentiation that he regarded as necessary for political, legal and social reasons. Gentz favoured a concept of the 'native' based on the level of 'civilization'. In his view, the decisive factor should not be whether a person of 'mixed' heritage had 'a somewhat higher or lower proportion of native blood in his veins', but rather whether, 'in accordance with the opinions prevailing in the country, he is worthy, in terms of his position, his manner of life, his upbringing and his attitudes to be accepted into the ranks of the Europeans'. In view of the great differences within the 'mixed'-heritage population, he did not feel it made sense to make a general rule as to whether 'mixed-race' people should be accepted into the circle of the Whites or else be relegated to the category of 'Natives'. There was, for

example, 'the dark-complexioned, woolly-haired native on the lowest level of civilization, with hardly any identifiable trace of European blood', but also the representative of the 'blue-eyed, fair-haired Germanic type, in whom nothing betrays his descent on his mother's side'. The 'illegitimate child of a soldier and a coloured prostitute, raised in a native pontok' was to be set against the 'child born to a highly regarded German or English settler, joined in a legal marriage blessed by the church to a wife who may be of native descent, but has been brought up as a European'. F. Gentz, *Die rechtliche Stellung der Bastards in Deutsch-Südwestafrika* [The Legal Status of the Bastards in German South West Africa], a supplement to *Kolonialpolitik und Kolonialwirtschaft*, n.d., 90–92. Copy of the article in NAW ZBU F.IV.R.1., 61ba (spec. pag.). It was Gentz's article that provided the direct occasion for Tecklenburg's expatiations.

149. Report by Tecklenburg (transcript), 24 September 1903.
150. So Gentz maintained in his article.
151. Report by Tecklenburg (transcript), 24 September 1903.
152. IGW to FO-CD, 20 February 1904.
153. On the prohibition of 'mixed' marriages after the war against the Herero and Nama, see also Bley, *Kolonialherrschaft*, 249–56. However, Bley wrongly reduces the motives for this policy to the nationality issue and the question of maintaining colonial rule. He does not consider biological or medical/anthropological arguments to have carried any weight. Ibid. 251–52.
154. Hintrager later claimed to have been the person responsible for putting through the prohibition of civil marriages in 1905. IGW to ICO, 20 June 1910, BAL R 1001/2059, 44a–47b.
155. Circulated Order, IGW to Register Offices, 23 September 1905, NAW ZBU F.IV.R.1., 22a. Hintrager was one of those who signed off this Circulated Order, which explains the positive assessment of the measure that is to be found in his memoirs, where the order is also reproduced. Hintrager, *Südwestafrika in der deutschen Zeit*, 75.
156. Imperial Chancellor Hohenlohe, *Bekanntmachung wegen Redaktion des Schutzgebietgesetzes* [Proclamation concerning the Amendment of the Colonies Act], 10 September 1900, reproduced in DKG 5 (1899/1900), 143–46.
157. Tecklenburg to FO-CD, 23 October 1905, NAW F.IV.R.1., 24a–34a.
158. Tecklenburg to FO-CD, 23 October 1905.
159. Here Tecklenburg contradicts his own statement of 24 September 1903, quoted above, according to which the British had not pursued racial segregation strictly enough.
160. Tecklenburg to FO-CD, 23 October 1905.
161. IGW to FO-CD, 12 August 1906, NAW F.IV.R.1., 36b–39a.
162. Ibid. The acceptance of Tecklenburg's argumentation and the mention of the 'threat arising out of miscegenation' in the draft originated from Hintrager, and confirm his role in helping racial segregation to prevail, a role he later pursued even more determinedly.
163. Leutwein, *Elf Jahre*, 233–34.

164. Judgment of Windhoek District Court, 26 September 1907 (executed copy of 25 April 1908), NAW ZBU F.IV.R.1., II-37a–40b (spec. pag.). Original of the judgment in NAW GWI 530 [R 1/07], 23a–26a.
165. The relevant section of the Colonies Act did not, however, fundamentally exclude marriage, but offered the possibility of issuing an Ordinance to permit it. Amendment to the Colonies Act, 143–146. However, no such ordinance was issued.
166. Judgment of Windhoek District Court, 26 September 1907 (executed copy of 25 April 1908), NAW ZBU F.IV.R.1., II-37a–40b (spec. pag.). Original of the judgment in NAW GWI 530 [R 1/07], 23a–26a.
167. Memo of Hintrager's on an executed copy of the judgment, 9 May 1908. Judgment of Windhoek District Court, 26 September 1907.
168. Superior Court to lower courts, 16 May 1908, NAW F.IV.R.1., 41a.
169. Circulated Decree, IGW to DOs, 16 May 1908, NAW F.IV.R.1., 41a f.
170. IGW to ICO, 2 October 1908, BAL R 1001/2086, 62a–65a.
171. Keetmanshoop DO to IGW, 19 June 1908, NAW F.IV.R.1., 42a.
172. Judgment of Windhoek Superior Court, 10 November 1909, NAW F.IV.R.1., 52a–55a.
173. By far the majority of children with White fathers and African mothers had been a consequence of extramarital relationships or of rape. On this, and above all on the contribution of White women to the campaign against 'mixed' marriages and extramarital relationships, through which they sought to rid themselves of African rivals, see also Smidt, 'Germania', 146–71.
174. Imperial Chancellor, *Verordnung betr. die Selbstverwaltung in Deutsch-Südwestafrika* [Ordinance concerning Local Self-Government in German South West Africa], 28 January 1909, reproduced in DKG 13 (1909) 19–34.
175. On the matter of local self-government, see Bley, *Kolonialherrschaft*, 223–34.
176. Imperial Chancellor, *Verordnung betr. die Selbstverwaltung.*
177. Imperial Chancellor, *Verordnungsentwurf betr. die Organisation der Selbstverwaltung in Deutsch-Südwestafrika* [Draft Ordinance concerning the Organization of Local Self-Government in German South West Africa], n.d., BAL R 1001/2057, 22a–38a. This was sent by IGW to ICO on 1 February 1908. IGW to ICO, 1 February 1908, BAL R 1001/2057, 20a–21a. Von Schuckmann even warned explicitly that the Germans 'living in state-recognized marriages with natives' could not 'be subjected to prejudicial legal measures'. IGW to ICO, 4 May 1908, BAL R 1001/2057, 67a–75a.
178. ICO, Section C2, Position statement on the Local Self-Government Ordinance, 19 March 1908, BAL R 1001/2057, 53b–55b.
179. Position statement of Golinelli's on the Local Self-Government Ordinance, 17 March 1908, BAL R 1001/2057, 52a–53a. Draft of the ordinance, with corrections by Golinelli in pencil. BAL R 1001/2057, 77a–94b. Golinelli confirmed in a letter that the corrections were his. Golinelli, ICO, to Meyer-Gerhard, ICO, 18 July 1908, BAL R 1001/2057, 113a f.
180. The ICO was apparently not yet aware of the annulment of these marriages by the court in Windhoek, which had occurred only a few weeks before.

181. ICO to IGW, August 1908, BAL R 1001/2057, 118a–122a.
182. For examples, see Bley, *Kolonialherrschaft*, 253–56.
183. IGW to ICO, 20 June 1910, BAL R 1001/2059, 44a–47b.
184. This was chosen as the effective date because as late as 1908 a District Officer had married a farmer named Schubert to a 'mixed-race' woman called Bowe, the daughter of an Englishman of that name, despite the fact that such marriages had already been forbidden in 1905. IGW to ICO, 20 June 1910, BAL R 1001/2059, 44a–47b.
185. Application from the Territorial Council, 2 May 1910, quoted according to IGW to ICO, 20 June 1910, BAL R 1001/2059, 44a–47b.
186. Imperial Chancellor, *Verordnung zur Abänderung der Verordnung vom 28.1.09, betr. die Selbstverwaltung in Deutsch-Südwestafrika* [Ordinance amending the Ordinance of 28 January 1909 concerning Local Self-Government in German South West Africa], 28 March 1912, BAL R 1001/2059, 112a f.
187. IGW, *Verordnung über die Mischlingsbevölkerung* [Ordinance concerning the Mixed-Race Population], 23 May 1912, NAW F.IV.R.1., 128a f.
188. Only in cases of 'mixed' marriages, which no longer really existed by law, or if it was the father himself who reported the birth, were his personal details to be recorded as well. Circulated Decree, IGW to DOs, 19 July 1912, NAW F.IV.R.1., 146a f.
189. Imperial Chancellor, Instruction concerning the Act of 4 May 1870, *Gesetz betr. die Eheschließung und die Beurkundung des Personenstandes von Bundesangehörigen im Ausland* [Act concerning Marriages of Nationals of the Federation Abroad and the Notarization of their Civil Status], reproduced in DKG 1 (up to 1892), 58–79.
190. IGW, *Verordnung über die Mischlingsbevölkerung*, 23 May 1912, 128a f.
191. In this respect, Hintrager refers to explicit resolutions of the Territorial Council.
192. Circulated Decree, IGW to DOs, 31 July 1912, NAW F.IV.R.1., 140a–141b.
193. IGW to Wandres, 14 May 1910, NAW F.IV.R.1., 51a f.
194. Statement by Wandres, n.d., NAW F.IV.R.1., 58a–60a. Wandres sent it to Hintrager on 24 May 1910. Wandres to IGW, 24 May 1910, ibid. 57a. Emphasis (underlining) as in the original.
195. *Bemerkungen über Mischehen und Mischlinge aus der Praxis für die Praxis* [Remarks on Mixed Marriages and Mixed-Race People, from Practical Experience for Practical Application], Missionary Carl Wandres (transcript), n.d., NAW F.IV.R.1., 143b–145b. Wandres' remarks were circulated to the DOs by Hintrager on 12 July 1912.
196. IGW to DOs, 12 July 1912, NAW F.IV.R.1., 142a.

3

Demographics, Economics and Institutions
Basic Factors after the War

Population and Economic Development

During the last ten years of German colonial rule, the demographic and economic fundamentals of South West Africa changed substantially. Whereas the African population had been reduced substantially as a result of the large number of victims claimed by the war, and amounted on 1 January 1913 to only 69,003, plus 1,746 people with both White and African ancestors and 2,648 foreign Africans,[1] sustained immigration had increased the White population from 4,640 on 1 January 1903[2] to 14,830 on 1 January 1913.[3] Sales of farms to settlers reflected this development: whereas only 480 farms had been sold up to the beginning of 1907,[4] this figure increased to 1,331 by the year 1913, of which 1,138 farms with a total area of 11,514,029 hectares were actually in productive use.[5] Stock breeding, by far the most important sector of agriculture, also showed a considerable recovery after the war: the numbers of cattle, meat sheep and goats increased fourfold between 1907 and 1913, while the stock of Angora goats increased eightfold and that of wool sheep fifteenfold.[6] Despite this, the relative importance of agriculture within the South West African economy declined as a result of the exploitation of additional copper deposits from 1907 onwards, and above all of the discovery of the first diamonds in 1908. Annual diamond production rose from 38,273 carats in 1908 to 846,695 carats in 1910, and some 1.5 million carats in 1913.[7] Of total exports with a sales value amounting to about M70,302,830 in the year 1913, diamonds and copper accounted for over M66,839,000, whereas agricultural produce such as cattle, skins, fleeces, wool and ostrich feathers accounted for only about M3.5 million. The proceeds from copper exports, despite amounting to only about 10 per cent of the value of diamond exports, were nevertheless almost three times those from agricultural exports.[8] Thus diamond production was by far the most important sector of the economy of South West Africa, and of all the territories constituting Germany's colonial empire 'South West' was by far the most important trading partner for the motherland.[9]

The economic upturn was reinforced by ambitious railway construction projects. Whereas in 1902 there had been only one railway line in the colony, the 382-km Swakopmund–Windhoek State Railway, by the end of 1913 a network of 2,104 km had been constructed, including lines connecting Tsumeb to Swakopmund and Windhoek to Lüderitzbucht via Keetmanshoop.[10]

This economic development also had an impact on state finances: between 1909 and 1913 diamond production was responsible for 66 per cent of all the colony's revenues.[11] This meant that towards the end of German rule South West Africa was in a position to meet at least the costs of its civil administration – excluding those of the Schutztruppe, the military force stationed in the colony – out of its own pocket.[12] The territory's revenues, which in 1901 amounted to a mere M1,879,000, had risen to M6,908,000 by 1908[13] and to no less than M17,621,000 by 1909, reaching their peak value of M18,098,000 in the following year.[14] These revenues, however, were outbalanced by expenditure of M12,624,000 in 1901, M119,078,000 in 1908,[15] M29,387,000 in 1909 and M40,148,000 in 1910.[16] The shortfall was covered by subsidies from the Imperial Government for military expenditure, by Imperial Government loans and above all by colonial bonds issued to finance the building of the railways.[17]

The rise of the mining industry and the consequent decline in the relative importance of agriculture led to conflicts within the White population of the colony. These did not relate only to the dispute over the creation of a monopoly in respect of prospecting and mining rights (on the initiative of Colonial Secretary Bernhard Dernburg) and the centralization of the diamond trade,[18] which led to the formation of the state-supervised consortium known as the Diamantenregie, through which the White population of South West Africa felt itself excluded from participation in the diamond boom.[19] Controversies also arose in relation to the urgent labour question, and these persisted until the end of German rule. The shortage of African workers grew more and more acute; indeed it was not alleviated until long after 1915.

The mining industry, which was so important to exports and thus to the colony's public sector finances, had to compete for workers with agriculture, which, while its production for export was far smaller, was of crucial importance to South West Africa's future as a settler colony. Agriculture enjoyed particular support from the Colonial Government,[20] and farmers increasingly articulated their claim to be the sole representatives of the whole White population, as they considered themselves to be the 'true' settlers who were safeguarding the colony's long-term economic future, while regarding the diamond boom as being only a passing phenomenon. The system of local self-government introduced in 1909, which provided for elected councils to be set up in all districts and for the colony as a whole, endowed them with additional political weight.[21] In the Territorial Council that had been set up to advise the Governor, for example, the agricultural interest was overrepresented in comparison with the mining industry and the railways.[22] The first Territorial Council of 1910 included fifteen farmers, but only seven representatives of the Deutsche Kolonialgesellschaft, the Otavi Railway and the Municipalities of Lüderitzbucht and Swakopmund, which held considerable direct stakes in the mines. Alongside these there were four representatives of the Administration and four of the other municipalities. Despite their loss of relative economic importance, therefore, the farmers were able to make themselves heard very effectively.

General Administration, the Territorial Police and the Military Presence

In the years after the Herero and Nama War, the expansion of German administration in South West Africa proceeded according to plan. Whereas in 1903 there had been only six autonomous District Offices,[23] their number had risen to sixteen by 1914, both as a result of the establishment of new offices and through the conversion of previously non-autonomous districts into autonomous ones.[24] Immediately after the war there was no separate Native Administration, and it was only from 1911 onwards that the first steps were taken towards creating one. Until then, all executive, legislative and judicial functions affecting the African population were exercised by the civil administration that was also responsible for the White population, although there was an independent judicial structure for the Whites.

There were four tiers of administration in the colony: the Colonial Government in Windhoek, the autonomous District Offices, the non-autonomous District Offices and the subordinate police stations. The highest authority in the colony was the Governor in Windhoek, whose office formed the effective government of the territory. It received instructions from the Colonial Department of the Foreign Office or later the Imperial Colonial Office,[25] issued Decrees and Ordinances of its own after obtaining approval for them from the superior authority in Berlin,[26] and collated information received from its own subordinate authorities for onward transmission to the Imperial authority. In addition, the Governor's Office adjudicated disputes between subordinate offices and officers, and possessed the competence to interpret whatever Ordinances and Decrees had been promulgated, issuing Implementation Regulations that laid down in detail how they were to be applied. It also had the power to correct decisions made by the District Offices.

Regional administration centred on the District Offices. It was their task to implement directives coming from the Governor's Office in Windhoek and to pass on information that they had collected to the higher authority. With regard to the implementation of the measures that were to be put into force, they were allowed to issue implementation regulations of their own, called District Police (i.e. Administrative) Ordinances. It was they who bore the main burden of Native Administration; being the tier of the Administration responsible for the implementation of Native Policy at a local level, they had been assigned judicial, executive and – to a lesser extent – even legislative competences. In the event of disputes between Africans and Whites they were the first and fundamental point of contact for adjudication for the African population, who unlike the Whites had no right of appeal to the colony's courts. With regard to disputes between Africans, the District Offices exercised judicial powers as well, as they also did if Africans infringed the rules and regulations of the instruments of Native Policy that they were subject to. In this field the District Offices combined the functions of prosecutor and judge, and were also able to impose punishments, though in the case of death sentences and severe corporal punishment these had to be confirmed by the Governor.[27]

The position of the District Officers within their districts was such that it was difficult for the central colonial authorities to exercise surveillance over them, and this frequently led to tensions between them and the Governor's Office. In some cases, they would interpret the instructions handed down to them in a very wayward manner, or would ignore them completely. The Governor's Office, on the other hand, was for its part always attempting to extend the degree of its control, especially over the more remote District Offices, by an ever-increasing measure of bureaucracy, displayed for example in demands for reports or statistics. The Governor's Office was also the supervisory authority in personnel and disciplinary matters, able to influence the future careers of subordinate officers by its staff appraisals. Thus an officer who displayed an attitude or held an opinion that deviated from that of the Governor's Office could be brought into line by means of such a staff appraisal. This was a risk that very few of the lower-ranking officials were willing to take, as is demonstrated by their overwhelmingly positive responses to whatever proposals they received from Windhoek.

Despite all this, the tensions between the central and local colonial administrations often opened up areas of personal freedom for the African population; but they also, where the local chief administrator saw fit, allowed regulations to be implemented with a degree of strictness going beyond what was actually contained in the Ordinances. Such cases were customarily camouflaged by stereotyped reports that measures had been properly implemented, which the occasional inspections often discovered to be a misleading representation of the situation. Thus it is not possible to conclude, from the formal nature of the legal instruments of Native Policy that were adopted, either that they were implemented smoothly at the local level, or that they functioned as intended; rather, before any conclusions can be drawn as to what Native Policy looked like in real life, all the areas covered by it have to be investigated in detail at the local level.

The activities of the Administration were restricted to the centre and south of the colony, the so-called Police Zone, whereas the northern area was for the time being excluded from German administration. There had been plans for the military occupation of Ovamboland as early as the governorship of Theodor Leutwein, but these had been vetoed by the Colonial Department in Berlin; this authority was reluctant to incur the costs of such a military adventure, the outcome of which, in view of the strength of the Ovambo and the degree of resistance that could be expected, would have been at best uncertain.[28] Finally, in January 1906, Governor von Lindequist ordered that the borders to Ovamboland should be closed. The import of firearms, ammunition, horses and liquor was prohibited, and other trade was only permitted with a limited-period licence. Beyond this, the Governor forbade everybody except Africans domiciled in Ovamboland and the missionaries who lived there to enter the area.[29] In particular, he wanted to restrict the recruitment of migrant workers to those with special authorization, which would be granted only to 'absolutely reliable persons'.[30]

This closing of the borders of Ovamboland, which came into force in 1906, was only intended to be a provisional measure[31] until German rule had been consolidated in the southern and central areas of the colony and there were sufficient forces available to change the status quo in Ovamboland. But the reductions in the strength of the military that began immediately after the end of the Herero and Nama War meant that the conquest of Ovamboland had to be postponed to some indefinite and far-off future. Throughout the German colonial period, this part of the colony remained outside the area of direct rule, and it was only under the South Africans that a campaign to conquer Ovamboland was undertaken.[32]

In 1908 the Colonial Government in Windhoek also excluded the Caprivi Strip from more intensive penetration by direct German rule, and restricted access to the area.[33] In 1909, in order to advertise the German claim to sovereignty to the local population, counter the increasing influence of British and Portuguese interests and document internationally that the area was part of German South West Africa, the German Imperial authorities merely established a small presence, the Residency at Schuckmannsburg; it did not, however, pursue any effective administration.[34] In addition to these areas, the Kaokoveld in the north-west of the colony and the Kalahari on the borders to the Cape Colony and the Bechuanaland Protectorate were also excluded from the administrative system.[35] Apart from financial issues, the decisive reason for these limitations on the extension of effective German administration was no doubt an appreciation of the enormous military commitment that an occupation of the areas outside the Police Zone would have demanded.

For enforcement support in respect of their administrative responsibilities the central Colonial Government and the District Offices could call upon both the Territorial Police and the Schutztruppe. The latter's day-to-day effectiveness in this field was limited, however, by the demands of its own primary task, which was to secure the colony against threats, both internal[36] and external.[37] The territory's police force, on the other hand, was of great importance, since unlike the Schutztruppe it was an arm of 'the civil authorities responsible for administering the colony'.[38] Up until 1905 it had been almost exclusively members of the Schutztruppe who had been entrusted with policing tasks, but as this had resulted in repeated friction and disputes between the military and civil administrations, Governor Leutwein proposed to the colonial authorities at home as early as 1900 that a Police Executive should be set up. By 1902 the planning had progressed to such an extent that he was able to make concrete proposals for a police force completely detached from the Schutztruppe;[39] and the process culminated in the issue on 1 March 1905 of the 'Territorial Police Regulations'. These laid down that members of the police force, being civil servants, were 'subject to the disciplinary provisions applicable to such', and were subordinate not only to the Governor but also to the District Officers.[40] However, with the outbreak of the Herero War and the resulting enormous expansion of the Schutztruppe, the establishment of a Territorial Police Force no longer seemed so urgent, the military forces being entrusted with the upholding of public order for the time being. It was not until Governor von Lindequist took office that steps were taken to push ahead with the build-up of the Territorial Police, and the number of establishment posts provided for in the budget grew from 80 in the years 1904 and 1905 to 160 for the year 1906.[41] This expansion was all the more important in view of the massive reduction in the size of the Schutztruppe after the ending of the State of War on 31 March 1907 and its resulting imminent withdrawal from the places and military posts that it had controlled until then. What is more, the introduction of the Native Ordinances, which was planned for August 1907, increased the staffing requirement enormously. This was reflected in the 1907 budget, which provided for the Territorial Police to be strengthened to 720 men.[42] However, as in reality there were only 119 police officers available on 1 April 1907, there was a shortfall of 601. The theoretical strength of 720 was never achieved in the subsequent years either, since far fewer members of the Schutztruppe were prepared to switch over to the police than had been expected, and recruiting attempts in Germany did not bring the desired success either.[43] The greatest strength ever achieved under German Administration was the 569 policemen serving in 1912, who were supplemented by a further 370 African 'police servants', or auxiliary policemen.[44]

The consequence of the inadequate level of manpower was that while as of 1 February 1909 there were sixty-nine police stations in the colony as a whole, thirty-three of these were staffed by only two policemen and nineteen by only one; only nine had three police officers, and only eight had four or five.[45] In some cases the distance between stations might be as much as 140 km, so that each had a vast area to exercise surveillance over. Although the number of stations had increased to 108 by 1914, staffed by 393 men, the total strength of the Territorial Police had fallen to 470 men,[46] and there was never any time when all the police officers were available for duty: on average a quarter of them were either on leave or sick.[47] And not all the policemen were available to keep check on the African population, as they were also responsible for policing the White community, which included undertaking measures of veterinary surveillance or executing attachment orders issued by the courts.[48] The very circumstance of the rapid increase in the White population after the war led to more and more police being required in the larger centres of population,[49] who were therefore unavailable to exercise surveillance over the scattered African settlements.

The military was not able to adequately compensate for the shortage of police manpower either, as its effectiveness had been reduced by the cuts in its personnel that began soon after the end of the war. The size of the Schutztruppe was reduced from 3,988 men in the years 1907–08 to 2,431 in 1909, and to a mere 1,970 men by 1912.[50] The reason for this reduction in the size of the forces was the enormous cost of the military presence, which in 1909, for example, required a subsidy of M16,252,000 from the Imperial Government.[51]

The police and the Schutztruppe also had different types of task to perform: the police had to be dispersed throughout the country in order to exercise surveillance over the individual Africans, whereas the Schutztruppe were concentrated at a small number of centres to facilitate their better training and to ensure that they were able to respond massively to curb any unrest.[52] Moreover, cooperation between the civil administration and the Schutztruppe did not always function without friction, as the District Officers had no direct power to command the military personnel stationed in their districts. Although the Schutztruppe was officially subordinate to the civil administration, it retained its own organizational and command structure; that is to say, instructions from the Governor had to be communicated to the Commander of the Schutztruppe, who then passed them on to the individual units.[53]

Moves towards Creating a Separate 'Native Administration'

The subjection of thousands of Africans to direct German rule substantially increased the amount of administrative activity required, and so demanded structural changes within the Administration. It was not long before the realization took hold that it was impossible to 'have Native Affairs dealt with just on the side by one of the departments in the Governor's Office'; so in July 1910 the Colonial Government decided to set up a separate Department of Native Affairs 'as an expert unit to assist the Governor in administrative matters concerning the Natives'.[54] The new department, the Referat für Eingeborenen-Angelegenheiten,[55] which was also to concern itself with all 'decisions of the Governor regarding sentences pronounced in criminal cases involving Natives' and with the 'lists of punishments imposed, which are to be submitted by the District Offices',[56] was established on 7 February 1911. Furthermore, the Head of the Department was to supervise the system of migratory labour,[57] and also to maintain relations with those South West African ethnic groups living outside the Police Zone, for which purpose he had to undertake regular journeys into Ovamboland to collect information and to organize relief supplies in years of drought.[58] Simultaneously with the appointment of this Head of Native Affairs, Native Commissioners[59] were also appointed on a trial basis; these latter had to 'fulfil the same functions in respect of the local authorities as the former in respect of the Governor's Office'.[60]

Previously, in the Control Ordinance of 1907 and the Local Self-Government Ordinance of 1909, the creation of such Native Commissioners had already been held out as a prospect.[61] Thus their establishment was directly linked to the introduction of the Native Ordinances. The concept of the 'semifree' labour market could only function if it was possible to guarantee that the Africans would actually be able to enjoy the rights they were entitled to; and this could only be done by putting an intermediary in place who was responsible solely for their concerns. Colonial Secretary Bernhard Dernburg had pointed this out in the Reichstag on 19 May 1908:

> This person [the Native Commissioner] is first and foremost to ensure that the regulations in force with regard to employed workers, of whatever kind these regulations may be, are altogether implemented correctly and strictly, and thus to act in the Territory as a kind of arbiter or referee in disputes arising in relation to conditions of employment. For the rest, it is not intended to withdraw jurisdiction over the affairs of the black population from the regular courts.

> But in addition, because there are such extraordinary difficulties incumbent on representing black people against whites in the regular courts, the Native Commissioners are to assume ex officio the representation of black people in actions against whites in the regular courts, insofar as they are convinced that the matter in dispute is not of a frivolous nature.[62]

The Native Commissioners were to be 'the advocates of the coloured people in all their vital interests', and also to represent the Africans' interests towards the Administration. They thus became a connecting link between the Administration and the African population. But winning the confidence of the Africans required a lot of time and effort, and also demanded constant contact with them. For this reason, the function had to be separated from that of the District Officer. This also appeared to be necessary in order to avoid conflicts of interest, as the District Officers, having the power to impose punishments, were in this respect 'on the opposite side of the fence from the Commissioners'.[63]

The Native Commissioner had a difficult task to perform in acting as an intermediary between Whites and Africans. He also needed to enjoy a modicum of confidence among the Africans if he was to be able to fulfil this task, so candidates for the position had to fulfil particular requirements in terms of their personal qualifications. Care had to be taken 'to find people who, apart from having adequate knowledge of the laws of the territory, of administrative issues and of commercial operations, and leading exemplary lives, also have some knowledge of the languages spoken here and have a feeling for the way the Native mind works'.[64]

By the end of 1912 Native Commissioners had been appointed in the particularly overburdened Districts of Lüderitzbucht and Windhoek, and also in Warmbad and Keetmanshoop,[65] and Service Instructions had been issued to regulate their activities.[66] These all matched with each other in their descriptions of the fundamental rights and duties, varying only in respect of the specific areas of responsibility in the different districts.[67]

The tasks of a Native Commissioner embraced 'monitoring the healthy nutrition, clothing and accommodation of the Natives', ensuring that they were correctly paid and 'properly treated by their employers'.[68] Over and above this he was also responsible, except in the case of the Native Commissioner of Lüderitzbucht, for the registration of the Africans, the inspection of the werfs in accordance with the Control Ordinance and the distribution of workers between the employers in his area of responsibility.[69] The Native Commissioner was 'to receive all complaints from employers about their Natives and from Natives about their employers and to investigate these thoroughly', and to remedy them 'where necessary in consultation with the District Officer'. He was to investigate all 'crimes and misdemeanours' committed by Africans within his area of responsibility if requested to do so by the responsible District Officer.[70] Only the Native Commissioner of Lüderitzbucht was entitled to undertake such investigations ex officio, and even in his case only to the extent that the matter concerned entailed no more than disciplinary penalties: court proceedings remained a matter for the District Officer, who also possessed the competence – in other words, it was he who decided whether a case was to be treated as a disciplinary one or as a matter for the courts.[71] In court proceedings involving Africans, the Native Commissioner acted as their legal counsel. Just as the absence of a strict division of competences between the police and the Native Commissioner could potentially have a negative impact on the Native Commissioner's work, so too the division of tasks between the District Officer and the Native Commissioner inevitably involved a danger of even further tensions. For this reason, and to guarantee the independence of the Native Commissioner, he was not subject to the disciplinary authority of the District Officer concerned.

The Native Commissioners had an important role to play in solving the labour question. The trust that it was the Commissioner's task to earn among the Africans, and his interventions to enforce the protective provisions of the 1907 Native Ordinances, were intended to contribute towards reducing conflict between employees and employers and in particular to prevent Africans from deserting their places of work. The Service Instructions for Lüderitzbucht explicitly emphasized this aspect of the Native Commissioner's task: he was to carry out regular inspections of the diamond fields and to remedy any malpractices, but also at the same time to exhort the Africans 'particularly to fulfil their duties towards their employers'.[72]

The Native Commissioners also had the important function of supplying the Governor's Office in Windhoek with information on conditions in the often remote districts. In this way the Governor sought to keep an overview of the situation of the Africans, while at the same time supervising the Native Commissioners in the same way as he did the District Officers. There was however, too much explosive material in the Commissioners' reports for the Colonial Administration to consider publishing them, as they often depicted the situation in unvarnished terms, not pulling their punches even when it came to describing misconduct committed by Whites. For this reason Deputy Governor Hintrager had already rejected a suggestion from the Reichstag in 1912 that the reports of the Native Commissioners should be published.[73] He was only willing to approve the publication of a summary of the reports (i.e. a version sanitized by the Governor's Office) in the Annual Report.[74] The Governor's Office, though itself making use of the reporting obligation to keep tabs on the subordinate tiers of the administration, had no interest in disclosing its own activities or the success or otherwise of its policies to the Reichstag, or to a public that in some quarters was critical in its attitude to colonial activities.[75]

The appointment of Native Commissioners was thus not linked to any kind of criticism or modification of Native Policy;[76] on the contrary, the Commissioner played a crucial role in implementing the principles laid down in the Native Ordinances, which were congruent with his own three main tasks of maintaining a supply of workers, monitoring their conditions and caring for their welfare. It did mean, however, that in those districts where it was introduced an at least partially autonomous authority was set up alongside the District Officers, whom it had scarcely been possible to monitor until then; although in their everyday activities the commissioners had no alternative but to cooperate with the District Officers, they were not answerable to them in disciplinary terms, and so were in a position to exercise surveillance over them in respect of their Native Policy.

Two Native Commissioners, those of Warmbad and Keetmanshoop, had broader fields of responsibility, as their districts both contained communities – the Bondelswarts and the Nama of Berseba respectively – that had not been dissolved as a result of the war.[77] In respect of these, the Native Commissioners had not only the usual surveillance obligations but also particular duties of care.

This is particularly noticeable in the case of the Bondelswart Commission, which to a certain extent had occupied a special position right from the start, as it had originally been set up by the Schutztruppe.[78] This must have been one of the factors contributing to the fact that the Bondelswart Commission managed to get down to work considerably more quickly than the civil Native Commissioners' Offices, although the decision to establish it was taken at the same time as consideration was being given to setting up the latter. Its level of manpower was initially also more generous than that of the later Native Commissioners' Offices, since it was staffed by several Commissioners and not just one.[79] Its responsibility extended to all Bondelswarts, including those living outside the reservation, and thus to the entire southern area of the colony. It found them employment both inside Warmbad District and outside – for example, in the diamond mines at Lüderitzbucht and in railway construction work.[80] At the same time, it also helped the Bondelswarts to be economically self-sufficient, to a certain degree, by providing them with oxcarts so that they could earn money as carriers, and by making agricultural equipment and seed available, which in addition contributed to persuading the Bondelswarts to lead a sedentary existence.

The Governor's Office in Windhoek long harboured reservations with regard to the Bondelswart Commission, in view of its having been set up by the Schutztruppe. It was only when the authorities came to realize that most Bondelswart men were looking for employment and that they had been successfully 'pacified' that the civil administration was able to bring itself to recognize the achievements of that Commission, which was taken over by the civil administration at the end of 1910.[81] At the same time, the number of Commissioners was reduced to one. A year later, more or less at the same time as it established a legal framework for the activities of the other Native Commissioners, the Governor's Office also regularized the status of the Bondelswart Commission, which until then had not been unambiguously legally defined, by issuing a Service Instruction that showed distinct parallels with those applying to the other Commissioners.[82]

The Bondelswart Commissioner continued to be responsible for all the Bondelswarts who had submitted to the Germans in the Treaty of Ukamas, irrespective of whether they lived inside or outside the locations assigned to their group. He had to see to their registration and ensure that they earned their livelihoods; this he was to do in particular 'by finding them employment and exhorting them to live prudent and economically well-ordered lives'. He was also to attend to ensuring that 'the Bondels make progress economically, so that they will no longer need support from the Government' and would gradually 'lose their warlike characteristics'. Contracts of employment inside the Bondelswart Reservation could only be concluded by the Commissioner; outside the reservation they required at least his retrospective confirmation. As an extension of his previous field of activity, he was also made responsible for the 'surveillance and welfare' of all other Africans domiciled in Warmbad District.[83] But with regard to those Africans who were not Bondelswarts, the final decision-making competence in cases of dispute remained, as was the case with the other Native Commissioners, with the District Officer. The Bondelswart Commissioner thus had two different superiors: in respect of the Bondelswarts he reported directly to the Governor, but in his function as Native Commissioner for Warmbad District in respect of all other Africans he was subject to supervision by Warmbad District Office.[84]

The Native Commissioner of Keetmanshoop, who was responsible for the Nama of Berseba, had similar competences. He was also to ensure 'that the Berseba Hottentots can find a livelihood'. This he was to do above all by finding the Africans jobs with employers outside the areas they lived in, particularly in the diamond mines, but also by 'training them to work and to practise horticulture'. Thus apart from the task of recruiting workers, the predominant aspect of his work was the security aspect, as it was intended that the Berseba Nama too should gradually 'lose their warlike characteristics' through work, and in particular work on the land. In view of the unusual political situation there, the Native Commissioner was 'in consultation with the District Officer to care for the welfare of the Berseba Hottentots living in their tribal area and for the administration of their tribal affairs, to the extent that these are not political by nature'. 'Affairs that are political by nature' remained, however, 'the sole responsibility of the District Officer', although the latter was required to 'keep the Commissioner informed' and 'where necessary to seek as far as possible his collaboration'. Measures were 'always to be implemented in consultation with the Chief and his Council', whereby the Chief's standing was always to be respected. In order to keep this agreement on mutual consultation effective, the Native Commissioner was to travel to Berseba every two months, taking the opportunities afforded by these expeditions to get to know the whole area.[85]

As Native Commissioners were only introduced relatively late on, and then only in four Districts, the District Officers remained the most important players in the field of Native Policy on the ground. How they went about fulfilling their role in this respect will be examined in more detail in the following chapter. Since the instruments of Native Policy analysed in the previous chapter were not implemented in the areas outside the Police Zone, or at most in a highly indirect manner, those areas will only occupy a marginal place in this examination. Within the Police Zone, on the other hand, direct control over the African population living there was intensified after the war; and the policy that the authorities sought to follow may be regarded as being indicative of what German Native Policy would have looked like in the long term outside the Police Zone as well, had German rule been maintained.

Notes

1. The figures are based on a headcount, plus an estimate of a further 9,807 Africans, more than 80 per cent of them San or Himba. They relate to the Police Zone, i.e. the central and southern areas of the colony, excluding the areas outside effective German administration. The figure does include 5,705 Ovambo who were inside the Police Zone on the day of the count, but not those living in Ovamboland. *Die deutschen Schutzgebiete*, Vol. 4, 1912/13, Statistical Section, 46–57.
2. Leutwein, *Elf Jahre*, 232.
3. *Die deutschen Schutzgebiete*, Vol. 4, 1912/13, Statistical Section, 22.
4. Drechsler, *Südwestafrika unter deutscher Kolonialherrschaft*, Vol. I, 235.
5. *Die deutschen Schutzgebiete*, Vol. 4, 1912/13, Report Section, 143.
6. Hintrager, *Südwestafrika in der deutschen Zeit*, 175.

7. Ibid., 115. Total production between 1908 and the end of 1913 amounted to around 5 million carats; Hintrager later gave the figure of 4.6 million carats. Ibid., 170. Drechsler states that production in this period amounted to 4.7 million carats, to a value of M150 million. Drechsler, *Südwestafrika* II, 281. Drechsler's book also contains a detailed overview of the development of the mining industry.

8. Hintrager, *Südwestafrika*, 177–78.

9. Gründer, *Geschichte der deutschen Kolonien*, 126.

10. Hintrager, *Südwestafrika*, 174–75.

11. Gründer, *Kolonien*, 126.

12. Hintrager, *Südwestafrika*, 177. Apart from taxation and export duties, the colony's revenues included, for example, income from the Ports and Railways Administration.

13. *Die deutschen Schutzgebiete*, Vol. 1, 1909/10, Statistical Section, 254.

14. Ibid., Vol. 4, 1912/13, Statistical Section, 404–5. The draft budget for 1914 even predicted revenues of M23,299,000.

15. Ibid., Vol. 1, 1909/10, Statistical Section, 255. The high figure for 1908 was apparently a still persisting consequence of the enormous military expenditure during the war.

16. Ibid., Vol. 4, 1912/13, Statistical Section, 405.

17. On the colonial bonds and their development, see Schiefel, *Bernhard Dernburg*, 89–90.

18. Imperial Ordinance, *Verordnung betr. den Handel mit südwestafrikanischen Diamanten* [Ordinance concerning the Trade in South West African Diamonds], 16 January 1909, reproduced in *Die Deutsche Kolonialgesetzgebung* (DKG), Vol. 13 (Berlin: Mittler, 1909), 14–15.

19. On the diamond policy, see Schiefel, *Dernburg*, 101–108.

20. According to Oskar Hintrager's memoirs, for example, Governor Schuckmann had said in 1908 that the most important task of the Administration was to ensure that agriculture flourished. Hintrager, *Südwestafrika*, 108–9. At the same time, however, he wanted to ensure that the colony's finances were on a sound footing, for which the revenues from diamond production were of vital importance. Schuckmann, Speech of 28 March 1908, in *Deutsches Kolonialblatt*, Vol. 19 (1908), 467–68.

21. Imperial Chancellor, *Verordnung betr. die Selbstverwaltung in Deutsch-Südwestafrika* [Ordinance concerning Local Self-Government in German South West Africa – the 'Local Self-Government Ordinance'], 28 January 1909, reproduced in DKG 13 (1909), 19–34. On the realization and success of municipal self-government in South West Africa and on the farmers' self-image and their view of their role, together with their ever more aggressive attitude, see Bley, *Kolonialherrschaft und Sozialstruktur*, 223–39.

22. See the Table in Hintrager, *Südwestafrika*, 126. The various economic interests led to council members with shared attitudes forming themselves into groups: ibid., 128 and 130.

23. The earlier and larger subdivisions of the colony were named *Bezirke*, which might be more accurately translated as 'Regions'; most of these contained subordinate areas that were called *Distrikte* (districts) – see Chapter 1, Note

69. Later and progressively, other areas were formed out of the *Bezirke* and made autonomous of them; these were, however, also named *Distrikte*. In this translation, for the sake of simplicity and clarity, all these three types of area are called 'districts', their authorities 'District Offices' ('DOs') and their chief officials 'District Officers'. Thus the term 'autonomous districts' covers both the *Bezirke* and the *selbständige Distrikte* [translator's note]. In addition, there were two autonomous military districts. Rafalski, *Vom Niemandsland zum Ordnungsstaat*, 45.

24. *Handbuch für das Deutsche Reich*, 1914, 403–4. See also Map 0.2 in the Front Matter. An overview of the history of the administration, which also outlines briefly the development of the individual district offices, is to be found in Hubatsch, *Grundriß zur deutschen Verwaltungsgeschichte*, 425–50.

25. In 1907 the Colonial Policy Department of the German Foreign Office (FO-CD) in Berlin was converted into the Reichskolonialamt (Imperial Colonial Office – ICO), headed by an independent Staatssekretär (Colonial Secretary). For the circumstances leading up to the establishment of the Reichskolonialamt, see Schiefel, *Dernburg*, 31–66.

26. Such approval does not appear to have been mandatory, but it was the wish of the Imperial Colonial Office that it should be sought. In 1901, for example, its predecessor the Colonial Department of the Foreign Office (FO-CD) had called upon the Governors of the colonies, 'in all cases in which it appears expedient and possible without deleterious effects on the matter in question, to present drafts of Ordinances that are to be issued to this office for approval', and in general to make sparing use of their right to issue Ordinances. FO-CD, *Runderlaß betr. die Handhabung des Verordnungsrechts* [Circulated Decree concerning the Use of the Right to Issue Ordinances], 14 March 1901, reproduced in DKG 6 (1901/02), 287.

27. On 'native' criminal law, see Zimmerling, *Die Entwicklung der Strafrechtspflege*; and Schröder, *Prügelstrafe und Züchtigungsrecht*.

28. On the various German initiatives to conquer Ovamboland and the reactions of the Ovambo to these, see Eirola, *The Ovambogefahr*.

29. IGW, *Verordnung betr. den Verkehr in und nach dem Amboland* [Ordinance concerning movements within and to Ovamboland – the 'Ovamboland Ordinance'], 25 January 1906, reproduced in DKG 10 (1906), 25–27.

30. IGW, 'Implementation Regulations to the Ordinance regarding Movements within and to Ovamboland', 25 January 1906, reproduced in DKG 10 (1906), 27–30.

31. In a letter to the Rhenish Missionary Society, von Lindequist stated that the closing of the borders of Ovamboland was a reaction to Nehale's attack on Namutoni, and that when Nehale had paid the penalty imposed on him (and if the other Chiefs so wished), he would permit trade with them again. IGW to Rhenish Missionary Society, 2 January 1906, ELCIN II.11.5.A. (no page number).

32. On the military campaign against the Ovambo King Mandume, see Silvester, *My Heart Tells Me*.

33. IGW, *Verordnung betr. den Verkehr in und nach dem Caprivizipfel* [Ordinance concerning Movements within and to the Caprivi Strip], 16 October 1908, reproduced in DKG 12 (1908), 436–37.

34. On the history of the Caprivi Strip during German colonial rule in South West Africa, see Fisch, *Der Caprivizipfel*.
35. Hintrager, *Südwestafrika*, 99–100.
36. This included above all the immediate suppression of any renewed resistance, as the Commander of the Schutztruppe, Joachim von Heydebreck, set out in a Memorandum in 1912. *Denkschrift über die Möglichkeit einer Verminderung der Schutztruppe für Deutsch-Südwestafrika und einer Verringerung der Ausgaben des Militär-Etats* [Memorandum on the Possibility of Reducing the Size of the Schutztruppe for South West Africa and of the Military Budget and Expenditure). CSW, Heydebreck, to ICO, 14 July 1912, NAW ZBU *Geheimakten* (Classified Documents) IX.B. Vol. 1, 57a–79b.
37. The Governor's Office expected to have to defend the colony in the event of war with Great Britain. Seitz, *Vom Aufstieg und Niederbruch deutscher Kolonialmacht*, 21–22, 27.
38. IGW, *Bestimmungen betr. die Organisation der Landespolizei für das deutsch-südwestafrikanische Schutzgebiet* [Regulations concerning the Organization of a Territorial Police Force for the Colony of German South West Africa – the 'Territorial Police Regulations'), 1 March 1905, in DKG 9 (1905), 64–69.
39. Rafalski, *Niemandsland*, 53.
40. IGW, Territorial Police Regulations, 1 March 1905, 64–69. In addition, the organization of the police in the colony was in accordance with the Memorandum on the Second Supplementary Budget of 1907, the *Allerhöchste Verordnung* (Imperial Ordinance) of 4 October 1907, and the Governor's 'Implementation Regulations on Acceptance and Appointment, Structure, Deployment, Clothing and Equipment. Rafalski, *Niemandsland*, 61. The *Verordnung betr. die Rechtsverhältnisse der Landespolizei in Deutsch-Südwestafrika* [Ordinance concerning the Legal Status of the Territorial Police in German South West Africa], 4 October 1907, is reproduced in DKG 11 (1907), 395–96.
41. Rafalski, *Niemandsland*, 56–58.
42. Ibid., 61. On the relationship between the planned and actual strength of the police, see Table A.1 in the Appendix.
43. Ibid., 70–71.
44. *Die deutschen Schutzgebiete*, Vol. 4, 1912/13, Report Section, 133. Here the strength of the police force is stated to be 600 German officers: this figure clearly relates to the planned strength. The African police auxiliaries, like the African members of the Schutztruppe, were forbidden to carry rifles, though they could, if only exceptionally and if accompanied by White officers, be equipped with pistols. In addition, the 'use of mounted native patrols ... [was) to be restricted as far as possible'. Circulated Order, IGW to 'DOs, Police Barracks and the Police Stations in Swakopmund and Aus' (transcript), 10 June 1910, BAL. R 1002/2608, 1a. An order to the same effect had also been sent to the Schutztruppe. But this meant that the African auxiliary forces were not equipped to play a part in the effective control of the colony either. Disciplinary authority over the Africans employed by the police lay with the Inspector of the Territorial Police and all officers of the Inspectorate. Circulated Order, IGW (transcript), 5 August 1911, BAL R 1002/2596, 5a.

45. Rafalski, *Niemandsland*, 90.
46. Ibid., 74–75. Here there is also a detailed list of the police stations established. The 393 policemen were deployed at these police stations or police posts; this accounts for the difference from the total strength of 470 men, which also included the reserve manpower stationed at the police barracks.
47. Ibid., 72.
48. Seitz, *Aufstieg*, 19.
49. Rafalski, *Niemandsland*, 59–60.
50. Hintrager, *Südwestafrika*, 122. The figures relate to German soldiers only; there were also African auxiliaries, numbering 635 in 1910. Eirola, *Ovambogefahr*, 274. In 1913–14 the number of soldiers remained static at 1,967.
51. *Die deutschen Schutzgebiete*, Vol. 4, 1912/13, Statistical Section, 405. The subsidy declined to M14,426,000 in 1910 and M11,416,000 in 1911, but rising again to M13,828,000 in the following year.
52. Heydebreck, *Denkschrift* (Memorandum), 14 July 1912, 57a–79b.
53. *Organisatorische Bestimmungen für die kaiserliche Schutztruppe in Afrika* [Organizational regulations for the Imperial Forces in Africa), 25 July 1898, in DKG 3 (1897/98), 49–112. Even the Governor could not give orders to subordinate units himself, except in exceptional circumstances.
54. IGW to ICO, July 1910, NAW ZBU W.II.A.4. Vol. 1, 23a–24a.
55. The person appointed as the first – and only – Head of Department was Kurt Streitwolf, a Captain in the Schutztruppe. Internal Instruction, IGW (transcript), 7 February 1911, BAL R 1001/2235, 54a. The payment of Streitwolf's salary was taken over by the Governor's Office as from 1 April 1911. CSW to IGW, 27 July 1911, BAL R 1002/1709, 5a. On Streitwolf himself and his activities, see Stals, *Kurt Streitwolf*.
56. Internal instruction, IGW (transcript), 7 February 1911, BAL R 1001/2235, 54a.
57. Eirola, *Ovambogefahr*, 273.
58. Hintrager, *Südwestafrika*, 100.
59. For a more detailed treatment of the topic of the Native Commissioners, see Abun-Nasr, 'Eingeborenenkommissare'.
60. IGW to ICO, July 1910, NAW ZBU W.II.A.4. Vol. 1, 23a–24a.
61. IGW, *Verordnung betr. Maßregeln zur Kontrolle der Eingeborenen* [Ordinance concerning Regulations for the Control and Surveillance of the Natives – 'Control Ordinance'], 18 August 1907, reproduced in DKG 11 (1907), 345–47. Imperial Chancellor, Local Self-Government Ordinance, 28 January 1909.
62. Dernburg before the Reichstag on 19 March 1908: Reichstag, sten. rec. 231, quoted according to Abun-Nasr, 'Eingeborenenkommissare', 61.
63. ITP to IGW, 11 September 1908, NAW ZBU W.II.A.4. Vol. 1, 7a–8a.
64. IGW to ICO, July 1910, NAW ZBU W.II.A.4. Vol. 1, 23a–24a.
65. Ibid. Although Swakopmund was also considered to be particularly overburdened, no Native Commissioner was appointed there. This could be because there was already a Native Commissioner appointed by the municipality, and the Administration was satisfied with his work. See also the Report on Paper 13, Native Commissioners, for the Territorial Council 1910, ITP to IGW, 28 May 1910, NAW ZBU W.II.A.4. Vol. 1, 20a–21a.

66. *Dienstanweisung für den Kommissar des Bondelszwartsreservates und den Eingeborenenkommissar des Bezirks Warmbad* [Service Instruction for the Commissioner of the Bondelswart Reservation and Native Commissioner of Warmbad District], 2 November 1911, NAW W.II.A.9. Vol. 1, 24a–25b. *Dienstanweisung für den Eingeborenenkommissar von Lüderitzbucht* (transcript), 23 April 1912, BAL R1001/2235, 74a–76a. *Dienstanweisung für den Eingeborenekommissar des Bezirks Windhuk* (transcript), 29 May 1912, BAL R 1001/2235, 62a–63a. *Dienstanweisung für den Eingeborenenkommissar für Keetmanshoop und Berseba* (transcript), 9 November 1912, BAL R 1001/2235, 81a–82b.

67. The Native Commissioner of Lüderitzbucht, for example, was responsible only for the African workers employed in the diamond fields there, while all other Africans were outside his area of responsibility. NCO Lüderitzbucht to IGW, 23 July 1914, NAW ZBU W.IV.A.5. Vol. 1, 22a f. The activities of the other three Native Commissioners embraced all Africans in their respective Districts.

68. Service Instruction, NC Windhoek, 29 May 1912.

69. The Native Commissioner of Lüderitzbucht did not need to concern himself with the registration of the Africans as they were recruited and registered by the mining companies. Service Instruction, NC Lüderitzbucht, 23 April 1912.

70. Service Instruction, NC Windhoek, 29 May 1912.

71. Service Instruction, NC Lüderitzbucht, 23 April 1912.

72. Ibid.

73. ICO to IGW, 16 July 1912, NAW ZBU W.II.A.4. Vol. 1, 31a. The Imperial Colonial Office required the Governor's Office to provide a statement of opinion 'on this issue, which is to be treated with great circumspection'.

74. Hintrager gave a warning that 'the Native Commissioners have been appointed so recently' that it was advisable 'to be very cautious for a few years about drawing conclusions from the Native Commissioners' reports'; 'only in part and only with caution' were they suitable for publication. The reason he gave, namely that 'the reports would have an unfavourable effect on the natives', would appear to be merely an excuse. IGW to ICO, 29 August 1912, BAL R 1001/2235, 65a f.

75. The Reichstag Budgetary Commission passed a renewed resolution on this matter in its session of 2 July 1914. The Imperial Colonial Office then once again called upon the Governor in Windhoek to submit the required reports by 1 October of each year. ICO to IGW, 2 July 1914, NAW ZBU W.II.A.4. Vol. 1, 35a f.

76. In its decision to create a Department of Native Affairs and to appoint Native Commissioners, the Governor's Office explicitly declared that 'changes to the existing native regulations, which have proved themselves well, … are not necessary'. IGW to ICO, July 1910, 23a–24a.

77. In its Report in response to the Paper to be presented to the Territorial Council, the Police Inspectorate expected Native Commissioners also to be appointed in those Districts 'in which there are Locations or Native Reservations'; Keetmanshoop and Omaruru were explicitly mentioned.

The idea of establishing a special Commissioner's Office for the Basters of Rehoboth was rejected as 'mistaken' and 'dangerous', without any precise reasons being given. Nor was the Police Inspectorate in favour of any changes to the administration of the Bondelswarts, as it was being 'excellently handled' by the Schutztruppe at the time. ITP to IGW, 28 May 1910, 20a–21a. IGW, however, was of the opinion that it was not likely to be worthwhile having a Native Commissioner for Okombahe. Internal memorandum, IGW, 29 June 1910, NAW ZBU W.II.A.4. Vol. 1, 29a.

78. The establishment of a Commission had already been provided for in the Treaty of Ukamas in 1906, and was implemented in the following year. *Unterwerfungsabkommen zwischen Oberstleutnant von Estorff und den Bondelszwart-Hottentotten* [Submission agreement between Lieutenant Colonel von Estorff and the Bondelswart Hottentots), 23 December 1906, reproduced in DKG 11 (1907), 234.

79. On the organization and activities of the Bondelswart commissioners, see R. Hitz, 'Die Bondelszwarts', 47–58, on which the following description is based.

80. Apart from satisfying the demand for labour in these labour-intensive enterprises, this also had a military policy aspect, as it served to disperse those men who were capable of bearing arms 'as workers outside the areas they are familiar with', so that there were never more than a few present in their home locations. Bondelswart Commission to Schutztruppe Southern Command, Keetmanshoop (transcript), 13 March 1910, NAW ZBU W.II.F.2. Vol. 1, 102a.

81. Von Estorff, *Wanderungen und Kämpfe*, 156. First Lieutenant Ebeling, who was already serving as a Bondelswart Commissioner, was taken over into the civil administration on 29 December 1910. ICO to IGW, 29 December 1910, NAW ZBU W.II.A.4. Vol. 1, 25a–26b.

82. Service Instruction, Bondelswart Commissioner and NC Warmbad, 2 November 1911.

83. This was done at the suggestion of Warmbad DO. Warmbad DO to IGW, 18 July 1911, NAW ZBU W.II.A.9. Vol. 1, 21a–22a.

84. IGW to Warmbad DO, 2 November 1911, NAW ZBU W.II.A.9. Vol. 1, 23a f.

85. Service Instruction, NC Keetmanshoop and Berseba, 9 November 1912.

4

Securing Colonial Rule

The aim of German Native Policy was to establish complete control over the African population of the colony. A seamless system of surveillance, designed to be devoid of any loopholes, was devised, the major aims of which were to ensure that the whole of the working-age population was available as labour, to provide a basis for changing the nature of African societies through measures of social discipline summarized under the slogan 'education to work', and to guarantee the security of the White population of South West Africa. This meant that the Africans ceased to be free inhabitants of the territory and instead became subject peoples, who except for the few still intact societies were directly subjected to German law and regulations, and could be deployed as the German authorities saw fit in accordance with their ideas on how the colony should develop. The basic prerequisite for this was the complete registration of the entire African population, without which it would be impossible to implement the distribution of labour, the settlement of the population, the compulsion to work and the measures of social discipline. The principle of bureaucratic rule, as expressed in the attempts of the central authorities in Windhoek to exercise supervision over the subordinate administrative offices, also required surveillance of the Africans if it was to function properly. The Governor's Office, being so far distant, could only undertake sensible decision-making and thereby curb the initially largely autonomous status of the District Officers if it was able to obtain reliable statistics regarding the Africans, and information on the mood prevailing among them. Furthermore, careful observation of the African population was intended to allow the authorities to spot at an early stage any fall into too deep a state of desperation, so that any centres of potential resistance could be eliminated in good time.

The District Officers had welcomed the Native Ordinances and their attempt to organize the future coexistence of Whites and Africans in accordance with German ideas of what such coexistence should look like, concurring with their intentions and provisions to a high degree. One reason for this was that they eliminated what the Germans saw as the ill-defined legal status of the Africans; for the system of indirect rule that had been practised before the war contradicted European attitudes to law and the state, which saw all citizens as being subject to unambiguously defined legal provisions that were the same for everybody in a particular category. The local administrative officers therefore set about zealously implementing the new Ordinances, and after a year submitted reports that presented their achievements as being almost free of blemish, and apparently fulfilling all expectations. If at that time the officials were already aware that there were shortcomings in their arrangements, and that these were likely to make themselves felt in future, then they were either made light of or else completely ignored, due to an inability to even contemplate the expression of any criticism of instructions issued by superior authorities.

But the goal of achieving 100 per cent surveillance was completely illusory, in view of the vastness of the country and the utterly inadequate staffing levels of the Administration and the police. What was required was no less than to track down more than 65,000 people in a country that covered an area of over 700,000 km^2, register them and issue them with pass tokens. Furthermore, many of them were still on the run, and the guerrilla war that was still going on in the south of the territory had made it plain to everyone how many areas of refuge and of escape from control the colony offered to the Africans, who knew their country backwards.

The Ordinances had moreover to be implemented in a colony that was still widely lacking in infrastructure, still had comparatively few White settlers, and had been utterly disrupted by the recent war. It soon became apparent that there was no way in which the Ordinances could be fully implemented, their success being dependent on the civil and military authorities cooperating smoothly with each other, and on the White population also playing their part. Compartmentalized thinking by different areas of the Administration and the egoism of the settlers together undermined the implementation of the measures; and the vastness of the colony and the lack of any procedural basis for determining Africans' identities also detracted substantially from their effectiveness. But this endangered the functionality of the entire German colonial project, which was built on a system of registration. For the African population, by contrast, gaps in the surveillance system opened up areas in which they could still enjoy a certain degree of freedom.

The Control System: The Regulations and the Reality

The African population of the colony was supposed to be registered and supervised using a uniform procedure developed at Windhoek District Office, and which Deputy Governor Oskar Hintrager distributed to the other autonomous District Offices for their scrutiny in a circular accompanying the Native Ordinances when he sent out them out on 13 May 1907.[1] Since Windhoek was among the administrative districts with the most developed and best equipped administrative apparatus, the circular tells more about how the Governor's Office imagined that the surveillance of the African population should take place in the future than it does about its actual implementation throughout the colony. But at the same time, it makes clear the intention to set up a 'perfect' surveillance system:

> As far as Windhoek District is concerned, the intention is to divide it up into individual 'police wards', within which the responsible police officer is to inspect all places where natives live once a month. Every police ward will be allocated pass tokens with numbers of a particular series, which however is big enough to provide for any later growth in the native population. This has the advantage that if a native is stopped and checked it is possible to determine immediately which police ward he belongs to. ... The Governor's Office will consult with the Commander of the Schutztruppe in order to ensure the support of the military authorities in any given area for the implementation of the native control legislation.

> It is intended to prescribe that Native Registers should be kept not only at District Offices, but also at police stations and at those military posts that are invested with police powers in respect of the natives under their supervision. ...

> Every time a native is entered in the Native Register, enough space should be left for all changes of employer etc. to be entered subsequently. In order to ensure that the registers are always up to date, the natives are to be instructed that any births and deaths and any movements into or away from the area ... are to be reported to the responsible police or military post immediately.

> It is considered by this office to be highly desirable that the heads of police stations should submit monthly reports to their superior authorities on any changes in the numbers of natives living in their areas, so that information is available at any time on the number and distribution of native workers.[2]

Thus the objective was total surveillance, on the one hand to ensure 'law and order' and on the other as a prerequisite for the efficient utilization of the available labour. If the monitoring had worked properly, unsupervised movements of the African population would have been impossible, as the Administration would have been able to determine at any time from the differing number series if anyone had left his place of abode, even if he had only moved within one of the more extensive Districts.

In furtherance of this all-embracing aspiration that the Native Ordinances would make it possible to control the population completely, the Native Registers were to contain as much information as possible about each individual African: in addition to the serial number in the register, the number of the pass token, the 'tribal' affiliation and the sex, name – if possible also the first name – and age of the African concerned, the registers were also to record the degrees of his relationship to other Africans entered in the register, his place of abode, his employment with the date of any employment contract that had been registered with the police, his place of origin, his destination and any remarks, punishments, travel passes already issued and the like.[3] It is interesting to see 'tribal' identity included among the details required; this made identification easier, but also kept alive a consciousness on the part of the African of his group identity, even making it into a part of the new identity conferred upon him by the Germans.

The number on the pass token was the connecting link between the different instruments of control, being common to the register, the pass token itself and the travel pass.[4] The last-mentioned document was to contain the following details: the name of the holder, his 'tribal' affiliation, his place of abode and, if the African concerned was intending to return, the number of his pass token and details of his employment. In addition, the destination of the journey (with a note indicating whether the holder intended to return), its route and purpose, the time and date of departure and an endorsement 'is taking with him (number and type of livestock etc.)' were to be recorded.

In order to make it possible for a comprehensive picture of the distribution of the Africans and their movements to be obtained from the individual Native Registers, it was necessary to have a sophisticated reporting system through which up-to-date figures could be notified to the superior authority and collated there. Individual police stations had to report to the non-autonomous District Offices every month[5] or even every week,[6] which then transmitted the information to their superior autonomous District Offices every quarter; these in their turn summarized the reports and sent them to the Governor's Office every six months.[7] In Districts where Native Commissioners had been appointed, there was an additional parallel reporting obligation through that hierarchy.

But even these rigorous measures of surveillance were not enough to satisfy some officials, so that the District Officer of Karibib, for example, ordered an even stricter application of the travel pass requirement within his District. In this, he provides a good example of the bureaucratic zeal that some officials applied to the implementation of the control system, attempting to out-bureaucrat even the Governor's Office:

> I have extended the provisions of Section 3 [of the Pass Ordinance: the requirement to obtain a travel pass when leaving the District] to apply to the individual police wards; for in view of the fact that each such ward has received a certain series of tokens, it has not been necessary for these to be specially labelled. Thus every native who leaves the police ward must be able to identify himself by means of a travel pass – issued by the responsible police station or by his employer – whereas within the police ward the pass token alone is sufficient identification. If this is to be the case for the entire District, then on the one hand the registers kept by the individual police stations of the natives living in their area can never be correct, as natives who are not in employment do not need to report when they leave the ward; while on the other hand, the supervision of these people, who are precisely the ones that constitute the unstable elements among them, will be made substantially more difficult or even impossible.[8]

In order to keep themselves up to date with regard to how many Africans were eployed by farmers – often in remote locations – the officers posted to a police station were to patrol these locations at regular short intervals, the intention being once a month.[9]

In addition to the 'inspections of the private werfs', which were apparently only intended to allow the police to receive a report from the werf foreman, 'searches' were to be undertaken 'at three to six monthly intervals in order to identify any Africans who are unemployed or have run away from their place of work'.[10] The lists kept by the employers were clearly not considered to be reliable enough. But apart from merely searching for Africans, these checks also served the purpose of creating a climate of fear and evoking a feeling of total surveillance, as District Officer Schenke of Swakopmund reported:

> The natives in Swakopmund itself are continually kept under the impression, by frequent police inspections and unannounced checks of the werfs, that they are under constant observation as soon as they do anything to violate the Ordinances they are familiar with [the three Native Ordinances of 1907].

> For this reason it is no seldom occurrence that natives themselves require their employers to register them with the police immediately, and will not take up their employment until they are in possession of the pass token or the employment logbook.[11]

In the Neuer Kamp ('New Compound') location near Lüderitzbucht, for example, where up to three thousand families lived,[12] there was even a police officer living 'in a permanent house erected in a prominent position', directly in or immediately adjacent to the werf.[13]

This feeling of being under constant observation had a profound impact on the African population. They knew the obligations imposed on them by the Native Ordinances, and due to the threat of punishment hanging over them they even insisted themselves that their employers should observe the regulations. This also prepared the ground for the pass token and the employment logbook to become a part of their own identity, thus leading to an internalization of the identity attributes ascribed to them by the German colonial state, and in the case of the pass token reducing every individual person to a mere number.

Such surveillance of almost totalitarian proportions could only function, however, in the centres of population and the big werfs that were set up close to them, but not out in the country. In the Keetmanshoop and Gobabis Districts, for example, the practical implementation of the Native Ordinances had to be limited. As only one-third of Gobabis District lay within the Police Zone, the 'idea of implementing the Control and Pass Ordinances is something that can only be taken with a pinch of salt'.[14] Apparently it was impossible to prevent free movement between the areas inside the Police Zone and those outside it, which opened up numerous opportunities to take refuge in areas that were not subject to surveillance.

In Keetmanshoop District, the Governor's Office postponed the introduction of the Control Ordinance, stating as its reason that 'in view of the current political situation in that District, it does not appear to be expedient to proceed against the natives with drastic regulations'.[15] This shows that even after the end of the war the German authorities still regarded their power base in the south of the colony as being fragile. Whereas the Governor's Office had originally planned to ensure that the Africans living there should at least be registered, it had second thoughts about implementing this as it did not want to alarm them.[16]

Irrespective of these exceptions, right from the beginning registration also embraced those Ovambo who entered the Police Zone from Ovamboland as migrant labour, as ever greater numbers were doing, and who thus became subject to the provisions of the Native Ordinances. In 1906, when the borders to Ovamboland were closed, Governor von Lindequist had already decreed that pass tokens should be issued to those crossing the border, which they were then to keep when they returned home.[17] Although in fact no individual pass tokens were then distributed after all, the Ovambo were given group identity documents 'containing only brief details of the migrants', which were handed out to the foreman of the group for him to take to the place of destination. Only if the Ovambo travelled by train were they issued with 'full passes',[18] which they needed to have as it would otherwise have been forbidden to sell them train tickets.[19] Thus even the Ovambo found their freedom of movement restricted within the Police Zone, and they were subject to the general control measures. No resistance seems to have been offered to this pass requirement, thanks to the efforts of the missionaries in Ovamboland. They had done their best to get the population accustomed to the identity document requirement in advance by giving workers who travelled into the Police Zone a pass issued by the Mission, which then only needed to be endorsed by the District Office.[20] In this way, the missionaries played their part in bringing about the penetration of Ovamboland by the disciplinary measures applying inside the Police Zone, despite its lying outside it.

In the same way, Africans from other countries were also subject to the Native Ordinances while they were in South West Africa. In order to ensure that they did not enjoy any possible additional freedoms, a special regulation was even introduced for the African workers employed on the construction of the railways in Lüderitzbucht and Keetmanshoop Districts. They posed a problem for the system as envisaged, since they were constantly on the move between these two districts as the construction work progressed. They were therefore provided with the construction company's own 'tokens with serial numbers, of a different shape to the government tags'. The company was also responsible for further control measures, having to present 'lists of names of the coloured people entering and leaving the District' to the District Office.[21] When workers were discharged within the colony they were instructed to report immediately to the nearest police station, which ensured their integration into the control system.

By the end of 1908, the introduction of the Pass and Control Ordinances had largely been completed to the satisfaction of the District Officers, the existence of regional Pass Ordinances in a number of districts having facilitated registration and the distribution of pass tags. District Officer Schenke of Swakopmund had to admit in 1908 that there had been 'violations of [the Native Ordinances] both on the part of employers and on the part of natives', which 'will always occur'; but he thought that the Ordinances were functioning 'quite well on the whole', and had also 'found acceptance among the natives', which would doubtless become more widespread as time went on.[22] The District Officer of Bethanie, Georg Wasserfall, also observed that the Pass Ordinance had 'not been met by any reluctance on the part of the natives', so that 'in principle there is no reason at all to doubt that they will submit to it and observe it'.[23]

This positive evaluation of the Ordinance was repeated in the first reports of the year 1907. There is once again no single mention of the devastating consequences for the African population, although the Administration appears to have been thoroughly aware that there were also some critical voices, in particular from the Mission. As District Officer Narciß of Windhoek District therefore explicitly emphasized:

> The three Ordinances have essentially proved themselves to be thoroughly expedient. For once, this is an assessment that the authorities, the population and the Mission all agree on. The natives too have all in all grown accustomed to the implementation of the ordinances surprisingly quickly, and appear to feel quite comfortable under their regime.[24]

The officials were convinced that they were acting in the interests of the Africans too, seeing no contradiction between the settlers' demands for cheap labour and the well-being of the Africans. They ignored the fear and alarm spread by their constant checks and the relentless sanctions imposed when the Ordinances were violated, or else they never even became aware of them. For them, the forced obedience of the Africans confirmed the 'expediency' of the Ordinances:

> The Native Ordinances have proved themselves well in practice. The more they are implemented, the more their advantages will become apparent. In particular, the natives have become well accustomed to the Control Ordinance and the Pass Ordinance. They have themselves realized that the pass token and the travel pass afford them protection against everyone, and they themselves strive to come into possession of these means of identification.[25]

The District Office of Sesfontein also reported that the Africans there were gradually learning to recognize the advantages of the passes, as they enabled them to demonstrate to any Whites that they were entitled to be where they were.[26] When District Officer Hölscher of Rehoboth remarks that the Basters, although themselves 'natives', see 'no hardship' in the Ordinances either, it sounds almost as if he is attempting to convince himself.[27]

There were only a few heads of Districts who did not share this optimism. They advised caution, and pointed out, as the District Officer of Gibeon did, that no final assessment of how well the Ordinances were working was yet possible, and that it was still necessary for the Africans to be given 'frequent instruction'.[28] But even he did not fundamentally question the measures imposed, and was quick to explain that he had 'for the time being no reason to doubt that the Ordinances will prove themselves in practice'. The inhibitions against raising any fundamental criticisms of arrangements originating from Colonial Secretary Bernhard Dernburg or Governor von Lindequist were simply too great. Only Victor Franke, the Outjo District Officer, confirmed in November 1908 the pessimistic forecast that his deputy Hungels had made on 27 May 1907[29] with regard to the implementation of the Ordinances in that District:

> In view of the small number of officials available, it has not yet been possible for the District Office to implement the Ordinances in question completely. If one takes into account the considerable extent of the District, one can only come to the conclusion that under the circumstances described it is not likely to prove feasible to do this successfully as set out in the Instructions of 18 August 1907 within the foreseeable future.[30]

Franke was the only District Officer who dared to report the difficulties that had arisen to the Governor's Office without beating about the bush. There were problems in other Districts too, as can be concluded from the reports they submitted, which indicate that the officials had not succeeded in registering the entire African population. But the District Officers concealed this fact behind optimistic forecasts that complete implementation of the Ordinances would be achieved in the near future, and instead expressed in rosy terms how well the Native Ordinances were proving themselves.

So an illusion of complete surveillance and control was built up, leading Deputy Governor Hintrager to remark as late as 1910: 'The reports do not indicate the necessity for special measures of any kind'.[31] At the same time he removed the requirement for six-monthly reporting that was laid down in the Ordinances, 'now that the natives have generally come to accept, to a satisfactory degree, the legal situation created by the Ordinances of 18 August 1907'. Instead, the situation of the Africans was to be dealt with in greater detail in the Annual Report.[32]

How misleading this portrayal of the smooth functioning of the Ordinances was is shown by the fact that in both of the following two years the Governor's Office had to concern itself with considerations relating to the setting up of collection points for Africans, and with a discussion of the unsatisfactory situation with regard to the means of identification of the African population. Furthermore, problems had arisen as early as the first few months of the implementation of the Native Ordinances which in some cases remained unsolved right to the end of German rule.

Logistical Problems, Slipshod Implementation and an Uncooperative White Population

Although the Governor's Office had been working on the legal codification of Native Policy since as early as 1905, and in doing so had been able to draw on considerations raised in previous discussions of the matter in the prewar period, the practical implementation of the Native Ordinances began with a logistical disaster. Despite the length of time that had been spent debating the legal aspects of the measures and discussing them with the District Offices, it turned out that no adequate quantities of pass tokens, registers, travel pass documents or employment logbooks were available at the end of 1907. Although the Pass Ordinance clearly laid down that all those subject to the pass requirement were to 'report to the police station responsible for their place of abode without delay upon this Ordinance coming into force, in order to be issued with a pass token',[33] in fact it was not possible for the tokens to be issued everywhere.

Gibeon District, for example, had to wait until April 1908 – that is to say, six months after the Ordinances had come into force and almost a year after the first discussions of the draft Ordinances in the colony – for pass tokens, travel passes and employment logbooks to be delivered. The registration process then took a further six months.[34] The Keetmanshoop[35] and Lüderitzbucht District Offices[36] had to wait even longer to receive their supplies. The documents had to be ordered from printers in Germany via the Imperial Colonial Office in Berlin, which was a slow and tedious process.[37] At the time when the Ordinances were being formulated, nobody in either the Governor's Office in Windhoek or the Imperial Colonial Office in Berlin appears to have spared a thought for the little matter of how the Administration in the colony was to be supplied with the necessary materials.

And when the long-awaited consignments of registers, employment logbooks and travel passes at last reached the colony in June 1908, it did not take long for the District Offices to find out that there were far too few of them to meet even their most urgent requirements.[38]

Of the 61,500 pass tokens ordered, none had arrived, and of the 31,500 employment logbooks only half. Only 10 per cent of the registers and 20 per cent of the travel passes were delivered.[39] The Governor's Office called upon the District Offices to improvise, for example by making forms of their own.[40] In addition, the District administrations themselves often had little idea as to how many Africans they had to register, and in some cases had to revise their initial figures and order additional materials immediately.[41] These problems are another good indication of the extent to which the Ordinances had been drawn up by bureaucrats far removed from the 'coal face', of how little consideration had been given to how they were actually to be implemented, and of how few preparations had been made.

As the realization of the inadequacy of the resources provided by the Governor's Office sank in among the middle tiers of the Administration, a parallel fall-off in motivation was to be observed among the officials themselves. They were by no means always zealous in their efforts to implement the procedures introduced; rather, they obstructed the proper functioning of the Ordinances by the slipshod manner in which they went about their duties. This can be seen clearly in the way reports were frequently submitted late. The Governor's Office was compelled to remind the District Offices time and time again of the importance of these reports, which were essential to the whole system of controlling the African population and its administration. On 17 October 1908, for example, the Governor's Office was obliged to send a circular to all the District Offices (except Lüderitzbucht and Sesfontein), calling upon them to finally submit the required report on how well the Native Ordinances were proving themselves in practice.[42] The District Officers in turn immediately passed the buck to the police stations, claiming not to have received any reports from them yet.[43] They also reminded the Governor's Office that they were overstretched and asked to be relieved of the requirement to submit six-monthly reports, since the statistical details that were called for represented 'a large amount of additional work' and kept 'a whole number of officials' occupied.[44] So it proved impossible for the Administration to obtain in reality the overview of the situation of the Africans that the Native Ordinances were designed to provide.

In some cases, the District Officers simply did not implement certain provisions of the Native Ordinances. This was revealed in 1912 when the Governor's Office, in view of the lack of success in mobilizing workers, set about checking the implementation of Sec. 7 of the Control Ordinance (which made it necessary to obtain approval for more than ten families to live in a private werf) and obtaining detailed reports on the extent to which this had been enforced.[45] Okahandja District Office was taken completely by surprise, and had to admit that this provision 'has not been implemented here, since the big enterprises and farm operations had already had more than ten families settled with them for many years'. In order to remedy this failure, the District Officer announced that 'a strict inspection' would be carried out, but that he was not in a position to say which enterprises or farms would be subjected to it. He promised to submit the results of the inquiries that were immediately ordered at a later date.[46] After two months he then reported that he had instructed eleven farms 'to immediately obtain the required authorization'.[47] Zealous declarations that particularly strict and rigorous control was now to be exercised were clearly intended to conceal the earlier sin of omission.

But this was not simply a one-off case. The District Officer of Maltahöhe, for example, tried to talk himself out of his embarrassing position by declaring that 'in the few cases in this district where there are more than ten native families living on a farm or other location, tacit authorization has been granted'. He further attempted to justify himself by stating that no case was known 'in which an employer has kept more natives on his farm than are required to meet his most urgent requirements'.[48]

Although the Native Ordinances had provided for White employers to be subjected to control as well, in the way this issue was handled it is possible to observe a certain rapprochement between the Administration and the settlers. The economically successful ones among them, who were the only ones affected by Sec. 7 of the Control Ordinance, were not monitored, and the officials seem to have relied on the fact that they and the settlers were committed to achieving the same objectives.

Warmbad District Office also had to own up to having 'tacitly' made an exception: '193 natives including women and children' were living on the Heirachabis Mission Station in 1912 without any express approval. To excuse his negligence, District Officer Beyer pointed out that this werf was subject to separate inspection by the Native Commissioner, who took care to see 'that the men who are capable of working do actually seek work'.[49] Bearing in mind the ardour with which Kurt Streitwolf, in view of the fears he had entertained, had opposed making any exception for the Mission in 1907, this negligence is astonishing. It seems as if the original enthusiasm of the officials had very quickly given way to a certain degree of resignation.

If one takes into account the extent to which Native Policy was bound up with attempts to alleviate the labour shortage in those years, it is all the more astonishing how careless the middle-tier administration was about implementing it. But it does show how far the image of a perfectly functioning German administrative apparatus is from the reality. The chronic understaffing and the immense distance between many of the District Offices and the Central Administration made it almost impossible for the senior officials in Windhoek to keep a strict eye on their subordinates. And as, in addition, the reports of the District Officers were imprecisely formulated and superficial, or did not go beyond general statements about how magnificently all the provisions had been put into effect, there was scarcely any chance that the Governor's Office would be able to gain any real insights into the true situation[50] – and the occasional tours of inspection that officials from Windhoek undertook through the colony were apparently not sufficient to compensate for this.

Right from the beginning there was friction between the civil administration and the Schutztruppe, and this had an enormous impact on the surveillance of the African population immediately after the war. Cooperation was impeded by class consciousness, by officers who stood on their rank or position and by the petty egoisms of the different departments. As a result, conflicts soon began to develop with regard to the demarcation of competences between the District Offices and the commanders of the various units of the Schutztruppe. The Schutztruppe Command in Windhoek therefore demanded to be invested with police powers in respect of 'the issuance of employment contracts and logbooks to the natives serving with the forces', and of 'the supervision of the natives serving with the forces and of their werfs'.[51] The Schutztruppe was unwilling to reconcile itself to the fact that since the official ending of the state of war 'the relationship of the military authorities that employ natives' to those 'natives' was 'precisely the same as that of any private employer', as the District Officer of Swakopmund formulated it,[52] and was keen to emphasize its special status with regard to maintaining security in the colony.[53] The occasion that caused this dispute to come to a head was a quarrel between the commanding officer of the Schutztruppe in Swakopmund and the local District Office, whose officials wanted to pick up an African prisoner of war in order to interrogate him; the duty officer refused to allow this as he had not been informed in advance.[54] The Schutztruppe claimed that it had to insist on prior consultations between the civil authorities and the local commandant, 'simply in order to safeguard the standing of the military power in relation to the natives';[55] but in fact it was more concerned with fundamentally underlining its own autonomy from the District administration. The dispute between the authorities would scarcely have come to the notice of the African prisoners of war if the military officers had not blown it up out of all proportion themselves, as they did in the case here described. The responsible officer, who was present in the werf, refused the civil official access to the person he was looking for, in full view of everybody.

The Schutztruppe attempted to defend its own autonomy by pointing out how important the military mission was that it had to fulfil. Commander in Chief Ludwig von Estorff complained that the civilians had no understanding of military requirements:

> Furthermore, if the police authority were to be given the right to have access to the natives attached to the forces at will, the forces would no longer be in a position to carry out their duties at any time with the native manpower they need for that purpose. Their ability to carry out their military duties would be at the pleasure of the police authority.[56]

The Governor did not, however, grant von Estorff his wish to have 'the powers of these authorities [i.e. the Schutztruppe and the civil administration] over natives completely separated',[57] and pointed out to him that although a transfer of 'police powers in respect of the issuance of employment logbooks and of the supervision of the werfs' to the Schutztruppe would be possible, the District Office concerned was under an obligation 'to undertake checks on the situation of the natives in the military werfs at certain intervals of time'.[58] This would ultimately have meant the subordination of the military authority to the civil administration; but this was precisely what the Schutztruppe was seeking to prevent. Since 'the existing prisoners of war still need to be under military guard', a compromise was reached under which 'the natives in military service will remain in the military werfs under the supervision of the military authorities until further notice',[59] while the military command ordered all local commanders to cause all Africans to be entered forthwith in the District Office registers, and to inform these offices of any changes in the 'native inventory'. In all other respects, all the 'natives with the forces' were to remain in the military werfs under the supervision of, and guarded by, the military authorities.[60]

But this did not bring about a complete end to the frictions between the Administration and the military authorities, as is evidenced by a renewed complaint from the Commander of the Schutztruppe to the Governor about the conduct of Windhoek District Office in 1912: he accused that office of having repeatedly caused the batman of a certain Captain von Strube to be taken away for punishment without the Captain having been notified in advance. The Schutztruppe attempted to claim immunity for him in respect of the civil authorities by arguing that as an officer's batman he was not privately employed but a member of the Schutztruppe staff.[61] This case, banal as it was in itself, demonstrates how strained the relations were between the civil officials and the officers of the Schutztruppe on the middle level of administration. Under these circumstances, smooth cooperation between the civil and military authorities was impossible.

The slipshod work of the administrative officials and the strained relations with the military were not, however, the only circumstances hindering the complete implementation of the Native Ordinances. The settlers themselves also stood in the way of their effective implementation through their unwillingness to cooperate with the authorities.

Possible though it was, through the imposition of constant measures of control, to discipline a large part of the African population to the extent that they 'as a general rule anxiously make every effort to always have their pass tokens with them', the actions of the Whites themselves contributed towards rendering the system of control less than fully effective. In order to make it impossible for African servants to escape from their places of employment, it 'was no rare occurrence' for employers to infringe the Ordinances by taking their pass tags away and so 'prevent them from leaving their service', as Windhoek District Office complained.[62] While the authorities were disseminating propaganda in an attempt to free the pass tokens and travel passes from the stigma of being instruments of repression, that was precisely how the settlers were using them. The Windhoek District Officer therefore demanded that these Whites should be punished, and complained that the White population was affording insufficient assistance – and that only reluctantly – to the implementation of the provisions on pass tokens and travel passes, and moreover was displaying a lack of interest in the 'concerns of the natives', as was 'noticeable in particular in the way they perform those duties imposed on private individuals by the present Ordinance'.[63] As early as the year 1900, the District Command in Gobabis had reported, on the basis of its experience with the pass requirement that had been introduced in the District in February of that year, that such difficulties with the settlers were only to be expected, and had pointed out that in many cases the settlers were simply unwilling to go to the trouble of issuing their employees with a written order when they gave them tasks to perform that entailed their leaving the farm.[64] Even the experience of the war, which one might have thought would have enhanced the awareness of the need for security on the part of the settlers, does not appear to have brought about any change in their attitude.

But the Karibib District Officer did not attribute this inadequate support on the part of the White settlers merely to a lack of will on their part; he thought that the poor record-keeping was due to the fact that 'some of the farmers are too unskilled in writing, and some of them are too negligent, to keep the lists in such a way that they always present a clear picture of the number of natives in their employment, particularly as there is quite a high degree of fluctuation'.[65] By picking up on the feeling of superiority that had always been latently present in the Administration with regard to the Whites living in the colonies, and instrumentalizing it to put the blame on them for the difficulties with the introduction of the control system, he was indirectly admitting the failure of the surveillance apparatus that had been conceived by the Administration in such a perfectionist manner, but which could not function without the assistance of the settlers.

The severe shortage of labour also led to individual employers abusing the privileges conferred on them by the Native Ordinances to get hold of workers illegally. Sec. 4 of the Pass Ordinance, under which Africans did not need a travel pass if they were travelling in the company of Whites, left a gap in the control system that was exploited by unscrupulous Whites. District Officer Schenke of Swakopmund, for example, complained to the Governor's Office about cases in which

> native women have been abducted by white men without the knowledge of their masters. Similarly, it is often the case that natives are recruited here by whites and travel to another place in their company without a travel pass. In such cases the police at the place of destination do not know whether the natives who arrive without travel passes have ended their previous employment in a proper manner or not, and in order to avoid any further repercussions are compelled to believe what the accompanying whites tell them.[66]

These Africans had slipped through a hole in the surveillance net, because in respect of their identities as well, the authorities had no other choice but to believe what they or the Whites accompanying them said. Yet one aim of the Native Ordinances had been precisely to ensure that every section of the African population was both registered and under surveillance. In reality, however, the ever more serious labour shortage had, from the beginning, not only led to such infringements of the law by some Whites, but had also generated resentment amongst employers against the registration requirement itself. It cost them working time, and some employers were not prepared to pay this price for the implementation of the Control and Pass Ordinances.

Even government employees joined in the protest. On 7 June 1907, for example, the Department of Works in Windhoek registered a complaint with the Governor's Office against the local District Office, which that morning, without any prior notice, had kept twenty-seven Africans employed by the Department away from work in order to register them. As a result they had come to work an hour late, and the Department was afraid that the enterprises to which it supplied workers would claim compensation for the lost working time. In this way the control measures frustrated the efforts of the entrepreneurs and settlers to make use of every minute of the Africans' working time. The District Office's argument in its own defence that 'such checks in the werfs occur only very rarely, and the Department of Works [could] easily put up with such a slight disturbance to its operations' was not shared by everybody in the Governor's Office, as a note written in the margin of the document testifies: '27 men means 27 working hours. I don't consider that to be only a slight disturbance'.[67]

District Officer Narciß justified the fact that the action had been kept under cover, which was one of the factors heavily criticized in the complaint, by arguing that only in this way had it been possible to get hold of those 'elements that for whatever reason are reluctant to come into contact with the police'. Nor was it possible to inform the employers in advance, since the Africans would have learnt of this immediately, as he himself knew from experience; because confidential cooperation simply did not work, even in respect of the military:

> I have known this procedure [absolute secrecy with even the police being informed only at the last moment] to be necessary ever since an occasion when my intention to search a werf for weapons, which had been agreed <u>very circumspectly</u> between me and the military, inexplicably came to the knowledge of the natives concerned in advance.[68]

Thus instead of being able to count on the cooperation of other authorities and the settlers, the civil administration was obliged to keep its planned actions secret, even from them.

The lack of a willingness to cooperate among the Whites was particularly apparent in relation to the Master and Servant Ordinance. The information contained in the Employment Logbook represented an important link in the unbroken chain of surveillance measures, as it was only from this that the Administration was able to obtain a complete overview of employment relationships. However, since the Ordinance provided for some of the fundamental rights of the African workers in relation to their employers to be explained to them when the Employment Logbook was issued, and some of the crucial conditions of the employment contract, such as its term and the amount and type of remuneration, were required to be set out in it in writing, it was boycotted by the employers. Far from displaying the identity of interests between the bureaucracy and the settlers that is so often invoked by commentators, the employers stood in opposition to the prescribed measures, and the overwhelming majority of them evaded the logbook requirement by avoiding the conclusion of employment contracts with a term of more than one month, for which a logbook was mandatory. 'The reason is to be found in the fact that when the native is issued with his Employment Logbook the police are required to explain to him not only his duties but also his rights. This point is not to the liking of many farmers', the Gobabis District Office reported.[69] In Keetmanshoop,[70] Lüderitzbucht,[71] Karibib[72] and Bethanie[73] things were much the same.[74] In Gibeon, taking the figures for August 1908 as an example, only ninety-six of the 1,768 Africans employed there had an employment contract with a term of more than one month.[75] This was a situation in which no improvement was noticeable anywhere in the colony over the following years, as Bethanie District Office remarked in 1910, explaining it by the fact that the employers 'do not want to enter into commitments to natives for too long a period'.[76] By acting in this way the Whites were not only holding out against the implementation of a minimum degree of protection for African workers, but were throwing a spanner into the works of the entire control system.

The Failure of Control

Right from the beginning, the Native Ordinances had aimed to encompass not merely those Africans living in the larger centres of population, those who were prisoners of war and those who were employed by Whites, but all Africans living in the colony, including 'Hereros, Berg Damaras and Bushmen [San] living wild in the mountains, on the veld and in the bush'.[77] With the aim of getting these people to give up their nomadic way of life and become settled, the District Office at Namutoni, a non-autonomous District in the Grootfontein *Bezirk*, set up a collection camp for them, where they were to be accustomed to work and 'educated' to comply with the pass regulations. The degree of success was only modest, as the San, though happy to use the camp over the winter, ran away from it again afterwards.[78] As was the case with the matter of equipping the offices with pass tokens, here too the complicated and tedious bureaucratic procedure to some extent nullified the efforts of the District Office. At the beginning of 1909 the remaining San had to be released, 'as no decision had yet reached the camp as to whether they should be provided with food'.[79]

Nor did it prove possible to compel those San who were employed by Whites to stick to their jobs. In mid-1909, for example, they all disappeared precisely at harvest time when their labour was most urgently required by the farmers, without the authorities being able to do anything to prevent it. The degree of official impotence is made clear by reports from farmers that the San simply laughed at threats to call the police, and just ran away. The Whites too doubted whether the Administration was at all in a position to be able to make any show of strength. If initially they complained to the police about the disappearance of the San, in the end they simply had to resign themselves to such behaviour. When the San returned, not a single farmer applied to the District Office to have them punished; some even explicitly refused to do so, apparently so as not to jeopardize the voluntary return of the deserters.[80]

The 're-education measures' did not produce the desired success either, as the following report from Namutoni indicates – yet another example of a report of a failure being presented as a success:

> They have all been exhaustively instructed as to the importance of the tokens they have been issued with, and they appear to have understood. This is shown by a few cases in which individual Bushmen did disappear again, but before doing so gave their pass tags to other Bushmen to be handed in at the District Office.[81]

In Sesfontein, a non-autonomous District in Outjo *Bezirk*, the Pass Ordinance was even suspended again in respect of the Berg Damara and the San, since the District Officer declared it to be impossible to implement; his superior, the District Officer of Outjo District, thereupon ordered that the pass tokens already distributed should be collected in again.[82]

This was in spite of the Colonial Administration's urgent desire to control the San and to persuade them to give up their nomadic way of life, not only because of the prevailing labour shortage but also because of the prevalence of livestock thefts, which they were mainly blamed for: 'Stealing livestock is the Bushmen's trade, no matter whether the cattle belong to a white farmer or to a native. The political attitude of the Bushmen is therefore a hostile one', the District Officer of Maltahöhe declared.[83] Bethanie too reported an increase in cattle rustling at the end of 1908, which it blamed on the San.[84]

The Administration attempted to proceed against cattle thieving by force of arms, but apparently with only moderate success, as the farmers were not willing to rely on the organs of the state. The farmers, so the District Office in Maltahöhe reported, protected themselves 'by entering into barter transactions with the Bushmen, from which it is the Bushman who gains the most'.[85] The failure of state power and authority could scarcely have been more clearly expressed, even if there were some isolated successes in arresting so-called 'gangs'.[86] The Whites had to find a way of getting along with the San, as the authorities were unable to protect their property.

But it was not only San who disappeared from their werfs or their places of work and absented themselves either temporarily or permanently from the White settlements. The Namutoni District Officer reported that a number of Herero who had been working in the mines at Tsumeb had terminated their employment there in a regular manner, and so, according to the provisions of the Native Ordinances, should have made their way by a predefined route to their next employers. What they actually did was to first 'spend about four weeks in the bush recuperating, before reporting to the authorities in Namutoni'.[87] The Administration was not in a position to prevent behaviour of this kind either.[88]

The Governor had to get on top of this situation, both in order to relieve the general shortage of labour and also to justify the very existence of his police force. In January 1911 the Governor's Office drew up a new plan and circulated it to the District Offices for discussion:

> In order to get the natives who are still roaming about out on the veld to take up a settled existence and to register themselves, it appears necessary to send out police patrols to collect these natives up again and bring them to collection points.

> At the collection points, which would be best located close to a police station and placed under the supervision of a police officer, these natives should construct their werfs under the direction of a foreman, and be assigned to farmers as workers should there be any demand.[89]

The reactions of the recipients of this plan proved to be crushing for the Governor's Office in two respects: they made clear the scale of the prevalent shortage of labour, and they also showed how pessimistic officials in the Districts had become in their estimates of the chances of being able to exert any effective control over the entire African population. The proposal that the Districts should set up 'native collection points' of their own was universally rejected by all District Officers except for those of Bethanie and Gibeon,[90] since the huge shortage of workers meant that 'every native should be immediately be put to use as a worker',[91] and therefore no collection point was necessary. In Windhoek District alone one hundred employers had been recorded as requesting to be allocated African workers in February 1911, and the District Office feared that the provision of free meals would even create an incentive for other Africans to run away from their places of work:

> If they were now to be accommodated at a collection point and given food at the expense of the state, then no doubt they would have nothing against this in principle. Because not having to do any work but nevertheless being given food is something that suits the natives fine. ...
> The natives run away from their masters, throw away their pass tokens, move away quietly into a different District and present themselves at the collection point there as having been living out on the veld ever since the war.[92]

In this, however, the Windhoek District Office found itself taking an opposite position from the District Office in Grootfontein, which proposed, since the San's 'thirst for freedom ... is unconquerable' and it would not be possible to hold them at any collection point, that the distribution of food, and above all of tobacco, should be used to lure them there.[93] These contradictory proposals show that the District Officers were increasingly coming to feel themselves to be at their wits' end.

A further factor was that the many inaccessible places of refuge could not be systematically and permanently kept under surveillance, either by the police or by the Schutztruppe. Although the District Offices repeatedly reported that Africans had been brought in and immediately distributed to Whites as workers, such successes occurred more or less by chance, as the District Officer of Karibib openly admitted:

> In this District, however – and predominantly, as has already repeatedly been reported elsewhere, in the thinly populated mountainous and inaccessible areas in the south-west of the District – there are indeed individual natives and occasionally also smaller bands of vagrant natives wandering around on the veld. But these are almost exclusively runaway *Bambusen* [African army servants] or workers who all, to a greater or lesser extent, bear grudges and therefore will not give themselves up voluntarily under any circumstances. How extraordinarily difficult it is to lay hands on them has been demonstrated by numerous patrols – some of them patrols of this District's police, some of them strong combined patrols of this and the adjoining Districts – most of which, however, did not produce any results.[94]

The Africans were obviously taking advantage of the division of the colony into administrative areas, and were to be found 'almost always close to the District boundaries, so that if they are pursued they can vanish into the neighbouring District'.[95] Much the same thing was also to be found on the external borders of the colony, the borders with British territory having already proved porous during the guerrilla war.

The head of the Department of Native Affairs in the Windhoek government, Kurt Streitwolf, who received the reports for evaluation, nevertheless put his faith in stronger mounted patrols, and would have liked to entrust the task of carrying them out to the Schutztruppe. Their task would be to 'clean up' the *sandveld*, the open arid area where the greater proportion of the free Africans were presumed to be holding out most of the time. But as in the days when he had been District Officer of Gobabis, Streitwolf again showed himself to be a proponent of brutal measures of compulsion, closing his report to the Governor with the words: 'The more ruthlessly we proceed against the natives out on the veld, the more successful we will be. Not only will we gain hundreds of workers, but we will also put an end to the desertions by working natives.'[96]

Four years after the introduction of the Native Ordinances, which were intended to solve the problem of keeping the African population under control and to bring about their complete integration into the work process, Streitwolf's demand was equivalent to an admission that the Ordinances were not fit for purpose. How wrong he was in his forecast that a policy of harshness would serve to stem the flight of the Africans is demonstrated by the debate on how to control the Africans in the years 1912 and 1913, a debate that became more and more radicalized in particular with regard to the matter of means of identification, which right from the beginning had been one of the main obstacles to implementing the Ordinances.

In March 1911, as a result of the numerous complaints he had received, Governor Seitz had to admit 'that the identification of the natives is made extraordinarily difficult by arbitrary changes of name'.[97] This had been preceded by a complaint from Pastor Johannes Olpp, the head of the Rhenish Mission in South West Africa, 'that the natives love to take different names, in which they are further strengthened by the fact that masters also often confer new names on their servants. This makes it very difficult, and in some cases impossible, to keep track of who is who'.[98] The solution proposed in response by a clerical officer in the Governor's Office named von Schwerin testifies unambiguously to the desperate situation of the control measures introduced with such great enthusiasm in 1907:

> For this reason, a name register for natives is now to be set up at the District Offices, which every native in the District is to be entered in and which is to be kept constantly up to date. In the case of unbaptized natives, the surname and first name are to be entered, in the case of

baptized natives, the surname and the Christian name given at baptism. The natives should be particularly instructed at the time when this entry is made that from that time on it is forbidden for them to use any other name. A penalty must be determined for deliberately using a false name.[99]

As these very measures had already been provided for in the Control Ordinance of 1907, von Schwerin was basically demanding that the registration of the Africans should be begun all over again – further proof that the Control Ordinance had failed. The Governor's Office did point out in its reply to Olpp that at the District Offices 'the natives are to be registered as precisely as possible, … both by their pass token and by name';[100] but the 'successes' that had been achieved in this respect had apparently not established themselves in the public consciousness.

In addition, the lack of respect for the individuality and the personality of the Africans on the part of White employers, who were both able to give their workers whatever names they liked and then also to change these names arbitrarily, proved to be a serious factor detracting from the functionality of the control system, as Olpp himself had made clear. It was often the case that employers who had several servants with the same name would summarily change their names, not infrequently simply because the employer did not like the worker's actual name, or because he thought it was too long. By contrast, Olpp maintained, the reproach also raised against the Mission that it was contributing to the confusion by giving Africans other names when they were baptized was not tenable, as the missionaries gave the Africans those Christian names 'by which they are, for example, entered in the police register'.[101]

Olpp's complaints were apparently justified, as despite the placatory letter to him drawing attention to the existing system of registration, Governor Seitz did see a need for action:

> I therefore request that all means should be applied to ensure that the native retains the name he has once taken, and furthermore that the master should not simply give his native some other name. If the master has several natives with the same name, then he would be well advised to add a number to the name in order to distinguish them. In the Native Registers the native's own name and the name of his father is always to be noted in addition to the number of the pass token, so that the custom of using family names as surnames will gradually become established among the natives.[102]

Seitz was attempting to rescue the control practice as it had been applied up until then through the adoption of a measure of social discipline, namely that of introducing surnames among the Africans. If the allocation of pass token numbers had led to a depersonalization of the Africans, this new move was at least a small step towards seeing them as individuals, as human beings.

These measures were not sufficient, however, to satisfy the more and more radical demands of the settlers for stricter control of the African population, or to stand up to the growing pressure of public opinion. In April 1912 the Governor's Office therefore recommended that 'every native who is found without a pass token is to be punished for contravening the Pass Ordinance'.[103] This was obviously intended to prevent Africans who had deserted their places of employment from talking themselves out of the situation by claiming never to have been registered.

On 29 March 1912 the Governor's Office had circulated to all District Offices an 'instruction for undertaking physical descriptions', and further ordered on 25 June 1912: 'On all official identity documents, passes etc. for natives, the holder's right thumbprint is always to be impressed, so that identification is possible.' This measure, adopted in imitation of the measures customary in British South Africa and Portuguese East Africa, was intended to 'provide for the certain identification of the person', since the 'easily exchangeable pass token does not ensure this'.[104] The Administration was thus obviously attempting to calm down the farmers, who for some considerable time had already been demanding more drastic actions such as the tattooing of the Africans. This was a measure that was rejected by the Administration, as 'no ... colonial nation makes use of such methods',[105] and furthermore it would 'cause great anxiety among the natives and be met with great resistance' and 'be exploited at home by anti-colonial elements to justify wild agitation'.[106]

The farmers, however, were not prepared to accept this rejection, and the Farmers' Associations of Waterberg,[107] Gobabis[108] and Okahandja demanded once again a few months later that 'natives who display an inclination to run away should be identified by a tattoo'.[109] In the view of the farmers from Gobabis, this was the only way in which effective control would be possible, since 'as has been emphasized in the press on various occasions, the runaways throw away their pass tokens and if captured claim never to have worked for a farmer'. The reason given for this inhuman proposal was the expectation that it would 'do at least a little to remedy the shortage of labour'.[110]

Although some individual District Officers, such as District Officer Runck of Gobabis, did show some sympathy for this demand, they too in the end came down in favour of the Colonial Government's paying heed to the mood in Germany, and particularly in the Reichstag, and remaining true to its attitude of rejection, 'quite irrespective of the fact that it [the Government] would perhaps itself be in favour, in principle, of the harsher treatment of native employees'.[111]

The farmers refused to be placated, however, and took the matter up repeatedly in the Territorial Council. The Farmers' Association of Grootfontein demanded that in addition to the tattooing 'a stricter registration requirement and a poll tax should be introduced to improve control', as 'the pass requirement for natives that has existed up until now has proved unsuccessful'.[112] The Governor remained unyielding in the matter of tattooing, but promised to at least consider issuing an Ordinance concerning a registration requirement such as had existed in Windhoek District since 1913;[113] however, this never seems to have reached the stage of implementation.

Six years after the promulgation of the Native Ordinances, the Colonial Government was practically at a loss with regard to how it might be possible to prevent Africans from deserting their workplaces and how to track down those who were in hiding. On the one hand, the labour shortage demanded that recruiting should be more comprehensive; but on the other hand, the Colonial Government could not bring itself to adopt all too barbarous methods. The only thing that was certain was that no watertight surveillance of the Africans could be achieved with the control measures introduced in 1907. The outbreak of the First World War in 1914 and the German surrender of South West Africa a year later meant that any further planning was in vain.

Unrest and Fears of Resistance

The passive resistance of individual Africans and of small groups, as expressed in their desertion of their places of work, their throwing away of their pass tags or their flight into inaccessible areas of the colony where there were scarcely any roads, was damaging to the colonial economy, and it aroused fear among the White population. Not only were Africans who had managed to escape state control and whose whereabouts was unknown economically unproductive, but the situation nourished White fears of new organized resistance. However, this never represented any real threat to the foundations of German colonial rule.

The groups that became known as 'gangs', on the other hand, appeared to be a much greater danger: Africans acting collectively in an organized manner to attack farms and police or Schutztruppe patrols. It is very difficult to determine retrospectively whether in any individual case such an attack represented an act of political resistance, or whether it was more economically motivated.[114] The distinction between the two was blurred, as a deterioration in the economic situation of the African population was factored into the colonialist programme. Furthermore, it was one of the peculiar features of the colonial situation that any action that in the eyes of the colonial state constituted a breach of the law, and in particular any attack on the lives or property of colonists, could appear in the eyes of the colonized to have the character of a legitimate action against the colonial oppressors. Even contemporaries could not make up their minds about the motives of such groups, sometimes referring to them as bands of robbers or 'marauders', but sometimes speaking of a continuation of the war.

Even at their zenith in the year 1908, however, such disturbances never represented any real threat to colonial rule. The reason for the astonishingly high level of attention that they nevertheless attracted from the German side, and which led to extreme reactions from the colonial state, was to be found in the real or imagined link to the guerrilla war that had only just come to an end. Apart from the proximity in time to the shooting of Morenga on 17 September 1907 and the flaring up again of raids by Simon Kopper and his people at the turn of the year 1907/08,[115] this was also related to the form that the resistance took, namely that of surprise attacks on farms and small military units.

In order to counter the danger that the conflict would spread, the Germans acted ruthlessly against any manifestation of opposition. As especially in the south of the colony the border to the Cape Colony offered the gangs a convenient escape route, cooperation with the Government of the Cape Colony was of great importance. To deprive the Africans of this possibility of withdrawing to a safe haven the German Government insisted that any people accused of complicity in such raids who had taken refuge in the Cape Colony should be extradited. But cooperation between the German and British authorities was anything but smooth, since the Government of the Cape Colony insisted on faultless extradition proceedings, as is made clear by the example of Abraham Rolf and his 'gang'.

Although there was no serious danger to the German population, the situation simply would not calm down. The prevailing atmosphere of often hysterical fear found its expression in ever new rumours of a revival of the organized resistance. The responsible people in the Administration, the police and the Schutztruppe reacted with military force. The traumatic experience of having been taken by surprise by the outbreak of war in 1904 was still very much alive and very potent, and nobody wanted to expose himself to a reproach of having been too casual in his approach to the situation.

Moreover, officials with a radical agenda exploited the climate of fear in order to propagate their plans to eliminate those few nations in the south whose structures were still intact after the war. Apart from the resettlement of the Stuurmann people, however, these plans never came to anything, due to the reluctance of the Colonial Government to give its approval to an action that would doubtless have occasioned heavy casualties.

Gang Activities in the South and the Border Problem: The 'Rolf' Case

The gang raids were concentrated above all in the south of the colony, where numerous areas in the Kalahari and in the borderland to the Cape Colony offered many places of refuge that the gangs could retreat to. The climax was in the year 1908, when the fact that three different gangs, the Ortmann Gang, the Klein-Jacobus Gang and the Rolf Gang, were all active simultaneously gave rise to widespread alarm.

At the end of January 1907, seven Bondelswarts led by Wilhelm Ortmann had escaped from German colonial rule by fleeing to the Cape Colony. Although the incident they were responsible for was actually a fairly insignificant one,[116] the German Administration would not allow the case to rest but sought to make an example of the men concerned. As a deterrent to others, it filed a request for extradition with the British authorities in March 1908.[117] The Government of the Cape Colony acceded to the request,[118] and Wilhelm Ortmann and his companions were extradited; they were imprisoned in Grootfontein, where they had to spend their days 'working out of doors under strict supervision'. An escape attempt was foiled; but the conditions of their imprisonment were so harsh that by March 1909 both Wilhelm and Karl Ortmann were dead.[119]

But Wilhelm Ortmann's gang was not the only one that escaped to British territory. At the same time that it requested their extradition, the German Administration also filed requests for the extradition of a group led by Klein-Jacobus Christian and of two Herero named Paul and Abraham from Rietfontein.[120] While the latter were accused of horse theft, Klein-Jacobus, Koos, Jan and David Christian and Jan Kurazie were charged with the misappropriation of forty-six items of small livestock and of stealing food, tobacco, merchandise and cattle from two farmers.[121] They too were extradited.[122]

In December 1908 there then occurred the most serious incident of the postwar period in the south of the colony, when a group of Bondelswarts under the leadership of the Baster Abraham Rolf, having previously assembled on British territory, attacked a number of farms and a Schutztruppe patrol; three soldiers and four settlers were killed.[123] That a raid was in the offing had already been reported to Ukamas police station in early December by the South African farmer Joseph Isaak: he had made a statement to the effect that the gang had assembled on British territory[124] and was intending 'to restart the war in the German colony'.[125] This, however, was merely the uncorroborated statement of an individual; so although the Commander of the Schutztruppe was informed, he failed to pass the information on to the Colonial Government.[126] This indicates that the military were convinced they would be able to get a grip on the situation quickly enough. The responsible Southern Command of the Schutztruppe reacted promptly and resolutely by assembling a largish number of troops, and even redeploying soldiers from the north of the colony, as 'it was to be feared that they [the gang] would be able to attract more and more people if they continued to achieve successes, and in addition, in the relatively well-populated area of the Great Karras Mountains, many people's lives were at stake'. Above all, it was feared that further Africans would join in the disturbances, 'as there were also rumours in circulation that the Berseba people were eager for war, and the loyalty of the Bondels, even though they had remained completely quiet until then, could at least be severely tested'.[127]

As things turned out, the reinforcements from the north were not required, since by the time the 10th Company had arrived in Keetmanshoop on 26 December 1908[128] the matter had already been decided in a couple of skirmishes[129] – and on the same day, Abraham Rolf and his men had withdrawn across the border back into British territory, allegedly in order to meet up with Simon Kopper.[130] Although the disturbances triggered by Abraham Rolf remained 'restricted to a local area'[131] and the Commander of the Territorial Police, Joachim von Heydebreck, could see 'no reason to be alarmed', patrols in the area were strengthened as a precaution.[132]

Thus, even if the actual threat emanating from the raids carried out by the Abraham Rolf Gang was relatively small, their real significance lay in the general atmosphere of fear they gave rise to outside the military and police forces, where alarm was spread by 'exaggerated rumours'.[133] In addition, the fundamental vulnerability of the southern area of the colony was brought home to the German Colonial Administration and to the settlers, a major contributor to this being the proximity of the border between German and British territory, across which the Africans could withdraw with ease. The German authorities were quick to hold the British responsible. District Officer Karl Schmidt of Keetmanshoop, for example, identified not only the 'warmongering' of the Cape Colony merchants, who profited from the weapons trade, but also the lack of cooperation from the Cape Colony Government as being the main obstacles to a rapid and permanent pacification of the colony:

> A second contributory factor is the fact that the Cape Government allows people who are in rebellion against a friendly white nation to repeatedly cross backwards and forwards across the frontier unhindered, instead of rendering them harmless, i.e. either extraditing them or transplanting them to an area far enough away from the border. The Cape Government says it is neutral, but by allowing the rebels to cross the border unhindered and to remain close to the border it is in fact not remaining neutral but is directly supporting them, and that extremely actively. The German troops have to respect the border, and they have no station nearby where they and their animals can go to recuperate, whilst every rebel is safe and secure as soon as he has crossed the 20th parallel. If the rebels were not able to take refuge again and again in this way, they would have been overcome and put out of action by the German troops years ago.[134]

Commanding Officer Baerecke of the Schutztruppe Southern Command was also of the opinion that the 'very inadequate police surveillance of the British border area' and the fact that Africans living on the British side such as the 'Rietfontein Basters to a great extent sympathize with the rebels ... makes it completely impossible even to precisely determine who all the people are who are involved, never mind to get our hands on them'. Even though it was unlikely, in view of the 'undoubted failure in which the incursion so quickly ended', that others would feel encouraged to make similar attempts, it nevertheless could not be completely ruled out 'that there might be a recurrence of such plundering expeditions into German territory, which appear to be professionally organized and equipped by Jews from Upington and the surrounding area'.[135]

The only way to largely put a stop to this was to institute even stricter surveillance of the border area, to which end Baerecke proposed building up a permanent espionage network. In addition, he gave orders that no further passes were to be issued to the Bondelswarts for travel to the Cape Colony or into the border area.[136] Furthermore, it appeared to him that the decisive factor would be the rapid suppression and crushing of even the smallest disorders, in order to create precedents that would deter others. In this respect, the action against Abraham Rolf – and in particular the rapid redeployment of

Schutztruppe units from the north to the south by train – was regarded as a success, even though in the end those troops were not required. Baerecke was convinced that their rapid appearance 'will not have failed to make an impression on the natives and their behaviour, and that for the future as well'.[137]

Just as important to the Colonial Administration in Windhoek as the strengthening of border surveillance in order to deter any further raids was the punishment of those Africans who had fled to British territory. In order to ensure that they would be subject to prosecution even across the border, the Governor's Office notified the Government of the Cape Colony and the German High Commission in Johannesburg even before the end of December 1908.[138] On Cape Colony territory the local police took up the pursuit of Abraham Rolf and his gang,[139] not least because they were also accused of having raided a farm there as well, and stolen livestock.[140] Of the sixty-seven men that originally constituted the Rolf Gang, twenty-two reached Rietfontein on British territory, where at first they were allowed to move around freely.[141] But once the Germans had filed their request for extradition, seventeen of them – the rest had disappeared in the meantime – were brought to Upington at the end of January 1909,[142] and a short time later interned near Cape Town.[143]

It had not originally been intended to request their extradition; Colonial Secretary Dernburg would have been satisfied if they had been disarmed, the stolen livestock returned, and Abraham Rolf and his men resettled elsewhere on British territory, far away from the German border.[144] This conciliatory attitude met with resistance, however, from Deputy Governor Hintrager, who wanted to make an example of the gang and use their extradition and sentencing as a deterrent, since in his view the 'failure to punish such murderers and robbers would be a direct invitation to other natives to repeat their actions', as they would feel confident that they would enjoy the protection of the British government.[145] So Dernburg finally left it up to the Colonial Government in Windhoek to decide whether extradition proceedings should be pursued.[146] There, Hintrager prevailed over Governor Bruno von Schuckmann – who would apparently also have been content with the resettlement of the Rolf Gang in South Africa as Dernburg had initially envisaged[147] – and only one day later requested the German Consul General in Cape Town to apply to the Government of the Cape Colony for the extradition of Abraham Rolf and his fellow prisoners.[148]

Far from presenting a picture of smooth cooperation between the British and the German authorities, as Drechsler wrongly claims,[149] the extradition proved to be a tedious and long-winded undertaking, since the Cape Government insisted on properly conducted proceedings. The Africans had far more legal resources available to them than they would have had in German territory. The Government of the Cape Colony repeatedly raised new demands that the German side was forced to fulfil. The fact that the German Colonial Administration, and above all Deputy Governor Hintrager, was prepared to submit itself to this process shows what great importance it attributed to a legal precedent of this kind. The German side wanted to demonstrate at all costs that there was no escape from German criminal justice, not even by crossing into foreign territory. This alone is sufficient to make clear what a major problem the border represented for German control.

Hintrager was very much aware that the extraditions he was seeking were by no means going to take place more or less automatically as an act of cooperation between the two colonial powers. Simultaneously with the filing of the request for extradition, therefore, he also requested the District Officer of Keetmannshoop, who was responsible in his other capacity as a Native Judge, to collect evidence relating to the offences committed by the persons concerned, since this had to be submitted to the British authorities within two months of their arrest.[150]

The allegation that the gang had already robbed and murdered on British territory before starting to carry out raids in the German colony, and that consequently the case 'involved only a band of robbers, and not *orloyg* people [*sic*: orlog = war]', developed into a central plank of the German argumentation.[151]

Before it could contemplate ordering extradition, the Department of Justice of the Cape Colony first of all had to be satisfied that the accused had been unambiguously identified. This meant that witnesses had to confirm not only that each of the accused was a member of the gang, but also that he had actually taken part in its crimes. The Cape Government insisted on this, since in the extradition proceedings against Klein-Jacobus Christian some innocent people had been arrested as well and had subsequently been successful in suing the Cape Government for damages. If the accused had not been identified beyond all doubt, the Cape Government would have released them.[152]

In response to this requirement, the Government of South West Africa sent three African witnesses to Cape Town under guard in early May 1909.[153] But even then, the proceedings still did not seem to get properly under way, as the Germans first had to prove that a State of War no longer prevailed in the south of the colony; because if there had been any political background to Rolf's actions, such as an intention to wage war against the Germans, there could have been no question of his being extradited. This explains why the German Administration, which had initially spoken of a revival of the war, now avoided all reference to any such thing.

The extradition proceedings took place in Cape Town in June 1909. The Cape Colony Department of Justice appointed the Cape Town prosecuting counsel Nightingale to represent the German Government, whilst a lawyer by the name of Struben, a member of the House of Assembly, the Lower House of the Cape Colony Parliament, undertook the defence of Abraham Rolf and his fellow accused. The fact that in the Cape Colony Africans had the vote and that Struben would also be able to mobilize political opinion if there were any shortcomings in the procedure is likely to have contributed to the fact that 'the extradition proceedings were conducted with extraordinary thoroughness'.[154] The whole matter was also made more difficult by the fact that in the meantime, as a result of a lack of witnesses, the accused had been acquitted of the charge of 'public violence' in respect of the alleged offences committed in the Cape Colony. The chief prosecution witness having gone down with malaria and being unable to appear at the trial, the presiding judge had refused to postpone the case since the accused could not be held in custody for an unlimited period; for 'though these people were Hottentots they were entitled to the rights of civilized people'. As he could therefore find no evidence of 'public violence', he pronounced the accused not guilty of this charge. He would not make any statement with regard to the extradition proceedings as he was not familiar with them, but he did declare that he did not know 'whether it was purely a political offence or not, or whether they are prisoners of war. The offence may have been done in the act of fighting.'[155] According to the German Consul General, the judge had even stated in the grounds for his judgment that 'the accused had at the time in question been at war with the German Government'.[156] If the judge in the extradition proceedings were to take that view as well, he would be bound to refuse to grant the application.

Despite this, the German Consulate General judged the chances for a favourable outcome to the proceedings to be good – from the German point of view – although it feared that in that case there would be an appeal to the Supreme Court. It attested that the Cape Government had so far applied itself to the matter with 'the greatest degree of objectivity'. Its concern had been 'exclusively to achieve a faithful interpretation and rational application of the existing extradition treaty'.[157]

During the extradition proceedings the evidence presented concentrated on the question of whether or not a State of War had prevailed in South West Africa at the time of the alleged offences – in other words, whether Rolf and his men were simply armed bandits 'or whether they were fighting German authority, believing that the war in Damaraland, which it was officially announced was concluded two years ago, was still in progress'.[158] The German side now presented evidence that included both testimonies given under oath by Keetmanshoop District Officer Karl Schmidt[159] and Schutztruppe Commander Ludwig von Estorff,[160] which were submitted in writing; and also a statement from Joachim von Heydebreck, the Commander of the Territorial Police,[161] who had come to Cape Town to appear in person as a witness. All three of these testified to the fact that there had been peace in the colony for years, and their statements appear to have convinced the judge that peace did indeed prevail in South West Africa. On 5 July 1909 the court decided that the following members of the Rolf Gang should be extradited: Abraham Rolf, Isaak Petrus, Boy Boysen, Piet Adam, Jan April, Isaak Links, Gert Swartbooi, Jan Jantze and Abraham Christian.[162] Thus nine of the fourteen men whose extradition had been applied for were to be deported to South West Africa.[163] They immediately filed a petition against the decision, on the grounds of formal errors by the German government in the attestation of the statements given under oath, and because they claimed that the offences had been of a political nature.[164] In order to influence the proceedings in the direction desired by the German authorities, the Consulate General in Cape Town supplied the lawyer representing the German side in the extradition proceedings, the prosecuting counsel Nightingale, with some aids to argumentation which went in the direction of calling upon the authorities in the Cape Colony not to apply different standards when assessing Germany's Native Policy from those applied in relation to Great Britain:

> As to the alleged political character of the crimes of Abraham Rolf's gang, I would only refer to two incidents of recent British history. Doubtlessly the Zulus in their repeated disturbances during the last 3 years have been actuated at least to some degree as Rolf and his men by political motives. Nevertheless, the murder of, e.g., the Resident Magistrate in 1906 was, as a matter of course, regarded as an ordinary murder by British and Colonial Authorities alike.

> The murderous attack of Dhinagri (Dhingra) on Sir [C]urzon Wyllis, a few weeks ago, in London had undisputedly none other but political motives. Nevertheless, we all read in the Papers at the time of Dhinagri's trial that the presiding judge explicitly pointed out that his dead [*sic*]

had to be treated as ordinary murder. And, as you know, as common murderer has he been executed yesterday [*sic*].[165]

The implication of this statement was that in assessing crimes by colonized people against their colonizers it was not a question of whether political or criminal motives predominated, but of the interests of the colonial power, which was obliged to punish attacks of any kind, simply in order to secure its own domination.

On 26 August, the Supreme Court of the Cape Colony finally confirmed the extradition of the accused.[166] In the grounds of his judgment, Chief Justice Henry de Villiers stated that the formal shortcomings in the attestations were not of a serious enough nature to allow the petition. He also rejected the proposition that Abraham Rolf and his men had been politically motivated:

> This brings me to the third and main ground relied upon in support of the petition, namely, that the crimes, if any, committed by the petitioners are of political nature. They belonged to the tribe of the Bondelzwarts, with whom peace had been made by the German Government about two years previously. Not one of them occupied any position of importance in the tribe, and they all acted the part of marauders, and not of patriots fighting for the independence of their country.[167]

He then went into the offences in the Cape Colony that they had been charged with. Although they had not been convicted of the murder of a man called Olivier, a Cape farmer, there was evidence that they had belonged to the gang that had killed Olivier. But Olivier had not been a German, although it was against the Germans that the hostilities had allegedly been directed. The farmers murdered in South West Africa had also been peaceful civilians, thus the crimes of the accused had been 'wanton acts of violence committed, not against officials of the state, but against peaceful and harmless citizens, and without any apparent political object in view.'[168]

The successful extradition proceedings also attracted international attention. The Amsterdam newspaper *De Zuidafrikaansche Post*, for example, welcomed the decision of the Supreme Court in Cape Town as marking a turnaround in British policy towards Africans who had fled from South West Africa.[169] Very decisively taking the part of the 'Boers', who wished to see any offences against White rule punished in the same manner by all the colonial powers, the article confirmed German views that 'the extradition of the Rolf Gang has very clearly brought the natives to an awareness that they can no longer, as in the past, rely on finding refuge and immunity from punishment in British territories if they have robbed or murdered German farmers'.[170]

But the Supreme Court in Cape Town also linked the confirmation of the extraditions to a demand that the Government of South West Africa should ensure that those extradited received a fair trial, and that all rules of procedure should be minutely observed. Henry de Villiers had declared in the grounds of his judgment that he was

> naturally totally convinced that the individual persons extradited would not be tried for any other acts but those because of which they are being extradited. It goes without saying that the decision of this Court is not a finding that these people committed the crimes they are accused of. The task of the extradition proceedings was merely to investigate whether there were sufficient grounds for suspicion to justify an application for extradition. The Court is convinced that the South West African Court will examine the evidence in detail, and that it will only bring convictions if the guilt of the accused is proven beyond doubt.[171]

The Governor's Office in Windhoek wanted to avoid any possibility of the legal procedure being open to criticism, and immediately forwarded this admonition from the Consulate General in Cape Town to the District Officer of Keetmanshoop, before whom the trial proper was to take place.[172] It is nevertheless impossible to speak of a fair trial, as the outcome was never in doubt at any time. Even before the extradition proceedings, District Officer Schmidt had written that he was expecting 'the condemnation of the gang of murderers to exercise a beneficial effect on the attitude of any natives here who are thinking of rebelling'.[173] The Governor's Office too was concerned first and foremost with the deterrent effect, and wanted to accelerate the carrying out of the sentences; it therefore took measures to see that they were implemented as expeditiously as possible. As the expected death sentences would have to be confirmed by the Governor, Deputy Governor Hintrager had already made arrangements on 4 October for the verdicts to be relayed from Keetmanshoop to Windhoek, 450 km away as the crow flies, as quickly as possible. To achieve this, the administrative posts along the route were required to set up relay stations, each being staffed by at least one police sergeant and one auxiliary policeman, and equipped with three horses.[174]

The nine extradited persons having reached Lüderitzbucht on 2 October 1909,[175] they were immediately transferred to Keetmanshoop, where they were tried in just three days, from 4 to 6 October. As early as 9 October the Governor confirmed the five death sentences against Abraham Rolf, Isaak Petrus, Piet Adam, Booi Boysen and Jan April,[176] and the sentences of life imprisonment in chains and twice twenty-five lashes on Isaak Links, Abraham Christian, Jan Jantze and Gert Swartbooi.[177] On 13 October 1909, only eleven days after they had been returned to South West African soil, the five condemned men were executed.[178] It seems as if the Governor, after the long-drawn-out extradition proceedings in Cape Town, wanted to show the world that he at any rate knew how to make short work of proceedings against Africans.

There then occurred what looks superficially like an alleviation of the punishment of those sentenced to life imprisonment. Governor von Schuckmann 'exercised clemency', commuting their sentences to fifteen or ten years' imprisonment in chains, and above all setting aside the corporal punishment. As he added in confidence, he had come to this decision because the latter punishment 'was not mentioned among the punishments listed in the arrest warrant, and because the Hottentots' defence lawyer Struben, being a Member of Parliament, has already taken this as a pretext for asking a question in the Cape Parliament'. The fifty lashes did not seem to him to be 'important enough to give this gentleman' a further excuse to 'comment on our native justice'. That it was not done out of pity for the prisoners was made clear by his explicit wish 'that the prisoners in chains will come to feel the full rigour of the punishment, and that any violations of prison regulations or discipline will be dealt with most severely through disciplinary channels'.[179] By the end of November of the same year, Abraham Christian and Gert Swartbooi had already died in prison.[180]

Once the gang members had been convicted, the next problem was that there was no way in which it was possible to keep them securely locked up. Keetmanshoop District Office therefore requested that they should be deported to another colony, or at least relocated further north, as it feared that in view of prison conditions in the colony they might well succeed in escaping. The District Office declared that in the south they were well known, and so would soon be able to gather a following and embark once more on their campaign of robbery and murder.[181] In December 1909 the two surviving prisoners were therefore transferred to Karibib, but almost immediately, in the night of 17/18 January 1910, they succeeded in escaping, even though Karibib Prison was 'a robust structure by local standards' and the Administration had applied 'every conceivable security measure to prevent their getting away'. As in the meantime rainfall had 'washed away all traces', there was no longer any hope of recapturing the fugitives,[182] and neither the Pass Ordinance nor the Control Ordinance could make any difference to that. And so the deterrent effect that the authorities had hoped the extradition would give rise to was transformed into the very opposite, with the Administration having to fear that the successful escape would give rise to undesirable copycat effects among other African prisoners, as Hintrager wrote to the Imperial Colonial Office.[183] In April 1910 the Cape Colony Police had to concern themselves with the last survivors of the Rolf Gang again, as the Governor of the Cape Colony instructed them to arrest the fugitives immediately if they should turn up on British territory.[184] But even the offer of a reward of 1,000 marks for each fugitive[185] did not lead to any result.

The great effort that the German Administration put into obtaining the extradition of the Rolf Gang shows how anxious it was to nip in the bud any stirrings of resistance on the part of the African population. From the German point of view, the possibility that Africans could escape over the border to British territory represented a constant source of danger. And as it was not possible to close the border permanently, it was decided to pursue a policy of deterrence by demonstrating that fugitives were not safe from the German authorities, even on the other side of the border. But the cooperation with the authorities in the British territories of southern Africa did not proceed without friction. Before any extradition could be carried out, there had to be proper proceedings in which the Africans had recourse to far more legal possibilities than they would have had on German territory.

Justified Fears and Hysterical Reactions

Although it soon became clear that the Rolf Gang's raids did not constitute any real threat to German colonial rule, they did provoke hysterical reactions among the settlers. The first to feel the repercussions of these exaggerated fears were the Bondelswarts, a few of whom had joined up with Rolf. Bondelswart Commissioner Ebeling reported completely 'unfounded rumours, e.g. that the Bondels were intending to kill all the whites, and to all run away on a particular night and make *orlog* [war]'. In the night of 29/30 December 1908, for example, it had been rumoured that 'all the Bondels have taken themselves off and are going to attack Warmbad'. Ebeling immediately went out to inspect the werf and discovered 'that this rumour was completely unfounded; all the Bondels were fast asleep'.[186] As by virtue of his office he had become a particularly attentive observer of the political mood among the Bondelswarts, Ebeling explicitly emphasized that their leaders had had no connection with Rolf, had themselves condemned his actions and had even demanded that the British should extradite him. Apart from those Bondelswarts taken prisoner by Abraham Rolf and his people, not one of them had left the location and gone to join the 'gang'.

But Ebeling was not really quite as certain of the peaceable disposition of the Bondelswarts as these statements sought to make people believe; he had after all, as a precautionary measure, had those Bondelswarts 'who, with the permission of the Commission because of the bad pasture in the locations, had been staying in Umeis and Eendorn when the unrest began, ... immediately summoned back to the locations by patrols sent out by the Commission, and had had the werfs in the locations moved closer together so that they could be more easily monitored'. And when, in addition, two transports of workers whose employment contracts with the railway had expired came back to Warmbad, the reservation was no longer able to sustain all the people, as there was not enough work for them all. Ebeling nevertheless still did not dare to send them to workplaces outside the Bondelswart area again, but instead decided to put them on government work and distribute food to them. Only the rapid suppression of the unrest allowed him to send men who were fit to work back to the railway again on 11 January 1909, 'in order to put an end to the most extreme need'.[187]

So Ebeling did not want to take any risks, and preferred to fall back on the 'proven' methods of control and intimidation within his area of decision-making. After the completely unexpected outbreak of the Herero War only five years previously, even the Bondelswart Commissioner's confidence in the loyalty of the Africans – or at least in his own ability to recognize what the prevailing mood among the African population was really like – was badly shaken.

Soon it was the turn of the Berseba Nama to have 'rebellious' intentions attributed to them. In January 1909, Commandant Baereke of the Schutztruppe's Southern Command gave orders for the Petter machine-gun unit (Petter being the name of the officer commanding it) to be relocated to the 'Deutsche Erde' farm, as the farmers living on the borders of the Berseba area had been complaining about 'conspicuously insubordinate behaviour on the part of the Berseba people', and feared that a catastrophe was looming.[188] The owner of the farm, a certain Dr Kaempfer, reported that Berseba was almost empty of people, but that there were constant comings and goings of people on horseback, and footprint trails crossing his farm. Women and children could be seen heading north, as if 'non-combatants' were being got out of the way. Some of the Africans were acting recalcitrantly, refusing to obey commands for days at a time. One had spat on the ground in front of his wife before carrying out the order she had given him. As he was not in a position to defend his homestead alone, he announced that he was going to get his family and livestock away if he did not get police or military cover, since he had already had to leave his farm on foot once before and had only been able to escape 'with my bare life through particularly fortunate circumstances'. He 'lacked the resolution' to go through something like that 'a second time', and to risk the lives of his wife and children and the goods and chattels he had acquired with so much effort into the bargain. In support of his fears he pointed out that the farmers Bake, Kaese and Prenzlow judged the situation in the same way as he did.[189]

In the same month, rumours of an imminent 'uprising' of the Berseba people, planned for 27 January, were so widespread in Gibeon District 'that the Naude family in Kamelhaar and the Melchior family in Rietrevier felt themselves obliged to leave their farms'. They reached Gibeon on 26 January, but then left again 'as things had remained peaceful on the following day'.[190] The 'conspicuous observation' that precisely at this time 'the Hottentots and the Herero were very friendly in their dealings with each other' was also enough to worry Gibeon District Office. But by the end of January the rumours had died down again.[191]

When the Administration looked more closely into the rumours of resistance put about by Kaempfer and his colleagues, they proved to be unfounded. It turned out that, apart from a few insignificant observations of their own, the rumours circulated by the farmers Bake, Kaese, Prenzlow, Hafs and Kaempfer could all be traced back to Hans and Fritz Kriehs, who had been seeking to damage the reputation of the District Officer of Berseba (a non-autonomous District in Keetmanshoop *Bezirk*), Lieutenant von Linsingen. Hans Kriehs was annoyed with von Linsingen because the latter had forbidden his soldiers to enter Kriehs's public house and had also sought and received 'permission from the Government to sell provisions from official stocks', which had apparently had a negative effect on Kriehs's own business. The superordinated District Office in Keetmanshoop suspected 'that Kriehs is accustomed to inflating the behaviour of those disaffected elements that always exist into rumours of *orlog*, in order to achieve his own ends'.[192]

In the situation of unrest arising out of the activities of the Rolf Gang, such rumours fell on fertile soil. The reactions of the affected farmers, and in particular their uncritical acceptance of the rumours and their unthinking further dissemination of second-hand information, display clear signs of hysteria.[193] All of this was a delayed reaction to the completely unexpected outbreak of the Herero War, in advance of which many threatening signs had been overlooked. The immediate massive military reaction – in the form of the redeployment of a machine gun unit – shows that the commanders of the Schutztruppe were not prepared to take any risks where security was concerned.

But there were also times when the system of scouts and informers maintained on British territory by the German side to collect information on possible attacks by Africans had a counterproductive effect as far as any realistic assessment of the threat was concerned. In the spring of 1909, for example, a First Lieutenant Trainer passed on to the Commandant of the Southern Command a report from his informer Kock, who was staying with one Abraham Morris in the Cape Colony, in which he reported that an attack on German territory by a band of some fifty to seventy men was imminent. Kock asked for an advance of a thousand marks for this information.[194] The report was passed on up through the administrative hierarchy until it reached the Governor's Office, whereupon the Government of the Cape Colony was asked for assistance. The latter reacted immediately, as the German side had requested it to, but soon sent a report from the Resident Magistrate in Springbokfontein that was embarrassing to the authorities in Windhoek, stating as it did that 'Abraham Morris is living peacefully at Steinkopf, about one hundred miles from Rozynbosch, that he owes no money at Steinkopf and that there is apparently no foundation in fact for the rumours of a contemplated raid into German territory'.[195]

Annoyed at this embarrassment, which could only make him appear excessively anxious in the eyes of the British, and might lead to their not responding so promptly next time to an enquiry that might then turn out to be justified, von Schuckmann forbade the Commandant of the Southern Command to have any more contact with this spy, whom he now considered to be an unreliable person 'whose efforts have only been directed towards cashing in on our credulity'. At the same time he placed a general prohibition on obtaining information about Africans on British territory and announced that in future the Government would itself do whatever was necessary to obtain the information it required.[196] The network of spies set up to observe Africans who had fled to British territory had not fulfilled its function, as the informants had not only invented or inflated rumours of rebellion in order to earn their pay, but had also stoked up hysteria among the population. But this ran contrary to the aims of the Administration, which had in the meantime recognized 'that if we are to develop the country, what we need first and foremost in the south is a situation of calm, and we should therefore do everything we can to counter any alarming reports, notwithstanding which it goes without saying that the commanders of the troops should of course remain prepared for any eventuality'. The military and administrative officers in particular were therefore called upon, 'in view of the general addiction to invention and exaggeration in the colony ... to keep absolutely calm, and thereby also to calm the population'.[197]

At the end of 1910, rumours arose once again that a large-scale African rising was imminent. This time, however, the alleged centre was across the border in the British Bechuanaland Protectorate. The 1st Company of the Schutztruppe reported that according to information received from, amongst others, the Catholic missionary Father Weiler, a rising was in the offing among the British Bechuana. There had almost been such a rising three years previously, but the British Government had been able to suppress it at the very last moment. Now, with the Bechuana Chief Khama III expected to die shortly, there were fears that his death would be followed by a repetition of this scenario.[198] The threat appeared to be particularly serious because the authorities could potentially have found themselves faced by several hundred thousand adversaries.[199]

In view of the military capability that this figure implies, one can only wonder at the calmness with which the German Administration reacted. Although the 1st Company reported the rumours to Windhoek, it at the same time cast doubt on their reliability, and warned that they should be scrutinized with great caution with regard to their credibility, as it had already been the case in 1908 that 'wildly exaggerated and sometimes even completely false information' had been received from the Mission at Aminuis.[200] And as the Commander of the Schutztruppe did not see any reason to 'attribute any particularly serious significance' to the reports either,[201] and the Colonial Government was explicitly quite prepared to share this assessment,[202] the whole matter was soon forgotten without having given rise to actions of any importance.

But this sober and realistic assessment of the security situation did not bring about any change with regard to the policy of not tolerating even the smallest organized action by Africans, but of punishing them in the customary extremely harsh manner. In September 1912 some Africans belonging to the group around Simon Kopper were taken prisoner while apparently on a hunting expedition, and then sentenced to many years in prison – two were even condemned to death. The reasons given for this degree of harshness were the usual ones: the people concerned were considered to be a threat to the security of the colony.[203]

Violent acts were not always only directed against Whites. In August 1912 some Nama attacked a San werf near Gaus and tried to carry the inhabitants off into British territory. But a Schutztruppe patrol was able to catch up with them and capture them without a fight. They were allegedly on their way to join Simon Kopper, who was living on British territory.[204] Kopper also played a part in other incidents, although an actual link with him could not always be proved, as often there was a lack of reliable information. In September 1912, for example, when a Corporal Müller was shot dead to the west of Hunirob,[205] Gibeon District Office was not able to discover whether the deed had been committed by Kopper's people, by San or by some other party.[206] But the incident helped to nourish rumours of every possible kind.

It was no coincidence that San were among those held responsible, as they represented a constant problem for the German Administration. They were the people who were the least susceptible to being made subject to the Control and Pass Ordinances, they 'ran away' from their places of work practically whenever they wanted to, and drove the Administration to despair with their cattle rustling. After the end of the Herero and Nama War, the Administration had tried in vain to solve this problem by increasing the number of Schutztruppe patrols, but then abandoned this plan again; in the meantime, it was prepared to allow the San to continue to live their traditional way of life. If the San for their part would only give up stealing livestock, Governor von Schuckmann would be willing, he declared in 1909, to allow them to occupy 'places that at the moment are not suitable for white settlement, and where they cannot do any harm'. He therefore ordered the Schutztruppe 'not to undertake any further expeditions against the Bushmen'. Only if thieves were caught red-handed were they to be pursued or punished. In addition, he made money available for the care of 'Bushmen in need', but on condition that they were prepared to stay 'at a place determined by an authority or police station for at least some of the time'.[207] But the deep mistrust with regard to the San remained. District Officer von Vietsch of Rehoboth ordered his police to only distribute the rations made available by the Government if the San really were prepared 'to remain at the places assigned to them by the police, without taking the opportunity to spy or perform other services for their fellow tribespeople'.[208]

Although this change in policy proved effective in certain areas, for example in the Namib, where the San remained quiet and the number of livestock thefts declined,[209] the situation in general became more acute. In October 1911, 'the attitude of the Bushmen towards other natives, white settlers and police officers has become so hostile' that the situation even led to the deaths of a settler and a police officer. In order to 'combat this danger with all available means', Governor Theodor Seitz even modified the 'Regulations on the Use of Weapons by the Territorial Police' specifically with regard to the San. The police were now explicitly instructed 'to keep their firearms always ready for immediate use' when on patrol or when breaking up a werf. They were to use their weapons 'in the event of the slightest degree of recalcitrance', or if a person running away did not stop and stand still when called upon to do so. In the conflict with the San, even the African police auxiliaries were, exceptionally, to be equipped with rifles.[210] But as the Government apparently did not believe it would ever be able to subject all the San to the control system, even by applying these harsher measures, von Schuckmann's strategy of leaving the San alone as long as they remained peaceable also continued to find application at the same time. Measures were only to be taken against those San settlements guilty of thefts of livestock or even 'attacks carried out on Europeans or their native workers'. However, if in the course of such measures, 'strong men capable of working' were taken prisoner, they were to be sent to Lüderitzbucht District Office to work in the diamond fields.[211] These measures were thus intended not only to eliminate the 'plague' that the San had become 'in some parts of the country',[212] but also to gradually bring about their integration into the general system of labour recruitment.

In general, the question of the security of German rule and that of the mobilization of all available labour went hand in hand. If Africans were able to get out of their obligation to work, it meant that they were also able to slip through the loopholes in the established control network. This in turn made them, in the eyes of the German colonizers, a danger to the entire colonial system. So the German administrative and military officers were able to regard themselves as acting in the interests of the colony's security, while at the same time satisfying the requirement of the colonial economy for workers, yet without seeing themselves as agents of the employers.

Basically, the San represented no more of a threat to German rule than the so-called 'gangs' in the south. Above all, however, it was the memory of how the Herero War had broken out so unexpectedly that led the responsible people in the German Administration to adopt a completely uncompromising attitude towards even the smallest disturbances. The general nervousness of the White population also made its contribution to the adoption of ever more radical measures. Even though the administrative and military officers on the ground, if they stopped to consider the situation soberly, were themselves often convinced that the rumours of rebellion that circulated so freely were exaggerated, none of them wanted to run any risk. The fate of the African population carried little weight in their eyes compared to the assumed consequences of any military reaction being too little or too late. Furthermore, the members of the Schutztruppe were under pressure to justify their continued presence in the colony, and so sought to maintain a level of activity that would stifle any moves to reduce the force's manpower level even further. In this way, the general hysteria also served their interests.

Seeking to Change the Status Quo

Even though most 'tribal' structures had already been dismantled during the war, some officials exploited the climate of fear evoked by the unrest at the turn of the year 1908/09 to propagate their plans to do away with the special statuses of the Bondelswarts, the Berseba Nama and the Stuurmann people in the south of the colony. Among the factors leading to this, apart from the latent feeling of being under threat, was a fundamental aversion among the bureaucrats to any kind of special status that ran counter to the desired situation of all Africans being treated equally.

In October 1908 the District Officer of Keetmanshoop, Karl Schmidt, reported to Windhoek about 'lively disaffection among the Berseba people and rumours that disturbances are about to start'. The causes of this dissatisfaction were to be found in the numerous court cases relating to the repayment of loans, and to foreclosures undertaken against the Berseba Nama. In order to put an end to these, the Governor's Office banned the granting of loans to Africans, and then, in response to an application from Schmidt, was forced to combat the famine that broke out as a result (since without credit the Africans were not able to buy anything) by granting food subsidies. Although this succeeded in eliminating the acute danger of a 'rebellion', Hintrager's report on the situation to the Imperial Colonial Office showed that he did not really trust the peace. His mistrust also encompassed the Bondelswarts:

> The Bondels demand no less caution than do the Berseba people. It is useless to waste words on whether one should trust them or not. I will merely stick to the facts: that they did not suffer defeat at the time of the war, that they run away whenever they feel inclined, and plot against us together with the rabble on the other side of the border ... The Bondels and the Berseba people are the two open gunpowder barrels in the south. We need to watch out to make sure no spark falls into them.[213]

This meant taking rigorous action against any attacks, strictly controlling the African population and avoiding to the greatest possible extent anything that might upset them.

Schmidt, however, drew up a new plan to safeguard the peace. Although it was his own office that had applied to be allowed to subsidize foodstuffs for the Berseba Nama, such willingness to compromise with the Africans went against the grain for him. The starting point for his considerations, and for Hintrager's too, was the assessment that the Bondelswart settlements in particular were the source of a 'constant threat to the country', as their 'undisturbed existence ... incites the natives on the other side of the border – their relatives and fellow tribespeople – to repeatedly undertake new incursions'. He therefore proposed that they should be completely resettled:

> In my view, therefore, the Bondels living in the locations must be deported to the north, to Grootfontein, where they will no longer be a danger, and this must be done forcibly, and the sooner the better. It may prove a difficult task, and it may be that it can only be carried out at the cost of bloodshed, but even that would still be better than the present situation of constant uncertainty and insecurity.[214]

He took as a model the deportations of the Khauas and Swartbooi Nama to Windhoek in 1896 and 1898; it was thanks to these, in his view, that neither 'tribe' had taken part in the last war: 'Displaced from his country and taken to a different area, the native no longer represents a danger of war; he learns to work and obey.' The Bondelswarts would then be followed by the Stuurmann people from Spitzkopp, whom he considered to be, 'if it is possible, even more unreliable'. In Schmidt's view, however, this would only be the first phase of a comprehensive resettlement programme embracing all the colony's ethnicities, one that would change the entire structure of settlement within the Police Zone: 'As has often been reported, the people from these locations will have to be followed northwards by all the Hottentots in the south as soon as they show any signs of being unreliable, while Hereros are relocated to the south'. The reason for Schmidt's fear and for his rigorous plans lay in his astonishingly profound insights into the impact of German colonial rule, which had been clearly revealed by the Herero and Nama War:

> According to my knowledge of the natives, it is a great mistake to believe that the Bondels living in the locations or indeed any other natives in the country are content with the turn that their history has taken as a result of the war. And it would be scarcely comprehensible from a human point of view if it were not so; because from being the masters of the country, as they were before the rebellion, they have been relegated to being people who have to respect the dominion of the whites and their laws, and above all have to work if they want to live.[215]

Since the Africans had lived predominantly from hunting before the Germans came, Schmidt went on, they would only undertake dependent employment unwillingly and under compulsion. To remould them 'overnight' was not possible; it would require 'a new generation to grow up'. And although the Nama was the 'worst, laziest and falsest native of all the African tribes, he must also be the cleverest and the most cunning'. He would therefore 'attempt again and again to throw off the yoke that we have to impose on him if German South West Africa is to be a German colony for whites.' Thus Schmidt believed that policy should not be determined by '*Humanitätsduselei*' ('sloppy humanitarian sentimentalism') but must be 'utilitarian', and above all 'must be applied against the constant danger in the south, the Bondel locations, before it is again too late, and we are again those who have to suffer and pay the price'.

> But if the government does not wish to make use of what may well be a two-edged sword by compulsorily relocating them to the north of the colony, the only way out that would remain, with extremely doubtful prospects of success, would be to pay the *Kaptein* and the Big Men of the Bondels high annual salaries ... and to provide the other Hottentots in the locations with sufficient food and clothing, without requiring them to work for wages (railway construction etc.). Leaving them sitting hungry in the locations will arouse thoughts of *orlog* [war].[216]

Hintrager explicitly backed Schmidt's proposals, as did von Heydebreck, the head of the Territorial Police. Hintrager prophesied that the Bondelswart locations in the south would never 'calm down', and expressed himself in favour of 'removing' them. He thought, however, that it was still too soon to do this, as the railway to Kalkfontein needed to be completed first; without it 'no secure transportation of the prisoners would be possible'. Even then it would still be difficult to capture them all. The planned 'transplantation' of the Bondelswarts was not to be compared with the resettlement of the Khauas and Swartbooi Nama, as they had been defeated and leaderless, whereas the former were 'undefeated' and had learnt that 'one could break treaties with the German government with impunity', and so would 'not submit so easily to their fate'. For the moment, therefore, there was no alternative but simply to maintain an increased level of watchfulness in order to avoid being taken by surprise. So the police had been instructed 'to maintain active patrol operations with all the forces they have available', military and police operations on a largish scale being important so that the Bondelswarts would 'get used to the massing of largish assemblies of troops' such as those that would be required to 'settle the Bondel issue'.[217] Thus both Hintrager and von Heydebreck were protagonists of the planned resettlement, which was only prevented for the time being by their realistic assessment of their own weakness.

Despite Hintrager's coming down on the side of postponement, Schmidt put his proposal forward again a month later, as the last two years had shown 'that leniency does not get you anywhere with the Hottentots', and that only 'just severity' and deportation to the north could bring about a change for the better with 'this degenerate, workshy and untruthful nation'. Peace in Namaland would not be secured 'until the last Hottentot has been removed to the north of the colony'. But for every Nama sent north, a Herero would have to be sent south, sinceAfricans were required as workers there too.

> A systematic and purposefully executed removal of the yellow and black peoples of the colony from their locations will do more to ensure peace in the country than any amount of support and compensation for the war, the granting of which in my opinion would not unjustifiably meet with bitter resistance among a large part of the white population of the colony.[218]

It is noticeable that these plans related above all to the Bondelswarts and the Nama of Berseba – that is to say, to two ethnic groups in the south whose social organization had not been destroyed in the Herero and Nama War. Their concentration in autonomous settlement areas – a situation that in respect of the Herero and most of the Nama had been done away with by the Native Ordinances – provoked equal levels of anxiety among settlers, civil administrators and army officers, even though the Administration was well aware that there was no real threat to German rule. And so the resettlement plans that had first found expression during the war were revived again, and the general feeling of agitation that had arisen among large parts of the administration and the settler population as a result of the unrest of 1908–09 served as a pretext for people such as Schmidt and Hintrager to put the status quo in the south into question.

It was only a few days later that Schmidt seized the opportunity to implement his resettlement plans, at least on a small scale. Those affected were the Stuurmann people, a small group of forty-two Africans, including thirteen women and nine children,[219] who lived at Spitzkopp, some 25 km to the east of Keetmanshoop. There were general complaints from the farmers living nearby that the Stuurmann people were reluctant to work. When seven men left their workplaces without permission and did not come back, District Officer Schmidt of Keetmanshoop suspected that they had been involved in the raids perpetrated by Abraham Rolf, even though, as he himself admitted, he had no evidence of this.[220] As the Stuurmann people continued to be 'recalcitrant and insolent'[221] – an expression often used by both officials and settlers if Africans did not immediately comply with all the orders given them or expressed annoyance with them – Schmidt considered 'the situation, after all that has gone before, to be worrying enough' to justify 'an application for the whole location to be taken into custody'.[222] This was approved by the Governor's Office. As Hintrager also assessed 'the situation to be critical and rapid action to be necessary', the Keetmanshoop District Office, with his approval, requisitioned a Schutztruppe unit consisting of one officer and thirty men, who on 17 February 1909 arrested the whole werf, eighty people in all.[223] In addition to the Stuurmann people, these included the thirty-eight followers of Klein-Hendrik Witbooi (six men, fifteen women and seventeen children) whose deportation had already been called for in October 1908. No one escaped. The Commandant of the Southern Command, who had been asked to provide military assistance, had 'responded to the request for support immediately and most readily'.[224]

Hintrager having felt obliged, in view of the power factor that they represented, to reject the proposal to deport the Bondelswarts and the Berseba Nama put forward by the Keetmanshoop District Officer, Karl Schmidt, the latter now turned to making an example of the Stuurmann and Klein-Hendrik Witbooi people, forcibly displacing them with the Deputy Governor's approval. It seems as if Schmidt, and Hintrager too, had only been waiting for a pretext to be able to take such action. But as it was only such a comparatively small number of Africans that were involved, the question still remains as to what they had done to deserve being treated in this way. In particular, the reference to an immediate threat that could not be eliminated except by rapid action is only explicable against a background of the feeling of insecurity triggered by the Rolf Gang. Schmidt above all took advantage of the unrest in the south in order to be able at long last to implement his plans for the economic exploitation of the population. Security considerations are likely to have been involved as well; but so was his fundamental obsession with the fact that traditional African forms of society and ways of life continued to exist. If one takes into account that Schmidt was one of the few German officials who was fully aware of the extent of the changes that had been wrought among the Africans by the Herero and Nama War, and who therefore considered that some form of desperate resistance was inevitable, his paranoia is explicable. He seems to have been on the lookout everywhere for any signs of the expected 'uprising'. The slightest irregularities, such as people refusing to work or running away from the settlement, immediately took on a degree of significance for him that went far beyond their real nature, assuming the dimensions of a fundamental threat to German colonial rule. This was why he was in favour of eliminating all the reservations and all special conditions applicable to individual ethnicities. In Hintrager he found a superior who thought in similar terms. The Schutztruppe too was only too ready to play its part, as by doing so they could demonstrate their importance for the colony's security, after having failed to prevent the Rolf Gang raids.

Schmidt's action against the Stuurmann and Klein-Hendrik Witbooi people was targeted equally at the Bondelswarts and the Berseba Nama, even though he had been forbidden to resettle them. He therefore notified the District Offices at Berseba and Warmbad of the dissolution of the Stuurmann werf, so that they could inform the local African population 'in order to avoid any alarm'.[225] This circumlocution was a euphemism for the intimidatory effect the measure was intended to have on the Bondelswarts and Berseba Nama. According to Hintrager's report, they were told that the deportation had taken place 'because the Stuurmann Hottentots had behaved recalcitrantly and rebelliously'.[226] This made it unmistakably clear to them that the same could happen to them at any time if their conduct was contrary to what the German colonial 'masters' desired.

But Schmidt's own actions in connection with the deportation of Klein-Hendrik Witbooi and his people reveal an odd combination of drastic measures that appeared to him to be justified for reasons of security policy, as he saw it, and a strongly legalistic attitude to less important points of private law connected with the resettlement. When the followers of Klein-Hendrik Witbooi were deported, their livestock was left behind; but in contrast to what happened to the animals left behind by the Stuurmann people, which became the property of the military, he obtained permission from the Governor's Office to sell the livestock and send the proceeds to Grootfontein District Office, which could then use the money to buy livestock for Klein-Hendrik Witbooi's people.[227] Hintrager having given permission for this,[228] the Africans' property was auctioned and the proceeds amounting to 729 marks were sent – after the deduction of postage – to Grootfontein.[229] There the money was initially held in safekeeping, since Klein-Hendrik Witbooi had expressed the wish that the purchase of livestock should be delayed 'until there is an opportunity to buy it cheaply'.[230]

Schmidt thus made fine distinctions with regard to the ownership rights of the livestock. The Witbooi had been deported, it was true; but it was not his intention, in terms of the rule of law, to expropriate them. Such 'correct' procedure in relatively subsidiary matters, at the same time as a brutal and ruthless policy was being implemented that would occasion far more harm to those concerned than the loss of their livestock could ever have done, no doubt gave the officials involved a feeling that they were acting impartially and fairly, thus enabling them to deceive themselves with regard to the impact of their own actions.

The subsequent fate of the deportees took on the character of a self-fulfilling prophecy: the Africans expelled from Spitzkopp offered resistance to their resettlement, which the German side immediately took as proof of how dangerous they were, providing justification for the claim that it was essential to banish them to other German colonies. Having been resettled to Grootfontein because 'they had behaved extremely mutinously and had threatened to run away',[231] they refused to accept their fate without resistance, particularly as on top of everything else the so-called 'ringleaders' among them had been punished.[232] 'Despite the strict supervision' that they were subjected to in Grootfontein, they had attempted to break out shortly after their arrival, an attempt 'that could only be prevented by virtue of a lucky chance'. Because of the 'primitive conditions of their accommodation', a 'permanently strong guard' was necessary, which demanded a 'disproportionate' amount of manpower and accordingly occasioned high costs. Despite all this trouble and expense, however, even the Governor's Office itself did not believe that it would be able 'to prevent the escape of some individuals among these natives'. And now the Administration in Grootfontein also began to fear that 'trouble would be fermented among natives who have been peaceful up until now', and therefore applied for them to be deported to Cameroon, Togo or East Africa. This was a measure that von Schuckmann too considered to be 'absolutely essential in the interests of security'.

In the meantime the Veldskoendraer Nama, a total of forty-four people including twenty men, had also been deported to Grootfontein, which was gradually developing into a collection camp for detained Africans; and as they had 'torn off their leg irons and made a renewed escape attempt in January of that year', they were also to be removed from the country as soon as possible – although the women and children were to be allowed to remain in Grootfontein if they so wished.

Banishment to other colonies was seen as a measure that could enable 'peace to be further safeguarded in the colony at little expense'.[233] But in view of the fact that 'the Witbooi Hottentots who had been banished to Togo and Cameroon previously had suffered very much under the climatic conditions, an issue that was also taken up by the press', Colonial Secretary Dernburg did not consider it to be 'advisable' to deport them there. He did, however, agree to address an inquiry to the Governor of German East Africa.[234]

But Governor von Rechenberg refused to accept the prisoners for precisely the same reasons that the Government of South West Africa had given for wanting to deport them. Precisely because they were so dangerous, and would attempt to escape from their captivity in East Africa as well, he came down against deportation; the prisons in German East Africa too were 'still very primitive and cramped', so that it would not be possible to guard the prisoners securely. But he saw any escape as being a threat to German rule there, as the Nama knew how to handle weapons and had successfully resisted German rule for years. The renown that they had acquired as a result, von Rechenberg feared, would also exert an 'unfavourable and very dangerous influence' on other prisoners, and if they should succeed in escaping it would encourage the local African population also to practise resistance to German rule:

> If disaffected elements who continue to view the ending of German rule as something to be worth striving for learn from the mouths of eyewitnesses that the Germans had to fight for several years – and by no means always successfully – against a few tribes that taken all together made up no more people than the Wachagga alone, then in view of how easily the imaginations of the Negro tribes precisely in Moshi District are stimulated, this could have consequences for which I cannot bear the responsibility. Our power in the colony is largely based on the fact that the natives have not yet begun to realize what strength in numbers they possess. Those Hottentots would be just the people to teach them.[235]

As Dernburg too now associated himself with von Rechenberg's 'serious misgivings' with regard to a transfer of the Stuurmann and Veldskoendraer Nama to German East Africa,[236] the idea of deporting them there was dropped. But Hintrager was not prepared to allow the matter to rest there, and in March 1910, after a further escape attempt, he addressed himself once again to the Imperial Colonial Office, reminding it that South West Africa had accepted people banished from Cameroon, and requesting it to 'free the colony from the danger that these Hottentot prisoners represent to the territory'.[237]

By exaggerating how dangerous the Stuurmann people were in order to justify their deportation, the German Administration succeeded in demonizing this rather insignificant and by no means dangerous group – their original offence having been only a matter of running away to escape the obligation to work, and in any case, the people who were deported were precisely those who had not run away – to the extent that ultimately they were presented as being a potential threat not only to the South West Africa colony but to East Africa as well.

Thanks to Hintrager's insistence, the Imperial Colonial Office ultimately agreed to the Africans' deportation. Despite Dernburg's earlier reservations, it was Cameroon they were now sent to after all. The impact on the deportees was just as devastating as it had been on the Witbooi Nama six years before. Only a few months after the arrival of the ninety-three Nama (twenty-six men, forty women and twenty-seven children),[238] eleven had died and forty were in hospital. This led the Governor of Cameroon to demand that the survivors should be sent back, but Hintrager refused to accept them. By August 1912 fifty-six of the deportees were already dead, and after the case had attracted the attention of the Reichstag and the parliament had adopted a resolution calling upon the Chancellor to send the survivors back home, the Imperial Colonial Office at last instructed the Government in Windhoek to arrange for their return.[239] Thus after three years of deportation, a human tragedy was finally brought to an end that had actually begun quite harmlessly with the flight of seven men from Spitzkopp, without there being any evidence of their having taken part in any raids. Despite the fact that each such deportation had ended with the deaths of many of the displaced people, the Colonial Government still favoured banishment as a form of punishment for undesirable Africans. As deportation to the other German colonies in Africa was no longer viewed as practicable, new plans provided for the creation of a penal colony in the South Pacific instead.[240] But these plans came to nothing due to the outbreak of the First World War.

Schmidt and Hintrager had been serious in their intention to resettle the Herero and Nama, as is demonstrated by the example of the Stuurmann people. The Bondelswarts came to experience this as well, as their resettlement was only postponed. When the First World War broke out their deportation to the north was set in train.[241] Although there had been no change in the power relationships, the emergency situation meant that all misgivings were now set aside.

Notes

1. IGW, Circular to DOs, 13 May 1907, NAW ZBU W.III.A.1. Vol. 1, 15a–18a.
2. Ibid.
3. Specimen of a Native Register: NAW ZBU W.III.B.3. Vol. 1, 2b–3a.
4. Specimen of a travel pass: NAW ZBU W.III.B.3. Vol. 1, 71a–72b.
5. Gibeon DO to IGW, 19 July 1907, NAW ZBU W.III.A.1. Vol. 1, 38a–40b.
6. Lüderitzbucht DO to IGW, 12 July 1907, NAW ZBU W.III.A.1. Vol. 1, 33a–36a.
7. IGW, *Runderlass zu den Verordnungen betr.die Kontrolle und Paßpflicht der Eingeborenen sowie die Dienst- und Arbeitsverträge mit diesen* [Circulated Decree accompanying the Ordinances concerning the Control of and Pass

Requirement for the Natives and Employment Contracts with them – the 'Native Ordinances'], 18 August 1907, reproduced in DKG 11 (1907), 352–57. The autonomous districts apparently also reported every six months themselves: this case is not set out precisely in the Circulated Decree.

8. Karibib DO to IGW, 26 November 1908, NAW ZBU W.III.A.3. Vol. 1, 52a–59a.
9. IGW, Circular to DOs, 13 May 1907, 15a–18a.
10. Windhoek DO to IGW, 25 November 1908, NAW ZBU W.III.A.3. Vol. 1, 60a–69a. Emphases in the original (underlining).
11. Swakopmund DO to IGW, 24 November 1908, NAW ZBU W.III.A.3. Vol. 1, 47a–51a.
12. Rafalski, *Vom Niemandsland zum Ordnungsstaat*, 88.
13. The last point is not unambiguously clear from the letter. Lüderitzbucht DO to IGW, 15 February 1910, NAW ZBU W.III.A.3. Vol. 1, 138a–140b.
14. Gobabis DO to IGW, 17 June 1907, NAW ZBU W.III.A.1. Vol. 1, 30a–31b.
15. IGW to Keetmanshoop DO, 6 September 1907, NAW ZBU W.III.A.1. Vol. 1, Bl.71a–72a.
16. IGW to CSW, 31 August 1907, NAW ZBU W.III.F.4. Vol. 1, 9a–10b.
17. IGW, *Verordnung betr. den Verkehr in und nach dem Amboland* [Ordinance concerning Movements within and to Ovamboland – the 'Ovamboland Ordinance'], 25 January 1906, reproduced in DKG 10 (1906), 25–27. IGW, *Ausführungsverfügung zur Verordnung, betr. den Verkehr in und nach dem Amboland* [Implementation Regulations to the Ovamboland Ordinance], reproduced ibid., 27–30.
18. Namutoni DO to Grootfontein DO, 1 July 1909, NAW ZBU W.III.A.3. Vol. 1, 111a–114a.
19. IGW, *Verordnung betr. die Paßpflicht der Eingeborenen* [Ordinance concerning the Pass Requirement for Natives – the 'Pass Ordinance'], 18 August 1907, in DKG 11 (1907), 347–50.
20. Namutoni DO to Grootfontein DO, 1 November 1908, NAW ZBU W.III.A.3. Vol. 1, 73a–77a.
21. Lüderitzbucht DO to IGW, 1 July 1908, NAW ZBU W.III.A.3. Vol. 1, 7a–23a.
22. Swakopmund DO to IGW, 24 November 1908, NAW ZBU W.III.A.3. Vol. 1, 47a–51a.
23. Bethanie DO to IGW, 20 November 1908, NAW ZBU W.III.A.3. Vol. 1, 70a–71b.
24. Windhoek DO to IGW, 25 November 1908, NAW ZBU W.III.A.3. Vol. 1, 60a–69a.
25. Keetmanshoop DO to IGW, 24 May 1909, NAW ZBU W.III.A.3. Vol. 1, 106a–107a.
26. Sesfontein DO to IGW, 1 July 1908, NAW ZBU W.III.A.3. Vol. 1, 2a–6a.
27. Rehoboth DO to IGW, 28 October 1908, NAW ZBU W.III.A.3. Vol. 1, 36a–41a.
28. Gibeon DO to IGW, 23 October 1908, NAW ZBU W.III.A.3. Vol. 1, 33a–34b.
29. Outjo DO to IGW, 27 May 1907, NAW ZBU W.III.A.1. Vol. 1, 21a–24a.
30. Outjo DO to IGW, 28 November 1908, NAW ZBU W.III.A.3. Vol. 1, 72a.
31. Memorandum of Hintrager's, 4 March 1910, NAW ZBU W.III.A.3. Vol. 1, 164a.
32. IGW, Circular to DOs, 5 March 1910, NAW ZBU W.III.A.3. Vol. 1, 165a.

33. IGW, Pass Ordinance, 18 August 1907.
34. Gibeon DO to IGW, 23 October 1908, NAW ZBU W.III.A.3. Vol. 1, 33a–34b.
35. Keetmanshoop DO to IGW, 3 November 1908, NAW ZBU W.III.A.3. Vol. 1, 45a.
36. The registers, travel passes and employment logbooks had not yet arrived on 1 July 1908. Lüderitzbucht DO to IGW, 1 July 1908, NAW ZBU W.III.A.3. Vol. 1, 7a–23a.
37. Note by IGW on an inquiry about the materials from Gibeon DO, February 1908, NAW ZBU W.III.B.3. Vol. 1, 14a.
38. IGW, Circular to DOs, June 1908, NAW ZBU W.III.B.3. Vol. 1, 22a–23a.
39. On the requirements for, and deliveries of, pass tokens, employment logbooks etc., see Table A.2 in the Appendix.
40. IGW, Circular to DOs, June 1908.
41. Omaruru DO to IGW, 25 July 1908, NAW ZBU W.III.B.3. Vol. 1, 43a. Swakopmund DO to IGW, 13 October 1908, NAW ZBU W.III.B.3. Vol. 1, 49a. Lüderitzbucht DO to IGW, 28 May 1909, NAW ZBU W.III.B.3. Vol. 1, 61a. Rehoboth DO to IGW, 7 September 1911, NAW ZBU W.III.B.3. Vol. 1, 66a.
42. IGW, Circular to DOs except Lüderitzbucht and Sesfontein, 17 October 1908, NAW ZBU W.III.A.3. Vol. 1, 24a.
43. Windhoek DO to IGW, 22 October 1908, NAW ZBU W.III.A.3. Vol. 1, 25a.
44. Keetmanshoop DO to IGW, 24 May 1909, NAW ZBU W.III.A.3. Vol. 1, 106a–107a.
45. IGW, Circulated Order, 20 January 1912, NAW ZBU W.III.B.4. Vol. 1, 2a.
46. Okahandja DO to IGW, 13 February 1912, NAW ZBU W.III.B.4. Vol. 1, 6a.
47. Okahandja DO to IGW, 10 April 1912, NAW ZBU W.III.B.4. Vol. 1, 17a–18b.
48. Maltahöhe DO to IGW, 17 February 1912, NAW ZBU W.III.B.4. Vol. 1, 11a.
49. Warmbad DO to IGW, 22 March 1912, NAW ZBU W.III.B.4. Vol. 1, 16a.
50. There also appear to have been problems with information processing within the Governor's Office, as can be seen from the sometimes chaotic files; correspondence that belongs together can be found in different file volumes. This will certainly not have been helpful towards obtaining a quick overview.
51. CSW to IGW, 27 August 1907, NAW ZBU W.III.F.4. Vol. 1, 8a f.
52. Swakopmund DO to the local commandant of the Schutztruppe, Swakopmund (transcript), 19 July 1907, NAW ZBU W.III.F.4. Vol. 1, 2b.
53. CSW to IGW, 12 August 1907, NAW ZBU W.III.F.4. Vol. 1, 4a f.
54. See the correspondence between Swakopmund DO, the local commandant of the Schutztruppe, Swakopmund, CSW and IGW, 25 July – 13 September 1907, NAW ZBU W.III.F.4. Vol. 1, 1a–12b.
55. CSW to IGW, 12 August 1907.
56. Ibid.
57. Ibid.
58. IGW to CSW, 31 August 1907, NAW ZBU W.III.F.4. Vol. 1, 9a–10b.
59. IGW, Circular to DOs, 13 September 1907, NAW ZBU W.III.F.4. Vol. 1, 12a f. In addition, the police were instructed 'that if they have to negotiate with natives who are accommodated at military werfs, they should inform the

officer or military person entrusted with the supervision of the werf of this in good time'.

60. CSW to IGW, 4 September 1907, NAW ZBU W.III.F.4. Vol. 1, 11a.

61. CSW to IGW, 25 January 1912, NAW ZBU W.III.F.4. Vol. 1, 13a f.

62. Windhoek DO to IGW, 25 November 1908, NAW ZBU W.III.A.3. Vol. 1, 60a–69a.

63. Ibid. The District Office pointed out that 'natives are regularly required … to produce their travel passes when they leave the District'. On the other hand, 'the handing in of the travel pass and pass token in the cases prescribed by the Ordinance [had] not yet become second nature to the natives. Here too, it would be desirable if the white masters would do more to cooperate.'

64. Gobabis District Commandant to IGW, 15 October 1900, NAW ZBU W.III.B.1. Vol. 1, 3b.

65. Karibib DO to IGW, 26 November 1908, NAW ZBU W.III.A.3. Vol. 1, 52a–59a.

66. Swakopmund DO to IGW, 24 November 1908, NAW ZBU W.III.A.3. Vol. 1, 47a–51a.

67. Windhoek Department of Works to IGW, 7 June 1907, NAW ZBU W.III.B.2. Vol. 1, 5a.

68. Windhoek DO to IGW, 10 June 1907, NAW ZBU W.III.B.2. Vol. 1, 6a–7a. Emphasis (underlining) in the original.

69. Gobabis DO to IGW, 31 October 1908, NAW ZBU W.III.A.3. Vol. 1, 42a.

70. Keetmanshoop DO to IGW, 24 May 1909, NAW ZBU W.III.A.3. Vol. 1, 106a–107a.

71. Lüderitzbucht DO to IGW, 1 July 1908, NAW ZBU W.III.A.3. Vol. 1, 7a–23a.

72. Karibib DO to IGW, 26 November 1908, NAW ZBU W.III.A.3. Vol. 1, 52a–59a.

73. Bethanie DO to IGW, 10 January 1910, NAW ZBU W.III.A.3. Vol. 1, 131a–133a.

74. Only Grootfontein DO reported that it was the Master and Servant Ordinance that 'had best proved itself by a long chalk', since both sides had recognized the advantages accruing to them from it. Grootfontein DO to IGW, 24 October 1908, NAW ZBU W.III.A.3. Vol. 1, 43a–44a.

75. Gibeon DO to IGW, 23 October 1908, NAW ZBU W.III.A.3. Vol. 1, 33a–34b.

76. Bethanie DO to IGW, 10 January 1910.

77. Grootfontein DO to IGW, 26 August 1907, NAW ZBU W.III.A.1. Vol. 1, 69a–70a.

78. Namutoni DO to Grootfontein DO, 1 November 1908, NAW ZBU W.III.A.3. Vol. 1, 73a–77a.

79. Namutoni DO to Grootfontein DO, 1 January 1909, NAW ZBU W.III.A.1. Vol. 1, 79a–82a.

80. Namutoni DO to Grootfontein DO, 1 July 1909, NAW ZBU W.III.A.3. Vol. 1, 111b–114a.

81. Namutoni DO to Grootfontein DO, 1 November 1908, NAW ZBU W.III.A.1. Vol. 1, 73a–77a.

82. Sesfontein DO to IGW, 1 October 1909, NAW ZBU W.III.A.3. Vol. 1, 115a–118a.

83. Maltahöhe DO to Gibeon DO, 1 April 1909, NAW ZBU W.III.A.3. Vol. 1, 101a–105a.

84. Bethanie DO to IGW, 20 November 1908, NAW ZBU W.III.A.3. Vol. 1, 70a–71b.
85. Maltahöhe DO to Gibeon DO, 2 January 1909, NAW ZBU W.III.A.3. Vol. 1, 101a–105a.
86. Lüderitzbucht DO to IGW, 8 March 1909, NAW ZBU W.III.A.3. Vol. 1, 83a–92a.
87. Namutoni DO to Grootfontein DO, 1 July 1909, NAW ZBU W.III.A.3. Vol. 1, 111a–114a.
88. And it was not just a matter of a few individual cases. For the years 1911 and 1912 alone (for which we have official figures), the statistics record more than 3,500 cases in which Africans had deserted their workplaces. *Die deutschen Schutzgebiete*, Vol. 4, 1912/13, Statistical Section, 50–51.
89. IGW, Circulated Order to DOs and Police Barracks, 26 January 1911, NAW ZBU W.III.B.5. Vol. 1, 8a f.
90. Letters in response from the DOs of Windhoek, Karibib, Omaruru, Grootfontein, Bethanie, Outjo, Gobabis, Lüderitzbucht, Okahandja, Keetmanshoop and Hasuur, 14 February – 16 March 1911, NAW ZBU W.III.B.5. Vol. 1, 9a–24a.
91. Windhoek DO to IGW, 14 February 1911, NAW ZBU W.III.B.5. Vol. 1, 9a–10a.
92. Ibid.
93. Grootfontein DO to IGW, 16 February 1911, NAW ZBU W.III.B.5. Vol. 1, 12a.
94. Karibib DO to IGW, 15 February 1911, NAW ZBU W.III.B.5. Vol. 1, 11a f.
95. Okahandja DO to IGW, 8 March 1911, NAW ZBU W.III.B.5. Vol. 1, 18a f.
96. IGW, Section F (Native Affairs), to Governor, 6 May 1911, NAW ZBU W.III.B.5. Vol. 1, 26a–27b.
97. IGW, Circulated Order to DOs, 29 March 1911, NAW ZBU W.III.B.1. Vol. 1, 26a.
98. So reported by the clerical officer, von Schwerin. IGW, internal memorandum of von Schwerin, 24 January 1911, NAW ZBU W.III.B.1. Vol. 1, 21a–22b.
99. Ibid.
100. IGW to Pastor Olpp, 9 March 1911, NAW ZBU W.III.B.1. Vol. 1, 23a f.
101. Pastor Olpp to IGW, 13 March 1911, NAW ZBU W.III.B.1. Vol. 1, 24a f.
102. IGW, Circulated Order to DOs, 29 March 1911, NAW ZBU W.III.B.1. Vol. 1, 26a.
103. IGW to Outjo DO, 9 April 1912, NAW ZBU W.III.B.1. Vol. 1, 30a.
104. IGW, Circulated Order to DOs, 25 June 1912, NAW ZBU W.III.B.1. Vol. 1, 34a f. This contains the reference to the Instruction of 29 March 1912. Why the Instruction had to be repeated is not known.
105. IGW to a farmer named von Gossler, chairman of the *Landwirtschaftlicher Verein* (Farmers' Association) of Okahandja, 31 December 1912, NAW ZBU W.III.B.1. Vol. 1, 36a.
106. Outjo DO to IGW, 4 March 1912, NAW ZBU W.III.B.1. Vol. 1, 29a. The fact that these remarks also reflected the opinion of the Colonial Government can be deduced from the comment 'very true' in the margin.
107. Waterberg Farmers' Association to IGW, 2 February 1913, NAW ZBU W.III.B.1. Vol. 1, 37a.

108. Gobabis Farmers' Association to IGW, 9 February 1913, NAW ZBU W.III.B.1. Vol. 1, 39a.
109. Okahandja Farmers' Association to IGW, 16 December 1912, NAW ZBU W.III.B.1. Vol. 1, 35a.
110. Gobabis Farmers' Association to IGW, 9 February 1913.
111. Gobabis DO to IGW, 25 February 1913, NAW ZBU W.III.B.1. Vol. 1, 39b.
112. Grootfontein Farmers' Association to Territorial Council, 1 September 1913, NAW ZBU W.III.B.1. Vol. 1, 41a.
113. IGW to Grootfontein Farmers' Association, 24 November 1913, NAW ZBU W.III.B.1. Vol. 1, 42a.
114. On this point, see also Prein, *Guns*, 106–7.
115. Drechsler, *Südwestafrika* I, 201–6.
116. They were being investigated in a case of misappropriation. Warmbad DO to Keetmanshoop DO, 9 April 1908, NAW ZBU *Geheimakten* (Classified Documents) VIII.K. Vol. 2, 18a.
117. Keetmanshoop DO to SSC, Keetmanshoop, 30 March 1908, NAW ZBU *Geheimakten* VIII.K. Vol. 2, 14b.
118. Drechsler, *Südwestafrika* I, 229.
119. Grootfontein DO to IGW, 10 March 1909, NAW ZBU *Geheimakten* VIII.K. Vol. 1, 251a.
120. Keetmanshoop DO to SSC, Keetmanshoop, 30 March 1908.
121. Arrest warrant, Keetmanshoop DO, 24 April 1908, NAW ZBU *Geheimakten* VIII.K. Vol. 2, 19a–20b.
122. IGW to ICO, 6 January 1909, NAW ZBU *Geheimakten* VIII.K. Vol. 1, 86a. Klein-Jacobus Christian was killed before this could be done: he was shot trying to escape while still in the Cape Colony. IGW to Keetmanshoop DO (telegram), 23 December 1908, NAW ZBU *Geheimakten* VIII.K. Vol. 2, 32a.
123. ITP to Outjo DO, 26 December 1908, NAW ZBU *Geheimakten* VIII.K. Vol. 1, 69a f.
124. Keetmanshoop DO to IGW, 22 December 1908, NAW ZBU *Geheimakten* VIII.K. Vol. 1, 20a–28b.
125. Record of the testimony of the Baster Joseph Isaak, taken down in Ukamas, 31 December 1908, NAW ZBU *Geheimakten* VIII.K. Vol. 1, 135a–136a.
126. Keetmanshoop DO to IGW, 22 December 1908, NAW ZBU *Geheimakten* VIII.K. Vol. 1, 20a–28b.
127. SSC, Keetmanshoop, *Bericht über die Operationen gegen die Bande Abraham Rolfs im Dezember 1908* [Report on the Operations against the Abraham Rolf Gang in December 1908 – the 'Rolf Gang Report'] (transcript), 5 April 1909, NAW ZBU *Geheimakten* VIII.K. Vol. 1, 199a–206a.
128. Ibid.
129. ITP to Outjo DO, 26 December 1908, NAW ZBU *Geheimakten* VIII.K. Vol. 1, 69a f.
130. SSC, Keetmanshoop, to CSW (transcript of telegram), 28 December 1908, NAW ZBU *Geheimakten* VIII.K. Vol. 1, 60a f.
131. ITP to Outjo DO, 26 December 1908.
132. ITP to Gibeon DO, 30 December 1908, NAW ZBU *Geheimakten* VIII.K. Vol. 1, 73a.

133. Outjo DO to IGW (telegram), 26 December 1908, NAW ZBU *Geheimakten* VIII.K. Vol. 1, 68a.
134. Keetmanshoop DO to IGW, 22 December 1908, NAW ZBU *Geheimakten* VIII.K. Vol. 1, 20a–28b.
135. SSC, Keetmanshoop, Rolf Gang Report.
136. Ibid.
137. Ibid. Hintrager too emphasized in his letter to the Imperial Colonial Office the 'salutory impression' that the rapid redeployment of the troops was likely to have made on the Africans. IGW to ICO, 31 December 1908, NAW ZBU *Geheimakten* VIII.K. Vol. 1, 77a–79b. The same applies to Bondelswart Commissioner Ebeling. Bondelswart Commission, Warmbad, to SSC, Keetmanshoop (transcript), 9 February 1909, NAW ZBU *Geheimakten* VIII.K. Vol. 1, 175a–176b.
138. IGW to ICO, 29 December 1908, NAW ZBU *Geheimakten* VIII.K. Vol. 1, 61a.
139. ITP to Gibeon DO, 30 December 1908, NAW ZBU *Geheimakten* VIII.K. Vol. 1, 73a.
140. SSC, Keetmanshoop, to CSW (transcript of telegram), 28 December 1908, NAW ZBU *Geheimakten* VIII.K. Vol. 1, 60a f.
141. Hasuur DO to Keetmanshoop DO (transcript of telegram), 6 January 1909, NAW ZBU *Geheimakten* VIII.K. Vol. 1, II–120a (page number appears twice). This information was provided by the veterinarian Struwe, who had been staying in Rietfontein.
142. SSC, Keetmanshoop, to CSW (transcript of telegram), 28 January 1909, NAW ZBU *Geheimakten* VIII.K. Vol. 1, II–124a (page number appears twice).
143. GCG Cape Town to IGW, 15 March 1909, NAW ZBU *Geheimakten* VIII.K. Vol. 1, 148a–149a.
144. ICO to IGW (telegram), 5 January 1909, NAW ZBU *Geheimakten* VIII.K. Vol. 1, 82a.
145. IGW to ICO, 6 January 1909, NAW ZBU *Geheimakten* VIII.K. Vol. 1, 86a.
146. ICO to IGW (telegram), 8 January 1909, NAW ZBU *Geheimakten* VIII.K. Vol. 1, 95a f.
147. IGW to ICO, 23 December 1908, NAW ZBU *Geheimakten* VIII.K. Vol. 2, 174a–175b.
148. IGW to GCG Cape Town (telegram), 9 January 1909, NAW ZBU *Geheimakten* VIII.K. Vol. 1, 96a.
149. Although Drechsler mentions the extradition proceedings, he does not give any details of the tortuous procedure itself. Drechsler, *Südwestafrika* I, 229–31.
150. IGW to CSW (telegram), 9 January 1909, NAW ZBU *Geheimakten* VIII.K. Vol. 1, 97a f.
151. IGW to the Government of the Cape Colony, 13 February 1909, NAW ZBU *Geheimakten* VIII.K. Vol. 1, 137a–138a.
152. GCG Cape Town to IGW, 29 April 1909, NAW ZBU *Geheimakten* VIII.K. Vol. 1, 265a–266a.
153. IGW to GCG Cape Town (telegram), 3 May 1909, NAW ZBU *Geheimakten* VIII.K. Vol. 1, 195a.

154. GCG Cape Town to IGW, 29 June 1909, NAW ZBU *Geheimakten* VIII.K. Vol. 2, 74a–75a.

155. 'Relied on British Justice. Armed Hottentots' Offence Near Border', *South African News*, 10 June 1909. Article retrieved from NAW ZBU *Geheimakten* VIII.K. Vol. 2, 76a f. Quoted in the original English.

156. GCG Cape Town to IGW, 29 June 1909, NAW ZBU *Geheimakten* VIII.K. Vol. 2, 74a–75a. [Translator's note: The consulate general gives the quotation from the judgment in German; it has been retranslated back into English as the original is not available.]

157. At least one person who read this letter in the Governor's Office in Windhoek had his doubts about the degree of objectivity, however, as is revealed by a question mark drawn in the margin.

158. 'Life on German Border. Strange Stories in the Extradition Case', *South African News*, 29 June 1909. Article retrieved from NAW ZBU *Geheimakten* VIII.K. Vol. 2, 80a. Quoted in the original English.

159. Schmidt, testimony given under oath, 17 June 1909, NAW ZBU *Geheimakten* VIII.K. Vol. 2, 59a–60a.

160. IGW to GCG Cape Town, 18 June 1909, NAW ZBU *Geheimakten* VIII.K. Vol. 1, 286a f.

161. Heydebreck's testifying in person is mentioned in 'Was it War? A Troublous Territory', *Cape Times*, 3 July 1909. Article retrieved from NAW ZBU *Geheimakten* VIII.K. Vol. 2, 95a. The sending of the two written testimonies given under oath had not been enough to satisfy the judicial authorities in Cape Town, as the counsel defending Rolf and his men had demanded that a German adminstrative or military officer with a good knowledge of the situation in the south should be sent to Cape Town as a witness. GCG Cape Town to IGW (telegram), 23 June 1909, NAW ZBU *Geheimakten* VIII.K. Vol. 1, 287a.

162. Heydebreck, Cape Town, to IGW, 6 July 1909, NAW ZBU *Geheimakten* VIII.K. Vol. 2, 92a.

163. GCG Cape Town to IGW, 30 June 1909, NAW ZBU *Geheimakten* VIII.K. Vol. 2, 93a–94b. The proceedings against two of the accused were suspended because they were too ill to take part in the trial and had to be moved to an area with a healthier climate. What became of the other three is not apparent from the documents.

164. Heydebreck to IGW (telegram), 18 July 1909, NAW ZBU *Geheimakten* VIII.K. Vol. 2, 84a–86a.

165. GCG Cape Town to prosecuting counsel Nightingale, 17 August 1909, NAW ZBU *Geheimakten* VIII.K. Vol. 2, 130a–133a. Quoted in the original English.

166. GCG Cape Town to IGW (telegram), 26 August 1909, NAW ZBU *Geheimakten* VIII.K. Vol. 2, 115a.

167. Quoted in the original English according to 'Hottentott Extradiction Case [*sic*]. Court of Appeal's Judgement', *Cape Times*, 27 August 1909. Article retrieved from NAW ZBU *Geheimakten* VIII.K. Vol. 2, 124a.

168. Ibid. Quoted in the original English.

169. This article appeared in *De Zuidafrikaansche Post*, Amsterdam, on 23 October 1909, and extracts from it were reprinted in the *Windhuker Nachrichten*. '*Das Asylrecht der Eingeborenen*' [The Natives' Right of Asylum] in *Windhuker Nachrichten* No. 102 of 22 December 1909 (cutting), NAW ZBU *Geheimakten* VIII.K. Vol. 2, 176b f.

170. Governor von Schuckmann therefore sent the article to the Imperial Colonial Office as confirmation. IGW to ICO, 23 December 1909, NAW ZBU *Geheimakten* VIII.K. Vol. 2, 174a–175b.

171. GCG Cape Town to IGW, 30 August 1909, NAW ZBU *Geheimakten* VIII.K. Vol. 2, 123a f. [Translator's note: The Consulate General gives the quotation from the judgment in German; it has been retranslated back into English as the original is not available.]

172. IGW to Keetmanshoop DO, 16 September 1909, NAW ZBU *Geheimakten* VIII.K. Vol. 2, 125a.

173. Keetmanshoop DO to IGW, 22 May 1909, NAW ZBU *Geheimakten* VIII.K. Vol. 1, 272a f.

174. IGW to Gibeon DO and to Kub and Kupferberg Police Barracks (telegram), 4 October 1909, NAW ZBU *Geheimakten* VIII.K. Vol. 2, 157a–158a.

175. Lüderitzbucht DO to IGW (telegram), 2 October 1909, NAW ZBU *Geheimakten* VIII.K. Vol. 2, 148a.

176. Death sentence, IGW, 9 October 1909, NAW ZBU *Geheimakten* VIII.K. Vol. 2, 151a f. This is the confirmation of the sentence by IGW.

177. IGW to Keetmanshoop DO, 9 October 1909, NAW ZBU *Geheimakten* VIII.K. Vol. 2, 151a.

178. Keetmanshoop DO to IGW (telegram), 13 October 1909, NAW ZBU *Geheimakten* VIII.K. Vol. 2, 153a.

179. IGW to Keetmanshoop DO, 19 October 1909, NAW ZBU *Geheimakten* VIII.K. Vol. 2, 155b–156b.

180. Keetmanshoop DO to IGW, 23 January 1910, NAW ZBU *Geheimakten* VIII.K. Vol. 2, 170a.

181. Keetmanshoop DO to IGW, 7 October 1909, NAW ZBU *Geheimakten* VIII.K. Vol. 2, 149a f.

182. IGW to ICO, 1 March 1910, NAW ZBU *Geheimakten* VIII.K. Vol. 2, 189a–191b.

183. Ibid.

184. Government of the Cape Colony to IGW, 20 April 1910, NAW ZBU *Geheimakten* VIII.K. Vol. 2, 205a.

185. IGW to GCG Cape Town, 23 May 1910, NAW ZBU *Geheimakten* VIII.K. Vol. 2, 206a.

186. Bondelswart Commission, Warmbad, to SSC, Keetmanshoop (transcript), 9 February 1909, NAW ZBU *Geheimakten* VIII.K. Vol. 1, 175a–176b.

187. Ibid. Ebeling was one of those who had been in favour of Rolf's extradition.

188. SSC, Keetmanshoop, to CSW (transcript of telegram), 28 January 1909, NAW ZBU *Geheimakten* VIII.K. Vol. 1, II–124a (page number appears twice).

189. Farmer Dr Kaempfer, Deutsche Erde, to Gibeon DO (transcript), 21 January 1909, NAW ZBU *Geheimakten* VIII.K. Vol. 1, 144a–145b. Gibeon DO also forwarded the letter to SSC, Keetmanshoop, ibid., 142a.

190. Gibeon DO to IGW, 26 March 1909, NAW ZBU *Geheimakten* VIII.K. Vol. 1, 261a f.

191. Gibeon DO to IGW, 18 April 1909, NAW ZBU W.III.A.3. Vol. 1, 95a–100a.

192. Keetmanshoop DO to IGW, 19 March 1909, NAW ZBU *Geheimakten* VIII.K. Vol. 2, 39a–41b.

193. On similar reactions among settlers in South Africa, see Krikler, 'Social Neurosis'.

194. Trainer, Warmbad, to SSC, Keetmanshoop (transcript), 23 May 1909, NAW ZBU *Geheimakten* VIII.K. Vol. 2, 70a f.

195. Government of the Cape Colony to IGW, 4 June 1909, NAW ZBU *Geheimakten* VIII.K. Vol. 2, 64a.

196. IGW to CSW, 19 June 1909, NAW ZBU *Geheimakten* VIII.K. Vol. 2, 72a–73a.

197. Ibid.

198. 1st Company, Arahoab, to SNC, Windhoek (transcript), 7 December 1910, NAW ZBU *Geheimakten* VII.D. Vol. 1, 25a f.

199. Document attached to: 1st Company to SNC, 7 December 1910, 26a f.

200. 1st Company to SNC, 7 December 1910, 25a f.

201. CSW to IGW, 30 December 1910, NAW ZBU *Geheimakten* VII.D. Vol. 1, 24a.

202. IGW to CSW, 11 January 1911, NAW ZBU *Geheimakten* VII.D. Vol. 1, 27a f.

203. Drechsler, *Südwestafrika* I, 235.

204. Report on the Patrol of 29 August – 5 September 1912, First Lieutenant Kirchheim (transcript), 9 September 1912, NAW ZBU *Geheimakten* VIII.I. Vol. 3, 69a–77a.

205. SSC, Keetmanshoop, to CSW (memorandum of telephone message), 27 September 1912, NAW ZBU *Geheimakten* VIII.I. Vol. 3, 79a.

206. Gibeon DO to SSC, Keetmanshoop (transcript of telegram), 1 October 1912, NAW ZBU *Geheimakten* VIII.I. Vol. 3, 83a f.

207. IGW to Rehoboth DO, 16 August 1909, NAW BRE E.3.E., 7a f.

208. Rehoboth DO, Circulated Decree to the Police Stations, 25 October 1909, NAW BRE E.3.E., 9a.

209. IGW to ICO, 8 February 1910, BAL R 1001/8086, 149a–150a.

210. IGW, Circulated Order to DOs, 24 October 1911, NAW BRE E.3.E., 10a–11a.

211. Ibid.

212. IGW to ICO, 13 May 1912, BAL R 1001/2087, 86a f.

213. IGW to ICO, 23 December 1908, NAW ZBU *Geheimakten* VIII.K. Vol. 1, 38a–40a.

214. Keetmanshoop DO to IGW, 22 December 1908, NAW ZBU *Geheimakten* VIII.K. Vol. 1, 20a–28b.

215. Ibid.

216. Ibid. Drechsler wrongly ascribes this report of Schmidt's to Hintrager. Drechsler, *Südwestafrika* I, 232–33. But in fact Hintrager had merely forwarded it to the ICO. IGW to ICO, 31 December 1908, NAW ZBU *Geheimakten* VIII.K. Vol. 1, 77a–79b.

217. Ibid. Heydebreck had signed the letter off as well. However, the Governor's Office apparently feared that the Imperial Colonial Office would react negatively to the news that preparations were currently being made to forcibly resettle the Bondelswarts, and so the last sentence was deleted from the draft of the letter again.

218. Keetmanshoop DO to IGW, 25 January 1909, NAW ZBU *Geheimakten* VIII.K. Vol. 1, 215a f.

219. Keetmanshoop DO to IGW, 28 January 1909, NAW ZBU *Geheimakten* VIII.K. Vol. 1, 214a.

220. Ibid. Schmidt himself confirmed that the idea of there being a connection with Rolf was no more than a suspicion of his, and that only the men's extradition could clear the matter up. It is also unclear what led him to the conclusion that they were on British territory.

221. *'widerwillig und frech'* – this is how Hintrager expressed himself in his letter to the Imperial Colonial Office justifying the arrests. He considered it a further indication of how dangerous they were that the seven men had openly declared that they would disregard the German instructions and simply take themselves off if they were not allowed to go to Warmbad on vacation. IGW to ICO, 5 March 1909, NAW ZBU *Geheimakten* VIII.K. Vol. 1, 216a–217b.

222. Keetmanshoop DO to IGW, 18 February 1909, NAW ZBU *Geheimakten* VIII.K. Vol. 1, 243a–244a.

223. IGW to ICO, 5 March 1909.

224. Keetmanshoop DO to IGW, 18 February 1909, NAW ZBU *Geheimakten* VIII.K. Vol. 1, 243a–244a. And on the same date: Keetmanshoop DO to IGW, NAW ZBU *Geheimakten* VIII.K. Vol. 1, 246a–248a.

225. Keetmanshoop DO to IGW, 18 February 1909, NAW ZBU *Geheimakten* VIII.K. Vol. 1, 243a–244a.

226. IGW to ICO, 5 March 1909, NAW ZBU *Geheimakten* VIII.K. Vol. 1, 216a–217b.

227. Keetmanshoop DO to IGW, 19 February 1909, NAW ZBU *Geheimakten* VIII.K. Vol. 1, 249a.

228. IGW to Keetmanshoop DO, 22 March 1909, NAW ZBU *Geheimakten* VIII.K. Vol. 1, 250a.

229. Keetmanshoop DO to IGW, 27 April 1909, NAW ZBU *Geheimakten* VIII.K. Vol. 1, 263a.

230. Grootfontein DO to IGW, 19 June 1909, NAW ZBU *Geheimakten* VIII.K. Vol. 2, 83a.

231. IGW to Grootfontein DO, 19 February 1909, NAW ZBU *Geheimakten* VIII.K. Vol. 1, 242a.

232. IGW to ICO, 26 April 1909, NAW ZBU *Geheimakten* VIII.K. Vol. 2, 61a–62a.

233. Ibid.

234. ICO to IGW, 20 June 1909, NAW ZBU *Geheimakten* VIII.K. Vol. 2, 183a.

235. Governor of German East Africa to ICO (transcript), 24 July 1909, NAW ZBU *Geheimakten* VIII.K. Vol. 2, 187a–188b.

236. ICO to IGW, 20 August 1909, NAW ZBU *Geheimakten* VIII.K. Vol. 2, 186a.

237. IGW to ICO, 1 March 1910, NAW ZBU *Geheimakten* VIII.K. Vol. 2, 189a–191b.
238. Apparently not all of the Stuurmann and Hendrik Witbooi people and Veldskoendraer Nama were deported, or else some of them had already died on the journey or had escaped.
239. Drechsler, *Südwestafrika* I, 234.
240. On this, see the correspondence between IGW, ICO and the Governor of New Guinea. IGW to ICO, 12 August 1913, BAL R 1001/2091, 11a f.

ICO to Governor of New Guinea, 6 November 1913, BAL R 1001/2091, 12a f.

Governor of New Guinea to ICO, 13 March 1914, BAL R 1001/2091, 20a f.

Governor of New Guinea to ICO, 5 June 1914, BAL R 1001/2091, 23a f.
241. In August 1914 the Bondelswarts were taken north in several trainloads, in some cases under inhuman conditions, and were there forced to work on the construction of the Amboland Railway. The missionary Hermann Nyhof was put in charge of taking care of them. These circumstances can be derived from the following letters:

Nyhof to IGW, 5 September 1914, NAW ZBU W.II.F.2. Vol. 1, 188a–189a.
IGW to Nyhof, 9 September 1914, NAW ZBU W.II.F.2. Vol. 1, 190a.
Keetmanshoop DO to IGW, 28 August 1914, NAW ZBU W.II.F.2. Vol. 1, 199a–200b.
Keetmanshoop DO to IGW, 2 September 1914, NAW ZBU W.II.F.2. Vol. 1, 188a–189a.
IGW to Keetmanshoop DO, 9 September14, NAW ZBU W.II.F.2. Vol. 1, 198a.

5

THE LABOUR MARKET
Recruitment and Working Conditions

Native Policy as pursued after the Herero and Nama War did not seek merely to secure German rule, but also aimed to recruit as far as possible the whole of the African population as labour for the colonial economy. The economy was completely dependent upon there being an adequate number of cheap African workers available to work in the mines, to develop the country's infrastructure and to pursue extensive animal husbandry. The recruitment of labour and the regulation of working conditions therefore played a major role within the German Colonial Government's overall Native Policy. The measures employed to obtain workers and those for the surveillance of the Africans were closely linked, interlocking with each other in many ways: control measures assisted recruiting as well, and working Africans were easier to keep under surveillance.

The 'semifree' labour market that was introduced had the aim of gradually replacing the system of mobilizing African manpower on the basis of forced labour with one of 'voluntary' employment. What officialdom wanted was not the forced labourer but the working subject: the man who, having been re-educated to accept the European work ethic, defined himself through his status as a worker. Indirect measures such as the expropriation of the Africans' land, which severely restricted the opportunities for them to pursue independent economic activity other than by selling their labour, together with the legally imposed compulsion to take up employment, ensured that the supply of workers was maintained. But instead of the State having to organize the compulsory allocation of workers to particular employers, it was intended that it should gradually become possible to leave the task of distributing workers, in short supply as they were, to the market forces of supply and demand. The determination of the economic value of an African labourer, as expressed in the level of his wages, was also supposed to take place in an environment of largely free competition between employers. This, however, assumed as a prerequisite that the workers would enjoy the freedom to negotiate, with regard both to the choice of their employer and to the amount of payment.

In order to ensure that the Africans actually did enjoy such liberty to freely negotiate their working conditions, compliance with contracts of employment was to be subject to state control. Such state control was thus intended to be exercised in two directions, aiming to monitor both the workers and the employers; but as a result the Administration found itself subject to two contrary forces: on the one hand its own liberal ideas of the rights of the Africans, and on the other the demands of the Whites for stricter measures of compulsion. Individual officials reacted in quite different ways to this. District Officers interpreted the regulations divergently: some displayed solidarity with the interests of the employers, while others did their best to uphold the rights of the Africans. It depended on these individual attitudes of the administrative officers whether the elements of compulsion or the Africans' right to dispose freely of their labour were able to predominate – or in other words, whether the system tended more in the direction of forced labour or of a 'semifree' labour market.

The decimation of the population in the war of 1904–08 meant that the requirement for labour within the Police Zone could not be met, despite the most rigorous efforts to mobilize as many workers as possible. This shortage, indeed this severe shortage, of labourers continued right up to the end of German colonial rule. In 1911, for example, the gap between supply and demand was estimated at 15,000,[1] equivalent to more than 75 per cent of the working male African population of 23,227.[2] The Administration therefore actively supported the attempts of employers to recruit labourers in Ovamboland and from outside the colony, especially from the British territories that later came to constitute the Union of South Africa. But such migrant workers could provide no more than a minor augmentation to the supply of labour; the number of incoming workers was simply too small.

In addition, the use of migrant labour had some severe drawbacks from the employers' point of view. As it was not possible to exert direct pressure either on the Ovambo or on South African labourers to take up employment, they had to be lured by higher wages. This made labour more expensive. The primary aim therefore remained to meet the requirement for workers from within the Police Zone. During the last years of German colonial rule a relatively constant 70 per cent of the workers employed by Whites originated from there. The rest mostly came from Ovamboland or from South Africa.

This chapter deals in three separate sections with the three main categories of workers: those from the Police Zone, those from Ovamboland and those from South Africa. It was the workers' origins that essentially determined what type of work they would be employed in: while farmworkers came predominantly from the Police Zone, the Ovambo and the South African labourers worked mainly in the diamond and copper mines or on railway construction. The farmworkers were scattered across the whole country in small groups, living for the most part with their families under the watchful eyes of the farmers, whereas the railway construction and mine labourers often lived – several hundred together – at a small number of centres, and were employed under the supervision of White foremen.

The following investigations concentrate in each case on the question of how workers were recruited, and the extent of the role played by the Administration both in this and in the determination of conditions of employment. In particular, the questions of how far the Executive was able or willing to guarantee minimum levels of rights, and whether it fulfilled its duties of supervision, are gone into.

Compared with the South West African workers, the South Africans were more self-assured, more experienced in dealing with White people, and better organized. To the colonizers this represented a particular threat. In 1910 the Schutztruppe shot dead fourteen South African labourers on a railway construction site. As this 'Massacre of Wilhelmstal' attracted international attention, every attempt was made to sweep the details of the event under the carpet. This example is used to show how the Administration reacted to the illegal use of force by its own executive organs.

The Labour Market within the Police Zone

Workers originating from within the Police Zone were by far the most important pillar of the colony's labour economy. The Colonial Government regarded the population of the territory as its property, and therefore did everything it could to prevent people leaving for elsewhere. The view expressed in this proprietorial attitude that the African population represented a purely economic factor was further reflected in the categorization of the African 'tribes' according to what was seen as their 'ability to work' and the amount of work it was possible to extract from each individual.

The essential prerequisite for the 'semifree' labour market was that African workers should be free to choose for whom they wished to work. Only if they were in a position to look for a new employer and also to actually accept a job that was more attractive, whether because the wages were higher or because the working conditions were better, could market forces play their part. The same applied to freedom of movement between the various Districts within the colony. It was above all the higher wages in the mines that were a substantial incentive to workers to leave those areas whose economic structures were purely agrarian; as a result, the farmers in such areas inevitably grumbled about the freedom of movement enshrined in the Native Ordinances. Some District Officers themselves adopted the positions represented by the demands of the agricultural sector and introduced restrictions on freedom of movement. As time went on, the Governor's Office in Windhoek found itself unable to resist this growing pressure.

Fundamental departures from the principle of freedom of movement were to be found on the one hand in the system whereby 'vagrants' were compulsorily assigned to work for a particular employer, and on the other hand in the way 'runaways', Africans who had left their places of work without permission, were returned to them. As some employers, due to the ubiquitous labour shortage, refused to allow their workers to leave their employment, and it proved to be very difficult for Africans to demonstrate that they had given proper notice and had terminated their employment in accordance with the law, the workers quite often simply deserted. This is a clear indication that working conditions were often not such as had been agreed in the employment contract. But by bringing 'runaways' back to their employers, the Administration undermined the Africans' most effective form of resistance.

There certainly were occasions on which officials showed themselves to be in sympathy with the employers of their respective districts in this issue; and this was also a problem in respect of the Administration's duty to exercise supervision over the rights accorded to Africans, whether under the Native Ordinances or in their individual employment contracts. It is not possible, however, to determine how typical such behaviour was, as the only cases that got documented were those in which the Administration saw itself obliged to intervene. Thus the extent to which it basically gave its placet to illegal conduct on the part of the Whites, or simply chose to ignore the abuses and look the other way, remains unclear. But general complaints about abuses in the colony, and indeed documented cases in which the Administration intervened in favour of Africans, show that both kinds of behaviour did exist. Not all German officials by any means were blind accessories to the settlers' interests, as can also be seen from the fact that the employers themselves accused the Administration of disregarding their interests.

Exclusive Recruitment and Utilitarian Assessment

Long before the year 1907, when the Colonial Secretary in Berlin, Bernhard Dernburg, described the 'natives' as the 'most important asset' of the colonies,[3] the first Imperial Administrator, Curt von François, had realized that the Africans were a valuable economic factor and had attempted to prevent workers emigrating to the British territories to the South. Only six years after Germany had taken possession of South West Africa he forbade 'the recruitment of Berg Damaras or other natives of the colony of German South West Africa to be taken out of the territory as labourers, or the causing of such natives to emigrate'.[4] His intention was to put an end to the lucrative trade in labourers that had been strongly promoted since the middle of the century by the Herero chiefs in Omaruru, who received weapons and ammunition from the Cape Colony in exchange for manpower.[5] Behind the official pretext of humanitarian motives – those recruited were only reimbursed the cost of the one-way journey, so many of them could be left stranded in what later became the Union of South Africa – von François was in fact seeking to reserve the labour of the Berg Damara for exclusive use in South West Africa.

In 1901 a new version of the 1891 Ordinance was promulgated. The occasion for this was a Circulated Decree sent out by the Colonial Department of the Foreign Office in Berlin in 1899 in response to cases in which African servants had been taken from the colonies to Germany by their employers, but once there were soon abandoned to their fate. From then on, only such Whites who had entered into an obligation to provide for the maintenance of their employees would be permitted to take them to Germany in this way.[6] The question of forbidding the recruitment of workers for other countries was not dealt with in the Decree: whether or not this was in the German interest remained a matter of dispute. One place where the two opposing views came into collision was in the *Kolonialrat*, a council advising the Colonial Department in Berlin: while some members declared themselves in favour of a prohibition, others such as the lawyer Dr

Scharlach pleaded for 'the greatest possible degree of freedom in the "intercolonial" exchange of workers'.[7] But all this did nothing to modify the fundamental claim of proprietorship over the African population, as it merely turned them into objects of barter.

The new Ordinance[8] subjected both the emigration and the recruitment of labourers to work in other countries to strict governmental control. In particular, approval could be linked to certain conditions or to the putting down of a deposit of up to 20 marks per person. This, however, turned emigration by African labourers into a lucrative business for the colonial state, which then received monetary compensation for the loss of labour.[9]

That the population should be regarded as an important asset of the State whose emigration was therefore to be restricted, or at least subjected to a charge that would benefit the State's finances, was not a new idea as it had been common practice in the German states before the Revolution of 1848–49[10] – and in the German colonial empire it was by no means restricted to South West Africa. Between 1887 and 1896 Ordinances were promulgated in all of Germany's African colonies that either completely prohibited the emigration of the African population, or at the very least subjected it to restrictive control.[11]

But in the particular case of South West Africa, where laments about the lack of 'indigenous labour' were one of the major factors in debates between the settlers and the mining companies on the one side and the Administration on the other, and were also very present in the public domain, the recruitment of Africans for neighbouring territories, in particular South Africa, was almost completely stopped.[12] Only three exceptions were made. The earliest of these was a regional measure affecting only the south-west of the colony: in 1897 the District Officer of Keetmanshoop, Angelo Golinelli, had given permission to the British companies exploiting guano deposits on the British islands near Lüderitzbucht to recruit African labourers. However, approval by the authorities on the spot was required in each individual case,[13] so that the German Administration retained control. Two other exceptions were introduced in the years shortly before and after the outbreak of the German–Herero War. Firstly, the Witwatersrand Native Labour Association was given permission to recruit labourers in 1903, leading to around a thousand people leaving the country; but this approval was valid for only one year and was not renewed.[14] And secondly, in January 1904 Herero were deported to British southern Africa as a consequence of the outbreak of war; but this practice was soon brought to an end as well, the favoured measure to replace it being to transfer the people concerned to other

German colonies, so that the German colonial empire was at least able to retain the benefit of their labour.

Thus almost from the beginning, the African workers were as far as possible reserved exclusively for deployment within the colony itself, as it had been recognized that they represented an important factor in the economic development of the territory. This assessment of the African population primarily in terms of economic factors was also reflected in the attribution of particular properties and characteristics to the individual ethnicities. In the regular reports that were required under the Native Ordinances, the District Offices were requested to explain 'which occupations the various nations show the most inclination towards and ability for', and 'what the situation is with regard to their willingness to work and their physical capabilities'.[15] Thus not only were all ethnic groups categorized by their supposed usefulness to the colonial economic system, but they were also discussed in terms of the most efficient way of making use of them in accordance with their 'characteristics'.[16]

How questionable such utilitarian assessments were could be seen in the contradictory nature of the replies to such enquiries. While one District Office, for example, found that the men of all the 'tribes' were 'willing to work', and declared only the Nama women to be lazy,[17] another thought that both the Herero and the Nama were lacking in such willingness. It was said, for example, that a Herero would start to complain very quickly if there was rather more work to be done, while it was 'only by means of strict measures' that a Nama, 'due to his workshy nature', could be forced into producing 'even a low level of performance'. The Berg Damara, it was said, though basically really good workers, could 'easily become insolent'.[18] There was also disagreement with regard to the different nations' inclination and ability to undertake particular types of work. Whereas Swakopmund District Office did not think that it was possible to determine any 'particular inclination or ability' towards certain types of employment as between the different peoples of South West Africa,[19] Windhoek District Office declared that the Nama were particularly suitable to be cattle drovers, house servants or handicraft workers, while the Herero and the San could best be used as cowherds, and the Berg Damara for heavy physical work.[20] How the San should be assessed was also a matter of controversy. They were said to be 'unsuitable for heavy work' as they lacked the necessary physical strength; they were 'unreliable' as herdsmen as they 'keep watch badly, although as a result of their outstandingly sharp senses they are able to find lost animals again'. But as they did not 'understand the sense of the work at all' they were 'only to be used under supervision'. They were therefore only to be employed to help out in order to alleviate the shortage of Herero, Berg Damara or Nama, who were difficult to recruit.[21] But whereas Bethanie District Office reported that San could only be got accustomed 'to regular work with great difficulty',[22] Grootfontein District Office reported that in its experience, 'if they have to deal with whites for any length of time, they get acclimatized relatively quickly and become willing workers'.[23]

These completely diverging assessments of the 'utility' of the various ethnicities, depending on who was reporting,[24] were based far more on preconceived ideas and stereotypes that the officials found confirmed in practice – though only by closing their eyes to the social and political causes – than they were on actual observation. The fact that African workers were treated differently in different parts of the country can also be taken to explain their varying degrees of 'ability to work' in practice. That there were shortcomings with regard to their treatment is involuntarily revealed by one terse sentence in the report from Okahanja District Office, in which the Herero is declared to be very suitable for use, even for hard physical labour, 'as long as he gets enough to eat'.[25] That was not always the case, however.

From Forced Labour to a 'Semifree' Labour Market

There had already been forced labour in South West Africa before 1904 – it had, for example, been imposed in connection with the military suppression of so-called 'risings', serving as a punishment for the defeated and as a deterrent to those who had not been involved;[26] but as has already been shown, during the war against the Herero and Nama it was practised on a large scale. It was not restricted to work that benefited the State treasury directly, but also included the provision of contingents of labourers to private employers for which the Colonial Administration received a fee in return. In this way the State had income and the employers cheap labour, but the forced labourers were not remunerated at all.[27]

When prisoner-of-war status was terminated on 27 January 1908, many of the forced labourers initially remained at their workplaces, some of them for several years,[28] because although they were officially free to leave they often first had to earn the money to be able to travel back home.[29] Thus it was the forced labour imposed during the war that laid the foundation for the 'semifree' labour market based on the free choice of employer that was instituted in the postwar period. At the same time, it meant that this was launched with one of its basic principles already severely compromised, as the original employer had not been freely chosen but had been the outcome of compulsory assignment. It was only in the course of the years that this was compensated for by the high degree of mobility among the African population. Thus in the year 1912 alone, 7,618 Africans (including 3,182 Herero, 2,581 Berg Damara and 952 Nama) moved to other districts – and that out of a total population of 69,003.[30]

The ending of prisoner-of-war status subjected the more liberal provisions of the Native Ordinances to their first major test, as the former prisoners sought to make use of their right to give notice and move away to other areas. Among the White population voices were immediately raised to demand that the released prisoners should be forced to stay longer in the places where they had been held captive. The Herero in Lüderitzbucht, for example, felt drawn back to their home area, so that in Lüderitzbucht District the fear grew that there would be a substantial shortage of cheap labour. But District Officer Rudolf Böhmer felt himself bound by the strict wording of the Native Ordinances, and therefore rejected the suggestion made by the local District Judge, Adolf Schottelius, that the Herero should be forbidden to leave the District by virtue of Section 5 of the Pass Ordinance, arguing that this Section provided for a prohibition only for political reasons. But it was not for political reasons that the Herero wanted to move away; they did not feel comfortable in the cold climate, they missed their grazing lands, and they simply longed to go back home. He considered that 'to forbid them to move there if they have given notice in proper form' would be 'a hardship' that he did 'not wish to be responsible for'. Instead, he declared, more Ovambo needed to be recruited.[31]

Thus the political reasons mentioned in the Ordinance as a condition for prohibiting movement did not in their narrow interpretation include the economic concerns of the Whites, but rather covered unrest and the threat of rebellion. But this example also shows that other Germans considered economic grounds to be sufficient, and completely ignored the passages in the Native Ordinances that contradicted this view. As the proposal to limit freedom of movement was made by a judge, one can presumably exclude the possibility of its having been made in ignorance of the provisions of the Ordinances. But if not even representatives of the law felt themselves bound by those provisions, then it has to be asked how other officials dealt with the situation, to say nothing of the rest of the population.

Not all of them felt obliged to uphold the principle of freedom of movement in the way Böhmer did. This can be seen, for example, from the argument between Lüderitzbucht and Bethanie District Offices about a prohibition on leaving the District imposed by the latter. Böhmer submitted an objection to this to the Governor's Office in 1911, claiming it was contrary to Sec. 5 of the Pass Ordinance and deleterious to the interests of Lüderitzbucht District, as Africans from Bethanie District frequently sought work in Lüderitzbucht.[32] The quarrel had been triggered by an African, Sem Seister, who had moved from Bethanie to Lüderitzbucht to look for work there. Bethanie District Office had requested Lüderitzbucht District Office to send Seister back, because in Bethanie District it had been forbidden since 20 March 1909,[33] 'due to the shortage of labour, for natives to move away from the district', and exceptions to this would be permitted 'only in urgent exceptional cases'.[34]

At first the Governor's Office agreed with Böhmer's objection and sent a Circulated Order to all District Offices instructing them that they were 'not entitled to generally prevent natives from leaving their Districts'. The Offices could 'only forbid individuals to leave the District pursuant to Sec. 5 of the Pass Ordinance, and that only for good cause'. Economic motives were explicitly excluded from the category of 'good cause', and it was pointed out that an African who wished to move to another District 'because he can find better wages there' could 'not be refused leave' to move.[35] The quarrel thus appeared to have been decided in Böhmer's favour. The fact that the Governor's Office used the instrument of a Circulated Order to settle the issue indicates that it must have been one that arose frequently.

However, the Bethanie District Officer, von Roebern, considered the matter to be of such importance that he queried the decision of the Governor's Office. According to von Roebern, the proximity of two largish centres of population, Lüderitzbucht and Keetmanshoop, made it difficult for the District Office to supply people living in the District with sufficient workers, as the Africans preferred to live in larger places where there was more social life, the wages were higher and they could shirk work more easily. That was why his predecessor had 'made a principle of applying' the prohibition on leaving the district that was provided for in the Pass Ordinance, 'as there is no other way of controlling the flight from the land'. The labour situation in the district was already bad, and if he were to be deprived of the means to restrict the Africans' freedom of movement it would become precarious. Furthermore, no farmer in Bethanie was in a position to pay 'anything like the wages that are paid in Lüderitzbucht'. In addition, after working in Lüderitzbucht for even a short time, the Africans were 'spoilt for farm work', since they lost their characteristics as 'a nation of herdsmen'.[36] In his annoyance that Böhmer had 'given a native to understand that his District Office, in the view of a third party official, had been acting illegally against him for years', von Roebern refused to see 'any illegality in the general application of the paragraph', even though the Governor's Office was of a different opinion. In an attempt to rid himself of the reproach of having acted illegally, he applied some legalistic hair-splitting, pointing out 'that no general order ... to the effect that no travel passes at all are to be issued' had been promulgated, and that he and his predecessor had 'merely come to the conclusion that in view of the particular economic and political situation in Bethanie, natives should in every individual case be forbidden to move away from the District until further notice', although short periods of leave were permitted.[37]

Von Roebern was not to be persuaded in any way that precisely this suspension of freedom of movement was against the law. Instead, he even went beyond economic arguments to claim that he was acting in what he saw as the interests of the Africans:

> I am certainly the last person who would want to begrudge the natives their place in the sun, and all my efforts are directed towards helping even the most wretched Bushman to enjoy his rights; but I also believe I am only acting in the natives' own interests if I keep them in the healthy conditions of a farm environment, even if as a result they earn a few marks less a month.[38]

If one bears in mind that agricultural labourers occupied the lowest rung of a wage scale that was in any case low, and if one also considers the frequent maltreatment and excessive beatings that they had to suffer, then these remarks appear to be nothing less than cynical. But they provide a typical example of the way the interests of the colonized were presumed to be identical to those of the White colonialists, without any concern for the real needs or the rights of the African population. Faced with the growing problems that employers in the agricultural districts – and not only in Bethanie – saw themselves confronted with as a result of the mining boom, von Roebern identified with the economic requirements of the White population of his District. As a result, the original intentions of the Native Ordinances were pushed into the background.

Hintrager, acting in the name of the Governor's Office, now suddenly turned the previous policy completely on its head, approving von Roebern's measures on the grounds that the Order of Bethanie District Office dated 8 October 1909 was an internal service instruction that certainly did provide for the possibility of giving an African permission to move away from the District. The misgivings of the Governor's Office were thereby satisfied, he declared, although the District Office must take care to see that the Order was not applied in such a way as to conflict with the wording of the Pass Ordinance. In addition, the District Office should set out the political reasons once again,[39] in spite of the fact that von Roebern had left not a shadow of doubt that his concern was to make it fundamentally difficult to leave the District for economic reasons. The decision of the Governor's Office was thus a case of unadulterated legal positivism.

Von Roebern's conduct in this dispute shows how completely incapable a Wilhelminian civil servant could be of self-critically admitting that he had made a mistake, and how indignant he was at having had an error pointed out to him by a colleague. The fact that Böhmer had reported this to a superior authority is moreover likely to have only strengthened von Roebern's unbending insistence on his position.

The rejection of Böhmer's objection, which also represented the approval of von Roebern's actions, also signified a victory of agriculture over the mining industry, which despite its steadily increasing importance to the colony's economy was apparently not yet in a position to exert sufficient influence in Windhoek to prevent a decision from being taken that was disadvantageous to it but beneficial to Bethanie District Office. At the same time, with the growing attractiveness of the mines to African labourers, the principles of freedom of movement and free choice of employer were increasingly coming under pressure, and were soon threatened with complete extinction.

It was normal practice for lobbyists working on behalf of the farmers to attempt to persuade the Governor's Office in Windhoek to give state-sanctioned preferential treatment to their sector. In 1911, for example, the Territorial Council, which was dominated by farmers' representatives, passed a resolution by twelve votes to eleven that would have forbidden practically all Africans except the Ovambo to work in the mines.[40] However, as the mining industry too was complaining about the inadequate supply of labour, the Governor was obliged to pay some attention to its interests as well, and so could not bring himself to introduce such a prohibition. Although recognizing that the Territorial Council's application had 'a certain justification in view of the shortage of workers in the rural areas', he decided to take internal measures to benefit the farmers, and sent out a Circulated Order to all District Offices instructing them to 'exert their influence to ensure that those natives who are suited to working on farms' did indeed 'seek employment on farms', and to do whatever they could to prevent as far as possible the migration 'of natives who are required on the land from the country districts, not only to the mining enterprises, but to any of the larger centres of population'.[41]

Thus even the Governor himself pursued that pattern of behaviour that was so often to be observed whereby a policy that was contrary to the letter of the Native Ordinances, while not exactly being officially approved, was taken internally as a guideline for action. He nevertheless avoided legalizing discrimination against the mining enterprises, which would not only have led to fiercer conflicts with them but would also have laid the Colonial Government open to having its policy challenged in the courts.

Despite the Governor's willingness to give the farms preference in the allocation of workers, this did nothing to change the general shortage of labour in agriculture. The mines continued to be highly attractive to African workers. And so in October 1913 Governor Seitz saw himself once again confronted with complaints from the farmers 'that the mining enterprises are drawing the necessary farmworkers away from the farms', in response to which he renewed his original instruction 'that Hereros and Kaffirs, to the extent that they are not already employed in such enterprises, should be assigned not to mining enterprises but to farms'.[42]

Agriculture was also similarly placed in relation to the railway construction companies, and so in August 1912 the Gibeon Farmers' Association applied to the Governor's Office to 'reduce the wages of the local natives working in railway construction gangs', as the farmers were of the opinion that the Africans were 'being spoilt' there, that the higher payment 'made operations more expensive for the farmers', and that 'workers were being drawn off from them'.[43] The Governor's Office took this reproach seriously, but having no idea of the wage rates or food allowances that were customary in the railway construction sector it enquired about them from the responsible Railway Commissioner for the Southern Region.[44] The Commissioner's Office thus found itself in the strange position of having to demonstrate, despite the customary government rhetoric about the need to treat Africans well so that they would do good work, that it did not treat its labourers all that well after all. The circumstance that the food allowances laid down in 1906 'for natives debilitated by the war' had since been reduced was now put forward as a positive factor. The proposal that the amount of food provided should be further reduced was rejected 'in view of the fact that it is necessary to maintain a healthy native population, and that the people involved in railway construction have to do very exhausting heavy work'. The Railway Commissioner's findings that wage rates and food allowances were by no means too high and that the 'natives' were not being spoilt[45] were expressly accepted by the Governor's Office,[46] so that the application from the Gibeon Farmers' Association was turned down. The logical conclusion that was to be drawn from this – namely, that if the farmworkers were worse paid and fed than their fellow workers on the railways, but the latter received no more than the necessary minimum, then the farmworkers were quite clearly not well enough provided for – was never explicitly mentioned.

Other factors too caused an uneven distribution of labour. Freedom of movement and the free choice of employer could lead to too many Africans congregating on particular farms, whether because the farmers concerned paid better wages or offered better working conditions, or because they were able to live there in their old family and social structures. According to the Native Ordinances, however, 'the accumulation of an unnecessarily large number of natives at a single place' was to be prevented in the 'interests of achieving as far as possible a regular distribution of workers across the colony'.[47] It was for this very reason that it had been laid down in the Control Ordinance that private werfs with more than ten families or individuals required the approval of the authorities,[48] a provision that had set limits to the free choice of employer right from the beginning.

A survey carried out by the Governor's Office at the beginning of 1912 showed that there were 112 farms or enterprises employing more than ten families and allowing these to live together in a single werf.[49] As the Ordinance concerned had never been completely implemented, these figures represent only an approximation and say nothing about the size of the werfs – and in any case, the responses to the survey did not distinguish between farms, businesses and the Rhenish Mission. Despite this, it is clear from them that larger werfs only existed on less than 10 per cent of the 1,144 farms operating as of 1 April 1912.[50] They were unequally distributed, depending on the attitude of the responsible District authorities: there were none in Lüderitzbucht[51] or Gobabis;[52] Rehoboth,[53] Warmbad[54] and Keetmanshoop[55] each had one; and Omaruru,[56] Maltahöhe and Gibeon[57] each had four; but there were five in Bethanie,[58] eight in Grootfontein,[59] eleven in Okahandja[60] and twelve in Windhoek. In Swakopmund no less than sixteen large werfs had received approval,[61] but in Karibib as many as forty-five.[62] As of 1 January 1912, of the overall total of 23,227 African men,[63] 7,292 were working in larger enterprises, 2,307 of these in Lüderitzbucht District alone, 1,380 in Grootfontein, 1,165 in Karibib, 856 in Windhoek and 644 in Swakopmund;[64] many of them will presumably have been accommodated on the larger werfs. But that still left two-thirds of the African men working for employers who had only a small number of African workers; complaints about workers being concentrated in the mines or on the railways therefore had no basis in reality. The complaints were nonetheless a clear sign of the increasing concern about the shortage of labour that prevailed everywhere. In addition, the demand of the Farmers' Associations that it should be a particular concern of the State's to protect the supply of workers to the farms was an expression of a clear attitude of entitlement with regard to the colonial state. The farmers saw themselves as the 'true masters' of South West Africa – the task of the Colonial Administration being to serve them. The Administration's attitude that it should only have to lay down a framework of fundamental conditions and guarantee the observance of these, and that within this framework the various parties – the farmers, the mining companies and also the African labourers – should pursue the satisfaction of their respective requirements through market mechanisms, was foreign to the farmers' way of thinking.

As late as 1914 Governor Seitz was still complaining that people who had bought farms from the Government were invoking an alleged obligation on the Government, as it had sold them their farms under the prevailing conditions, to make workers available to them. As the administration was not able to fulfil this condition it instructed all government agencies to make a disclaimer to would-be purchasers when they put in their offers to the effect that 'the government can give no guarantee' that 'the purchaser concerned will also find workers', and that neither the 'responsible District Office nor the Colonial Government will be in a position in the foreseeable future' to change this situation. In order to guard against any legal claims being raised by purchasers, this disclaimer had to be expressly recorded when the Contract of Purchase was presented. Seitz offered purchasers who had already bought government farms the possibility of withdrawing from their contracts 'in view of the labour situation'.[65]

But it was not only new settlers who regarded the administrative officers as being there to promote their interests; long-established colonists also raised the demand for workers to be assigned to them by the State.[66] The Administration was helpless in the face of the farmers' complaints about the lack of workers, and when farmers complained that the shortage was particularly acute in their own area,[67] the officials were only able to answer tersely: 'We acknowledge fully and completely that there is an acute shortage of workers, but this is the case not only in that District but in all Districts'.[68] This was an implicit admission that it was not possible to supply all employers with workers from the Police Zone, which intensified dissatisfaction with the Administration among the farmers. As late as 1914 the Governor's

Office had to point out that the decision as to 'who such people are to be assigned to' was 'under no circumstances to be left to the lower tiers of the administration'. For there had been occasions on which 'farmers have been held out the prospect of being assigned workers, but in the end, when the farmers came to collect them, some or all of them were no longer available, although the head of the Administration was not able to get any information as to where they had gone'.[69]

But the Colonial Administration was itself not completely free of blame with regard to this attitude of expectation on the part of the farmers. The 'semifree' structure of the labour market was compromised in two respects by the principle of even distribution across the market: on the one hand by the forced assignment to farmers of so-called 'vagrants' and of Africans found hiding out in the bush, and on the other hand by the provision for 'runaway' Africans to be returned to their employers.

The strict control provisions of the 1907 Native Ordinances had not been able to guarantee in the long term that all able-bodied African men and women would be registered and recruited. Again and again, the Schutztruppe or the Territorial Police would break up so-called 'wild werfs', or would undertake expeditions into remote parts of the colony in order to capture Herero, Nama and San who were hiding there. The security aspect, i.e. the need to combat 'bandits and marauders', went hand in hand with the necessity to mobilize all potential labour. In accordance with the directives from Windhoek,[70] Africans who were captured by the patrols were assigned to farmers by the individual District Offices[71] – either immediately or after a short time of internment – until the employers concerned could be informed that new workers were available for collection from the police station or military post.[72] Whenever rumours arose that there were Africans living out on the veld, they were 'immediately gone after and distributed to the farms, all of which were suffering from a shortage of labour'.[73] In some cases, though, they were first imprisoned and 'punished for vagrancy'.[74]

Such forced assignments contravened the principle of the free choice of employer, so in practice this principle only applied to those Africans who allowed themselves to be integrated into the labour market system willingly. If they absolutely refused to submit to the requirement to take up employment, they became victims of the forced allocation mechanism that had developed above all during the war. This could only strengthen the settlers' feelings of entitlement.

Furthermore, the Administration played a major role in bringing back workers who had deserted or 'run away'. As early as 1894 the 'District

Police Ordinance concerning the Relationship between Employers and Workers' for Otjimbingwe District,[75] and the corresponding Ordinance of Gibeon District Office,[76] described the bringing back of workers who had illegally left their places of work as being one of the principal tasks of the District Offices. The Master and Servant Ordinance of 1907[77] also took up the same idea, and made it mandatory for the whole of the area in which the Native Ordinances applied; thus the Administration was directly involved in cementing low wages and working conditions that in some cases were extremely bad. The Africans often reacted to intolerable working conditions and mistreatment by simply leaving. According to the official statistics, 1,998 Africans deserted from their places of work in 1911, and 1,607 in 1912; the numbers of such fugitives recaptured in the same years were 1,177 and 1,650 respectively.[78] By bringing the fugitives back, and in some cases first punishing them, the Administration prevented any improvement of their working conditions to meet the general standards, low as these were in any case, as it deprived the African population of their theoretical basic possibility of showing resistance by withdrawing their labour.

The authorities lent their assistance to White employers, even if they knew that the desertion had been caused by ill-treatment on the employer's part. Two examples can be used to illustrate this, one from the time immediately after the Herero and Nama War and before the promulgation of the Native Ordinances, the other from the year 1913.

In 1907 all the female employees of the innkeeper Hülsmann, who lived in Windhoek district, ran away several times within only two months; they were brought back by the police five times, although the District Officer knew that the innkeeper himself was to blame. In the view of the District Office Secretary, Friedrich Wilhelm Lang, his 'manner and way of life are not in the least of a kind to evoke the respect of the natives'.[79] What exactly was to be understood by this was expressed in more concrete terms by the District Officer, Heinrich Narciß:

> The fact that the natives have run away from the innkeeper Hülsmann so often is due not to any lack of severity on the part of the authority, but to the way the natives have been treated by Hülsmann, who is known to be a brutal person.

> The three women who last ran away on 4 July have all stated, in a credible manner and concurring with each other, that they ran away because Hülsmann had constantly beaten them with the sjambok.[80]

Thus Narciß himself admitted that the claim that Hülsmann had mistreated his servants was convincing; nevertheless, the fugitives were repeatedly returned to him. Immediately after the events referred to in the passage quoted above, Hülsmann was even informed that he could come and collect two further women.

The dispute between Hülsmann and Windhoek District Office, which was fought out shortly before the three Native Ordinances came into force, already shows clear parallels with the further conflicts between employers and the Administration that continued to occur right up to the end of German colonial rule. The employers lacked any sense of being in the wrong; they responded to remonstrations that they mistreated their staff by reproaching the Administration with being insufficiently severe, as Hülsmann did in a reader's letter to the *Windhuker Nachrichten;*[81] it was only thanks to this that the dispute found its way into the official files at all. The reason for Hülsmann's extreme annoyance was that the District Office had not allowed him to chastise his 'natives' himself, but merely notified him that he could prosecute them before the District Officer. Having been informed of the punishments that might be imposed, namely 'that the men should be flogged or beaten and the women locked up', he responded that 'locking them up would be no use to him, as then he really would have no workers at all'; whereupon District Office Secretary Lang, according to his own account, replied that he 'was unable to help him, as it was not allowed to beat women'. When Hülsmann, who was described as being very much on edge, and the trader Berger who accompanied him and was already drunk, then launched into 'polemics on Native Policy' and on the way Africans were treated by the Government, Lang broke off the interview.[82]

But Hülsmann's appeal to public opinion now put District Officer Narciß under pressure. He was forced to react and defend himself against the reproach of being too lenient, because he was afraid that this would give his superiors, and in particular the Undersecretary in the Imperial Colonial Office, von Lindequist, who was still present in the colony, a false picture of his attitude to the question. Narciß therefore sent a statement of his own position, together with Lang's report, to the Governor's Office, with the request that it should also be communicated to von Lindequist 'in the interests of the most rapid rectification of the picture presented'. To vindicate himself, Narciß pointed out that in the previous fourteen weeks he had imposed disciplinary punishments on Africans in fifty-seven different cases.[83] Although the Administration's officers were independent of the population of the colony, the White population was in a position to exercise pressure by 'going public'. The officials had to take this very seriously, for fear of a false impression being created in the Governor's

Office or the Imperial Colonial Office which could possibly have had a disadvantageous effect on the career prospects of the official concerned. Emphasizing the fact 'that everything has been done by the District Office and the police that could possibly have been done in accordance with the legal provisions',[84] Narciß sought to deflect the reproach of a lack of severity by putting the blame on the rigid framework of law, and suggesting that he personally would certainly have been willing to display a harsher attitude. This, however, is a revealing statement in itself, as it demonstrates that irrespective of the personal opinions of the individual officials concerned the Administration was faithful to the law and took seriously the limits imposed on it by the legal provisions.

The fact that no sanctions of any kind were imposed on Hülsmann, either in the form of a prosecution or even of a decision to stop bringing his 'runaway' workers back to him, gives one a sense of how potentially explosive disputes between the Administration and the employers could be when it was a question of concrete measures taken by, or expected of, the Administration. Such differences were particularly critical when the Administration refused to provide certain Whites with any more African workers, in most cases because of the suspicion that the employers concerned had exceeded the limits of the 'parental powers of chastisement', generously interpreted though these were, and did not wish to encourage cases of distinctly brutal maltreatment by appearing to give them official backing.

An example of this is provided by the dispute between Outjo District Office and the farmer Baron von Wangenheim. On 21 February 1913 von Wangenheim had 'boxed the ears' of the Herero Elisabeth, who was pregnant, after she had failed to carry out immediately an order that he had given her, 'until she fell to the ground, bleeding heavily from the nose'. In consequence, the responsible District Officer of Outjo, Hans Schultze-Jena, ordered the District Office not to assign any more African workers to von Wangenheim, but decided to refrain from pressing charges against him.[85]

However, von Wangenheim was not willing to accept this and complained to the Governor's Office. He countered Schultze-Jena's accusation that he 'did not know how to treat' his African workers with the argument that he had been in the colony since 1908, had done his service with the Schutztruppe, and had got on well with 'natives' wherever he had had to deal with them. Instead, he put the blame on the Africans, whom he had been having difficulties with for a year. All the complaints that they had made against him had 'turned out to be unfounded, or to be malicious calumnies', and in no single case had court proceedings been instituted against him. He felt himself 'most seriously prejudiced and hindered in the pursuit of his activities' by Schultze-Jena's order, as he had more than two hundred head of large livestock and quite a few small animals, and did not know how he was to run his farm without suitable workers. All in all, he felt himself obliged to reproach Schultze-Jena with the fact that his way of treating 'natives … did not demonstrate the seriousness or severity that is shown in other Districts'. It was not, he averred, in accordance 'with the interests either of the settlers or of the natives themselves for them to be treated with all too much leniency and forbearance'.[86]

As in the Hülsemann case described above, the Administration's criticism of the way the workers were treated was met by the person accused with the reproach of excessive forbearance and leniency. And just as in the other case, the authority concerned was obliged first of all to dispose of this apparently dangerous accusation by referring to the punishment statistics. The 'punishment records themselves prove the contrary', replied the District Officer's deputy on behalf of his boss, who was on home leave. He defended the order forbidding any further assignment of workers to von Wangenheim, declaring that 'von Wangenheim was well known to be a person who treated his natives brutally', and also indicated that he had actually got off lightly, since 'criminal proceedings would probably have ended more unpleasantly' for him.[87]

On receiving Outjo District Office's description of how the pregnant woman had been maltreated, Governor Seitz unambiguously backed Schultze-Jena's decision and rejected the complaints against him as being 'unfounded'. In addition, he emphasized that there was 'no obligation on the District Office to assign natives to the farmers as workers', even if officials were in general happy to support 'the economic interests of the farmers and settlers' by being of assistance to them with the recruitment of African labourers. Seitz wanted to 'continue in future to leave it up to the District Office' to decide whether it would assign workers or not. But he explicitly pointed out to von Wangenheim that he was free 'to recruit natives independently for himself' at any time.[88]

So the Governor's Office did not forbid von Wangenheim to employ Africans, but even pointed out to him explicitly that a free labour market existed; however, nor did it explicitly confirm Schultze-Jena's decision, but merely emphasized that the District Officer was autonomous in his decision-making; thus it would be quite possible for a successor in the office to revise the decision. In this way, the District Officer's action was prevented from assuming the status of a binding precedent.

Although Schultze-Jena was convinced that von Wangenheim had indeed maltreated the pregnant woman, he did not bring a prosecution for causing bodily harm. He only seems to have intervened at all because it was clearly contrary to his understanding of his office to assign workers to a person who mistreated pregnant women; on the other hand, he was not so fundamentally upset by such conduct as to bring a prosecution that would have led to an exemplary punishment being imposed. But even this degree of concession to his duty of care exposed him to the reproach of lacking severity, which he could only refute by drawing on the punishment statistics.

Even a District Officer, largely autonomous though he was in his decision-making, did not take such decisions as a solitary figure shut up in his office, but in an atmosphere of public controversy between settlers and the Administration. He lived and worked for the most part in a social environment of settlers with more extreme views, whose susceptibilities he had to take account of. The staff of the Governor's Office and even the Governor himself also moved in the same social and public milieu, and constantly had to defend themselves against the reproach that Africans were treated all too leniently. It was precisely this vulnerable point that von Wangenheim was targeting with his complaint, in that he attempted to discredit Schultze-Jena's action as the shortcoming of an individual official by pointing out that Africans were treated more severely in other districts.

The reproach of a lack of severity towards the Africans was one that was constantly being raised by White employers. They were generally in favour of strengthening the elements of compulsion in Native Policy as against the more liberal elements, as became clear from the demand already mentioned, raised by the Farmers' Associations but rejected by the Colonial Government, for Africans who 'ran away' from their employment to be tattooed.

The Native Ordinances provided for the Administration to intervene in relationships between employers and workers, not only in the matter of bringing back 'runaway' employees, but also in relation to the monitoring of compliance with contract conditions. An important prerequisite for this latter function was that it should be possible to check what level of wages had been agreed. This was why the Governor's Office pressed for the introduction of police scrutiny of employment contracts. The police had the explicit duty to ensure when employment logbooks were issued that the wage was unambiguously determined as 'a certain amount of money or a quantity of rations precisely laid down in German weights and measures', and that the African knew and understood what the agreed wage was. This was intended above all to prevent wages being paid in kind in the form of goods whose value could be arbitrarily determined by the employer, or workers being forced to buy at their employers' shops. In the Government's view, the Africans needed particular protection against this so-called 'truck system', as many employers used it to recover the wages they had paid out to their employees by selling them overpriced goods. This control obligation was justified in terms of the 'primitiveness' of the Africans: in the Circulated Decree accompanying the 1907 Native Ordinances it was stated that 'even more than is the case at home, for the protection of the white worker, ... all available means must be brought to bear here to counter the truck system, for the protection of the native who is in a less favourable position due to his lesser intelligence and his lack of knowledge of the German language'.[89]

Registration with the police was only mandatory, however, for contracts with a term exceeding one month,[90] but such longer employment contracts remained the exception. Even in 1912 verbal contracts with a term of one month were the rule.[91] If it had originally been the farmers who had boycotted longer-term contracts, later it was the majority of Africans, who rejected the written employment contracts as they saw in them a 'noose to tie them for longer periods of time to such employers as they would otherwise soon have given notice to and left', as is stated in a report by the Rhenish Mission. Furthermore, there were some employers who failed to comply with the contractual agreements, even if they were set out in the employment logbook. If the workers then complained about this – for example, that they were not being given the agreed amount of food – the White employer would simply deny what they said. And as the missionary Johannes Olpp commented, it was well known that 'what the white person says is given more credence than what the native says'.[92] Thus in disputes over wages or rations, the Administration was faced with enormous problems in finding out the truth of the matter. In 1908 the Gobabis District Officer, Kurt Streitwolf, lamented that there was 'still a very great deal that needs to be put right' in the area of wage payments, but that it was very difficult to check whether the agreed quantities of rations had actually been distributed.[93]

Nothing changed in this respect in the course of the years. As the Native Commissioner for Keetmanshoop was still obliged to report in 1913:

> It is only with difficulty that one is able to come to a sound conclusion with regard to the remuneration and treatment of native workers. What

the one side says is abruptly contradicted by the other. The employers for their part complain about laziness and insubordination, the workers about bad treatment, inadequate rations and a refusal to pay them the wages they have earned, or to pay them out in cash.[94]

As the possibilities for Africans themselves to give notice were limited, many saw no other way of escape but to leave their workplaces illegally. But as has already been shown, that made them liable to punishment and to being forcibly brought back – and this even though the Governor's Office and many District Officers were well aware that such desertion was the result of intolerable working conditions or shortcomings in the food provided:

> According to our observations here, it may be assumed with certainty that when natives run away this is due in by far the great majority of cases to improper treatment and inadequate food; but determining the facts in such cases is made difficult by the way the settlers, when sounded out about such matters, generally paint everything in the rosiest of colours, and then it is one person's word against the other.[95]

Whether an official took the Africans' complaints seriously or not depended on his own personal view of the African character. Did he, as the Omaruru District Officer Victor von Frankenberg shows he did in the above quotation, consider Africans to be credible witnesses, or did he regard them as notorious liars? The latter would appear to have been the view of the Windhoek District Officer Narciß, for whom the complaints that 'runaway natives' had 'deserted their workplaces because they had been frequently beaten and given too little food' were pure inventions for their own protection. In his view, it was 'always possible to determine that such claims are mere excuses'.[96]

But the constant cases of African workers 'running away' must surely have opened the officials' eyes to the fact that things were badly wrong with the Africans' living and working conditions on some of the farms. But even if it did, this did not lead to any fundamental questioning of Native Policy as set out in the 1907 Native Ordinances. Instead, attempts were made to explain the glaring abuses as being due to the failings of individual Whites – employers, of course, not the officials themselves. According to this theory, it was the inexperience of settlers who were new to the country that was to blame,[97] or else it was the 'Boers', who were notorious for treating 'the natives mostly very severely, and in many cases brutally'.[98]

The extent to which complaints from Africans were recorded by the Administration and passed on to the responsible courts is a question that cannot be answered with any certainty. Although there are cases recorded in the files in which investigations were conducted against employers, it is not possible to say how representative these are, as we do not know the overall extent to which breaches of contract occurred. This cannot be determined from the available sources since only those cases that for one reason or another particularly attracted the attention of the Administration are preserved in the archives. Despite the apparently widespread consensus that it was either shortcomings in their rations or physical maltreatment that were responsible for hundreds if not thousands of Africans deserting their workplaces every year, it is only in a few individual cases that there is any evidence of alleged breaches of contract being investigated. It seems that the great majority of such cases were not investigated by the authorities, so either they must have been ignored or else they never came to the attention of the Administration at all.

In most cases, the officials appear to have taken sides with the employer. This is demonstrated by the numerous convictions of Africans for breach of contract or insubordination.[99] Although in reality it ought to have been just as difficult to find proof in favour of the Whites as in favour of the Africans, Africans were punished considerably more frequently, as the Whites were more likely to be believed. Thus it can be seen that in a society of racial privilege, even rights that are defined by law in what appears to be a watertight fashion do not guarantee legal protection. As a result, the 'semifree' labour market only functioned in practice to a strictly limited extent. This explains why, despite the appeals of the Colonial Government to the District Officers to fulfil their supervisory duties,[100] and despite the appointment of officials whose duty it was 'to represent the interests of the natives in enforcing their claims in court',[101] even the efforts of the more well-meaning ones among them did not in fact lead to any substantial changes in the Africans' situation.

The different views held by different officials with regard to how they should fulfil their supervisory duties, and the resistance that even the more committed ones amongst them saw themselves exposed to, will be illustrated in the following section by some examples of the efforts made to prevent Africans from being maltreated by their employers. Attempts to help workers to obtain the wages due to them also met with the same responses.

Efforts to Combat the Maltreatment of Africans

The Colonial Government had recognized at an early stage that the intention of the Native Ordinances to achieve a situation in labour relations that reconciled the interests of the Whites and those of the

Africans would be under severe threat if the employers were not subjected to supervision as well. It was precisely with this in mind that the institution of the Native Commissioner was planned, and a few years later indeed also realized. This did not, however, in any way relieve the District Officers of their supervisory duties. And the District Office had in any case sole responsibility for the protection of the African population in those Districts where no Native Commissioner had been appointed.

As early as January 1908, that is to say immediately after the Ordinances had come into effect, Governor Seitz had to react to complaints that settlers had been guilty of 'gross maltreatment of their natives'. He therefore required all District Offices to submit a report on this matter, pointing out that 'only even-tempered, consistent and just treatment can make the native into a willing and contented worker'. Otherwise, Seitz went on, it had to be feared that African workers would run away in droves. If, on the other hand, 'the native had once gained the conviction that he was not merely regarded as a slave, but that his justified claims would be met' and that he stood 'under the protection of the law', then he would 'not have so much of an inclination to run away from his master'.[102]

But beyond regulating the duty of supervision and occasionally sending exhortations to the District Offices regarding the fulfilment of their protective functions, there was little that the Governor's Office could do. It was the subordinate tiers of the Administration that decided whether or not they should intervene on behalf of Africans. And as it was these subordinate tiers that were also the main sources of information for the central Administration, the latter had scarcely any way of keeping a close eye on their activities. One may assume that a District Officer who failed to fulfil his supervisory duties was unlikely to report this fact to Windhoek; and the same is also likely to have applied as between the police and the District Offices. Cases of turning a blind eye were not recorded in the files.

The whole gamut of difficulties associated with the practical fulfilment of the State's duty of supervision is already apparent in the District Offices' reports in response to the Circulated Order of January 1908. These responses show three things. Firstly, they demonstrate that not all the District Officers were indifferent to the wretched situation the Africans found themselves in, but that some did indeed take their supervisory duties seriously. Secondly, they document that in any interventions on behalf of the labourers, the officials were able to exercise a very wide degree of discretion as to what was legal and what was illegal, and that some officials were more punctilious than others in fulfilling their duty. And thirdly, it becomes clear that the Administration could only act within very narrow limits, above all because in criminal proceedings against Whites it only exercised the prosecuting function, whilst the decisions lay with the courts, over which the Administration had no control.

A total of seven out of the fifteen autonomous District Offices reported cases of maltreatment, but all of these claimed to have taken action to remedy them. District Officer von Frankenberg of Omaruru, for example, reported that he no longer assigned Africans to employers who were guilty of such offences.[103] In Maltahöhe District an employer had hit an African man on the head with a rifle and severely injured him, for which he was sentenced to a fine of 100 marks or ten days' imprisonment.[104] Warmbad District Office had reported several cases of maltreatment, but only one led to criminal proceedings, while most of the others were settled by the farmers making monetary gifts to the mistreated Africans before the authority became aware of the case.[105] Rehoboth District Office also reported knowing of several cases of maltreatment; the two that are described in detail are notable for the fact that it was the African women concerned who had themselves gone to the police to seek help.[106] This indicates that the Africans knew that the authorities had a duty of care and also knew their rights, and that they had at least a minimum degree of confidence in the police.

The Lüderitzbucht District Officer, Rudolf Böhmer, reported several cases of maltreatment, committed, however, not by farmers but by railway employees. In the majority of the cases he filed a charge with the local District Court. This, though, 'only rarely led to any punishment, as in the great majority of cases the only available witnesses were natives, whose testimonies were not considered sufficient proof by the Court'. Despite this, he was able to enclose five judgments given against Whites with his report.[107] They were all cases of bodily harm arising out of an alleged refusal to work or to obey orders. In June 1906 the carrier Alfred Heilbrunner was fined 50 marks because he had hit the Herero prisoner-of-war Eduard 'over the head several times with a thick whip handle, even when he was already down on the ground'. As the accused had no previous conviction for causing bodily harm and 'the Herero had not suffered any injury from the blows', mitigating circumstances were allowed.[108] In March 1907 the District Court convicted the cook Joseph Balsis of having on several occasions 'chastised the Herero women employed by him with blows of the hand', and had once hit a girl called Katharina 'on the right-hand side of her head' with a broomstick 'in such a way that she began to bleed on that side'. In the grounds of his judgment, Judge Schottelius declared that even if 'employers might not be denied the right to punish minor offences of the native workers under their authority on the spot', such punishment must not 'degenerate into the infliction of physical injury'. In view of the fact that the girls had been 'disobedient' and that 'the injury was only slight', the judge considered a fine of 25 marks to be appropriate. It appears that Schottelius sentenced Balsis contrary to his own personal convictions, as in the grounds of the judgment he mentioned almost apologetically that it was necessary to punish the accused because it was District Officer Böhmer, as guardian of the four Herero girls, who had applied for his prosecution.[109] Judge Schulze also found mitigating circumstances when he sentenced the clerk Gustav Tümmler to a fine of 25 marks because he had 'hit the Herero woman Elisabeth several times on the back and the arm with a walking-stick when she allegedly refused to carry out the work of watering plants that had been assigned to her'. Schulze did not consider the chastisement to be 'demonstrably very severe or disproportionate', even though it was illegal. Nor, in his opinion, could the stick used by the accused be regarded 'as a dangerous instrument within the meaning of Sec. 223 of the Imperial Penal Code'.[110]

The case against the engineer Georg Rost led to appeal proceedings before the Superior Court in Windhoek. He had been sentenced by Lüderitzbucht District Court, which allowed extenuating circumstances, to three months' imprisonment for 'causing grievous bodily harm leading to death', whereupon he appealed, seeking a 'not guilty' verdict. The Superior Court under Judge Bruhns, however, increased the sentence to four months' imprisonment.[111]

How many accused persons were acquitted by the courts cannot be determined from the archives, but even the few convictions that are recorded are enough to show that District Officer Böhmer did intervene in cases of maltreatment, and that he interpreted that term relatively broadly. Not all the District Officers, however, were as willing as Böhmer to categorize the acts of White employers as maltreatment, as can be seen from the report from Gibeon District. District Officer von der Gröben had taken a farmer's workers away from him because he had beaten several Africans so brutally with an ox-hide whip and with sticks, while two other Whites held them, that they were scarcely able to walk afterwards. Von der Gröben did construe this case as maltreatment, but in another case, in which a 'Boer' employer had beaten his worker with a stick because he had allegedly repeatedly stolen meat, he judged differently. In his view there had been no maltreatment in this case, even though the employer had 'exceeded the measure covered by the parental power of chastisement'.[112] So von der Gröben made distinctions between one case of maltreatment and another in a way that was legally highly questionable: because if the accused had exceeded the extent of his disciplinary rights as an employer, as the District Officer himself admitted that he had, then this could only mean that it was a case of inflicting bodily harm, which could not be anything else but maltreatment. But von der Gröben was not alone in making such questionable differentiations. Swakopmund District Office, for example, reported that the haulage contractor Junkereit had been sentenced by the court to a fine of 50 marks at the end of 1907 because he had 'beaten a native, who had refused to perform his work, with a piece of a horse's harness', while at the same time stating that no cases of 'brutal maltreatment' had occurred.[113] Keetmanshoop District Office also reported that there had been no cases of 'gross' maltreatment, only to go on to recount a case that had been reported to Windhoek, but which it then immediately sought to play down by describing the action that had given rise to it as merely 'light physical chastisement because of neglect of duty'.[114] Karibib and Windhoek District Offices also reported that there had been no cases of 'gross maltreatment', or at least that none were known to them.[115]

The excessive vagueness of the term 'gross maltreatment' renders the reports submitted by these offices largely worthless, as it led to a large number of cases of 'simple' maltreatment being ignored.[116] By submitting reports that did no more than respond in very narrow terms to Seitz's question about cases of 'gross maltreatment', the officials concerned were able to present unblemished records that allowed the situations in their own respective districts to appear in the best possible light.

But the reports from Gibeon, Swakopmund and Keetmanshoop do throw light on the dilemma that the Colonial Government found itself facing in its attempts to combat the maltreatment of Africans. Many cases of bodily harm inflicted on them by Whites were not perceived as such, either by the officials or by the settlers. District Officer Karl Schmidt of Keetmanshoop adopts a markedly apologetic tone when describing how in his opinion such acts came to occur:

> Experience shows that most cases of chastisement of natives occur ... as a result of misunderstandings with new settlers who understand neither the nature of the natives nor their language. The master gives his order, he may even repeat it a few times, adding a few fragments of Dutch or of a native language that he has himself not digested properly; the native says yes, goes away, and because he has understood either nothing or only a few individual words, and these wrongly, he either does nothing at all or else something quite different from what he was ordered to do.

So it comes to blows, which the native, quite rightly, cannot see that he has deserved. The master, however, believes that the native is being obstinate, that he has intentionally failed to carry out the order, which he had repeated three times, so that the native must either have understood it quite well or else did not wish to understand it. However, the longer the white master is in the country, and the more he tries to get to know the nature of his natives and to understand them, the less frequently such collisions between them will occur, particularly if the native is able to see that the white man has a heart for him and treats him just as well as he does one of his livestock, which any sensible owner also takes good care of, feeding it and not driving it too hard.[117]

So according to Schmidt it was only the inexperience of the farmers and not their brutal attitudes or their view of themselves as a 'master race' that triggered such excessive beatings. This reference to the inexperience of the employers furnished the official with sufficient excuse for ignoring excessive beatings, since he could justify his inactivity with the argument that cases of maltreatment would automatically become less frequent as time went by. But even he distanced himself from the 'brutal and cruel natures that incline to commit maltreatment', who were to be found everywhere and against whom action had to be taken, even if only to ensure that the supply of labourers was not jeopardized.[118]

But the great vagueness attaching to the term 'maltreatment' was also related to the fact that corporal punishment was not fundamentally prohibited. The overwhelming majority of employers claimed for themselves a 'parental power of chastisement' in respect of their African workers, a concept rooted in Master and Servant law of the early modern period. According to this concept, the master had a right to inflict physical chastisement on his servants. The 'Allgemeine Landrecht für die Preußischen Staaten' (General Legal Code for the States of Prussia) of 1791 attempted to limit the use and degree of corporal punishment, but it remained fundamentally admissible, particularly among landowners. The Prussian Master and Servant Ordinance of 1810 also provided for it, and indeed it was not until the twentieth century that this right of physical chastisement was abolished in Germany.[119] In South West Africa it was never anchored in the law,[120] but was considered to be a common law right sanctioned by the courts and justified by the mission of the Whites to educate and train the Africans. For this purpose, it was argued, the Whites had to be allowed to use those forms of chastisement that were also admissible at home. The application of corporal punishment was restricted, however, by the condition that it must not lead to any damage to health.[121] Officials and settlers shared the racist stereotypes of 'lazy' and 'insubordinate'

Africans who needed a 'firm hand', and who were not affected by corporal punishment because of their 'lower level of civilization'. This was even justified in terms of the different physiology of the Africans, whose 'particularly hardened and largely insensitive skin' led to their suffering 'at the most superficial abrasions of the skin, even when they are severely punished'.[122] This had far-reaching consequences for the Administration's efforts to combat the mistreatment of Africans. From the point of view of the Whites, corporal punishment did not always represent maltreatment, and not even injuries were proof of it. And as Africans were accorded little credibility, it was even more difficult to prove the case in court.

The Colonial Government was well aware of the connection between the 'parental power of chastisement' and excessive beatings, and therefore refused to have the former enshrined in law, although it was the wish of the White population that it should be. When the Territorial Council demanded this in a 1913 resolution, the Colonial Government refused to countenance it. In the view of Deputy Governor Hintrager, the numerous excesses that occurred were little encouragement to the Governor's Office to see things differently, and he feared that if the right of private White individuals to inflict corporal punishment on Africans were guaranteed in law, such excesses would be promoted rather than restricted. He therefore recommended that the Imperial Colonial Office should subject the whole issue to delaying tactics.[123]

However, the Administration did not fundamentally reject corporal punishment for Africans, seeing in it an important instrument in disciplinary and criminal proceedings.[124] The number of cases in which corporal punishment was imposed by the courts rose continuously after the war, from 534 in the 1907/08 reporting year to 1,713 in 1912/13.[125] How often it was used as a disciplinary measure is unknown, but the figure is likely to have been substantially higher. A factor that no doubt also contributed to the acceptance of corporal punishment for Africans among both the German colonial officials and the White inhabitants of the colony was that although it had been abolished as a criminal punishment in Germany with the introduction of the Imperial Penal Code in 1871, it could still legally be used as a disciplinary measure in prisons and workhouses right up to 1923.[126]

But this basic acceptance of the use of corporal punishment against the African population had far-reaching consequences for relations between Whites and Africans, as it contributed to a culture of violence that also fostered abuse of the 'parental power of chastisement'. The German Administration did not succeed in effectively bringing the maltreatment of Africans under control, either because many of the

District Offices or the police under their authority did not fulfil their supervisory duties adequately, or because the courts did not support the efforts of the Administration to pursue a stricter line in the matter.

The Colonial Government was getting more and more concerned, however, about the growing brutalization of working conditions, which was an existential threat to a Native Policy that aimed at reconciling the interests of Africans and Whites. In May 1912, therefore, Governor Seitz, alarmed at reports that a 'mood of desperation' was spreading 'among the natives in certain areas of the colony', sent out a secret circular calling upon the Administration to take up the struggle against maltreatment once more. He was afraid there might be unrest, as the number of cases of 'brutal excesses by whites against natives', which sometimes even involved policemen, were increasing 'to an alarming extent, and are often not expiated before the courts in a manner that satisfies the natives' sense of justice', so that the Africans 'despaired of the impartiality of our legal system'. And he went on:

> It is obvious that such feelings of hatred among the natives will sooner or later, to the extent that no determined measures are taken to remedy them, lead to a renewed desperate rebellion on the part of the natives, and thus to the economic ruin of the country. It is therefore in the interests of the entire white population that every available means should be used to bring under control those elements who vent their fury on the natives with the violence of madness and see their white skins as giving them carte blanche to commit brutal crimes. Because a nation that lays claim to being regarded as a master race must above all ensure that it keeps its own ranks clean.[127]

Seitz had to qualify this with an admission that the Governor had no competence to influence the jurisdiction of the courts over Whites, but he did announce that he would 'use administrative procedures' to ensure that wherever possible 'action is taken to counter the abuses that indubitably exist at present'. From case to case, therefore, he was prepared to order 'that such whites as are guilty of continued acts of brutality against their natives may not be allocated any further natives as workers', thereby proposing a measure that District Officers had already been recommended to apply since immediately after the war, and which had thus already proved ineffective. In addition, Seitz himself admitted that state controls alone could not bring about the cessation of abuse. It would only be possible to remedy the situation effectively 'if the white population itself, which, as I know, most sharply condemns such acts of brutality committed by rough elements among it, adopts attitudes towards those individuals, constituting as they do a public menace, that leave them in no doubt as to its opinion, and actively cooperates in order to prevent such crimes and, should they occur, to cause them to be punished'. In view of this, the content of this circular was to be made known to members of District Councils under conditions of strict confidentiality. It would then be up to them to influence their fellow citizens in such a way that the Africans would recover the confidence 'that they too will receive assistance from the whites against the brutal excesses of a few individuals'.[128]

A year later the Territorial Council also associated itself with the Governor's demands, at the same time rejecting, as Seitz himself had done, any wholesale condemnation of the White population, and instead holding 'black sheep' responsible for the colony's bad reputation in this respect:[129]

> The attacks on natives by whites that have led to repeated convictions in recent years are likely to give outsiders a false picture of the conditions here. They are exceptional cases in which individual people have committed serious offences. The Territorial Council condemns most severely any maltreatment of natives, and sees in the people who commit such acts a great danger to the public. ... The opinions published in some organs of the territory's press, seeking to gather support for such acts to be treated leniently, have not always displayed the right attitude either. The territory's press has a duty to point out that taking matters into one's own hands is bound to lead to conflict with the law. It would be more beneficial to warn those involved that the maltreatment of natives is unacceptable than to reinforce their mistaken understanding of the parental power of chastisement. The Territorial Council proposes that employers who have repeatedly been guilty of ill-treating their natives should not, if so judged by the District Council, be assigned any further workers. But alongside such determined action against whites, equally energetic action should be taken against coloured cattle thieves and vagabonds. Excessive leniency of the authorities towards coloured people has in many cases been the occasion for the offences committed by whites.[130]

Seitz's concern about the threat to the colony's internal stability is sufficient proof that, contrary to the way the issue was depicted by the Territorial Council, it was more than a matter of a few exceptional cases. It is impossible, however, to determine how common such abuses actually were. The Colonial Government was at any rate not prepared to tolerate employers' taking the law into their own hands, nor did it restrict itself to simply trying to use persuasion on them. There were court cases involving the maltreatment of Africans by Whites throughout the whole of the postwar period.

Two further examples,[131] both from the year 1912, will serve to illustrate both the wide range of the offences and the nature of the argumentation employed by judges. On 19 July 1912 Windhoek District Court, with Judge Weber presiding and District Officer Todt prosecuting, sentenced the farmer Friedrich Schneidewind to a total of two years and three months' imprisonment for bodily harm resulting in death, and for grievous bodily harm. The following is a description of the more serious of these two offences. On 18 December 1911 Schneidewind had threatened an African woman called Goras, who allegedly was not doing her work, with the sjambok, whereupon she ran away. He then pursued her with his dogs, caught up with her after some 600 or 800 metres and drove her back, 'striking her repeatedly with the sjambok':

> In doing so he shoved her violently several times, so that she fell very heavily. When he got close to the ox cart, he first grabbed the girl, who was lying completely exhausted on the ground, by the left foot and dragged her a distance of 20 m, then placed an ox strap around her neck, dragged her by it another 12 m or so to the cart and tied her firmly to it. When she tried to crawl into the shadow of the cart, he pulled her back into the sun [*The occurrence took place in December, at the height of summer*]. Finally he threw several heavy rocks at her, striking her on the thigh and the upper arm. This was in the morning. She died in the afternoon, at about 4 o'clock. It was later possible to determine from the body that an upper arm and several ribs were broken.[132]

This description is based on the affidavits filed by Police Sergeant Stallinger, who had exhumed the body and performed the first interrogations, and the 'Boer' Louw, who had witnessed the mistreatment of Goras.

The Court found that only a longish term of imprisonment would serve to adequately atone for these crimes, as Schneidewind had behaved 'in a thoroughly inhuman manner'. Nevertheless, extenuating circumstances were allowed, since the maltreatment was deemed to be an exceptional case, and it was confirmed by Louw and a number of Africans that Schneidewind did not tend to act violently. In addition, the accused had, according to his own credible assertion, been in a 'state of great nervous excitement' due to the loss of four hundred items of small livestock, representing a third of his wealth, which had escaped – as a result of the negligence of 'his natives', as the Court found.

> The Court has thus come to the conclusion that the Goras case was not an act of deliberate cruelty, but an outbreak of violent temper, though admittedly one that was terrifying in its degree. There was thus no cause to subject the accused to a sentence of imprisonment with hard labour that would dishonour him. On the contrary, further mitigating

circumstances have also been allowed him, in addition to the factors stated above also his unblemished record until now. Despite this, his inhuman behaviour, the consequences of which can no longer be undone, demands that the penalty imposed should lie not too far below the minimum punishment provided for by the law where there are no extenuating circumstances.[133]

For the offence of inflicting bodily harm resulting in death he was therefore sentenced to two years and two months in prison, and for the substantially less serious case of inflicting bodily harm to three weeks in prison.[134]

Three months previously, the same court had sentenced the farmer Franz Würzberger to one month's imprisonment on a charge of causing bodily harm. According to the grounds of the judgment, Würzberger had been provoked when undertaking the carriage of freight by the repeated 'disobedience' of his two workers, who had also caused him financial loss, and when he then discovered that the cotter pin was missing from one wheel of his cart he had interpreted this as an attempt on his life and that of his housekeeper. He thereupon attacked one of his workers:

> The accused, in a state of extreme rage, confronted the Herero Thimoteus. When the latter denied the accusation, he struck him on the head with his hand in his agitation, and when Thimoteus threw himself to the ground, he kicked at him with the point of his shoe. By chance he kicked Thimoteus in the right eye, which was seriously injured and subsequently had to be removed in order to save the left eye.[135]

The Court was of the opinion that even if 'the accused person's action of striking his worker with his hand ... might be construed as the exercise of his parental power of chastisement, the kicking could never be construed as such, but as the deliberate infliction of bodily harm'. The heavy shoe that the accused was wearing constituted 'a dangerous instrument'. Mitigating circumstances were allowed in that the accused had a previously unblemished record and had made an open and remorseful confession. In addition, he had been in a 'state of justified agitation'.

The judge considered it appropriate to impose the most lenient permissible penalty, since the accused had otherwise been a good employer, as all the Africans who had been interviewed had admitted, and because he, being otherwise much too lenient (as the Court found), had been provoked by the 'laziness and insubordination' of the 'natives' and was agitated due to the fear for his life. In addition, the severe injury inflicted on Thimoteus had not been intentional.[136]

The District Office in Okahandja further ordered Würzberger to pay compensation to Thimoteus in the form of fifteen goats.[137] When Würzberger refused to comply, Deputy Governor Hintrager instructed the District Office to bring a new case against Würzberger in order to force him to pay Thimoteus a monetary pension.[138] Würzberger thereupon declared that he was prepared to pay his debt after all, and since Thimoteus also indicated that he was satisfied with this, the District Office asked to be allowed not to pursue the case. In the view of the official, Würzberger had already been very severely punished, and the payment of a pension, in addition to his prison sentence and the high court costs, would ruin him; and Thimoteus too was satisfied. He was 'scarcely hindered' in his work by the loss of his eye, and the 'detriment to his appearance was not likely to matter much to the native'.[139] The Governor's Office accepted this.[140]

The Court did not regard Würzberger's behaviour as being unmotivated, but it convicted him nevertheless. Against this background it is particularly amazing that both the District Office and the Governor's Office were determined to obtain compensation for Thimoteus, even though Würzberger had to go to prison anyway. As in the Schneidewind case, the Court accepted mitigating circumstances. The 'violent temper' of the accused in the one case, and the 'great agitation' in the other, were accepted as extenuating factors. The Court also hinted in both cases that the victims were themselves partly to blame – which can only be seen as arising out of the racist attitudes of the judges and their assessors.

Although it was a matter for the District Offices to prosecute in cases of alleged maltreatment, in view of its concern about the prevalence of such cases the Colonial Government did not want to have to rely on them alone. In cases in which it suspected that a criminal offence had indeed been committed, therefore, it took the initiative and itself instructed the District Office concerned to pursue investigations. From an article in the 7 March 1913 edition of the newspaper *Südwest*, for example, the Governor's Office learnt that there had been a case of maltreatment of an Ovambo in Rehoboth District. It thereupon instructed the District Office to investigate the matter and, insofar as the results of the investigation were able to support the allegation, to bring a prosecution for causing bodily harm.[141] District Officer von Vietsch responded to the request and reported that a White woman had set her two dogs on an Ovambo called Kuck, who had 'suffered a minor wound'. The woman had immediately called the dogs back. The Ovambo had not taken the matter too seriously and had asked to be allowed to continue working for the woman. A prosecution for causing bodily harm was therefore not justified; but the woman concerned had been issued with a police penalty notice in the amount of fifteen marks.[142]

The Administration can thus be seen to have been active in cases of maltreatment; but Governor Seitz's confidence that the majority of the settlers would show an understanding of the reprehensible nature of such conduct was disappointed. As the members of the Territorial Council were themselves forced to admit, many in the colony, rather than unambiguously condemning these excesses, made light of them.[143] The sanction, which the Territorial Council had itself proposed, of not supplying further workers to employers who were guilty of such offences, failed because it was too rarely implemented by the responsible officials. A year after Seitz had issued his appeal there was no notable change in the situation. As a senior official in the Governor's Office named Kohler bluntly stated in the draft for a new Circulated Order, Africans were still being assigned to employers 'who were devoid of any proper understanding of their rights and duties towards the natives'. Generally in such cases, difficulties were placed in the way of their giving notice, so that they found themselves 'in a state of dependency' and were 'as a rule completely at the mercy of their masters'. Kohler openly expressed his fear of an increasing 'brutalization' of the White population. Yet even he did not fundamentally call the 'parental power of chastisement' into question, but only wanted to see cases 'of unjust, too frequent or too severe chastisement' prevented.[144] What exactly was to be understood by these categories he did not go into in any more detail. His efforts did nothing to change the degree of reliance on the officials' subjective discretion.

But not all farmers made light of the excesses of corporal punishment that Africans were subjected to. In a letter to the Colonial Government in 1913, a farmer, Captain (ret'd) Georg Engelhard, wrote ironically:

> There are cases known to me in which whites, without being in any employment relationship with a particular black person, have fallen upon the latter totally without cause and beaten him, without the black person being able to have any idea of why. In such cases: is the black person allowed, before he dies, to defend himself, or to hold the white person fast until other whites come to protect him? Or must he wait until <u>after</u> his <u>death</u> has occurred or he has fallen into a state of unconsciousness?

> Am I allowed to force the wife of one of my workers to work for me without giving her food or wages or any other remuneration? Am I considered legally to be her master? May I hit her on the head if in my – incontrovertible – opinion she carries out my orders too slowly?[145]

At the same time, this letter indicates that there was a widespread attitude that all Africans were to be physically at the disposition of Whites, irrespective of whether any employment relationship existed or not – and that this attitude was very familiar in settler circles.

The Governor's Office appears to have taken offence at this implicit reproach that it was doing nothing to prevent maltreatment, and answered tersely: 'The Governor's Office does not regard itself as being under any obligation to respond to inquiries of a purely theoretical nature. You are recommended to report any occurrences of the type you describe to the competent court with a view to prosecution.'[146]

To summarize, it is clear that the Colonial Government did in principle make efforts to get a grip on cases of maltreatment. But it failed, just as it did in its efforts to constrain the employers, and not only the African workers, to comply with the obligations they had entered into. Ultimately, the issue as to whether the District Officers should intervene on behalf of an African was subject to much too broad a degree of discretion on their part. In addition, some of them showed too much solidarity with the interests of the White population. If an official simply shared the view that nothing Africans said was to be believed, it was scarcely to be expected that he would help them to obtain justice. Nor was there any way out of the dilemma that the Administration was bound by the law, and in cases of proceedings against Whites had to leave the decision to an independent court, which often put paid to the initiatives of well-meaning officials. To give the Africans any chance of being treated equally by the courts, the colonial situation itself – that is to say, the way the colonized were discriminated against in all aspects of everyday life – would have had to have been set aside. But there was nobody who wanted that.

Migrant Workers from Ovamboland

Despite the German Colonial Administration's intense efforts to recruit all the able-bodied African men living within the Police Zone to work on White-owned farms, in railway construction or in the mines, it was unable to relieve the shortage of labour. The only way out was to increasingly employ labourers from elsewhere: primarily from Ovamboland, but also from British southern Africa. These people were known as 'migrant workers': they worked in the Police Zone on limited-term contracts, and then returned home.

Most of them were employed in major enterprises: in the mines or in railway construction. Unlike the workers originating in the Police

Zone, however, they could not be recruited through the exercise of direct compulsion, so that employers had to pay much higher wages in order to attract them. These wages in their turn were then substantially higher for labourers from the British territories to the South than for Ovambo, because the mines in South West Africa had to compete with those on the Witwatersrand in their home country. In respect of their working conditions, however, they cannot be said to have been any better off. Precisely because they would be returning home after a relatively short time, their labour was if anything exploited even more ruthlessly and with even less consideration than on the farms. There was no incentive to treat them better with a view to building up a permanent and contented workforce.

In its efforts to maintain minimum standards of treatment for the Africans working in the mines and on the railways, the Administration was faced with similar problems to those existing on the farms; but they were rendered even more intractable by the fact that the officials were up against bigger and far more powerful employers, who moreover in the case of the mining companies had come together to form the Lüderitzbucht Chamber of Mines, and were thus able to form a united front against critical officials.

The following account of the world of migrant labour concentrates on working conditions in the diamond mines, as the majority of the migrant workers were employed there and it was there that the conflicts between the Administration and the employers became most acute, focusing on the person of the Lüderitzbucht Native Commissioner, Hermann Tönjes. The section of the chapter concerning labourers from the British territories will present an example illustrating conditions on the railway construction sites. But as the migration of workers from Ovamboland gave rise to characteristic structures, which as a result of the specific form of recruitment and the long distances between the workers' homes and their places of work were different from those on the labour market within the Police Zone, the first section consists of a brief account of these.

Reasons for the Migrant Labour System, the Organization of Recruitment and the Journey to the Workplaces

Thanks to its large population, Ovamboland had attracted the attention of the Colonial Government as a reservoir of potential labour as early as 1884.[147] A little later, Ovambo did indeed start to be employed in significant numbers on major construction projects, such as the railway line from Swakopmund to Windhoek in the years 1897 to 1902, the

Swakopmund–Otavi line from 1903 onwards, or the construction of the port at Swakopmund in the years 1899 to 1903.[148]

The war against the Herero and Nama increased the requirement for migrant workers substantially. The wartime turbulences and the deaths of so many Herero and Nama led to a considerable shortage of workers, especially at a time when the demand was increasing rapidly due to the exploitation of the copper deposits at Tsumeb from 1906 onwards and the discovery of the first diamonds in 1908.[149] This led to an intensification of attempts to recruit labourers from Ovamboland. Whereas in 1908 scarcely more than two thousand migrant workers had made their way southwards, this number rose rapidly to reach up to ten thousand per year between 1910 and 1914.[150] As the typical contract was only concluded for a period of six months, however, there were never this many of them in the Police Zone at one and the same time. The official statistics reported the following numbers of Ovambo on 1 January of the respective years: 896 in 1909, 2,790 in 1910, 5,122 in 1911, 5,136 in 1912 and 5,557 in 1913.[151]

The decision not to occupy Ovamboland but to use it as a reservoir of labour outside the area of direct rule was taken during the Herero and Nama War. As has already been described, it was Governor von Lindequist who introduced the first measures to protect Ovamboland against the dynamics of colonial settlement such as had ultimately led to the outbreak of war in the south. In 1906 he basically closed the borders of Ovamboland to Whites, requiring them to obtain official authorization either to enter the area or in particular to recruit labourers from it.[152] Such authorization was to be granted only to 'absolutely reliable persons', in order to prevent abuse and so 'to preserve the valuable stock of manpower … and persuade more and more Ovambo to leave their tribal areas at least for a time and to seek a livelihood in the service of the whites'.[153] Furthermore, migrant labour was to be kept under state control. Recruiting agents were therefore obliged, under the threat of high penalties, to present the workers to the police at one of the two major border crossing points – the only places where it was permitted to enter or leave the area – when they left Ovamboland, so that they could be issued with the prescribed pass tokens.[154] It was to be explained to the Ovambo at the time what 'advantages' the pass tokens conferred on them. Although the obligation to use one of these two border stations did not apply when they returned home, they were to be indirectly encouraged to do so by the prospect of being able to make complaints about their employers there if they so wished. The main purpose of this measure, however, was not to protect the workers but to implement an 'undercover' extension of the measures of surveillance and control. Governor von Lindequist explained it as follows:

> The District Officer will above all be required to do everything in his power to receive the people and to take care of them, so that they grow accustomed to using the crossing points [Namutoni or Okaukweyo] voluntarily when they go back home. When the return migration takes place, it will be his duty to enquire where this or that person is, if for example he is not to be found among the people returning home, and in particular whether he has voluntarily extended his employment. In any case, the Ovambo are to be given the feeling that this surveillance is an act of care for them, and the impression is to be avoided that it is detrimental to them in any way.[155]

Thus both the recruiting agents and the labourers were to be subject to control by the authorities: the former in order to counter the political dangers that could arise out of too unscrupulous practices being applied among the still intact 'tribes' of Ovamboland, and the latter so that they too could be subjected to the system of watertight control that was to be applied within the Police Zone – this being just the time when the authorities in Windhoek were working on the Pass and Control Ordinances.

This met with resistance among potential employers, as they wanted to have unhindered access to the Chiefs ruling in Ovamboland and the potential labourers living there, or even favoured a military conquest of the northern area of the colony, so that its population too could be subjected to the requirement to take up employment. They were not susceptible to the argument that such a military occupation would be enormously expensive, as it would have been the State treasury that would have had to bear the costs. The resulting conflict between the Administration and the Chamber of Mines remained unresolved right up to the end of German colonial rule. The Chamber of Mines put forward its demand for military conquest again and again, which the Administration again and again rejected, or else evaded by hinting at the possibility of military undertakings at some time in the future.[156] Thus there was no way in which direct pressure could be exerted on the Ovambo to accept dependent employment with Whites in the central and southern areas of the colony. The fact that there were nevertheless times when up to six thousand Ovambo were working in the Police Zone is explained by a whole range of exogenous and endogenous factors.

The principal 'push factor' was that traditional agriculture in Ovamboland was vulnerable to repeated crises. Enormous fluctuations in the annual rainfall – in the period from 1886/87 to 1910/11, for example, it varied between a minimum of 181.0 mm and a maximum of 928.3 mm – led to frequent flooding, alternating with disastrous droughts. The particularly devastating climatic conditions that prevailed during the last fifteen years in which the area was formally under German colonial rule were intensified by the rinderpest outbreak of 1897, which had a major impact in Ovamboland as well, destroying a large proportion of the cattle herds. With parts of the population being rendered destitute as a result, the pressure to emigrate was increased precisely at the time when the demand for labour in the southern part of the colony was increasing. It was a feature shared by Herero and Ovambo culture that the ownership of cattle not only represented material wealth but was also indicative of the owner's social status, the loss of which weakened the sense of self-worth of men in particular. Volunteering to become a migrant labourer appeared to be a way out of this wretched economic and socio-psychological situation, reflecting as it did the concepts of mobility and risk that were dominant features in the vision that young Ovambo in particular had of the lives they sought to lead, being vital components of the phase of proving oneself as one entered adult life. Thus 'manly' virtues were linked above all to ideas of prevailing over dangers and trials such as were incident upon hunting expeditions, for example, and that far away from one's family. These concepts could be transferred to the life of a migrant worker; and they were supplemented by the Christian work ethic propagated by the Missions, which sought to integrate the value of work into the ideal life pattern of the Ovambo. As the Finnish Mission that had been active in Ovamboland since 1870, and even more so the Rhenish Mission that had been present there since 1891, operated in close cooperation with the German colonizers, the emphasis given to the value of individual work acted as a signpost pointing beyond the borders of Ovamboland and in the direction of dependent employment in the south of the colony.

In addition to these 'push factors', there were also a number of 'pull factors' that had developed out of the contacts with White merchants, which had existed since the mid-nineteenth century. While the first contacts had been with traders operating out of Portuguese Angola, Damara traders from the south soon began to appear in greater numbers too. They brought highly coveted items such as weapons and horses, which became important status symbols for the traditional elites, and also consumer goods, among which alcohol occupied pride of place. While these had originally been traded above all for ivory, cattle later became the predominant trading commodity – at least up to the time when the herds were destroyed by the rinderpest epidemic. And it was precisely at this time, around the turn of the century, that the Ovambo started to sell their labour as migrant workers, a phenomenon that grew in scale as a result of the increasing destitution caused by the frequent famines.[157]

The elites promoted the model of working outside Ovamboland to some extent, as they received a cut of the wages paid or were rewarded by the prospective employers for persuading their subjects to migrate. This provided them with the financial means they needed to pay their growing debts to the traders and to buy new goods. The German Administration deliberately speculated on this link between the consumption of European goods and the willingness to become migrant workers, which gave the Ovambo continued access to the trading network despite the closing of the borders to Ovamboland. The restrictions on access would have been counterproductive in this respect, so von Lindequist attempted to compensate for them by recommending that markets should be held in Okaukweyo and Namutoni twice a year, in which proposal he explicitly had in mind the aim of promoting the sales of European goods among the Ovambo. Von Lindequist expressly stated that the intention of the Ovambo Ordinance was 'not to restrict intercourse with the Ovambo, but on the contrary to enhance it and to protect it against factors that would interfere with it'.[158]

After plans to establish a German Residency in Ovamboland had been abandoned in 1909 due to objections from the Imperial Colonial Office,[159] migrancy could only be promoted through individual expeditions. The Administration therefore carried out recruiting expeditions through the territory in the years 1911, 1912 and 1913. The results were disappointing, the willingness to be involved in migrant labour apparently being dampened by Ovambo returning home and spreading information about how wretched the working conditions in the diamond fields were. The Colonial Government did not therefore succeed in bringing about any increase in the number of Ovambo willing to become migrant workers.[160]

Right up to the end of the German colonial period, Ovamboland remained outside the area subject to direct German rule, and the migrant labour phenomenon was based on the interplay of endogenous and exogenous factors. But migrancy had repercussions back in Ovamboland too; it made the precarious economic situation in the labourers' home area more acute, as the labour of those who migrated was then lacking back home. Those who did sign up as migrant workers therefore did all they could to at least be back on their own land for harvest time, and so concluded contracts with terms of not more than six months.[161] This explains the high fluctuation in the numbers of the migrant workers:

the number of incoming workers was always particularly high in the first quarter of the year, whereas six months later the number of those returning home was at its highest.[162]

When the Ovambo set out, they had a long journey in front of them and many hardships to overcome before they reached their workplaces in Tsumeb or Lüderitzbucht. First, they had to get from their home areas to one of the two border crossing points, Namutoni or Okaukweyo. To do this they had to negotiate a route some parts of which were largely without water, and in years of drought these claimed the first fatalities. At the border crossings the recruiting agents were lying in wait for them – private entrepreneurs looking for labourers particularly for the mines. They were paid according to the number of people they recruited, and so were willing to resort to practically any means to win over as many Ovambo as possible. They exploited the hunger and above all the thirst of people worn out by the long distances they had already had to cover, and often lured the Ovambo into signing contracts by distributing food and drink to them. Furthermore, the recruiting agents often painted a completely false picture of working conditions in the diamond fields – a tactic that was particularly effective with those coming for the first time. As many of the Ovambo could not read, to say nothing of being able to speak German, they placed their fingerprints in lieu of signatures under contracts whose content they generally did not understand.[163] But once they had done that, they were caught up in the clutches of bureaucracy and it was only too easy for them to become guilty of breach of contract, whereupon they would be pursued by the State's enforcement agencies. The fact that Outjo District Office proposed in 1911 that at least two interpreters should be available at each of the border crossings shows that the Administration was aware of the problem and was attempting to do something about it. It is not clear, however, whether the proposal was ever implemented. All in all, State control over the recruiting agents left much to be desired – and as the Administration complained again and again, there were never enough police officers available to do anything about it.

Despite this, it would be wrong to present the Ovambo simply as passive victims deprived of any freedom to make decisions for themselves. Increasing experience of migrant work, whether that experience was their own or what they were told by friends and acquaintances, led them to be able to make more deliberate use of their opportunities to make choices, at least up until 1911 when those opportunities were restricted (see below).

Their initial freedom of choice received nourishment from the fierce competition between the recruiting agents, which in turn was a reflection of the competition between the employers, the copper mines in Tsumeb being in strong competition with the diamond mines in the south of the country. The Otavi Company with its mining operations in Tsumeb had the geographical advantage on its side, however. Situated in the north of the Police Zone, it was popular with the migrant workers because of the shorter distances they had to travel: it was easier for them to return home from there when they had completed their contracts. In addition, the Otavi Company proved itself to be rather more liberal in the way it treated its labourers. It deliberately paid attention to their needs as a way of enhancing its competitiveness in the recruitment of workers, and to the extent that the recruiting agents were aware of this – and as time went by, knowledge about working conditions was spread by word of mouth by the returning workers – it became a further distinct locational advantage. As a result, from 1912 onwards some 30 per cent of all Ovambo migrant workers were employed in the copper mines, and this was enough to completely meet their requirements.[164]

Once the Ovambo had signed a contract at one of the two border stations, they would make their way to their places of work. Tsumeb was comparatively close, but the labourers recruited for the diamond mines in the south still had more than 1,000 km to travel. From Namutoni and Okaukweyo they trekked to the railway stations at Kalkveld or Otjiwarongo. But the hardships of the journey continued unabated, as there was no accommodation, they were inadequately clothed for nights out in the open, and on this stage of the journey water too was in short supply. Things were much the same at the railway station, as they often had a long wait for a train heading south. As they were not allowed to travel on passenger trains, they had no choice but to ride on open goods wagons. The railway companies saw the Ovambo simply as an ancillary source of income; they loaded their trains with goods in the normal way, and only thereafter were the Ovambo allowed to climb up on top of the loads. Not only were they exposed to the vagaries of the weather on the open wagons; the journey was also dangerous. Travellers quite often fell to their deaths from the overloaded trains, so that the Administration was forced to limit the loading of the trains in order to offer a minimum degree of protection and reduce the danger of accidents. Before the railway line to the south was completed in 1911, they had to transfer from rail to water transport at Swakopmund. The accommodation and the travelling conditions were just about as bad as they had been during the rail journey. Above all, the inadequately clothed Ovambo were at the mercy of the harsh weather conditions in Swakopmund, where there were sometimes enormous temperature differences between day and night. There was also an inadequate supply of food. As the recruiting agents were given a fixed sum per worker by the future employers, but also had to pay the workers' fares and the costs of feeding them out of this, every mark they could save represented higher profits for themselves. They thus pursued a strict policy of cost minimization, and it was the Ovambo who had to suffer. The fact that as a result they often arrived at their employers sick and exhausted was of little concern to the recruiting agents.[165]

In its struggle against these dreadful conditions, the German Administration was in a hopeless position. It intervened in minor aspects again and again, trying at least to impose minimum standards for the equipment the recruits were to be provided with. But in this they met with resistance from both the recruiting agents and the Chamber of Mines, which resorted to delaying tactics with regard to implementing the conditions laid down and attempted to water down any improvements. As has been shown in the previous chapter, the German Administration was not all-powerful.[166] It cannot therefore be concluded from the failure or the inadequate effectiveness of its efforts to intervene on behalf of the Ovambo that it was totally indifferent to their fate. As will be shown below by the example of the attempts to exercise supervision over the diamond fields, the Administration was by no means in a position to do whatever it wanted without restriction, but was limited in its ability to exert control over the situation by the bitter resistance of the employers.

The Colonial Government started to consider introducing an Ordinance to regulate the recruiting of Ovambo and to eliminate the most serious abuses in 1909; but due to resistance from the mine operators it was not until December 1911 that such an Ordinance was in fact promulgated. Contrary to the wishes of the employers for the recruitment of labourers to be completely deregulated, it was to continue to be centralized and concentrated at a 'recruiting point under State supervision', which all employers were obliged to make use of. For every worker recruited a fee had to be paid to the State treasury. The employers were subjected to an obligation to provide certain services, including, and above all, care for the sick and payment of the fares for the workers' return journeys. The Native Commissioner for Lüderitzbucht was equipped with far-reaching competences: he was not only to monitor compliance with the obligations mentioned above, but could also, upon presentation of a doctor's certificate, order that a sick worker should be sent home prematurely at the employer's expense. In addition, contract extensions were only valid if they had received his approval.[167]

The Director of the Recruiting Point and all his staff had to be approved by the Colonial Government. Any employees the Governor's Office thought to be unsuitable for this task had to be dismissed. They and the head of the station were forbidden to undertake any trading or other ancillary activities, which clearly throws light on the past practice of the private recruiting agents. The recruiting point was obliged to assign workers in accordance with the order in which the employers' applications were received, a provision intended to prevent any preference being given to certain firms. However, 'in cases where there is an inadequate supply of labourers' the Governor could order that 'individual employers are to receive preference in accordance with the general public interest in the maintenance of their operations': this was a provision that clearly violated the principle of free choice of employer that had prevailed up until then, since the Ovambo were being deprived of the opportunity to choose where they would prefer to work. The aspect of supervision and control was also a central aspect of the Ordinance: it prescribed a precise route by which the labourers who had been recruited were to travel to the mines in Tsumeb or to Lüderitzbucht, which they were only allowed to do in work gangs under the leadership of a foreman, who had to carry a list of all the workers with him. The same applied to the return journey as well. In order to eliminate the obvious inadequacy of the Africans' clothing, the Government prescribed that before they started out on the journey by rail they were to be provided with a suit of clothes and a blanket, or even two in the case of those who were destined to work in the coastal regions .[168]

The Recruitment Ordinance was thus the Administration's reaction to the most glaring abuses the labourers were exposed to while travelling to their places of work, and above all to the chaos unleashed by the competition between different recruiting agents. Despite this, the attempt to centralize recruitment proved in practice to be a vain undertaking. Although the Colonial Government immediately advertised the position of Director of the Recruiting Point,[169] the post remained vacant right up to the end of German colonial rule.[170]

Social Conditions in the Diamond Fields and the Administration's Efforts to Protect Workers

The Recruitment Ordinance not only regulated the recruitment of migrant workers and their journeys to and from their place of employment, but also laid down minimum standards for their treatment at their workplaces. The employer, for example, had to provide his workers with 'accommodation and rations fulfilling all the requirements for promoting good health', and also with any medical treatment that might be necessary for a period of up to six weeks, even if this continued after the end of the contract. Enterprises with more than twenty-five workers had to provide for their food to be cooked for them if they so desired, and to make the necessary water and fuel available. If there were more than fifty employees, a separate sickroom had to be provided, and if there were more than two hundred a trained White paramedic had to be employed and an African cook made available who worked only for the enterprise concerned. Every employer had to keep a properly stocked and equipped pharmacy. The employers were also under an obligation to keep precise records of the days worked, the wages paid and any deductions from wages. Any fatalities were to be notified immediately to the Native Commissioner. He was also required to monitor the labourers' accommodation and food, how they were treated, the payment of wages, and the arrangements for their journeys home, and to be prepared at any time to receive any complaints the workers might have, and to contact the employer about them. If no consensus could be reached, the matter was to be presented to the Governor.[171]

These provisions were the Colonial Government's reaction to the kinds of abuse and irregularity that most often occurred. There are no reliable statistics about conditions in the diamond fields; but the information that is available is sufficient to demonstrate that wage deductions, unsatisfactory food, inadequate provision in cases of sickness and sadistically excessive beatings, often leading to death, were not merely isolated occurrences.[172] The cases described below give some insight into working conditions, without being able to claim to be representative of all mining companies.

The working day lasted up to twelve hours, in most cases including Sundays. The lack of rest breaks led to health problems that were intensified by the inadequacy of the food. Deductions from rations and from wages were methods of punishing labourers for alleged laziness, and were frequently applied even though this was illegal. In addition, corporal punishment was used, as on the farms, to punish employees who were alleged to be 'workshy' or who refused to obey orders. In some cases, Ovambo were literally beaten to death. The causes for these excesses of violence were to be found both in the feelings of racial superiority of the overseers, for whom an African life hardly counted, and also in the tough working conditions that the Whites too had to endure, even though theirs were far better than those of the Africans. In addition, in the more remote fields the Whites were hardly subject to any surveillance. They too were merely employees of the diamond companies, and they often cared little if their behaviour impaired the ability of their African subordinates to work efficiently or affected the supply of migrant workers altogether, as they had no sense of ownership of the business (as we would say nowadays), and nor were they confronted directly with the negative consequences of their actions on the supply of labourers.

The result was health problems for many workers. At the operation of the 'Koloniale Bergbau-Gesellschaft' (Colonial Mining Company) in the northern fields, for example, almost 30 per cent of the workforce was ill. Scurvy in particular was rampant as a result of the bad food, as were bronchial complaints: the climate was raw, the nights were very cold, and the workers had poor clothing and often completely inadequate accommodation. Medical care was often inadequate too: labourers who reported sick were generally accused of malingering and forced to work until they collapsed. Mortality in the diamond fields was consequently high. In 1911 alone, according to the official figures, no less than 181 migrant workers out of a total workforce of 2,300 (i.e. three or four a week) died in the mining areas south of Lüderitzbucht. Mortality rates varied substantially between the individual enterprises. Whereas in the last two months of 1911 the death rate at the Koloniale Bergbau-Gesellschaft lay at around 3 per cent, in the Kolmanskoppe Diamond Mines it was just over 10 per cent.[173] No reliable figures are available for the following years, but the numerous protests from the Native Commissioner and the Lüderitzbucht District Officer indicate that there had been no substantial improvement in the conditions, at least in some of the fields.

The appointment of Hermann Tönjes to the position of Native Commissioner represented the beginning of stricter State surveillance of the diamond fields;[174] although in view of the size of the area concerned and the thousands of labourers who were employed there – the scope of his responsibility covered all the diamond fields in Lüderitzbucht District – even his work could not be more than superficial and had to be limited to random checks.[175] But the reports he submitted on his tours of inspection did serve to bring the horrific conditions at some places of work to the attention of both the Lüderitzbucht District Office and the Colonial Government.

Without in any way seeking to cast doubt on the fact that it was Tönjes's own personal integrity, his sense of justice and his personal revulsion at the conditions prevailing in the diamond fields that led him to stand up for the interests of the labourers, the circumstance that his field of responsibility also included promoting the recruitment of migrant workers in Ovamboland must inevitably have played a part as well. The bad food, the health situation – which in some places was catastrophic – and the high level of mortality among the migrant workers impeded this task, as tales of the conditions prevailing in Lüderitzbucht got about in Ovamboland and threatened to hinder continuing recruitment. In his view – one shared by Lüderitzbucht District Office and the Governor's Office – the mining companies were pursuing false economies, since the policy of paring down the costs of labour as far as possible was a danger to the whole of the migrant labour system, which was based on voluntary participation. The heart of the matter was the question of who was to bear the higher costs. Whereas some mine operators were content to follow the course of exploiting their labourers without any regard for their health, accepting the fact that this would turn many of them into invalids who were unable to work – whereupon the companies would then simply bring in new labourers and demand that the Colonial Government should take more and more drastic measures to promote migrant labour – the Administration stood up for minimum standards in order not to jeopardize the supply of labourers.

As was also the case with regard to farmworkers, the Governor's Office saw the key to promoting stable working relationships and solving the problem of the labour shortage as lying in good treatment of the workers. And this was a solution that did not require it to undertake any additional tasks, and therefore did not create any additional expense either. Here too, however, a policy of bringing criminal prosecutions against White offenders proved to be more or less ineffective. In most cases the offenders got off scot-free or with relatively light punishments. The efforts of Lüderitzbucht District Office, as outlined below, to persuade the diamond companies to comply with at least a minimum level of protection for the Africans is typical both of the good intentions of District Officer Rudolf Böhmer and Native Commissioner Hermann Tönjes, and also of the reactions of the employers and their attempts to draw a veil over the real situation. Unlike the expressions of discontent on the part of individual farmers, the opposition that Tönjes encountered from the employers' side took the form of organized resistance, as the diamond companies had a body to represent them in the form of the Chamber of Mines. In addition, they were by far the most important sector of the economy, employing several thousand labourers concentrated in Lüderitzbucht District and the south of Swakopmund District, and were up against only a single Native Commissioner, who became the focus for all their grumbles.

At the beginning of May 1912 Tönjes complained to the Governor's Office about renewed cases of maltreatment in the diamond mines, and spoke openly about the likely consequences for the recruitment of labourers.[176] The Governor's Office took his warning that it was impossible for him under these circumstances to recruit new workers during his tour of Ovamboland very seriously. It was particularly alarmed by his assessment that while the Ovambo would put up with 'any kind of treatment' in the diamond fields, when they got home they would then 'simply beat up the first white who interfered with them in any way'. The Governor felt that under these circumstances it was actually quite remarkable that the Ovambo had not already resorted to taking the law into their own hands within the Police Zone. He was forced to conclude that the way they were treated in the diamond mines was not calculated to contribute to 'making the Ovambos more willing to move to our areas of work'. The Colonial Government would therefore only allow any access to Ovamboland 'with misgivings', since it was feared 'that the Ovambo, who had a strong tendency to harbour revengeful feelings', would 'repay whites in Ovamboland for the treatment that has been meted out to them here'. Seitz was thus fully aware of the direct threat to the recruitment of labourers. In order to defuse this dangerous situation, he appealed to the Chamber of Mines to ensure that 'such whites' as had been guilty of the gross maltreatment of Africans were 'immediately dismissed'.[177]

The Administration appears to have believed that the continuing cases of maltreatment could be laid at the door of a few notoriously thuggish individuals. It therefore attempted to persuade the mining companies to dismiss Whites who had repeatedly drawn attention to themselves in this way, or at least to transfer them to somewhere else. As the Lüderitzbucht Deputy District Officer Heilingbrunner wrote to the Chamber of Mines, there were some mines that had already said they were prepared to do this. The District Office now attempted to exert pressure on the others. Heilingbrunner pointed out to the Chamber of Mines that it was in their own interests to bring an end to the continued maltreatment, as Africans who had been victims of ill treatment were entitled to give immediate notice, and the companies would then have to pay for their return journeys home. In addition, there was no doubt that Ovambo would be deterred from deciding to take up migrant work if labourers returning home reported having suffered beatings. However, the Deputy District Officer clearly no longer believed that he could rely on voluntary cooperation from the mines. He therefore announced that he was engaged in consultations with the Office of Mining about the introduction of a Police Regulation that would give the police powers to instruct companies in individual cases 'not to employ unsuitable people in positions (e.g. as managers or sorters) in which they are entitled to supervise natives directly'.[178]

The controversies that then surrounded this Police Regulation show how powerless the District Office was to exert any real pressure on the mining companies. The President of the Chamber of Mines, Emil Kreplin, replied immediately and declared that his organization was quite prepared to exhort the individual companies 'either to dismiss people who have been proved to have maltreated natives without justification or else to employ them in positions in which they have no direct supervision of natives'. However, he rejected the idea of a binding Police Regulation, which would represent serious interference with private rights and therefore be illegal, and took the view that the companies could not permit the authorities to lay down which people they could employ and which not. The criminal law was there to deal with supervisors who maltreated 'natives' without reason, and that was sufficient; 'everything else' should be 'left to the employers, who are best able to judge whether one of their employees was more useful or harmful to their operations'.[179] A month later, the Colonial Government also confirmed that such a Police Regulation would be legally inadmissible, even though both Deputy Governor Hintrager and Lüderitzbucht District Office saw a need to take action. In Hintrager's view, the supervisory personnel concerned should be deported from the colony as a general danger to public order.[180] In the essence of the matter, therefore, the Colonial Government supported Heilingbrunner's position, but its ability to take action was limited by the principle, which applied at least in the case of Whites, that the rule of law must prevail.

The recommendation that Whites who maltreated Africans should be deported did not prove to be very useful, as Lüderitzbucht District Office reported in a letter almost a year later. German nationals could not be deported if they had not been convicted of any offence; and that stage was not usually reached. It was difficult even to deport foreigners, and such measures could seldom be implemented; and as in addition the requisite proceedings took a very long time, that factor alone would be sufficient to nullify their 'effectiveness and success'.[181]

This entire letter reflects the powerlessness and frustration of Lüderitzbucht District Office, which was unable to make any progress in its efforts to achieve better treatment of the African labourers; indeed, it was even forced to take note of a considerable deterioration in the situation. After a period during which an encouraging improvement had taken place, the District Office reported, the number of cases of Africans being maltreated had recently begun to increase again. Whereas in May 1912 the companies had threatened that anyone inflicting corporal punishment on Africans would be immediately dismissed, they had now taken to countering reports of sorters who were constantly beating Africans with the assertion that there had been complaints about them too. In District Officer Böhmer's view, this 'shift in opinion' was due to the fact that the mining companies now had enough workers, and so 'did not think they needed to pay so much attention to them'. The Courts too were totally failing in their responsibility. Where there was an irrefutable level of proof it might be possible to obtain a conviction with a fine in individual cases in the District Court; but then an appeal would be lodged. A Judge of the Superior Court who did not know the conditions in the diamond fields would preside over the proceedings, the African witnesses would long ago have departed, straight after the first trial, and the accused White man would have learnt from the first trial the direction in which he ought to steer his defence. What Africans said would simply not be believed, whereas any statement made by a White under oath, however dubious, would be given credence, and so the whole affair would end with a splendid acquittal – and there was no more thankless task than to represent the prosecuting authorities in such cases. It was useless to negotiate with the Chamber of Mines, as they would simply deny everything; and in any case, they did not have anything like the influence over their members that they were popularly believed to possess. The fact that the Colonial Government had refused to issue a Police Regulation prohibiting Whites who were guilty of maltreating Africans from occupying supervisory positions had left the District Office completely powerless. It therefore demanded once again that the proposed Police Regulation should be adopted.[182]

The Colonial Government again refused to do this, because of uncertainty about its legal admissibility. It confirmed, however, that there had been an increase in the number of maltreatment cases, and it also shared the criticism of the judicial system. In the original draft of the letter it said: 'Here too we have often not been able to escape the impression that the courts frequently fail to deliver in cases brought against whites for the maltreatment of natives'. In the end, however, Hintrager could not bring himself to declare the dysfunctionality of the court system in such frank terms, and the whole sentence was deleted from the draft.

Despite his critical attitude towards the Police Regulation demanded by the District Office, Hintrager recognized the need for the Administration to take action to prevent the mistreatment of Africans.

As a way out of the deadlock he pointed out that the Governor's Office had decided, with the approval of the Territorial Council, not to assign any more workers to employers whom the District Office considered to be guilty of maltreatment. This would in future also be applied to mining companies 'that keep supervisors who are known for their tendency to commit aggressive acts against natives'. If the issue of formal warnings should prove to be insufficient to get such supervisors dismissed or transferred to other positions, these businesses would no longer be supplied with labourers by the agents recruiting Ovambo.[183] But like the previous suggestion that people found guilty of committing offences should be deported, this proposal too reveals the extent to which the Colonial Government was at a loss to know how to deal with the problem, and shows the ignorance that prevailed about conditions in the diamond fields. As Böhmer wrote, the threat to forbid the assignment of labourers to certain employers was an empty gesture:

> As the Imperial Colonial Government must be well aware, having had the issue of employment both in Ovamboland and in this District investigated by the Head of the Department of Native Affairs, neither the District Office nor the recruiting agent has any influence at all on the assignment of labourers. The workers who come to the diamond fields are all recruited on behalf of the Chamber of Mines, and only when they are on their way, at Keetmanshoop or even only when they arrive here, are they assigned to the individual employers. Thus there is no way in which an instruction to the recruiting agents not to supply labourers to a particular company could be effective, as the agent has nothing to do with the individual companies. But the Chamber of Mines, which arranges the distribution, would scarcely comply with any such instruction.[184]

Böhmer also rejected the idea of making the assignment of labourers to a particular company conditional on the prior agreement of the District Council, and that for two reasons. Firstly, he did not believe that the District Council could judge 'how every one of the three hundred white employees in the diamond fields treats the natives', and secondly because he had severe doubts regarding its impartiality, as the District Council in Lüderitzbucht was composed 'to a substantial degree of diamond interests' (at the time, indeed, all three members were associated with the mining industry). He also had fundamental doubts about 'making an activity of the District Offices that is purely a public order function dependent upon the adoption of a resolution by a body that meets seldom, is made up of interested parties and was created for completely different purposes'. If the police were to be effective at all, he thought, they must be able to intervene immediately and directly. It was the District Officer who bore 'responsibility for this from the civil law, criminal law and disciplinary points of view', and his actions were subject to the supervision of his superior authority; but he could not let his actions be dependent upon the decisions of a 'collective body made up of buddies'. Böhmer's mention of the 'interested parties' comprising the District Council indicates his fundamental reservations with regard to lobbies representing particular interests, implicitly contrasting these with the Wilhelminian civil servant who fulfils the duties of his office objectively and is responsible only to the general good.

Böhmer therefore continued to insist on his proposal that a Police Regulation should be issued that would prevent a White person who had maltreated Africans from being allowed to exercise supervision over 'natives', as this was the only way in which it was possible to bring about the effective protection of Africans:

> If the police continue to be refused this instrument, then they are completely powerless with regard to the maltreatment of natives, as the courts fail to provide any protection or are far too late in doing so, ... and the District Office is then no longer in a position to take any responsibility for ensuring that the natives in the diamond fields are properly treated.[185]

But as the Colonial Government continued to refuse to accept this position and once again pointed out that dealing with the maltreatment of Africans was a matter for the criminal courts,[186] the hands of the District Office were as firmly tied as ever.

Despite this, the efforts of Böhmer, Heilingbrunner and Tönjes were not totally in vain; in particular the inspections and reports of the Native Commissioner were felt by the mining companies to be a troublesome nuisance. This is demonstrated by their attempts to discredit him. The Native Commissioner was deliberately smeared, and the mining companies, turning reality completely on its head, tried to make him responsible for the deterioration of conditions in the diamond fields. The conflicts between the Koloniale Bergbau-Gesellschaft and the Lüderitzbucht Chamber of Mines on the one hand and Tönjes on the other illustrate the tense relationships that had come to prevail between the Administration and the diamond companies. All the cases of maltreatment reported by Tönjes were rejected by the employers as being false accusations by the Ovambo: 'All in all, we are forced to emphasize again and again ... that the Ovambo are thoroughly untruthful, and that the testimony of a white person who understands the significance of an oath is worth ten times that of an Ovambo'. At the same time, they accused Tönjes of being himself responsible for those cases of maltreatment that did take place, as he had 'not always gone about things in the way that might have been expected'. He had, for example, failed to inform the companies promptly about cases of maltreatment that had come to his attention. But if the Native Commissioner acted like that, then they would 'never reach a position in which maltreatment is stopped'. It was the primary task of the Commissioner to inform the company first of all and immediately of any abuses, so that they could take measures against their employees. But they had known nothing of the many cases of maltreatment he had reported.

> This is perfectly understandable, as a white employee will never mistreat a black person in the presence of his superior. The Native Commissioner, through his dealings with the blacks, is in a much better position to learn about such abuses. But he should not keep these to himself, but, as has already been stated, must report them to the companies.[187]

It apparently never occurred to the writer of this letter that any representative of the management could question workers just as easily as the Native Commissioner could, or that the failure of the internal control of employees, which he admitted in this letter, could have been avoided. There was one obvious fundamental difference, however, between the company staff and Tönjes: the former assumed that all Africans were liars, whereas Tönjes took their complaints thoroughly seriously.

Only a few days later, the Chamber of Mines also found itself defending the Koloniale Bergbau-Gesellschaft against renewed accusations that there had been cases of maltreatment. In doing so, it presented the conditions in the company's mining areas as being nothing less than exemplary, since there were 'many fewer cases of maltreatment than might be expected with a workforce normally amounting to 1,200 men, a large number of whom are workshy and insolent. ... No diamond company in German South West Africa affords its native labourers better treatment, food and accommodation than the Koloniale Bergbau-Gesellschaft'. Tönjes's accusations were attributed to a lack of objectivity:

> If this gentleman, the Native Commissioner, were not guided by an exaggerated idealism that it would be quite impossible to implement in practice, then his reports on the aforesaid company would have to say that in view of the large workforce and the <u>character of the natives with their inclination to laziness</u>, the cases of maltreatment that occur are relatively very few.[188]

The Chamber of Mines implicitly attributed responsibility for the Ovambo's refusal to work and for their insubordination to Tönjes, and so tacitly also blamed him for the need to inflict corporal punishment:

> We cannot refrain from taking this opportunity to point out that all our members engaged in mining have been complaining for months that the discipline of the labourers has declined markedly and that cases of disobedience and direct insolence on the part of the natives are becoming more and more numerous. The activities of the Native Commissioner in questioning the boys in order to bring to light any complaints they may have seem to have given rise to an opinion among the natives that they are not obliged to take any notice of what the white supervisors say, and that it depends entirely on their own goodwill whether they work or not.[189]

But it was not only for the mining companies that Tönjes's unvarnished revelations of conditions in the diamond fields were a thorn in the flesh. Even Governor Seitz gradually came to feel that the Native Commissioner's detailed annual reports went too far. He did not think they were 'suitable' to be presented to the Imperial Colonial Office and the Reichstag, and required Tönjes to rewrite his report for 1912/13. He was to limit it to providing general statistical information, and in the section on the health situation in particular to give merely a 'general overall picture' and 'avoid ... details'. In the section on working conditions too, he was only to describe whether any 'detrimental circumstances of a more general nature' had arisen, how these had been dealt with and whether the Africans had demonstrated any appreciation of the fact that government agencies were making every effort to improve their conditions of work. In order to draw attention to the Administration's commitment to this, Seitz suggested that Tönjes should report on the fact that the Ovambo were prepared to extend their employment contracts.[190] In this way, Seitz was indirectly instructing the Native Commissioner to report progress in the combating of abuses. Seitz's instruction need not be regarded as placing any kind of limitation on Tönjes's activities; but it did prevent him from being able to mobilize public opinion, particularly in Germany, against the mining companies responsible for the abuses by reporting on them candidly. The Governor did not want to deliver any new ammunition for the criticisms of Germany's colonial activities that were being expressed in the Reichstag and elsewhere.

The truth of the situation, however, is that the Native Commissioner and the Lüderitzbucht District Administration did not automatically take the side of the workers against the employers. In 1912, for example, Africans were sentenced to corporal punishment in at least

106 cases and to imprisonment in seven.[191] Despite their efforts to remedy the grossest abuses in the mines, none of them – not Tönjes, not Böhmer and not Heilingbrunner – were fundamental opponents of the migrant worker system; but neither were they cat's paws of the mining industry, as is demonstrated by the opposition they faced from the employers. They punished workers who broke the terms of their contracts; but at the same time, they also took action against breaches of contract on the part of the employers. The reason why their efforts in the latter field achieved so little long-term success was to be found in the legal security guaranteed to the Whites living in South West Africa. The fact that the law and its interpretation by the courts protected them against interventions from the Administration led to a situation in which it was not possible to protect the Africans effectively against maltreatment. The law as it existed tied the Administration's hands, and so exacerbated the Africans' lack of rights.

The Colonial Government's realization, which found expression in the Recruitment Ordinance, that only better treatment of the Ovambo who went to work in the south could ensure that sufficient numbers of labourers could be recruited – a standpoint that applied equally to the treatment of the Herero, Berg Damara, Nama and San, who for the most part worked on the farms – found little acceptance among the mine operators. The Ordinance was thus not able to do anything to redress the fundamental shortage of labour either, and the colonial economy of South West Africa remained dependent on an inflow of labourers from other German territories and the colonies of other nations.

Labourers from South Africa

The biggest group amongst the Africans originating from outside the colony were the labourers from the British colonies which united to form the Union of South Africa in 1910. The number of the so-called 'Cape Boys' rose from 1,247 in 1909 to 2,540 in 1910 and 6,439 in 1911, then falling off again to 3,625 in 1912 and 2,089 in 1913. By comparison, the total 'non-native coloured population' – including women and children – amounted to 1,429 in 1909 and 2,825 in 1910, reached a high point of 7,026 in 1911, and then fell again to 4,173 in 1912 and 2,648 in 1913. Thus the South Africans represented something between 80 and 90 per cent of the 'non-native coloured' population. The other foreigners came from West Africa – the German colonies of Cameroon and Togo – and also from Abyssinia, India and the West Indies.[192]

Migrant workers from British southern Africa thus constituted an important element in the supply of labour to German South West Africa. On occasions the number of South Africans even exceeded that of Ovambo: at the beginning of 1911, for example, there were 6,439 South Africans registered within the Police Zone, but only 3,372 Ovambo.[193] This situation had arisen out of the Herero and Nama War, which had not only led to a major shortage of labour, but had also increased the requirement of the rapidly growing Schutztruppe for auxiliary personnel.[194] A few hundred migrants from British southern Africa came to South West Africa as early as June 1904 to support the Schutztruppe as ox-drivers and transportation workers. Only a year later the Bachstein-Koppel company, which had been awarded the contract to build the railway to Otavi, also started to recruit labourers in the eastern Cape, and above all in Cape Town.

In those areas there was no shortage of people willing to take up employment in German South West Africa, since the natural disasters of the 1880s and 1890s had had a heavy impact on agriculture. Initially, the South African War was able to absorb some of those who had become unemployed as a result. As was the case in the war in South West Africa only a few years later, they were employed in the army's supply units and in railway construction, which was expanded at the same time, and so acquired precisely the skills that were later in demand in German South West Africa. After the end of the South African War, most of these opportunities to earn a living disappeared again. In 1903 an economic recession began in the Cape Colony, which made it more difficult for those made redundant to find alternative employment, so that new jobs were greatly in demand. At the same time, work in South West Africa offered better opportunities for earning good wages than the mines in the Transvaal, which were also looking for labourers. One outstanding advantage of working in South West Africa rather than in the gold mines on the Witwatersrand was the fact that the mining was opencast, whereas in South Africa the miners had to work underground and in addition were subjected to rigorous social control through the system of compounds where the miners were obliged to live. The recruiting agents working on behalf of the German companies therefore had no problem at first in finding enough labourers.

After the end of the war in South West Africa, the Schutztruppe's requirement for auxiliary manpower was reduced. At the same time the Bachstein-Koppel company, the biggest civilian employer of South Africans, decided it had recruited enough labourers from the Cape and would largely be able to satisfy its remaining requirement from within South West Africa, so that recruitment in the British colonies flattened off and even declined. But working in South West Africa was so attractive that even after the decline in organized recruitment some jobseekers took it upon themselves to walk over 1,000 km to South West Africa. They then sought work on the spot, though at wage rates that were lower than those previously offered by the recruiting agents in Cape Town. Subsequently, however, a further expansion of the railway network in German South West Africa led to an increased requirement for labourers from 1910 onwards. The labour shortage within the Colony made it necessary to expand recruitment in South Africa again, and as a result, the number of labourers from the Cape employed in South West Africa rose to over 6,000 in 1911.

Resistance to this export of labour began to mount in South Africa, however, and the mine operators on the Rand sought to eliminate the competition from South West Africa – or else, as a counterweight to it, demanded the removal of the prohibition on their own recruiting on German territory. Complaints about the bad treatment of Africans by German employers supplied the opponents of German recruitment with valuable arguments. And above all, the Wilhelmstal Massacre of October 1910, in which fourteen Africans from the Cape Colony were shot dead by the Schutztruppe, was a major topic of public discussion in South Africa.

Labour Relations Military Style: The Wilhelmstal Massacre

At the beginning of October 1910 there occurred the most serious violent incident between the State authorities and African workers of the postwar period, when Schutztruppe soldiers shot dead fourteen South African labourers on the railway construction site of the Bachstein-Koppel company in Wilhelmstal, between Okahandja and Karibib. This incident was symptomatic of the atmosphere prevailing in South West Africa: the victims were South African labourers, who were more self-assured in their manner than their South West African colleagues, and in addition were able to organize themselves to fight for their rights. Both of these factors aroused alarm among the German Colonial Government and the White population in general, immediately evoking the prospect of a new 'rebellion' and appearing to make it a matter of existential importance for the Colony that the authorities should react with determination. The colonial state confronted the workers in military guise, because although it was really a matter for the police, the Schutztruppe, contrary to Army Regulations, intervened in a labour dispute.

The incident is very revealing with regard to the military authorities' understanding of their role. They saw themselves as the guarantors of the colonial order, yet they showed no concern for the assignment of competences or the following of chains of command as prescribed by law. The civil administration in its investigations of the massacre immediately recognized that the military intervention had been illegal, and also expressed this openly in its internal communications. It could not, however, bring itself to make any public criticism of the military players in the incident, but instead denied that there had been any wrongdoing. The various reports written on the massacre allow the Administration's cover-up strategy to be reconstructed step by step. Despite the indubitably illegal nature of the military action, both Governor Seitz and Colonial Secretary von Lindequist publicly defended the army's role.

The sequence of events leading up to the catastrophe can best be followed in the original depiction by the Colonial Government, which was able to draw upon a report from Deputy District Officer Franz of Karibib, who had been sent to the scene immediately after the event. According to this report, there had already been a dispute on 29 September 1910 between a group of eighty men from the Cape Colony working at Wilhelmstal and the railway construction company about wages. The section engineer, named Hanssen, had rejected their complaints 'without granting them any further hearing or examining their complaints at all closely', and so they started out to march to Windhoek in order to negotiate with the construction manager there. On the way, however, they met the Deputy District Officer of Okahandja, who succeeded in persuading them to return to their work. On 4 October there was a renewed increase in tension, and threats were made from the African side when Hanssen sought to send three 'ringleaders' to Wilhelmstal for interrogation. The workers refused to hand over their leaders; whereupon a Lieutenant Albrecht, who happened by chance to be present, reported the incident to his superior, Captain Willeke, who then came to the construction site with thirty-eight mounted troopers to pick up the 'ringleaders'. According to the Colonial Government's report, the conflict then escalated:

> When the workers, in response to Hanssen's demand that they should hand over the ringleaders, started to make a loud commotion and in some cases to swing their *kieries* in the air, Captain Willeke ordered them to lay their sticks down on the ground. As they did not obey, he ordered his soldiers to fix their bayonets and to surround the boys at a jog-trot, whereupon some of the boys ran away. When the boys had been encircled, Willeke once again called upon them to lay down their sticks.

This order too was disregarded, so he ordered his troopers to advance. In the close confrontation that followed, a small number of soldiers fired their rifles; the others jabbed at the workers with their bayonets or hit out at them with their rifle butts. The kaffirs then broke through the circle and ran away, whereupon the officers immediately ordered the soldiers to stop firing, which they did.[195]

A total of fourteen Africans lost their lives in the massacre. In the view of the Colonial Government, the disaster could have been averted if those involved had adhered to the provisions of the Army Regulations. The Administration saw the blame as lying mainly with the construction company, as it had not taken the labourers' complaints seriously. In addition, Hanssen had turned to Lieutenant Albrecht 'in a totally unjustified manner' with the request for military assistance.

There was not the slightest occasion to call for military assistance. Up to that time, the Cape Boys had not shown the slightest sign of a threatening attitude; and the so-called ringleaders whom Hanssen demanded they should hand over had done nothing more than address a few improper expressions to him and to the overseer, Herr Hümpel, during the preceding days, for which he should have reported them to the responsible District Office for punishment if he wanted them punished.[196]

It was also impossible to condone the fact that Albrecht, a young officer who had only been in the colony for a short time, should have responded to the request for military intervention, as he was not authorized to do so. Interestingly enough, the Governor's Office condemned the actions of Hanssen and Albrecht precisely because resistance was to be expected from the Africans. Thus it did not regard the military as being an instrument to immediately suppress any recalcitrance, and so would have preferred a de-escalation strategy. Rather contradictorily, however, it judged that Willeke had acted properly, though for him too it would not have been too late to avoid the bloody outcome, as the 'Cape Boys' had been seeking a peaceful solution.

In order to prevent any repetition, the construction company was informed that in the event of any further disturbances it should turn exclusively to the police. In addition, at the request of the Governor's Office, the Commander of the Schutztruppe instructed the troops not to respond in future to any requests from private individuals to intervene in such situations, but to wait for a request for assistance from the police.

With regard to the conditions on the construction sites too, the Administration took action. It tried to remedy the abuses, but did not seek to punish the Africans – a clear sign that it did not blame them for the escalation. The monitoring of working conditions was put in the hands of von Roebern, who was Adjutant to the Commander of the Territorial Police at the time, since he had 'been particularly conspicuous for his calmness and skill in handling the situation during these weeks'. He was now to inspect the construction sites every week and 'to receive mutual complaints and mediate them'. As the construction company's site manager had to share the blame for the conditions prevailing there, his role was to be investigated, and if necessary the company was to be instructed to dismiss him.[197]

It was only after the catastrophe had occurred that the Governor's Office started to take an interest in working conditions on the railway construction sites. The newly appointed State Inspector, von Roebern, wrote a confidential report that presented a desolate picture of the conditions prevailing there. He declared that the construction company's responsible inspector of operations, a man called Lichtenfels, had 'responded to the discontent that existed among the natives with sovereign indifference, even in the very critical days after Wilhelmstal', and viewed 'the natives as no more than beasts of burden'. He regarded people 'who concerned themselves with the natives' interests only as troublemakers who disturbed the orderly progress of construction operations', thereby preventing the company's Labour Commissioner from fulfilling his responsibilities. There had been cases of maltreatment of Africans, the reason for which in von Roebern's view was to be found 'in the white overseers, who stand in low regard and are therefore of inferior quality'. They were themselves badly treated and badly paid; anyone who applied for the position could become a foreman without any training. Complaints from the Africans were not listened to, and instead they were threatened with military intervention. The Operations Manager, *Baurat* Schönherr, had tolerated these abuses, seeking to conceal 'his insecurity, arising out of his lack of knowledge of the colonial situation' by 'ruling despotically', and he was unsuitable to manage such an enterprise.[198]

Governor Seitz, in his own statement, associated himself with von Roebern's accusations, adding self-critically that the Administration shared responsibility since it had not exercised sufficient surveillance over the company. He saw a 'principal reason for the prevailing abuses' in the fact 'that right from the beginning there has been a lack of the necessary state surveillance', and neither a Native

Commissioner nor a government medical officer had inspected the lines under construction. Changes would now be introduced in this respect. He also admitted that calling in the army had been a mistake, and promised to do everything he could 'to make both administrative officers and company managers aware that neither the Schutztruppe nor the police are there to remedy mistakes in the way coloured people are treated by shooting at them'.[199]

In respect of the responsibility of the construction company, there were consequences. The company's Berlin headquarters responded to the wishes of the Colonial Secretary by ordering that the foreman Hümpel should be dismissed and the engineer Hanssen recalled to Germany to be employed elsewhere. At the same time, however, it emphasized that it did not see any call to blame Hanssen for his behaviour, as it was 'at the very most to be described as ineptitude on the part of Herr Hanssen' that he 'did not immediately respond to the kaffirs' complaints and comply with their wish to send for a particular interpreter'.[200]

With regard to the clearly improper action of the military, on the other hand, nothing was done, although it was indisputable, even in the view of the Windhoek Military Court that investigated the incident, 'that Lieutenant Albrecht had had no authority to appear before the natives in an official service capacity on the morning of 4 October 1910', as it was 'purely a matter of a wage dispute', no request for assistance had been submitted by a civil authority, and 'the preconditions for the military to intervene on its own authority ... did not exist on that day':

> Lieutenant Albrecht should therefore have refused Engineer Hanssen's request. Initially he did restrict himself to lecturing the natives and trying to influence them by persuasion, but in the end he attempted to get them to hand over the people Engineer Hanssen described as ringleaders by the threat of force. To this extent, his actions were objectively contrary to the law.

> Subjectively, however, it was his conviction that he was not only entitled but obliged to grant Hanssen's request and take the ringleaders into custody. After the events already described that had gone before, he believed it to be his duty to intervene without further orders in the interests of the authority of the State and the standing of the white race, being confirmed in this error by something his superior, Captain Willeke, had said on the previous day.

> Lieutenant Albrecht's actions thus did not go beyond the limits of the authority that he believed himself to possess. Thus he lacked that awareness of the illegality of an action that is required to constitute a punishable offence.[201]

Thus the subjective feeling of being obliged to protect the standing of the White race was enough to excuse an infringement of binding regulations. The very fact that the Africans had contradicted Whites and had presented their complaints, and also did not do as they were told to do by an officer, had been seen by Albrecht as insubordinate behaviour. For the Court, this way of thinking made complete sense.

But this still does not explain why the conflict had to end in bloodshed. It was Willeke who was to blame for this, even if no guilt under the law could be demonstrated. His uncompromising attitude was determined by a racist view of the world. This is unambiguously revealed by a letter of self-justification in which he sought to counter the accusation of having reacted wrongly, and emphasized that 'from neither a military nor a political point of view could [he] have acted differently':

> I saw it as my task to prevent a breach of public order and security, which were under serious threat from the way the kaffirs had come together in a mob. There were no police available on the spot, and none could have been brought in immediately, so it was my duty to intervene immediately. As soon as I saw that Herr Hanssen was not able to prevail against the mob, which was threatening him with clubs, knives etc., I knew that the moment had come to order them to lay down their weapons. Their refusal then led to their being encircled by the company, a measure which I still believed would lead them to lay down their weapons. It was not until after the kaffirs had started to hit out at the riders that weapons were used. ... After my many years of experience in dealing with natives, I could not have come to any other decision. There could have been no question of South West African natives acting in such a manner as these kaffirs did. But the kaffirs thought that as 'free citizens of South Africa and subjects of His Majesty the King', which is what they regarded themselves as, according to the way they also addressed Lieutenant Albrecht, they could disregard the laws and customs of this territory and let themselves in for a trial of strength with the troops, as they had done earlier with the police. ... If I had allowed the threatening attitude of the kaffirs to cause me to withdraw the armed company without forcing them to lay down their weapons, I would have severely damaged the authority of the German Government and of the troops and the standing of the white race, and endangered the life and safety of the civil persons employed on constructing the railway.[202]

In the face of such a prejudiced attitude on the part of the responsible officers, who automatically saw the Africans as being in the wrong and completely identified with the interests of the employers, no peaceful solution to the conflict was possible.

But in contrast to the conciliatory attitude pursued by the Colonial Government, Willeke's forceful stance was applauded in settler circles where official Native Policy had long been regarded as too 'wet'. They saw in the officer a man who, unlike a government whose policy it was not to disturb the Africans at any cost, had upheld 'the honour of the German nation in the world', but particularly among the 'natives', as Carl Schlettwein wrote in the newspaper *Südwest*:

> To the honour of the German nation (*Zur Ehre des Deutschtums*) there was a man present who did not first ask what the diplomats would say, but simply: What have I to do as a German soldier? His rifles spoke a language that even English kaffirs will have understood: anyone who dares to get involved with German soldiers, or even to go so far as to play with them, is risking his life.[203]

Schlettwein's attitude was that the question as to whether or not the Africans might have been in the right did not arise: their duty was simply to obey. He followed this up with an attack on anti-colonialist circles in Germany, who would perhaps have preferred to have seen a different kind of military leader on the spot who would have handed out presents instead of shooting; but leniency and concessions would only be interpreted by the Africans as weakness. The people back home might well be acting in good faith, he declared, but they did not know the situation. The settlers in the colony, however, who understood the situation better, would not be deterred 'by philosophizing professors or fanatical humanitarianists' from doing what they had recognized as being the right thing. Finally, he made undisguised threats that the colony might break away from the mother country and go it alone, writing that South West Africa was 'faithful to the home country (*Heimat*) and every South West African [was] ready to give his all for the Fatherland if called upon to do so; the mother country could not succeed in throwing off and throwing away this affectionate dependency except by violence – but it could!'[204]

Governor Seitz assured Schlettwein in a personal interview that Willeke would not be made to answer for his actions, but that the Colonial Government would not be influenced by such articles, and that such reports that made internal matters public were more harmful than useful to those concerned.[205]

The events in Wilhelmstal not only polarized opinions in the colony, but also made a sensation in Germany and in South Africa, where the victims came from. By contrast to the critical internal assessment of the Schutztruppe's intervention, the Administration attempted to sweep the misconduct under the carpet as far as outsiders were concerned. In a letter of 24 October 1910, the Governor's Office had already reported to the Imperial Colonial Office in Berlin that the British

Consul in Lüderitzbucht was persuaded 'that the Government had done everything in the interests of the kaffirs that could reasonably be expected'. The letter then went on: 'Towards him we naturally took the line that the behaviour of the military had been irreproachable from the start'. Colonial Secretary von Lindequist himself noted in the margin: 'So we must take that line too!'[206] This was also the version that was maintained in the following weeks. When von Lindequist was asked about events in Wilhelmstal by the anti-colonialist Centre Party deputy Matthias Erzberger during the Reichstag debate on the 1911 budget for the colony, and was confronted with the accusation that the proper procedures and chains of command had not been followed and that a peaceful resolution would have been possible – as was indeed the case according to the Colonial Government's own reports – he declared that the company had acted properly. The labourers' actions had been instigated by three of their colleagues, whereupon the company had turned to an officer of the Schutztruppe who had happened to be on the spot; as no police had been present, the officer had assumed their responsibilities. The question of guilt had been investigated by both the military and the civil administrations, but the inquiries had not been pursued since it was not possible to show that any blame was attributable to those concerned.[207]

The wish to appear blameless in the eyes of the British authorities is likely to have been a further factor contributing to the way the errors of the Schutztruppe and the construction company were concealed in public. Both the individuals concerned and the Administration had very soon realized that the massacre would have serious consequences for the further recruitment of South African labourers for the colony.[208]

The newspapers in South Africa in particular concerned themselves 'in a very lively manner' with the events in Wilhelmstal, as the German Consul General, von Humboldt, reported in alarm to the Imperial Chancellor, with versions of the story obtained from private sources being embroidered with 'some pretty sharp marginal notes'. The *South African Review* even printed a picture 'in which German soldiers are to be seen shooting with rifles and machine guns at unarmed kaffirs', and which bore the caption 'German South West. Great Battle between Soldiers and Cape Boys'.[209] Only two weeks later he had to report to Berlin that the *Cape Times* of 31 October 1910 had printed 'a big photo of the heap of bodies'.[210] The Wilhelmstal Massacre thus provided additional ammunition to the opponents of German recruitment of labourers in South Africa precisely at a time when the Parliament there was discussing prohibiting it altogether.

Debate in South Africa about the Recruitment of Labourers for South West Africa

In the meantime, a movement to oppose the export of labourers to South West Africa had formed in South Africa. This was occasioned first and foremost by the increased requirement for labourers in the mines in South Africa itself, above all on the Witwatersrand, where the number of Africans working in the Transvaal mines had risen between 1904 and 1908 from four thousand to over fifty thousand. And when the Chinese 'indentured' or contract labourers, who together with the Mozambicans made up the majority of the mineworkers, left South Africa after the expiry of their contracts there was an acute labour shortage in the mines there.[211] Increased recruiting at the Cape took workers away from the farms there, which was why it was above all the farmers who sought to get Parliament to forbid recruiting for the German colony.

On 23 October 1910 the Senate of the Union Parliament at last began to debate a motion from Senator Antonie Viljoen that 'the renewal of licences for the recruitment of natives and others to work outside the Union when they expire should be declared to be undesirable', and 'the issue of new licences should not be permitted'. But the feared prohibition on recruitment was not in fact imposed. The German Consul General, von Humboldt, had done a lot of lobbying in advance of these parliamentary proceedings and had talked to a number of major political figures, including the Minister of Native Affairs, Henry Burton, the Minister of the Interior, Jan Smuts, and the former Prime Minister of the Cape Colony, John Xavier Merriman, and had declared his support for the granting of new recruiting licences, 'even if there is no reciprocity from the German side'. Above all, he had succeeded in the meantime in mitigating the harmful impact of the events in Wilhelmstal on the politicians. He was able to report to Berlin with satisfaction that the massacre was now viewed without prejudgement by all the relevant people, and was likely 'to have hardly any influence on the question of recruitment'. It was now proving to be a 'favourable circumstance' that only 'kaffirs from the remoter eastern parts of the Province were involved, and not also Cape Boys, who are already very different from them in the kind of individualism they display, and are able to make their weight felt and get influential people interested in their affairs'. Reporting on the parliamentary debate, von Humboldt commented that although the farmers' representatives had given their support to Viljoen's motion, contrary positions had also been expressed by people who had pointed out that it would be dangerous for the Union, which itself required so many foreign labourers, to prohibit recruiting from outside. Although at the time it was only for South West Africa that recruiting was taking place, the idea of prohibiting recruitment for that territory alone had been rejected as it could have been regarded as an unfriendly act. In addition, several speakers had recognized 'that the Cape Province in particular had been greatly advantaged and was still drawing advantages from its relations with the German colony, and working there was very popular among both natives and coloureds'. Despite all this, deleterious effects on German recruitment had to be reckoned with. Burton, for example, had stated that he himself was personally against the adoption of the resolution, but had nevertheless announced that the Government would wish to 'discourage' the recruitment of African workers by other countries and would soon ask Parliament for the power to forbid it completely. Having inquired directly of the Ministry of Native Affairs, von Humboldt had received a highly confidential answer that 'the Government would no longer support or encourage recruitment for South West Africa among the natives as it had done in the past, but would seek to restrict it as far as possible'; it would not, however, prohibit it altogether.[212]

Once again, the more liberal forces in the South African Government had prevailed and preference had been given to the regulation of the labour question by market forces rather than by administrative measures. An article in the *South African News* summarized this position:

> It is perfectly true that we ourselves require all the native labour available within the Union, but the way to get it is by offering it the best market, not by [en]deavouring to restrict [the] market. The latter course is not fair to the native himself, and the moral and economic injustice which it involves would only react against our own interests. And, as Mr Burton pointed out, we should lose control over the traffic altogether by withdrawing the recruiting licenses, for as long as the conditions of employment in German South West Africa remain attractive to our natives – as they admittedly are – they will continue to go there.[213]

This emphasis on the rights of the Africans involved consequences for employers and the Administration in South West Africa that they were less than happy about, however, as it increased the pressure from the South African Government to be allowed to have a say in the way South Africans employed in the German colony were treated. At the beginning of 1911 an independent South African Commission of Inquiry headed by Dr Rubusana, the only African member of the Provincial Council of Cape Province, toured German South West Africa and also inspected the railway construction sites, where – though in the presence of engineers, overseers and foremen – they interviewed some three hundred African labourers from Cape Province. The report that they produced after this visit was astonishingly positive in its conclusions:

> We found the <u>nature of the work</u> very good, and the Consortium most anxious to meet the reasonable wants of the natives. We also found that there had not been a satisfactory middleman to investigate complaints and rectify same. Mr. Quandt, who acted as Native Commissioner, in our opinion, was a complete failure, and most of the trouble is due to this fact. Nor could he speak the kaffir language, which is essential. We are very glad to have learned during our stay that Herr Baurat Schoenherr had accepted the resignation of Mr. Quandt and that different arrangements will be made.[214]

Only a few individual proposals for improvements were made, the implementation of which, the report concluded, would lead to a further enhancement of working conditions, so that the Commission would not hesitate to recommend 'Cape natives' to work in South West Africa.[215]

This did not, however, bring the dispute between South Africa and South West Africa to an end; indeed, in the following months it even acquired a new dimension, as the Government in London now also got involved and entered into direct contacts with the German Government. The demands that had been raised gained more weight, in that they were now the subject of official exchanges between the British ambassador and the Foreign Office in Berlin. The basis for the British complaints was not Rubusana's more conciliatory report, but a far less favourable one from the British Consul in Lüderitzbucht, a German citizen named Müller, who had been stationed in the town since 1909 – and who, despite being a German citizen, was a declared critic of German colonial policy. Taking as his starting point complaints that had been expressed repeatedly in the previous years about Cape labourers being cheated in respect of their wages, the British ambassador, Sir Edward Goschen, in a letter to the German Foreign Secretary, Alfred von Kiderlen-Waechter, first referred to a report from Consul Müller stating 'that the grievances of labourers as regards pay were well founded'. Then, however, he went on to raise the burning issue of mutual permission for recruitment. If British recruiting agents were not to be allowed to recruit labourers in South West Africa, 'the Union Government will feel bound to consider the withdrawal of the facilities now given to German agents to recruit within the Union'; such was the ambassador's undisguised threat. A further point of criticism was the subjection of the Cape labourers to the Native Policy regulations applying in South West Africa:

> At the present the Cape natives and coloured labourers are placed on the same level as the Hereros, notwithstanding the fact that disciplinary regulations possibly suitable to the latter are by no means suitable to free labourers from a neighbouring and friendly country who are playing an important part in the development of German South West Africa.[216]

Nine months later, Goschen then returned to the Wilhelmstal Massacre and presented a demand from the British Government that the German Government should ask Bachstein-Koppel to pay compensation of £50 for every worker killed, and £25 for every one wounded. He expressly mentioned that Foreign Secretary Sir Edward Grey had authorized him to ask whether the responsible people at Bachstein-Koppel really had been dismissed, as Dr Rubusana had written in his report.[217] The indignation over events in Wilhelmstal had initially calmed down somewhat, thanks to the unruffled way in which they were handled in the South African Parliament; but now the whole matter became a foreign-policy issue quite detached from the actual events, which after all had related to a private company. After Goschen, in his letter of 11 December 1911, had dropped the demand for a 'reciprocal arrangement with regard to labour recruiting',[218] the second point at issue was also cleared up through the willingness of the Bachstein-Koppel company to make a voluntary payment of 15,000 marks in compensation for the Africans killed or wounded in the 'Wilhelmstal disaster'. This readiness to pay was in response to a request from the Imperial Colonial Office, and explicitly excluded any admission of an obligation or of any blame on the part of the company's staff for the occurrences.[219]

There thus remained only one point at issue, namely the legal position of the Cape labourers. Here, however, there were substantial differences, as the British Government had compiled a comprehensive catalogue of requirements which Goschen sent to the German Foreign Office Undersecretary Zimmermann. Among other things, 'coloured' British subjects should not be subject to the 'parental powers of chastisement', nor should they be subject to corporal punishment imposed by the authorities except with the approval of the Colonial Government. Furthermore, as long as neither a 'recognized penal code for natives' nor a published set of rules of procedure 'for the guidance of magistrates in trying native offenders' existed, the authorities should be instructed 'to follow the procedures laid down for the guidance of judges of the Imperial Courts'. Proceedings against British subjects were to take place in public hearings, and any accused person who expressed the wish to be legally represented should have adequate opportunity to approach the British Consul or another 'approved person for assistance'. In view of the limited time for which Cape labourers stayed in the territory, all legal proceedings involving them were to be carried out with the greatest possible expedition, to the extent that this could be reconciled with the demands of justice.[220]

Only thinly disguised behind this catalogue of demands lay fundamental criticism of German Native Policy. German policy was contrasted with South African, which was presented as a model for the 'proper' treatment of Africans. In addition to these demands, a few weeks later the British embassy sent von Kiderlen-Waechter three labour regulation documents from the Cape Colony that could be taken as models, with the request that similar regulations should be adopted in South West Africa for the benefit of both the employers and the African labourers.[221] This was done at the express wish of the South African Government. Although the embassy counsellor, Granville, declared that this was not intended as a demand that the Government of South West Africa should adopt the regulations of a foreign power, it could not really be understood as anything else. The German side was correspondingly annoyed. Even the clerical officer processing the correspondence in the Imperial Colonial Office noted angrily:

> I cannot consider it to be right that we should adopt a position towards the British Government that suggests we are willing to receive instruction of any kind. Although maintaining all due courtesy in the external forms, the British Government is presuming to act as a praeceptor Germaniae in a manner that I personally find intolerable.[222]

A few months previously, South West Africa's Governor, Theodor Seitz, had dismissed South Africa's constant interference as being completely unacceptable. His reaction clearly displays wounded pride. He rejected both the punishment of those guilty of the Wilhelmstal Massacre that the South Africans demanded, and also the payment of compensation to the victims; and for his part raised accusations against Consul Müller, the British Consul in Lüderitzbucht, since in his discussions with the Colonial Government he had apparently expressed a completely different opinion from that expressed afterwards in his report to the British Government, and had declared the actions of the Schutztruppe to be justified. Seitz demanded that it should be precisely defined what role Müller was supposed to be playing, as one could not carry on official business with a man who first expressed to the German authorities his complete agreement with their actions, and then reported the contrary to his own government. The idea of treating the Africans from the Cape differently from those from South West Africa he considered to be impossible to implement 'without its leading to extreme abuses'. In South West Africa the settlers were already complaining that the Administration was 'too lenient towards the natives' and were constantly demanding that 'the strict treatment of the natives prevalent in South Africa' should be adopted. Finally, Seitz recommended that the colony should make itself independent of labourers from South Africa. The 'demanding and spoilt Cape Boys and Transkei Kaffirs' got so little work done that it would be better to dispense with them completely. They also exerted a bad influence on the colony's own 'natives'. The best solution to the labour shortage in South West Africa was to recruit labourers from the other German territories of Cameroon and East Africa. South West Africa should make itself free of foreign African labourers, particularly British ones, 'so that the eternal whingeing of the British authorities about alleged bad treatment of their subjects' would finally cease. 'If Britain does not wish to understand' that 'South Africa receives many thousands of marks annually' from Germany 'for the provision of labourers, then it would simply have to do without these revenues'.[223]

Thus the British protests achieved what the farmers' representatives and the mining companies had failed to achieve in the South African Parliament, namely a reduction in the scale of German recruiting from the Cape Province. Instead of being subjected to a prohibition, which would have been felt internationally to have been an unfriendly gesture, the German Colonial Administration was put into a position in which it itself no longer sought to promote this recruitment. The harshness of tone evident in the protests from London gives rise at least to the suspicion that over and above the justified desire to protect South African citizens there was also a deliberate intention to discourage the Germans from recruiting South African labourers. For the German side, managing without such recruitment offered a way out of what was felt to be the inadmissible interference of a foreign power. Internal assessments assumed in any case that the South Africans would soon no longer be needed: 'With the forthcoming completion of the railway, the recruitment of any larger quantities of labourers for German South West Africa from the British territories will no longer be required for the foreseeable future,' the Imperial Colonial Office informed the German Foreign Office in a confidential memorandum.[224] When from 1912 onwards the South African Government made good its threat and refused to renew recruiting licences any more,[225] the migration of labour from South Africa to South West Africa ended, apparently without there having been any further dispute on the subject between the German Colonial Administration and the South African or the British Government.

This example of migrant labour from South Africa shows how dependent the German colonial economy was on foreign labourers, but also indicates the drawbacks associated with this dependence in the form of the substantially higher wages that needed to be paid and British interference in South West African affairs – drawbacks that led to constant pressure from South West African employers for the process of recruiting Herero, Nama and Ovambo to be made ever more efficient.

Notes

1. Estimate made by a farmer named Schlettwein. Müller, 'Die deutsche Eingeborenenpolitik', 97.
2. As of 1 January 1912. *Die deutschen Schutzgebiete*, 1911/12, Statistical Section, 44–45.
3. Dernburg, *Zielpunkte*, 6–7.
4. Imperial Commissioner, *Verordnung betr. das Verbot der Anwerbung und Fortführung von Berg-Damara des südwestafrikanischen Schutzgebietes* [Ordinance concerning the Prohibition on Recruiting and Removing Berg Damara from the Colony of South West Africa], 17 May 1891, reproduced in *Die Deutsche KolonialGesetzgebung*, Vol. 1 (until 1892), 322.
5. On recruiting practices, collaboration on the part of local chiefs, the fate of those recruited and the importance of the Berg Damara as workers within the German colony, see Gewald, *Towards Redemption*, 78–81 and 91.
6. FO-CD, *Runderlass betr. Auswanderung der Eingeborenen aus den Schutzgebieten* [Circulated Decree concerning the Emigration of Natives from the Colonies], 16 August 1899, reproduced in DKG 4 (1898/99), 92–93.
7. Minutes of the meeting of the *Kolonialrat* (Colonial Council) (transcript), 10 November 1900, NAW ZBU W.I.F.1. Vol. 1, 3a–9b.
8. IGW, *Verordnung betr. die Ausführung und Auswanderung Eingeborener aus dem südwestafrikanischen Schutzgebiet* [Ordinance concerning the Removal and Emigration of Natives from the Colony of South West Africa], 30 November 1901, NAW ZBU W.I.F.1. Vol. 1, 10a–11b, reproduced in DKG 6 (1901/02), 427–28.
9. Minutes of the meeting of the *Kolonialrat*, 10 November 1900.
10. This is why the 1848–49 National Assembly, meeting in St Paul's Church in Frankfurt, included the following item in the Catalogue of Basic Rights that it adopted (Article 1 No. 5): 'Emigration shall not be restricted by the State. Charges may not be imposed for leaving the country.' Gründer, '"…da und dort ein junges Deutschland gründen◻', 15.

11. Government of Cameroon, *Verordnung betr. die Anwerbung und Ausfuhr von Eingeborenen aus dem Schutzgebiet* [Ordinance concerning the Recruitment and Removal of Natives from the Colony], 6 June/7 October 1887, reproduced in DKG 1 (until 1892), 253. Togo Commissioner's Office, *Verordnung betr. die Anwebung von Eingeborenen des Togogebietes zu Diensten außerhalb des Schutzgebietes* [Ordinance concerning the Recruitment of Natives of the Togo Territory for Service outside the Colony], 24 December 1891, reproduced ibid., 280. Government of Cameroon, *Verordnung betr. die Auswanderung der Eingeborenen des Kaiserlichen Schutzgebietes von Kamerun* [Ordinance concerning the Emigration of Natives from the Imperial Colony of Cameroon), 11 December 1893, reproduced in DKG 2 (1893–97), 64–65. Government of German East Africa, *Verordnung betr. das Verbot der Anwerbung von Arbeitern zum Zwecke der Ausfuhr derselben aus Deutsch-Ostafrika nach fremden Gebieten* [Ordinance concerning the Prohibition on Recruiting Workers for the Purpose of Removing them from German East Africa to Foreign Territories], 20 March 1896, reproduced ibid., 214.

12. The British Ambassador in Berlin, Sir Edward Goschen, for example, complained in 1911 about the fact that the recruitment of Africans for South Africa was forbidden. British Embassy Berlin to German FO, 14 March 1911, BAL R 1001/1235, 30a–32a.

13. Keetmanshoop DO, *Verordnung betr. Anwerbung und Ausfuhr eingeborener Arbeiter im Südbezirk* [Ordinance concerning the recruitment and removal abroad of native workers from the southern region], 1 March 1897 (content deduced from the covering letter), NAW ZBU W.IV.A.3. Vol. 1, 81a.

14. Beinart, '"Jamani"', 169.

15. IGW, *Runderlass betr. die Kontroll- und Paßpflicht der Eingeborenen sowie Dienst- und Arbeitsverträge mit diesen* [Circulated Decree concerning the Control and Pass Requirements for the Natives and Employment Contracts with them – 'Decree accompanying the Native Ordinances'], 18 August 1907, reproduced in DKG 11 (1907), 352–57.

16. On the image of the 'native', see Scheulen, *Die 'Eingeborenen' Deutsch-Südwestafrikas*.

17. Bethanie DO to IGW, 20 November 1908, NAW ZBU W.III.A.3. Vol. 1, 71b. And again in 1910: Bethanie DO to IGW, 10 January 1910, NAW ZBU W.III.A.3. Vol. 1, 131a–133a.

18. Maltahöhe DO to IGW, 2 January 1909, NAW ZBU W.III.A.3. Vol. 1, 102a–105a.

19. Swakopmund DO to IGW, 24 November 1908, NAW ZBU W.III.A.3. Vol. 1, 47a–51a. Similarly with regard to the Herero, Berg Damara and Nama, see Namutoni DO to IGW, 1 November 1908, NAW ZBU W.III.A.3. Vol. 1, 74a–77a. Namutoni DO regarded the members of all three nations as being suitable to undertake heavy work, but Gibeon DO disgreed about the Nama. Gibeon DO to IGW, n.d., NAW ZBU W.III.A.3. Vol. 1, 95a–100a.

20. Windhoek DO to IGW, 25 November 1908, NAW ZBU W.III.A.3. Vol. 1, 60a–69a.

21. Namutoni DO to IGW, 1 November 1908.

22. Bethanie DO to IGW, 10 January 1910.

23. Grootfontein DO to IGW, 24 October 1908, NAW ZBU W.III.A.3. Vol. 1, 43a–44a.
24. There should not really have been any regional differences. As Karibib DO put it: 'Otherwise, depending on which individual tribe they [the Africans] belong to, the capabilities of which are the same here as throughout the colony, they are more or less suitable to be used for any kind of physical work.' Karibib DO to IGW, 26 November 1908, NAW ZBU W.III.A.3. Vol. 1, 52a–59a.
25. Okahandja DO to IGW, 26 October 1908, NAW ZBU W.III.A.3. Vol. 1, 26a–32a.
26. The Swartbooi people, for example, consisting of some 150 men and 400 women and children, had been brought to Windhoek after the suppression of their 'rising' in 1898 and there engaged on public works. Leutwein, *Elf Jahre*, 152–53.
27. Surprisingly, perhaps, there were some employers who were opposed to the unpaid employment of the forced labourers. The Arthur Koppel company, for example, declared itself to be against this system and that it would rather pay five marks to the workers directly. The reasons can only be speculated about: perhaps the company thought the workers would be more productive if they were remunerated, or perhaps it wanted to make the Africans bear their own living costs on the grounds that they were being paid. It is also conceivable that it thought it would be able to recover the money paid to the workers through company-owned shops. Arthur Koppel A.G. – Otavi Eisenbahnbau to Finance Officer Pahl, IGW, 5 December 1905, NAW ZBU *Geheimakten* (Classified Documents) VI.A. Vol. 1, 23a–26a. The archived documents do not show whether or not the proposal was accepted.
28. The Railway Commissioner's Office, Southern Region, for example, had been assigned prisoners of war in 1906 who were still working for it in 1912. Railway Commissioner's Office, Southern Region, to IGW, 7 September 1912, NAW ZBU W.IV.A.2. Vol. 1, 62ca f. (special pagination).
29. Lüderitzbucht DO to IGW, 1 July 1908, NAW ZBU W.III.A.3. Vol. 1, 7a–23a.
30. *Die deutschen Schutzgebiete*, 1912/13, Statistical Section, 49–51. The figures relate to Africans – men, women and children – originating in the colony (i.e. excluding those who came from other German territories or from foreign colonies). The 4,880 Ovambo were not included either, as they were migrant workers included under the figures for immigration and emigration. A figure of 4,181 is also given for 'departures'. This discrepancy is probably explained by the fact that many Africans left their former places of abode without deregistering. Further additions were an excess of births over deaths amounting to 1,314, and those Africans who had not been registered in the previous year. People who were captured by the patrols are listed separately and are not included in the figures given.
31. Lüderitzbucht DO to IGW, 8 March 1909, NAW ZBU W.III.A.3. Vol. 1, 83a–92a.
32. Lüderitzbucht DO to IGW, 20 October 1911, NAW ZBU W.III.B.5. Vol. 1, 29a.
33. 'Only in urgent exceptional cases are travel passes to be issued to natives who wish to leave the District. In all other cases the prior approval of

the District Office is to be obtained. … In view of the shortage of labour prevailing in the District, an exodus of natives must be avoided under all circumstances.

Only cases of the death or severe illness of next of kin living in another district are to be considered urgent exceptional cases within the meaning of the above, in which the police stations may issue travel passes to natives on their own authority. The police station shall first take steps to verify precisely that the details given are correct.' Bethanie DO, Order (transcript), 8 October 1909, NAW ZBU W.III.B.5. Vol. 1, 37a f. Emphasis (underlining) in the original.

34. Bethanie DO to Lüderitzbucht DO, 16 October 1911, NAW ZBU W.III.B.5. Vol. 1, 30a.
35. IGW Circulated Order, 18 November 1911, NAW ZBU W.III.B.5. Vol. 1, 31a.
36. Bethanie DO to IGW, 18 November 1911, NAW ZBU W.III.B.5. Vol. 1, 34a f.
37. Ibid.
38. Bethanie DO to IGW, 30 November 1911, NAW ZBU W.III.B.5. Vol. 1, 36a f.
39. IGW to Bethanie DO, 9 January 1912, NAW ZBU W.III.B.5. Vol. 1, 38a f.
40. Minutes of Territorial Council meeting, 1911 (transcript, n.d.), NAW ZBU W.IV.A.1. Vol. 1, 10a–12a.
41. IGW Circulated Order to DOs, 13 June 1911, NAW ZBU W.IV.A.1. Vol. 1, 13a f.
42. IGW Circulated Order to DOs, 31 October 1913, NAW ZBU W.IV.A.1. Vol. 1, 28a f.
43. Gibeon DO to IGW, 10 August 1912, NAW ZBU W.IV.A.2. Vol. 1, 62aa (special pagination).
44. IGW internal memorandum, 24 August 1912, NAW ZBU W.IV.A.2. Vol. 1, 62ab (special pagination).
45. Railway Commissioner's Office, Southern Region, to IGW, 7 September 1912 (underling by a clerical officer in the original).
46. IGW to Gibeon DO, 17 September 1912, NAW ZBU W.IV.A.2. Vol. 1, 62da (special pagination).
47. IGW, Decree accompanying the Native Ordinances, 18 August 1907. This clause is at the same time a clear example of how security and economic interests were interlinked. The Decree refers explicitly to the dual purpose of enhancing control and distributing workers.
48. IGW, *Verordnung betr. Maßregeln zur Kontrolle der Eingeborenen* [Ordinance concerning Regulations for the Control and Surveillance of the Natives – the 'Control Ordinance'], 18 August 1907, reproduced in DKG 11 (1907), 345–47.
49. There were other farmers as well who employed more than ten families but did not accommodate them all on the same werf; however, there are no precise figures relating to these. Nor are there any comprehensive figures relating to those werfs maintained by the Territorial Police, the Schutztruppe or the Administration.
50. *Die deutschen Schutzgebiete*, 1911/12, Statistical Section, 78.

51. Lüderitzbucht DO to IGW, 18 April 1912, NAW ZBU W.III.B.4. Vol. 1, 22a. The fact that Lüderitzbucht DO did not report any large werfs indicates that the diamond mines were not included in its report.
52. Gobabis DO to IGW, 22 March 1912, NAW ZBU W.III.B.4. Vol. 1, 15a.
53. Rehoboth DO to IGW, 6 February 1912, NAW ZBU W.III.B.4. Vol. 1, 3a. In addition there was one Baster who employed such a large number of workers.
54. Warmbad DO to IGW, 22 March 1912, NAW ZBU W.III.B.4. Vol. 1, 16a.
55. Keetmanshoop DO to IGW, 28 July 1912, NAW ZBU W.III.B.4. Vol. 1, 23a.
56. Omaruru DO to IGW, 4 March 1912, NAW ZBU W.III.B.4. Vol. 1, 9a.
57. Gibeon DO to IGW, 19 March 1912, NAW ZBU W.III.B.4. Vol. 1, 12a.
58. Bethanie DO to IGW, 21 February 1912, NAW ZBU W.III.B.4. Vol. 1, 7a.
59. Grootfontein DO to IGW, 5 February 1912, NAW ZBU W.III.B.4. Vol. 1, 4a.
60. Okahandja DO to IGW, 10 April 1912, NAW ZBU W.III.B.4. Vol. 1, 17a–18b.
61. Swakopmund DO to IGW, 13 February 1912, NAW ZBU W.III.B.4. Vol. 1, 5a.
62. Karibib DO to IGW, n.d., NAW ZBU W.III.B.4. Vol. 1, 13a–14a. As only 59 farms had been sold or leased in the district, and the number of farms actually operating was even lower, this means that practically every farm had special authorization. For the number of farms, see *Die deutschen Schutzgebiete*, 1911/12, Statistical Section, 78.
63. This figure does not include Africans from other German colonies or foreign territories.
64. *Die deutschen Schutzgebiete*, 1911/12, Statistical Section, 44–45.
65. IGW, Circulated Order to DOs, 16 July 1914, NAW ZBU W.IV.E.1. Vol. 1, 7a.
66. For example: Letter from a farmer named Strobell of Farm Felseneck, Post Okasise, to IGW, 25 May 1914, NAW ZBU W.IV.E.2. Vol. 2, 14a f.
67. For example: Resolution of the Karibib Farmers' Association to Karibib DO, 2 February 1914, NAW ZBU W.IV.A.1. Vol. 1, 33a–36a.
68. IGW to Karibib DO, 11 March 1914, NAW ZBU W.IV.A.1. Vol. 1, 37a–38a.
69. IGW, Circulated Order to DOs, 16 July 1914, 7a.
70. Note of the clerical officer at IGW on the report from Windhoek district office. Windhoek DO to IGW, 14 February 1911, NAW ZBU W.III.B.5. Vol. 1, 9a–10a.
71. Outjo DO to IGW, 6 March 1911, NAW ZBU W.III.B.5. Vol. 1, 21a. Gobabis DO to IGW, 15 March 1911, NAW ZBU W.III.B.5. Vol. 1, 22a f.
72. Omaruru DO to IGW, 14 February 1911, NAW ZBU W.III.B.5. Vol. 1, 13a f.
73. Grootfontein DO to IGW, 16 February 1911, NAW ZBU W.III.B.5. Vol. 1, 12a.
74. Windhoek DO to IGW, 14 February 1911.
75. Otjimbingwe DO, *Bezirks-Polizei-Verordnung betreffend das Verhältnis der Arbeitgeber zu den Arbeitern* [District Police Ordinance concerning Relations between Employers and Workers], 3 July 1894, reproduced in DKG 2 (1893–97), 104.
76. Gibeon DO, *Verordnung betr. Regelung der Dienstboten- pp. Verhältnisse* [Ordinance concerning the Regulation of Service and Similar Relationships] (transcript), 23 March 1896, NAW ZBU W.IV.A.3. Vol. 2, 41ea–41fa (special pagination).

77. IGW, *Verordnung betr. Dienst- und Arbeitsverträge mit Eingeborenen* [Ordinance concerning Contracts of Service and Employment with Natives – the 'Master and Servant Ordinance'], 18 August 1907, reproduced in DKG 11 (1907), 350–52.
78. *Die deutschen Schutzgebiete*, 1912/13, Statistical Section, 50–51.
79. Report by District Office Secretary F.W. Lang, Windhoek DO, 12 July 1907, NAW ZBU W.III.B.5. Vol. 1, 2a.
80. Windhoek DO to IGW, 12 July 1907, NAW ZBU W.III.B.5. Vol. 1, 1a f.
81. This is revealed by the District Office's letter, ibid.
82. Report by District Office Secretary F.W. Lang, Windhoek DO, 12 July 1907.
83. Windhoek DO to IGW, 12 July 1907. The Governor's Office immediately sent the report on to von Lindequist, who was in Keetmanshoop at the time. IGW to von Lindequist, 14 July 1907, NAW ZBU W.III.B.5. Vol. 1, 3a. Von Lindequist ultimately stated that he 'consented to the rectification'. Von Lindequist to IGW, 2 August 1907, NAW ZBU W.III.B.5. Vol. 1, 6a.
84. Windhoek DO to IGW, 12 July 1907.
85. Outjo DO to IGW, 10 December 1913, NAW ZBU W.IV.E.2. Vol. 1, 193b–194b.
86. Von Wangenheim to IGW, 11 November 1913, NAW ZBU W.IV.E.2. Vol. 1, 189a–192b.
87. Outjo DO to IGW, 10 December 1913.
88. IGW to von Wangenheim, 28 December 1913, NAW ZBU W.IV.E.2. Vol. 1, 195a f.
89. IGW, Decree accompanying the Native Ordinances, 18 August 1907.
90. IGW, Master and Servant Ordinance, 18 August 1907. IGW, Decree accompanying the Native Ordinances, 18 August 1907.
91. IGW to Bethanie DO, 9 September 1912, NAW ZBU W.III.N.1. Vol. 1, 19a.
92. Synod Chairman Olpp, Rhenish Mission, Karibib, to IGW, 3 October 1912, NAW ZBU W.III.O.1. Vol. 1, 4a f.
93. Gobabis DO to IGW, 29 January 1908, NAW ZBU W.III.R.2. Vol. 1, 12a–13a.
94. Annual Report of Keetmanshoop Native Commissioner, IGW, 1 September 1913, NAW ZBU A.VI.A.8, 31a–39b.
95. Omaruru DO to IGW, 12 January 1908, NAW ZBU W.III.R.2. Vol. 1, 5a–6a. District Officer Victor Franke of Outjo argued similarly. Outjo DO to IGW, 22 January 1908, NAW ZBU W.III.R.2. Vol. 1, 10a f.
96. Windhoek DO to IGW, 19 February 1908, NAW ZBU W.III.R.2. Vol. 1, 25a.
97. Bethanie DO to IGW, 13 March 1908, NAW ZBU W.III.R.2. Vol. 1, 29a–30a.
98. Gibeon DO to IGW, 7 March 1908, NAW ZBU W.III.R.2. Vol. 1, 26a f.
99. On the use of corporal punishment as a penalty in criminal law, see Schröder, *Prügelstrafe und Züchtigungsrecht*, 92–98.
100. For example, the IGW Circulated Order of 2 January 1908, NAW ZBU W.III.R.1. Vol. 1, 1a–2a.
101. IGW Circulated Order (transcript) 24 September 1912, BAL R 1001/2235, 89a f. This was intended first and foremost to be the Native Commissioner. He or a deputy was to determine the facts of the case and the evidence for it, obtain power of attorney from the potential African plaintiff, and then do whatever was necessary. If it was a difficult legal matter, 'he will be able to limit his activity to applying to the court for legal aid under the

Poor Law so that a solicitor can be instructed'. The official was, however, responsible for ensuring 'that only such claims are raised that appear to have a prospect of success'. And these arrangements did nothing to solve the problem of the plaintiff's credibility: it remained a problem for Africans to prove that their claims were justified.

102. IGW, Circulated Order, 2 January 1908.
103. Omaruru DO to IGW, 12 January 1908, NAW ZBU W.III.R.2. Vol. 1, 5a–6a.
104. Maltahöhe DO to IGW, 28 February 1908, NAW ZBU W.III.R.2. Vol. 1, 27a f.
105. Warmbad DO to IGW, 3 March 1908, NAW ZBU W.III.R.2. Vol. 1, 31a f.
106. Rehoboth DO to IGW, 24 January 1908, NAW ZBU W.III.R.2. Vol. 1, 11a f.
107. Lüderitzbucht DO to IGW, 31 January 1908, NAW ZBU W.III.R.2. Vol. 1, 14a.
108. Judgment of Lüderitzbucht District Court against Alfred Heilbrunner (transcript), proceedings of 26 October 1906, NAW ZBU W.III.R.2. Vol. 1, 22a f.
109. Judgment of Lüderitzbucht District Court against Joseph Balsis (transcript), proceedings of 15 March 1907, NAW ZBU W.III.R.2. Vol. 1, 19a–20a.
110. Judgment of Lüderitzbucht District Court against Gustav Tümmler (transcript), proceedings of 6 July 1907, NAW ZBU W.III.R.2. Vol. 1, 23a f.
111. Judgment of the Superior Court, Windhoek, against Georg Rost (transcript), proceedings of 9 January 1908, NAW ZBU W.III.R.2. Vol. 1, 15a–18a.
112. Gibeon DO to IGW, 7 March 1908.
113. Swakopmund DO to IGW, 26 January 1908, NAW ZBU W.III.R.2. Vol. 1, 9a.
114. Keetmanshoop DO to IGW, 15 March 1908, NAW ZBU W.III.R.2. Vol. 1, 28a f.
115. Karibib DO to IGW, 25 January 1908, NAW ZBU W.III.R.2. Vol. 1, 8a f. Similarly: Windhoek DO to IGW, 19 February 1908, NAW ZBU W.III.R.2. Vol. 1, 25a.
116. Only five District Offices reported no cases of maltreatment. Grootfontein DO to IGW, 20 January 1908, NAW ZBU W.III.R.2. Vol. 1, 7a. Outjo DO to IGW, 22 January 1908, ibid., 10a f. Gobabis DO to IGW, 29 January 1908, ibid., 12a–13a. Okaukweyo DO to Outjo DO, 31 January 1908, ibid., 24a. Bethanie DO to IGW, 13 March 1908, ibid., 29a–30a.
117. Keetmanshoop DO to IGW, 15 March 1908.
118. Ibid.
119. Koselleck, *Preußen zwischen Reform und Revolution*, 641–52.
120. The Master and Servant Ordinance promulgated for Otjimbingwe district in 1894 did, however, provide for a right of chastisement by the employer in the case of workers aged under eighteen. Otjimbingwe DO, *Bezirkspolizei-Verordnung betr. Verhältnis der Arbeitgeber zu den Arbeitern* [District Police Ordinance concerning relations between Employers and Workers], 3 July 1894, reproduced in DKG 2 (1893–97), 104.
121. On the debate concerning, and on the application of, the 'parental power of chastisement', see Schröder, *Prügelstrafe*, 101–20.
122. IGW to ICO, 30 December 1907, quoted according to Gründer, *Junges Deutschland*, 279.

123. IGW to ICO, 29 August 1913, NAW ZBU W.IV.A.1. Vol. 1, 24a–25a.

124. On corporal punishment as a sanction in all African colonies, see Schröder, *Prügelstrafe*.

125. The individual figures were: 151 (1900/01), 257 (1901/02), 473 (1902/03), 340 (1903/04), 187 (1904/05), 294 (1905/06), 336 (1906/07), 534 (1907/08), 703 (1908/09), 928 (1909/10), 1,262 (1910/11), 1,655 (1911/12), 1,713 (1912/13). These figures do not include disciplinary measures. Ibid., 94.

126. Ibid., 5–8.

127. IGW Circulated Order to DOs, 31 May 1912, NAW ZBU W.III.R.1. Vol. 1, 7a–8a.

128. Ibid.

129. The practice of corporal punishment prevailing in South West Africa had been repeatedly criticized, particularly in the Reichstag. Schröder, *Prügelstrafe*, 99.

130. *Landesrat* (Territorial Council) 1913, extract from minutes, NAW ZBU W.IV.A.1. Vol. 1, 18a f.

131. Further examples can be found in Drechsler, *Südwestafrika unter deutscher Kolonialherrschaft*, Vol. I, 227–28; and Bley, *Kolonialherrschaft und Sozialstruktur*, 294–300. Bley's depiction of a series of criminal trials between 1911 and 1913 gives the incorrect impression that there had not been any prosecutions for maltreatment before then. The above examples from the preceding years prove the contrary.

132. Judgment of Windhoek District Court against Friedrich Schneidewind, proceedings on 19 July 1912, NAW ZBU W.III.R.2. Vol. 1, 130a–132a.

133. Ibid.

134. Ibid.

135. Judgment of Windhoek District Court against Franz Würzberger, proceedings on 26 April 1912, NAW ZBU W.III.R.2. Vol. 1, 125a–127a.

136. Ibid.

137. Okahandja DO to IGW, 17 October 1912, NAW ZBU W.III.R.2. Vol. 1, 14a f.

138. IGW to Okahandja DO, 28 October 1912, NAW ZBU W.III.R.2. Vol. 1, 144a.

139. Okahandja DO to IGW, 4 December 1912, NAW ZBU W.III.R.2. Vol. 1, 146a f.

140. IGW to Okahandja DO, December 1912, NAW ZBU W.III.R.2. Vol. 1, 146b.

141. IGW to Rehoboth DO, 11 March 1913, NAW ZBU W.III.R.2. Vol. 1, 148a.

142. Rehoboth DO to IGW, 27 March 1913, NAW ZBU W.III.R.2. Vol. 1, 150a.

143. The trials conducted in the years 1911 to 1913 also demonstrate that public opinion, at least in as far as represented by those expressions of it published in South West Africa, took the part of the accused employers. Bley, *Kolonialherrschaft*, 298–301.

144. Circulated Order to DOs and Native Commissioners (draft), 4 August 1913 (date it was initialled by Kohler), NAW ZBU W.IV.A.1. Vol. 1, 20a–22a. It cannot be determined from the files whether this draft was ever actually circulated; Hintrager and Blumhagen were opposed to it, as is shown by the marginal notes.

145. Georg Engelhard to IGW, 7 April 1913, NAW ZBU W.III.R.2. Vol. 1, 151a f. Emphases (underlining) as in the original (underlined by the processing officer in the original, with a question mark in the margin).

146. IGW to Engelhard, Ferdinandshöhe Farm near Omaruru, 16 April 1913, NAW ZBU W.III.R.2. Vol. 1, 153a.

147. Strassegger, 'Wanderarbeit', 35–36.

148. Eirola, *Ovambogefahr*, 213.

149. On the development of the mines, see Drechsler, *Südwestafrika unter deutscher Kolonialherrschaft*, Vol. II, 193–283.

150. Clarence-Smith and Moorsom, 'Underdevelopment and Class Formation', 183.

151. These figures relate only to men; estimated figures were not included. *Die deutschen Schutzgebiete*, 1909/10, Statistical Section, 24; ibid., 1910/11, Statistical Section, 38; ibid., 1911/12, Statistical Section, 42; ibid., 1912/13, Statistical Section, 48.

152. IGW, *Verordnung betr. den Verkehr in und nach dem Amboland* [Ordinance concerning Movements within and to Ovamboland – the 'Ovamboland Ordinance'], 25 January 1906, reproduced in DKG 10 (1906), 25–27.

153. IGW, *Ausführungsbestimmungen zur Verordnung betr. den Verkehr in und nach dem Amboland* [Implementation Regulations to the Ovamboland Ordinance], 25 January 1906, ibid., 27–30.

154. IGW, Ovamboland Ordinance, 25 January 1906, ibid., 25–27. This reference to the pass requirement dates from a year and a half before the promulgation of the Pass Ordinance.

155. IGW, Implementation Regulations to the Ovamboland Ordinance, 25 January 1906, ibid., 27–30.

156. Strassegger, 'Wanderarbeit', 49–62.

157. Ibid., 17–80. Clarence-Smith and Moorsom, 'Underdevelopment', 178–83.

158. IGW, Implementation Regulations to the Ovamboland Ordinance, 25 January 1906, reproduced in DKG 10 (1906), 27–30.

159. Eirola, *Ovambogefahr*, 243–45.

160. Strassegger, 'Wanderarbeit', 68–75.

161. Clarence-Smith and Moorsom, 'Underdevelopment', 184. The Chiefs too generally only permitted their subjects to conclude contracts with a six-month term, for the same reason.

162. Strassegger, 'Wanderarbeit', 82.

163. Ibid., 85–93.

164. Ibid., 83.

165. Ibid., 94–100.

166. Strassegger's work appears to be based on the assumption that it was. As a result, she wrongly attributes the very limited success of attempts to improve the situation of the Ovambo to a lack of political will on the part of the Colonial Government.

167. IGW, *Verordnung betr. Anwerbung und Arbeitsverhältnisse der eingeborenen Arbeiter* [Ordinance concerning the Recruitment and Working Conditions of Native Workers – the 'Recruitment Ordinance'], 16 December 1911, reproduced in *Amtsblatt für das Schutzgebiet Deutsch-Südwestafrika* [Official Gazette of the Colony of German South West Africa], Vol. 3 (1912), Windhoek 1913, 2–4.

168. IGW, *Dienstanweisung für die Anwerbestelle von Ovambo* [Service Instruction for the Ovambo Recruiting Point], 16 December 1911, reproduced in *Amtsblatt*, Vol. 3 (1912), Windhoek 1913, 4–5.

169. IGW, *Bekanntmachung* (Announcement), 16 December 1911, reproduced in *Amtsblatt*, Vol. 3 (1912), Windhoek 1913, 5.

170. Strassegger, 'Wanderarbeit', 67.

171. IGW, Recruitment Ordinance, 16 December 1911.

172. Regina Strassegger is not able to furnish any reliable statistical data in her work either. She quotes a mass of individual examples that clearly demonstrate that offences were committed by employers quite frequently, but she is not able to show convincingly how representative these cases are. Although she herself refers to the unreliability of the contemporary statistics, she presents the worst example as being the norm in each case, without giving any further explanation of why she does so. Strassegger, 'Wanderarbeit', 111–65.

173. Ibid., 145–62. Strassegger points out that the mortality figures to be found in the Archives are contradictory. The Administration itself does not appear to have had any clear picture of the overall situation. However, the disparity between the mortality figures given for the Koloniale Bergbau-Gesellschaft and those for the Kolmanskoppe Diamond Mines demonstrates that they were closely linked to the conditions in the various individual diamond fields.

174. Ibid., 114–17. Strassegger's statement that District Officer Böhmer displayed an attitude of solidarity with the employers and therefore did not admit any criticism of conditions in the diamond fields is not convincing. The shortcomings in surveillance may also have been due to the fact that he was overworked; this was after all one of the reasons for the appointment of Native Commissioners. As can be seen from the following, he supported Tönjes in his efforts on the workers' behalf, so it cannot by any means be claimed that he was particularly well disposed towards the employers.

175. The scope of his duties was extended even further in 1913 when he was also made responsible for the surveillance of the Northern Fields, i.e. those lying to the north of Lüderitzbucht, which were located partly in Swakopmund District. Abun-Nasr, 'Eingeborenenkommissare', 103.

176. Lüderitzbucht Native Commissioner to IGW, 9 May 1912, NAW ZBU W.III.R.2. Vol. 1, 101a–111a.

177. IGW to Lüderitzbucht Chamber of Mines, 25 May 1912, NAW ZBU W.III.R.2. Vol. 1, 112a–113a.

178. Lüderitzbucht DO to Lüderitzbucht Chamber of Mines (transcript), 10 May 1912, NAW ZBU W.III.R.2. Vol. 1, 65a–66a.

179. Lüderitzbucht Chamber of Mines to Lüderitzbucht DO (transcript), 11 May 1912, NAW ZBU W.III.R.2. Vol. 1, 67a–68a.

180. IGW to Lüderitzbucht DO, 13 June 1912, NAW ZBU W.III.R.2. Vol. 1, 69a.

181. Lüderitzbucht DO to IGW, 21 April 1913, NAW ZBU W.III.R.2. Vol. 1, 156a–159a.

182. Ibid.

183. IGW to Lüderitzbucht DO, 26 May 1913, NAW ZBU W.III.R.2. Vol. 1, 160a f.
184. Lüderitzbucht DO to IGW, 13 June 1913, NAW ZBU W.III.R.2. Vol. 1, 169a–170b.
185. Ibid. Emphasis (underlining) as in the original.
186. IGW to Lüderitzbucht DO, 11 July 1913, NAW ZBU W.III.R.2. Vol. 1, 171a–172.
187. Koloniale Bergbau-Gesellschaft to Lüderitzbucht Chamber of Mines (transcript), 12 June 1912, NAW ZBU W.III.R.2. Vol. 1, 118a–122a.
188. Lüderitzbucht Chamber of Mines to IGW, 18 June 1912, NAW ZBU W.III.R.2. Vol. 1, 116a–117a. The emphasis (underlining) represents underlining added to the original by the clerical officer who processed the document at IGW.
189. Lüderitzbucht Chamber of Mines to Lüderitzbucht DO (transcript), 11 May 1912, NAW ZBU W.III.R.2. Vol. 1, 67a–68a.
190. IGW to Lüderitzbucht Native Commissioner, 9 October 1913, NAW BLU E.K. 34 (no page number).
191. There is, however, a period of three-and-a-half months for which details are missing from the statistics. Strassegger, 'Wanderarbeit', 204.
192. *Die deutschen Schutzgebiete*, 1909/10, Statistical Section, 24–25; ibid., 1910/11, Statistical Section, 40–41; ibid., 1911/12, Statistical Section, 46–47; ibid., 1912/13, Statistical Section, 52–53. All figures relate to 1 January of the year concerned. In the 1909/10 Annual Report, the Bechuana are erroneously listed as foreign Africans: I have corrected this error and recalculated the figures accordingly. Although most of the Bechuana lived in the (British) Bechuanaland protectorate, there was also a small group living within South West Africa; only these have been included here. The figures for 'Cape Boys' only relate to men, as it was they who were integrated into the colonial economy as workers. This is not to suggest that the women did not work as well; but they were not recruited as migrant workers. The proportion of women and children amounted to 5 per cent or less. The figures do not include ninety-two 'Cape Coloureds' ('Kapbastards') who were listed separately in the 1910/11 Annual Report but do not appear again in the following years, being then included under the heading 'Foreigners of mixed race'.
193. *Die deutschen Schutzgebiete*, 1910/11, Statistical Section, 38–40. In addition to these, there were further Ovambo for whom only an estimated figure of 1,750 is given. Here too, only the men were included.
194. On the following passage, see Beinart, '"Jamani"', 169–82.
195. IGW to ICO, 24 October 1910, BAL R 1001/1234, 53a–57b.
196. Ibid.
197. Ibid.
198. Report by von Roebern (transcript), 21 November 1910, BAL R 1001/1234, 100a–104a.
199. IGW to ICO, 4 December 1910, BAL R 1001/1234, 98a–99a.
200. Bau- und Betriebskonsortium Bachstein-Koppel, Berlin, to ICO, 24 December 1910, BAL R 1001/1234, 77a–78a.

201. Court Order, Imperial Schutztruppe for South West Africa – Court of the Schutztruppe Central Command (transcript), 5 December 1910, BAL R 1001/1234, 95a–97b.
202. Willeke to CSW (transcript), 9 January 1911, BAL R 1001/1235, 25a–26b. Emphasis (underlining) as in the original.
203. Carl Schlettwein, 'Soldat und Diplomat' [Soldier and Diplomat], in *Südwest – Unabhängige Zeitung für die Interessen des Schutzgebietes*, 14 March 1911, 1a f. Copy of the newspaper in BAL R 1001/1235, 87a.
204. Ibid.
205. IGW to ICO, 5 June 1911, BAL R 1002/1235, 85a f.
206. IGW to ICO, 24 October 1910, BAL R 1001/1234, 53a–57b.
207. Reichstag, Session 1909/1911 – Imperial Budget Commission, 94th Meeting, Berlin 22 March 1911, 1–14. Copy of the minutes in BAL R 1001/1235, 66a–72b.
208. IGW to ICO, 24 October 1910. Similarly: von Roebern's report (transcript), 21 November 1910, BAL R 1001/1234, 100a–104a.
209. GCG Cape Town to Imperial Chancellor Bethmann Hollweg (transcript), 17 October 1910, BAL R 1001/1234, 29a–30a. The photo caption is in English in the original.
210. GCG Cape Town to Imperial Chancellor Bethmann Hollweg (transcript), 2 November 1910, BAL R 1001/1234, 71a–74b.
211. Beinart, '"Jamani"', 177–80.
212. GCG Cape Town to Imperial Chancellor Bethmann Hollweg (transcript), 27 November 1910, NAW *Geheimakten* VII.I. Vol. 1, 1a–5a. [Translator's note: The Consulate General gives the – presumably originally English – quotation from the Ministry's reply in German; it has been retranslated back into English as the original is not available.]
213. 'Wilhelmstal and After' in *South African News*, 25 November 1910 (cutting), NAW *Geheimakten* VII.I. Vol. 1, 6a. Quoted in the original English.
214. *Report on visit to German S. W. Africa*, by Dr. Rubusana, Enoch Mamba, Charles Wakeford, H. Jungheinrich (sent to ICO by the German FO), 13 January 1911, BAL R 1001/1235 92a–96a. Quoted in the original English. Emphasis (underlining) as in the original.
215. Ibid.
216. British Embassy Berlin to German FO (transcript), 14 March 1911. Quoted in the original English.
217. British Embassy Berlin to German FO (transcript), 11 December 1911, BAL R 1001/1235, 103a–104a.
218. Ibid. Quoted in the original English.
219. Bau- und Betriebskonsortium Bachstein-Koppel, Berlin, to ICO, 16 January 1912, BAL R 1001/1235, 110a.
220. British Embassy Berlin to German FO (transcript), 29 January 1912, BAL R 1001/1235, 117a–118b. The quotations are in the original English.
221. British Embassy Berlin to German FO (transcript), 1 March 1912, BAL R 1001/1235 124a–125a. Act to Amend Act No. 15, 1856, intituled: An Act to amend the Laws regulating the relative Rights and Duties of Masters, Servants, and Apprentices (Assented to 26th June, 1873). Act to Amend

the Law relating to Masters, Servants, and Apprentices (Assented to 30th June, 1875). Act to Amend the Law relating to Masters, Servants and Apprentices (Assented to 12th August, 1889). The texts are to be found ibid., 126.

222. Note on file, ICO, 9 May 1912, BAL R 1001/1235, 127a.
223. IGW to ICO, 14 October 1911, BAL R 1001/1235, 98a–100a.
224. ICO to German FO, 20 January 1912, BAL R 1001/1235, 105a–108a.
225. Beinart, '"Jamani"', 182–83. Despite this, some workers remained in South West Africa for a considerable time: in 1913 there were still more than two thousand South Africans working in the German colony. *Die deutschen Schutzgebiete*, 1912/13, Statistical Section, 52.

6

SOCIAL DISCIPLINE, EDUCATIONAL POLICY AND THE TAXATION OF THE AFRICANS

The objective of German Native Policy after the Herero and Nama War was as far as possible to mould the entire African population into a willing and efficient labour force for the colonial economy. The aim was that the imposition of forced labour should give way in the long term to the 'voluntary' acceptance of employment. The elements of compulsion, it was thought, would gradually fade into the background as the result of a successful process of subjecting the Africans to measures of social discipline: measures that would culminate in the appearance of a new type of African, one who complied uncomplainingly with the requirement to undertake work as a dependent employee, who indeed even defined himself through his function as a worker. The most important instrument in this 'education to work' was the compulsion to accept employment as described in the foregoing chapters. This programme of social and cultural transformation was closely linked to attempts to make labour more efficient through education and training. A crucial role was ascribed to the school system, which was not only to furnish the Africans with the knowledge of the German language – essential if they were to 'function' perfectly as workers – but also to inculcate in them 'values' such as discipline and the will to work. All of this was intended to fill the vacuum left behind by the destruction of traditional African social structures.

The African who found his fulfilment in dependent employment, and was thus able to earn enough to enjoy a secure livelihood, was ultimately also to be an important element in the wider project of making the colony financially self-sufficient. Only then would the build-up of the colonial economy be complete, and the colonial state be viable from its own resources. This aim was also to be pursued by taxing the Africans – a much-debated topic that provides a further instructive illustration of the long-term concept behind German Native Policy. Taxation was to be imposed in a manner appropriate to the economic resources of the African population, and was by no means intended to exploit them 'beyond measure'. In addition, the contribution to the public purse raised in this way was to be applied to meeting the needs of the Africans, so that the tax would serve to make Native Policy self-financing.

Trained in school to understand and accept their new dependent social situation, and making a financial contribution to the economic development of the Colony through taxation: it was through such measures that the new Africans were to be formed and the social and cultural transformation of the territory brought to its consummation.

Educational Policy

The provision of schooling for the African population of German South West Africa was a task for the missions; in contrast to the other German colonies, there were no state schools for Africans in South West Africa right up to the end of German colonial rule.[1] In 1903 there were already fifty-three Protestant mission schools with a total of 2,457 pupils;[2] but this figure fell markedly due to the turmoil of the war and the resulting drastic fall in the population. In 1913 there were thirty-five mission schools, twenty of them Protestant, with a total of 2,791 pupils; of these 2,198 attended the schools of the Protestant Rhenish Mission, while the rest attended Catholic schools.[3] This means that some 15 per cent of all the African children living within the Police Zone were receiving schooling.[4] In order to train African teaching assistants, who had to bear the brunt of the teaching work during the frequent absences of the missionaries from their mission stations, the Rhenish Mission set up a training college of its own in Gaub in 1911.[5] In addition, as early as 1909 there were 'half-white residential training institutions' for young people of 'mixed' heritage in Windhoek and Okahandja, and a training workshop for the teaching of handicrafts at the Catholic mission in Windhoek.[6]

It is very difficult to put together a coherent picture of what everyday life in the schools was really like. Educational success suffered under irregular attendance and the fact that 'in many cases children of school age' already had to work, which made it 'extraordinarily difficult for regular, consistent and determined progress of the kind envisaged in the curriculum to be made in the subjects taught', as the Rhenish Mission complained. However, a model school timetable drawn up by the Rhenish Mission in 1913 gives some indication of the content of the tuition. The children were to receive three lessons on each of five school days, made up of five lessons in religious knowledge, four lessons in their mother language, two in German, two in arithmetic and one in each of two other subjects such as singing, handwriting or real science. The aim was to contribute to 'the mental improvement of the natives' and, 'by influencing them religiously, to progressively train young people to display diligence, loyalty, conscientiousness, discipline and good order'.[7]

The Catholic Mission described the idea behind its activities in similar terms. It regarded schooling as an appropriate way 'of educating the natives in the <u>best interests of the country</u>' (as seen through German eyes, of course), and considered that 'an initially moderate level' of schooling for Africans would benefit 'the entire <u>economic</u> life of the colony'.[8]

The schools were financed first and foremost from the resources of the missionary societies, although there were state grants from the fund 'for the Propagation of the German Language in the Colony' amounting to M7,900 in 1910, M8,000 in 1911 and M9,000 in 1912.[9] As even in the government's own eyes these amounts represented no more than a very minor level of assistance, scarcely any supervision was exercised from the Administration side, apart from occasional visits by District Officers to the mission schools in their districts.[10]

The German Administration long paid hardly any attention to the question of schooling for Africans; but in 1913 a resolution of the Budget Committee of the Reichstag[11] that held out the prospect of higher subsidies for schools at last triggered discussion of the topic in German South West Africa as well. As there were no government schools for Africans there – and it was considered that it would cost too much to set them up – the plan was to provide more support than had previously been afforded to the schools maintained by the missionary societies.[12] In return, however, these were to be subjected to more intensive state supervision.

But fond as the Administration was of praising the contribution made by the missionary societies to the establishment and consolidation of German colonial rule, in other respects there prevailed in official circles a fundamental distrust of the missionaries' objectives, which the authorities sought to relativize by putting forward concepts of their own. Higher grants were therefore tied to the introduction of a school curriculum that had a firmly determined content. Whereas the missionary societies of both denominations had hitherto focused their curricula on religious knowledge, the Colonial Government laid great stress on how important it was to teach the children German. It was considered essential for the Africans to learn to speak and understand German better, simply in order 'to avoid the many conflicts between whites and blacks that result from misunderstandings arising out of a lack of knowledge of the language'.[13]

Although the missionary societies were prepared to allow the Administration a right of supervision in exchange for the proposed state subsidies, they insisted that this should be restricted to those subjects for which assistance was granted. If, for example, money was to be made available only to support the teaching of German, then that was the only subject that the state would be allowed to have a say on.[14]

Working out a state curriculum for the Native Schools turned out to be a difficult matter, however. The educational issue having been neglected for such a long time, there was – according to the Head of the Native Affairs Department, Kurt Streitwolf – no one in the Administration in 1913 who had any experience with African education, and so it remained dependent upon the cooperation and expertise of the missionary societies.[15] The model school timetable that had been drawn up by the Rhenish Mission, as mentioned above, therefore remained the focus of deliberations.[16]

The plans to expand African schooling were not, however, uncontested within the Colonial Administration: in some quarters there was fundamental opposition. According to the draft of a letter to the Imperial Colonial Office, for example, the results produced by teaching German up until then 'scarcely make it appear desirable to further promote the elementary schooling of the natives with state funding'. The reason given for this was that the Africans 'frequently misused the knowledge they had acquired, particularly in written German'. It had 'happened on numerous occasions that natives had sent notes to shops on which they had forged their masters' signatures, in order to obtain alcoholic drinks'. Furthermore, such 'half-educated natives' had started to display a 'reluctance to work' arising out of 'arrogance and pride'. The 'training of the natives as craftsmen' too had, with few exceptions, 'so far only led to their being used as assistants': 'an ability on the part of the natives to work and think independently' had 'not yet been achieved, and in view of the character of the Colony is not likely to be in the general public interest'. There was therefore no desire for the level of funding for Native Schools to be increased.[17]

Apparently as a result of bitter resistance from Native Affairs Officer Streitwolf, who expressly refused to sign off this draft letter,[18] the passages quoted were all struck out. Who originally composed this draft cannot be determined, but the author was not alone in his opinion. Deputy Governor Oskar Hintrager also wrote to Berlin rejecting the proposed increase in funding.[19]

However, the opponents were unable to get their way. It was Native Affairs Officer Streitwolf who set himself up as the strongest protagonist of an expansion of African schooling. Indignant at the 'absurd manner, which is not to be reconciled with the principles of colonization by a civilized nation', in which the Governor's Office had wanted to reply to the Imperial Colonial Office's proposals to support African education, he wrote a memorandum setting out his own ideas, unrestrainedly castigating the school policy that had prevailed in South West Africa until then. He described as 'absurd ... the view that the natives here are not capable of being educated, and the allegations that education would only seduce them into arrogance, laziness, forging signatures etc.', as up to that time 'nobody has taken the trouble to do anything at all for the improvement of the natives', and the Administration's involvement in education had been restricted to the payment of 'minuscule' sums to the mission schools.

He considered it would be impossible in the long term to 'continue to uphold the view that the natives as our labourers (or rather, to put it bluntly, our serfs) do not need any schooling at all, irrespective of the fact that the contrary opinion will soon come to prevail at home'. Nor, he maintained, were there any grounds for reservations with regard to allowing Africans 'the rudiments of elementary education (reading, writing, arithmetic, German)', as this would certainly not 'be accompanied by the evil consequences of overhasty attempts at personality formation'. With education being limited to those who lived in places where there were schools, 'this education, which so many people here in the territory regard as being a particularly malign influence on the natives', would in any case 'only trickle down slowly, drop by drop, into the wider population'.

Streitwolf then went on to consider the question of whether 'the improvement of the natives' was in fact in the interests of the Colony. Although one might justifiably argue, he maintained, 'that it is not in the interests of an increase in the white population for a large number of natives to be put in the position of being able to take jobs with the Post Office or in other offices or shops etc. away from whites', so that there were 'justified reservations with regard to over-extensive education such as is being given to the natives in East Africa and

Cameroon', it was nevertheless urgently necessary to achieve 'a better and more thorough learning of <u>the German language</u> by the natives'. In the southern areas of South West Africa, he observed, 'something that is supposed to be Cape Dutch, but could better be described as double Dutch (*Kauderwelsch*), is spoken in transactions between whites and blacks, and in the north a corrupt form of German that often makes a mockery of our mother tongue'. And what the north and the south had in common was that 'despite that twisted and unintelligible double Dutch, and despite that mockery of our own language, white and black are still not able to understand each other'. This resulted in 'misunderstanding after misunderstanding, leading in many cases to the maltreatment of natives by whites because of alleged disobedience'. In Streitwolf's view, many cases 'of improper treatment and of brutal maltreatment of natives by whites' could have been avoided if there had not been these difficulties of communication. But as the Whites were unwilling to take the trouble to learn African languages, it was necessary to teach the Africans German. This was not, however, the only reason why he considered language teaching to be important; it would also serve to make the Africans aware 'that we do not merely want to exploit them as beasts of burden, but that we are also seeking to do something for their intellectual and moral improvement'. But as yet, he went on, nothing had been done in this respect. The Germans had always heard complaints, and also complained themselves, 'that the natives are getting worse from year to year'; but nobody had considered it necessary 'to undertake any educational measures (except 15 to 25 strokes of the sjambok)'. This was the situation that the schools now had to take up, and it was 'in the compelling interest' of the colony to support them in their task. They had to teach the Africans German 'and also discipline and good order', just as they taught these things to Whites, and thereby provide something to replace the 'tribal' organizations that had been destroyed.

Streitwolf pleaded for the mission schools to be granted sufficient funding; he estimated the requirement at M54,000, far more than had been granted in the past. This financial subsidy should be linked, however, to the strict condition that 'reading, writing and arithmetic should be taught in German, and the German language taught as well'. The number of lessons to be given in the individual subjects every week should be precisely determined, in order to guarantee that the curriculum of the mission schools 'should no longer be made up predominantly of religion, singing etc. ... but of basic subjects'. At the same time Streitwolf demanded that the mission schools should be subjected to state supervision; though he did not think it would be possible to make education compulsory.

Streitwolf was against the setting up of handicraft schools, however, as he thought there were enough White craftsmen in South West Africa and it would be unreasonable 'to artificially create black competition for them'. Instead of providing craft training in special schools, he wanted to make it compulsory for the mission schools to train their pupils in practical work such as horticulture or handicrafts one day a week, 'so that native children do not only receive theoretical training, but also learn to do practical work. This was, after all, 'the most important thing in the education of the natives'.[20]

Thus Streitwolf was himself not primarily guided, any more than other officials were, by philanthropic motives, but by considerations relating to the consolidation of colonial rule and the development of the economy. But Streitwolf, who had been Native Affairs Officer since 1908 and so must have been thoroughly familiar with the situation of the Africans, was the one person to give clear expression to the realization that the Africans could neither be controlled nor integrated into the colonial economy by pure compulsion. The intended transformation of the Africans into a working class orientated towards fulfilling German needs required a conscious effort to educate them if it was to be sustainable in the long term. The fact that Streitwolf rejected craft training shows that he had no more desire than anyone else to present Africans with a way of avoiding working in dependent employment.

Governor Seitz, in his reply to the Imperial Colonial Office, associated himself with Streitwolf's views, and also argued in favour of improved education for Africans:

> Improved schooling for the natives has increasingly shown itself to be an essential requirement. On the one hand, the discipline of the natives, and in particular of the children, has been very much relaxed since the disappearance of the tribal organizations in the form of the chieftaincies, so that it is urgently necessary to put something else in the place of the tribal organization and tribal discipline – that something else being schooling, with the inculcation of a sense of duty and discipline in respect of the state; while on the other hand it is an inescapable necessity for native children to be better prepared for their later occupation in the employment of whites by teaching them German, so that the constant conflicts between workers and employers as a result of mutual misunderstandings arising out of a lack of knowledge of the language are progressively eliminated.[21]

He explicitly contradicted his Deputy, Oskar Hintrager, stating that he considered the money that had been made available in the past to have been too little, and demanding state support for the mission schools to the tune of M60,000 – even more than Streitwolf had proposed. In view of the high costs of setting up government schools, he agreed totally with Streitwolf's plea for the mission schools to be granted funding, wanted to see them subjected to state supervision, and rejected separate craft schools, giving as his reason the opposition that was to be expected in the population and in the Territorial Council. He sent the Imperial Colonial Office a school organizational plan drawn up in collaboration with the Mission.[22]

As well as laying down German or the African language customary in the area as the language of tuition, this plan also provided for a degree of compulsion in school attendance for the pupils. The parents of children who wished to attend a mission school were to enter into an obligation, insofar as the children were not yet eight years old when first registered, to ensure that they remained in school for the whole of the four-year course. To break off their schooling prematurely they would require the approval of the school's management, although the responsible District Officer would have the power to overrule a headteacher who refused his approval. If children then failed to attend school without permission, they were to be compelled to attend by the local administrative authorities. A fine could be imposed upon parents, werf elders or employers with whom the pupils were in a dependent personal relationship, if they 'deliberately caused a registered pupil not to attend school'. In return for the state support they were to receive, the mission schools were to accept the obligation to keep to the curriculum and were to be subject to an annual inspection by the District Officer and a government teacher. State control was only to extend, however, to the subjects set out the curriculum; other subjects, such as religious education, were not to be subject to state influence.[23]

The curriculum prescribed by the authorities encompassed the following learning targets:

(a) a proper understanding and clear speaking of simple colloquial German, (b) moderately fluent reading of German handwriting and printing, (c) the writing of simple sentences from dictation and if possible the free writing of interconnected thoughts from the native's own area of experience, and (d) the performance of arithmetical operations in German, covering the range of figures from 1 to 100.[24]

The children, aged around 7 to 11, were to be taught in four year-groups, with six German language lessons and two arithmetic lessons also conducted in German every week.[25] In this way, it was hoped, the school would 'first and foremost educate young natives in a sense of duty, in discipline with regard to the State, and in working', and secondly 'teach native children the rudiments of school subjects and the German language'.[26]

But the need for labourers not only influenced the syllabuses but also persuaded the Colonial Government not to seek to impose universal compulsory education, as the missions had repeatedly demanded, but instead, 'in order to take account to the greatest possible extent of the shortage of labour in the colony', to introduce only 'conditionally compulsory schooling'.[27] This meant that only those pupils who had been properly registered should be compelled to attend school, while children older than eight would no longer be admitted to the complete four-year course.[28] Thus in this respect too, the Colonial Government had to yield to the immediate pressure of the demands of the labour market, and postpone the fulfilment of its longer term plans.

The Imperial Colonial Office having approved both the school organizational plan and the curriculum, and also the application for increased funding for 1915,[29] the organizational plan and the curriculum were presented to the Territorial Council.[30] Although this body also gave its approval, it does not appear to have been possible to fully implement the reorganization of African education before the outbreak of war, as the missions first wanted to have the issue of supervision that was bound up with the acceptance of public funding and the introduction of the school organizational plan clarified in more detail. The money that had already been made available was therefore initially distributed to the schools without conditions being attached.[31]

This approach to school policy represented an attempt to replace the compulsion to work by measures of social disciplining in the long term. The plan was that the Africans, re-educated as the Whites thought appropriate, would 'voluntarily' accept the labourer role ascribed to them. In this way, conflicts between the colonizers and the colonized were to be defused, and the society of privilege placed on a permanent basis. Enhanced performance at work brought about by better education was to make the colonial economy more efficient and so benefit development in the colony.

Taxation of the Africans

Alongside the three Native Ordinances of 1907, the imposition of a Native Tax was one of the central pillars of German policy towards the Africans, even if its belated implementation, followed only a few years later by the loss of the Colony, meant that its effects were almost imperceptible. Although the direct taxation of the African population was not implemented in South West Africa until very late as compared with the other German colonies, debate on the issue had begun as early as the Governorship of Theodor Leutwein. It was taken up again after the ending of the Herero and Nama War. The debate was a very controversial one, both within the local administration and the Colonial Government, and also within the Imperial Colonial Office; and this discussion on what the purpose of direct taxation should be and on whether it would be possible to actually implement it reveals a lot about the thought processes of the civil servants involved, and about the conscious or unconscious strategies that existed for the legitimization of colonial rule. As the debate involved fundamental considerations with regard to how South West African society was to be organized in future, it is appropriate to go into these in some detail. At the same time, they demonstrate the degree of attentiveness that the Colonial Administration applied to observing and assessing the experience of other colonial powers.

Fundamentals and Models

Once German rule had been consolidated after the Herero and Nama War, and once the three 1907 Native Ordinances had made any organized resistance on the part of the Africans impossible, the primary objective of the Administration was to promote the economic recovery of South West Africa. This included, as explicitly demanded by the Imperial Colonial Office, making the colony financially self-sufficient, i.e. relieving it of its dependence on subsidies from the Imperial Government, as Governor Bruno von Schuckmann emphasized in a programmatic speech at the opening of the second session of the Government Council on 28 March 1908. Von Schuckmann forecast that the colony would 'also prove itself to be capable of collecting taxes and so providing revenue for the Administration'. In order to provide for this, he presented to the Government Council a draft plan for a tax on real estate, turnover and beer, and for the raising of the customs duties on a few items. Furthermore, 'in accordance with the wishes of the population', he presented for discussion a 'draft document on the establishment of local self-government in the Districts and Municipalities'.[32] The latter was then indeed introduced by means of the 'Ordinance of the Imperial Chancellor concerning Local Self-Government in German South West Africa', promulgated on 28 January 1909.[33]

Of great significance in connection with the issue of taxing the Africans was the transfer of responsibility for a variety of tasks to the District and Municipal Authorities *(Bezirks- und Gemeindeverbände)* that were to be created. They were to be made responsible for the construction and maintenance of public highways, the public water supply, the public health service 'including care of the sick' and the prevention of epidemics, and also for the welfare of the poor, education and the 'protection and promotion of general well-being'. In this way the field of African welfare, an area that was just beginning to develop, was made a responsibility of local government. In order to cover the costs arising from their being allocated these tasks, the local authorities were given the power 'to supplement the funding assigned to them by the Governor by raising taxes from the inhabitants of their areas'.[34] For Governor von Schuckmann, the opportunity to spread the costs incurred for the development of the colony across the population had been a major factor driving his plans to expand local government administration right from the beginning[35] – and this included the possibility of subjecting the Africans to taxation.

The 'Ordinance of the Governor of German South West Africa concerning the Taxation of Real Estate in the Colony of German South West Africa', which had been presented to the Government Council at the same time as the Local Self-Government Ordinance, then came into force on 1 April 1909. Through this Ordinance, all 'improved and unimproved real estate' was subjected to 'a land tax and a turnover tax' (on land sales). Not only did this mean that settlers were made subject to direct taxation, but the Ordinance also represented the beginning of the taxation of the Africans, its provisions being explicitly also 'applicable to the real estate of the Rehoboth Basters'. In addition, the Governor was to have the power to determine to what extent 'other natives should be subject to these provisions'.[36]

But this land tax affected only that minority among the African population who still possessed any real estate after the expropriations of 1906 and 1907. The Administration therefore considered introducing a separate tax applying specifically to the African population. It was no mere coincidence that these matters were being considered at a time so close to that of the introduction of the 1907 Native Ordinances, since a crucial prerequisite for imposing a direct tax on the Africans was that they should have been comprehensively registered.

On 24 November 1908, Deputy Governor Hintrager called on the District Offices to state their positions with regard to the direct taxation of the Africans that the Colonial Government was intending to introduce, and to make proposals:

> By contrast to British southern Africa, no direct taxation of the natives has so far been introduced in German South West Africa. As there is a

prospect at the present time of the white population being subjected to direct taxation in connection with the introduction of local self-government in the colony, it is time to look more closely at this question too, particularly as the experience gathered in the British colonies speaks clearly in favour of getting the natives too to share the burden of public expenditure through direct taxation; and the Native Affairs Commission that deliberated there between 1903 and 1905 expressly stated that it recognized the necessity of imposing direct taxation on the natives ...

Under these circumstances, I intend to ask the next Government Council to concern itself with this matter and to submit to it the question of whether it is appropriate at this time to proceed with the direct taxation of the natives, and if so, in what form (poll tax, hut tax, livestock tax?). And if this is done, at what level would it be most expedient to set the tax?[37]

Hintrager's considerations thus focused on the hope of providing relief for the state treasury, as the introduction of local self-government had in any case made reform of the colony's finances essential. He was apparently very impressed by the yields that Native Taxes were producing in the colonies of other European states, and in support of his proposal he attached detailed tables of the sums that had flowed into the public purse from the Native Taxes in the Transvaal and Bechuanaland.[38]

Hintrager's initiative was the result of deliberations that had preoccupied him over some considerable length of time, and which deliberately also embraced the experience of the British colonies. Not only were Governors von Lindequist and von Schuckmann comparatively well acquainted with British colonial practice, having both held the office of German Consul General in Cape Town,[39] but the Colonial Government also set about collecting information on the policies of other countries via the German Empire's diplomatic channels or by studying colonial documents available in Germany. The Governor's Office had been collecting information on the direct taxes levied on Africans in the British colonies, especially Natal and the Transvaal, since at least 1906. In some cases this was the result of prompting from the Colonial Department of the Foreign Office in Berlin, which in February 1906, for example, forwarded to the Governor's Office in Windhoek a transcript of a report it had received from London. This told of unrest that had broken out among the Zulus in Natal[40] in reaction to the introduction of a poll tax. Extensive details were given about the various forms of poll tax or hut tax that the administration in Natal was experimenting with, and about the

'Report of the South African Native Affairs Commission, 1903–05', a commission whose task it was to promote the introduction of a hut tax.[41] How important the British model was to the Germans can be seen from the fact that Hintrager, in his Circulated Order, explicitly referred to the recommendations of this commission.

But Rhodesia was also being kept under observation, as a newspaper cutting from the *Deutsch-Südwestafrikanische Zeitung* of 31 October 1908 about tax income in that territory indicates. In this article, the entire revenues of Rhodesia were stated to amount to M11,081,640, with the Native Tax contributing M3,883,160. This was the most important information extracted from the article, as the underlining in the original confirms. Hintrager himself had also added the corresponding figures for Natal in a handwritten note underneath; there, taxes had first been raised from the Africans as long ago as 1849. Alarmed by the reports sent from London by Henrich Schnee, the Colonial Attaché at the German Embassy there, Hintrager added a comment: 'This tax was collected without any untoward occurrences'.[42] The Administration may have been seeking to extract as much money as possible from the Africans; but this nevertheless remained an area that needed to be handled particularly sensitively in view of the very recent experience of the surprise resistance of the Herero and Nama.

How attentively the Colonial Government continued to follow developments in this field in the British territories is demonstrated by an article on 'The Taxation of the Natives in the British African Colonies' that is to be found in the files in the form of a cutting from the *Deutsch-Südwestafrikanische Zeitung* of 23 October 1909. The author of this article, a person named von König, provided an overview in tabular form of most of the British African colonies and the types of direct taxation imposed on the Africans there, and of the total annual tax income of each colony. He analysed in detail the example of Sierra Leone, where there had been unrest after the introduction of the hut tax, but also sought to allay any fears by quoting the report of the responsible minister, Joseph Chamberlain, who saw the causes of the unrest as lying not only in the introduction of the hut tax, but also in the 'cruelty' that lies in the 'nature' of the 'natives', and in the changes brought about by the progressive penetration of civilization, the benefits deriving from which the Africans were not able to appreciate. Drawing on Chamberlain's report, von König further wrote that the unrest had soon died down and that the introduction of the tax was to be regarded as a success. Von König also presented the Governor of Sierra Leone, Sir Charles King-Harman, as a keen advocate of direct taxation of the Africans. He quoted extensively from a speech of Sir Charles's in which he had declared that every nation has to pay for its government, including the British nation and that of Sierra Leone, and that the tax collected would not flow out of the country but would be used for the benefit of the Africans, through investment in 'the government of the colony, the administration of justice or the infrastructure'.[43] The arguments put forward by British colonial politicians are reproduced almost word for word in discussions of a Native Tax in South West Africa, demonstrating that this was by no means a singularly German phenomenon.

Even after the colony had introduced its own tax, the Colonial Government continued to collect information about the revenues raised in neighbouring countries. In 1914 the German Legation in Lisbon sent a report to Chancellor von Bethmann Hollweg that contained information and figures relating to a tax increase in Angola, and this was immediately forwarded to the Colonial Government in Windhoek.[44] Hintrager, having learnt from the press of new tax legislation in the Transvaal, used diplomatic channels to get more precise information as quickly as possible. He wrote directly to the German Consulate in Pretoria and asked to have a copy of the new law sent to him.[45] Thus the Colonial Government in Windhoek made every effort to learn from the experience of other colonial powers, and so to avoid making the same mistakes.

There had already been moves in the direction of introducing direct taxation of the Africans in South West Africa before the Herero and Nama War; but each time the proposals had been set aside by the Governor's Office as being 'impossible to implement for the time being'.[46] So it took pressure from the Colonial Council in Berlin, at a meeting of which on 18 May 1903 Privy Councillor (ret'd) Simon had proposed 'universal taxation' of the Africans in South West Africa,[47] to get the Colonial Government to finally take the issue up and report back to the Colonial Department in Berlin. In making his proposals, however, Simon had been less concerned with the level of revenues that the tax would bring in than with the 'aim of giving useful instruction in economics':[48]

> My only concern is to ensure that the issue of the taxing of the natives, in whatever form, should be given serious consideration at all, though I would like to mention that in German South West Africa in particular a general tax that was purely a poll tax would be particularly difficult to implement in view of the fact that to a large extent the population still tends to be nomadic. I see the main value of direct taxation of the natives

as lying not in the revenues that it would generate, as the amounts raised from such taxes will continue to be insignificant for a long time to come, but in the education to work, which the natives will need to perform if they are to be able to raise the tax.

The views of Dr Peters and others that the natives have to be compelled to work by the application of a greater or lesser degree of force, I cannot concur with. Education remains the only possibility, which I can see no better means of inculcating than by imposing a tax in the form of a moderate charge to pay for the services performed for the natives by the Government, and in general by the fact that the whites have a higher level of civilization.[49]

Leutwein responded to Simon's proposals in September 1903, but emphasized that he was merely expressing his personal opinion, as he would have to hear what the views of the District Officers were before he could recommend any course of action. He considered a hut tax to be impossible to implement, as the majority of the Africans living in South West Africa did not have permanent houses, but lived in 'lightly constructed "pontoks", which they would simply abandon if there was any threat of their being taxed'. Thus there remained only the poll tax, the introduction of which he thought would be counterproductive in view of the low level of development that had been attained in the colony up to that time:

It would no doubt be a nice idea to compel the natives to work by means of this type of tax. But the nomadic lives led by our natives in this thinly populated territory stand in the way of this as well. Only those few natives would be affected by the tax who have settled down either on the mission stations or where there are other white settlements. Instead of keeping them there, where it is to our advantage to have them, we would reawaken in them the longing to join up again with their fellow tribesmen who live more freely.

It is true that the care provided by the white government brings the natives a number of advantages. Whether they have come to appreciate this is doubtful. But on the other hand, these advantages are balanced by a number of disadvantages that the influx of numerous whites, some of them of dubious character, into their tribal areas in the train of the white government must certainly have brought in the eyes of the natives.[50]

Thus Leutwein recognized that the tax would function as a means to force the African population to undertake wage-earning work, and he welcomed this. He too wanted to see the number of Africans working for wages increased; but in view of the still inadequate structures of the state administration he thought it would be detrimental to the economic development of the colony if a Native Tax were to be introduced prematurely. He did, however, hold out to the Colonial Department the prospect that further ideas for a 'tax system directed at the natives' would be developed once the epidemics of livestock disease, which represented a major threat to the colony's prosperity, had been overcome.[51]

Leutwein's assessment that it would still be premature to introduce a tax on the Africans was shared by the District Officers of Omaruru, Gibeon and Karibib.[52] The motives for rejecting Simon's proposals set out in these statements in 1903 already foreshadowed some of the major arguments in the poll tax debate that would be conducted within the Administration after 1908, when the main focus would once again be on the realization that a universal tax would still be impossible to implement. The Karibib District Officer thought it would only make sense to impose a tax if all the Africans could be subjected to it equally; but in fact, with police resources still far from adequate, nobody would be able to prevent Africans from withdrawing into inaccessible parts of the colony. For the time being, therefore, the tax would only affect those Africans who were employed by Whites or at the mission stations. He also thought that the general state of impoverishment made it inappropriate to impose a tax.[53] An objection that was also shared by Omaruru District Office was that 'the great drought' had led to famine in the most densely populated areas. It furthermore pointed out that the 'usual wage rates for ordinary workers are in fact already so low that simply being appointed to a job might well be regarded as a form of direct taxation'. This could be seen from the fact 'that our natives are deserting in droves to the agents for the South African' [*sic*].[54] The many benefits 'that the natives derive from orderly administration' were 'quite sufficiently paid for by the monstrous taxes imposed on those same natives by the white traders'.[55] The District Officer of Gibeon weighed up the negative effects the tax would have on farmers, 'who would be obliged to pay the natives in cash so that they could pay their tax, whereas at the moment they are able to pay their workers to a large extent in clothing' or otherwise in kind; but it was not out of consideration for the interests of the Africans that he rejected the introduction of direct taxation. He saw it as something that might be introduced in some five to ten years' time, 'after the natives have been pushed back into the reservations'.[56] However, the changes that came about as a result of the Herero and Nama War, and the promulgation of the Native Ordinances immediately thereafter, lent urgency to the issue as early as 1908.

The 'Native Tax' Debate of 1908–09

In contrast to the positive assessment of a direct tax on the Africans formulated by Hintrager, the opinions of the District Officers questioned remained predominantly negative in their 1908 responses too. This, however, was less a matter of rejecting the tax in principle than a view that it was not a sensible measure at that point in time, especially as it was one that could not yet be effectively implemented. Grootfontein and Outjo District Offices pointed out in their reports that conditions in the German colony were not to be compared with those in South Africa. The Outjo District Officer, Captain Victor Franke, for example, declared:

> The positive results in the Cape Colony are a result of the well-ordered conditions there, which cannot be compared with the situation here, which is still developing. British South Africa has been under the influence of white colonization for almost a hundred years; our colony for a mere twenty-four years.[57]

The District Officers of Grootfontein,[58] Keetmanshoop,[59] Gibeon,[60] Bethanie[61] and Okahandja[62] also thought it would be premature to introduce a universal tax; in particular, they were afraid of the additional workload. Franke, too, considered that the tax would require a disproportionate amount of additional work, and also feared it would make it even more difficult to find workers for the farms.[63] Gibeon District Office also considered that in view of the 'unstable nature' of labour relationships there would inevitably be an increase in the amount of bureaucratic paperwork.[64] This was something the District Officers generally sought to avoid, as had already been shown by the complaints that had arisen in connection with the introduction of the Native Ordinances in 1907.

The argument most frequently raised against the immediate introduction of a tax, however, was the economic situation of the Africans, which was still desperate after the war.[65] The District Officer of Grootfontein, for example, argued as follows:

> By far the greater number of the natives are completely without possessions; they live from the food they receive from their employers, and their wages are generally barely sufficient to cover their requirements for clothing, tobacco, etc. Collecting a tax would therefore require the employer to deduct the appropriate sum from the wages, a procedure that appears to me to be very questionable.[66]

This mention of the fact that the introduction of a tax on the Africans might involve legal problems also shows up a fundamental dilemma:

the Colonial Administration was bound by law in the measures it adopted, or at least in any measure that impinged on German citizens. But as the Africans working for wages in dependent employment represented a fundamental element of the colonial economy, the interests of the German settlers and entrepreneurs were almost always affected as well.

District Officer Georg Wasserfall of Bethanie also pointed out that the Africans living in his district 'have with few exceptions been rendered completely destitute by the war', and that a tax would not make sense until 'secure livelihoods have been restored, i.e. until the natives' stocks of small livestock have been replenished to such an extent that they can stand being taxed'.[67] Here he was indicating a fundamental conflict between the competing objectives of, on the one hand, compelling Africans to work for extremely low wages by denying them the opportunity to earn an independent living, and on the other hand demanding the highest possible taxes from them. The imposition of an income tax would have to lead either to higher wages or to reductions in the Africans' net incomes. District Officer Schenke of Swakopmund set this out very clearly: 'Another circumstance that speaks against such a tax here is that it would essentially turn out to be a tax on the employers rather than on the natives.'[68] Gibeon District Office also pointed out that the prerequisite 'for the introduction of the tax would be an improvement in the pitiable conditions that the natives are currently living under here, with more stable employment relationships and proper regular wages'. Years would have to pass, however, before these preconditions could be achieved. Under the present circumstances he found himself 'compelled to reply in the negative' to the question of whether such a tax could be a financial success.[69]

Among some officials, the discussion on the tax even led to suggestions that there should be a cautious reversal of the policy initiated after the war. In 1906 and 1907 the Herero and Nama had been almost completely dispossessed; but Police Sergeant Springborn, the Director of Waterberg Police Barracks, made the following suggestion in respect of the financial yield:

> The taxing of the Herero and the Hottentots, who have been economically ruined by the war, and the imposition of the tax on other natives is likely to produce little in the way of a successful outcome for the time being. It would even increase the danger of their leaving their jobs and going back into the veld. It would be advisable, if possible, to allow some of the natives to have small plots of land and to tax the yields they produce.[70]

It should be made clear to the Herero and Nama, however, that although they were provisionally exempted from such taxation, 'they would be brought into the scope of the tax later on'.[71]

The only officials to reply with unqualified approval were the three District Officers of Lüderitzbucht, Warmbad and Maltahöhe, and the representatives of the Territorial Police; whereby in the case of District Officer Runck of Warmbad, the fact that he had apparently only taken up his post a short time before, and so was not fully acquainted with the real situation in his District when he answered Hintrager's questionnaire, may well have influenced his attitude.[72] The District Officer of Maltahöhe pointed out in his statement that apart from taxing the wage-earning workers there was above all a need to impose a livestock tax on the numerous herds of small livestock that thrifty Africans had already been able to acquire again out of their wages.[73] He wanted to see limits imposed on these herds. The fact that Lüderitzbucht District Office applauded the proposals was no doubt due to the special situation the District found itself in as a result of the discovery of diamonds and the intensification of mining there. In its statement it expressly mentioned the 'very many highly paid coloureds from the Cape' and the existence of 'self-employed tradesman among these coloured people, such as washers, who also earn a lot of money'.[74]

The head of the Territorial Police, Chief Inspector Joachim von Heydebreck, also showed himself to be a vehement protagonist of taxing the Africans, without, however, going into detail as to how this could be implemented in concrete terms. Writing completely from the point of view of the central administration, he only expressed himself in general terms on the usefulness of a Native Tax. His statement corresponds to a large extent to those of his subordinates from the Kupferberg and Kub Police Barracks. Only Police Sergeant Springborn from Waterberg referred not only to the poverty of the Herero and most of the Nama but also to difficulties that might arise in taxing the Nama of Berseba and the Reheboth Basters, as only very few of them were employed as wage-earning workers and it was very difficult to assess their income from livestock trading.[75] No doubt the Territorial Police were pursuing a different agenda from the District Officers with their predominantly positive assessments of the taxation issue. They were an instrument of the state executive, whose very existence was dependent on the Colonial Government having adequate financial resources. They had simply no choice but to support any possible initiative that would fill the colony's coffers, purely out of self-interest. Equally, when assessing the feasibility of such measures, they were obliged to present practically every proposal as being possible to implement, in order to emphasize what valuable service they performed. In addition, they did not need to pay any regard to the possibly disadvantageous effects of the tax on the supply of labour to the farms and the mines, as this was not something they were responsible for.

Thus of the sixteen District Offices, only three were in favour of immediately introducing a direct tax on the Africans. On the other hand, none of them explicitly stated that they were against such a tax in principle. They were all fundamentally in favour, but did not want to see it introduced at that point in time, or at least not in the areas for which their respective offices were responsible. A similar pattern had emerged during the discussions of the Native Ordinances of 1907: the measures proposed by the Governor's Office had not been criticized fundamentally, but rather declared to be good in principle. Apart from the District Officers' knowledge of the real situations existing in their districts and their appreciation of the difficulties attaching to the practical implementation of a general tax on the Africans, a further motive may have played a part as well: a tax on the African population imposed universally by the colonial authorities in Windhoek would have robbed the District Officers of any possibility of reacting flexibly to the specific situations on the ground in their respective districts. The fact that they considered it essential to retain this possibility can be deduced from their detailed proposals with regard to the form such a tax should take. Moreover, a tax rate imposed 'top-down' would have involved much more intensive bureaucratic supervision from the central Colonial Government, whereas the District Officers sought to retain as much freedom of action as possible with regard to the central authority.[76] In this connection it is indicative that the practical implementation of the Native Tax did not take place until the Colonial Government had given up its plans to impose a uniform tax rate throughout the Colony, and had opened up the way for the tax to be adapted to meet local conditions.

Most of the District Officers went into the various possible types of tax – hut tax, livestock tax, poll tax or land tax – in detail in their statements, weighing up their advantages and disadvantages. Their argumentation gives valuable insights into the intentions that each associated with the tax, and into the legitimation strategies that the colonial officials used to justify this further financial exploitation of the African population.

A hut tax after the model of German East Africa was generally regarded as being 'unsuitable', since in South West Africa the possession of a pontok was 'no measure of the ability to pay tax'. This was 'different in East Africa, where more or less every hut owner has a *shamba* [farming plot] of his own'.[77] It was also considered to be a not very good idea in view of the Africans' semi-nomadic lifestyle,[78] as it would be susceptible to tax evasion: 'a hut tax would fail to achieve its objective since the Hottentots, who are fond of communal living, would all pack themselves degradingly into a single pontok in order as far as possible to avoid the hut tax'.[79] Springborn also raised legal reservations with regard to whether such a tax was admissible, pointing out that a hut tax would 'be likely to be considered a disagreeable matter, since the pontoks stand on the owners' own land and the owners take the necessary building material from their own stocks'. But he was against it for practical reasons as well, as it would be very difficult to make any distinction between the better off and the less well off.[80] But without such differentiation, the tax would be a flat-rate charge that it would not be possible to adapt to take account of the individual's assumed ability to pay; and most of the District Officers wanted the tax to be variable in this way, as was shown in their proposals for a progressive income tax.

There was, on the other hand, fundamental acceptance of the idea of a poll tax, as it was assumed that the 1907 Pass and Control Ordinances had led to there being sufficient surveillance instruments available to allow every individual African man and woman to be subjected to the tax directly. The Gibeon District Officer expressed this openly: 'The introduction of a hut tax is not something that ought to be considered for this colony, since here every native is registered and is under constant control.' A hut tax, by contrast, was appropriate only 'where it is difficult, if not impossible, to keep the natives under supervision because of the unrestricted freedom of movement they enjoy'.[81]

Knowing where every individual African lived was a necessary prerequisite for a poll tax, as the tax would relate to each specific person. The very intention of such a tax was to give the Colonial Administration access to every individual member of the colonized population, and so to ensure the highest possible financial yield from the available 'fiscal resources'. Where such a tax is completely implemented, every member of African society makes his contribution to the total revenues raised from society as a whole. However, this presents the entity raising the tax with a dilemma. Its objective is to achieve the highest possible financial yield; but when setting the tax rate it has to take care not to destroy the economic resources that the taxpayer needs to survive – otherwise, in order to achieve a higher level of revenues in the short term, it would be depriving itself of future tax income. The District Officers and representatives of the

Territorial Police who were required to give their opinions were well aware of this, which is why they devoted such exhaustive discussion to the issue of what rate of tax would be appropriate.

Tax was to be paid – on this there was universal agreement – by all able-bodied adult male Africans. Whether a person might be considered to be not able-bodied and therefore to be incapable of working was to be decided by the authorities in any given case,[82] although there was also a proposal that a general maximum age should be laid down.[83] As was already the case with the Pass Ordinance, all Africans were to be regarded as 'adult' who were older than fourteen or 'whose physical development corresponds to that of a person of this age'.[84] What counted, then, was their ability to work. But the taxing of Africans who were not yet of full age was not undisputed. Springborn, for example, would have preferred to have seen a reduced tax rate for those aged between fourteen and eighteen,[85] whilst Windhoek District Office would have liked to have seen the tax obligation imposed only from the age of twenty[86] – but then on women as well. While most of the statements of opinion agreed in proposing that unmarried African women should be taxed – and Maltahöhe District Office explicitly demanded that this should also apply to prostitutes[87] – there remained a certain measure of disagreement on the matter of whether married women should be exempt from tax. These differences in opinion were particularly acute with regard to the tax position of a man's second or third wife. Paying no regard at all to the polygamous basis of African society, Police Chief von Heydebreck stated tersely: 'The tax-paying man has one wife tax-free'.[88] This was an unambiguous statement which particularly attracted the attention of the official processing the document in the Governor's Office, as the marginal notes indicate.[89]

Namutoni District Office adopted a contrary position. As it pointed out, 'Taxing men who have more than one wife more heavily would give rise to permanent tax evasion, while at the same time being regarded by the natives as unwelcome interference in their private relationships'.[90] Apart from the admission that such elaborate tax regulations would be impossible to keep check on, this reference to Africans actually having a private sphere is astonishing in view of the massive interference represented by the Native Ordinances and the existing compulsion to work, which Namutoni District Office expressed itself in favour of in the same report. It is clear, however, that the official was doing his best to hit upon a tax rule that he thought would be regarded as reasonable by the Africans.

The fact that any consideration at all was given to exempting certain groups of people from the tax indicates that, from the point of view of the officials, a Native Tax had to fulfil certain criteria if it was to be justifiable. It was not to be merely an arbitrary instrument for taxing all Africans to the same extent; rather, there was to be a certain degree of fairness and equitableness about it, as is demonstrated by the rejection of a hut tax by Waterberg Police Barracks, and by the justification strategies put forward by the District Officers, which will be analysed below.

Also discussed in detail was the rate of the tax, with the proposals ranging from five to twenty marks per annum for adult men.[91] If women were to pay any tax at all, then a reduced rate was proposed for them. The question of the rate of tax being graduated in accordance with income occupied a lot of space in the discussion. Von Heydebreck, for example, considered that it would be very difficult to introduce a tax graduated by income, 'because for employers here the term income is extremely elastic'.[92] This was a reference to the problem of getting employers to actually pay wages in cash, which the introduction of an income tax assumed; because only if the worker received cash would he be able to pay the tax in cash. But this was often not the case:

> Of the natives employed on farms or by private persons, only very few receive wages in cash in addition to their rations; it would therefore scarcely be possible to tax them. In such a case, it might be possible to introduce a tax that the farmer would have to pay per family.[93]

In addition, African workers were often forced to purchase the goods they needed for their everyday lives at the farmer's own shop, which enabled their employers to recuperate a proportion of the wages they had paid out. As a result, their actual income, which any attempt to set an appropriate level of tax had to aim to determine, was lower than the amount of wages contractually agreed, as Omaruru District Office pointed out:

> In view of the current levels of the natives' wages and rations on the one hand, and the high store prices for poor quality kaffir goods on the other, I feel the natives could not be subjected to taxation without imposing an unintended element of hardship on them.[94]

Instead of an overall scheme of graduated tax, von Heydebreck would have liked to see the foreign Africans who came into the country as wage labourers, and were substantially better paid than the locals, taxed additionally by means of a transit fee that they would have to pay when they crossed the border. He was seeking to avoid the major objection against a flat-rate poll tax, namely that it would be unjust since the South African workers earned an average of ninety to one hundred marks per month, but the South West Africans only twenty marks. He thought such an additional tax was justified 'because these coloureds, e.g. the Cape Boys, spend the greater part of their income not here in the colony, but back in their home country'.[95]

The District Officer of Swakopmund also appears to have been expressing a fundamental rejection of any progressive tax, and therefore also of any kind of percentage income tax, when he reasoned as follows:

> Wages vary between five and up to a hundred marks (Cape Boys, Togo Negroes). But if the tax is fixed at a certain percentage of wages, then there will be difficulties in collecting it if wages are increased or fall, or if the natives are unemployed or sick at the time when the tax is collected. These difficulties would for the most part be eliminated, however, if the tax were collected monthly, or perhaps even if it were to be collected every quarter.[96]

Police Sergeant Springborn took precisely the opposite point of view; he would have liked to simply collect 4 per cent of the 'annual cash income', with the worse-paid Africans on the farms having half of their tax paid by their employers, as the latter were employing their workers relatively cheaply.[97] As has already been mentioned, however, in his position he was not directly confronted with the practical implications of his ideas.

In addition to the 'reasons of equity', for which, as District Officer Narciß thought, Africans who earned more should also pay more tax than their worse-off colleagues,[98] there was also the argument that higher revenues would be achieved in this way, since otherwise the tax rate would have to be set in accordance with the ability of the lowest income groups to pay. District Officer Böhmer shared this view as well: 'If the tax is to bring in a good level of revenue but at the same time to be fair, it must in my opinion be graduated in accordance with the level of income'.[99] Otherwise there would be a danger of the tax imposing such a burden on the Africans that they would have no opportunity to earn an adequate amount of money. The Administration would then have to be prepared to see them 'deserting their jobs and going back into the veld', as Police Sergeant Springborn prophesied.[100] The whole discussion does show that at least some of the officials questioned were in favour of a tax that took account of the Africans' situation and their low levels of wages.

The general opinion was that there was no need to set a minimum level of wages from which the tax would be due, 'as in view of the constantly increasing demand for native workers, anyone who makes a serious effort can find a relatively well-paid position'.[101] District Officer Schenke of Swakopmund argued similarly, adding that under the conditions prevailing in South West Africa an income tax for wage earners would be very much the same thing as a flat-rate poll tax:

> As there are practically no unemployed natives in the coastal districts, and probably will not be any in the future either, the tax could simply be imposed on every native, as long as he is not, in the opinion of the administrative authorities, incapable of working.[102]

But this rejection of a minimum income as a prerequisite for tax liability also arose to some extent out of the anxiety that collusion between employers and servants might lead to tax evasion. There was a fear that Africans could very easily avoid their tax liability by 'agreeing a wage that is just a little lower than the lowest level of taxable income'.[103]

Thus as in the discussions of the Native Ordinances, so once again in this case the deliberations were influenced by feelings of mistrust towards the Whites harboured by the officials. The Okahandja District Officer, Fromm, for example, warned:

> Many whites are unhappy with the Authority, because it concerns itself (as it is required to do by the regulations) with the native workers. Farmers with any sense will make sure themselves that their people are properly registered, and so will pay the tax themselves and recover it from their workers.
>
> It cannot, however, be excluded that an employer will tighten the tax screw to his own advantage, that he will employ people and not register them, but nevertheless withhold tax from their wages. Such possibilities must also be taken into account.[104]

Thus the officials saw the farmers as being capable of both colluding with the Africans and also of embezzling tax money.

While a poll tax would have targeted all Africans irrespective of whether they were in dependent employment or had income from independent economic activity, a land tax or a livestock tax would have been a charge only on those who did have property of their own. In von Heydebreck's opinion, such a tax could only be countenanced 'for the owners of larger herds of livestock and for those tribes that still have tribal lands of their own or to whom government land has been allocated as pasture'.[105] But this would be a substantially smaller category of people, and a tax of this kind was therefore not acceptable as a sole source of revenue. In addition, a projected land tax would have faced the Administration with an additional problem, as the African societies had a fundamentally different concept of land ownership from what Whites understood by the term. It generally meant a right of common utilization for all members of a social grouping.[106] Von Heydebreck therefore suggested a procedure that he hoped would serve to bring European legal concepts into harmony with African reality. He thought it ought to be 'laid down how much pastureland is required on average for one item of large or small livestock, and the land tax then levied on the amount of pasture required for the quantity of livestock owned by the natives concerned'.[107] In this way, the livestock tax became a component of the land tax. In von Heydebreck's view, those 'tribes' that still had intact structures and territories of their own should form exceptions:

> Coloured people who possess defined areas of pastureland (e.g. the Rehoboth Basters) should pay for the entire area. That may sound hard, but it would force the natives to make better use of their broad acres than they have done up until now. They could also lease out the land they do not use.[108]

This proposal sought to impose a European concept of efficiency on African agriculture: von Heydebreck wanted to make land that, by European standards, was not intensively utilized available to other livestock breeders. The argument that land was not adequately exploited had already served as a justification for further expropriations in the Native Ordinances; this process was now to be continued using tax instruments.

The Herero and Nama having been largely expropriated, the attitudes of the District Officers to the land and livestock tax depended very strongly on the peculiarities of their own individual districts. Only the 'Berseba Hottentots' and the 'Rehoboth Basters' possessed 'tribal lands' and 'larger herds of livestock'.[109] Accordingly, Berseba District Office was of the view that the livestock tax might be well worthwhile.[110] In other districts, however, there were hardly any herds of cattle in African ownership, and even herds of small livestock were fairly rare. Maltahöhe District Office, for example, reported thirty-five herds of up to fifty items of small livestock and five even larger herds, but only eleven head of cattle that Africans had been able to buy out of what they had saved from their wages.[111] But this was already enough to make the District Office favour a livestock tax. In Gobabis District, there was only one Herero who had livestock in any quantity worth mentioning, together with the Bechuana in Aminuis and Epukiro. But as in these cases it was the Kaptein who was the real owner of the herd, the District Officer proposed 'a monetary tax to be imposed on the Kaptein'.[112]

Namutoni District Office also favoured a tax on all Africans who owned large livestock, without any distinction of 'standing, age, occupation or sex'. The tax rate should amount to two marks per item of livestock per year, which would mean that if ten animals were owned, that being the size of herd from which an African was able to 'live without any ancillary income', the tax would be twenty marks – in other words, twice as much as the proposed poll tax. This was a level that the District Office saw as being justified, 'as the labour of these well-off people is lost to the colony'.[113]

Although Swakopmund District had scarcely any Africans 'who are not in regular employment, but instead keep livestock and live from it and from their own crops',[114] District Officer Schenke was also in favour of 'applying other principles to the taxation of natives who are not in employment but possess cattle than to those natives who are in regular employment', as this 'would be more in accordance with the natives' own views of things' than a hut tax, for example. His concern was to ensure that the tax would be in line with the Africans' actual ability to pay, and demanded: 'As the utilization value of the livestock depends on the quality of the pastureland, lower tax rates should be set for the Namib districts.'[115] In arguing like this he was adopting a principle from the Land Tax Regulations of 1909, which had essentially been conceived for Whites. These regulations explicitly provided for plots of land in the Namib and in the southern districts, which produced lower yields, to be taxed at only half the standard rate.[116] Thus Schenke too wanted to take due account of the economic situation of the Africans. In the Grootfontein, Windhoek, Gibeon and Bethanie Districts there was scarcely any livestock in African ownership, so that these District Offices took a much more negative view of the idea of a livestock tax.[117] Waterberg District Office was opposed to such a tax on principle, as in the opinion of District Officer Runck 'every native should keep livestock, and making a herd of livestock liable to tax would be detrimental to the public interest in seeing livestock breeding developed'.[118] This was a view that contradicted the intention to force the African population to accept wage-earning jobs by destroying their traditional ways of life.

A livestock tax was generally regarded as a way of getting those Africans who still had property of their own, and were therefore in a position to continue living an economically independent life, into the tax system. Above all, it was a way of extending the system to embrace those parts of the African population whose community social structures had not been destroyed. Although these people were not to be directly forced into paid employment, they were at least to be made to contribute financially to the colonial state. This also marked the beginning of their gradual incorporation into the colonial system of wage-earning labour, because in order to be able to pay their tax they would have to either sell or lease out land, sell livestock or make payments in kind to the Administration, thereby weakening their own economic substance, or else seek work with Whites in order to earn cash to pay the tax. The District Officers and the representatives of the Territorial Police were well aware of this, as an analysis of the objectives that they associated with the Native Tax shows.

Alongside the financial contribution to the Colony's budget that was to be expected, the District Officers' considerations and those of the Territorial Police were very clearly focused on the tax's function of being a further means of forcing able-bodied Africans to take up dependent work. Gibeon District Office was alone in putting forward the following view:

> In all German colonial territories in which the natives have been subjected to direct taxation the motive has been to educate the blacks to work. This motive does not apply here, as the natives of this colony, with the exception of the members of the few self-sufficient tribes, are forced to work in any case, because they own no property and have no resources, and the Native Ordinances prescribe that they should be obliged to work.[119]

The majority of the District Officers, on the other hand, did not consider that the Native Ordinances had been as successful as they ought to have been in forcing the Africans to take up employment, and therefore favoured measures to reinforce them, while still leaving room for the play of market forces. Windhoek District Office, for example, favoured the poll tax because it represented a 'gentle compulsion to work'.[120] In order 'to do more to educate African women into work' too, Swakopmund District Office expressly favoured the imposition of a tax on women as well.[121]

The tax had the further intention of preventing Africans from regaining their economic independence:

> I consider it to be urgently necessary to introduce a Native Tax, as only through this compulsive measure can all natives be forced into work.

> It is my experience that the Herero in particular invest almost every penny they earn in livestock, with the aim, as I have myself been told by ones who have been able to purchase large numbers of animals out of their savings, of not having to work any more.

> An appropriate level of taxation will, however, force them to seek employment, or else to see themselves lose their livestock again, one animal after another.[122]

The intensifying labour shortage compelled the Administration to apply the criterion of efficiency to the use of African labourers on the farms as well. The Control Ordinance of 1907 had already provided for the number of African families to be limited to ten per farm; but this measure was not enough to produce the desired effect. As the workers often received hardly anything in wages, Gobabis District Office wanted to see the tax imposed on the farmer per family employed. In addition to the financial yield, this was regarded as offering a further positive side effect in that 'the farmer would not keep more people on his farm than were absolutely necessary. This would mean that the natives were better distributed and the shortage of workers would be relieved, if only to a certain extent'.[123]

The reasons given by Warmbad District Office, on the other hand, evoke matters of principle, with their emphasis on the connection between nationhood and taxation:

> In this District, direct taxation of the natives is considered to be a real necessity, as it would force the natives to finally recognize their duties towards the government of the country and the state in which they live; and it is furthermore to be expected that these measures will substantially strengthen the self-assurance of the Hottentots when they find themselves called upon to share the burdens with the whites – seeing that they do, after all, like to flirt with European ways.[124]

Quite apart from any direct functionality of the tax, it was also, in the view of the officials, legitimated by the 'benefits' that would accrue to taxpayers as a result of the dues they paid. While Warmbad District Office, in the above quotation, regarded the 'benefit' as a psychological one, other District Officers saw it in material terms. Furthermore, many attempted to link the advantage to the Whites of being provided with cheap labour to a 'benefit' for the Africans as well. As Namutoni District Office stated:

> The native has to pay tax:
>
> (a) because he enjoys the protection of the government and makes use of the institutions created for that purpose (administration, military, police);
>
> (b) because he is to be caused to devote his labour to the well-being of the country, which in its turn secures him an income in cash and in food, clothing and the like;
>
> (c) because if he is the owner of a herd of cattle, on the one hand all or part of his labour is withheld from benefiting the country, while on the other hand he possesses capital which must also be made to yield a return for the government.[125]

This mention of the protection that the German Colonial Administration afforded the African population was something that had been an issue right from the beginning of the colonial conquest, when Protection Treaties were concluded with the various ethnicities. The view that the 'savage' Africans, who formerly had constantly been fighting each other, had been 'pacified' and had been brought 'law and order' and protection against their enemies was one of the familiar basic topoi of colonialist propaganda. This and the theme of the need to develop the country through infrastructure measures also played their part in the discussion of the Native Tax. As 'performance by the government' in return for the taxes collected, Waterberg Police Barracks mentioned the way the government took care of 'the administration of the country, the highways, the watering places, improving the livestock and protecting the herds, building schools, etc.' In the view of Police Sergeant Springborn, the tax levy was 'only a token recompense for the costs incurred by the government', but it was necessary to educate the Africans with regard to how 'the money paid always comes back to benefit those who pay it'.[126] Maltahöhe District Office argued similarly that it was only fair towards the White population to tax the Africans, since 'the natives enjoy the advantages of state amenities and particular protection by the authorities just as much as the non-natives do'.[127] Karibib District Office was in favour of only imposing a tax on those 'natives', apart from the ones still living in their own 'tribal' areas, 'who live at larger places provided with public welfare amenities ... because they share in the benefits and advantages of these amenities in the conduct of their lives'.[128] Those among the Africans who had not yet been able to enjoy 'the blessings of civilization' should not, in its view, have to pay taxes for them.

The Territorial Police Inspectorate, on the other hand, pointed out that Whites had been placed under an obligation to pay taxes, so that it was a matter of equity in taxation matters that the Africans should be subjected to it as well:

> If the white population is made to pay for the costs of administration to an increased extent, then it appears only right that the coloured population should do the same, especially if the plan to appoint special Commissioners for the Natives is implemented. These Commissioners will have to be paid salaries that will be a further burden on the Administration, which it is only fair that the natives should play their part in bearing, as it is in their interests that the Commissioners will be working.[129]

Thus the benefits that accrued to the colonizers from the economic and infrastructural development of the colony were equated with benefits accruing to the Africans too. As had been the case in the debate on the 1907 Native Ordinances, during which the compulsion to work had been justified in terms of its educational function for the Africans and the contribution it would make to their 'cultural improvement', so too now in relation to the introduction of the Native Tax the colonial officials displayed a complete lack of insight into the actual situation in the country.

It would be wrong, however, to suppose that the officials wished to introduce the tax only in a calculating way for the sake of its financial and employment market benefits. One line of argument for the legitimacy of direct taxation sought to demonstrate that it was in line with traditional law:

> The native has never known anything else but that he owes tribute to his rulers. When the natives still all had tribal chiefs of their own, those chiefs even dealt pretty arbitrarily with the possessions of their subjects. The native took this for granted, so that in earlier years he would even pay a certain level of tribute to representatives of the government voluntarily on particular occasions, in the form of gifts of livestock or foodstuffs.

> Rulers to whom there is no need to pay tribute are, in the natives' perception of what is right and proper, not proper rulers at all.[130]

Through such arguments, the elimination of the arbitrariness of the taxation imposed by the former African elites and its replacement by a properly regulated tax collection system under German rule, under which the same rules applied to everybody, were thus themselves presented as examples of the 'benefits' that the African population, in the view of the officials, had received from their new 'masters'. District Officer Fromm followed a similar line when he pointed out that the Herero, Nama and Berg Damara 'had from time immemorial paid tribute to their Kapteins, in livestock, cash or labour, depending on their standing and the amount of their possessions'. Even now that the 'tribes' had been dissolved these mechanisms still functioned, and the former 'Big Men' still received such tribute from the members of their 'tribes'. In order to show that this earlier form of taxation was arbitrary by nature, Fromm drew on the example of Hendrik Witbooi, who imposed undeserved punishments on his subjects in order to get hold of money.[131] In contrast to this, Fromm proposed a fixed rate of tax for all able-bodied adult Africans, graduated only according to sex.[132]

But the fact that the officials were not merely concerned to find a simple justification for the tax for practical reasons can be seen from the statements submitted by those two District Offices that did not agree with the idea of imposing a direct tax on the African population. Berseba District Office put forward some legal misgivings; it did consider that a tax would be an appropriate way of forcing Africans to work, but at the same time pointed out 'that the natives here are still living as a free native tribe under the protection of the German Empire, and the District Office has its doubts as to whether they can legally be made subject to such taxation'.[133]

Windhoek District Office came out against the immediate introduction of a tax on the 'natives' with the moral argument that Whites and Africans should be treated equally in respect of their liability to pay tax, even though it considered such a tax 'to be in principle opportune and fair, and also to be feasible with regard to its implementation at the present time':

> Nevertheless, I believe I ought to make my endorsement of the introduction of a tax on the natives dependent on the precondition that first of all those natives who remained loyal should be compensated for their war losses in the same way the white settlers have been. Because in my view it is not equitable to impose burdens upon these natives before they have been appropriately compensated for the losses that they suffered as a result of their pro-German attitude.[134]

A year later, when the District Office's statement of opinion was reviewed again, apparently in connection with the drafting of the Native Tax Regulations, the Governor's Office rejected this objection as no longer holding water, adding a marginal note 'has already happened'.[135]

In 1909 the officials went in great detail into the advantages and disadvantages of the different types of tax, and the question of whether it would actually be possible, in principle, to implement universal direct taxation. They attempted to come up with taxation of a type that in their view was fair both in relation to the tax obligation on Whites and in respect of the Africans' ability to pay. They were convinced that the Africans should make their contribution to the 'blessings' of colonialism, such as protection, administration and the development of the colony's infrastructure. They showed no awareness of the fact that they were actually conquerors in a foreign country, or that for the local population the 'achievements' of the colonial state in practice meant economic destitution and the compulsion to undertake wage-earning employment.

But apart from these insights that the 1909 discussion on the introduction of direct taxation of the Africans affords into the mentalities and manners of thinking of the colonial officials, it is also important with regard to the tax regulations that were actually put into force in the subsequent years, in which many of the proposals made in 1909 were realized in practice in a variety of ways. There was no such broad-based discussion again at any later time.

The Colonial Government's 1911 Plan

At the turn of the year 1910/11,[136] the Colonial Government in Windhoek undertook a renewed attempt to bring in a system of taxing Africans that could be implemented uniformly throughout the colony, and presented its draft of an 'Ordinance concerning the Taxation of the Natives'.[137] The declared aim of this was 'primarily to educate the natives to work', and to create a further source of income for the local authorities in order to recompense them for the growing expenditure they were incurring for the 'benefit' of the African population. A further reason given was the success of the Native Taxes in the British colonies in southern Africa, where 'Native Taxes have already existed for a long time', with 'the experience collected there ... being thoroughly favourable to the intention to cause the natives to bear a proportion of the burden on the public purse through direct taxation'.[138]

This draft was essentially the Colonial Government's regurgitation of the insights it had gained in the 1909 discussion; it proposed a uniform poll tax on all 'able-bodied adult natives, male and female',[139] as it did not consider a hut tax or a livestock tax to be suitable for South West Africa. No exception was made for women, even for married women; rather, they were deliberately included 'because they are scarcely less able than the men to work and to earn a living, but as a rule still substantially exceed them in their disinclination to work'.[140]

The assessment of tax liability was to be performed 'in municipal areas by the Municipalities, [and] outside the municipal areas by the District authorities', and the tax revenues were to be credited to the local authority concerned. Tax revenues were 'to be applied first and foremost in the interests of the natives'.[141] In this way, the Colonial Government was seeking to provide the additional resources required by the local authorities, 'which have had substantial obligations imposed on them in the field of native welfare by the Local Self-Government Ordinance'.[142]

The rate of tax provided for was fifty pfennigs per month, with the local authorities being empowered 'to determine an increase for natives who are not farmworkers through the promulgation of an Ordinance approved by the Governor'.[143] This determination of a minimum tax rate was intended to ensure that the tax situation would be similar throughout the colony, since it was feared that if there were 'substantial differences in the tax rates, the natives would move from the Districts with high rates of tax to those with low rates of tax'. The tax rate of fifty pfennigs per month was considered to be appropriate for 'natives ... in most of the rural areas, especially on the farms'.[144]

This exception of farmworkers from any prospective increase in the tax rate was also a measure of structural policy. In view of the grave shortage of labour, a lower rate of tax would give the farmers a certain advantage in the competition for African workers as against the big enterprises and mining companies, some of which paid substantially higher wages. The Colonial Government appears to have been afraid that for the sake of higher tax revenues in the short term the Districts and Municipalities would have been quite prepared to risk precipitating a migration of workers from agriculture to industry. But to have harmed the agricultural economy in such a way would have run contrary to the importance attributed to agriculture within the social structure it was intended to create in South West Africa, and would also have provoked opposition from the influential farmers in the local self-government bodies, in particular the Territorial Council, to whom this draft was to be presented for discussion. Such self-denial can only be explained in political terms; otherwise, had it simply been a matter of keeping the Municipalities under control, it would have been sufficient to make all tax increases subject to a general requirement for approval by the Governor's Office. Higher rates were explicitly to be allowed only in respect of 'natives in municipal areas and those employed in railway construction, the diamond sector and other commercial operations, and in particular foreign coloured workers'.[145] Where Africans were employed in the service of Whites, the White employer was responsible for ensuring that the Africans paid their taxes. If the Africans were unable to pay, they were threatened with 'tax labour', whereby thirty days' 'tax labour' was considered to be equivalent to a year's taxation – although the 'tax labourer' had to be fed by the Municipality or District that benefited from his work for this period of time.[146]

The 'Basters and Ovambos living in their tribal areas' were exempted from the tax;[147] in the former case this was stated to be for political reasons, and in the latter case because it would have been 'impossible to collect the tax'.[148] Those Ovambo who entered the Police Zone as migrant workers were, however, subject to the poll tax. 'Territorial Police servants' were also to be exempted from the tax,[149] 'so that particularly able natives can be won for this responsible service'.[150] As African landowners were subject to the general land tax, they and 'their family members living in community with them'[151] were to be exempted from the poll tax, as it was a question of 'equity' that 'those natives who are treated like whites in respect of the land tax (which applies mainly to some Basters living outside the tribal area) should not be treated as natives in respect of the poll tax, and thereby subjected to double taxation'.[152]

Whereas these strictly limited exceptions were still in line with a general and equal tax liability for all African men and women, an element of arbitrariness was introduced by the power invested in the Governor to order further exceptions at any time,[153] 'in order to take account of cases in which further exemptions could become necessary in future for purely political or economic reasons'.[154] Apparently the Colonial Government wanted to keep open the possibility of suspending the tax if it was found to have occasioned too great hardships in any particular region. The fear of possible unrest and resistance activities may also have played a role.

The Colonial Government's intention was to bring the Ordinance into force as of 1 April 1911, with the 'regulations required for its implementation ... to be promulgated as Ordinances by the Municipalities and District Authorities empowered to collect the taxes'.[155] But the Colonial Government's plan to present the draft Ordinance to the Territorial Council was countermanded by the Imperial Colonial Office 'for political reasons' on 18 March 1911, even though Colonial Secretary von Lindequist had expressly declared himself to be 'in agreement with its tenor'.[156] It was apparently so important to the Imperial Colonial Office to prevent the publication of the draft that it repeated its objection on 2 April 1911.[157] A renewed request from Governor Seitz for permission to present the paper to the Territorial Council[158] was also turned down.[159]

The Imperial Colonial Office later agreed to permit a discussion of the tax regulations in the Territorial Council, but only if 'secrecy can be guaranteed'.[160] Governor Seitz thereupon decided to abandon completely the idea of having the controversial draft discussed in the Territorial Council, 'as it is impossible to negotiate and to decide on a measure of this kind, which will have such a major impact on the economic life of the whole country, behind closed doors'. In any case, it was very difficult to keep matters discussed in the Territorial Council secret, as had become clear on earlier occasions:

> I therefore think it better to treat as few things as possible as 'secret', and as far as possible only those things that I desire to become known to the public as quickly as possible and to be discussed as widely as possible in the press. As I do not consider it to be desirable that the issue of taxing the natives should occupy too much space in the public arena, I prefer to do without any confidential or even secret discussions of the matter, and will restrict myself to examining any applications from Municipalities or District Authorities to introduce a Native Tax, and to ensuring that such taxation is as far as possible imposed in the same manner everywhere.[161]

This meant that there was no longer any chance of the issue of Native Taxation being dealt with by means of uniform tax regulations applying throughout the colony, and the way was opened up for the introduction of tax bylaws at local level. But the Imperial Colonial Office still had reservations in this respect as well, and exhorted the Governor to ensure 'that any applications from Municipalities and District Authorities that wish to introduce a Native Tax should be approved only <u>after thorough scrutiny</u>.[162]

Thus the Colonial Government preferred to avoid broad public discussion of a Native Tax, because it feared that a majority of the settlers would be against it. The reasons for this assumption are likely to have lain in the rise in wage costs that the settlers would inevitably have expected to be faced with, and in the fact that employers would have been forced to pay out a larger proportion of wages in cash, in order to make it possible for the Africans to pay their tax at all. It was for this reason that the District Officers had already declared themselves to be against the direct taxation of the Africans in 1908. Another factor that is likely to have played a part is the settlers' fear that they might lose their workers for a while if they were to be requisitioned by the authorities to do 'tax labour' in the event of their being unable to pay.[163]

A further obstacle to the introduction of a uniform tax throughout the colony was no doubt to be found in the varying levels of economic development in the individual regions. Depending on whether there were mining operations or only agriculture, quite different levels of wages prevailed, so that uniform taxation did not appear to make too much sense. At the same time, local self-government had given the Districts a new momentum in getting to grips themselves with the issues that immediately affected them. The draft Ordinance, on the other hand, represented a failed attempt by the Colonial Government to intervene at local government level in order to achieve uniformity.

Although no uniform tax system for the whole colony came into being, the Colonial Government's draft Ordinance did make a sustained impact, the text having apparently been circulated to the District Offices.[164] In this way it provided the Districts and Municipalities with at least a rough guide as to which tax provisions appeared to be acceptable to the Colonial Government, and which not. A comparison between the provisions included in the Government draft and those that afterwards appeared in the individual local tax bylaws reveals those respects in which the draft drawn up by officials in the rarefied atmosphere of colonial headquarters was modified by the practitioners on the ground in the District Offices, and the advisory councils attached to them.

Local Tax Bylaws

The Ordinance of 1909 on Local Self-Government in South West Africa granted the local authorities, as already described, the right to impose charges on residents. The first District to take advantage of this provision in order to impose direct taxes on Africans was Lüderitzbucht, which as early as 30 September 1910 – more or less the same time that the Colonial Government was drafting its own proposed tax regulations – promulgated an 'Ordinance concerning the Raising of a Native Poll Tax'. This made every 'male native of the colony and such as have migrated from abroad', living in Lüderitzbucht District but outside the town of Lüderitzbucht, liable to pay tax 'insofar as he is capable of earning his livelihood'. The tax rate was graduated in accordance with wage levels: Africans with an income of less than 10 marks per month were exempted from the tax; the rate for wage levels of 10–40 marks per month was fifty pfennigs; for wages of 40–80 marks it was one mark; for 80–120 marks it was two marks; and for wages of over 120 marks it was three marks. 'Free accommodation and rations' were not taken into consideration. The employer was liable for ensuring that tax payments were made regularly; he had to keep wage lists, deduct the tax amount from the wages and pay it over to the District Office. In the event of failure to pay, twice the amount became due, and the debtor could be forced to work in lieu of payment. Revenues were 'to be applied first and foremost to the benefit of the natives'.[165]

From 1912 onwards other Districts followed suit. The District Authorities of Maltahöhe,[166] Omaruru,[167] Outjo,[168] Gobabis,[169] Okahandja,[170] Gibeon,[171] Swakopmund[172] and Windhoek[173] all promulgated tax regulations of their own, which essentially corresponded to those of Lüderitzbucht. In Swakopmund the tax rate was graduated in exactly the same way as in Lüderitzbucht, while Omaruru and Gibeon distinguished between farm labourers, who had to pay twenty-five pfennigs a month, and other workers whose tax rate was fifty pfennigs per month. In the other Districts' tax regulations, a flat rate of fifty pfennigs per month was provided for, in accordance with the Colonial Government's own draft. However, contrary to the Colonial Government's express wish 'not to burden natives who are economically independent with any special supplement',[174] the District Authorities of Omaruru, Gibeon, Maltahöhe, Okahandja and Swakopmund required every able-bodied African who was not actually earning wages to pay the double rate of one mark. In addition, Gobabis and Maltahöhe also imposed the tax on able-bodied women;

in Gobabis an annual tax rate of four marks for men and one mark for women applied.

Although the Colonial Government in its draft tax regulations had expressly demanded that women should be subject to taxation as well, it was not able to impose this against the interests of most of the Districts. Bethanie District Office did welcome the provision explicitly: 'Among the Hottentots here it is particularly the women who are workshy, so I have a very particular interest in making use of all possible means to combat the women's reluctance to work'.[175] But most of the District Offices apparently shared the opinion of the Windhoek office: it had reported to the Governor's Office that, in the view of the District Council, 'it cannot equitably be required of a married woman to go to work', and that such women should therefore be exempt from taxation.[176] Karibib District Office reported that the Municipal Council there 'believes that this [the taxing of women] constitutes a hardship' and considered it right to exempt married women from the tax.[177] Maltahöhe, having initially imposed the tax on women, revoked the provision again in the revised version of its tax regulations issued on 1 January 1914. The Governor's Office too had already revised its position in a Circulated Order of 19 June 1912, stating that 'married women and women who have children to care for are always to be regarded as being unable to work and to be exempt from taxation'.[178] In January 1913 the Governor's Office had gone a step further and had laid down:

> In Municipal Authority areas, those women who have children to take care of are to remain exempt from tax; in District Authority areas, on the other hand, all women are to be exempt. This latter provision appeared to be necessary as it has become noticeable that particularly the women on the farms are tending to move into larger townships, so that the farmworkers are complaining that they lack the opportunity to get married.[179]

In this respect the Governor's Office had to accept dilutions of its original concept, since developments in the various Districts demanded that concessions should be made to agriculture for reasons of structural policy.

In Omaruru District an additional Livestock Tax was applied to the Berg Damara of Okombahe, at a rate of fifty pfennigs per year per head of large livestock and five pfennigs per item of small livestock. In Outjo District the rates were twice as high; but this tax was imposed without differentiation on all 'persons, whether natives or non-natives, who keep livestock in the District without owning or leasing land'.[180] Gobabis District Office imposed a tax of fifty pfennigs per year per head of large livestock, but exempted from it those Africans who were already subject to the poll tax.

Some of the tax bylaws explicitly indicated that revenues from the Native Tax were only to be applied in the interests of the Africans. In the view of the Governor's Office, however, this should have applied automatically in all districts. In a Circulated Order of 9 June 1912 it was emphasized once again that 'revenue from the Native Tax' was to be used '<u>exclusively</u> for the benefit of the natives'.[181] Only if this was the case did the Colonial Government view it as being legitimate to tax the Africans. But this hypothecation of the Native Tax was apparently not always respected, so that in 1914 the Governor's Office had to send out another reminder:

> Under the provisions of the Native Tax Regulations, revenues from Native Taxes are to be applied exclusively in the interests of the natives.
>
> One District Authority failed to implement expenditure on behalf of the natives that had been envisaged in one year, and then in its budget proposals for the following year posted the amount thereby saved as 'savings from the previous year' and applied it to general expenditure, so that this amount was diverted from its original purpose of being applied in the interests of the natives.
>
> I therefore request all District Offices in future, should any surpluses from previous years appear in the budgets of the District Authorities, to state whether these or any part of them originate from Native Tax revenues of the previous year that have not been spent on behalf of the natives.
>
> If this should be the case, such revenues are to be applied to expenditure in the interests of the natives in the new accounting year.
>
> In the event of any failure to demonstrate that funds have been correctly applied in this way, no further approval for the raising of Native Taxes will be granted in future.[182]

A further condition for the granting of approval for a local tax on the Africans was that the White population too should be subject to direct taxation in the District concerned.[183] This condition was fulfilled everywhere.[184] The Colonial Government clearly did not want to see the Native Tax turned into a convenient sole source of income for the local authorities. Rather, the tax was intended to furnish local authorities with the resources they needed to do justice to the tasks assigned to them in the developing field of 'native welfare'.

It was the Administration's intention to use the Native Tax to place the finances of the Colony, and in particular the expenditure on Native Policy, on a stable financial footing for the longer term. Getting the Africans to make their own direct contribution to the

Colony's expenditure was intended to be a step towards making South West Africa financially independent of Imperial subsidies. But the Governor's Office had to take more and more account of political opinion in the Municipal and District Councils, which were sometimes quite happy to see their tax revenues reduced if they were thereby able to strengthen agriculture in its competition with the mining enterprises to obtain African labour.

But the handling of the tax issue also confirms that German Native Policy in South West Africa should not be viewed merely as a policy of pure exploitation in which the local population was regarded as being completely without rights. In the discourse on taxation it is possible to discover what the colonial officials saw as their long-term objectives, which they hoped to achieve when a 'normal situation' prevailed in the Colony. At the same time, the debate on taxation also illustrates the limits of the Administration's ability to put through its proposals in the face of political opposition, as local interest groups of farmers and mining enterprises had gained in influence as a result of the local self-government introduced in 1909. These lobbies forced the Colonial Government to revise some of its own ideas – for example, that of taxing African women – and to subordinate them to the economic interests of the Whites. Thus the Government in Windhoek was unable to impose the uniform tax throughout the Colony that it would have preferred. Instead, developments within South West Africa could be seen to be beginning to lead the various regions in different directions.

Notes

1. IGW to Kolonial-Institut Hamburg, 11 March 1913, NAW ZBU I.X.A.2. Vol. 1, 10a.
2. Leutwein, *Elf Jahre*, 282. Leutwein gives no information regarding the Catholic Mission.
3. IGW to ICO, 10 December 1913, NAW ZBU I.X.A.1. Vol. 1, 50a–52b. See also Cohen, '"The Natives Must First Become Good Workmen"', 117–23; although the figures compiled by Cohen from secondary sources differ, in some cases substantially, from those given by the Governor's Office itself.
4. The number of African children registered in the Police Zone as of 1 January 1913 totalled 19,876; this does not include children from other countries. *Die deutschen Schutzgebiete in Afrika und der Südsee*, Vol. 4, 1912/13, Statistical Section, 46–49. Outside the Police Zone there were a further twelve Protestant schools and one Catholic school in Ovamboland and on the Okavango River. Internal Memorandum of Streitwolf, IGW, 10 June 1913, NAW ZBU I.X.A.1. Vol. 1, 30a–33b.

5. Rhenish Mission, Karibib, to IGW, 9 July 1913, NAW ZBU I.X.A.1. Vol. 1, 39a–40b.

6. *Bericht über die Reise Conzes und Fischers nach Südafrika, Mozambik und Südwestafrika* [Report on the journey to South Africa, Mozambique and South West Africa by Conze and Fischer], 5 October 1909, BAL R 1001/1500, 49a–80b.

7. Rhenish Mission, Karibib, to IGW, 9 July 1913.

8. Catholic Prefecture, Windhoek, to IGW, 4 July 1913, NAW ZBU I.X.A.1. Vol. 1, 37a–38b. Emphases (underlining) as in the original.

9. IGW to ICO, 29 August 1913, NAW ZBU I.X.A.1. Vol. 1, 24a–25a.

10. IGW to ICO, 10 December 1913, NAW ZBU I.X.A.1. Vol. 1, 50a–52b. In some cases it was sufficient to provide a written certificate that the state subsidies had been properly applied. See e.g. Omaruru DO to Rhenish Mission, Omaruru, 16 March 1910, ELCIN II.11.1. (n.p.) and Rhenish Mission, Omaruru to Omaruru DO, 31 March 1910, ELCIN II.11.1. (n.p.).

11. The Reichstag gave its approval in plenary session on 8 March 1913. The ICO also lent its support to the proposals. ICO to IGW, 15 April 1913, NAW ZBU I.X.A.1. Vol. 1, 22a–24b.

12. Ibid.

13. IGW to the Head of the Herero Mission, Karibib, the Head of the Nama Mission, Keetmanshoop, the Prefect of the Catholic Mission, Windhoek, and the Prefect of the Catholic Mission to Namaland, Heirachabis, 20 June 1913, NAW ZBU I.X.A.1. Vol. 1, 34a–35a.

14. Catholic Prefecture, Windhoek, to IGW, 4 July 1913.

15. Streitwolf, IGW, to Head of Section 1, IGW, 14 August 1913, NAW ZBU I.X.A.1. Vol. 1, 27a.

16. Bernhard Voigt, IGW Territorial Inspector of Schools, to IGW Section 8, 23 August 1913, NAW ZBU I.X.A.1. Vol. 1, 41a f. Voigt was actually responsible for the schools for White children.

17. IGW to ICO, June 1913, NAW ZBU I.X.A.1. Vol. 1, 28a–29b.

18. Ibid.: note written by Streitwolf on the document.

19. IGW to ICO, 29 August 1913.

20. Internal Memorandum of Streitwolf's, IGW, 10 June 1913. Emphases (underlinings) as in the original.

21. IGW to ICO, 10 December 1913.

22. Ibid.

23. *Entwurf einer Schulordnung für die Missionsschulen, die Staatliche Beihilfe erhalten* [Draft of a School Organizational Plan for the Mission Schools that Receive State Grants], n.d., NAW ZBU I.X.A.1. Vol. 1, 64a–65a. A first draft of the plan is dated 3 September 1913: ibid. 74–76a.

24. *Lehrplan für den deutschen Unterricht an den Eingeborenenschulen der Missionen, die bei der Verteilung der Schulbeihilfen berücksichtigt werden sollen* [Curriculum for German-Medium Teaching at the Missions' Native Schools that are to be Considered in the Distribution of School Grants], n.d., NAW ZBU I.X.A.1. Vol. 1, 65a–66a. A first draft of the Curriculum is dated 3 September 1913, ibid. 77 f.

25. Ibid.

26. *Begründung zum Entwurf der Schulordnung und des Lehrplanes* [Reasoning behind the Draft School Organizational Plan and Curriculum], n.d., NAW ZBU I.X.A.1. Vol. 1, 66a–67a.
27. IGW to ICO, 10 December 1913.
28. Reasoning behind the Draft School Organizational Plan.
29. ICO to IGW, 27 February 1914, NAW ZBU I.X.A.1. Vol. 1, 68a.
30. IGW to Territorial Council, 12 April 1914, NAW ZBU I.X.A.1. Vol. 1, 69a.
31. IGW to ICO, 19 June 1914, NAW ZBU I.X.A.1. Vol. 1, 72a f.
32. Von Schuckmann, speech of 28 March 1908, *Deutsches Kolonialblatt* 19 (1908), 467–68. [Translator's note: The emphasis here shown by underlining (as also in the German version of the book) takes the form of letterspacing in the original. As letterspacing is a specifically German form of emphasis, not used in English, underlining has been used instead]
33. Imperial Chancellor, *Verordnung betr. die Selbstverwaltung in Deutsch-Südwestafrika* [Ordinance concerning Local Self-Government in German South West Africa – the 'Local Self-Government Ordinance'], 28 January 1909, reproduced in *Die Deutsche Kolonialgesetzgebung* (DKG), Vol. 13, 19–34. On the setting up of local self-government in South West Africa and its success, see Bley, *Kolonialherrschaft und Sozialstruktur*, 223–34.
34. Local Self-Government Ordinance.
35. Bley, *Kolonialherrschaft*, 230.
36. IGW, *Verordnung betr. die Besteuerung des Grundeigentums im deutsch-südwestafrikanischen Schutzgebiete* [Ordinance concerning the Taxation of Real Estate in the Territory of German South West Africa – the 'Real Estate Taxation Ordinance'], 19 March 1909, *Deutsches Kolonialblatt* 20 (1909), 479–81.
37. IGW, Circulated Order, 24 November 1908, NAW ZBU W.II.I.2. Vol. 1, 9a f.
38. Ibid.
39. Hintrager, *Südwestafrika in der deutschen Zeit*, 81 and 99.
40. When Natal found itself in a recession after the expiry of British reconstruction aid in 1905, the Government tried to put its finances in order by introducing new taxes on the Africans. The attempt to collect these met with resistance from the Zulus at the beginning of 1906. The Government's attempt to break this resistance by exerting massive state repression claimed some 3,500–4,000 victims on the African side. It was not until 1908 that the protest was finally quashed. See Fisch, *Geschichte Südafrikas*, 221.
41. FO-CD to IGW, 13 February 1906, NAW ZBU W.II.I.2. Vol. 1, 3a–4b.
42. Cutting from the *Deutsch-Südwestafrikanische Zeitung*, 31 October 1908. Remark added by Hintrager 3 November 1908, NAW ZBU W.II.I.2. Vol. 1, 8a.
43. Cutting from a supplement to the *Deutsch-Südwestafrikanische Zeitung*, 23 October 1909, NAW ZBU W.II.I.2. Vol. 1, 25a.
44. German Legation, Lisbon, to Imperial Chancellor (transcript), 4 June 1914, NAW ZBU W.II.I.2. Vol. 1, 101a.
45. IGW to German Consulate in Pretoria, 3 January 1909, NAW ZBU W.II.I.2. Vol. 1, 15a.

46. IGW to FO-CD, 26 September 1903, NAW ZBU W.II.I.1. Vol. 1, 1da–1ea (special pagination).
47. FO-CD to IGW, 8 August 1903, NAW ZBU W.II.I.1. Vol. 1, 1b.
48. Reinhard, *Geschichte der Europäischen Expansion*, 98.
49. This was how Simon retrospectively justified what he had said during the session of the Colonial Council. Simon to IGW (transcript), 6 December 1903, NAW ZBU W.II.I.2. Vol. 1, 1la–1ma (spec. pag.).
50. IGW to FO-CD, 26 September 1903, NAW ZBU W.II.I.1. Vol. 1, 1da–1ea (spec. pag.).
51. Ibid.
52. Leutwein wrote to the district offices, calling on them to submit statements of opinion; but only Omaruru, Gibeon and Karibib responded. IGW Circular to DOs, 26 September 1903, NAW ZBU W.II.I.1. Vol. 1, 1da–1ea (spec. pag.).
53. Karibib DO to IGW, 15 October 1903, NAW ZBU W.II.I.1. Vol. 1, 1ga–ha (spec. pag.).
54. This must refer to recruiting agents offering jobs in South Africa.
55. Omaruru DO to IGW, 26 January 1903, NAW ZBU W.II.I.1. Vol. 1, 1ia f. (spec. pag.).
56. Gibeon DO to IGW, 19 November 1903, NAW ZBU W.II.I.1. Vol. 1, 1ka f. (spec. pag.).
57. Outjo DO to IGW, 11 January 1909, NAW ZBU W.II.I.2. Vol. 1, 24a f.
58. Grootfontein DO to IGW, 5 December 1908, NAW ZBU W.II.I.2. Vol. 1, 22a.
59. Keetmanshoop DO to IGW, 30 January 1909, NAW ZBU W.II.I.2. Vol. 1, 36a.
60. Gibeon DO to IGW, 28 January 1909, NAW ZBU W.II.I.2. Vol. 1, 39a f.
61. Bethanie DO to IGW, 16 January 1909, NAW ZBU W.II.I.2. Vol. 1, 38a f.
62. Okahandja DO to IGW, 9 March 1909, NAW ZBU W.II.I.2. Vol. 1, 48a-49a.
63. Outjo DO to IGW, 11 January 1909.
64. Gibeon DO was above all afraid of the increased administrative workload relating to 'the frequent cases of native labourers who run away from their workplaces'. Gibeon DO to IGW, 28 January 1909.
65. Bethanie DO to IGW, 16 January 1909. Gibeon DO to IGW, 28 January 1909. Karibib DO to IGW, 27 February 1909, NAW ZBU W.II.I.2. Vol. 1, 47a f. Karibib thought it would be possible to tax those Africans living in the 'special tribal areas'; but there were no such areas in that district.
66. Grootfontein DO to IGW, 5 December 1908.
67. Bethanie DO to IGW, 16 January 1909.
68. Swakopmund DO to IGW, 11 May 1909, NAW ZBU W.II.I.2. Vol. 1, 52a–53b.
69. Gibeon DO to IGW, 28 January 1909.
70. Waterberg Police Barracks to ITP, 10 January 1909, NAW ZBU W.II.I.2. Vol. 1, 30a–32b.
71. Ibid.
72. Runck states in his letter that he is replying to a 'letter I have found here which has not yet been dealt with'. Warmbad DO to IGW, 7 May 1909, NAW ZBU W.II.I.2. Vol. 1, 54a.
73. Maltahöhe DO to IGW, 10 January 1909, NAW ZBU W.II.I.2. Vol. 1, 40a–41b.
74. Lüderitzbucht DO to IGW, 15 August 1909, NAW ZBU W.II.I.2. Vol. 1, 55a.
75. Waterberg Police Barracks to ITP, 10 January 1909.

76. Trutz von Trotha has gone into this in exemplary fashion in his study of Togo. Von Trotha, *Koloniale Herrschaft*, 346–73.
77. Swakopmund DO to IGW, 11 May 1909.
78. Berseba DO to IGW, 24 February 1909, NAW ZBU W.II.I.2. Vol. 1, 50a f.
79. Warmbad DO to IGW, 7 May 1909.
80. Waterberg Police Barracks to ITP, 10 January 1909.
81. Gibeon DO to IGW, 28 January 1909.
82. Swakopmund DO to IGW, 11 May 1909. Namutoni DO to IGW, 1 February 1909, NAW ZBU W.II.I.2. Vol. 1, 43a–46a.
83. This can be deduced from the report from Waterberg police barracks, where it says: 'At what age (maximum) the average native becomes unable to work, so that he would no longer be liable to pay the tax from then on, I am not able to judge'. Waterberg Police Barracks to ITP, 10 January 1909.
84. Namutoni DO to IGW, 1 February 1909.
85. Waterberg Police Barracks to ITP, 10 January 1909.
86. Windhoek DO to IGW, 22 January 1909, NAW ZBU W.II.I.2. Vol. 1, 33a–35a.
87. Maltahöhe DO to IGW, 10 January 1909.
88. 'Der steuerpflichtige Mann hat eine Frau steuerfrei.' ITP to IGW, 29 January 1909, NAW ZBU W.II.I.2. Vol. 1, 26a–27b.
89. There are marking strokes drawn in the margin by this sentence, and at the phrase *'eine Frau'* (one wife) the word *'eine'* (one) is even underlined. Ibid.
90. Namutoni DO to IGW, 1 February 1909.
91. For the tax rates proposed by the District Officers, see Table A.3 in the Appendix.
92. ITP to IGW, 29 January 1909.
93. Gobabis DO to IGW, 3 February 1909, NAW ZBU W.II.I.2. Vol. 1, 42a f.
94. Omaruru DO to IGW, 20 January 1909, NAW ZBU W.II.I.2. Vol. 1, 37a.
95. ITP to IGW, 29 January 1909.
96. Swakopmund DO to IGW, 11 May 1909.
97. Waterberg Police Barracks to ITP, 10 January 1909. This should not be interpreted, however, as paying due regard to the social situation of the Africans, since as Springborn added, the farmers would be able to recuperate the tax by paying even lower wages.
98. Windhoek DO to IGW, 22 January 1909.
99. Lüderitzbucht DO to IGW, 15 August 1909.
100. Waterberg Police Barracks to ITP, 10 January 1909.
101. Windhoek DO to IGW, 22 January 1909.
102. Swakopmund DO to IGW, 11 May 1909.
103. Windhoek DO to IGW, 22 January 1909.
104. Okahandja DO to IGW, 9 March 1909. Emphasis (underlining) as in the original.
105. ITP to IGW, 29 January 1909.
106. On this, see Gründer, *Geschichte der deutschen Kolonien*, 116.
107. For this purpose he suggested a standard rate of 30 ha per large animal and 5 ha per small animal. As the tax rate, he proposed ten pfennings per hectare per annum, with up to twenty items of small livestock tax free. ITP to IGW, 29 January 1909.

108. Ibid.
109. For 1907, Waterberg Police Barracks gave the following figures for the stock of the Rehoboth Basters: 428 horses, 5,937 items of large livestock and 17,549 items of small livestock. But these figures did not include ordinary goats, Angora goats, donkeys, mules or hinnies. Waterberg Police Barracks to ITP, 10 January 1909.
110. Berseba DO to IGW, 24 February 1909. There is no statement from Rehoboth DO on file, the issue having been discussed personally in Windhoek. Rehoboth DO to IGW, 1 May 1909, NAW ZBU W.II.I.2. Vol. 1, 51a f.
111. Maltahöhe DO to IGW, 10 January 1909.
112. Gobabis DO to IGW, 3 February 1909.
113. Namutoni DO to IGW, 1 February 1909.
114. The only exception was Kuiseb, which was home to a number of Basters, San and Topnaar Nama 'who possess greater or smaller numbers of small livestock, in some cases also large livestock'. Swakopmund DO to IGW, 11 May 1909.
115. Ibid.
116. IGW, Real Estate Taxation Ordinance, 479–81.
117. The District Offices of Outjo, Karibib, Keetmanshoop, Lüderitzbucht, Namutoni, Omaruru and Okahandja gave no details of livestock quantities.
118. Warmbad DO to IGW, 7 May 1909.
119. Gibeon DO to IGW, 28 January 1909.
120. Windhoek DO to IGW, 22 January 1909. Berseba District Office argued in a very similar way: it too favoured a poll tax as a way of compelling the Africans to work. Berseba DO to IGW, 24 February 1909. The same applies to the Inspectorate of Police. ITP to IGW, 29 January 1909.
121. Swakopmund DO to IGW, 11 May 1909.
122. Kub Police Barracks to ITP, 6 January 1909, NAW ZBU W.II.I.2. Vol. 1, 29a f.
123. Gobabis DO to IGW, 3 February 1909.
124. Warmbad DO to IGW, 7 May 1909.
125. Namutoni DO to IGW, 1 February 1909.
126. Waterberg Police Barracks to ITP, 10 January 1909.
127. Maltahöhe DO to IGW, 10 January 1909.
128. Karibib DO to IGW, 27 February 1909.
129. ITP to IGW, 29 January 1909.
130. Ibid. Emphasis (underlining) added to the original by the clerical officer processing the document at IGW.
131. 'Old Hendrik Witbooi collected taxes from time to time. He had his own way of doing it: "I need this or that", and then X would provide this and Y that. Or he would send his Sub-Kaptein Samuel Isaak or one of his counsellors around the country with a patrol to hold court. His favourite way – always the same – was to ask on the farms if "his people" had been behaving well. The court patrol would then "punish" the *Witkamp* [delinquent] concerned according to his deserts, or in fact according to his possessions. The "fines" were then handed over to the Kaptein.' Okahandja DO to IGW, 9 March 1909.

132. Ibid.
133. Berseba DO to IGW, 24 February 1909.
134. Windhoek DO to IGW, 22 January 1909.
135. Marginal note on the report from Windhoek DO with the date 1910. Ibid.
136. The precise date of this first draft cannot be determined from the sources. It must have been before 18 March 1911, however, as there is a telegram of that date from the ICO referring to the draft. ICO to IGW, 18 March 1911, NAW ZBU W.II.I.1. Vol. 1, 11a.
137. IGW, *Verordnung betreffend die Heranziehung der Eingeborenen zu Steuerleistungen* [Ordinance concerning the Taxation of the Natives – the 'Native Taxation Ordinance'] (draft, n.d.), NAW ZBU W.II.I.1. Vol. 1, 13a–14a. A handwritten draft of this text, identical to the typewritten version quoted here, is to be found ibid., 4a–6a. An earlier version with numerous corrections is to be found in ibid., 9a–10b.
138. IGW, *Begründung des Verordnungsentwurfs* [Reasoning behind the Draft Ordinance], n.d., NAW ZBU W.II.I.1. Vol. 1, 15a f.
139. IGW, draft Native Taxation Ordinance.
140. IGW, Reasoning behind the Draft Ordinance.
141. IGW, draft Native Taxation Ordinance.
142. IGW, Reasoning behind the Draft Ordinance.
143. IGW, draft Native Taxation Ordinance.
144. IGW, Reasoning behind the Draft Ordinance.
145. Ibid.
146. IGW, draft Native Taxation Ordinance.
147. Ibid.
148. IGW, Reasoning behind the Draft Ordinance.
149. IGW, draft Native Taxation Ordinance.
150. IGW, Reasoning behind the Draft Ordinance.
151. IGW, draft Native Taxation Ordinance.
152. IGW, Reasoning behind the Draft Ordinance.
153. IGW, draft Native Taxation Ordinance.
154. IGW, Reasoning behind the Draft Ordinance.
155. IGW, draft Native Taxation Ordinance.
156. ICO to IGW (extract from collective telegram), 18 March 1911.
157. ICO to IGW (extract from collective telegram), 2 April 1911, NAW ZBU W.II.I.1. Vol. 1, 16a.
158. IGW to ICO (telegram), 5 April 1911, NAW ZBU W.II.I.1. Vol. 1, 12a.
159. ICO to IGW (extract from collective telegram), 8 April 1911, NAW ZBU W.II.I.2. Vol. 1, 19a.
160. This can be deduced from a letter from the ICO to the IGW, in whch the latter is requested to report on the discussions. ICO to IGW, 18 September 1911, NAW ZBU W.II.I.1. Vol. 1, 22a–23b.
161. IGW to ICO, 29 October 1911, NAW ZBU W.II.I.1. Vol. 1, 22a–23b.
162. ICO to IGW, 8 December 1911, NAW ZBU W.II.I.1. Vol. 1, 24a. Emphasis (underlining) added to the original by the clerical officer processing the document at IGW.
163. Müller, 'Die deutsche Eingeborenenpolitik', 131.

164. This can be deduced from opinions submitted by Windhoek and Gibeon District Offices, which put forward suggestions for amendments to the text. Windhoek DO to IGW, 21 March 1911, NAW ZBU W.II.I.2. Vol. 1, 82a–83a. Gibeon DO to IGW, 29 March 1911, NAW ZBU W.II.I.2. Vol. 1, 97a f.

165. Lüderitzbucht DO, *Verordnung über die Erhebung einer Eingeborenen-Kopfsteuer* [Ordinance concerning the Raising of a Native Poll Tax], 30 September 1910, reproduced in *Amtsblatt für das Schutzgebiet Deutsch-Südwestafrika* [Official gazette of the Colony of German South West Africa], Windhoek: IGW (1910–1914), Vol. 3 (1912), 196.

166. Maltahöhe District Authority, *Satzung betr. Erhebung einer Eingeborenenkopfsteuer* [Regulations concerning the Raising of a Native Poll Tax], 29 June 1912, reproduced in *Amtsblatt* 3 (1912), 273–74. On 1 January 1914 the District Authority issued new Regulations, reproduced in *Amtsblatt* 5 (1914), 170.

167. Omaruru District Authority, *Satzung betr. Erhebung einer Eingeborenen-Personalkopf- und Viehsteuer* [Regulations concerning the Raising of a Native Poll and Livestock Tax], 8 July 1912, reproduced in *Amtsblatt* 3 (1912), 289–90. On 20 March 1913 the district authority issued new regulations: Omaruru District Authority, *Satzung betr. Erhebung einer Eingeborenen-Personalkopfsteuer* [Regulations concerning the Raising of a Native Poll Tax], reproduced in *Amtsblatt* 4 (1913), 102–3.

168. Outjo District Authority, *Satzung betr. Erhebung einer Viehkopfsteuer im Bezirk Outjo* [Regulations concerning the Raising of a Livestock Poll Tax in Outjo District – 'Outjo Native Tax Regulations'], 15 April 1912, reproduced in *Amtsblatt* 3 (1912), 315–16.

169. Gobabis District Authority, *Satzung betr. Erhebung einer Eingeborenenkopfsteuer* [Regulations concerning the Raising of a Native Poll Tax], 24 September 1912, reproduced in *Amtsblatt* 3 (1912), 427. On 17 February 1913 the district authority issued new regulations: Gobabis District Authority, *Satzung betr. Erhebung einer Eingeborenenkopfsteuer für das Rechnungsjahr 1913* [Regulations concerning the Raising of a Native Poll Tax for the 1913 Accounting Year], 17 February 1913, reproduced in *Amtsblatt* 4 (1913), 181.

170. Okahandja District Authority, *Satzung betr. Eingeborenen-Besteuerung* [Regulations concerning the Taxing of the Natives], 1 May 1913, reproduced in *Amtsblatt* 4 (1913), 163.

171. Gibeon District Authority, *Satzung betr. Erhebung einer Eingeborenen-Personalkopfsteuer* [Regulations concerning the Raising of a Native Poll Tax], 25 September 1913, reproduced in *Amtsblatt* 4 (1913), 350.

172. Swakopmund District Authority, *Satzung betr. Erhebung einer Eingeborenenkopfsteuer* [Regulations concerning the Raising of a Native Poll Tax], 14 March 1914, reproduced in *Amtsblatt* 5 (1914), 143.

173. This can be deduced from an internal IGW document. IGW, Internal Document, 10 December 1912, NAW ZBU W.II.I.1. Vol. 1, 27a. No Regulations for Windhoek were published in the *Amtsblatt*.

174. IGW to Bethanie DO, 30 November 1911, NAW ZBU W.II.I.2. Vol. 1, 93–94a.

175. Bethanie DO to IGW, 30 October 1911, NAW ZBU W.II.I.2. Vol. 1, 89a–90a.
176. Windhoek DO to IGW, 21 March 1911, NAW ZBU W.II.I.2. Vol. 1, 82a–83a.
177. Karibib DO to IGW, 21 March 1911, NAW ZBU W.II.I.2. Vol. 1, 69a.
178. IGW, Circulated Order to DOs, 19 June 1912, NAW ZBU W.II.I.2. Vol. 1, 26a f.
179. IGW, Circulated Order, 16 January 1913, NAW ZBU W.II.I.2. Vol. 1, 33a.
180. 'Outjo Native Tax Regulations'.
181. IGW, Circulated Order, 19 June 1912. Emphasis (underlining) as in the original.
182. IGW, Circulated Order, 20 March 1914, NAW ZBU W.II.I.2. Vol. 1, 35a.
183. This can be deduced from an application from Bethanie District Office for the approval of tax regulations for that District, in which the District Officer requests that this condition should be set aside. He wrote: 'I was aware of the fact that the taxing of the natives is only agreeable to the Imperial Governor's Office if the white population is taxed as well'. Bethanie DO to IGW, 30 October 1911.
184. Maltahöhe District Authority, *Satzung betr. Erhebung einer Personenkopfsteuer* [Regulations concerning the Raising of a Personal Poll Tax], 25 April 1912, in *Amtsblatt* 3 (1912), 226. Omaruru District Authority, *Satzung betr. Erhebung einer Viehsteuer, eines Zuschlags zur staatlichen Grundsteuer und einer Personalsteuer* [Regulations concerning the Raising of a Livestock Tax, a Surcharge on the State Land Tax and a Personal Tax], 25 July 1911, in *Amtsblatt* 2 (1911), 166. Gobabis District Authority, *Satzung betr. Bezirkssteuern für Nichteingeborene für das Rechnungsjahr 1912* [Regulations concerning District Taxes on Non-Natives for the 1912 Accounting Year], 25 June 1912, in *Amtsblatt* 3 (1912), 316. Gibeon District Authority, *Bezirksgesetz betr. Erhebung eines Zuschlags zur staatlichen Grundsteuer für den Bezirk Gibeon* [District Bylaw concerning a Surcharge to the State Land Tax for Gibeon District], 10 January 1911, in *Amtsblatt* 1 (1910/11), 284. Windhoek District Authority, *Satzung betr. Erhebung einer Personen-Kopfsteuer* [Regulations concerning the Raising of a Personal Poll Tax], 22 February 1913, in *Amtsblatt* 4 (1913), 147. Only for Okahandja District were no tax regulations published in the *Amtsblatt*.

Conclusion

With the outbreak of the First World War and the conquest of South West Africa by the forces of the Union of South Africa in 1915, German colonial rule in southern Africa came to an end after only thirty years. Short though this period was, it had seen the country – a country newly created by the fiat of the colonial powers – undergo a profound transformation. The fact that the Colony's various ethnic groups, which up until then had never belonged to any shared polity, had been incorporated into a state created by treaties between European powers, was far from being the only legacy of colonialism. Another was the influx of almost fifteen thousand White people, who farmed the land, set up businesses, built railways and exploited natural resources. And those who bore the brunt of that transformation were the Africans; it was their land that was taken away from them to be farmed by the new settlers, it was their toil that was exploited in the construction of the railways and to extract the diamonds and copper from the earth, and it was they who had to work as housemaids, farm servants and labourers.

This process of displacing and subjugating the local population was the outcome not of uncontrolled developments, but of planned policy. The massive changes in the social and economic structures of the local societies living within the Police Zone, which led to the confiscation of the land of almost the entire African population and forced the Africans who lived on it to undertake dependent work for wages, were the results of state administrative action: the government's Native Policy. That the various ordinances implementing this Native Policy were not merely a collection of separate and unconnected legislative measures, introduced as reactions to specific 'problems' as they arose without any inner relationship to each other, can be seen from two findings of this work. One is that the regulations promulgated can be traced back to a small circle of initiators – basically only four people: von Lindequist, Golinelli, Tecklenburg and Hintrager; the other is that almost from the very beginning of German colonial rule there was a relatively high level of consistency in the aims and measures introduced.

Thus in the concepts underlying Native Policy, continuity had prevailed since the mid-1890s: the differences had been only in respect of the methods by which they were implemented, because the first Governor, Theodor Leutwein, lacked the military strength and the administrative manpower he would have needed to establish direct rule over the African population. His policy towards the Chiefs – that is, his attempt to use a 'divide-and-rule' policy through which he could find allies among those Africans who were willing to collaborate, and so prevent the establishment of a unified resistance front embracing all the Africans – was simply a matter of making a virtue out of necessity.

Native Policy, as it was conducted during the Herero and Nama War that raged from 1904 to 1908, was pursued in the face of exceptional circumstances, of a state of emergency. The conduct of the war, waged as it was with genocidal objectives, was quite at variance with Native Policy as the colonial authorities had intended to pursue it, since it threatened to bring about nothing less than the extermination of the African population. By destroying their autonomous social and economic structures, however, it did in fact at the same time paradoxically create the conditions required for the rapid implementation of the Government's underlying Native Policy. The mass internment of Herero and Nama prisoners of war, who during the 'race war' and its prolongation as a guerrilla war also included women and children, exemplifies at one and the same time the two contrary poles around which the war aims orbited: while on the one hand some of those responsible knowingly and deliberately pursued a course of extermination through work and neglect as a foetid emanation of the wartime policy of genocide, on the other hand the use of the prisoners of war as forced labour foreshadowed a major feature of the postwar order.

The Ordinances promulgated after the Herero and Nama War represented the distilled essence of the first moves towards subjecting the Africans to direct rule that had already been manifested in the prewar period. The expropriation of land, the prohibition of 'mixed' marriages, the compulsion to enter into employment and the direct taxation of Africans were all measures that had already been sounded out under Leutwein. The three Native Ordinances of 1907 were even based directly on the earlier Pass Ordinance and Master and Servant Ordinance which had already been promulgated in some Districts in the years since 1894: all that was new was that these regulations were now extended to apply throughout the Colony, except for those areas outside the Police Zone. Precisely in view of the anarchic conditions that had prevailed during the war, the officials in the Administration saw the Native Ordinances as putting day-to-day relations with the Africans on that sound legal footing that appeared to them to be necessary after a period of such great upheavals.

This leads on to the question of *Herrschaftsutopie*, governmental and administrative utopia – the utopian concept that the Colonial Government and Administration had of the social order they felt themselves called upon to create, and of the role attributed therein to the African population. The aim of German Native Policy was to build up an efficient economic system whose functionality was to be ensured by the establishment of a social order derived from premodern concepts such as that of a system of distinct 'estates', in which the Administration, the settlers and the African population were all to have their fixed roles. The local population was to be registered and kept under surveillance by a watertight system of control, integrated into the economic system as cheap labour and, as part of a process of social disciplining, re-educated to accept compliantly their role as workers. In this way, the Colonial Government sought to press ahead speedily with the economic development of the Colony so that minerals could be extracted and the territory's development into a settler colony could proceed in an orderly fashion. The intention of Native Policy was to transform South West Africa into a single economic area across which an African workforce could be evenly distributed in a manner that would meet the needs of the colonial economy. Nevertheless, the Africans were not regarded as being completely without rights in this process. They were to be able to choose their own employers, and also to be entitled to change their jobs if they were offered better conditions elsewhere. At the individual level, the distribution of workers was to be left to the market forces of supply and demand. As the compulsion to enter into employment kept the supply of labour high, the situation on the labour market may be described as 'semifree', combining a compulsion to undertake dependent work of some kind with a free choice of employer. Although the corporal chastisement of Africans was not completely forbidden, 'severe' maltreatment was to be prevented. As a result, German officialdom believed, the Africans would come in the course of time to accept their place in this society and so readily fulfil their function as cheap labour. Physical compulsion would then give way to voluntary acceptance, arising out of measures of social discipline.

Educational policy, too, was directed towards serving this objective of social discipline. In addition to the teaching of practical skills such as a command of the German language and the basic arithmetical operations, 'German values' such as orderliness and hard work were also to be inculcated. These were not only seen as a means to increase efficiency; they also went hand in hand with the 'civilizatory mission' that the officials felt themselves called to pursue.

The society of racial privilege such as was created above all by the Native Ordinances demanded a precise definition of who belonged to the privileged group and who did not. In the initial years of German colonial rule a culturalist definition of the term 'native' had predominated: it had been possible for individuals to break through racial barriers if they were able to demonstrate that their level of 'civilization' or 'culture' entitled them to be considered members of White society. In practice, this was relevant above all to people of 'mixed race', the children of marriages between White men and African women. Although initially encouraged, such 'mixed' marriages became a target for criticism as early as under Leutwein's governorship. After the outbreak of the war – although it was not the war that caused it – the Administration forbade all civil marriages between Whites and Africans; and in 1907 even those marriages that had been duly entered into earlier were retrospectively declared invalid. Sexual relations of any kind between Whites and Africans were increasingly stigmatized and subjected to sanctions for purely racist reasons. This undisguisedly racist turn of events was accompanied by a redefinition of the terms 'native' and 'non-native': anybody with even a 'drop' of African blood was now a 'native'. Thus the culture-based definition yielded to the biological one, and the society of privilege thereby sealed itself off completely against the nonprivileged.

A curious feature of German Native Policy was the way it blended premodern objectives with modern methods of achieving them. This is shown in the concept on which the *Herrschaftsutopie* was based, that of a society made up of what were effectively different 'estates' – a premodern concept that was combined, however, with thoroughly modern elements such as the economic structure it was intended to create. Native Policy was based on the desire to make the colonial system, and above all the colonial economy, efficient. The dominant values in this case were therefore not the outdated military values of an atavistic caste of warriors – values that Joseph A. Schumpeter saw as being the driving forces behind colonialism[1] – but the modern values of a bureaucracy that sought to regulate all areas of life. The Administration set up by this bureaucracy was not old-fashioned or irrational in its methods, but modern and rational. The Africans were considered to be the colonies' 'most important assets'. The Native Ordinances were intended not only to control them and force them to take up dependent employment, but also to ensure that within this framework they were 'well treated'. In this way they met the conditions that Bernhard Dernburg, for example, demanded should be fulfilled by Native Policy. No reform phase, such as has been identified in German colonial history in general for the years from 1910 onwards, is to be observed in South West Africa; whatever reforms might have been introduced had already been anticipated by the Native Ordinances.

In terms of the constitutional situation, however, the structures of the form of dominion that the colonial regime sought to impose recall the term coined by Ernst Rudolf Huber to describe the preconstitutional Prussia of the period between 1820 and 1840: the term *Gesetzesstaat*,[2] the 'state under the rule of legislation', in contrast to the *Rechtsstaat*, the state under the rule of law and orientated towards upholding fundamental rights. According to Huber, this 'state under the rule of legislation' was characterized by the fact that state interventions impacting on the liberties and the property of its subjects, which in our case means the Africans, were not arbitrary but were always legitimized by legislation. But the sole legislator was the monarch; and in the colonies the Emperor still exercised this function, delegating his competence through the Imperial Chancellor to the Governor. This concept explains the sophisticated network of regulations governing how the Africans were to be treated – and also exploited. Arbitrary robbery was replaced by expropriation legitimized by the state. And the concept of the *Gesetzesstaat* is again a backward-pointing one, relating to the premodern era of German history. The 'proper order' depicted by Huber as being the principle on which the state was based, and which in preconstitutional Prussia was acknowledged to take precedence over liberty, was reincarnated as the pre-eminent value in society in South West Africa under German colonial rule.

Another prominent feature of German Native Policy, however, was the yawning gap between the regulatory aspirations of the Colonial Government and their practical implementation. State surveillance was defeated by the vastness of the colony and the impossibility of monitoring it in its entirety, by logistical problems, by inadequate staffing levels in the Administration, the police and the military, by officials who acted as they saw fit without due authority, and by the lack of cooperation among the White population. The Administration did not succeed either in exercising watertight control over the whole of the African population, or in recruiting all its members into the colonial labour market. There were sections of the African population that succeeded again and again in escaping from German control. The colonial state was not all-powerful, and was at no time able to reduce the African population to being merely the objects of administrative decisions. This was not the least of the factors that afforded the African population a degree of leeway to preserve their own traditions at least in part.

Comprehensive implementation of Native Policy was also compromised by the behaviour of the bureaucrats themselves. Although in their official statements most officials welcomed the proposals made by their superiors, they often did not implement them in practice, or else they interpreted them as they themselves saw fit. The principle of the 'semifree' labour market in particular was impaired by the way individual officials at local level showed themselves to be sympathetic to the interests of the local White population. Crucial elements of the intended 'semifree' labour market – such as, for example, freedom of movement between Districts – suffered as a result.

Nor was the bulk of the White population outside the Administration by any means completely behind official Native Policy; on the contrary, they boycotted any measures they did not like, particularly if they saw them as being economically detrimental, even if only in the short term, to the White population. On the one hand they found the state surveillance measures, which required the cooperation of the White population, too much trouble to implement fully; while on the other hand they considered Native Policy to be not strict enough. The constant shortage of workers, which persisted right up to the end of German colonial rule despite the influx of migrant labour from Ovamboland and South Africa, led to their ignoring the principle of free choice of employer and the right of the Africans to give notice. In particular, agriculture and the mining industry were in fierce competition with each other for workers. Whereas the former was generally considered to be the backbone of South West Africa as a settler colony, it was above all the diamond companies that were responsible for a major part of the colony's revenues. The two were constant rivals in their efforts to exert influence on the Colonial Government; but as their respective demands often contradicted each other, the Administration was not always able to satisfy both. For that reason alone, the perception of there having been a general identity of interests between the Administration and the White population does not reflect the situation accurately.

In particular, the idea that Africans had certain minimum rights met with little acceptance among the White population. Working on remote farms or in remote mining areas, the African workers were at the mercy of their employers. Largely unsupervised and convinced of their own superiority in both racial and civilizatory terms, the farmers and the mining and construction companies' White supervisors developed feelings of being all-powerful, and these were expressed in arbitrary behaviour against which the workers had no protection. These fantasies of omnipotence, together with a latent sense of being threatened by the African majority of the population, led to a culture of beating and chastisement that crossed the line into sadism. This nullified all the effort that the bureaucracy put into attempting to achieve stable labour relations by ensuring that the African workers were generally content with their lot.

To some extent, the officials ignored such abuses, as they shared the prejudice regarding allegedly lazy Africans, and so concurred with the view of the White population in their districts that the 'natives' would not work properly unless they were beaten into it. While several District Officers did try to intervene in cases where Africans had suffered unjust treatment, for the most part they were less than successful in their efforts. There were essentially two reasons for this: on the one hand resistance from the employers, and on the other the limits placed on the Administration's scope for action by the law applying to the Whites. With regard to the first of these factors: both the farmers and the powerful mining companies lobbied widely to further their interests, campaigned against those officials who defended the Africans' rights, and mobilized public opinion in the colony against what they saw as too lenient a policy towards the African population. And the Colonial Government had no option but to pay due regard to the farming and mining lobbies, especially after the introduction of local self-government in 1909. Social pressure on the officials was a further factor that prevented them from taking up all too critical positions: the officials, after all, lived and worked in a social environment in which the employers set the tone. Perhaps even more important in this context was the second factor: the limits placed on the Administration's ability to take effective action by the law and by the independence of the judicial system to which Whites were subject. For Whites to be punished for maltreating Africans required a sentence imposed by a court. But the courts were much more ready to believe what a White said than what an African said, and so either refused to punish Whites at all or else imposed punishments that were excessively lenient. The officials were scarcely able to exert any influence on the courts. The modern elements of Native Policy – for example, legal protection for Africans too – were cancelled out by the premodern elements – the disadvantaged status of the Africans in a society of racial privilege. In the colonial context, which was based on a racial hierarchy as between the colonizers and the colonized, there was no way in which this disadvantage, which also encompassed the refusal of Whites (including judges) to give credit to statements made by Africans, could be remedied.

The officials' eyes were closed to this dilemma, so they did not question the Native Policy that gave rise to it and which they were responsible for administering. On the one hand, they shared the settlers' and the courts' mistrust with regard to Africans' credibility, and so were able to simply deny the reality of acts of cruelty carried out against Africans, and the often inhuman way they were exploited. On the other hand, the arrogant sense of superiority that the Wilhelminian civil servants harboured towards the White population caused them to close their eyes to their own failures as well. Abuse of the 'parental power of chastisement', for example, was attributed to only a few 'black sheep' among the employers, and these, moreover, were assumed to come from lower social backgrounds; and there was a lurking conviction that the employers too first needed to get accustomed to their new role as members of a 'master class'.

An investigation of these legitimation strategies raises the issue of the officials' perceptions of themselves and of other people, and of how they justified their own actions. The bureaucrats saw themselves, as representatives of the colonial state, as impartial agents of social and economic change in the direction of a modern society and an efficiently functioning economy – as agents who were only answerable to the general good. It was their task, as the guarantors of 'law and order', to put in place the fundamental factors necessary to ensure it. They themselves, or so they saw it, acted rationally and efficiently, and were bringing culture and civilization to the Africans. In line with the idea of asymmetrical counter-concepts described by Reinhart Koselleck,[3] the local population was by contrast perceived as being lacking in culture and civilization, as premodern, inefficient and irrational. The civil servants had a worldview fuelled by the conviction that there was a wide differential in levels of development, a cultural divide between themselves and the African population. Despite all the distinctions that can be identified in the attitudes of individual civil servants to individual issues, there was a common basis underlying them all: namely, the view of the African as being on a lower cultural level, at a stage of development comparable to that of a child, and incapable of leading his life autonomously without a benevolent guardian – his colonial 'master'. He first needed to be educated, and that could best be done by placing him in the service of the Whites, whether as a house servant or as cheap labour on the farms, in railway construction or in the mines. Thanks to an ideology that viewed the colonized as inferior, the officials saw no contradiction between what they considered to be their mission to civilize and educate, and the economic benefit that they drew from colonial rule. Education to work and education through work meant one and the same thing to them.

For both officials and settlers, their own cultural superiority was clearly manifest in the objective superiority of the German military and of German organization, as appeared to have been demonstrated by the successful outcome of the Herero and Nama War. The factors that facilitated that victory were thus at the same time seen as legitimizing colonial rule; the prerequisites for success became objectives of the process of colonization. This line of thought was still further strengthened by the high costs occasioned by the war, as the expenditure now also had to be justified to government and public opinion at home. If maximum profit was to be achieved, the highest possible degree of efficiency was required. Everything else was subordinated to this, and the permanent interference with the African population's way of life was thereby justified. In the view of the officials, the Africans were, after all, only being required to reimburse the costs they had occasioned their colonizers by their 'rebelliousness'. And at the same time they were being 'educated': that is to say, in the view of the colonizers they were themselves benefiting from foreign rule.

This was made absolutely clear by the issue of Native Taxation. A direct tax brought money into the government's coffers and accustomed the African population to taking part in the money-based economy. At the same time, it made it easier for the Administration to check that the Africans did indeed receive their wages in cash. The tax could be justified in terms of the civilizatory 'blessings' that the Africans were able to partake of in the form of infrastructure measures and welfare provisions. Thus the 'modernization project' was to be self-financing, which at the same time was itself a contribution to 'modernization'. The fact that the colonized population had never asked for these 'blessings', the greater part of which only contributed to their exploitation, did not register with anyone in the Administration.

The conviction of the superiority of their own culture, their own administrative tradition – the awareness that in setting up a modern state they were in harmony with the laws of history – led to this form of administration being deployed to cover the entire African population without any concern for the consequences it would have for them. And these consequences were very grave: going beyond the compulsion to work for wages, the reshaping of the economic and social structures was an attempt to subject the entire local population to the requirements of the colonial economy and the modern state. The re-education of the Africans was ultimately intended to force them to submit compliantly to the new situation. This would have culminated in the creation of a 'new' African who was totally uprooted from his own traditions and only served the needs of the colonial state. The early loss of the colony in the First World War prevented this programme from being fully implemented; but the seed had been sown. And this, together with the losses among the population caused by the war, was a further legacy of German colonialism.

Notes

1. Schumpeter, 'Zur Soziologie der Imperialismen', 282–85.
2. Huber, *Deutsche Verfassungsgeschichte*, 16–19.
3. Koselleck, 'Zur historisch-politischen Semantik asymmetrischer Gegenbegriffe', 211–18.

Appendix

Diagrams and Tables

Emperor
Sovereign

Imperial Chancellor
representing the Emperor

Imperial Colonial Office
acting under instructions from the Chancellor

Department A	**Department B**	**Department C**	**Department M**
Political matters, general administration and law	Finance	Personnel	Military administration
Legislation, organization of administrative authorities, supervision of the administration of justice, judicial assistance, policing, internal administration, population registration/births, marriages and deaths, granting of citizenship, revenue and customs legislation, research, cartography and survey, health and veterinary matters, agriculture and forestry, mining, border control, licences and concessions, settlement, missionary activity and education, shipping, posts and telegraphy, banking, economic statistics, annual reports, colonial gazette etc.	Construction, railways and transportation, budget, payments and accounting, currency and coinage, insurance, civil engineering, mechanical engineering, shipbuilding, waterways and other public works, ports and coastal protection, procurement.	Organization of central administration, personnel and disciplinary matters, management of the Office's facilities etc.	Operations, mobilization, defence of the colonies, observation of the colonies of foreign powers, field signalling, post, telegraphy and railways, transportation, organization of the colonial forces, supply of weapons, munitions and equipment, accommodation and catering, hygiene, health and veterinary matters, military courts.

Diagram A.1 Imperial Colonial Office (*Reichskolonialamt*) – structure 1913.
Note: Translated from U. Jäschke, 'Der Aufbau der Verwaltung der deutschen Zeit', in H. Lamping and U. Jäschke (eds), *Aktuelle Fragen der Namibia-Forschung: Rundgespräch in Zusammenarbeit mit der Deutsch-Namibischen Gesellschaft* (Frankfurt: Institut für Wirtschafts- und Sozialgeographie, 1991), 21.

I Colonial Government (Governor's Office) in Windhoek

Governor
First Secretary (Deputy Governor)
Heads of Section
Assistants
Expert officers:
Cattle breeding
Fruit-growing, viticulture
Tobacco cultivation
Wool sheep breeding
Agriculture
Financial officer
Supervisors:
Comptroller
Offices
Main store
Cashier
Secretaries
Mechanics 1st and 2nd class
Materials administrator

II Local Administration

a) **District Offices (*Bezirksämter* with subordinate *Distriktsämter*)**
Windhoek *Bezirksamt*
Swapokmund *Bezirksamt*
Lüberitzbucht *Bezirksamt*
Criminal Department for Diamond Offences
Keetmanshoop *Bezirksamt*
Hasuur *Distriktsamt*
Gibeon *Bezirksamt*
Karibib *Bezirksamt*
Outjo *Bezirksamt*
Grootfontein *Bezirksamt*
Warmbad *Bezirksamt*
Rehoboth *Bezirksamt*
District Office secretaries
Clerical assistants, 1st and 2nd class

b) **Autonomous District Offices**
Omaruru *Distriktsamt*
Gobabis *Distriktsamt*
Okahandja *Distriktsamt*
Bethanie *Distriktsamt*
Maltahöhe *Distriktsamt*
Caprivi Strip *Distriktsamt*
Native Commissioners

c) **Swakopmund Harbour Office**
Director of Marine Construction
Government Construction Manager
Master of Works
Technician
Harbourmaster
Food and Materials Administration Swakopmund
Food and Materials Administration Lüderitzbucht

d) **Mining Authorities**

Mines Office Lüderitzbucht
Mines Office Windhoek

e) **Government Medical Officers**

Windhoek	Swakopmund
Okahandja	Grootfontein
Gibeon	Karibib
Lüderitzbucht	Omaruru
Maltahöhe	Rehoboth
Gobabis	

f) **Local Technical Officers and Authorities**
Windhoek Survey Administration
Omaruru Survey Office
Windhoek Survey Office
Keetmanshoop Survey Office

g) **Veterinary Institutes**
Gamams   Fredrichsfelde

h) **Stud Administration**

i) **Teachers**

k) **Foresters**

l) **Horticultural Research Gardens**
Windhoek   Okahandja

m) **Inspectors of Well Construction**

III Judicial Administration
Windhoek Superior Court
Swakopmund Regional Court
Lüderitzbucht Regional Court
Keetmanshoop Regional Court
Omaruru Regional Court
Solicitors and Notaries Public

IV Customs Administration
Windhoek Customs Office
Keetmanshoop Customs Office
Swakopmund Customs Office
Lüderitzbucht Customs Office
Karibib Customs Office
(operating through District Office)

V Railway Administration

a) **Operations Management in Windhoek**

b) **Railway Construction Commissioner South**

c) **Railway Construction Commissioner North**

VI Territorial Police

Diagram A.2 Administration of the *Schutzgebiet* – structure 1913.
Note: Translated from Jäschke, *Aufbau*, 33.

Table A.1 Relationship between planned establishment and actual strength of the Territorial Police.

Date	Planned Establishment	Actual Strength
1.4.1907	720	119
1.4.1908	720	162
1.4.1909	720	429
1.4.1910	716	439
1.4.1911	716	552
1.4.1912	600	569
1.4.1913	525	510
1.4.1914	500	470

Source: H. Rafalski, *Vom Niemandsland zum Ordnungsstaat: Geschichte der ehemaligen Landespolizei für Deutsch-Südwestafrika*. Berlin: Wernitz, 1930, 72.

Table A.2 Orders for pass tokens, employment logbooks etc. and actual deliveries.

	Pass Tokens	Employment Logbooks	Travel Passes	Registers
Ordered by District Offices	61,500	31,500	23,000	22,850
Delivered by June 1908	(-)[a]	15,000	5,000	2,000

Source: IGW's lists of the Pass Tokens, Employment Logbooks, etc. ordered and received, June 1908, NAW ZBU W.III.B.3. Vol. 1, 24a.

Note:
[a] The pass tokens had been ordered from a different supplier and so were not received with the other consignments of stationery.

Table A.3 Rates of taxation proposed by the administration during the 1908–09 discussions.

Adminstrative Office[a]	Men	Women
Inspectorate of the Territorial Police	M 20[b]	M 10
Kupferberg Police Barracks	M 6 for wages between M 60 and M 180 with free board (w.f.b.) M 12 for wages above M 180 w.f.b.	no proposal
Kub Police Barracks	M 12 for wages between M 120 and M 360 M 18–24 for wages above M 360	no proposal
Waterberg Police Barracks	M 5 for workers aged 14–18 M 10 for workers aged over 18 or 4% of the cash income[c]	no proposal
Windhoek DO	M 10 M 5 more for every M 240 of wages exceeding M 480	M 5
Maltahöhe DO	M 10 for wages between M 60 and M 120 w.f.b. M 15 for wages between M 120 and M 240 w.f.b. M 20 for wages above M 240 w.f.b.	no proposal
Namutoni DO	M 10	no proposal
Okahandja DO	M 10	M 3
Berseba DO	M 10	no proposal
Warmbad DO	M 5	no proposal
Lüderitzbucht DO	M 40[d]	no proposal

Source: Statements of Opinion from the District Offices and the Territorial Police. NAW ZBU W.II.I.2. Vol. 1 (1908/09), 22a–24a, 26a–55a.

Notes:
[a] Grootfontein, Outjo, Keetmanshoop, Gibeon, Karibib, Swakopmund, Omaruru, Bethanie and Gobabis District Offices did not make any proposal regarding the rate of taxation.
[b] All wage levels and rates of taxation are stated per annum.
[c] The employer might have had to pay half of the tax due.
[d] This amount relates to Africans from Cape Province earning up to M 600 per annum. No proposal was made for South West African workers.

Glossary

Colonial language was full of racist and derogatory terms and phrases. In a study concerning the colonizers' mindsets and policies it is almost impossible to avoid problematic or discriminatory language without substantially altering the meaning of the discourse – which would, if such a thing were at all possible, constitute a form of whitewashing insofar as it would mask the cruel intentions and racist mindsets of the colonizers. The use of such terms and phrases is a form of quotation. This glossary explains key terms and their use in translation, including technical terms. It points to the most blatant racist terms, and why and how they have been used or translated in this text where necessary.

For all cities, towns, places and Districts, see Maps 0.1 and 0.2 (located in the Front Matter).

African: Term used for the colonized population of South West Africa (SWA), in contemporary sources often referred to as 'Eingeborene' ('Natives' – see below).

Black: Capitalized to emphasize that 'race' is not a biological category but a social construct employed by the colonizers to create a hierarchy among the population.

'Boers': 'Buren', White non-German settlers from Southern Africa, usually from Dutch backgrounds via the former Dutch Cape Colony.

Captain: Equivalent to the rank of 'Hauptmann' in the German Military (e.g. Curt von François); not to be confused with 'Kaptein' (Nama Leader).

Chief: Term for the political leader of an African group, which could vary in size. Used today by, for example, the Herero (see Paramount Chief). The equivalent German term 'Häuptling' is today considered derogatory.

Colonial Department: 'Kolonialabteilung', Imperial Office for the Colonies in Berlin, until 1907 a department of the Foreign Office, then independent as the Imperial Colonial Office, 'Reichskolonialamt'.

Colonial Secretary: 'Staatssekretär im Reichskolonialamt', the head of the Imperial Colonial Office.

District Captaincy, 'Bezirkshauptmannschaft'; District Captain, 'Bezirkshauptmann'; after 1898 District Officer, 'Bezirksamtmann', and District Office, 'Bezirksamt', respectively: the administrative authority and its head for each district. The term 'Captain', taken from the military rank, was later replaced by 'Officer'.

Districts: 'Bezirke' and 'Distrikte', the administrative divisions of the colony (see Map 0.2). As the Administration continued to develop, the number of Bezirke and Distrikte continued to increase; many of the latter were autonomous (i.e. not part of a Bezirk but answering directly to the Governor), while the Bezirke, as larger administrative units, might have been divided into non-autonomous districts. [Translator's note: Accordingly, and for the sake of simplicity, both Bezirk and Distrikt are translated as 'District' in this work.]

employment logbook: 'Dienstbuch', a document each African who worked for a White farmer was supposed to receive, containing their name, 'tribal' affiliation and information on their employment.

Governor: 'Gouverneur', head of the German Colonial Administration. The name of the office was changed from 'Kaiserlicher Kommissar' (Imperial Commissioner) to 'Kaiserlicher Landeshauptmann' (Imperial Administrator) in 1893, and then to 'Kaiserlicher Gouverneur' (Imperial Governor) in 1898.

Herero and Nama War: Denomination used for the conflict as a whole from 1904 to 1908.

Herero: In accordance with general use in English, 'Herero' is used throughout this book not only as the singular form but also the plural, rather than the technically more correct 'Ovaherero'.

Imperial Commissioner: 'Kaiserlicher Kommissar'; from 1893 onwards Imperial Administrator, 'Kaiserlicher Landeshauptmann'; and from 1898 onwards Imperial Governor, 'Kaiserlicher Gouverneur' – successive terms for the officer heading the Colonial Administration.

Indigenatsgesetz: The German Nationality Act, which was not generally applied to the colonies and their African inhabitants.

Kaptein: 'Captain' or 'Chief' of a Nama group, not to be confused with the military rank 'Captain' as a translation of 'Hauptmann'.

Local Self-Government Ordinance: 'Selbstverwaltungsverordnung', a legal provision giving White Germans political rights in SWA.

'mixed': Placed in quotation marks to indicate that 'race' is not a biological category but a social construct employed by the colonizers to create a hierarchy among the population, and that 'races' are therefore not separate entities that can be 'mixed'.

Nama: In contemporary sources referred to as 'Hottentotten' ('Hottentots'). In accordance with general use in English, 'Nama' is used throughout this book not only as the singular form but also the plural, rather than the technically more correct 'Namaqua'.

'native': 'Eingeborene', the denomination used by colonial officers for the African population of SWA, not including Black working migrants from the Cape Colony. To reflect the negative and racist implications, 'native' is in quotation marks throughout the book unless the term is part of a capitalized phrase or a longer quotation.

Native Administration: 'Eingeborenenverwaltung', capitalized to represent the historical use as a technical and legal term.

Native Commissioners: 'Eingeborenenkomissare', capitalized to represent the historical use as an administrative position.

Native Ordinances: 'Eingeborenenverordnungen', capitalized to represent the historical use as a legal term.

Native Policy: 'Eingeborenenpolitik', capitalized to represent the historical use as an administrative term.

Native Register: 'Eingeborenenregister', capitalized to represent the historical use as an administrative term.

Paramount Chief: A chief of the Herero claiming the authority of a 'chief of chiefs' over the other Herero chiefs – a claim disputed by others.

Pass Ordinance: 'Paßverordnung', capitalized to represent the historical use as a legal term.

pass tokens: Referred to as 'Passblechmarken', 'Passmarken' or 'Marken' in source texts; metal discs the African population were forced to wear as a means of identification. Also referred to as 'pass tags'.

Police Zone: 'Polizeizone', the central and southern areas of the colony where the Colonial Administration attempted to enforce its Native Policy. Some German settlements or police stations were situated outside this area.

'race': Placed in quotation marks to indicate that 'race' is not a biological category but a social construct employed by the colonizers to create a hierarchy among the population.

Reichstag: The Parliament of the German Empire.

Resistance: In this book, resistance generally refers to deliberate actions against the German colonizers, which in contemporary sources is synonymous with 'uprising' or 'rebellion'.

Rhenish Missionary Society: 'Rheinische Missionsgesellschaft', German Missionary Society active in the region since 1842.

San: In contemporary sources referred to as 'Bushmen' (Buschleute).

Sandveld: Part of the Omaheke desert, in which Herero died by the thousands during the Herero and Nama War.

Schutzgebiet: The German colonies were officially called 'Schutzgebiete' ('Protectorates); however, contrary to the use of the term 'Protectorate' in British imperial history, the German 'Schutzgebiete' had no status that distinguished them from colonies, and the two terms are in effect interchangeable (cf. the terms 'Kolonialabteilung' and 'Reichskolonialamt', designating the responsible government department).

Schutztruppe: 'Protection Force', effectively the colonial army; use of the term generally mirrors the term 'Schutzgebiet' in its euphemistic meaning.

Schutzvertrag: 'Protection Treaty', a treaty between an African leader and the German colonial power.

society of racial privilege: 'Rassische Priviliegengesellschaft', a term utilized to describe the new social order that the Colonial Government attempted to establish based on a racist hierarchy and strict segregation.

'tribe': 'Stamm', denomination used by colonial officers for certain groups of the African population of SWA. The German term carries associations of backwardness, primitiveness and a lack of civilization, and it played an important part in constructing the colonized Other. To reflect the negative implications, 'tribe' is in quotation marks throughout the book unless the term is part of a capitalized phrase or a longer quotation.

Vagrancy Section: 'Landstreicherparagraph', a legal provision that enabled colonial authorities to force people without visible means of support to work in positions assigned to them (i.e. to perform forced labour).

White: Capitalized to indicate that 'race' is not a biological category but a social construct employed by the colonizers to create a hierarchy among the population.

Bibliography

Archive Sources Referenced

German Federal Archives, Lichterfelde, Berlin
(Bundesarchiv Berlin-Lichterfelde – BAL)

Imperial Colonial Office (Reichskolonialamt) (R-1001)

R-1001/1220	Confiscation of African Assets
R-1001/1234	Labour Disturbances in Wilhelmstal
R-1001/1235	Labour Disturbances in Wilhelmstal
R-1001/1461	State Secretary Dernburg's Journey to GSWA and British South Africa, 1908
R-1001/1462	State Secretary Dernburg's Journey to GSWA and British South Africa, 1908
R-1001/1464	State Secretary Dernburg's Journey to British South Africa, 1908
R-1001/1496	State Secretary Dr Solf's Journeys to GSWA, 1912
R-1001/1497	State Secretary Dr Solf's Journeys to GSWA, 1912
R-1001/1498	Study Tours to GSWA by Members of the Reichstag
R-1001/1500	Information Collecting Journey to GSWA and South Africa by *Ministerialdirektor* Dr Conze

R-1001/2057	Establishment of Local Self-Government in GSWA
R-1001/2058	Establishment of Local Self-Government in GSWA
R-1001/2059	Establishment of Local Self-Government in GSWA
R-1001/2086	General Matters in GSWA
R-1001/2087	General Matters in GSWA
R-1001/2089	Differences between Lieutenant General v. Trotha and Governor Leutwein on the relationship between political and military measures to end the war
R-1001/2090	Transfer of prisoners of war from GSWA to other German territories
R-1001/2091	Transfer of prisoners of war from GSWA to other German territories
R-1001/2097	Restriction on the keeping of large livestock by the Native population
R-1001/2111	Rebellion of the Herero
R-1001/2117	Rebellion of the Herero
R-1001/2124	The Basters of Rehoboth
R-1001/2235	Matters relating to Native administration in GSWA
R-1001/5099	Criminal records of non-Natives
R-1001/6541	Memoranda relating to GSWA
R-1001/6551	Memoranda relating to the financial development of the German *Schutzgebiete* and to German capital interests in the German *Schutzgebiete*

German South West Africa Schutzgebiet (R-1002)

R-1002/221	Personnel file B-31, Rudolf Böhmer: Administrative civil servant

R-1002/222	Personnel file B-31, Rudolf Böhmer: District Officer
R-1002/223	Personnel file B-31, Böhmer confidential documents
R-1002/1709	Personnel file 123, Captain Kurt Streitwolf, Head of Section
R-1002/2596	Authorities in GSWA, Case Files of the Territorial Police: Disciplinary punishments imposed on Natives
R-1002/2598	Authorities in GSWA, Inspectorate of the Territorial Police, Windhoek: Natives in the Inspectorate
R-1002/2599	Authorities in GSWA, Case Files of the Territorial Police: Natives in the Inspectorate
R-1002/2606	Authorities in GSWA, Case Files of the Territorial Police: Native Wages, Gen.
R-1002/2608	Authorities in GSWA, Inspectorate of the Territorial Police, Windhoek: Arming of Natives, Gen.

National Archives, Windhoek (NAW)
Central Office of the Governor (ZBU)

ZBU A.II.C.1.	Colonial Office incl. High Command of the *Schutztruppe*: Organization
ZBU A.II.C.2.	Colonial Office incl. High Command of the *Schutztruppe*: Personnel matters
ZBU A.II.C.5.	Colonial Office incl. High Command of the *Schutztruppe*: Journeys by State Secretary Dernburg
ZBU A.II.C.6.	Colonial Office incl. High Command of the *Schutztruppe*: Journeys by the Commander in Chief of the *Schutztruppen*
ZBU A.II.C.7.	Journey of State Secretary Dernburg to the *Schutzgebiet*, 1908

ZBU A.II.C.8.	Journey by Head of Section in the Colonial Office, Dr Conze, 1909
ZBU A.II.C.9.	Journey of State Secretary Solf to the *Schutzgebiet*, 1912
ZBU A.II.C.10.	Journeys by Officials of the Imperial Colonial Office
ZBU A.III.D.8.A. Vol. 1	Session of the Territorial Council 1911: Papers and other matters
ZBU A.VI.A.5.Vol. 3	Annual Reports of the Specialist Departments by years, 1913/14
ZBU A.VI.A.7.	Annual Reports of the Missions and Church Parishes
ZBU A.VI.A.8.	Annual Reports of the Native Commissioners
ZBU D.III.W.3.	Military Service Treaty with the Basters of Rehoboth
ZBU D.III.W.4.	Exercises of the Natives liable to Military Service
ZBU D.IV.L.2. Vol. 5	Herero Rebellion 1904, Campaign: political matters
ZBU D.IV.L.2. Vol. 6	Herero Rebellion 1904, Campaign: political matters
ZBU F.IV.R.1.	Mixed marriages and their Progeny: Gen.
ZBU F.IV.R.2. Vol. 1	Mixed marriages and their Progeny: Spec.
ZBU F.IV.R.2. Vol. 2	Mixed marriages and their Progeny: Spec.
ZBU F.IV.R.2. Vol. 3	Mixed marriages and their Progeny: Spec.
ZBU F.V.A.1. Vol. 1 (MF)	Administration of Criminal Justice vis-à-vis Natives, criminal cases and punishment: Gen.

ZBU F.V.A.2. Vol. 1 (MF)	Administration of Criminal Justice vis-à-vis Natives, criminal cases and punishment: Spec.
ZBU F.V.A.3. Vol. 1 (MF)	Administration of Criminal Justice vis-à-vis Natives, criminal cases and punishment: Murder of Dürr and Claasen
ZBU F.V.B.1. Vol. 1 (MF)	Administration of Criminal Justice vis-à-vis Natives, final imposition of death penalty on Natives: Gen.
ZBU F.V.B.2. Vol. 1 (MF)	Administration of Criminal Justice vis-à-vis Natives, final imposition of death penalty on Natives: Spec.
ZBU F.V.C.1. Vol. 1 (MF)	Administration of Criminal Justice vis-à-vis Natives, approval of criminal sentences: Gen
ZBU F.V.C.2. Vol. 1 (MF)	Administration of Criminal Justice vis-à-vis Natives, approval of criminal sentences: Spec.
ZBU F.V.C.2. Vol. 2 (MF)	Administration of Criminal Justice vis-à-vis Natives, approval of criminal sentences: Spec.
ZBU F.V.C.2. Vol. 3 (MF)	Administration of Criminal Justice vis-à-vis Natives, approval of criminal sentences: Spec.
ZBU F.VII.C.1. Vol. 1 (MF)	Credit transactions of Natives: Gen.
ZBU F.VII.C.1. Vol. 2 (MF)	Credit transactions of Natives: Gen.
ZBU F.VII.C.2. Vol. 1 (MF)	Credit transactions of Natives: Spec.
ZBU F.VII.C.3. Vol. 1 (MF)	Credit transactions of Natives: Loan agreements
ZBU F.VII.D.1. Vol. 1 (MF)	Foreclosure against Natives: Gen
ZBU F.VII.D.2. Vol. 1 (MF)	Foreclosure against Natives: Spec.
ZBU F.VII.F.1 Vol. 1 (MF)	Reports on Civil Suits against Natives: Gen.
ZBU F.VII.F.2 Vol. 1 (MF)	Foreclosure against Natives: Spec.

ZBU G.IV.D.1. — Police and Vice Squad, Measures against licentious behaviour: Gen.

ZBU G.IV.D.2. — Police and Vice Squad, Measures against licentious behaviour: Spec.

ZBU G.IV.M.2. — Measures against the falling birth rate among Natives resulting from forbidden means: Spec.

ZBU H.VII.F.2. Vol. 1 (MF) — Native Infirmary Windhoek: Spec.

ZBU H.VII.G.1. Vol. 1 (MF) — Native Infirmary Keetmanshoop: Gen.

ZBU H.VII.G.2. Vol. 1 (MF) — Native Infirmary Keetmanshoop: Spec.

ZBU H.VII.H.1. Vol. 1 (MF) — Native Infirmary Karibib: Gen.

ZBU H.VII.H.2. Vol. 2 (MF) — Native Infirmary Karibib: Spec.

ZBU H.VII.I.1. Vol. 1 (MF) — Native Infirmary Outjo: Gen.

ZBU H.VII.I.2. Vol. 1 (MF) — Native Infirmary Outjo: Spec.

ZBU I.IX.D.3. Vol. 1 (MF) — Rhenish Missionary Society: Disputes with the Rhenish Missionary Society (old files)

ZBU I.IX.G.2. Vol. 1 (MF) — Missionary Oblates of Mary Immaculate: Spec.

ZBU I.X.C.2. Vol. 1 (MF) — Rhenish Mission Native Schools: Spec.

ZBU I.X.A.1 Vol. 1 (MF) — Mission Schools: Gen.

ZBU I.X.A.2. Vol. 1 (MF) — Mission Schools: Spec.

ZBU I.X.A.3. Vol. 1 (MF) — Mission Schools: Introduction of German writing in mission schools

ZBU I.X.B.1. Vol. 1 (MF) — Promotion of the knowledge of German among Natives and grants for that purpose: Gen.

ZBU I.X.B.2. Vol. 1 (MF) — Promotion of the knowledge of German among Natives and grants for that purpose: Spec.

ZBU I.X.C.3. Vol. 1 (MF) — Rhenish Mission Native Schools: Schools for the education of the Basters in Rehoboth

ZBU I.X.E.2. Vol. 1 (MF) Native Schools of the Missionary Oblates of Mary Immaculate: Spec.

ZBU W.I.A.2. Vol. 1 (MF) Description, Manners and Customs of the Natives: Spec.

ZBU W.1.B.1. Vol. 1 (MF) Language of the Natives: Gen.

ZBU W.1.B.1. Vol. 2 (MF) Language of the Natives: Gen.

ZBU W.1.B.2. Vol. 1 (MF) Language of the Natives: Spec.

ZBU W.1.B.3. Vol. 1 (MF) Language of the Natives: Herero

ZBU W.1.B.4. Vol. 1 (MF) Language of the Natives: Nama and Hill Damara

ZBU W.1.C.1. Vol. 1 (MF) Seminar for Oriental Languages: Seminar for Oriental Languages in Berlin

ZBU W.1.C.2. Vol. 1 (MF) Seminar for Oriental Languages: Colonial Institute Hamburg

ZBU W.1.D.2. Vol. 1 (MF) Trades of the Natives: Spec.

ZBU W.1.F.1. Vol. 1 (MF) Prohibition of the Export of Natives for Show Purposes: Gen.

ZBU W.1.F.2. Vol. 1 (MF) Prohibition of the Export of Natives for Show Purposes: Spec.

ZBU W.II.A.1. Vol. 1 (MF) Administration of Native Affairs: Gen.

ZBU W.II.A.2. Vol. 1 (MF) Administration of Native Affairs: Spec.

ZBU W.II.A.4. Vol. 1 (MF) Administration of Native Affairs: Native Commissioners' Offices: Gen.

ZBU W.II.A.5. Vol. 1 (MF) Administration of Native Affairs: Native Commissioners' Offices: Spec.

ZBU W.II.A.6. Vol. 1 (MF) Administration of Native Affairs: Windhoek Native Commissioner's Office

ZBU W.II.A.7. Vol. 1 (MF) Administration of Native Affairs: Lüderitzbucht Native Commissioner's Office

ZBU W.II.A.8. Vol. 1 (MF) Administration of Native Affairs: Keetmanshoop Native Commissioner's Office

ZBU W.II.A.9. Vol. 1 (MF)   Administration of Native Affairs:
                               Warmbad Native Commissioner's Office

ZBU W.II.A.10. Vol. 1 (MF)   Administration of Native Affairs:
                               Salaries of Captains and Headmen

ZBU W.II.B.1. Vol. 1 (MF)   Reports on the Situation of the Natives:
                               Gen.

ZBU W.II.B.2. Vol. 1 (MF)   Reports on the Situation of the Natives:
                               Spec.

ZBU W.II.B.2. Vol. 2 (MF)   Reports on the Situation of the Natives:
                               Spec.

ZBU W.II.C.3. Vol. 2 (MF)   Affairs of the Autonomous Tribes:
                               Basters of Rehoboth

ZBU W.II.C.3. Vol. 3 (MF)   Affairs of the Autonomous Tribes:
                               Basters of Rehoboth

ZBU W.II.C.3. Vol. 4 (MF)   Affairs of the Autonomous Tribes:
                               Basters of Rehoboth

ZBU W.II.C.4. Vol. 1 (MF)   Affairs of the Autonomous Tribes:
                               Berseba People

ZBU W.II.C.4. Vol. 2 (MF)   Affairs of the Autonomous Tribes:
                               Berseba People

ZBU W.II.C.4. Vol. 3 (MF)   Affairs of the Autonomous Tribes:
                               Berseba People

ZBU W.II.E.1. Vol. 1 (MF)   Native Reservations and Locations: Gen.

ZBU W.II.E.2. Vol. 1 (MF)   Native Reservations and Locations: Spec.

ZBU W.II.E.3. Vol. 1 (MF)   Native Reservations and Locations:
                               Omburo and Otjihaenena Herero
                               Reservations

ZBU W.II.E.4. Vol. 1 (MF)   Native Reservations and Locations: Gen.
                               (old files)

ZBU W.II.E.5. Vol. 1 (MF)   Native Reservations and Locations:
                               Rietmond and Kalkfontein Witbooi
                               Reservation (old files)

ZBU W.II.E.6. Vol. 1 (MF)   Native Reservations and Locations:
                               Bethanie Native Reservation (old files)

ZBU W.II.E.7. Vol. 1 (MF)　　Native Reservations and Locations: Hoachanas Native Reservation (old files)

ZBU W.II.E.8. Vol. 1 (MF)　　Native Reservations and Locations: Nosob Herero Reservation (old files)

ZBU W.II.E.9. Vol. 1 (MF)　　Native Reservations and Locations: Waterberg Herero Reservation (old files)

ZBU W.II.E.10. Vol. 1 (MF)　Native Reservations and Locations: Otjimbingwe Herero Reservation (old files)

ZBU W.II.F.1. Vol. 1 (MF)　　Affairs of the Bondels Location: Gen.

ZBU W.II.F.2. Vol. 1 (MF)　　Affairs of the Bondels Location: Spec.

ZBU W.II.G.1. Vol. 1 (MF)　　Affairs of the Kopper People living in British Bechuanaland: Gen.

ZBU W.II.G.2. Vol. 1 (MF)　　Affairs of the Kopper People living in British Bechuanaland: Spec.

ZBU W.II.H.1. Vol. 1 (MF)　　Participation of the Natives in the Costs of Administration: Gen.

ZBU W.II.H.2. Vol. 1 (MF)　　Participation of the Natives in the Costs of Administration: Spec.

ZBU W.II.I.1. Vol. 1 (MF)　　Taxation of the Natives: Gen.

ZBU W.II.I.2. Vol. 1 (MF)　　Taxation of the Natives: Spec.

ZBU W.II.K.1. Vol. 1 (MF)　　Ovamboland Affairs

ZBU W.II.K.1. Vol. 2 (MF)　　Ovamboland Affairs

ZBU W.II.L.2. Vol. 1 (MF)　　Native Affairs of the Caprivi Strip: Spec.

ZBU W.II.M.1. Vol. 1 (MF)　Bechuana and Bakalahari Settlements in Gobabis District: Gen.

ZBU W.II.M.2. Vol. 1 (MF)　Bechuana and Bakalahari Settlements in Gobabis District: Spec.

ZBU W.II.M.2. Vol. 2 (MF)　Bechuana and Bakalahari Settlements in Gobabis District: Spec.

ZBU W.II.M.3. Vol. 1 (MF)　Bechuana and Bakalahari Settlements in Gobabis District: Bechuana in British territory

ZBU W.II.N.2. Vol. 2 (MF)   Hill Damara: Spec.

ZBU W.III.A.1 Vol. 1 (MF)   Ordinances and Regulations concerning the Natives: Gen.

ZBU W.III.A.2. Vol. 1 (MF)   Ordinances and Regulations concerning the Natives: Spec.

ZBU W.III.A.3. Vol. 1 (MF)   Ordinances and Regulations concerning the Natives: District Office Reports on the Practical Implementation of the Native Ordinances

ZBU W.III.B.1 .Vol. 1 (MF)   Measures for the Surveillance of the Natives: Gen.

ZBU W.III.B.2. Vol. 1 (MF)   Measures for the Surveillance of the Natives: Spec.

ZBU W.III.B.3. Vol. 1 (MF)   Measures for the Surveillance of the Natives: Procurement of Employment Logbooks, Travel Passes and Registers

ZBU W.III.B.4. Vol. 1 (MF)   Measures for the Surveillance of the Natives: Identification of operations with more than ten Native workers

ZBU W.III.B.5 Vol. 1 (MF)   Measures for the Surveillance of the Natives: Desertion and Vagrancy of the Natives, Limitations on Freedom of Movement

ZBU W.III.B.5. Vol. 2 (MF)   Measures for the Surveillance of the Natives: Desertion and Vagrancy of the Natives, Limitations on Freedom of Movement

ZBU W.III.B.6. Vol. 1 (MF)   Measures for the Surveillance of the Natives: Registration of Railway Construction Workers

ZBU W.III.D.1. Vol. 1 (MF)   Keeping of Animals for Riding or Large Livestock by Natives: Gen.

ZBU W.III.D.2. Vol. 1 (MF)   Keeping of Animals for Riding or Large Livestock by Natives: Spec.

ZBU W.III.D.2. Vol. 2 (MF)   Keeping of Animals for Riding or Large Livestock by Natives: Spec.

ZBU W.III.E.1. Vol. 1 (MF) Keeping of the Native Registers: Gen.

ZBU W.III.E.2. Vol. 1 (MF) Keeping of the Native Registers: Spec.

ZBU W.III.F.1. Vol. 1 (MF) Native Werf Settlements: Gen.

ZBU W.III.F.2. Vol. 1 (MF) Native Werf Settlements: Spec.

ZBU W.III.F.3. Vol. 1 (MF) Native Werf Settlements: Native werfs on private land

ZBU W.III.F.4. Vol. 1 (MF) Native Werf Settlements: Military werfs

ZBU W.III.K.1. Vol. 1 (MF) Pass Requirement and Pass Tokens for the Natives: Gen.

ZBU W.III.K.2. Vol. 1 (MF) Pass Requirement and Pass Tokens for the Natives: Spec.

ZBU W.III.K.3. Vol. 1 (MF) Pass Requirement and Pass Tokens for the Natives: Procurement of pass tokens

ZBU W.III.L.1. Vol. 1 (MF) Travelling, Pass Fees and Travel Passes for Natives: Gen.

ZBU W.III.L.2. Vol. 1 (MF) Travelling, Pass Fees and Travel Passes for Natives: Spec.

ZBU W.III.N.1. Vol. 1 (MF) Service and Labour Contracts for Natives (Master and Servant Ordinance): Gen.

ZBU W.III.N.2. Vol. 1 (MF) Service and Labour Contracts for Natives (Master and Servant Ordinance): Spec.

ZBU W.III.O.1. Vol. 1 (MF) Employment Logbooks for the Natives: Gen.

ZBU W.III.P.1. Vol. 1 (MF) Surveillance of Natives' Correspondence: Gen.

ZBU W.III.P.2. Vol. 1 (MF) Surveillance of Natives' Correspondence: Spec.

ZBU W.III.R.1. Vol. 1 (MF) Maltreatment of Natives by Whites: Gen.

ZBU W.III.R.2. Vol. 1 (MF) Maltreatment of Natives by Whites: Spec.

ZBU W.III.R.2. Vol. 2 (MF) Maltreatment of Natives by Whites: Spec.

ZBU W.IV.A.1. Vol. 1 (MF) Native Labour Relations: Gen.

ZBU W.IV.A.2. Vol. 1 (MF) Native Labour Relations: Spec.

ZBU W.IV.A.3. Vol. 1 (MF) Native Labour Relations: old files

ZBU W.IV.A.3. Vol. 2 (MF) Native Labour Relations: old files

ZBU W.IV.A.4. Vol. 1 (MF) Native Labour Relations: Workers and Servants registration cards and medical examinations

ZBU W.IV.A.5. Vol. 1 (MF) Native Labour Relations: Assignment of unmarried girls to bachelor masters

ZBU W.IV.B.1. Vol. 1 (MF) Native Labour Relations in Neighbouring States: Union of South Africa

ZBU W.IV.B.1. Vol. 2 (MF) Native Labour Relations in Neighbouring States: Union of South Africa

ZBU W.IV.B.1. Vol. 3 (MF) Native Labour Relations in Neighbouring States: Union of South Africa

ZBU W.IV.B.1. Vol. 8 (MF) Native Labour Relations in Neighbouring States: Union of South Africa

ZBU W.IV.B.2. Vol. 1 (MF) Native Labour Relations in Neighbouring States: Rhodesia

ZBU W.IV.B.3. Vol. 1 (MF) Native Labour Relations in Neighbouring States: Belgian Congo

ZBU W.IV.B.4. Vol. 1 (MF) Native Labour Relations in Neighbouring States: Portuguese West Africa

ZBU W.IV.B.5. Vol. 1 (MF) Native Labour Relations in Neighbouring States: Rest of West Africa

ZBU W.IV.B.6. Vol. 1 (MF) Native Labour Relations in Neighbouring States: India and Indo-China

ZBU W.IV.C.4. Vol. 1 (MF) Native Labour Relations in Other German Territories: Pacific Protectorate

ZBU W.IV.E.1. Vol. 1 (MF) Native Farm Workers: Gen.

ZBU W.IV.E.2. Vol. 1 (MF)   Native Farm Workers: Spec.

ZBU W.IV.E.2. Vol. 2 (MF)   Native Farm Workers: Spec.

ZBU W.IV.F.2. Vol. 1 (MF)   Native Mine Workers: Spec.

ZBU W.IV.P.2. Vol. 1 (MF)   Recruitment of Coloured Workers from other Foreign Territories: Spec.

ZBU W.IV.P.3. Vol. 1 (MF)   Recruitment of Coloured Workers from other Foreign Territories: Recruitment of Kru Negroes

ZBU W.IV.R.1. Vol. 1 (MF)   Recruitment of Asian Workers: Immigration of Chinese

ZBU W.IV.R.2. Vol. 1 (MF)   Recruitment of Asian Workers: Immigration of Indians

ZBU W.IV.U.1. Vol. 1 (MF)   Keeping of records of the workforce, cases of sickness and deaths in the larger enterprises: Gen.

ZBU W.IV.U.2. Vol. 1 (MF)   Keeping of records of the workforce, cases of sickness and deaths in the larger enterprises: Spec.

ZBU W.IV.U.3. Vol. 1 (MF)   Keeping of records of the workforce, cases of sickness and deaths in the larger enterprises: The diamond fields.

ZBU W.IV.U.4. Vol. 1 (MF)   Keeping of records of the workforce, cases of sickness and deaths in the larger enterprises: The mines, including marble works.

Geheimakten – Confidential Documents:

ZBU Geheimakten VI.A. Vol. 1 (MF)   Labour Relations and Wages

ZBU Geheimakten VI.B. Vol. 1 (MF)   Funds from the Welfare Lottery

ZBU Geheimakten VI.E. Vol. 1 (MF)   Study, Ovamboland and the Caprivi Strip

ZBU Geheimakten VI.F. Vol. 1 (MF)   Economy: General

ZBU Geheimakten VII.A. Vol. 3 (MF) Ovamboland

ZBU Geheimakten VII.D. Vol. 1 (MF) Bechuana

ZBU Geheimakten VII.G. Vol. 1 (MF) Mixed marriages

ZBU Geheimakten VII.H. Vol. 1 (MF) Okavango area

ZBU Geheimakten VII.I. Vol. 1 (MF)   Recruitment of Native workers

ZBU Geheimakten VIII.G. Vol. 1 (MF) Witbooi Hottentots

ZBU Geheimakten VIII.I. Vol. 1 (MF) Simon Kopper

ZBU Geheimakten VIII.I. Vol. 3 (MF) Simon Kopper

ZBU Geheimakten VIII.K. Vol. 1 (MF) Unrest in the South

ZBU Geheimakten VIII.K. Vol. 2 (MF) Unrest in the South

ZBU Geheimakten IX.A. Vol. 1 (MF)   Powers of the High Command
of the *Schutztruppe*

ZBU Geheimakten IX.B. Vol. 1 (MF)   Structure, Deployment
and Auxiliary Units of the
Schutztruppe

ZBU Geheimakten IX.D. Vol. 1 (MF)   Field hospital affairs

ZBU Geheimakten IX.F. Vol. 1 (MF)   Order for the Remission of
Punishments in Mobilization
Matters

ZBU Geheimakten IX.H. Vol. 1 (MF)   *Schutztruppe*: Miscellaneous

Keetmanshoop District Office (Bezirksamt Keetmanshoop – BKE)

BKE B.II.57.E.   Prostitution in Keetmanshoop

BKE UA 34/1.   Prostitution: Health Certificates

Lüderitzbucht District Office (Bezirksamt Lüderitzbucht – BLU)

BLU E.K. 30.   Native Commissioner: Correspondence
with Lüderitzbucht District Office

BLU E.K. 32.   Native Commissioner: Correspondence
with Companies

BLU E.K. 34.   Native Commissioner: Correspondence
with the Governor's Office

BLU G.4/2.   Sanitary Police: Medical Certificates for Prostitutes

BLU O.1.D.   Police and Vice Squad: Measures against Licentious Behaviour

BLU O.1.G.   Police and Vice Squad: The Wearing of Uniforms by Natives

BLU O.1.H.   Police and Vice Squad: Concubinage

District Office Omaruru (Bezirksamt Omaruru – BOM)

BOM 4/1.   Natives Living in the Township of Omaruru

BOM S.13.G.   Register Office Affairs: Mixed Marriages and their Progeny

Rehoboth District Office (Bezirksamt Rehoboth – BRE)

BRE E.2.A.   Provisions concerning Native Workers

BRE E.2.B. Vol. 2   Surveillance of Native Workers: Researches into Desertions and New Arrivals

BRE E.2.E.Vol. 2   Applications for the Assignment of Native Workers

BRE E.2.F.   Complaints of Native Workers

BRE E.2.H.   Recruitment of Ovambo

BRE E.3.E.   Bushmen

BRE E.3.H.   Basters: General Matters and Legal Status

BRE E.3.K. Vol. 1   Baster Affairs

BRE E.3.K. Vol. 2   Baster Affairs

BRE O.1.D.   Measures against Licentious Behaviour: Prostitution and Trafficking in Girls

Swakopmund District Office (Bezirksamt Swakopmund – BSW)

BSW UA 33/5.	Marriages
BSW UA 33/7.	Register Office Affairs: Births
BSW UA 33/9.	Register of Birth for People of Mixed Race

Windhoek District Office (Bezirksamt Windhuk – BWI)

BWI E.5.D. Vol. 5	Native Civil Jurisdiction: Trial Documents
BWI O.1.D.1.	Police and Vice Squad: Measures against Licentious Behaviour: Brothels
BWI O.1.D.2. Vol. 1	Police and Vice Squad: Measures against Licentious Behaviour: Brothels
BWI O.1.D.2. Vol. 2	Police and Vice Squad: Measures against Licentious Behaviour: Brothels
BWI O.1.H.	Police and Vice Squad: Concubinage

Okahandja District Office (Distriktsamt Okahandja – DOK)

DOK S.13.6.	Register Office Affairs: Mixed Marriages and their Progeny

Lüderitzbucht District Court (Bezirksgericht Lüderitzbucht – GLU)

GLU D. 40/13.	Criminal Proceedings against Christophel Goosen and Hermann Reupke on a Charge of Grievous Bodily Harm
GLU D.47/13.	Criminal Proceedings against Adam Stutzer, sorter, on a Charge of Grievous Bodily Harm
GLU D.48/13.	Criminal Proceedings against Walther Christiani, company assistant, on a Charge of Bodily Harm

Swakopmund District Court (Bezirksgericht Swakopmund – GSW)

GSW 218/08.	Civil Proceedings, Regina Elisabeth Hollenbach née Cloete v. Heinrich Hollenbach, conductor, to establish the existence of cohabitation
GSW D 25/13. Vol. 1	Criminal Proceedings against Operations Manager Stöcker on a charge of bodily harm leading to death
GSW D 25/13. Vol. 2	Criminal Proceedings against Operations Manager Stöcker on a charge of bodily harm

Windhoek District Court (Bezirksgericht Windhuk – GWI)

GWI 60/06.	Civil Proceedings. Plaintiff: Ida Leinhos of Okahandja. Defendant: The haulage contractor Leinhos, previously of Otjihavera
GWI A.2/05.	Conciliation Proceedings, Leihnos v. Leinhos
GWI D.164/08.	Criminal Proceedings against 1. Bruno Schönfeld, gardener, 2. Gustav Hermanson, metalworker, of Klein-Windhoek, on a charge of maltreating a Native
GWI D.169/08.	Criminal Proceedings against the haulage contractor Melcher of Windhoek on a charge of maltreating a Native
GWI R.1/07.	Civil Proceedings. Plaintiff: Ida Leinhos of Okahandja. Defendant: The haulage contractor Leinhos of Okahandja.

Archives of the Evangelical-Lutheran Church in the Republic of Namibia, Windhoek (ELCIN)

II.11.1.	District Offices: Orders, correspondence

II.11.3.	Letters to and from military bases, command posts, commandants, military officials
II.11.5.a.	Letters to and from Governor's Office, Governor, District Office and other authorities
II.11.6.	District Office etc.
V.16.	Chronicle of Lüderitzbucht Municipality

German Federal Archives, Military Archives in Freiburg (Bundesarchiv-Militärarchiv Freiburg – BA-MA)

RM 2/1852	Naval Cabinet, *Schutztruppe* for South West Africa: Organization and Personnel Matters
RM 3/10263	Imperial Naval Office, Revolt in GSWA: Herero Rebellion
RM 5/v 6241	Naval Admiralty Staff, Voyage of HIH the Crown Prince to India and East Asia; Voyage of HIH to GSWA and East Africa
RW 51/2	Imperial *Schutztruppen* and other German Land Forces Abroad: Expulsion of the Herero from German territory and reward for the handing over captured Captains of the Herero; Order of Lieutenant General v. Trotha to the troops and the Herero nation
MSg 1/2038	Notes, pictures and press cuttings on the activities of Lieutenant Colonel von den Hagen with the *Schutztruppe* in German South West Africa

Published Sources

Abun-Nasr, S. 'Eingeborenenkommissare in Deutsch-Südwestafrika'. University of Freiburg, unpublished MA thesis, n.d.

Adick, C. 'Bildungsstatistiken zum deutschen kolonialen Schulwesen', in P. Heine and U. van der Heyden (eds), *Studien zur Geschichte des deutschen Kolonialismus in Afrika* (Festschrift to mark the 60th birthday of Peter Sebald) (Pfaffenweiler: Centaurus, 1995), 21–42.

Albertini, R. von (with A. Wirz). *Europäische Kolonialherrschaft 1880–1940.* Zurich: Atlantis, 1976.

Amtsblatt für das Schutzgebiet Deutsch-Südwest-Afrika [Official Gazette for the Schutzgebiet of German South West Africa], Vols 1 (1910) – 5 (1914). Imperial Governor's Office, Windhoek.

Anderson, D. 'Masters and Servants Legislation and Labour in Colonial Kenya 1895–1939'. Basler Afrika-Bibliographien, Working Paper No. 8, 1996.

Arendt, H. *Elemente und Ursprünge totaler Herrschaft.* Munich: Piper, 1986.

Arnold, B. *Steuer und Lohnarbeit im Südwesten von Deutsch-Ostafrika 1891–1916: Eine historisch-ethnologische Studie.* Münster: LIT, 1995.

Bade, K.J. 'Enthusiasmus und Kalkül. Kolonialbewegung und Wirtschaftsinteressen in der Bismarckzeit'. *Scriptae Mercaturae* 30 (1996), 81–107.

———. 'Imperialismusforschung und Kolonialhistorie'. *Geschichte und Gesellschaft* 9 (1983), 138–50.

———. 'Die "Organisation des Arbeitsmarktes" im kaiserlichen Deutschland'. *Scripta Mercaturae* 27 (1993), 75–90.

Bald, D. 'Zum Kriegsbild der militärischen Führung im Kaiserreich', in J. Dülffer and K. Holl (eds), *Bereit zum Krieg: Kriegsmentalität im wilhelminischen Deutschland* (Göttingen: Vandenhoeck & Ruprecht, 1986), 146–60.

Bayer, M. *Der Krieg in Südwestafrika und seine Bedeutung für die Entwicklung der Kolonie.* Leipzig: Engelmann, 1906.

———. 'Die Nation der Bastards'. *Zeitschrift für Kolonialpolitik, Kolonialrecht und Kolonialwirtschaft* 8 (1906), 625–48.

———. *Mit dem Hauptquartier in Südwestafrika.* Berlin: Weicher, 1909.

Beck, H. *The Origins of the Authoritarian Welfare State in Prussia: Conservatives, Bureaucracy and the Social Question 1815–70.* Ann Arbor: University of Michigan Press, 1995.

Beinart, W. '"Jamani": Cape Workers in German South West Africa 1904–12', in W. Beinart and C. Bundy (eds), *Hidden Struggle in Rural South Africa: Politics and Popular Movements in the Transkei Eastern Cape 1890–1930* (London: University of California Press, 1987), 166–90.

Billig, M. *Die rassistische Internationale: Zur Renaissance der Rassenlehre in der modernen Psychologie.* Frankfurt: Neue Kritik, 1981.

Bitterli, U. *Alte Welt – neue Welt: Formen des europäisch-überseeischen Kulturkontaktes vom 15. bis zum 18. Jahrhundert.* Munich: dtv, 1992.

Bley, H. *Kolonialherrschaft und Sozialstruktur in Deutsch-Südwestafrika 1894–1914.* Hamburg: Leibniz, 1968.

Bourdieu, P. *Praktische Vernunft: Zur Theorie des Handelns*. Frankfurt: Suhrkamp, 1998.

Bridgman, J. *The Revolt of the Hereros*. Los Angeles: University of California Press, 1981.

Budack, K. 'Der "Bastardaufstand" in Deutsch-Südwestafrika'. *Afrikanischer Heimatkalender* (1974), 39–63.

———. 'Übersicht der Völker und Kulturen', in H. Lamping (ed.), *Namibia: Ausgewählte Themen der Exkursion 1988* (Frankfurt: Institut für Wirtschafts- und Sozialgeographie, 1989), 57–108.

Clarence-Smith, G., and R. Moorsom. 'Underdevelopment and Class Formation in Ovamboland 1844–1917', in B. Wood (ed.), *Namibia 1884–1984: Readings on Namibia's History and Society* (Lusaka: Namibia Support Committee and UNIN, 1988), 175–89.

Claussen, D. *Was heisst Rassismus?* Darmstadt: WBG, 1994.

Cohen, C. '"The Natives Must First Become Good Workmen": Formal Educational Provision in German South West and East Africa Compared'. *Journal of Southern African Studies* 19 (1993), 115–34.

Dedering, T. 'The German-Herero War of 1904: Revisionism of Genocide or Imaginary Historiography?' *Journal of Southern African Studies* 19 (1993), 80–88.

———. *Hate the Old and Follow the New: Khoekhoe and Missionaries in Early Nineteenth-Century Namibia*. Stuttgart: Steiner, 1997.

———. 'Missionare und Khoikhoi in Namibia 1806–1840: Sozialer Wandel in einer afrikanischen Gesellschaft', in W. Wagner (ed.), *Kolonien und Missionen* (Münster: LIT, 1994), 222–41.

———. 'The Prophet's "War against Whites": Shepard Stuurman in Namibia and South Africa 1904–1907'. *Journal of African History* 40 (1999), 1–19.

Demhardt, I. *Deutsche Kolonialgrenzen in Afrika: Historisch-geographische Untersuchungen ausgewählter Grenzräume von Deutsch-Südwestafrika und Deutsch-Ostafrika*. Hildesheim: Olms, 1997.

Denkschrift über Eingeborenen-Politik und Hereroaufstand in Südwestafrika (supplement to the *Deutsches Kolonialblatt* 1904). Berlin: Mittler, 1904.

Dernburg, B. *Südwestafrikanische Eindrücke: Industrielle Fortschritte in den Kolonien. Zwei Vorträge*. Berlin: Mittler, 1909.

———. *Zielpunkte des Deutschen Kolonialwesens. Zwei Vorträge*. Berlin: Mittler, 1907.

Deutsches Kolonialblatt. Official Gazette for the Schutzgebiete in Africa and the South Pacific, Vols 1 (1890) – 25 (1914). Published by the Colonial Department of the German Foreign Office, and from 1907 onwards by the Imperial Colonial Office. Berlin: Mittler, 1890–1914.

Deutsch-Südwestafrikanische Zeitung. Swakopmund, 1901ff.

Die Deutsche Kolonial-Gesetzgebung. Collection of the Statutes, Ordinances, Decrees and International Agreeements relating to the German Schutzgebiete, with Notes and an Index. Edited by Riebow, Gerstmeyer and Köbner, Vols 1 (up to 1892) – 13 (1909). Berlin: Mittler, 1893–1910.

Die deutschen Schutzgebiete in Afrika und der Südsee. Official Annual Reports published by the Imperial Colonial Office, Vols 1 (1909/10) – 4 (1912/13). Berlin: Mittler, 1911–1914.

Digre, B. *Imperialism's New Clothes: The Repartition of Tropical Africa 1914–1919*. New York: Lang, 1990.

Douglas, M. *Wie Institutionen denken*, 2nd edn. Frankfurt: Suhrkamp, 1998.

Dove, K. 'Bastards', in H. Schnee (ed.), *Deutsches Kolonial-Lexikon, Vol. 1* (Leipzig: Quelle & Meyer, 1920), 140–41.

Drechsler, H. *Aufstände in Südwestafrika: Der Kampf der Herero und Nama 1904–1907 gegen die deutsche Kolonialherrschaft*. Berlin: Dietz, 1984.

————. *Südwestafrika unter deutscher Kolonialherrschaft*. Vol. I: *Der Kampf der Herero und Nama gegen den deutschen Imperialismus 1884–1915*, 2nd edn. Berlin: Akademie, 1984.

————. *Südwestafrika unter deutscher Kolonialherrschaft*. Vol. II: *Die großen Land- und Minengesellschaften 1885–1914*. Stuttgart: Steiner, 1996.

Dubow, S. *Scientific Racism in Modern South Africa*. Cambridge: Cambridge University Press, 1995.

Duignan, P., and L. Gann (eds). *Colonialism in Africa 1870–1960*. Vol. I: *The History and Politics of Colonialism 1870–1914*. Cambridge: Cambridge University Press, 1969.

Dülffer, J. 'Deutsche Kolonialherrschaft in Afrika'. *Neue Politische Literatur* 26 (1981), 458–73.

Eckart, W. 'Medizin und kolonialer Krieg: Die Niederschlagung der Herero-Nama-Erhebung im Schutzgebiet Deutsch-Südwestafrika 1904–1907', in P. Heine and U. van der Heyden (eds), *Studien zur Geschichte des deutschen Kolonialismus in Afrika* (Pfaffenweiler: Centaurus, 1995), 220–35.

————. *Medizin und Kolonialimperialismus: Deutschland 1884–1945*. Paderborn: Schöningh, 1997.

Eckenbrecher, M. von. *Was Afrika mir gab und nahm: Erlebnisse einer deutschen Frau in Südwestafrika*. Berlin: Mittler, 1907.

Eckert, A. 'Grundprobleme und Forschungsfelder in der neueren afrikanischen Geschichte'. *Neue Politische Literatur* 42 (1997), 48–69.

Eirola, M. *The Ovambogefahr: The Ovamboland Reservation in the Making – Political Responses of the Kingdom of Ondonga to the German Colonial Power 1884–1910*. Rovaniemi, Societas Historica Finlandiae Septentrionalis, 1992.

Elias, N. *Studien über die Deutschen: Machtkämpfe und Habitusentwicklung im 19. und 20. Jahrhundert*. Frankfurt: Suhrkamp, 1992.

Engel, L. *Kolonialismus und Nationalismus im deutschen Protestantismus in Namibia 1907 bis 1945: Beiträge zur Geschichte der deutschen evangelischen Mission und Kirche im ehemaligen Kolonial- und Mandatsgebiet Südwestafrika*. Frankfurt: Lang, 1976.

————. 'Die Rheinische Mission und die deutsche Kolonialherrschaft in Südwestafrika 1884–1915', in K.J. Bade (ed.), *Imperialismus und Kolonialmission: Kaiserliches Deutschland und koloniales Imperium*, 2nd edn (Wiesbaden: Steiner, 1982), 142–64.

Essner, C. *Deutsche Afrikareisende im 19. Jahrhundert: Zur Sozialgeschichte des Reisens*. Stuttgart: Steiner, 1985.

————. 'Im "Irrgarten der Rassenlogik" oder nordische Rassenlehre und nationale Frage 1919–1935'. *Historische Mitteilungen der Ranke-Gesellschaft* 7 (1994), 81–101.

Estorff, L. von. *Wanderungen und Kämpfe in Südwestafrika, Ostafrika und Südafrika 1894–1910*, 2nd edn. Windhoek: Meinert, 1979.

Farwell, B. *The Great War in Africa 1914–1918*. New York: Norton, 1989.

Fenske, H. 'Imperialistische Tendenzen in Deutschland vor 1866: Auswanderung, überseeische Bestrebungen, Weltmachtträume'. *Historisches Jahrbuch* 97/98 (1978), 336–83.

————. 'Ungeduldige Zuschauer: Die Deutschen und die europäische Expansion 1815–1880', in R. Wolfgang (ed.), *Imperialistische Kontinuität und nationale Ungeduld im 19. Jahrhundert* (Frankfurt: Fischer, 1991), 87–140.

Fieldhouse, D.K. *Colonialism 1870–1945: An Introduction*. London: Macmillan, 1983.

Fisch, J. *Geschichte Südafrikas*. Munich: dtv, 1990.

Fisch, M. *Der Caprivizipfel während der deutschen Kolonialzeit 1890–1914*. Windhoek: Out of Africa, 1996.

Fischer, E. *Die Rehobother Bastards und das Bastardisierungsproblem beim Menschen: Anthropologische und ethnographische Studien am Rehobother Bastardvolk in Deutsch-Südwest-Afrika*. Jena: G. Fischer, 1913.

François, C. von. *Deutsch-Südwestafrika: Geschichte der Kolonisation bis zum Ausbruch des Krieges mit Witboi, April 1893*. Berlin: Reimer, 1899.

François, H. von. *Nama und Damara*. Magdeburg: Baensch, 1895.

Friedeburg, R. von. 'Konservativismus und Reichskolonialrecht: Konservatives Weltbild und kolonialer Gedanke in England und Deutschland vom späten 19. Jahrhundert bis zum Ersten Weltkrieg'. *Historische Zeitschrift* 263 (1996), 345–93.

Fröhlich, M. *Von der Konfrontation zur Koexistenz: Die deutsch-englischen Kolonialbeziehungen in Afrika zwischen 1884 und 1914*. Bochum: Brockmeyer, 1990.

Gann, L., and P. Duignan. *The Rulers of German Africa 1884–1914*. Stanford, CA: Stanford University Press, 1977.

Geiss, I. *Geschichte des Rassismus*. Frankfurt: Suhrkamp, 1988.

————. 'Kontinuitäten des Imperialismus', in R. Wolfgang (ed.), *Imperialistische Kontinuität und nationale Ungeduld im 19. Jahrhundert* (Frankfurt: Fischer, 1991), 12–30.

Gewald, J.-B. 'The Great General of the Kaiser'. *Botswana Notes and Records* 26 (1994), 67–76.

————. 'The Issue of Forced Labour in the Onjembo: German South West Africa 1904–1908'. *Itinerario* 14(1) (1995), 97–104.

————. 'The Road of the Man Called Love and the Sack of Sero: The Herero-German War and the Export of Herero Labour to the South African Rand'. *Journal of African History* 40 (1999), 21–40.

————. *Towards Redemption: A Socio-Political History of the Herero of Namibia between 1890 and 1923*. Leiden: Research School CNWS, 1996.

Gifford, P., and W.R. Louis (eds). *Britain and Germany in Africa: Imperial Rivalry and Colonial Rule*. New Haven, CT: Yale University Press, 1967.

Glocke, N. *Zur Geschichte der Rheinischen Missionsgesellschaft in Deutsch-Südwestafrika unter besonderer Berücksichtigung des Kolonialkrieges von 1904 bis 1907*. Bochum: Brockmeyer, 1997.

Goldblatt, I. *History of South West Africa from the Beginning of the Nineteenth Century*. Cape Town: Juta, 1971.

Gordon, R. 'Gehegt bis zur Ausrottung: Buschleute im Südlichen Afrika'. *Peripherie* 20 (1985), 18–35.

Gründer, H. *Christliche Mission und deutscher Imperialismus: Eine politische Geschichte ihrer Beziehungen während der deutschen Kolonialzeit 1884–1914 unter besonderer Berücksichtigung Afrikas und Chinas*. Paderborn: Schöningh, 1982.

————— (ed.). '…*da und dort ein junges Deutschland gründen': Rassismus, Kolonien und kolonialer Gedanke vom 16. bis zum 20. Jahrhundert*. Munich: dtv, 1999.

—————. 'Genozid oder Zwangsmodernisierung? – Der moderne Kolonialismus in universalgeschichtlicher Perspektive', in M. Dabag and K. Platt (eds), *Genozid und Moderne*. Vol. I: *Strukturen kollektiver Gewalt* (Opladen: Leske + Budrich, 1998), 135–51.

—————. *Geschichte der deutschen Kolonien*, 3rd edn. Paderborn: Schöningh, 1995.

—————. 'Mission und Kolonialismus: Historische Beziehungen und strukturelle Zusammenhänge', in W. Wagner (ed.), *Kolonien und Missionen. Referate des 3. Internationalen Kolonialgeschichtlichen Symposiums 1993 in Bremen* (Münster: LIT, 1994), 24–37.

Handbuch für das Deutsche Reich, 11 (1884) – 41 (1914). Berlin: Heymanns, 1884–1914.

Harten, H.-C. *De-Kulturation und Germanisierung: Die nationalsozialistische Rassen- und Erziehungspolitik in Polen 1939–1945*. Frankfurt: Campus, 1996.

Hayes, P., et al. (eds). *Namibia under South African Rule: Mobility and Containment 1915–46*. Oxford: James Currey, 1998.

Heine, P., and U. van der Heyden (eds). *Studien zur Geschichte des deutschen Kolonialismus in Afrika* (Festschrift to mark the 60th birthday of Peter Sebald). Pfaffenweiler: Centaurus, 1995.

Helbig, H., and L. Helbig. *Mythos Deutsch-Südwest: Namibia und die Deutschen*. Weinheim: Beltz, 1983.

Henrichsen, D. '"Ehi rOvaherero": Mündliche Überlieferungen von Herero zu ihrer Geschichte im vorkolonialen Namibia'. *Werkstatt Geschichte* 9 (1994), 15–24.

—————. *Herrschaft und Identifikation im vorkolonialen Zentralnamibia: Das Herero- und Damaraland im 19. Jahrhundert*. University of Hamburg, unpublished doctoral thesis, 1997.

Herbert, U. 'Traditionen des Rassismus', in idem, *Arbeit, Volkstum, Weltanschauung: Über Fremde und Deutsche im 20. Jahrhundert* (Frankfurt: Fischer, 1995), 11–29.

Hesse, H. *Die Schutzverträge in Südwestafrika: Ein Beitrag zur rechtsgeschichtlichen und politischen Entwicklung des Schutzgebietes*. Berlin: Süsserott, 1905.

Heyden, U. van der. 'Die historische Afrikaforschung in der DDR: Versuch einer Bilanz der Afrika-Geschichtsschreibung', in U. van der Heyden,

I. Schleicher and H.-G. Schleicher (eds), *Die DDR und Afrika: Zwischen Klassenkampf und neuem Denken* (Münster: LIT, 1993), 108–30.

Hiery, H. *Das Deutsche Reich in der Südsee 1900–1921: Eine Annäherung an die Erfahrungen verschiedener Kulturen.* Göttingen: Vandenhoeck & Ruprecht, 1995.

Hildebrand, K. *Das vergangene Reich: Deutsche Außenpolitik von Bismarck bis Hitler 1871–1945.* Stuttgart: DVA, 1995.

————. *Vom Reich zum Weltreich: Hitler, NSDAP und koloniale Frage 1919–1945.* Munich: Fink, 1969.

Hintrager, O. *Südwestafrika in der deutschen Zeit*, 2nd edn. Munich: Oldenbourg, 1956.

Hintze, O. *Beamtentum und Bürokratie.* Göttingen: Vandenhoeck & Ruprecht, 1981.

Hitz, R. 'Die Bondelzwarts unter deutscher und südafrikanischer Herrschaft zu Beginn des 20. Jahrhunderts'. University of Freiburg, unpublished MA thesis, n.d.

Hobsbawm, E. *The Age of Empire.* London: Weidenfeld & Nicolson, 1987.

Hubatsch, W. *Grundriß zur deutschen Verwaltungsgeschichte 1815–1945.* Vol. 22: *Bundes- und Reichsbehörden.* Marburg: Herder, 1983.

Huber, E.R. *Deutsche Verfassungsgeschichte seit 1789.* Vol. 2: *Der Kampf um Einheit und Frieden 1830–1850*, 3rd edn. Stuttgart: Kohlhammer, 1988.

Hyam, R. *Empire and Sexuality: The British Experience.* Manchester: Manchester University Press, 1990.

Jäschke, U. 'Der Aufbau der Verwaltung der deutschen Zeit', in H. Lamping and U. Jäschke (eds), *Aktuelle Fragen der Namibia-Forschung: Rundgespräch in Zusammenarbeit mit der Deutsch-Namibischen Gesellschaft* (Frankfurt: Institut für Wirtschafts- und Sozialgeographie, 1991), 17–36.

Jessen, R. 'Polizei, Wohlfahrt und die Anfänge des modernen Sozialstaates'. *Geschichte und Gesellschaft* 20 (1994), 157–80.

Kaminski, A. *Konzentrationslager 1896 bis heute: Geschichte – Funktion – Typologie.* Munich: Piper, 1990.

Die Kämpfe der deutschen Truppen in Südwestafrika (Auf Grund amtlichen Materials bearbeitet von der Kriegsgeschichtlichen Abteilung I des Großen Generalstabes) [The fighting of the German Troops in South West Africa (complied on the basis of official sources by the Military History Department I of the Grand General Staff)], 2 vols. Berlin: Mittler, 1906/07.

Kennedy, D. *Islands of White: Settler Society and Culture in Kenya and Southern Rhodesia 1890–1939.* Durham, NC: Duke University Press, 1987.

Kennedy, P. *The Rise of the Anglo-German Antagonism 1860–1914.* London: Allen & Unwin, 1980.

Ki-Zerbo, J. *Die Geschichte Schwarzafrikas.* Frankfurt: Fischer, 1981.

Köhler, O. 'Dokumente zur Entstehung des Buschmannproblems in Südwestafrika'. *Afrikanischer Heimatkalender* (1957), 52–64.

König, H.-J., W. Reinhard and R. Wendt (eds). *Der europäische Beobachter außereuropäischer Kulturen: Zur Problematik der Wirklichkeitswahrnehmung.* Berlin: Duncker & Humblot, 1989.

Koselleck, R. 'Zur historisch-politischen Semantik asymmetrischer Gegenbegriffe', in idem, *Vergangene Zukunft: Zur Semantik geschichtlicher Zeiten*, 3rd edn (Frankfurt: Suhrkamp, 1995), 211–59.

——. *Preußen zwischen Reform und Revolution: Allgemeines Landrecht, Verwaltung und soziale Bewegung von 1791 bis 1848*. Munich: dtv, 1989.

Krikler, J. 'Social Neurosis and Hysterical Pre-cognition in South Africa: A Case Study and Reflections'. *South African Historical Journal* 28 (1993), 63–97.

Krüger, G. 'Der Deutsche Kolonialkrieg 1904–1907: Unterwerfung und Eigen-Sinn der Herero'. *Comparativ* 8 (1998), 10–26.

——. *Kriegsbewältigung und Geschichtsbewusstsein: Realität, Deutung und Verarbeitung des deutschen Kolonialkrieges in Namibia 1904–1907*. Göttingen: Vandenhoeck & Ruprecht, 1999.

——. 'Die Paßmarke im Archiv: Spuren einer Alltagsgeschichte nach dem Deutsch-Hererokrieg 1904–1907'. *Periplus* 4 (1994), 95–104.

——. '"(…) so schicke uns jemanden mit einem Brief von Dir": Alltagsgeschichtliche Quellen zur Nachkriegszeit des Deutsch-Hererokrieges 1904–1907'. Basler Afrika-Bibliographien, Working Paper No. 1, 1995.

Kühl, S. *Die Internationale der Rassisten: Aufstieg und Niedergang der internationalen Bewegung für Eugenik und Rassenhygiene im 20. Jahrhundert*. Frankfurt: Campus, 1997.

Kühne, H. 'Die Ausrottungsfeldzüge der "Kaiserlichen Schutztruppen in Afrika" und die sozialdemokratische Reichstagsfraktion'. *Zeitschrift für Militärgeschichte* 18 (1979), 206–16.

Külz, W. *Die Selbstverwaltung für Deutsch-Südafrika*. Berlin: Süsserott, 1909.

Lamping, H., and U. Jäschke (eds). *Föderative Raumstrukturen und wirtschaftliche Entwicklungen in Namibia*. Frankfurt: Institut für Wirtschafts- und Sozialgeographie, 1993.

Lau, B. (ed.). *The Hendrik Witbooi Papers*. Windhoek: National Archives of Namibia, 1989.

——. *Southern and Central Namibia in Jonker Afrikaner's Time*, 2nd edn. Windhoek: National Archives of Namibia, 1994.

——. 'Uncertain Certainties: The Herero-German War of 1904', in eadem, *History and Historiography – 4 Essays in Reprint* (Windhoek: Discourse/MSORP, 1995), 39–52.

Lenssen, H.E. *Chronik von Deutsch-Südwestafrika 1883–1915*, 5th edn. Windhoek: Namibia-Wiss. Ges., 1997.

Leutwein, P. *Afrikanerschicksal: Gouverneur Leutwein und seine Zeit*. Stuttgart: Union Deutsche Verlagsgesellschaft, n.d.

Leutwein, T. *Elf Jahre Gouverneur in Deutsch-Südwestafrika*, 3rd edn. Berlin: Mittler, 1908.

Lipton, M. *Capitalism and Apartheid. South Africa 1910–84*. Aldershot: Gower, 1985.

Loth, H. *Die christliche Mission in Südwestafrika: Zur destruktiven Rolle der Rheinischen Missionsgesellschaft beim Prozeß der Staatsbildung in Südwestafrika 1842–1893*. Berlin: Akademie, 1963.

Louis, W.R. *Das Ende des deutschen Kolonialreiches: Britischer Imperialismus und die deutschen Kolonien 1914–1919*. Düsseldorf: Bertelsmann, 1971.

Luhmann, N. *Funktionen und Folgen formaler Organisation*, 3rd edn. Berlin: Duncker & Humblot, 1976.

———. 'Funktion und Kausalität'. *Kölner Zeitschrift für Soziologie und Sozialpsychologie* 14 (1962), 617–44.

———. *Legitimation durch Verfahren*. Neuwied: Luchterhand, 1969.

———. *Soziale Systeme: Grundriß einer allgemeinen Theorie*. Frankfurt: Suhrkamp, 1984.

Mamozai, M. *Schwarze Frau, weiße Herrin: Frauenleben in den deutschen Kolonien*, 2nd edn. Reinbek: Rowohlt, 1989.

Marx, C. 'Afrikaaner Nationalismus und die Errichtung des Rassenstaates in Südafrika 1910'. *Geschichte und Gesellschaft* 17 (1991), 30–60.

———. 'Elitensozialisation und Gewalt: Das Beispiel der afrikaans-nationalistischen Machtelite in Südafrika', in R.P. Sieferle and H. Breuninger (eds), *Kulturen der Gewalt: Ritualisierung und Symbolisierung von Gewalt in der Geschichte* (Frankfurt: Campus, 1998), 215–40.

———. *Im Zeichen des Ochsenwagens: Der radikale Afrikaaner-Nationalismus in Südafrika und die Ossewabrandwag*. Münster: LIT, 1998.

———. 'Rassismus in Afrika'. *Asien, Afrika, Lateinamerika* 25 (1997), 609–27.

———. 'Völker ohne Schrift und Geschichte': Zur historischen Erfassung des vorkolonialen Schwarzafrika in der deutschen Forschung des 19. und frühen 20. Jahrhunderts. Stuttgart: Steiner, 1988.

Masson, J.R. 'A Fragment of Colonial History: The Killing of Jakob Marengo'. *Journal of Southern African Studies* 21 (1995), 247–56.

McGregor, R. *Imagined Destinies: Aboriginal Australians and the Doomed Race Theory, 1880–1939*. Carlton, VIC: Melbourne University Press, 1997.

Mecheril, P., and T. Teo (eds). *Psychologie und Rassismus*. Reinbek: Rowohlt, 1997.

Melber, H. 'Kontinuitäten totaler Herrschaft: Völkermord und Apartheid in Deutsch-Südwestafrika'. *Jahrbuch für Antisemitismusforschung* 1 (1992), 91–116.

———. *Namibia. Geschichte und Gegenwart: Zur Frage der Dekolonisation einer Siedlerkolonie*. Bonn: Informationsstelle Südliches Afrika, 1977.

——— (ed.). *Namibia: Kolonialismus und Widerstand*. Bonn: Informationsstelle Südliches Afrika, 1981.

———. *Schule und Kolonialismus: Das formale Erziehungswesen Namibias*. Hamburg: Institut für Afrika-Kunde, 1979.

Memmi, A. *Der Kolonisator und der Kolonisierte: Zwei Portraits*. Hamburg: EVA, 1994.

———. *Rassismus*. Hamburg: EVA, 1992.

Meyer, T. (ed.). *Reichs- und Staatsangehörigkeitsgesetz vom 22. Juli 1913: Unter Berücksichtigung der ergangenen Ausführungsvorschriften und unter Darstellung des früheren Reichs- und Landesrechts sowie des hauptsächlichen ausländischen Rechts*, 2nd edn. Berlin: Heymann, 1914.

Mogk, W. *Paul Rohrbach und das "Größere Deutschland": Ethischer Imperialismus im Wilhelminischen Zeitalter. Ein Beitrag zur Geschichte des Kulturprotestantismus.* Munich: Goldmann, 1972.

Mokopakgosi, B. 'Conflict and Collaboration in South-Eastern Namibia: Missionaries, Concessionaires and the Nama's War against German Imperialism, 1880–1908', in J.F. Ade Ajayi and J.D.Y. Peel (eds), *People and Empires in African History: Essays in Memory of Michael Crowder* (London: Longman, 1992), 185–96.

Mommsen, W.J. 'Europa und die außereuropäische Welt'. *Historische Zeitschrift* 258 (1994), 661–95.

Moorsom, R. 'Underdevelopment and Class Formation: The Origins of Migrant Labour in Namibia, 1850–1915', in T. Adler (ed.), *Perspectives on South Africa* (Johannesburg: African Studies Institute, University of the Witwatersrand, 1977), 17–44.

Mosse, G. *Rassismus, ein Krankheitssymptom in der europäischen Geschichte des 19. und 20. Jahrhunderts.* Königstein: Athenäum, 1978.

Müller, F.F. (ed.). *Kolonien unter der Peitsche: Eine Dokumentation.* Berlin: Rütten & Loening, 1962.

Müller, J. 'Die deutsche Eingeborenenpolitik in Südwestafrika 1905–1915'. University of Augsburg, unpublished MA thesis, 1984.

Nestvogel, R., and R. Tetzlaff (eds). *Afrika und der deutsche Kolonialismus.* Berlin: Reimer, 1987.

Newbury, C. 'Spoils of War: Sub-Imperial Collaboration in South West Africa and New Guinea 1914–20'. *Journal of Imperial and Commonwealth History* 16 (1988), 86–106.

Nipperdey, T. *Deutsche Geschichte 1866–1918.* Vol. 1: *Arbeitswelt und Bürgergeist.* Munich: Beck, 1990.

———. *Deutsche Geschichte 1866–1918.* Vol. 2: *Machtstaat vor der Demokratie.* Munich: Beck, 1992.

Norris, E.G. *Die Umerziehung des Afrikaners: Togo 1895–1938.* Munich: Trickster, 1993.

Norris, E.G., and A. Beuke. 'Kolonialkrieg und Karikatur in Deutschland: Die Aufstände der Herero und Nama und die Zeichnungen in deutschen satirischen Zeitschriften', in P. Heine and U. van der Heyden (eds), *Studien zur Geschichte des deutschen Kolonialismus in Afrika* (Pfaffenweiler: Centaurus, 1995), 368–98.

Noyes, J. *Colonial Space: Spatiality in the Discourse of German South West Africa, 1884–1915.* Chur, Switzerland: Harwood Academic Publishers, 1992.

Oelhafen, H. von. *Feldzug in Südwest 1914–1915.* Berlin: Safari, 1923.

Oermann, N.O. *Mission, Church and State Relations in South West Africa under German Rule (1884–1915).* Stuttgart: Steiner, 1999.

Onselen, C. van. *Chibaro: African Mine Labour in Southern Rhodesia 1900–1933.* London: Pluto, 1976.

Osterhammel, J. 'Jenseits der Orthodoxie: Imperium, Raum, Herrschaft und Kultur als Dimensionen der Imperialismustheorien'. *Periplus* 5 (1995), 119–31.

———. *Kolonialismus: Geschichte, Formen, Folgen.* Munich: Beck, 1995.

————. 'Kulturelle Grenzen in der Expansion Europas'. *Saeculum* 46 (1995), 101–38.

Osterhaus, A. *Europäischer Terraingewinn in Schwarzafrika: Das Verhältnis von Presse und Verwaltung in sechs Kolonien Deutschlands, Frankreichs und Großbritanniens von 1894–1914*. Frankfurt: Lang, 1990.

Ostertag, H. *Bildung, Ausbildung und Erziehung des Offizierskorps im deutschen Kaiserreich 1871 bis 1918: Eliteideal, Anspruch und Wirklichkeit*. Frankfurt: Lang, 1990.

Peters, W. 'Grundzüge des Städtebaus in Namibia', in P. Heine and U. van der Heyden (eds), *Studien zur Geschichte des deutschen Kolonialismus in Afrika* (Pfaffenweiler: Centaurus, 1995), 429–52.

Petter, W. 'Das Offizierskorps der deutschen Kolonialtruppen 1889–1918', in H. Hofmann (ed.), *Das deutsche Offizierskorps 1860–1918* (Boppard: Boldt, 1980), 163–74.

Philipps, J. *Deutsch-englische Komödie der Irrungen um Südwestafrika: Eine Studie zu Bismarcks Kolonialpolitik und deren Folgen*. Pfaffenhofen: Afrika-Verlag, 1986.

Poewe, K. *The Namibian Herero: A History of their Psychological Disintegration and Survival*. Lewiston, NY: Mellen Press, 1985.

Poliakov, L. *Der arische Mythos: Zu den Quellen von Rassismus und Nationalismus*. Hamburg: Junius, 1993.

Pool, G. *Samuel Maharero*. Windhoek: Gamsberg Macmillan, 1991.

Popitz, H. *Phänomene der Macht*, 2nd edn. Tübingen: Mohr Siebeck, 1992.

Prein, P. 'Guns and Top Hats: African Resistance in German South West Africa 1907–1915'. *Journal of Southern African Studies* 20 (1994), 99–121.

Rafalski, H. *Vom Niemandsland zum Ordnungsstaat: Geschichte der ehemaligen Landespolizei für Deutsch-Südwestafrika*. Berlin: Wernitz, n.d. [1930].

Ranger, T.O. (ed.). *Emerging Themes in African History*. London: Heinemann, 1968.

Reinhard, W. 'Einführung: Bewegung in der Imperialismusforschung', in idem (ed.), *Imperialistische Kontinuität und nationale Ungeduld im 19. Jahrhundert* (Frankfurt: Fischer, 1991), 7–11.

————. 'Eingeborenenpolitik in Südwestafrika: Der deutsche Weg zur Apartheid', in S. Weiss (ed.), *Historische Blickpunkte: Festschrift for Johann Rainer* (Innsbruck: Institut für Sprachwissenschaft, 1988), 543–56.

————. *Geschichte der Europäischen Expansion*. Vol. 4: *Dritte Welt, Afrika*. Stuttgart: Kohlhammer, 1990.

———— (ed.). *Hendrik Witbooi: Afrika den Afrikanern! Aufzeichnungen eines Nama-Häuptlings aus der Zeit der deutschen Eroberung Südwestafrikas 1884 bis 1894*. Berlin: Dietz, 1982.

————. *Kleine Geschichte des Kolonialismus*. Stuttgart: Kröner, 1996.

————. '"Sozialimperialismus" oder "Entkolonisierung der Historie"? Kolonialkrise und "Hottentottenwahlen" 1904–1907'. *Historisches Jahrbuch* 97/98 (1978), 384–417.

————. 'Von der Geschichtstheorie zur Theoriegeschichte: Eine Einführung'. *Periplus* 5 (1995), 72–84.

Report on the Natives of South West Africa and their Treatment by Germany (prepared in the Administrator's Office, Windhoek, 1918). London: His Majesty's Stationery Office, 1918.

Richter, E. *Die Expansion der Herrschaft: Eine demokratietheoretische Studie.* Opladen: Leske + Budrich, 1994.

Riehl, A. *Der 'Tanz um den Äquator': Bismarcks antienglische Bündnispolitik und die Erwartung des Thronwechsels in Deutschland 1883 bis 1885.* Berlin: Duncker & Humblot, 1993.

Robinson, R. 'Non-European Foundations of European Imperialism: Sketch for a Theory of Collaboration', in R. Owen and B. Sutcliffe (eds), *Studies in the Theory of Imperialism* (London: Longman, 1972), 117–42.

Rohrbach, P. *Aus Südwestafrikas schweren Tagen: Blätter von Arbeit und Abschied.* Berlin: Weicher, 1909.

———. *Das deutsche Kolonialwesen.* Leipzig: Gloeckner, 1911.

———. *Deutsche Kolonialwirtschaft: Kulturpolitische Grundsätze für die Rassen- und Missionsfragen.* Berlin: Hilfe, 1909.

———. *Deutsche Kolonialwirtschaft.* Vol. 1: *Südwest-Afrika.* Berlin: Hilfe, 1907.

———. *Die Kolonie.* Frankfurt: Rütten & Loening, 1907.

———. *Koloniale Siedlung und Wirtschaft der führenden Kolonialvölker.* Cologne: Schaffstein, 1934.

———. 'Siedlung und Wirtschaft der Weißen in Afrika'. *Marine-Rundschau* 18 (1907), 147–67.

———. *Unsere koloniale Zukunftsarbeit.* Stuttgart: Die Lese, 1915.

———. *Wie machen wir unsere Kolonien rentabel? Grundzüge eines Wirtschaftsprogrammes für Deutschlands afrikanischen Kolonialbesitz.* Halle: Gebauer-Schwetschke, 1907.

Rüdiger, K. *Die Namibia-Deutschen: Geschichte einer Nationalität im Werden.* Stuttgart: Steiner, 1993.

Rüdiger, K., and H. Weiland. '"Hart wie Kamelholzdorn": Der Weg der Deutschsprachigen von Südwest nach Namibia'. *Afrika Spectrum* 27 (1992), 343–65.

Rust, C. *Krieg und Frieden im Hererolande: Aufzeichnungen aus dem Kriegsjahre 1904.* Leipzig: Kittler, 1905.

Scheulen, P. *Die 'Eingeborenen' Deutsch-Südwestafrikas: Ihr Bild in deutschen Kolonialzeitschriften von 1884 bis 1914.* Cologne: Köppe, 1998.

Schiefel, W. *Bernhard Dernburg (1865–1937): Eine Biographie unter besonderer Berücksichtigung seiner kolonialpolitischen Tätigkeit 1906–1910.* Zurich: Atlantis, 1974.

Schinzinger, F. *Die Kolonien und das Deutsche Reich: Die wirtschaftliche Bedeutung der deutschen Besitzungen in Übersee.* Stuttgart: Steiner, 1984.

Schlosser, K. *Eingeborenenkirchen in Süd- und Südwestafrika, ihre Geschichte und Sozialstruktur.* Kiel: Mühlau, 1958.

Schluchter, W. *Aspekte bürokratischer Herrschaft: Studien zur Interpretation der fortschreitenden Industriegesellschaft.* Frankfurt: Suhrkamp, 1985.

Schmidt, G. *Der europäische Imperialismus.* Munich: Oldenbourg, 1985.

Schmidt-Lauber, B. *Die abhängigen Herren: Deutsche Identität in Namibia.* Münster: LIT, 1993.

Schnee, H. (ed.). *Deutsches Kolonial-Lexikon*. Leipzig: Quelle & Meyer, 1920.

Schröder, M. *Prügelstrafe und Züchtigungsrecht in den deutschen Schutzgebieten Schwarzafrikas*. Münster: LIT, 1997.

Schulte-Althoff, F.J. 'Koloniale Krise und Reformprojekte: Zur Diskussion über eine Kurskorrektur in der deutschen Kolonialpolitik nach der Jahrhundertwende', in H. Dollinger, H. Gründer and A. Hanschmidt (eds), *Weltpolitik – Europagedanke – Regionalismus* (Münster: Aschendorff, 1982), 407–25.

———. 'Rassenmischung im kolonialen System: Zur deutschen Kolonialpolitik im letzten Jahrzehnt vor dem Ersten Weltkrieg'. *Historisches Jahrbuch* 105 (1985), 52–94.

Schumpeter, J. 'Zur Soziologie der Imperialismen'. *Archiv für Sozialwissenschaft und Sozialpolitik* 46 (1918/19), 275–310.

Schwabe, K. *Im deutschen Diamantenlande: Deutsch-Südwestafrika von der Errichtung der deutschen Herrschaft bis zur Gegenwart (1884–1910)*. Berlin: Mittler, 1909.

———. *Der Krieg in Deutsch-Südwestafrika*. Berlin: Weller, 1907.

———. *Mit Schwert und Pflug in Deutsch-Südwestafrika*. Berlin: Mittler, 1899.

Seitz, T. 'Der Zusammenbruch in Deutsch-Südwestafrika', in idem, *Südafrika im Weltkriege* (Berlin: Reimer, 1920), 1–53.

———. *Vom Aufstieg und Niederbruch deutscher Kolonialmacht*. Vol. 3: *Die Gouverneursjahre in Südwestafrika*. Karlsruhe: Müller, 1929.

Selmeci, A., and D. Henrichsen. *Das Schwarzkommando: Thomas Pynchon und die Geschichte der Herero*. Bielefeld: Aisthesis, 1995.

Sharp, J., and E. Boonzaier. 'Ethnic Identity as Performance: Lessons from Namaqualand'. *Journal of Southern African Studies* 20 (1994), 405–15.

Siiskonen, H. *Trade and Socioeconomic Change in Ovamboland 1850–1906*. Helsinki: SHS, 1990.

Silvester, J. *My Heart Tells Me That I Have Done Nothing Wrong: The Fall of Mandume*. Windhoek: University of Namibia, 1995.

Sippel, H. '"Im Interesse des Deutschtums und der weißen Rasse": Behandlung und Rechtswirkungen von "Rassenmischehen" in den Kolonien Deutsch-Ostafrika und Deutsch-Südwestafrika'. *Jahrbuch für afrikanisches Recht* 9 (1995), 123–59.

———. 'Mission und Kodifikation: Der missionarische Beitrag zur Erforschung des afrikanischen Gewohnheitsrechts in der Kolonie Deutsch-Ostafrika', in W. Wagner (ed.), *Kolonien und Missionen* (Münster: LIT, 1994), 494–510.

Smidt, K. '"Germania führt die deutsche Frau nach Südwest": Auswanderung, Leben und soziale Konflikte deutscher Frauen in der ehemaligen Kolonie Deutsch-Südwestafrika 1884–1920. Eine sozial- und frauengeschichtliche Studie'. University of Magdeburg, unpublished doctoral thesis, 1995.

Smith, W.D. 'Colonialism and Colonial Empire', in R. Chickering (ed.), *Imperial Germany: A Historiographical Companion* (London: Greenwood Press, 1996), 430–53.

———. *The German Colonial Empire*. Chapel Hill: University of North Carolina Press, 1978.

————. *The Ideological Origins of Nazi Imperialism.* Oxford University Press, 1986.

Spiecker-Salazar, M. 'Mission und Kolonialherrschaft aus der Sicht eines Missionsinspektors: Das Tagebuch der Afrikareise von Pfarrer Johannes Spiecker, 1905–1907', in W. Wagner (ed.), *Kolonien und Missionen* (Münster: LIT, 1994), 426–39.

Spraul, G. 'Der "Völkermord" an den Herero'. *Geschichte in Wissenschaft und Unterricht* 39 (1988), 713–39.

Stals, E.L.P. *Kurt Streitwolf: Sy werk in Suidwes-Afrika 1899–1914.* Johannesburg: Perskor, 1978.

————. *Die Rol van Viktor Franke in Suidwes-Afrika 1896–1915.* Johannesburg: Randse Afrikaanse University, 1972.

Stoecker, H. (ed.). *Drang nach Afrika: Die koloniale Expansionspolitik und die Herrschaft des deutschen Imperialismus in Afrika von den Anfängen bis zum Ende des Zweiten Weltkrieges.* Berlin: Akademie, 1977.

Strassegger, R. 'Die Wanderarbeit der Ovambo während der Deutschen Kolonialbesetzung Namibias: Unter besonderer Berücksichtigung der Wanderarbeiter auf den Diamantenfeldern in den Jahren 1908–1914'. University of Graz, unpublished doctoral thesis, 1988.

Sudholt, G. *Die deutsche Eingeborenenpolitik in Südwestafrika: Von den Anfängen bis 1904.* Hildesheim: Olms, 1975.

Süle, T. *Preußische Bürokratietradition.* Göttingen: Vandenhoeck & Ruprecht, 1988.

Sundermeier, T. *Die Mbanderu: Studien zu ihrer Geschichte und Kultur.* St Augustin: Anthropos-Institut – Haus Völker und Kulturen, 1977.

Trotha, T. von. *Koloniale Herrschaft: Zur soziologischen Theorie der Staatsentstehung am Beispiel des 'Schutzgebietes Togo'.* Tübingen: Mohr Siebeck, 1994.

Ullmann, H.-P. *Das Deutsche Kaiserreich 1871–1918.* Frankfurt: Suhrkamp, 1995.

Vedder, H. *Das alte Südwestafrika:* Südwestafrikas Geschichte bis zum Tode Mahareros 1890. Berlin: Warneck, 1934.

Vietsch, E. von. *Wilhelm Solf. Botschafter zwischen den Zeiten.* Tübingen: Wunderlich, 1961.

Wagner, W. (ed.). *Rassendiskriminierung, Kolonialpolitik und ethnisch-nationale Identität.* Münster: LIT, 1992.

Wallach, J. *Das Dogma der Vernichtungsschlacht: Die Lehren von Clausewitz und Schlieffen und ihre Wirkungen in zwei Weltkriegen.* Frankfurt: Bernard & Graefe, 1967.

Weber, M. 'Der Nationalstaat und die Volkswirtschaftspolitik' (Inaugural lecture in Freiburg, 1895), in idem, *Gesammelte Politische Schriften*, 4th edn (Tübingen: Mohr Siebeck, 1980), 1–25.

————. *Wirtschaft und Gesellschaft*, 5th edn. Tübingen: Mohr Siebeck, 1980.

Wedi-Pascha, B. *Die deutsche Mittelafrika-Politik 1871–1914.* Pfaffenweiler: Centaurus, 1992.

Wege, F. 'Die Anfänge der Herausbildung einer Arbeiterklasse in Südwestafrika unter der deutschen Kolonialherrschaft'. *Jahrbuch für Wirtschaftsgeschichte* (1969), 183–221.

———. 'Zur Entstehung und Entwicklung der Arbeiterklasse in Südwestafrika während der deutschen Kolonialherrschaft'. University of Halle, unpublished doctoral thesis, 1966.

———. 'Zur sozialen Lage der Arbeiter Namibias unter der deutschen Kolonialherrschaft in den Jahren vor dem Ersten Weltkrieg'. *Jahrbuch für Wirtschaftsgeschichte* (1973), 201–18.

Wehler, H.-U. *Bismarck und der Imperialismus*, 4th edn. Munich: dtv, 1976.

———. *Deutsche Gesellschaftsgeschichte*. Vol. 3: *Von der 'Deutschen Doppelrevolution' bis zum Beginn des Ersten Weltkrieges 1849–1914*. Munich: Beck, 1995.

———. *Krisenherde des Kaiserreiches 1871–1918*, 2nd edn. Göttingen: Vandenhoeck & Ruprecht, 1979.

Weinberger, G. *An den Quellen der Apartheid*. Berlin: Akademie, 1975.

Weingart, P., J. Kroll and K. Bayertz. *Rasse, Blut und Gene: Geschichte der Eugenik und Rassenhygiene in Deutschland*. Frankfurt: Suhrkamp, 1992.

Wellington, J. *South West Africa and its Human Issues*. Oxford: Clarendon Press, 1967.

Werner, W. '"Playing Soldiers": The Truppenspieler Movement among the Herero of Namibia, 1915 to ca. 1945'. *Journal of Southern African Studies* 16 (1990), 476–502.

Wildenthal, L. 'Race, Gender and Citizenship in the German Colonial Empire', in F. Cooper and A.L. Stoler (eds), *Tensions of Empire: Colonial Cultures and a Bourgeois World* (Berkeley: University of California Press, 1997), 263–83.

Wirz, A. 'Missionare im Urwald, verängstigt und hilflos: Zur symbolischen Topografie des kolonialen Christentums', in W. Wagner (ed.), *Kolonien und Missionen* (Münster: LIT, 1994), 39–56.

Wolf, E. *Vom Fürsten Bismarck und seinem Haus*. Berlin: Fleischel, 1904.

Wolter, U. (with P. Kaller). 'Deutsches Kolonialrecht, ein wenig erforschtes Rechtsgebiet, dargestellt anhand des Arbeitsrechts der Eingeborenen'. *Zeitschrift für Neuere Rechtsgeschichte* (1995), 201–44.

Wunder, B. *Geschichte der Bürokratie in Deutschland*. Frankfurt: Suhrkamp, 1986.

Young, C. *The African Colonial State in Comparative Perspective*. New Haven, CT: Yale University Press, 1994.

Zimmerer, J. 'Das portugiesische Kolonialreich in der Außenpolitik des deutschen Kaiserreiches: Die deutsch-britischen Teilungspläne von 1898 und 1913', in H. Siepmann (ed.), *Portugal, Índia e Alemanha* (Lisbon: Narr Francke Attempto, 2000), 485–94.

———. 'Der totale Überwachungsstaat? Recht und Verwaltung in Deutsch-Südwestafrika', in R. Voigt (ed.), *Kolonialisierung des Rechts: Zur kolonialen Rechts- und Verwaltungsordnung – Schriften zur Rechtspolitologie, Vol. 11* (Baden-Baden: Nomos, 2001), 183–207.

———. 'Kriegsgefangene im Kolonialkrieg: Der Krieg gegen die Herero und Nama in Deutsch Südwestafrika (1904–1907)', in R. Overmans (ed.), *In der Hand des Feindes: Kriegsgefangenschaft von der Antike bis zum Zweiten Weltkrieg* (Cologne: Böhlau, 1999), 277–94.

————. 'Von der Bevormundung zur Selbstbestimmung: Die Pariser Friedenskonferenz und ihre Auswirkungen auf die britische Kolonialherrschaft im Südlichen Afrika', in G. Krumeich (ed.), *Versailles 1919: Ziele – Wirkung – Wahrnehmung* (Essen: Klartext, 2001), 145–58.

Zimmerling, J. *Die Entwicklung der Strafrechtspflege für Afrikaner in Deutsch-Südwestafrika 1884–1914: Eine juristisch-historische Untersuchung*. Bochum: Brockmeyer, 1995.

Supplementary Bibliography
(Works published after the German book was written)

Aitken, R. *Exclusion and Inclusion: Gradations of Whiteness and Socio-economic Engineering in German Southwest Africa, 1884–1914*. Berne: Lang, 2007.

Bachmann, K. *Genocidal Empires: German Colonialism in Africa and the Third Reich*. Berlin: Lang, 2018.

Baer, E.R. *The Genocidal Gaze: From German Southwest Africa to the Third Reich*. Detroit: University of Namibia Press, 2017.

Bauer, J. *Zwischen kolonialer Reproduktion und postkolonialer Neukonstruktion: Darstellung kolonialer Vergangenheit in 'Deutsch-Südwestafrika' in der deutschsprachigen Romanliteratur seit 1978*. Erlangen: Wehrhahn, 2015.

Bollig, M. 'Unmaking the Market: The Encapsulation of a Regional Trade Network: North-Western Namibia between the 1880s and the 1950s', in W.J.G. Möhlig (ed.), *Frühe Kolonialgeschichte Namibias, 1880–1930* (Cologne: Köppe, 2000), 11–29.

Botha, C. 'Internal Colonization and an Oppressed Minority? The Dynamics of Relations between Germans and Afrikaners against the Background of Constructing a Colonial State in Namibia, 1884–1990'. *Journal of Namibian Studies* 2 (2007), 7–50.

————. 'The Politics of Land Settlement in Namibia, 1890–1960'. *South African Historical Journal* 42 (2000), 232–76.

Brehl, M. *Vernichtung der Herero: Diskurse der Gewalt in der deutschen Kolonialliteratur*. Munich: Fink, 2007.

Bühler, A.H. *Der Namaaufstand gegen die deutsche Kolonialherrschaft in Namibia von 1904–1913*. Frankfurt: IKO, 2003.

Bürger, C. *Deutsche Kolonialgeschichte(n): der Genozid in Namibia und die Geschichtsschreibung der DDR und BRD*. Bielefeld: transcript, 2017.

Coalition Agreement between CDU, CSU and SPD for the 19th Parliament, March 2018, https://www.bundesregierung.de/breg-de/themen/koalitionsvertrag-zwischen-cdu-csu-und-spd-195906.

Duchhardt, H. *Herausforderung Südwest? Die deutschen Kulturwissenschaften und das 'Schutzgebiet' Deutsch-Südwestafrika*. Stuttgart: Steiner, 2013.

Dyck, K. 'Situating the Herero Genocide and the Holocaust among European Colonial Genocides'. *Przeglad Zachodni* 1 (2014), 153–72.

Eckl, A. 'The Herero Genocide of 1904: Source-Critical and Methodological Considerations'. *Journal of Namibian Studies* 3 (2008), 31–61.

————. *Herrschaft, Macht und Einfluß: Koloniale Interaktionen am Kavango (Nord-Namibia) von 1891 bis 1921.* Cologne: Köppe, 2004.

————. 'Mit Kreuz, Gewehr und Handelskarre: der Kavango 1903 im deutschen Fokus', in W.J.G. Möhlig (ed.), *Frühe Kolonialgeschichte Namibias, 1880–1930* (Cologne: Köppe, 2000), 31–75.

————. 'Reports from "Beyond the Line": The Accumulation of Knowledge of Kavango and its Peoples by the German Colonial Administration 1891–1911'. *Jornal of Namibian Studies* 1 (2007), 7–37.

————. 'Serving the Kavango Sovereigns' Political Interests: The Beginning of the Catholic Mission in Northern Namibia'. *Le Fait Missionaire* 14 (2004), 9–46.

————. '"Weiß oder Schwarz?" Kolonialer Farm-Alltag in Deutsch-Südwestafrika', in M. Bechhaus-Gerst and R. Klein-Arendt (eds), *AfrikanerInnen in Deutschland und schwarze Deutsche – Geschichte und Gegenwart* (Münster: LIT, 2004), 109–24.

Eckl, A., G. Hillebrecht and F. von Epp. *'S'ist ein übles Land hier': Zur Historiographie eines umstrittenen Kolonialkrieges. Tagebuchaufzeichnungen aus dem Herero-Krieg in Deutsch-Südwestafrika 1904 von Georg Hillebrecht und Franz Ritter von Epp.* Cologne: Köppe, 2005.

Eicker, S. *Der Deutsch-Herero-Krieg und das Völkerrecht: Die völkerrechtliche Haftung der Bundesrepublik Deutschland für das Vorgehen des Deutschen Reiches gegen die Herero in Deutsch-Südwestafrika im Jahre 1904 und ihre Durchsetzung vor einem nationalen Gericht.* Frankfurt: Lang, 2009.

Erichsen, C.W. *'The Angel of Death Has Descended Violently Among Them': Concentration Camps and Prisoners of War in Namibia, 1904–08.* Leiden: African Studies Centre, 2005.

————. *'What the Elders Used to Say': Namibian Perspectives on the Last Decade of German Colonial Rule.* Windhoek: Namibian Institute for Democracy, 2008.

Faber-Jonker, L. *More than Just an Object: A Material Analysis of the Return and Retention of Namibian Skulls from Germany.* Leiden: African Studies Centre, 2018.

———— (ed.). *Le premier génocide du XXe siècle: Herero et Nama dans le Sud-Ouest africain allemand, 1904–1908.* Paris: Éditions du Mémorial de la Shoah, 2017.

Fischer, F., and N. ▢upi▢. *Die Kontinuität des Genozids: Die europäische Moderne und der Völkermord an den Herero und Nama in Deutsch-Südwestafrika.* Berlin: AphorismA, 2015.

Förster, L. *Postkoloniale Erinnerungslandschaften: Wie Deutsche und Herero in Namibia des Kriegs von 1904 gedenken.* Frankfurt: Campus, 2010.

Gewald, J.-B. 'Chief Hosea Kutako: A Herero Royal and Namibian Nationalist's Life against Confinement 1870–1970', in M. de Bruijn, R. van Dijk and J.-B. Gewald (eds), *Strength beyond Structure: Social and Historical Trajectories of Agency in Africa* (Leiden: Brill, 2007), 83–113.

————. '"I was afraid of Samuel, therefore I came to Sekgoma": Herero Refugees and Patronage Politics in Ngamiland, Bechuanaland Protectorate, 1890–1914'. *Journal of African History* 43 (2002), 211–34.

Gordon, R.J. 'Hiding in Full View: The "Forgotten" Bushman Genocides of Namibia'. *Genocide Studies and Prevention: An International Journal* 4(1) (2009), 29–57.

Gustafsson, K. 'The Trade in Slaves in Ovamboland, ca. 1850–1910'. *African Economic History* 33 (2005), 31–68.

Hammerstein, K.v. 'The Herero: Witnessing Germany's "Other Genocide"'. *Contemporary French and Francophone Studies* 20(2) (2016), 267–86.

Hartmann, W. '"…als durchaus wünschenswert erachtet…": Zur Genese des "Mischehenverbots" in Deutsch-Südwestafrika', in L. Förster, D. Henrichsen and M. Bollig (eds), *Namibia – Deutschland, eine geteilte Geschichte: Widerstand, Gewalt, Erinnerung* (Wolfratshausen: Ed. Minerva, 2004), 182–93.

———. 'Urges in the Colony: Men and Women in Colonial Windhoek, 1890–1905'. *Journal of Namibian Studies* 1 (2007), 39–71.

Häußler, M. *Der Genozid an den Herero: Krieg, Emotion und extreme Gewalt in Deutsch-Südwestafrika.* Weilerswist: Velbrück, 2018.

———. '"Die Kommandogewalt hat geredet, der Reichstag hat zu schweigen": How the "Hottentottenwahlen" of 1907 Shaped the Relationship between Parliament and Military Policy in Imperial Germany'. *Journal of Namibian Studies* 15 (2014), 7–24.

———. 'Soldatische Hinterwäldler oder Avantgarde?: Über die einsatzbezogenen Erfahrungen der Kaiserlichen Schutztruppe in "Deutsch-Südwestafrika"'. *Militärgeschichtliche Zeitschrift* 71(2) (2012), 309–28.

———. 'Warum die Herero mit den Deutschen kooperierten: Zur "Pazifizierung" einer akephalen Gesellschaft'. *Mittelweg 36: Zeitschrift des Hamburger Instituts für Sozialforschung* 24(4) (2015), 86–108.

———. 'Zwischen Vernichtung und Pardon: Die Konzentrationslager in "Deutsch-Südwestafrika" (1904–1908)'. *Zeitschrift für Geschichtswissenschaft* 61(7/8) (2013), 601–20.

Häußler, M., and T.v. Trotha. 'Brutalisierung "von unten": Kleiner Krieg, Entgrenzung der Gewalt und Genozid im kolonialen Deutsch-Südwestafrika'. *Mittelweg 36: Zeitschrift des Hamburger Instituts für Sozialforschung* 21(3) (2012), 57–89.

Heinemann, P.O. 'Die deutschen Genozide an den Herero und Nama: Grenzen der rechtlichen Aufarbeitung'. *Der Staat* 55(4) (2016), 461–87.

Heinz, K.E. 'Die Entwicklung der Kolonialpolitik am Beispiel von Deutsch-Südwestafrika: Eine rechtstheoretische Analyse und Bewertung'. *Die öffentliche Verwaltung: Zeitschrift für öffentliches Recht und Verwaltungswissenschaft* 62(19) (2009), 805–10.

Henrichsen, D. '"Damara" Labour Recruitment to the Cape Colony and Marginalization and Hegemony in Late Nineteenth-Century Central Namibia'. *Journal of Namibian Studies* 3 (2014), 63–82.

———. *Herrschaft und Alltag im vorkolonialen Zentralnamibia: Das Herero- und Damaraland im 19. Jahrhundert.* Basel: Basler Afrika Bibliogr, 2011.

———. 'Ozombabuse and Ovasolondate: Everday Military Life and African Service Personnel in German South West Africa', in W. Hartmann (ed.),

Hues between Black and White: Historical Photography from Colonial Namibia,
1860s to 1915 (Windhoek: Out of Africa Publishers, 2004), 164–84.

———. 'Pastoral Modernity, Territoriality and Colonial Transformations in
Central Namibia, 1860s to 1902', in P. Limb, P. Midgley and N. Etherington
(eds), *Grappling with the Beast: Indigenous Southern African Responses to
Colonialism, 1840–1930* (Leiden: Brill, 2010), 87–114.

———. '"…Unerwuenscht im Schutzgebiet…nicht schlechthin unsittlich":
"Mischehen" und deren Nachkommen im Visier der Kolonialverwaltung
in Deutsch-Südwestafrika', in M. Bechhaus-Gerst and M. Leutner (eds),
Frauen in den deutschen Kolonien (Berlin: Ch. Links Verlag, 2009), 80–90.

Hermes, S. *'Fahrten nach Südwest': Die Kolonialkriege gegen die Herero und
Nama in der deutschen Literatur (1904–2004)*. Würzburg: Königshausen &
Neumann, 2009.

Jahnel, M.J. *Das Bodenrecht in 'Neudeutschland über See': Erwerb, Vergabe
und Nutzung von Land in der Kolonie Deutsch-Südwestafrika 1884–1915.*
Frankfurt: Lang, 2009.

Kaulich, U. *Die Geschichte der ehemaligen Kolonie Deutsch-Südwestafrika (1884–
1914): Eine Gesamtdarstellung.* Frankfurt: Lang, 2001.

Kellermeier-Rehbein, B. 'Sprache in postkolonialen Kontexten II: Varietäten
der deutschen Sprache in Namibia', in T. Stolz, I.H. Warnke and D.
Schmidt-Brücken (eds), *Sprache und Kolonialismus: eine interdisziplinäre
Einführung zu Sprache und Kommunikation in kolonialen Kontexten* (Berlin:
De Gruyter, 2016), 213–34.

Kiel, R.-M. 'Der Hereroaufstand in Deutsch-Südwestafrika: Zeitgenössische
Originalfotografien als Leihgabe des Historischen Vereins für Oberfranken
in der Universitätsbibliothek Bayreuth'. *Archiv für Geschichte von
Oberfranken* 85 (2005), 267–78.

Kinahan, J. 'Traumland Südwest: Two Moments in the History of German
Archaeological Inquiry in Namibia', in H. Härke (ed.), *Archaeology,
Ideology and Society: The German Experience* (Frankfurt: Lang, 2000), 353–74.

Kößler, R. *Namibia and Germany: Negotiating the Past.* Münster: Westfälisches
Dampfboot, 2015.

Kößler, R., H. Melber and H. Wieczorek-Zeul. *Völkermord – und was dann? Die
Politik deutsch-namibischer Vergangenheitsbearbeitung.* Frankfurt: Brandes &
Apsel, 2017.

Kotek, J. 'Le génocide des Herero, symptôme d'un Sonderweg allemand?'
*Revue d'histoire de la Shoah/Le monde juif: la revue du Centre de Documentation
Juive Contemporaine* 189 (2008), 177–97.

Kreienbaum, J. *A Sad Fiasco: Colonial Concentration Camps in Southern Africa,
1900–1908.* New York: Berghahn Books, 2019.

———. *'Ein trauriges Fiasko': Koloniale Konzentrationslager im südlichen Afrika
1900–1908.* Hamburg: Hamburger Edition HIS Verlagsges, 2015.

———. '"Vernichtungslager" in Deutsch-Südwestafrika? Zur Funktion der
Konzentrationslager im Herero- und Namakrieg (1904–1908)'. *Zeitschrift
für Geschichtswissenschaft* 58(12) (2010), 1014–26.

Krüger, G. 'Koloniale Gewalt, Alltagserfahrungen und Überlebensstrategien',
in L. Förster, D. Henrichsen and M. Bollig (eds), *Namibia – Deutschland,*

eine geteilte Geschichte: Widerstand, Gewalt, Erinnerung (Wolfratshausen: Ed. Minerva, 2004), 92–105.

Kundrus, B. 'Entscheidung für den Völkermord?: Einleitende Überlegungen zu einem historiographischen Problem'. *Mittelweg 36: Zeitschrift des Hamburger Instituts für Sozialforschung* 15(6) (2006), 4–17.

———. 'From the Herero to the Holocaust? Some Remarks on the Current Debate'. *Africa Spectrum* 40(2) (2005), 299–308.

Lundtofte, H. '"I believe that the nation as such must be annihilated...": Radicalization of the German Suppression of the Herero Rising in 1904', in S. Jensen (ed.), *Genocide: Cases, Comparisons and Contemporary Debates* (Copenhagen: Danish Center for Holocaust and Genocide Studies, 2003), 15–53.

Marouf, H. 'The German Konzentrationslager and the Debates about the Annihilation of the Herero, 1905–1908', in H. Marouf (ed.), *Restorative Justice, Humanitarian Rhetorics, and Public Memories of Colonial Camp Cultures* (London: Palgrave Macmillan, 2014), 90–127.

Melber, H. 'How to Come to Terms with the Past: Revisiting the German Colonial Genocide in Namibia'. *Afrika Spectrum* 40(1) (2005), 139–48.

Menzel, G. *'Widerstand und Gottesfurcht': Hendrik Witbooi – eine Biographie in zeitgenössischen Quellen.* Cologne: Köppe, 2000.

Miettinen, K. *On the Way to Whiteness: Christianization, Conflict and Change in Colonial Ovamboland, 1910–1965.* Helsinki: Suomalaisen Kirjallisuuden Seura, 2005.

Nuhn, W. *Feind überall: Der große Nama-Aufstand (Hottentottenaufstand) 1904–1908 in Deutsch-Südwestafrika (Namibia), der erste Partisanenkrieg in der Geschichte der deutschen Armee.* Bonn: Bernard & Graefe, 2000.

———. *Auf verlorenem Posten: Deutsch-Südwestafrika im Ersten Weltkrieg.* Bonn: Bernard & Graefe, 2006.

Olusoga, D., and C.W. Erichsen. *The Kaiser's Holocaust: Germany's Forgotten Genocide and the Colonial Roots of Nazism.* London: Faber and Faber, 2010.

Pohl, R. *Völkermord I: Deutschland, Namibia und die Herero und Nama*, 2nd edn. Kiel: Magazin-Verlag, 2018.

Sarkin, J. *Colonial Genocide and Reparations Claims in the 21st Century: The Socio-legal Context of Claims under International Law by the Herero against Germany for Genocide in Namibia, 1904–1908.* Westport, CT: Praeger, 2009.

———. *Germany's Genocide of the Herero: Kaiser Wilhelm II, His General, His Settlers, His Soldiers.* Cape Town: Currey, 2011.

Siebrecht, C. 'Seeing the "Savage" and the Suspension of Time: Photography, War and Concentration Camps in South West Africa, 1904–1908', in J. Evans, P. Betts and S.-L. Hoffmann (eds), *The Ethics of Seeing: Photography and Twentieth-Century German History* (New York: Berghahn Books, 2018), 37–56.

Silvester, J. 'Portraits of Power and Panoramas of Persuasion: The Palgrave Album at the National Archives of Namibia', in W. Hartmann (ed.), *Hues between Black and White: Historical Photography from Colonial Namibia, 1860s to 1915* (Windhoek: Out of Africa Publishers, 2004), 131–60.

————. '"Sleep with a Southwester": Monuments and Settler Identity in Namibia', in C. Elkins and S. Pedersen (eds), *Settler Colonialism in the Twentieth Century: Projects, Practices, Legacies* (New York: Routledge, 2005), 271–86.

Sobich, F.O. *'Schwarze Bestien, rote Gefahr': Rassismus und Antisozialismus im deutschen Kaiserreich*. Frankfurt: Campus, 2006.

Steinmetz, G. *The Devil's Handwriting: Precoloniality and the German Colonial State in Qingdao, Samoa, and Southwest Africa*. Chicago: University of Chicago Press, 2007.

Tiebel, A. *Die Entstehung der Schutztruppengesetze für die deutschen Schutzgebiete Deutsch-Ostafrika, Deutsch-Südwestafrika und Kamerun (1884–1898)*. Frankfurt: Lang, 2008.

Wallace, M., and J. Kinahan. *A History of Namibia: From the Beginning to 1990*. London: Hurst, 2011.

Wassink, J. *Auf den Spuren des deutschen Völkermordes in Südwestafrika: Der Herero-/Nama-Aufstand in der deutschen Kolonialliteratur. Eine literarhistorische Analyse*. Munich: M-Press, 2004.

Zeller, J. 'Images of the South West African War: Reflections of the 1904–1907 Colonial War in Contemporary Photo Reportage and Book Illustration', in W. Hartmann (ed.), *Hues between Black and White: Historical Photography from Colonial Namibia 1860s to 1915* (Windhoek: Out of Africa Publishers, 2004), 309–23.

Zimmerer, J. 'Das Deutsche Reich und der Genozid: Überlegungen zum historischen Ort des Völkermordes an den Herero und Nama', in L. Förster, D. Henrichsen and M. Bollig (eds), *Namibia – Deutschland, eine geteilte Geschichte: Widerstand, Gewalt, Erinnerung* (Wolfratshausen: Ed. Minerva, 2004), 106–21.

————. 'Kolonialismus und kollektive Identität: Erinnerungsorte der deutschen Kolonialgeschichte', in J. Zimmerer (ed.), *Kein Platz an der Sonne: Erinnerungsorte der deutschen Kolonialgeschichte* (Frankfurt: Campus, 2013), 9–38.

————. 'Rassenkrieg und Völkermord: Der Kolonialkrieg in Deutsch-Südwestafrika und die Globalgeschichte des Genozids', in H. Melber (ed.), *Genozid und Gedenken: Namibisch-deutsche Geschichte und Gegenwart* (Frankfurt: Brandes & Apsel, 2005), 23–48.

————. *Von Windhuk nach Auschwitz? Beiträge zum Verhältnis von Kolonialismus und Holocaust*. Münster: LIT, 2011.

Zimmerer, J., and J. Zeller (eds). *Genocide in German South-West Africa: The Colonial War (1904–1908) in Namibia and its Aftermath*. London: Merlin Press, 2008.

———— (eds). *Völkermord in Deutsch-Südwestafrika: Der Kolonialkrieg (1904–1908) in Namibia und seine Folgen*, 2nd edn. Berlin: Ch. Links, 2004.

Zollmann, J. *Koloniale Herrschaft und ihre Grenzen: Die Kolonialpolizei in Deutsch-Südwestafrika 1894–1915*. Göttingen: Vandenhoeck & Ruprecht, 2010.

Zöllner, C.W. *Deutsch-Herero-Krieg 1904: Eine Betrachtung unter dem Aspekt Völkermord*. Lorenz-von-Stein-Institut für Verwaltungswissenschaften an der Christian-Albrechts-Universität zu Kiel, 2017.

Index